VOLUME V

Gnosticism
in the
Early Church

edited with an introduction by

David M. Scholer

Garland Publishing, Inc.
New York & London
1993

Library of Congress Cataloging-in-Publication Data

Gnosticism in the early church / edited with an introduction by David
M. Scholer.
    p.   cm. — (Studies in early Christianity ; v. 5)
    Articles originally published 1964–1988.
    Includes bibliographical references.
    ISBN 0–8153–1065–X (alk. paper)
    1. Gnosticism.   I. Scholer, David M.   II. Series.
B638.G59   1993
273'.1—dc20   93–2815
                                                  CIP

Printed on acid-free, 250-year-life paper
Manufactured in the United States of America

Contents

Series Introduction

Christianity has been the formative influence on Western civilization and has maintained a significant presence as well in the Near East and, through its missions, in Africa and Asia. No one can understand Western civilization and the world today, much less religious history, without an understanding of the early history of Christianity.

The first six hundred years after the birth of Jesus were the formative period of Christian history. The theology, liturgy, and organization of the church assumed their definitive shape during this period. Since biblical studies form a separate, distinctive discipline, this series confines itself to sources outside the biblical canon, except as these sources were concerned with the interpretation and use of the biblical books. During the period covered in this series the distinctive characteristics of the Roman Catholic and Eastern Orthodox Churches emerged.

The study of early Christian literature, traditionally known as Patristics (for the church fathers), has experienced a resurgence in the late twentieth century. Evidences of this are the flourishing of a new professional society, the North American Patristics Society, a little over twenty years old; the growing number of teachers and course offerings at major universities and seminaries; the number of graduate students studying and choosing to write their dissertations in this area; the volume of books published in the field; and attendance at the quadrennial International Conferences on Patristic Studies at Oxford as well as at many smaller specialized conferences. This collection of articles reflects this recent growing interest and is intended to encourage further study. The papers at the International Conferences on Patristic Studies from the first conference in 1951 to the present have been published in the series *Studia Patristica,* and interested readers are referred to these volumes for more extensive treatment of the topics considered in this series of reprints and many other matters as well.

The volumes in this series are arranged topically to cover biography, literature, doctrines, practices, institutions, worship, missions, and daily life. Archaeology and art as well as writings are drawn on in order to give reality to the Christian movement in its early centuries. Ample attention is also given to the relation of Christianity to pagan thought and life, to the Roman state, to Judaism, and to doctrines and practices that came to be judged as heretical or schismatic. Introductions to each volume will attempt to tie the articles together so that an integrated understanding of the history will result.

The aim of the collection is to give balanced and comprehensive coverage. Early on I had to give up the idealism and admit the arrogance of attempting to select the "best" article on each topic. Criteria applied in the selection included the following: original and excellent research and writing, subject matter of use to teachers and students, groundbreaking importance for the history of research, foundational information for introducing issues and options. Preference was given to articles in English where available. Occasional French and German titles are included as a reminder of the international nature of scholarship.

The *Encyclopedia of Early Christianity* (New York: Garland, 1990) provides a comprehensive survey of the field written in a manner accessible to the average reader, yet containing information useful to the specialist. This series of reprints of Studies in Early Christianity is designed to supplement the encyclopedia and to be used with it.

The articles were chosen with the needs of teachers and students of early church history in mind with the hope that teachers will send students to these volumes to acquaint them with issues and scholarship in early Christian history. The volumes will fill the need of many libraries that do not have all the journals in the field or do not have complete holdings of those to which they subscribe. The series will provide an overview of the issues in the study of early Christianity and the resources for that study.

Understanding the development of early Christianity and its impact on Western history and thought provides indispensable insight into the modern world and the present situation of Christianity. It also provides perspective on comparable developments in other periods of history and insight into human nature in its religious dimension. Christians of all denominations may continue to learn from the preaching, writing, thinking, and working of the early church.

Introduction

Gnosticism has been a concern within the Christian Church virtually from the beginning. Although the details and date of the origins of Gnosticism are in dispute, many scholars believe that Gnosticism or some type of proto-Gnosticism was part of the problem or "heresy" addressed in various New Testament texts, such as Colossians, 1–2 John, or 1–2 Timothy and Titus. Certainly Gnosticism was a major issue in the second century of the ancient Church. One of the early church fathers who devoted himself to combatting Gnosticism was Irenaeus (ca. A.D. 115–202; see the articles on Irenaeus in Volume IV in this series, *Orthodoxy, Heresy, and Schism in Early Christianity*). The oldest Gnostic writings that have survived date from the second century.

Gnosticism (derived from the Greek word *gnosis* = knowledge) refers to a religious movement (or movements) in the ancient Hellenistic world. The Gnostic worldview was one of a radical anti-cosmic dualism: the created world and matter are inherently evil. Salvation comes through secret, revealed knowledge, brought by a heavenly redeemer. The Gnostic elect receive this knowledge and learn of their destiny: the return of their souls to the real God and divine realm, which completely transcends this world. Gnosticism was a syncretistic religion, clearly showing elements derived from current Hellenistic philosophy (mostly Platonic), Judaism, some traditional Egyptian religious motifs and, in its best known and predominant forms, early Christian theology. In Christian Gnosticism Christ was the Revealer of the secret knowledge necessary for salvation.

The study of Gnosticism experienced a major revival beginning almost fifty years ago with the discovery in 1945 near Nag Hammadi, Egypt of over fifty texts, most previously unknown Gnostic texts. The first published reports of this discovery began to appear in 1948. From that time through 1992 approximately 8,000 items have been published on Gnosticism and the so-called Nag Hammadi library (for a comprehensive bibliography see David M. Scholer, *Nag Hammadi Bibliography 1948–1969* (Nag Hammadi Studies 1; Leiden: E. J. Brill, 1971; updated annually [except for 1976 and 1991] in *Novum Testamentum*).

The entire Nag Hammadi library has been published in a facsimile edition. Many of the texts have also been published in critical editions, often with commentary. Numerous translations of various texts into many languages have also appeared (see the Scholer bibliography for details on all of this). The standard English translation today is that edited by James M. Robinson, *The Nag Hammadi Library In English: Translated and Introduced by Members of the Coptic Gnostic Library Project of the Institute for Antiquity and Christianity, Claremont, California* (Managing Editor, Richard Smith; 3d ed.; San Francisco: Harper & Row, 1988/Leiden: E. J. Brill, 1988; paperback edition, 1990).

Twenty-one important essays on Gnosticism originally published between 1964 and 1988 are collected here. Thus, all of these studies reflect knowledge of the Nag Hammadi library. Two-thirds of the essays come from *Festschriften* or collected essay volumes; one third come from periodicals, some of which are not readily accessible. Representative of recent significant Gnostic scholars, the seventeen authors of these articles discuss the fundamental questions of the study of Gnosticism today.

The classic question, and one of the most important, is that concerning the origins and components of Gnosticism. Arthur Darby Nock's article, one of the early ones after the Nag Hammadi texts began to appear, is considered a classic; it clearly shows both the Jewish and Greek components of Gnosticism. Yamauchi's article is a stout and able defense of the "traditional" view that Gnosticism originated in the second century as a Christian "heresy." In contrast, the article by Robinson is a strong case for understanding Gnosticism both as pre-Christian and as one of the beginning forms of early Christianity.

The Greek background and components of Gnosticism are ably explored in Armstrong's article. The Jewish contributions to the development of Gnosticism are thoroughly analyzed in the articles of Dahl, MacRae ("The Ego-Proclamation in Gnostic Sources") and Pearson. Wilson's article on Simon Magus ("Simon and Gnostic Origins") investigates one of the most difficult and important points of historical data for the possible origins of Gnosticism in the first century.

Another of the important and difficult historical and theological issues in the study of Gnosticism revolves around the concepts of "orthodoxy" and "heresy." Certainly the church fathers, as we call them, understood Gnosticism to be a heresy, but the historical realities of diversity within the early Church both in the first and second century mean that it is difficult and debatable whether and where such lines can be drawn (see Volume IV in this series, *Orthodoxy, Heresy, and Schism in Early Christianity*). The articles of Wisse ("The Use of Early Christian Literature as Evidence of Inner Diversity and Conflict"), MacRae ("Why the Church Rejected Gnosticism"), Robinson, Samuel, and Vallée directly discuss these complex problems from a variety of interpretive perspectives.

Part of the historical question about the identity and character of Gnosticism relates to the existence of various "schools" or movements within Gnosticism. The church fathers claimed that Gnosticism was divided into numerous sects or groups. The surviving Gnostic literature does not readily support this judgment. However, two Gnostic schools which seem clearly to have existed as definable movements are Sethian Gnosticism, named after the biblical Seth, who is seen as a redeemer figure, and Valentinian Gnosticism, named after Valentinus, a Gnostic teacher in the middle of the second century. Turner's article on Sethianism and Stead's article on Valentinus are especially fine studies of these movements (for more on the Valentinian school, see the article of Gilles Quispel, "La Lettre de Ptolémée à Flora" in Volume II in this series, *Literature of the Early Church*; Ptolemy was a teacher in the Valentinian school; part of a letter he wrote to Flora has been preserved by the church father Epiphanius).

Another of the important issues related to the study of Gnosticism is the attempt to give a social description of the Gnostic movement. There are many difficulties here, largely due to the limited number of Gnostic sources. There are very few references in the Nag Hammadi texts to the life and practices of the Gnostic communities. Green's article is an early and important introduction to some of these questions. The articles of Stead and Turner, already mentioned, also deal with these issues.

In seeking to provide a social description of Gnosticism, three important themes emerge: women, ethics, and worship and art. Gnostic texts abound in references to women and to feminine imagery. Was Gnosticism liberating for women? Did women have significant roles in Gnostic communities? In Gnostic ideologies? The seminal and often cited article of Pagels and those of Perkins and Wisse ("Flee Femininity: Antifemininity in Gnostic Texts and the Question of Social Milieu") address these questions with perception and depth (see also the article of J. E. Goehring, "Libertine or Liberated: Women in the So-called Libertine Gnostic Communities," in Volume XIV in this series, *Women in Early Christianity*).

The issues of Gnostic ethics often revolve around the assessment of whether gnostics were libertine, ascetic, or both. Wilson's two articles ("Ethics and the Gnostics" and "Alimentary and Sexual Encratism in the Nag Hammadi Tractates") address this issue well. Gnostic worship is discussed in the article of Tripp (for Gnostic art see the article of P. C.

Finney, "Did Gnostics Make Pictures?" in Volume XVIII in this series, *Art, Archaeology, and Architecture of Early Christianity*).

For further study of the primary sources related to Gnosticism, one may wish to consult an anthology that collects some of the writings of the church fathers on Gnosticism, including some of their presentations of otherwise lost early Gnostic texts. Two volumes in particular should be noted:

> Foerster, Werner. *Gnosis: A Selection of Gnostic Texts. I: Patristic Evidence*. Trans. R. McL. Wilson. Oxford: Clarendon, 1972.

> Grant, Robert M. *Gnosticism: A Source Book of Heretical Writings from the Early Christian Period*. New York: Harper & Brothers, 1961.

There are many good books on the history and theology of Gnosticism. The following volumes (limited to works available in English), representing various points of view, may be especially recommended for further study:

> Filoramo, Giovanni. *A History of Gnosticism*. Trans. Anthony Alcock. Oxford: Basil Blackwell, 1990.

> Jonas, Hans. *The Gnostic Religion: The Message of the Alien God and the Beginnings of Christianity*. 2d ed., 3d printing. Boston: Beacon, 1970.

> Couliano, Ioan P. *The Tree of Gnosis: Gnostic Mythology from Early Christianity to Modern Nihilism*. Trans. H. S. Wiesner. San Francisco: HarperSanFrancisco, 1992.

> Pétrement, Simone. *A Separate God: The Christian Origins of Gnosticism*. Trans. Carol Harrison. San Francisco: HarperSanFrancisco, 1990.

> Rudolph, Kurt. *Gnosis: The Nature and History of Gnosticism*. Trans. R. McL. Wilson. San Francisco: Harper & Row, 1983.

> Wilson, R. McL. *Gnosis and the New Testament*. Philadelphia: Fortress, 1968.

> Yamauchi, Edwin M. *Pre-Christian Gnosticism: A Survey of the Proposed Evidences*. 2d ed. Grand Rapids: Baker, 1983.

Pétrement and Yamauchi argue the case that Gnosticism is a second-century Christian heresy. Wilson takes a somewhat mediating position. The others represent the more likely position that Gnosticism has non-

Christian first-century origins. All seven of these books are very helpful and important in providing crucial perspectives and data for the study of Gnosticism in the early church.

For New Testament scholars, early church historians, Roman historians, and historians of religion, this volume provides a collection of important essays from a wide range of sources that enable one to understand clearly the issues in the study of ancient Gnosticism and the debates within post-Nag Hammadi Gnostic scholarship.

HARVARD THEOLOGICAL REVIEW

VOLUME 57 OCTOBER 1964 NUMBER 4

GNOSTICISM

ARTHUR DARBY NOCK †

HARVARD UNIVERSITY

[Shortly before his death Professor Nock asked me to arrange publication of the following lecture on Gnosticism (which had been read at the Harvard Divinity School and elsewhere). Of several unfinished lectures and papers he wished it alone to be printed. Anyone who knows his work or who could have seen the mass of material which he had already collected to supplement and annotate this paper will understand the hesitations which such a perfectionist must have overcome in order to authorize its appearance in so incomplete a form. He was clearly preparing to transform it into a major article with full augmentation and reference to other work. Though it remains only a sketch, however, it presents his final evaluation of a subject to which he had devoted frequent attention in articles and reviews for almost forty years. A few months before his death he wrote an important summary of recent work and of his own views on early gentile Christianity as an introduction to the recent paperback reprint of Early Gentile Christianity and Its Hellenistic Background (Harper Torchbooks, 1964). There he said that Gnosticism "may fairly be called the crucial issue today in the study of early Christianity." In his brief discussion the present lecture was evidently very much in his mind.

The lecture existed in two rather ragged copies, each annotated in the margins and each accompanied by a mass of small slips giving further notes and references. Some annotation was illegible, and of the rest very little could be referred usefully to specific discussion in the text. So only notes which Nock himself had written out or which were clearly intended have been included here, along with two or three brief supplements of my own in brackets. I should perhaps add that at the time of his death he had been sifting particularly the material in recent work of Colpe, Duchesne-Guillemin, Scholem, Schwabl, van Unnik, Waszink, and Wilson, but had not yet made use of it. The manuscript contained the concluding note "My warmest thanks are due to my colleagues, Frank M. Cross, Jr., and Helmut Koester, for generous and friendly aid." — Zeph Stewart]

1

1. An adequate discussion of the general theme of Gnosticism would require more than human powers of knowledge and of sympathy. Since my own main concern has been the attempt to understand something of the ethical and religious atmosphere of the Graeco-Roman world, all I shall try to do here is to give my impression of Gnosticism as seen from that point of view.

"Gnosticism," as currently used, denotes a phenomenon belonging to a particular situation in time and place. Nevertheless, it may fairly be related to certain human attitudes and predispositions which are extremely widespread. Three such suggest themselves at once: a preoccupation with the problem of evil, a sense of alienation and recoil from man's environment, and a desire for special and intimate knowledge of the secrets of the universe. Let us look at each of these three psychological factors.

To think of evil as residing in or produced by a specific supernatural power or powers, men do not need a Zoroaster. Ugo Bianchi finds myths of a dualistic stamp among a wide range of primitive peoples.[1] So earlier Paul Radin coined the brilliant phrase, "primitive man as philosopher," and used it as the title for one of his books.[2] Human beings — or at least some individuals in various societies — always ask and have asked the question, "Why?", and sickness and suffering and death are obstinate facts which can easily be thought to call for an explanation. Moreover, for some men, for some groups, evil is a personal, almost an obsessive concern.

Let us pass to the second factor, "a sense of alienation from man's environment." Man is a social animal, and the herd instinct may be thought to be an essential part of his constitution. Yet he remains an individual, not a stereotype. J. H. Driberg remarks:

> Observers have noticed, quite correctly, that there is a greater degree of conformity in a savage community than there is in our own: intellectual or moral rebels, sceptics, moral misfits, are far less frequent an occurrence. But what they have failed to notice is that they do occur.[3]

[1] Especially in his Il Dualismo Religioso: Saggio storico ed etnologico (Rome, 1958).

[2] 2nd ed. (New York, 1957).

[3] The Savage as He Really Is (London, 1929), p. 6.

If even under conditions which put so much of a premium on conformity in action (not, I suppose, in thought) there are rebels, we can be reasonably sure that in addition there are others who, however deeply rooted in their community, do, at least at times, feel a certain sense of estrangement from it. I am not comparing the city of Zenith, as depicted by Sinclair Lewis, with "the heathen in his blindness," but Zenith may serve as a type of a society in which everything makes for conformity and for a sense of satisfaction in conformity. And yet Babbitt, though he would have been a fish out of water if transported to another environment, at times could have said of Zenith, "The world is too much with us." More recently "the lonely crowd" has become a current phrase. In some individuals a sense of alienation is a pose; in some, a seemingly inescapable mood.

Now we come to the third internal factor. At the beginning of his Metaphysics Aristotle set the dictum, "All men naturally desire knowledge." Here we are concerned not with knowledge in general but with what is supposed to be esoteric knowledge. Belief in the existence and special value of such knowledge is a familiar phenomenon, and knowledge is power — at various levels. Let me quote from Franklin Edgerton's remarks:

> To the Hindu mind, "the truth shall make you free." Otherwise there is no virtue in it. This is quite as true of the later systems as of the early and less systematic speculations. To all of them knowledge is a means to an end. This attitude has its roots in a still more primitive belief, which appears clearly in the beginnings of Vedic philosophy and is still very much alive in the early Upaniṣads: the belief in the magic power of knowledge. . . . The Bhagavad Gītā and the later systems agree with the early Upaniṣadic thinkers in their practical attitude towards speculation. They all seek the truth, not because of its abstract interest, but because in some sense or other they think that a realization of the truth about man's place in the universe and his destiny will solve all man's problems . . . in short, bring him to the *summum bonum*, whatever they conceive that to be.[4]

The last words of this quotation are remarkably close to a definition of the Gnostic goal to which we come later.

[4] Bhagavad Gītā, II (Cambridge, 1944), 7f.

2. These three factors are all to be found in the world in which Gnosticism took its rise. The problem of evil had from earliest times concerned poets and thinkers in Greece, and something of their ideas filtered down to a wide public. From the fourth century B.C. some cultivated persons knew the outlines of Persian dualism; [5] further, while the word *daimon* was always neutral and did not have the associations which "demon" has for us,[6] we see under the Roman Empire a distinct tendency to believe in the existence of the *daimones* who are inferior or even evil supernatural beings. Within Judaism evil assumed for many a specific personalized form which we shall consider later. Again, in the hymn closing the Essene Manual of Discipline the words "in the dominion of fear and terror, the place of distress with desolation" [7] show what may fairly be called a sense of estrangement. For such a sense in the Graeco-Roman world one might quote Plato's picture of the philosopher as sheltering under a wall in a driving storm (Rep. 496D), or what Lucretius says of the frustrated lives of some contemporaries (3.1053ff.), or Manilius, "We always act like people about to live, and yet we never live" (4.5). In Greece the motif of the man who has come to hate the human race is as old as Iliad 6.202 (Bellerophon shunning the paths of men). Later we have the legend of Heraclitus (not indeed remote from the fact) and that of Timon. There is also the "inclination to retirement," finely discussed by A. J. Festugière [8]: in this indeed there is no recoil from society but a desire for concentration on inner well-being.

If these may seem slight indications for a sense of estrangement, there is certainly abundant evidence for an interest in esoteric knowledge. Above all, we have the fact that terms for mystery and initiation were freely applied even to rites which were open without reservation to all and which implied no sense of inwardness, not to speak of the more serious use of the terms in meta-

[5] [Nock planned to refer to the introductory chapters of C. Clemen, Religionsgeschichtliche Erklärung des Neuen Testaments (Giessen, 1924²)]

[6] [Nock felt that it might be necessary to modify this statement in view of Hippocrates, Morb. Sacr. 3, as discussed by A. J. Festugière, Les Moines d'Orient, I (Paris, 1961), 25]

[7] M. Burrows, The Dead Sea Scrolls (New York, 1955), p. 386. [1QSx.15]

[8] Personal Religion among the Greeks (Berkeley, 1954), pp. 53ff.

phor. The revival of interest in Pythagoreanism, or what was supposed to be such, provides yet another testimony.

3. From these general considerations we turn now to Gnosticism proper. Let us follow the example of the Odyssey and begin in the middle, in fact towards the end, of the story as a whole. At the beginning of the fourth century of our era the Neoplatonic philosopher Porphyry wrote a Life of Plotinus (to accompany his edition of the master's writings). We read in this (c. 16), "In his time there were many Christians, including sectarians trained in the old philosophy, Adelphius and Aquilinus and their followers. These men possessed a great many writings of Alexander the Libyan and Philocomus and Demostratus and Lydus, and brought forward Revelations of Zoroaster and Zostrianus and Nicotheus and Allogenes and Messos and other such persons. They led many astray, just as they had themselves been led astray, thinking that Plato had not plumbed the depth of Intelligible Being. Accordingly Plotinus in his lectures made many refutations of them and wrote a book to which I gave the title, In Answer to the Gnostics; he left the criticism of other matters (i.e., the details) to us." Porphyry proceeds to say that Amelius produced a work in 40 books against this writing of Zostrianus and that he, Porphyry, had proved the supposed "Zoroaster" to be a fake, composed by the founders of the sect in order to pass off their own ideas under the name of Zoroaster.

Now we possess the book written by Plotinus, with another title, also appropriate and quoted by Porphyry later (c. 24): it is (Enneads 2.9) In Answer to Those who Say that the Creator of the Universe is Evil and that the Universe is Evil. It is an impressive work, starting from first principles and remaining on a high level of discourse. Plotinus does not condescend to name his adversaries (just as later another Neoplatonist, Simplicius, wrote against the Manichees without naming them).[9] Yet clearly he regarded them as constituting a serious menace, even in the highly cultivated society which he addressed, and as being fully conversant with Platonism. In fact, he tells us (§ 10) of people who had encountered this doctrine before becoming his friends and

[9] Comment. in Epicteti Enchiridion, c. 27.

5

who still persisted in their adherence to it: he can do nothing more to win them over, but he is writing for the sake of his disciples. He speaks as a defender of the old philosophy, the Greek tradition which had flowered in Plato. As Richard Harder remarked, it is his only polemical writing.[10]

His argument, in brief, is that these Gnostics think very well of themselves and very ill of the universe. Each of them is a "son of God," superior even to heaven, and without any personal effort, each can apprehend the intelligible world, but they deny to heaven and to the stars a share in immortal soul; they teach that creation results from the fall of Soul; they draw a dramatic picture of terrors in the heavenly spheres and use spells for protection against them (presumably in the soul's ascent after death); they speak of a "strange earth" (should we say a "waste land"?); they bring men to despise the universe and its contents; they fail to produce any doctrine about *arete*, moral excellence; they bid you look towards God, without telling you how to do it; they profess to despise the beauties of this world: they would do well to despise the beauty of boys and women.

What Plotinus says about this menace to right thinking and to right conduct might leave us with the impression that it was an individual deviation from Platonism and not a system of thought with roots in an alien soil. But Porphyry has given us its *Sitz im Leben*.[11]

An earlier pagan reference by name to Gnostics likewise treats them as representing a deviation within Christianity. The True Word of Celsus was an onslaught on the Christian movement as an apostasy from the old tradition and includes a reference to difference within the new community (in Origen, Against Celsus 5.61): "Let no one suppose that I am unaware of the fact that some of them will agree that their God is the same as the God of the Jews, while others will say that their God is a different one,

---

[10] Die Antike 5 (1929), 79.

[11] In Porphyry the term *apokalypsis* ("revelation") as a book title has no known parallel among pagan book titles.

Note that Iamblichus (quoted in Stobaeus, I, 375 Wachsmuth), in listing various explanations of the activities which make the soul descend to earthly life, includes, "according to the Gnostics, madness or a deviation." A. J. Festugière, La Révélation d'Hermès Trismégiste, III (Paris, 1953), 210, n.2, remarks that the precise terms do not occur in Plotin. 2.9.

to whom the God of the Jews is opposed, and that the Son came from their God." Celsus proceeds to mention a third type of those who distinguish between *psychikoi* and *pneumatikoi* (people with soul and people with supersoul) and to tell of some who profess to be *gnostikoi*.

Accordingly, Gnostics, as seen through pagan eyes, were Christians of a kind, with a claim to intellectuality, with a passionate dualism, and with an extreme anthropocentricity. The term appears frequently in the Church Fathers and today serves to cover a wide range of groups sharing certain general features, a conglomerate which, like Puritanism, has for all its diversities a certain unity as seen from the outside.

What did the term *Gnostikoi* connote and suggest? Greek words are protean, and to transliterate them is liable to involve what Whitehead is quoted as calling "the fallacy of misplaced concreteness." The modern use of *kerygma* for "Apostolic Teaching" is a case in point. *Gnosis* is a verbal noun related to *gignosko*, "know," and applicable to any kind of apprehending or knowledge. In the Old Testament "to know God" is primarily to acknowledge what God has done for man and to man and to acknowledge what man owes to God in the way of obedience. As Frank M. Cross, Jr., remarks, the opposite is adultery, injustice, murder, etc. Cross further observes that in Qumran texts knowledge includes knowledge of what God is about to do and of proceedings in the Heavenly Council, and is increasingly eschatological. In Christian usage the noun had a wide range of meaning. Thus in the early prayer-type preserved in the Teaching of the Twelve Apostles (10.2) there is thanksgiving "for the knowledge and faith and immortality which thou didst make known to us through Jesus thy servant": here *gnosis* is the Gospel message. But it could also denote something esoteric, as in 1 Cor. 13:2, "if I have the gift of prophecy and understand all secrets and all *gnosis*." In either sense it was a gift. Earlier, on the question of meat that had been offered to idols (8:1), Paul conceded to the Corinthians, "We know that we all have *gnosis*," but warned them, "*gnosis* puffs up, but love builds up." This *gnosis* was not in substance incorrect, like the "falsely called *gnosis*" of 1 Tim. 6:20, some decades later, but it was a privilege which carried with it

7

the danger of spiritual pride. The Second Epistle to the Corinthians shows how anxious Paul was to avoid boasting: for him, as for Philo, any goodness of man is God's gift, not his achievement. So there was peril in taking or accepting *Gnostikoi*, which was new as a description of persons, as a sobriquet for your group. And yet we must remember that Clement of Alexandria did not, for all his modesty, shrink from using *gnostikos* as his term for the enlightened Christian.[12]

4. If we are to understand the development of early Christianity, we must always bear in mind its diversified Jewish background. In fact, the contribution of Greek thought to Christianity in its first hundred years came primarily through Hellenistic Judaism. The teaching of Jesus had its roots in a Palestinian culture of mainly Semitic speech, but teaching about the Christ had its roots largely in Greek-speaking Judaism such as we know primarily at Alexandria.

It was the duty of a Jew not only to observe the Law but also to study its meaning.[13] Not all were capable of study, and this fact could easily lead to a distinction between an élite and the masses — and perhaps especially among Hellenized Jews, for whom the highest insights of philosophers were to be found in Scripture by the methods of exegesis. For the masses a plain conformity to the letter of Scripture was enough, a Pass standard — but others went out for Honors. We see this in Philo, who in fact had to protest against the attitude of those who held that if they knew the inner meaning of the Law, they were dispensed from observance of its literal commands — a point of view which in a sense anticipates the antinomian tendencies of some Christian Gnostics. In Palestine, indeed, study was largely directed to Law as law, and the "ignorant of the land" were primarily those who did not know and observe its niceties. Yet there were those who deemed that they could avail themselves of special insights on other themes — notably the Essenes, who are so much better known since the discovery of the Qumran Scrolls.

In fact, Jerusalem and Alexandria were very far from presenting

[12] E.g., Strom. 4.21 (II, 305, line 21 Stählin). But he can object to people calling themselves *gnostikoi*: Paedagog. 1.6 (I, 121, line 9 Stählin).
[13] See G. F. Moore, Judaism, II (Cambridge, 1927), 239.

a neat antithesis. In the Judaism of both, Torah (the Biblical revelation which included Law but was far from being confined to it) was central, and (apart from matters which concerned only Palestine) the interpretation of the Law in practice may well have been very similar. Nevertheless, at the reflective and imaginative level there would appear to have been a marked contrast.

The Jews in Alexandria and up country in Egypt abhorred the worships of both Greeks and Egyptians no less than the prophets had abhorred Semitic paganism, but they found some Greek philosophy acceptable and in fact congenial. The Book of Wisdom (9:15) echoes Phaedo 81C, "For a perishable body weighs down the soul, and the earthy tabernacle is a burden to the thoughtful mind." In Philo the influence of Platonism is pervasive, and such approximation as he shows to dualism lies primarily in the contrast of body and soul (or mind). To be sure, when speaking of the two powers, the salutary and the destructive, which enter into every soul at its birth, he says, "Through these powers the world too was created" (Q. Ex. 1.23, tr. R. Marcus, II, 33); but in general his attitude towards the universe might be summed up in the text, "God saw everything that he had made, and, behold, it was very good" (Gen. 1:31). For him Adam's fall is not the tragic episode "wherewith the Face of Man is blacken'd," but a type of the enslavement of the senses by desire and of mind by the senses (Q. Gen. 1.47f.), and "evil angels" receive a moralistic interpretation (Gig. 17). Might one not say that for Philo there were temptations but no supernatural Tempter? Again, much as he discourses on abstractions and hypostases (e.g., the Wisdom and the Word of God), he shows no mythopoeic faculty.

In Palestine, indeed, the Greek language and Greek institutions were all around in the environment, and the higher gifts carried by the Greek language were, no doubt, not entirely lacking. Here too there was an element of dualism in the view taken of the human situation. In each man there was the good impulse and the evil impulse; the latter was not absolutely evil and was in any event, like the former, a creation of God. Attention has been drawn to the use of "flesh" and "flesh of evil" as found in the Qumran texts. In the Old Testament "flesh" is, at worst, man in his creaturely mortal quality. At Qumran "flesh" is sometimes used in a disparaging way, but the real antithesis is, I understand, between the personal warring Spirits of Truth and Perversion. Palestinian dualism is essentially supernatural and eschatological, not human and psychological.

Earlier Judaism had known of evil spirits, but they had no separate organization. Now there emerges the idea of a Satanic order, under its variously named head. Its principalities and powers had been, like all else, created in the beginning by God, but they had become an opposition which cast its shadow over the world which, for the time being, it dominated. For the time being, yes: and this may serve to introduce one more contrast. Among my memories of childhood is the confident and reassuring way in which the choir sang after each Psalm, "As it was in the beginning, is now, and ever shall be: world without end. Amen." This might represent Philo's prevailing mood. He can dream of a good time coming in which there will be universal peace and enmity will disappear from the animal world and from men;[14] but that is not one of the ideas to which his mind reverts, any more than is the hope which he mentions of the homecoming of the Jews from the Dispersion and of the humbling of their enemies. In Palestine, on the other hand, Pharisees and Essenes alike awaited a dramatic divine event, and so did probably many of the Jews who might be called theologically uncommitted. There would be war and tribulation, to be followed by a new order fulfilling the "hope of Israel."

Daniel claimed to have seen the court of Heaven, and subsequent Apocalyptic was by no means limited to the foretelling of what was to be:[15] so in 1 Enoch we have elaborate disquisitions on the heavenly bodies, the calendar, the winds, their portals, the rivers, the islands. Apocalyptic writing was esoteric as well as prophetic and dualistic. So are the Scrolls, with their emphasis on knowledge "as a revealed, especially eschatological knowledge."[16] We had known earlier from Josephus (B.J. 2.142) that the names of the angels were a secret which Essenes must on

[14] See Class. Philol. 43 (1948), 124 [in Nock's review of W. L. Knox, Some Hellenistic Elements in Primitive Christianity].

[15] On Jonah cf. Strack-Billerbeck, Kommentar zum Neuen Testament, I, 646.

[16] F. M. Cross, Jr., The Ancient Library of Qumran (rev. ed. New York, 1961), p. 207.

no account divulge to outsiders. All this is very much to the point for our approach to Gnosticism.

Further, what later crystallized as normative Judaism regarded certain parts of Scripture as unsuited for study by immature minds.[17] One was Ezekiel's vision of the Chariot, and another was the story of Creation. To be sure, Sirach 49:8 does not hesitate to speak of the former, and Josephus and Philo alike indicate that as to the latter no such caution was observed in the first century of our era. Now, if we look at the speculations associated with Gnostic sects, it is remarkable how many of them could be explained as arising from reflection upon the early chapters of Genesis. What was God doing during the unnumbered ages before creation? Again, "Let us make man" might suggest that two or more Powers were actively concerned. Then there is the first making of man by God in his own image, and "male and female," which in Rabbinic thought was repeatedly interpreted as the making of an original androgynous Adam;[18] then the second forming of man from the dust of the ground, God's breathing into his nostrils the breath of life, and the making of woman from Adam's rib. This God is a jealous God, who does not wish man to eat of the tree of the knowledge of good and evil, and the wise serpent plays a role slightly like that of Prometheus. After the eating of "that forbidden fruit" there is the shame which Adam and Eve feel at their nakedness, and the ordinance of childbearing with its accompanying curse of pain.

Before we continue with the Genesis story, let me remind you that in several noncanonical Sayings of the Lord a promise is attached to the time when the distinction of sex disappears, or when people doff their clothing and are unashamed (a precept which the Adamiani put into practice), or again when women cease bearing children. What is involved is precisely the restoration of the original conditions of Paradise.[19]

Returning to Genesis, we have thereafter Cain and Abel (and Cain could be and was represented as the worthy rebel); the

---

[17] See H. Loewe in Enc. of Rel. and Eth. VII, 622; and for an interesting example, L. Wallach, JBL 65 (1946), 393 ff.

[18] See L. Ginzberg, The Legends of the Jews (Philadelphia, 1910–38), V, 88 f.

[19] See Hennecke-Schneemelcher, Neutestamentliche Apokryphen, I (1959³), 111, and parallels in the Gospel of Thomas.

11

mysterious Seth and Enos and Enoch — Enoch who walked with
God and must have known secrets veiled from mankind in general; the sons of God who mated with the daughters of men; and
finally the Flood as an act of vengeful Divinity.

Apart from Genesis, an outstanding contribution of the Old
Testament and of intertestamental literature to the thought-
world of Gnosticism was the personification of Wisdom as a Power
of God, capable of assuming the role of an independent coadjutor
in creation and that of a factor in the higher life of men: so we
read in the Book of Wisdom, "In every generation she passes into
holy souls and makes them friends of God and prophets" (7:27,
RSV), and, what is more to our purpose, "She showed him ('a
righteous man,' Jacob) the kingdom of God and gave him knowledge of holy things (or 'holy men' — the angels seen on the
ladder)" (10:10). Of no less importance was the development of
angelology. The marshalled opposition of the fallen angels has
been mentioned.[20] On the other hand, Ezekiel stimulated speculation on the court of Heaven, as it remained without the rebels;
as Prof. Cross informs me, the angels were described at Qumran
as "knowers" and "spirits of knowledge."

5. We have considered some elements in Judaism which may
be thought to have contributed to the formation of Gnosticism.
Let us now turn to possible Greek components. Simone Pétrement, who has done ample justice to the Jewish substratum, has
nevertheless described Gnosticism as "un platonisme roman-
tique," [21] for which we might at times be tempted to substitute
"Platonism run wild." We saw how the Book of Wisdom echoed
Plato's idea of the soul as weighed down by a mortal body. Plato
had also spoken of the soul as immortal and as in bondage in the
body. He had again (Theaet. 176A) said that evils inevitably
hover about mortal nature and the earth, wherefore we ought to
try to escape hence to the dwelling of the gods as quickly as possible, and to escape is to become like God, so far as this is possible.
Further (Polit. 269E) he had raised the possibility that the uni-

[20] References in the Psalms to rulers who are hostile to God may have helped
to shape the picture of the "rulers of this world" as we see it in Paul. Cf. R. M.
Grant, Gnosticism and Early Christianity (New York, 1959), pp. 62f.

[21] Le Dualisme chez Platon, les Gnostiques et les Manichéens (Paris, 1947),
p. 129.

verse revolves under the control of two deities opposed to each other. Herein lay marked possibilities of dualism, and our present concern is not with what Plato meant, but with what he could suggest to other men centuries after his death. So again, few sayings echoed in men's minds more than, "To discover the Maker and Father of this universe is a task, and after discovering him it is impossible to tell of him to all men" (Tim. 28C).[22] Posterity evolved the idea of a remote Supreme Being, a *deus absconditus*, wholly separated from phenomena and not to be described save by the *via negativa*.

6. After this somewhat lengthy Preface to Gnosticism, let us now consider a Valentinian definition of *gnosis*: "What liberates us is not only baptism but also the knowledge of who we were, what we have become, where we were or into what we have been thrown, whither we are hurrying, whence we are being ransomed, what is birth, what is rebirth. . . ." (Clem. Alex., Exc. Theod. 78). If you subtract from this "into what we have been thrown," "are being ransomed," "birth," and "rebirth," the residuum is close to the demands which moral philosophy in the pagan world could make of its hearers. But the additions are crucial. This is a diagnosis, but in terms outside of human life; and this is a remedy, for those who can take it.

Do we find pagan analogies for the Gnostic doctrines as described by Irenaeus and others and as presented in our new original sources? Certainly not in Plutarch's work Concerning Isis and Osiris, which has been adduced in this connexion. Plutarch does indeed there represent knowledge, above all knowledge (so far as it is attainable) of the divine, as the highest blessing: yearning for truth is yearning for divinity (351E). Yes, but the ideal is precisely that of Aristotle: "The life according to the intellect is divine in comparison with human life. . . . We ought, so far as it is possible, to put ourselves on the plane of immortality" (Eth. Nic. 10.1177b30ff.). The knowledge of which Plutarch speaks is not esoteric or revealed; it is something to which the individual reason, aided by the deity, can attain (352C; cf. 374E, 378C). Above all, it is an end and not a means. In the

---

[22] [On some of the problems posed by the interpretation of this passage see A. D. Nock, Vig. Chr. 16 (1962), 79ff.]

body and in the soul of the universe the evil element is fighting the better (371B); but the myths are an expression of this, not an explanation. In this context Plutarch never leaves the plane of reverent reflective reason.

We are nearer to Gnosticism in the so-called Chaldaic Oracles, a collection of abstruse utterances in verse put together under Marcus Aurelius and probably expanded later. Unlike the Sibylline texts, they include no prophecies, but consist of revelations about the scheme of things and man's deliverance. We have only citations, but it is hard to see how the work, even when intact, cast such a spell over later Neoplatonists. According to these Oracles, man's soul is imprisoned in the body under the spell of drunkenness and forgetfulness (44–56 Kroll). In this condition it is subject to Fate and to the power of daimonic evil, but can be delivered by purifications and by rituals which raise men up. There was a technique which compelled supernatural beings to appear. The Oracles show a deep concern for man's plight, a pronounced dualism, a vulgarized Platonism, and a preoccupation with esoteric knowledge. Jewish influence is possible, but there is no Fall, no cosmic prehistory of the present state of things, and no prospect of any end to it. The picture of the universe in terms of a complicated structure of abstractions suggests Gnostic schemes, but the differences mentioned remain.

It is natural to turn next to the Hermetica, a literature composed in Greek in Egypt under the name which was the equivalent of Thoth, the scribe of the gods and the reputed author of the sacred literature preserved in the temples and containing ritual and astronomical lore. There were Greek Hermetica concerned with astrology and similar matters, but here we need consider only a number of dialogues and other works giving in the guise of revelation popular Greek philosophy (principally watered Platonism) with an admixture of Jewish elements. There are tractates with a monistic and optimistic world view, together with others which are dualistic and pessimistic in character; it is likely that those who treasured and preserved the literature did not notice these distinctions: all was revelation.

Three treatises may be mentioned. Firstly the Kore Kosmou (probably meaning "pupil of the eye of the universe") gives a

complicated account of the making of the universe and of man
(IV, 1–22 Festugière-Nock). There are constant echoes of the
Timaeus, but this is a dialogue of divinities in Egypt and not of
gentlemen at Athens, and there are dark shadows across the cosmic landscape: the inquisitiveness and willfulness of the souls
when participating in the work of creation (§ 24), their punishment by imprisonment in bodies, their subsequent lamentation,
audacity, and wrongdoing on the face of the earth (§ 53). Festugière has shown how the author of the work in its present shape
has blended various elements, including perhaps the story of the
Fallen Angels as we know it from 1 Enoch.[23] The work displays
far more sense of drama than of structure or purpose, and ends,
not with any message of deliverance, here or in the hereafter, from
the human predicament as such, but with the ending of lawless
disorder through the coming of Osiris and Isis (§ 64–): they are
praised in the now traditional style as the bringers of the blessings
of civilization.

The Poimandres, the first tractate in the Corpus Hermeticum,
is of a different character. Here too we have a creation story, and
here too there is willfulness on the part of a subordinate power,
the bisexual Primal Man. But there is also a Fall — a Fall of
Primal Man, who sinks into the embrace of Nature, and this Fall
explains the condition of present-day ordinary man, with his union
of the immortal and the mortal. Here, indeed, there is no cosmic
restoration of lost radiance: there is a Revealer, not a Redeemer;
and the individual, with the aid of Mind, can deliver himself here
and pass into divinity forever hereafter by awakening from
drunkenness and sleep, and by self-knowledge. Moreover, he can
help others to do likewise. This strange document, with its un-
mistakable Jewish element (including the song of the Powers, i.e.,
angels, to be heard by the soul after its ascent), as also the
thirteenth tractate, with its verbal sacrament of rebirth, somehow
conveys an impression of deep seriousness. The vision reads as if
it were an experience and not a fiction — the experience of a man
who, as he says, wanted "to learn about things that exist, to
understand their nature, and to know God," in other words, to
find through revelation what the sages had sought to fathom.

[23] In Hermès Trismégiste, III (Paris, 1954), clxxvii–ccxix.

Let me add that Hermetic treatises were found in the Coptic library to be considered later, just as were works of Allogenes, Messos, and Zostrianus — names mentioned by Porphyry (p. 259 above).[24] In point of fact, Hermetic writings enjoyed the favor of middle-of-the-road Christians also. This Egyptian god, like the Sibyl, was cited as a prehistoric witness from the outside to the truths of revealed religion, and while almost all the extant Sibyllina are Jewish or Christian compositions, the Hermetica quoted till the fifth century are, save Frag. 21, not influenced by Christianity. Again, the prayer ending the Poimandres was included in a Christian collection; our papyrus copy is assigned on grounds of script to the end of the third century.[25]

7. The Essenes held that the "Teacher of Righteousness" had received authority to reveal "the final phase of the end which was not made known to the prophet Habakkuk himself";[26] he "opened up the meaning of the ancient Scriptures."[27] His community continued to search the Scriptures: new light might come at any moment. So in the Synoptic Gospels no element is clearer than that Jesus expounded to his chosen band of disciples the secrets of the Kingdom of Heaven. The multitude might hear the parables, but the disciples were given the interpretation. "Many prophets and righteous men have desired to see those things which ye see, and have not seen them; and to hear those things which ye hear, and have not heard them" (Matt. 13:17).

In the succeeding Apostolic Age this consciousness of the possession of special revelation was reinforced by the belief that the Spirit of God was poured out on the community: "Your young men shall see visions and your old men shall dream dreams" (Acts 2:17). In considering this crucial period we are primarily concerned with the Apostle Paul, both for his teaching and for what he has to tell us about the communities which he had founded and which he sought to guide.

marked, "If Paul had ever had to get up his own theology for
Paul's whole way of thinking was complex. As John Lowe re-

---

[24] See J. Doresse, "Hermès et la Gnose," Novum Testamentum 1 (1956), 57.

[25] See Hermès Trismégiste, I (Paris, 1945), xxxvii.

[26] Quoted by K. Stendahl, The Scrolls and the New Testament (New York, 1957), p. 12.

[27] F. M. Cross, Jr., op. cit. (note 16), p. 160.

examination purposes, he might have produced a unified system
of Paulinism easier for us to grasp. Fortunately he left the whole
wonderful muddle unarranged and alive; we are the richer for
it." [28] Now Paul shows a pronounced dualism in two ways, in the
constant contrast of flesh and spirit as two planes of existence, and
in his overpowering conviction of the reality and activity of
(supernatural) principalities and powers: the human agents of
Calvary and in the opposition to the Gospel were but their instruments. He can speak of "the god of this world" (2 Cor. 4:4) —
bold language, which could be misunderstood. Paul's Christ had
taken our flesh and borne the lot of human servitude, but essentially he belonged to the heavenly places and not to Nazareth.
As for the Mosaic code, to him, as to Jesus, it was a second best:
"From the beginning it was not so" (Matt. 19:8). Further, he believed himself to have entered the third heaven and to have heard
"words that must not pass the lips, words that no man may utter"
(2 Cor. 12:4), and he had his high doctrine for which he did not
think the Corinthians were yet ready. Revelation had gone to
their heads, as it had to those of the Thessalonians, with their misunderstandings about the Resurrection, and to those of the Colossians, with their penchant for abstruse angelology.

Paul's sturdy moral sense and his passionate pastoral responsibility kept things in balance for him, but not for disciples such
as those. Moreover, while the imminence of the divine event
which should bring down the curtain on the drama of human history seems to wane a little during the short time span covered by
his writing, he had it always in his mind. After his death the
eagles gathered around Jerusalem, and the Temple was destroyed,
but the end was not yet. For the readjustment of Christians to
the situation we have evidence in the Epistle to the Hebrews: it
was no doubt gradual, but there was a change in things.[29] I do
not believe that the waning of the eschatological expectation was
a principal factor in the emergence of Gnosticism, for the raw
materials were all there before 70 A.D., but unquestionably it
added a new impetus.[30]

[28] JTS 42 (1941), 142.
[29] Cf. Matt. 25:1–13, with the remarks of A. Strobel, Novum Testamentum 2
(1958), 199 ff.
[30] [In this paragraph Nock had in mind the discussion of H. J. Schoeps, Paulus

8. We can picture the Christians of this time as decidedly isolated. If of Jewish origin, they were mostly now cut off from their own people and regarded as apostates; if of Gentile origin, they were set apart from the ordinary pleasures and small change of society, and they were liable to be looked on as very strange individuals, even stranger than those who had become Jewish proselytes, since proselytes were at least a known if not a popular type. This situation could easily lead some to an extreme concentration of interest on their religion. In the beginning its adherents numbered "not many wise men according to worldly standards" (1 Cor. 1:26). Later, men of cultivation came to be found in their ranks. Such men would be acquainted with what Festugière has called the spiritual *koine* of the time,[31] and some of them could hardly help finding questions rise in their minds.[32] Whence did evil arise? Why did the universe have so grave an imperfection? — to echo the language of Lucretius (5.199) in answer to those who believed that it was divinely made. How could the Supreme Being be himself the actual creator? How could he be directly linked to the world of the senses? Again, could a supernatural being literally assume our flesh and blood, accept the polluting embrace of matter, and physically suffer and die? What of the problems, mentioned earlier, in Genesis? What of the character ascribed to God in numerous other passages of the Old Testament? How was the supposedly divine origin of the Mosaic Law to be reconciled with the death of Jesus under the Law and with the teachings of Jesus and Paul? Why did some people receive the Gospel and others not? Even among those who did receive it why was there so great an apparent difference in spiritual capacity? What was the higher self (in those who were deemed to have a higher self) and what was it doing down here? Were the elect, after regeneration and enlightenment, obligated

---

(Tübingen, 1959), esp. pp. 102 and 121; Eng. ed. (London, 1961), pp. 103f. and 120f. Cf. also Nock's review of Schoeps, Gnomon 33 (1961), 581–90.]

[31] La Révélation d'Hermès Trismégiste II (Paris, 1949), p. 345.

[32] [In connection with these questionings Nock would have quoted and discussed the passage of Augustine on the Manichees (De Agone Christiano 1.4 = Augustini Opera, VI, 293, in Migne edition [Paris, 1841]): eligunt capitula de Scripturis, quae simplices homines non intelligunt; et per illa decipiunt animas imperitas, quaerendo unde sit malum (i.e., Rectores harum tenebrarum, et spiritualia nequitiae in coelestibus).]

by the ordinary rules of humdrum morality? Alternatively, should they renounce what seemed, in moderation, harmless enjoyments? Finally, were some of their own religious insights to be found under the trappings of pagan myth? If the Old Testament could be and had to be allegorized if it was to be accepted, why should not pagan myth be looked at in the same way, if God had "left not himself without witness?" [33] There was a further stimulus to the imagination in the tradition preserved in Acts 1:3 that the risen Jesus was visible to the Apostles for forty days and told them of the Kingdom of God. What might he have told them?

There were such questions which called for an answer. There was also the fact of religious lyricism: "When you come together, each one has a hymn, a lesson, a revelation, a tongue, or an interpretation" (1 Cor. 14:26, RSV). Such hymns, however artless, would inevitably develop a language of imagery which outran any such rudimentary formulations of doctrine as existed here or there. Is not this the background of much in the Epistles of Ignatius? Hymnology may sometimes lie behind theology, rather than vice versa.

In any event, what we call Gnosticism seems to me to be the aggregate of a series of individualistic responses to the religious situation — the responses, moreover, of men who in many cases cannot have thought of themselves as in any way deviationist. The crystallization of what came to be orthodoxy was a gradual process, a progressive elimination of ideas which proved unacceptable. It has been remarked that Valentinus seems to have stated his views without being in any way polemical. May not his personal scheme of thought have been originally an interpretation for those capable of receiving it, like the doctrine which Paul would not give to the Corinthians? So J. Scherer says of Origen: "Il est constant qu'il considérait une partie de son enseignement comme réservée à une élite d'esprits particulièrement exercés dans les problèmes religieux." [34]

Something will be said shortly about the Gospel of Truth, which

---

[33] Acts 14:17.
[34] Entretien d'Origène avec Héraclide (Sources Chrétiennes No. 67 [Paris, 1960]), p. 39.

is almost certainly the work of Valentinus. Here let me quote from its epilogue: "May the rest (of men) understand, therefore, in their places, that it beseems me not, having been in the place of rest, to say any more." [35] He had had his vision of Paradise. As an innovator in religion, he perhaps traveled farther than he knew he was traveling, and his second and final exclusion from the Roman community was likely to intensify this development. But he had qualities from which even Tertullian could not withhold a grudging tribute.

9. In considering the Gnostic answers to such questions as have been suggested, answers which often took the form of constructed myths and represented the world process in psychological terms, we had till recently only two early original documents of the movement, and we depended otherwise on the evidence of works written to confute its manifestations. The discovery in Egypt, the land where, incidentally, Gnosticism flourished and proliferated most, of a jar containing upwards of forty works in excellent condition was a most welcome surprise.[36] It should indeed be said in justice to Irenaeus, Hippolytus, and Epiphanius that we are still indebted to them for the anatomy of Gnosticism. They give us the bone structure; the new texts put much more flesh on it. This find represents a library, a collection comprising more than one school or type of thought. E. de Faye has remarked that between Gnostic sects there was a very active exchange of ideas and books.[37] So the alchemist Zosimus quotes Hermes and the supposed Zoroaster and above all Nicotheus [38] with a comprehensive hospitality like that of the Naassenes or of modern Theosophists. It will be some time before the new texts are all available in translation, but what is already at our disposal is remarkable.

Thus the Gospel of Truth proves to be not a narrative but a homiletic meditation addressed to a specific audience. The title employs the original meaning of the word *euangelion*, "good

---

[35] 42:39ff., K. Grobel, The Gospel of Truth (New York, 1960), p. 198.

[36] See J. Doresse, The Secret Books of the Egyptian Gnostics (New York, 1960).

[37] Gnostiques et Gnosticisme (Paris, 1925²), p. 490.

[38] His theology includes a bold development of the parallelism in Paul of Adam and Christ.

tidings," linked to specific happenings but not to their presentation in a biographic framework. Briefly, the theme is humanity's deliverance from its plight. It had been befogged and imprisoned, as though in a sleep haunted by dreadful nightmares of frustration. This description of the state of man has various parallels; but here there is a special explanation, the activity of Error, *Plane* — an abstraction having here at times the status of a "mythological person with a history of her own."[39] Error was in a fog concerning the father and sought to entice "Those-of-the-middle" — probably those who were of soul and not of spirit or of matter (17:29ff.; Grobel, p. 46). Deliverance comes not simply, as in the Poimandres, through moral exhortation and self-knowledge. It comes as a result of the historical suffering of Jesus on the Cross, a datum of vital importance to Valentinus even as to Paul. For Paul this suffering was the work of "the rulers of this world" (1 Cor. 2:8); for Valentinus it was the work of Error. The Good News meant the revelation of "the secret mystery; Jesus the Christ, through whom it has illumined those who by reason of Forgetting were in the darkness; it illumined them. It gave them a Way, and the Way is the Truth which it showed them. Because of this, *Plane* was enraged at it; she persecuted it: she was endangered by it and brought to nought; he was nailed to a tree" (18:15ff.; Grobel, p. 50). Furthermore, for Valentinus, as for Paul, deliverance comes from God the Father through the Son, or, as in the Fourth Gospel, through the Logos, or again through the Holy Spirit. The Supreme Being is not uninterested, let alone hostile. The only essential difference from Paul is that salvation is not from sin but from ignorance. Man returns to himself, like the Prodigal Son "coming to himself" (Luke 15:17, a normal idiom). Even so, repentance in the sense of "returning" is stressed (Grobel, p. 161, commenting on 35:23), and there is a strong insistence on the duty of having an ethical concern for others (Grobel, pp. 139, 141, commenting on 33:1). To judge from this work, which is full of echoes of the New Testament, Valentinus was at this time very close to the central tradition.

A sharp contrast in content is presented by the Gospel according to Thomas, which is a collection of Sayings of the Lord, in-

[39] Grobel, op. cit., p. 24.

cluding much that is familiar from the Synoptics, with variants in
the wording, as well as the Logia familiar from three Oxyrhynchus papyri and other Sayings previously known from quotations
as "winged words." [40] All the Sayings, the traditional and the
bizarre alike, are presented as "the secret words which the Living
Jesus spoke and Didymus Judas Thomas wrote." In the text as
it stands there is nothing about the resurrection of believers, and
the Kingdom is mainly present rather than future, but something
is still to happen (no. 111), and the disciples do not yet have full
vision (no. 37). Further, if the moral virtues are not stressed,
neither are they ignored (nos. 6, 14, 39).[41]

The relation of these and other new texts to the New Testament
seems to me to vindicate completely the traditional view of
Gnosticism as Christian heresy with roots in speculative thought.
Tertullian coupled heretics and philosophers as both concerned
with the same questions, "Whence is evil and why? Whence is
man and how?" To these he says Valentinus added, "Whence is
God?" (Praescr. haer. 7). We should make two additions. First,
much of the earliest of this "heresy" probably revolved around
varieties of Judaism and around reaction to Judaism. If the God
of the Law was the God of Creation, and if you rejected the Law,
might it not be that creation was a bad thing? Popular inklings of
Platonism would come to the support of this idea. Secondly, as
has been indicated, this "heresy" arose at a time when orthodoxy
had not yet taken shape by conflict and contrast.

Outside the Christian orbit we have seen in the Hermetica a
fusion of Platonism and Judaism which produced a scheme of
individual redemption without a personal redeemer and without
any final cosmic conclusion repairing the original fault (such a
conclusion as after all Manichaeism still provided). At this
point something must be said, however tentative it must necessarily be, about Simon Magus. The evidence of Justin Martyr
makes it clear that he was a figure of far more importance than
a casual reader of the Acts of the Apostles would suppose, though

[40] Edited by Guillaumont, Puech, Quispel, Till, Masīḥ (New York, 1959);
another translation in J. Doresse, The Secret Books . . . , and in R. M. Grant,
The Secret Sayings of Jesus (New York, 1960).

[41] [At this point Nock planned to make use of B. Gärtner, The Theology of
the Gospel according to Thomas (New York, 1961).]

even such a reader would remark that Simon is represented as active in Samaria before his contact with representatives of the Christian movement and as making claims at that time — which were amply accepted — to some sort of superhuman status. Palestine was at this time characterized by a religious ferment in which John the Baptizer bulked large, and various figures who professed to be prophetic leaders found a ready hearing.[42] The story in John 4 of the woman at the well in Samaria is distinctly suggestive. The tradition that Simon later said that God (with whom he identified himself) had appeared among the Jews as Son, had descended in Samaria as Father, and had come among the Gentiles as Holy Spirit may represent an attempt on his part to overtrump Christian claims after he became familiar with them. So, later, Mandaeism developed in opposition to Christianity.

10. But, you may ask, what of *die Gnosis*, as it is postulated by so many scholars today? What of the idea that not a few of Paul's converts succumbed to the lure of this supposedly rival movement? The plain truth is that you could not have found anyone in Corinth to direct you to a Gnostic church: the overwhelming probability is that there was no such thing.[43] It is at most possible that here (as certainly happened in Colossae) individual Christians came from or came into contact with esoteric Judaism.[44] The quasi-monastic Therapeutai described by Philo in his work On the Contemplative Life may very well have stemmed from the Essenes, and Apollos, an Alexandrian Jew who is described in Acts 18:24 as "a learned (so, rather than 'eloquent') man, well versed in the scriptures" and who had his special adherents at Corinth, may have come from this background. Be it added that Paul urged him to return to Corinth and cannot have objected to the content of his teaching. That is as far as I can go.[45]

[42] See Grant, op. cit., (note 20), p. 92.
[43] [See W. Schmithals, Die Gnosis in Korinth, FRLANT, NF 48 (Göttingen, 1956).] For excellent critiques of the Bultmann-Schmithals hypothesis see S. Pétremont, Revue de Métaphysique et de Morale 65 (1960), 385ff., and Joh. Munck, Stud. Theol. 15 (1961), 181ff.
[44] See W. D. Davies in K. Stendahl, The Scrolls and the New Testament, pp. 166ff.
[45] Corinth and Colossae were not like Rome and Alexandria, where any eccentricity might have had its representative cosmopolitan centers.

An eminent historian has been quoted as suggesting that there is a certain analogy between Gnosticism and existentialism, a mode of thought which can, it is said, be combined with points of view ranging from Catholicism to outright atheism. I should say that in general apart from the Christian movement there was a Gnostic way of thinking, but no Gnostic system of thought with its "place in the sun"; a mythopoeic faculty, but no specific Gnostic myth. Certainly it is an unsound proceeding to take Manichaean and other texts, full of echoes of the New Testament, and reconstruct from them something supposedly lying back of the New Testament.[46] So, with the rarest exceptions, it was the emergence of Jesus and of the belief that he was a supernatural being who had appeared on earth which precipitated elements previously suspended in solution. And at Corinth and elsewhere we have to reckon also with misunderstandings of Paul's teaching, for which there would have been no little excuse.

Gnosticism had its antecedents in Judaism and in Greek thought. As for the rest of the Near East, any contribution which Persia made was at second hand, as mediated through Greek and Jewish channels. The suggestion that the story of the imprisonment or that of the Fall of Wisdom, puzzling as it is, derived from the temporary misfortunes of Inanna or Ishtar seems to me eminently improbable.

Gnosticism was to have a long history, and for centuries it appealed to a great many individuals and produced a luxuriant abundance of schemes which I find incomprehensible in detail. Early Valentinianism has its complexities, but has also a certain charm and freshness. Some of the late developments convey a curious impression of auto-intoxication. Nevertheless, the temper of Gnosticism has reappeared in Judaism and Islam as well as in Christianity; it has even been maintained that there are analogies in psychoanalytic theory. The weakness of the Gnostic sects in Christian antiquity is, as Nilsson says, that they were broken up and unorganized.[47] Only with Mani, who had undeniable genius

---

[46] Ignatius, Eph. 19, on the star which appeared in the heavens and destroyed the operations of magic, etc., may, as has been suggested, give a story anterior to that of the Magi and the star. But Ignatius lived at a time when early floating material existed.

[47] Geschichte der Griechischen Religion, II (Munich, 1961²), 622.

and who, by the way, at the beginning of every letter called himself "Apostle of Jesus Christ," did such ideas find expression in a church — and it indeed spread as far as China. Against the individualism of the Gnostics stood the growing strength of episcopal organization, the idea of an apostolic succession of doctrine, and the formation of the Canon of the New Testament.

An historian should not, I believe, express value judgments, but it is hard to withhold admiration for the robust common sense of Irenaeus, with his insistence that people do not need to trouble themselves with unanswerable questions: leave them to Heaven.[48] In the last analysis, the Gnostics in general did not realize the truth contained in the remark of a Catholic priest, Robert Hugh Benson, "An immense agnosticism must be an element in every creed." [49]

[48] Adv. Haer. 2.41 (I, 349 and 351 Harvey). A similar attitude ascribed to Daniel Stylites in the anonymous Life: A. J. Festugière, op. cit. (note 6), II, 156f.

[49] Confessions of a Convert (London, 1913), p. 152.

I mention as well a passage (apropos of King Lear) from a letter which John Keats wrote to his brother George in December, 1817 (cited by Philip Wheelwright, Heraclitus [Princeton Univ. Press, 1959], p. 118): "It struck me what quality went to form a man of achievement, especially in literature, and which Shakespeare possesses so enormously. I mean *negative capability*; that is, when a man is capable of being in uncertainties, mysteries, doubts, without any irritable reaching after fact and reason."

Pre-Christian Gnosticism, the New Testament and Nag Hammadi in recent debate

Edwin Yamauchi

Dr Yamauchi, professor of history at Miami University in Oxford, Ohio, is chairman of the Insititute for Biblical Research, the American counterpart of the Tyndale Fellowship for Biblical and Theological Research. This article is a revised form of a lecture delivered to the IBR in Dallas, Texas, in December 1983, and is excerpted from the second edition of his book Pre-Christian Gnosticism *(Grand Rapids: Baker Book House, 1983) by permission of the publishers. The first edition appeared in 1973 (London: Tyndale Press, and Grand Rapids: Eerdmans). In the intervening decade, the stream of writings on Gnosticism, largely flowing from the discovery of the Nag Hammadi Coptic manuscripts in 1945, has mounted to a flood, high enough to daunt even the boldest of travellers into this difficult territory. Dr Yamauchi's second edition is 70 pages longer than the first, which indicates the quantity of fresh discussion to be taken into account. His assessment of recent writings and of the state of the argument, in a field where hazardous hypotheses too often belie the elusiveness of hard evidence, is always learned and level-headed. The new edition is an invaluable up-to-date guide, showing that the more adventurous or even sensational theories of scholars have failed to win the support of a consensus of their fellows. These edited extracts focus on two of the central areas in the debate – the New Testament, and the significance of the Nag Hammadi texts.*

1. Introduction

a. *Recent publications*

In the past decade numerous international conferences have focused on Gnosticism: at Stockholm (1973),[1] Strasbourg (1974),[2] Oxford (1975),[3] Cairo (1976),[4] New Haven (1978),[5] Quebec (1978),[6] Oxford (1979),[7] Louvain, (1980),[8] and Springfield (1983). Papers from all but the last are now available in print.

Festschrifts have been published in honor of three giants in the field of Gnostic scholarship: Hans Jonas,[9] Gilles Quispel,[10] and R. McL. Wilson.[11] Two valuable collections of essays have been edited by K.-W. Tröger, one on Gnosticism and the New Testament,[12] and the other on Gnosticism, the Old Testament and Early Judaism.[13]

Invaluable are the annual bibliographical surveys since 1971 (except for 1976) published by D. Scholer in *Novum Testamentum*. In his original monograph, *Nag Hammadi Bibliography 1948-1969* (Leiden: Brill, 1971) Scholer had listed 2425 items. In his latest supplement (XII) to his indispensable 'Bibliographia Gnostica', *Novum Testamentum*, 25 (1983), pp. 356-81, Scholer has listed the 5345th publication. In other words nearly 3,000 books, articles and reviews on Gnosticism have been published in the last decade!

From time to time articles have appeared which have attempted to assess current trends and interpretations of Gnosticism in general, and its relations to the New Testament and Christianity in particular. I would single out as especially valuable two recent essays. The first was the presidential address given by R. McL. Wilson to the Studiorum Novi Testamenti

26

Societas in Rome in 1981.[14] The second is an analysis by R. van den Broek of the salient trends as culled from over a hundred essays from recent conference papers and *Festschriften*.[15]

The major synthetic work is *Die Gnosis* published by K. Rudolph in 1977,[16] of which an English translation has just appeared. Also noteworthy as destined to serve as a standard textbook is the two-volume *Introduction to the New Testament* published by H. Koester in 1982.[17]

b. *Defining Gnosticism*

Scholars continue to experience difficulty in agreeing upon a definition of 'Gnosticism'.[18] Some such as H.-M. Schenke, K. Rudolph and G. Strecker have objected to the distinction urged at Messina in 1966 between 'proto-Gnosticism' and 'Gnosticism'.[19] They would prefer what I call the 'broad' definition of Gnosticism, emphasizing links of continuity over stages of development.[20]

On the other hand, Hans Jonas has insisted that an anti-cosmic dualism is the essential ingredient of Gnosticism. The same point has been stressed recently by K.-W. Tröger: 'Primarily the Gnostic religion is an *anti-cosmic religion*'.[21]

To underline the distinction between the apparently inchoate phenomena in the first century and the fully articulated systems in the second century Wilson has been urging that we use the term 'Gnosis' for the former and reserve 'Gnosticism' for the latter.[22]

2. New Testament exegesis on the basis of pre-Christian Gnosticism

a. *No pre-Christian documents*

When I first published *Pre-Christian Gnosticism* in 1973,[23] reviewers understandably reserved judgment as all of the Nag Hammadi tractates had not yet been published. But apart from the 'Trimorphic Protennoia' (see below) there have been no unexploded 'bombshells' in the Nag Hammadi corpus. Hence even the most ardent proponents of a Gnosticism earlier than or contemporary with the New Testament acknowledge that there are no Gnostic texts which date with certainty from the pre-Christian era.

J. M. Robinson declared at the congress at Yale in 1978, 'At this stage we have not found any Gnostic texts that clearly antedate the origin of Christianity'.[24] In his 1981 presidential address to the Society of Biblical Literature Robinson conceded, 'pre-Christian Gnosticism as such is hardly attested in a way to settle the debate once and for all'.[25] In a similar fashion G. W. MacRae declares, 'And even if we are on solid ground in some cases in arguing that the original works represented in the (Nag Hammadi) library are much older than the extant copies, we are still unable to postulate plausibly any pre-Christian dates'.[26]

Nevertheless there seems to be no lack of scholars who, undeterred by the lack of pre-Christian Gnostic documents, proceed to interpret the New Testament against a backdrop of a developed or developing Gnosticism. The view that Gnosticism is an essential element in the hermeneutical circle to understand the New Testament is maintained by MacRae,[27] Rudolph,[28] Koester,[29] and Schmithals.[30]

Following the concept of 'trajectories', which he and Professor Koester introduced,[31] Robinson in his SBL presidential address sketched two diverging trajectories which arose in primitive Christianity, both equally ancient and equally worthy of consideration. According to Robinson's schematization the 'orthodox' trajectory led from the pre-Pauline confession of 1 Corinthians 15:3-5 and the account of the empty tomb in the gospels to the Apostles' Creed in the second century. The 'left-wing' trajectory led from Paul's view of the resurrected Christ as a 'luminous appearance' and from Easter 'enthusiasm' to Gnosticism in the second century.[32] A further trajectory led from the Sayings Collection (Q) and the Gospel of Thomas to the Gnostic dialogues with the resurrected Christ.[33]

b. *The Gospel of John*

There is an enormous literature on this gospel and its possible

relations with Gnosticism.[34] In spite of doubts about Bultmann's reconstruction of Gnostic sources, many interpreters take the gospel either as a transformed Gnostic document or as an anti-Gnostic work.[35] For example, K. M. Fischer believes that one can understand John 10:1-18 *only* against the background of a Gnostic myth such as is found in the Nag Hammadi *Exegesis on the Soul*.[36]

Other scholars, however, have opposed this trend. Bultmann's reconstruction of a Gnostic background from Mandaean sources is sharply criticized by W. A. Meeks.[37] E. Ruckstuhl refutes Schottroff's recent Gnostic interpretation.[38]

Bultmann's formulation that the Johannine prologue was a pre-Christian Gnostic baptist hymn has not convinced even his own students – H. Conzelmann and E. Käsemann.[39] Most recently another former student, W. Schmithals, has repudiated his master's theory quite categorically: 'The hymn does not betray direct Gnostic influences. . . . The concept that the hymn was pre-Christian is rash. Bultmann's guess that it concerned an original baptismal hymn has rightly found no reception.'[40]

c. *1 and 2 Corinthians*

Because Paul speaks about *gnosis* and *sophia* and uses terminology found in later Gnostic literature in his letters to Corinth, the possibility of a Gnostic heresy looms the largest here. That this was the case has been most fully developed by W. Schmithals.[41] Rudolph believes that Schmithals' interpretation has thus far not been seriously refuted.[42]

But as a matter of fact an impressive number of scholars have now rejected the view that Gnosticism must be presupposed to understand Paul's opponents at Corinth. As Wilson points out, Rudolph was unaware that even U. Wilckens, whom he cites for support,[43] has recently changed his mind on this issue.[44]

S. Arai concluded his study on the subject as follows: 'The opponents of Paul in Corinth had therefore been inclined to be "Gnostic", they were, however, not yet Gnostic.'[45] This view has now been given considerable support by H. Conzelmann in his recent Hermeneia commentary on 1 Corinthians.[46] Wilson has come to very similar conclusions: 'What we have at Corinth, then, is not yet Gnosticism, but a kind of *Gnosis*.'[47]

In a series of articles R. A. Horsley has attempted to illuminate the 'gnosis' of Paul's opponents from Hellenistic Judaism as illustrated by Philo and the Wisdom of Solomon rather than from Gnosticism.[48] He argues, 'What Paul responds to, therefore, is not a Gnostic libertinism, as derived from Reitzenstein, elaborated on by Schmithals and still presupposed by commentators such as Barrett, but a Hellenistic Jewish *gnosis* at home precisely in the mission context'.[49]

d. *The Johannine epistles*

Because of the anti-Docetic polemic in the Johannine epistles the view is widespread that the opponents condemned were certainly Gnostics.[50]

But Docetism may have arisen from a Hellenistic prejudice against the body without necessarily implying a fully developed Gnostic theology.[51] Thus Wisse believes that 1 John is 'a tract dealing with the arrival of the eschatological antichrists rather than with a group of docetic Gnostics'.[52] K. Weiss also feels that 'The usual conclusion that these opponents there were Gnostics, however, goes too far.'[53]

3. The patristic evidence on Simon Magus

In view of the unanimous patristic view that Gnosticism began with Simon Magus, some scholars have continued to seek the roots of Gnosticism in Samaria. Jarl Fossum stresses the links of Simon to Dositheus,[54] and I. P. Culianu avers that Simon Magus borrowed the idea of a second Creator from the Magharians.[55] Unfortunately for such theories, the link with Dositheus is questionable[56] and the sources for the Magharians are quite late.[57]

As for whether or not we can take Simon Magus as an early Gnostic, there is a clear conflict between Acts 8, our earliest source which depicts him simply as a *magos*,[58] and the patristic accounts which depict him as a Gnostic.

Rudolph accepts the latter, dismissing Acts as a 'blur of contradictions and an idealization of primitive Christianity'.[59] Here he follows the lead of E. Haenchen who regarded the Acts account as untrustwrothy.[60] J. W. Drane, on the assumption that an early Gnosticism must have been current, suggests that Luke 'has deliberately omitted details in order that Simon may be seen as a sincere, if somewhat confused, believer in the Christian message'.[61]

But it makes more sense to recognize the accuracy of Acts [62] and to question the patristic accounts [63] as many scholars have done.[64] Two major studies which have recently upheld the view that the church fathers transformed Simon into a Gnostic are monographs by K. Beyschlag[65] and G. Lüdemann. Other scholars who have questioned the patristic accounts of Simon and Simonianism include S. Arai,[67] C. Colpe,[68] M. Elze,[69] and F. Wisse.[70] W. Meeks concludes his excellent summary of recent research on Simon by declaring, 'The use of reports about Simon Magus as evidence for a *pre*-Christian gnosticism has been effectively refuted'.[71]

4. The Gospel of Thomas

The Gospel of Thomas, which is preserved among the Coptic Nag Hammadi texts, and of which Greek fragments were found at Oxyrhynchus, is believed to have been composed *c.* AD 140 in Edessa, Syria.

There is still sharp disagreement as to whether the Gospel of Thomas represents an independent gospel tradition related to Q, as advocated by Koester and Robinson, or whether Thomas is essentially dependent upon the synoptic gospels. On the one hand, MacRae declares, 'It now appears that a majority of scholars who have seriously investigated the matter have been won over to the side of Thomas' independence of the canonical Gospels. . . .'[72] On the other hand, Kaestli writes, 'Today, the most widely accepted position is that of the dependence of the Gospel of Thomas on the canonical Gospels. . . .'[73]

Recently Quispel, who has written more prolifically on the Gospel of Thomas than any other scholar, has set forth his conclusions as to the sources of the Gospel of Thomas. Though maintainng that Thomas is independent from the synoptics, Quispel does not now agree with Koester that it represents a primitive tradition: 'The Gospel of Thomas, far from being a writing older than Q, is an anthology based upon two second-century apocryphal Gospels, and moreover a Hermetic writing which gave "Thomas" a seemingly Gnostic flavour.'[74]

Also opposed to the idea that the Gospel of Thomas represents pristine traditions of the Aramaic-speaking Christians in Palestine is Drijver's recent assessment. He would prefer to date the Gospel of Thomas about AD 200 on the assumption that the author knew and used Tatian's Diatessaron.[75]

If either Quispel or Drijvers is correct, we must relocate the Gospel of Thomas at a position much later on the trajectory from Palestine to Edessa than that assumed by Koester and Robinson.

5. The Coptic Evidence

a. *The Nag Hammadi Corpus*

The exciting story of the discovery of the Nag Hammadi texts[76] and the equally fasinating story leading up to their translation and publication in 1977[77] have been recounted in detail by J. M. Robinson, whose persistence and skill saw the task to its completion.[78]

It is probable that the codices were buried after the paschal letter from Athanasius in AD 367 banned such heteredox writings.[79] The books were discovered at the base of the Jabal at-Tarif cliffs north of the Nile river where it bends west to east, actually on the other side of the river from Nag Hammadi. B. Van Elderen was led to excavate the great basilica of Pachomius in the plain below Jabal at-Tarif beginning in 1975.[80] Scholars still debate about the nature of the library and the kind of monastic community which may have preserved it.[81]

b. *The Apocalypse of Adam*

The Apocalypse of Adam (ApocAd) continues to be touted by Robinson as an early, non-Christian Gnostic text which can help us understand the Gospel of John.[82] Rudolph asserts that the ApocAd 'certainly forms a witness of early Gnosticism' and that it has 'no Christian tenor'.[83] MacRae, who supports the non-Christian interpretation of ApocAd,[84] at least concedes that a Christian interpretation is possible.[85]

On the other hand, there has been an increasing number of scholars who have interpreted the ApocAd either as a Christian document or as a product of late rather than early Gnosticism. The Berliner Arbeitskreis für koptisch-gnostische Schriften notes that the figure 'upon whom the Holy Spirit descends' is clearly Jesus.[86] W. Beltz contends that the series of thirteen kingdoms and the kingless generation are all explanations for the birth of Jesus.[87] G. Shellrude presented evidence for a Christian provenance of the ApocAd at the 1979 Oxford conference.[88]

Hedrick suggests a redaction of the ApocAd 'in Palestine, possibly in Transjordan, before the second half of the second century AD'[89] He was not aware of my attempt to date the ApocAd on the basis of the allusion to the well-known Mithraic motif of the 'birth from a rock' (CG V, 80.24-25) in a paper which I presented at the IInd International Congress of Mithraic Studies at Teheran in 1975.[90] On the basis of the epigraphic and iconographic evidence collected by M. J. Vermaseren, I sought to demonstrate that this topos was not known before the second century AD and that the probable provenance for knowledge of such a motif for a Gnostic writer was Italy.

c. *The Paraphrase of Shem*

The Paraphrase of Shem (ParaShem) along with the ApocAd is one of the basic supports of the pre-Christian Gnosticism envisioned by Robinson.[91] MacRae believes that the ParaShem provides us with a striking example of a non-Christian heavenly redeemer who deceives the ignorant powers.[92] Koester assigns the work to 'a Jewish gnostic baptismal sect' since it contains 'no references to specific Christian names, themes, or traditions'.[93]

In my earlier expositions I had interpreted F. Wisse as holding that the ParaShem could provide us with evidence for a pre-Christian Gnosticism. As recently as 1977 he had written in the preface of his translation for the *NHL*: 'The tractate proclaims a redeemer whose features agree with those of New Testament Christology which may very well be pre-Christian in origin.' But Professor Wisse has recently written me, 'I still think it is basically non-Christian though most probably not pre-Christian.'[94]

Other scholars would emphatically disagree with the judgment that the ParaShem is without any trace of Christian influence. After analyzing the Coptic text, Sevrin concludes:

> Several features of this portrait of the redeemer have a Christological appearance: his origin in the light, of which he is the son, the ray and the voice, makes us think of the pre-existent Logos and of the Son of the Gospel of John, or also of Christ 'reflecting the glory of God' in Heb. 1:3; his descent 'into an infirm place' corresponds quite well to the coming of Christ into this world. . . .[95]

Fischer likewise concurs. 'Soldas seems once again to be a code name for Jesus, with whom the heavenly Christ (Derdekeas) is associated.'[96]

d. *The Trimorphic Protennoia*

Both at the international conference at Yale in the spring of 1978,[97] and at the fall conference of the Society of Biblical Literature at New Orleans that same year [98] Professor Robinson called attention to the views of the Berliner Arbeitskreis für koptisch-gnostische Schriften[99] and especially of Gesine Schenke,[100] regarding *The Trimorphic Protennoia* (TriProt). He also noted that Carsten Colpe had listed striking parallels in this tractate to the prologue of the Gospel of John.[101]

In the case of the parallels between the TriProt and the Johannine prologue, the Berlin group suggests that the light falls more from the former on the latter, that is, they believe that the setting of the same elements in the TriProt demonstrates its logical priority over the prologue.[102] It is quite clear that these scholars are working within a Bultmann framework.[103] Other scholars who do not share such presuppositions will have different perceptions of these parallels.[104]

Janssens, who has translated the work into French,[105] has argued that the TriProt reflects the priority of John's prologue.[106] The most striking parallel is that between John 1:14, 'And the Word became flesh and dwelt (*eskenosen*) among us' and (47, 14f.) 'The third time I revealed myself to them [in] their tents (*SKENE*)'.[107] As Helderman has demonstrated in detail, it is difficult to avoid the conclusion that the word *SKENE* in TriProt reflects the word *eskenosen* 'tented, tabernacled' of John 1:14.[108]

Janssens, Helderman, and Wilson are able to detect numerous New Testament allusions in the TriProt not only to John but to the other Gospel and Pauline texts. Wilson therefore concludes:

> In the light of all this it may be suggested that the Christian element in the text as it now stands is rather stronger than the Berlin group have recognised. This would in turn tend to weaken any theory of influence on the Fourth Gospel.[109]

6. The Jewish Evidence
a. *A Pre-Christian Jewish Gnosticism?*
Impressed by the great number of 'Jewish' elements such as the use of the Old Testament and midrashic interpretations in the Nag Hammadi texts a number of scholars are now maintaining the thesis of a pre-Christian 'Jewish' Gnosticism, that is, a Gnosticism which somehow developed from within Judaism itself. B. Pearson, the scholar who has been most effective in ferreting out traces of Jewish traditions in the Nag Hammadi texts, is convinced that Friedländer was correct in postulating 'that Gnosticism is a pre-Christian phenomenon which developed on Jewish soil'.[110]

Kurt Rudolph believes that Gnosticism proceeded from the sceptical and cynical Jewish wisdom tradition of Ecclesiastes, which he dates to *c.* 200 BC on the assumption that it had been influenced by Greek rationalism and early Hellenstic popular philosophy.[111] Pearson is quite impressed by Rudolph's arguments for a Jewish origin from Syro-Palestine Jewish circles.[112] MacRae believes that 'Gnosticism arose as a revolutionary reaction in Hellenized Jewish wisdom and apocalyptic circles'.[113]

B. *Doubts about an Early Jewish Gnosticism*
Opposed to scholars who presuppose a pre-Christian Jewish Gnosticism are others who have questioned the existence of such 'an animal' at least in the New Testament era. According to Gruenwald, 'Thus the views which hold that there was a Jewish Gnosis from which Gnosticism arose, or that Gnosticism arose from within Judaism, appear to me to infer too much from too little.'[114] Maier believes that the case for a Jewish Gnosticism has been prematurely presumed and that it cannot as yet be proven.[115] According to van Unnik one cannot find the roots of Gnosticism in Judaism.[116] Perkins doubts that there was 'a Jewish Gnosticism as such in the first century'.[117] Wilson concludes: 'In sum, the quest for a developed pre-Christian Gnosticism, even a Jewish one, which could be said to have influenced the Corinthians, or Paul himself, has not yielded any conclusive results.'[118]

A major difficulty in accepting an inner Jewish origin for Gnosticism is to account for the anti-Jewish use which most Gnostics seem to have made of the 'Jewish' elements. The anti-cosmic attitude of the Gnostics contradicts the Jewish belief that God created the world and declared it good. According to Tröger, 'But in my view, the hypothesis of a "revolt" *within* Judaism would hardly be sufficient in accounting for the fundamental and radical anti-cosmism in such a lot of Gnostic writings'.[119]

7. Conclusions
At the 1966 Messina conference on Gnostic origins Simone Petrément was almost the sole representative of the classical position which held that Gnosticism was none other than a Christian heresy.[120] In the last two decades the existence of a non-Christian Gnosticism has been amply demonstrated, but the existence of a pre-Christian Gnosticism in the first century or before, that is, a fully developed Gnostic system early enough to have influenced the New Testament writers, remains in doubt.

Gnosticism with a fully articulated theology, cosmology, anthropology, and soteriology cannot be discerned clearly until into the Christian era. According to Wilson, were we to adopt the programmatic definition of H. Jonas[121] 'then we must probably wait for the second century'.[122] Hengel would concur, 'Gnosticism is first visible as a spiritual movement at the end of the first century AD at the earliest and only develops fully in the second century.'[123]

At the Yale conference Barbara Aland emphasized the importance of Christianity for the understanding of Valentinianism. She would date the rise of Gnosticism in the first quarter of the second century.[124] Tröger would also underscore the role of Christianity for the development of at least certain branches of Gnosticism.[125]

Significantly, U. Bianchi, the editor of the conference volume from the Messina conference on the origins of Gnosticism,[126] has also come to the conclusion that Christianity is indispensable for understanding the full development of Gnosticism:

> In effect it is difficult to imagine in a purely Jewish environment, although penetrated by Greek thought, one would have been able to arrive at that extreme which is the demonization of the God of Israel. . . . Only the perspective of a messiah conceived as a divine manifestation, as a divine incarnate person, already present in the faith of the New Testament and of the Church, but interpreted by the Gnostics on the basis of ontological presuppositions of the Greek mysteriosophic doctrine of *soma-sema* ('body'-'tomb') and of the split in the divine, could allow the development of a new Gnostic theology where the God of the Bible, the creator, became the demiurge. . . .[127]

[1]G. Widengren (ed.) *Proceedings of the International Colloquium on Gnosticism* (Stockholm, 1977).
[2]J.-É. Ménard (ed.) *Les Textes de Nag Hammadi* (Leiden, 1975), [*Strasbourg*].
[3]M. Krause (ed.) *Gnosis and Gnosticism* (Leiden, 1977), [*Oxford*-1].
[4]R. McL. Wilson (ed.), *Nag Hammadi and Gnosis* (Leiden, 1978).
[5]B. Layton (ed.) *The Rediscovery of Gnosticism: I. The School of Valentinus* (Leiden, 1980), [*New Haven* I]; B. Layton (ed.) *The Rediscovery of Gnosticism: II. Sethian Gnosticism*, (Leiden, 1981), [*New Haven* II].
[6]B. Barc (ed.) *Colloque international sur les textes de Nag Hammadi* (Quebec/Louvain), 1981), [*Quebec*].
[7]M. Krause (ed.) *Gnosis and Gnosticism* (Leiden, 1981), [*Oxford*-2].
[8]J. Ries (ed.), *Gnosticisme et monde hellénistique* (Louvain-La-neuve, 1980), [*Louvain*].
[9]B. Aland (ed.), *Gnosis: Festschrift für Hans Jonas* (Göttingen, 1978), [*Jonas*].
[10]R. van den Broek and M. J. Vermaseren (eds.) *Studies in Gnosticism and Hellenistic Religions* (Leiden, 1981), [*Quispel*].
[11]A. J. M. Wedderburn and A. H. B. Logan (eds.), *The New Testament and Gnosis* (Edinburgh, 1983), [*Wilson*].
[12]K.-W. Tröger (ed.) *Gnosis und Neues Testament* (Berlin, 1973), [*GNT*].
[13]K.-W. Tröger (ed.) *Altes Testament-Frühjudentum-Gnosis* (Gerd Mohn, 1980), [*ATFG*].
[14]Nag Hammadi and the New Testament', *NTS*, 28 (1982), pp. 289-302.
[15]'The Present State of Gnostic Studies', *VigChr*, 37 (1983), pp. 41-71,
[16]*Die Gnosis* (Leipzig, 1977; Göttingen, 1978, 1980²). The English Translation by R. McL. Wilson was published at the end

of 1983. My references will be to the 2nd German edition, as I have not yet acquired a copy of the English version.

[17](Philadelphia, 1982).

[18]See my *Pre-Christian Gnosticism* (London/Grand Rapids, 1973), [*PCG*], pp. 13ff.; R. McL. Wilson, 'Slippery Words II.: Gnosis, Gnostic, Gnosticism', *ET*, 89 (1977/78), pp. 296-301; U. Bianchi, 'Le Gnosticisme: concept, terminologie, origines, délimitation', *Jonas*, pp. 33-64.

[19]See G. Strecker, 'Judenchristentum und Gnosis', *ATEG*, p. 265; K. Rudolph, '"Gnosis" and "Gnosticism" – the Problems of Their Definition and Their Relation to the Writings of the New Testament', *Wilson*, pp. 21-37.

[20]For a critique of Rudolph's position see R. McL. Wilson's review of his *Die Gnosis* in *Religion*, 9 (1979), pp. 231-33.

[21]'The Attitude of the Gnostic Religion towards Judaism as Viewed in a Variety of Perspectives', *Quebec*, p. 88.

[22]'Nag Hammadi and the New Testament', p. 292.

[23]For some reviews of the first edition see: W. H. C. Frend, *SJT*, 28 (1975), pp. 88-89: G. W. MacRae, *CBQ*, 36 (1974), pp. 296-97; E. H. Pagels, *TS*, 35 (1974), pp. 775-76; M. Peel, *JAAR*, 43 (1975), pp. 329-31; G. Quispel, *Louvain Studies*, 5 (1974), pp. 211-12; G. C. Stead, *JTS*, 26, (1975), p. 187; J. D. Turner, *JBL*, 93 (1974), pp. 482-84; and R. McL. Wilson, *ET*, 84 (1973), p. 379.

[24]J. M. Robinson, 'The Trimorphic Protennoia and the Prologue of the Gospel of John', *New Haven* II, p. 662.

[25]J. M. Robinson, 'Jesus: From Easter to Valentinus (Or to the Apostles' Creed)', *JBL*, 101 (1982), p. 5.

[26]G. W. MacRae, 'Nag Hammadi and the New Testament', *Jonas*, pp. 146-47. *Cf.* van den Broek, 'The Present State', p. 67, 'There are no gnostic works which in their present form are demonstrably pre-Christian'.

[27]G. W. MacRae, 'Why the Church Rejected Gnosticism', in E. P. Sanders (ed.), *Jewish and Christian Self-Definition I.: The Shaping of Christianity in the Second and Third Centuries* (Philadelphia, 1980), [hereafter *JCSD*], p. 127.

[28]Rudolph, *Die Gnosis*, pp. 319ff., especially p. 329.

[29]Koester, *Introduction to the NT*, *passim*.

[30]W. Schmithals, 'Die gnostischen Elemente im Neuen Testament als hermeneutisches Problem', *GNT*, pp. 359-81; *idem*, 'Zur Herkunft der gnostischen Elemente in der Sprache des Paulus', *Jonas*, pp. 385-414.

[31]J. M. Robinson and H. Koester, *Trajectories through Early Christianity* (Philadelphia, 1971).

[32]Robinson, 'Jesus: From Easter to Valentinus', pp. 6-10.

[33]*Ibid.*, p. 35. See P. Perkins, *The Gnostic Dialogue* (New York, 1980).

[34]See J. M. Lieu, 'Gnosticism and the Gospel of John', *ET*, 90, (1979), pp. 233-37; E. Yamauchi, 'Jewish Gnosticism? The Prologue of John, Mandaean Parallels, and the Trimorphic Protennoia', *Quispel*, pp. 467-86.

[35]Koester, *Introduction to the NT*, II, pp. 188-90; L. Schottroff, *Der Glaubende und die feindliche Welt* (Neukirchen-Vluyn, 1970).

[36]'Der johanneische Christus und der gnostische Erlöser', *GNT*, p. 256.

[37]'The Man from Heaven in Johannine Sectarianism', *JBL*, 91 (1972), p. 72.

[38]H. Baltensweiler and B. Reicke (eds.), 'Das Johannesevangelium und die Gnosis', *Neues Testament und Geschichte* [Oscar Cullman Festschrift] (Zürich/Tübingen, 1972), p. 155.

[39]See Yamauchi, 'Jewish Gnosticism?', p. 472.

[40]'Der Prolog des Johannesevangeliums', *ZNW*, 70 (1979), pp. 34-35.

[41]*Gnostics in Corinth* (Abingdon, 1971).

[42]*Die Gnosis*, p. 411, n. 131. E. Fascher, 'Die Korintherbriefe und die Gnosis', *GNT*, pp. 281-91, concludes that the identity of the opponents must remain disputed.

[43]M. D. Hooker and S. G. Wilson (eds.), R. McL. Wilson, 'Gnosis at Corinth', in *Paul and Paulinism* [C. K. Barrett Festschrift] (London, 1982), p. 108.

[44]See U. Wilckens, 'Zu 1 Kor. 2.1-16', C. Andresen and G. Klein (eds.) *Theologia Crucis – Signum Crucis* [E. Dinkler Festschrift], (Tübingen, 1979), p. 537.

[45]S. Arai, 'Die Gegner des Paulus in I. Korintherbrief und das Problem der Gnosis', *NTS*, 19 (1972/73), p. 437.

[46]H. Conzelmann, *I Corinthians* (Philadelphia, 1975), p. 15.

[47]Wilson, 'Gnosis at Corinth', p. 112. *Cf.* also F. T. Fallon, *2 Corinthians* (Wilmington, 1980), p. 8; F. Wisse, 'The "Opponents" in the New Testament in Light of the Nag Hammadi Writings', *Quebec*, p. 108.

[48]R. A. Horsley, 'Wisdom of Word and Words of Wisdom in Corinth', *CBQ*, 39, (1977), pp. 224-39; *idem*, '"How Can Some of You Say That There Is No Resurrection of the Dead?": Spiritual Elitism in Corinth', *NTS*, 20 (1978), pp. 203-31.

[49]R. A. Horsley, 'Gnosis in Corinth: I Corinthians 8.1-6', *NTS*, 27 (1980), pp. 48-49. *Cf.* also G. Sellin, 'Das "Geheimnis" der Weisheit und das Tätsel der "Christuspartie" (zu 1 Kor 1-4)', *ZNW*, 73 (1982), pp. 69-96.

[50]Koester, *Introduction to the NT*, II, pp. 195-96; R. Bultmann, *The Johannine Epistles* (Philadelphia, 1973), p. 38.

[51]On Docetism, see E. Yamauchi, 'The Crucifixion and Docetic Christology', *Concordia Theological Quarterly*, 46 (1982), pp. 1-20.

[52]F. Wisse, 'The Epistle of Jude in the History of Heresiology', M. Krause (ed.), *Essays on the Nag Hammadi Texts in Honour of Alexander Böhlig*, (Leiden, 1972), p. 142, n. 3.

[53]K. Weiss, 'Die "Gnosis" im Hintergrund und im Spiegel der Johannesbriefe', *GNT*, p. 356.

[54]J. Fossum, 'Samaritan Demiurgical Traditions and the Alleged Dove Cult of the Samaritans', *Quispel*, p. 160.

[55]I. P. Culianu, 'The Angels of the Nations and the Origins of Gnostic Dualism', *Quispel*, p. 86.

[56]S. Isser, *The Dositheans* (Leiden, 1976).

[57]See *PGCE*, pp. 158-59.

[58]On Simon as a magician, see J. D. M. Derrett, 'Simon Magus (Acts 8:9-24)', *ZNW*, 73 (1982), pp. 52-68; see my 'Magic in the Biblical World', *TB*, 34 (1983), pp. 169-200, for examples of magic from biblical and extra-biblical sources.

[59]Rudolph, *Die Gnosis*, pp. 312ff.

[60]E. Haenchen, 'Simon Magus in der Apostelgeschichte', *GNT*, pp. 267-79.

[61]J. W. Drane, 'Simon the Samaritan and the Lucan Concept of Salvation History', *EQ*, 47 (1975), p. 137.

[62]W. W. Gasque, *A History of the Criticism of the Acts of the Apostles*, (Tübingen/Grand Rapids, 1975); M. Hengel, *Acts and the History of Earliest Christianity* (Philadelphia, 1980).

[63]On the questionable value of the patristic accounts (with the exception of Irenaeus) see: F. Wisse, 'The Nag Hammadi Library and the Heresiologists', *VC*, 25 (1971), pp. 205-23; A. F. J. Klijn and G. J. Reinink, *Patristic Evidence for Jewish-Christian Sects* (Leiden, 1973); K. Koschorke, *Hippolyt's Ketzerbekämpfung und Polemik gegen die Gnostiker* (Wiesbaden, 1975); R. M. Grant, *Eusebius and Gnostic Origins', Paganisme, judäisme, christianisme* [Marcel Simon Festschrift], (Paris, 1978), pp. 195-205; G. Vallée, *A Study in Anti-Gnostic Polemics* (Waterloo, 1981).

[64]See, *e.g.*, R. Bergmeier, 'Quellen vorchristlicher Gnosis?' G. Jeremias *et al.* (eds.), *Tradition und Glaube* [K. G. Kuhn Festschrift] (Göttingen, 1971), pp. 203-206.

[65]*Simon Magus und die christliche Gnosis* (Tübingen, 1974).

[66]*Untersuchungen zur Simonianischen Gnosis* (Tübingen, 1974).

[67]'Simonianische Gnosis und die *Exegese über die Seele*', *Oxford*-1, pp. 185-203; *idem*, 'Zum "Simonianischen" in *AuthLog* und *Bronte*', *Oxford*-2, pp. 3-15.

[68]'Gnosis', *Reallexikon für Antike und Christentum* (Stuttgart, 1981), XI, col. 625.

[69]'Häresie und Einheit der Kirche im 2. Jahrhundert', *ZThK*, 21 (1974), p. 407.

[70]Wisse, 'The "Opponents"', p. 102, n. 13.

[71]'Simon Magus in Recent Research', *RelSRev*, 3 (1977), p. 141.

[72]MacRae, 'Nag Hammadi and the New Testament' (n. 26), p. 152.

[73]J.-D. Kaestli, 'L'évangile de Thomas', *Études théologiques*

et religeuses, 54, (1979), p. 383. *Cf.* J. Horman, 'The Source of the Version of the Parable of the Sower in the Gospel of Thomas', *NovTest*, 21 (1979), p. 326.

[74]Quispel, 'The *Gospel of Thomas* Revisited', *Quebec*, p. 223.

[75]Drijvers, 'Facts and Problems in Early Syriac-Speaking Christianity', *The Second Century*, 2 (1982), p. 173.

[76]J. M. Robinson, 'The Discovery of the Nag Hammadi Codices', *BA*, 42 (1979), pp. 206-24.

[77]J. M. Robinson, (ed.), *The Nag Hammadi Library* (San Francisco, 1977), [*NHL*]. See my 'New Light on Gnosticism', *Christianity Today*, 23 (Oct. 6, 1978), pp. 36-40, 42-43.

[78]J. M. Robinson, 'Getting the Nag Hammadi Library into English', *BA*, 42 (1979), pp. 239-48.

[79]F. Wisse, 'Gnosticism and Early Monasticism in Egypt', *Jonas*, p. 437; C. W. Hedrick, 'Gnostic Proclivities in the Greek *Life of Pachomius* and the *Sitz im Leben* of the Nag Hammadi Library', *NovTest*, 22 (1980), p. 93.

[80]B. Van Elderen, 'The Nag Hammadi Excavation', *BA*, 42 (1979), pp. 225-31; P. Grossman, 'The Basilica of St. Pachomius', *BA*, 42 (1979), pp. 232-36; C. Walters, *Monastic Archaeology in Egypt* (Winona Lake, 1974).

[81]T. Säve-Söderbergh, 'Holy Scriptures or Apologetic Documentations?: The "Sitz im Leben" of the Nag Hammadi Library', *Stra bourg*, pp. 3-14. *Idem*, 'The Pagan Elements in Early Christianity and Gnosticism', *Quebec*, pp. 71-85; F. Wisse, 'Language Mysticism in the Nag Hammadi Texts and in Early Coptic Monasticism I: Cryptography', *Enchoria*, 9 (1979), pp. 101-20; *idem*, 'Gnosticism and Early Monasticism in Egypt', *Jonas*, pp. 431-40.

[82]Robinson, *The Nag Hammadi Codices* (n. 74), pp. 13-14.

[83]Rudolph, *Die Gnosis*, p. 148.

[84]G. W. MacRae, 'The Apocalypse of Adam Rediscovered', L. C. McGaughy (ed.), *1972 SBL Seminar Papers* (n.p., 1972), II, pp. 574-75; *idem*, 'Adam, Apocalypse', *IDBS*, pp. 9-10.

[85]G. W. MacRae, 'Seth in Gnostic Texts and Traditions', P. J. Achtemeier (ed.), *1977 SBL Seminar Papers* (Missoula, 1977), p. 21.

[86]*GNT*, pp. 46-47.

[87]W. Beltz, 'Bemerkungen zur Adamapokalypse aus Nag-Hammadi-Codex V', P. Nagel (ed.), *Studia Coptica* (Berlin, 1974), pp. 159-62.

[88]G. Shellrude, 'The Apocalypse of Adam: Evidence for a Christian Provenance', *Oxford-2*, pp. 93-94.

[89]C. W. Hedrick, *The Apocalypse of Adam: A Literary and Source Analysis* (Missoula, 1980), p. 213.

[90]E. Yamauchi, 'The Apocalypse of Adam, Mithraism and Pre-Christian Gnosticism', J. Duchesne-Guillemin (ed.), *Études Mithraiques*, (*Acta Iranica* IV; Leiden/Teheran/Liège, 1978), pp. 537-63. For suggestions that the Adam Apocalypse dates even to the third or fourth centuries see Beltz, p. 162; F. Morard, 'L'*Apocalypse d'Adam* de Nag Hammadi', *Oxford-1*, pp. 35-42; *idem*, 'Thématique de l'*Apocalypse d'Adam* du Codex V de Nag Hammadi', *Quebec*, pp. 288-94.

[91]Robinson, *The Nag Hammadi Codices*, p. 7; *NHL*, p. 7.

[92]MacRae, 'Nag Hammadi and the New Testament', *Jonas*, p. 154.

[93]Koester, *Introduction to the New Testament*, II, p. 211.

[94]In a personal letter, 25 Jan. 1980. Professor Wisse also adds, 'I agree with you on the Apocalypse of Adam'.

[95]J.-M. Sevrin, 'À propos de la "Paraphrase de Sem"', *Le Muséon*, 88 (1975), p. 87.

[96]K.-M. Fischer, 'Die Paraphrase des Seem', M. Kause (ed.), *Essays on the Nag Hammadi Texts* [P. Labib Festschrift], (Leiden, 1975), p. 266.

[97]J. M. Robinson, 'Sethians and Johannine Thought: The *Trimorphic Protennoia* and the Prologue of the Gospel of John', *New Haven*, II, pp. 643-62.

[98]'The Prologue of the Gospel of John and the Trimorphic Protennoia', *SBL 1978 Abstracts*, ed. P. Achtemeier (Missoula, 1978), p. 29; *idem*, 'Gnosticism and the New Testament', *Jonas*, pp. 128-31.

[99]'Die dreigestaltige Protennoia', *ThLZ*, 99, (1974), cols. 733-34.

[100]G. Schenke, 'Die dreigestaltige Protennoia (NHC XIII)',

unpublished dissertation for Ristock University in 1977. It is worth noting that though she speaks of the work as 'nichtchristlich', she also designates parts of it as 'antichristlich' and others as presupposing 'christliche Gnosis' (pp. 131, 146).

[101]C. Colpe, 'Heidnische, Jüdische und christliche Überlieferung in den Schriften aus Nag Hammadi III', *JAC*, 17, (1974), pp. 122-24. Colpe holds that both the TriProt and the Prologue go back to Jewish Wisdom traditions. *Cf.* C. A. Evans, 'On the Prologue of John and the *Trimorphic Protennoia*', *NTS*, 27 (1981), pp. 395-401.

[102]*ThLZ*, 99 (1974), col. 733.

[103]*Ibid*. On Bultmann's presuppositions, see R. Kysar, 'R. Bultmann's Interpretation of the Concept of Creation in Jo 1, 3-4', *CBQ*, 32 (1970), pp. 77-85.

[104]Van den Broek, 'The Present State', (n. 15). p. 67, comments: 'In reading the gnostic treatise (TriProt) I absolutely do not get the impression of the Berlin group....'

[105]Y. Janssens, 'Le Codex XIII de Nag Hammadi', *Le Muséon*, 87 (1974), pp. 341-413; *La Prôtennoia Trimorphe (NH XIII.1)* (Quebec, 1978).

[106]Janssens, *La Prôtennoia*, p. 82: 'As for us, we remain convinced that it is a matter of the reminiscences of the New Testament in the TriProt and not the contrary'. *Cf. idem*, 'Une source gnostique du Prologue?' M. de Jonge (ed.), *L'Évangile de Jean* (Gembloux/Louvain, 1977), pp. 355-58. In her latest contribution, 'The Trimorphic Protennoia and the Fourth Gospel', *Wilson*, pp. 229-44, she leaves 'the last word to specialists in the Fourth Gospel'.

[107]See Yamauchi, *Quispel*, pp. 482-83; contrast Robinson, *New Haven*, II, pp. 660-62.

[108]J. Helderman, '"In ihren Zelten . . ." Bemerkungen bei Codex XIII . . . .', T. Baarda, A. F. J. Klijn, and W. C. van Unnik (eds.), *Miscellanea Neotestamentica*, (Leiden, 1978), I, pp. 181-211.

[109]R. McL. Wilson, 'The *Trimorphic Protennoia*', *Oxford-1*, p. 54.

[110]B. A. Pearson, 'Friedländer Revisited', *Studia Philonica*, 2 (1973), p. 35.

[111]K. Rudolph, 'Sophia und Gnosis', *ATFG*, P. 232; *idem*, *Die Gnosis*, pp. 298-301.

[112]B. A. Pearson, 'Jewish Elements in Gnosticism and the Development of Gnostic Self-definition', *JCSD*, p. 151.

[113]MacRae, 'Nag Hammadi and the New Testament', p. 150.

[114]I. Gruenwald, 'Aspects of the Jewish Gnostic Controversy', *New Haven*, II, p. 720.

[115]J. Maier, 'Jüdische Faktoren bei der Entstehung der Gnosis?', *ATFG*, p. 243.

[116]W. C. van Unnik, 'Gnosis und Judentum', *Jonas*, p. 84.

[117]Perkins, *The Gnostic Dialogue*, pp. 17-18.

[118]Wilson, 'Gnosis at Corinth', (n. 43), p. 111.

[119]Tröger, 'The Attitude', (n. 21), p. 93.

[120]S. Pétrement, 'Le Colloque de Messine et le problème du gnosticisme', *Revue de Métaphysique et de Morale*, 72 (1967), 344-73; *idem*, 'Sur le problème du gnosticisme', *Revue de Métaphysique et de Morale*, 85 (1980), pp. 145-77.

[121]H. Jonas, 'Response', J. P. Hyatt (ed.), *The Bible in Modern Scholarship* (Nashville, 1965), p. 293: 'A Gnosticism without a fallen god, without benighted creator and sinister creation, without alien soul, cosmic captivity and acosmic salvation, without the self-redeeming of the Deity – in short: A Gnosis without divine tragedy will not meet specifications.'

[122]Wilson, 'Gnosis at Corinth', (n. 43), p. 111; *idem*, 'From Gnosis to Gnosticism', *Mélanges d'Histoires des Religions offerts à Henri-Charles Puech* (Paris, 1974), p. 425.

[123]Hengel, *The Son of God*, p. 34.

[124]B. Aland, 'Gnosis und Christentum', *New Haven*, I, p. 340.

[125]Tröger, 'The Attitude', (n. 21), p. 98.

[126]U. Bianchi (ed.), *Le Origini dello Gnosticismo* (Leiden, 1967).

[127]U. Bianchi, 'Le gnosticisme et les origines du Christianisme', *Louvain* (n. 8), p. 228.

31

Arthur Hilary Armstrong

Gnosis and Greek Philosophy

1. Introduction

It gives me great pleasure to have been invited to join in honouring *Hans Jonas*. This is not only because of his unique contribution to our understanding of the subject of this volume, my appreciation of which will become apparent in the rest of this chapter. It is also because I have discovered in his writings on more modern topics something rare and precious in the modern world, which the ancients valued greatly and regarded as essential to a true philosopher, namely moral wisdom. I salute him, not only as a distinguished scholar in a field with which I am concerned, but as a genuine φιλόσοφος in the old sense, to whom one can go for good guidance in some of the most agonizing ethical dilemmas of contemporary life[1]. It is partly for this reason that, although in many areas of the vast and rapidly growing field of Gnostic studies I feel myself as alien as a Gnostic in the cosmos, I have decided to try to make such contribution to this volume as can be made by a sober historian of later Greek philosophy to whom the non-Greek-speaking world of the Eastern Mediterranean and adjoining lands in the first centuries of our era is unfamiliar, though increasingly fascinating.

As Socrates thought, it is as well to begin any serious discussion by trying to define what one is talking about. So I shall begin by asking myself "What do I mean by 'Gnosis?'" I cannot attempt (and it would be superfluous to do so) to characterize "Gnosis" with the depth, subtlety and precision of Jonas. Nor can I hope to produce any descriptive generalization about this strange and powerful way of faith which will do justice to all the complexities and varieties which are being revealed in ever greater detail by the progress of scholarship in this field. But it will at least be useful if I explain the senses in which I propose to use the term. I have found it convenient to use "Gnosis" and "Gnostic" in two different

---

[1] I refer, of course, to the essays on contemporary subjects collected in his Philosophical Essays (Prentice-Hall Inc. Englewood Cliffs, New Jersey, 1974). There is much to be learned from all of them, but the two which I would particularly choose to support my appreciation are, Philosophical Reflections on Experimenting with Human Subjects (No. 5) and, Against the Stream: Comments on the Definition of Death (No. 6).

33

senses, a wider and a narrower, each of which serves in a different way to distinguish this kind of religion from others. In the wider sense the use of the terms is intended to indicate that we are dealing with a belief that divine saving truth is contained in an esoteric revelation only accessible to a chosen few to whom it has been transmitted in secret and mysterious ways, without saying anything about the content of that revelation. In this sense Gnosis is clearly distinguished from all forms of what may be called "public religion". This latter may be philosophical, believing that God reveals himself to all men simply through their divine or God-given reason (in the large ancient sense) which all men have, though few use it, and the divine cosmos of which we are all inhabitants and in and through which, as well as within ourselves, we can discover him by the exercise of that reason, if we make the rare and extreme effort required to do so: or based on a particular revelation, given through a particular person or group, but universal in its message and intended to be proclaimed to all mankind. Gnosis in this sense is in a very special and distinctive way "private religion". It is the use of the terms in this sense which makes it possible to speak of the more cosmically optimistic treatises of the Hermetica[2] as containing a Gnosis and of their authors as "pagan Gnostics". And it may also be useful in this sense to the modern student of religions, for believers in esoteric revelations are still with us. Of course it must be used with caution, and the boundaries between the different kinds of belief must not be made too sharp: and we must realize that some doctrines which should be called "Gnostic" in the other sense, to be discussed next, may not be "Gnostic" in this sense. I do not think that Marcion could be called a Gnostic in this sense, and where does Manichaeism stand? Mani, surely, regarded his doctrine as a public and universal revelation.

The second sense in which I use the terms "Gnosis" and "Gnostic" is the more usual one in which the emphasis is on the attitude of mind of the believers and the content of their revelations more than on their esoteric character. I think it important to distinguish the two senses, both for the historical reasons briefly indicated in the last paragraph, and in order to make it as difficult as possible to use "Gnostic" in the deplorably loose and inaccurate way in which the term is sometimes employed, especially in controversial religious writing (where it often seems to mean "intellectual who presumes to disagree with the clergy, or the simple faithful, about religious doctrines"). A man should not be called a "Gnostic" unless he believes in an esoteric revelation or has the distinctively Gnostic attitude of mind which we are about to consider, or, preferably, combines both characteristics. A Gnostic in the second sense is a person who feels himself deeply alienated from this world in which we find ourselves and

---

[2] II. III. V. IX, XI, XII, XIV, XVI, Asclepius.

in revolt against the powers which govern it. He reverses the values which are implied for a Greek philosopher in the very word Cosmos, and utterly rejects that high esteem for God's good world and therefore for its maker which is central in the great public revelations of Judaism, Christianity and (later) Islam, and (in spite of its dualism, or rather because of its particular form of dualism) in the mainstream Iranian religious tradition which we call Zoroastrianism. The cosmos for him is an evil and alien place, a prison and a trap. His revelation explains to him why it exists and why he is here in it, and above all gives him the saving knowledge necessary to escape to his true, far-off home, the world of light, and the God of that other world who is his God whom he loves, worships and seeks. This description of the Gnostic state of mind is somewhat summary and sketchy, but at least it is sufficiently and deliberately vague enough at important points (as Gnostic scholars will appreciate) to cover most of the varieties of pessimistic Gnosticism known to us, and depth and accuracy can be added to it by simply reading the account of Gnosticism given with such fine precision and understanding by the scholar whom we are honouring[3].

It is with Gnosticism in this sense that we shall be mainly concerned in this chapter. The "pagan Gnosticism" of the cosmically optimistic treatises of the Hermetica is related to Greek philosophy very simply. The content of these treatises *is* for the most part popular Greek philosophy (what Theiler well called "proletarian Platonism", with its important Stoic elements). This of course does not exclude borrowings from non-Greek, mainly Jewish, sources[4]. And the whole is presented in the form of Egyptian revelations of immemorial antiquity, and given in a very pious tone by the devout authors. But there is nothing in these features, apart from the characteristically Gnostic (in my first sense) presentation of the treatises as esoteric revelations. to separate the optimistic Hermetica sharply from the general body of popular Greek philosophy. Most philosophers in the early centuries of our era were pious men and anxious to discover that the doctrines which they regarded as those of the ancient masters of Greek philosophy were in perfect accord with the im-

---

[3] See Hans Jonas. Gnosis und Spätantiker Geist I, 3rd. enlarged edition (Göttingen 1964): The Gnostic Religion, enlarged edition (Boston 1963). The profundity of Jonas' understanding of the Gnostic mind should be recognised by those who do not accept his earlier philosophical presuppositions (which are clearly stated and critically discussed with outstanding intellectual honesty in the Epilogue. Gnosticism, Nihilism and Intellectualism, to the 1963 edition of The Gnostic Religion, pp. 320–340).

[4] This Jewish influence is particularly marked in III (see the introduction and notes in the edition of A. D. Nock and H. J. Festugière (Paris 1945–54), which should be consulted throughout for a precise discrimination of Greek and non-Greek elements in the Hermetica.

memorial wisdom of the East, a discovery which their degree of knowledge of genuine Oriental sources and their methods of exegesis easily enabled them to make.

The relationship of Gnosticism in my second sense, the Gnosticism of alienation from and revolt against the cosmos and its maker, to the Greek philosophy of the first three centuries of our era is a great deal more complex and interesting, and the evidence is often very difficult to interpret. This is particularly true of the second, more subtle, and perhaps later, of the two types of explanation which the Gnostic revelations give of that deplorable occurrence, the formation of this evil cosmos of ours. The first is a form of straightforward Iranian dualism, with the "Zoroastrian" valuation of the cosmos reversed. There are two eternal opposed principles of good and evil, light and darkness, and this horrible world is the result of troubles on the frontier between them (variously described). This type of Gnosticism culminates in the great revelation of Mani. In this second type there is either no eternal principle of evil and darkness or it is of subordinate importance (in this confused and confusing world of imaginative religious thinking there are no clear frontiers between the different types of explanation, and they can blend in bewildering ways). The real cause of all the trouble is a pre-cosmic fault and fall of a being in the world of light itself, the consequences of which lead elaborately down to this dark prison of a world with its stupid and inferior Maker, the Demiurge and God of the Jews, and his sinister lieutenants the Archons who rule the heavens. The finest and most delicately and deeply imagined form of this is the Valentinian Gnosis, centering on that genuinely tragic figure, whom I call to myself, rather unkindly and irreverently, "naughty Sophie". (This is to some extent inspired by a venerable children's classic not altogether unknown to-day, Les Malheurs de Sophie. Does the name chosen by its authoress for her deplorably behaved but likeable little heroine represent some last lingering unconscious influence of the *Gnosis* in 19th century France? Or were Valentinus and the Comtesse de Ségur both inspired to some extent in their choice of name for their principal characters by the easily observable fact that names like Sophia, Angela, etc. do sometimes seem to have a shocking effect on the characters of those who are burdened with them?)

2. *Alienation from the world in Greek philosophy before Gnosticism*

It is with the problematical relations of this second type of Gnostic belief to the Greek philosophy of the first three centuries A. D. that most of the rest of this chapter will be concerned, though we shall later meet an interesting and rather significant adaptation to Hellenic purposes of straightforward Iranian (rather than particularly Gnostic) dualism in Plutarch. A necessary preliminary to considering these relations is to take note of forms of alienation from the world which are apparent in some Greek philosophers centuries before the earliest possible date for the origin of alienated Gnosticism.

The first form which I shall remark on is the Epicurean. This is the least relevant to our purposes, but it is perhaps worth mentioning to help us to remember, throughout our investigation, that it was possible for an ancient Greek (as for a modern man) to feel thoroughly alienated from the cosmos without having anything in common with the beliefs or state of mind of the alienated Gnostic. World-alienation is not in itself an infallible indication of Gnosticism. For the Epicureans, as is well known, there is no reason to feel any affection or admiration for this random, meaningless, transitory and very badly arranged cosmos[5]. It is not the work of, or ruled by, beneficent divine powers. If there were any world-ruling or world-making divine powers they would be as evil and terrible as any Gnostic Demiurge and Archons: but fortunately there are not: they are bogeys of the vulgar imagination, or the worse and more frightening superstitious fictions of the so-called philosophers who accept the cosmic piety of Plato, Aristotle and above all the Stoics (whose world-view seemed to Epicureans the ultimate in terrifying stupidity). The blessed gods of Epicurus are more complete strangers to the cosmos than the true God of the Gnostics: for they cannot and do not disturb their divine peace by doing anything to help their true worshippers to escape from this world to a better one. There is no escape, in the sense of a better future life, for any man. But the Epicurean philosopher can escape to beatitude here and now, and learn to manage very well in this alien and senseless universe, if he understands it by following the teaching of Epicurus which is the true gospel of salvation because it is the only rational philosophy, and in accordance with the doctrine of his master detaches himself in spirit from the cosmos and withdraws as far as possible from the common society of men. If members of these little

---

[5] The most succinct and forcible statement of Epicurean anti-cosmism is:
nam quamvis rerum ignorem primordia quae sint,
hoc tamen ex ipsis caeli rationibus ausim
confimare aliisque ex rebus reddere multis,
nequaquam nobis divinitus esse creatam
naturam mundi: tanta stat praedita culpa.
     (Lucretius II 177–181: repeated with slight variation and
     subsequent amplification at V 196–199).
This negation of the goodness and divine creation of the world always seem to appear in a context of Epicurean school-polemic against Stoic anthropocentric teleology. Hence the insistence that the world is a bad world *fos us men* (cp. also Cicero D. N. D. I 9–10, 23–24). The belief that the world was made and is governed by a good and wise divine power or powers who manipulate us for their own cosmic purposes and to whose will we must submit is for Epicurus and his followers the most effective cause of the *Angst* which is the supreme evil: cp: e. g: Epicurus Letter to Herodotus 76–81; Letter to Menoeceus 133–134; Κύριαι Δόξαι XII–XIII. He might have found in the Gnostic revolt against the cosmic powers a curious and irrational but striking illustration of the truth of his doctrine.

groups of true believers in very different anti-cosmic faiths had ever met, the Epicurean would have thought the Gnostic was reacting to the monstrous superstition of cosmic piety ultra-superstitiously (though not incomprehensibly, and in a way at least preferable to the whole-hearted world-acceptance of the Stoic or the qualified world-acceptance of the Platonist). The Gnostic, like the Platonist and orthodox Christian, would have thought of the Epicurean as a man without true light or hope: his own revelation would certainly have seemed to him a revelation of hope, not of despair, a true gospel, that is, good news, at least for the elect. And orthodox Christianity, too, has often been preached in forms which make it good news only for a chosen few, and the worst possible news for the vast majority of mankind. Of all those who have believed in salvation exclusively for a chosen few, only, perhaps, the great Gnostic Basilides has arrived at a really genial solution of the problem of what is to be done with the rest of them. His doctrine that when all the elect, those who belong to the Sonship, have returned to the highest, all those who are left, from the great Archons downwards, are confirmed in their several stupidities and spend eternity in blissful ignorance that there is any state happier than their own[6], is charmingly humane, and has a distinctly Hellenic flavour about it. This does not mean that I suppose Basilides was either influenced by or influenced any Greek philosophy. The difference between Epicurean and Gnostic forms of *Angst* and world-rejection may be due to the fact that Epicurus was a Hellene reacting against the ideas of contemporary Hellenes, while Gnosticism seems to have originated in an area strongly influenced by Judaism[7], and the Gnostics seem to be in black and furious revolt against the Jewish belief in their God as the good Creator of this good world. Gnosticism of this sort is primarily an anti-Semitic, and only secondarily and incidentally an anti-Hellenic religion.

It would of course be absurd to look for a spirit of world-alienation and rejection of the cosmos in Stoicism, especially the Old Stoicism of Zeno, Cleanthes and Chrysippus. But in considering alienated Gnosticism and its relationship to other, more Hellenic forms of world-alienation it is important to remember that alienation from the world goes closely with alienation from one's empirical, em-

---

[6] Hippolytus, Ref. VII, 27, 1–4.

[7] Again, the studied vagueness of this phrase may show Gnostic scholars that I am at least aware of the vigorous controversies about the origins of Gnosticism which still continue. Jonas has well brought out the intensely and consciously anti-Semitic character of alienated Gnosticism, and has convinced me that it is at least improbable that the first Gnostics were actually Jews, however unorthodox. See especially "The Hymn of the Pearl": Case Study of a symbol, and the Claims for a Jewish Origin of Gnosticism, in Philosophical Essays No. 14 pp. 277–289, a reply to G. Quispel, Gnosticism and the New Testament in the Bible in Modern Scholarship (Nashville 1965). The wild suspicion (probably easily refuted by Gnostic specialists) has sometimes crossed my mind that it might be plausible to look for the origins of Gnosticism (if any evidence was available) among the peoples forcibly Judaized by John Hyrcanus and Aristobulus in the 2nd. century B. C., the Idumaeans, Ituraeans or Peraeans. I admit to being influenced in my liking for this supposition by a desire to find an edifying τόπος more characteristic of an ancient rhetorician than a modern scholar. If (say) the Idumaeans, in return for their forcible conversion, had presented the Jewish people not only with the Herod family but with Gnostic anti-Semitism, it would be a most impressive warning against the dangers of religious coercion.

bodied, this-worldly self, whichever is the cause of the other[8]. And there is a very strange feature of Old Stoic doctrine which could have led (I do not say that it did lead, because of lack of relevant evidence[9]) to a profound sense of alienation from mankind in general and from oneself. To see this, one needs to consider several well-known Stoic doctrines in a single view, which is not always done. These are (i) the physical theology, with its necessarily unqualified cosmic optimism and world-acceptance: this is the best of all possible worlds because it is God. (ii) The doctrine of the equality of all vices: all men are equally wicked except the perfectly virtuous man, the σοφός or sage. (iii) The belief that sages are very rare indeed, even if one has ever existed: it does not seem that any Stoic philosopher worthy of the name ever claimed to be σοφός. (iv) The doctrine that virtue (which is almost unattainable) is the only good for man, and all other apparent and generally pursued "goods" in this perfect world are indifferent and empty. Put these doctrines together, and a distressing and paradoxical situation emerges. In this divinely good world, God in his cosmic phase, nearly all men, who are among God's most important living organic parts, and for whose benefit

---

[8] On the connection between the two see E. R. Dodds, Pagan and Christian in an Age of Anxiety (Cambirdge 1965), Chapter 1, a chapter which contains very much more which is highly relevant to the theme of this present chapter and of the greatest value. Dodds thinks that resentment against oneself, or at least one's empirical ego or one's body, is an "introjection" of resentment against the world (pp. 27 ff.). But I am inclined to think that the progression of hatred, contempt or disgust can sometimes go the other way. I have noticed that Platonists and Christians, in antiquity and in later centuries, are often much more hostile to their own bodies and lower selves than they are to the material cosmos, and can sometimes combine profound contempt and disgust for the mass of worldly men and (especially) women with a real delight in the beauty and goodness of the non-human cosmos. The process of alienation can develop either way, and stop at various points.

[9] Our evidence for the older Stoicism is not only scanty, but, as we are realizing more and more clearly, often biassed against the Stoics because so much of it comes from works of anti-Stoic polemic by members of other schools. It is certainly not sufficient to enable us to assess the range of moods or attitudes of mind possible to an early Stoic who was at all sensitive and introspective. Evidence from the Stoic moralists of the Roman Empire is generally unreliable for early Stoicism and not strictly relevant. Seneca's remarks on *displicentia sui* in De Tranquillitate II (to which Dodds refers, 1. c. p. 28) though psychologically penetrating, have nothing to do with the paradox I am here considering. Nor has his neurotic death-wish (on the relation of which to the true Stoic views on suicide see J. M. Rist's admirable chapter on Suicide in his Stoic Philosophy (Cambridge 1969) pp. 233–255). And I do not think that the extreme expressions of alienation from the world to be found in Marcus Aurelius (e. g: V. 33, VI. 13, and the really alarmingly depressed VIII. 24 – the "dirty bathwater" passage) should be regarded as expressions of Stoic philosophy or of some second-century *Zeitgeist*, Gnosticizing or otherwise; though the less extreme (e. g: VI. 13) may be inspired to some degree by the good Stoic spiritual exercise of trying to bring home to oneself the vanity and indifference of everything in the world except virtue, which is part of my paradox. But I would regard the tone of passionate disgust with the world in these passages as something very personal, perhaps the result of exhaustion and discouragement produced by the difficult and uncongenial business of conscientiously discharging his civil and military duties as Roman Emperor. And these passages are of course balanced by some of the noblest expressions of world-acceptance to be found in surviving Stoic literature (above all IV. 23 and X. 21). Marcus is not consistent in thought or mood.

the non-human cosmos has been arranged, are wicked, pretty well irredeemably. All the things in the world, which ought to be (and sometimes are) considered supremely beautiful and attractive as parts of God, and all human activities in pursuit and enjoyment of them, which should be considered as, in the last analysis, God's activities in his cosmic self-explication, are vain and valueless except the almost unattainable virtue. (Of course there is much ingenious Stoic casuistry to tone this down, but the paradox remains). On the strict principles of the physical theology Stoic morality should be thoroughly permissive, accepting with a rather indiscriminate delight all the beauties and enjoyments of the world. It certainly is not. There is a solid foundation here for alienation from oneself and the mass of mankind. Stoicism should not be presented as the absolute antithesis of Gnosticism simply on the strength of its physical theology, and the transition from Stoic acceptance to Gnostic revolt may have been easier than is generally supposed. It would have been facilitated by the fact that, like the Epicureans, at least some Stoics were body-soul dualists of a degree of sharpness and crudity only reachable by those who take a corporealist view of the soul. It is perhaps not possible to be a really thoroughgoing body-soul dualist unless one thinks that the soul is (or, as is often the case, imagines it as if it were) a material entity made of a different and superior stuff from the body[10]. Ryle's "ghost in the machine" would not be a bad general description of the doctrines of corporealist body-soul dualists from Democritus to the Manichees.

By far the most important form of alienation from this world to be found in any genuine Hellenic tradition is, of course, that to be discovered in the Pythagorean-Orphic tradition which became so influential in the first centuries of our era because it was accepted by Plato[11], though always, I think, with some reserve and with eventual vigorous modification in a more world-accepting direction. That an intense feeling of world-alienation did exist in this tradition hardly needs demonstrating. It might be described as a rather over-emphasized commonplace, whose emphasis often needs vigorous correction, especially when we are dealing with Plato, Plotinus and the later Neoplatonists. One of our best witnesses to how passionate this feeling could be is one of the earliest, Empedocles. There are fragments of the Καθαρμοί which can hardly be surpassed in Gnostic literature for the force with which they convey the misery of exile in this world[12]. (Perhaps we should remark in passing at this

---

[10] On body-soul dualism in the Stoics see the very careful examination of the evidence in J. Pepin, Idées Grecques sur l'Homme et sur Dieu, (Paris 1971) Part I, Chapters I–V.

[11] I do not think that "Neo-Pythagoreanism", in any of its more philosophically interesting forms, can at any stage be regarded as independent of Platonism. Many important ideas current among Platonists in the first three centuries may have been originated by persons calling themselves Pythagoreans, but not by Pythagoreans uninfluenced by the Old Academy and such records as survived of Plato's discussions therein.

[12] See expecially D K. 31. B 115. Of course Empedocles was an original and independent thinker, and should not be considered simply as a representative of the

point, to get our subject into perspective, that a decidedly gloomy view of this world is often expressed by classical Greek poets who were not in the least philosophical or other-worldly, and who sometimes in other moods appreciated and enjoyed it thoroughly[13]). It is extremely important, if we are to arrive at a just appreciation of the possibilities of mutual influence in the first centuries of our era, that we should not underplay the continuing strength of the influence of Platonic-Pythagorean tradition on Greek speakers or readers in these centuries and that we should understand as clearly as possible the differences between Platonic-Pythagorean and Gnostic world-alienation.

Let us therefore briefly consider these differences, referring back for the faith and mood of the alienated Gnostic either to my summary description above or to better sources elsewhere. First of all, for the Platonist or Pythagorean our lower world, though there is much evil in it, whose presence has to be explained, is predominantly a good world. It really is a cosmos, a thing of beauty and order, and even in its degree divine. It is brought into being and ruled by a good divine power or powers who are not responsible for the evil in it (this is one of the cardinal doctrines of Platonic theology: all θεοί are good and do good, not evil). There can therefore be no question of *total* rejection of the world or a spirit of revolt against its maker or rulers, even when there are believed to be higher divinities beyond them. (As Empedocles has been mentioned, it should be pointed out that his view of equipollent and alternatively, predominant powers, not so much of good and evil – though he certainly does not like Strife – but of unity and disunity, which are both necessary if there is to be a world, is entirely peculiar to his system). Secondly, the existence of the cosmos is necessary (and often thought to be eternal). It is not the result of an incursion of a positive evil principle or the lapse of a higher spiritual power. Even when there is a hierarchy of divinities the divine goodness flows down smoothly, without break or fault, to the demiurgic power. And if the cosmos is necessary, the essential principles required for its constitution are necessary: and the non-divine principle responsible for the existence of evil in it is as necessary as the divine principle responsible for its good. The life of the cosmos is an endless dialectic, and though the divine perennially gets the better of the argument, it never brings it to a triumphant conclusion and there is no resolution into a higher synthesis (even in Empedocles there is no final and

Pythagorean-Orphic tradition. But on this side at least of his complex (and still rather mysterious) thought he does seem to be fully in that tradition, and can legitimately be cited here as a witness.

[13] See, e. g: Mimnermus VI 1 (2) Diehl: and compare and contrast the first στάσιμον of Sophocles Antigone with the second, and the first στάσιμον of the Oedipus Coloneus with the third (with due regard to the dramatic contexts in both cases).

permanent synthesis). There can be no cosmos without the opposites: therefore both opposites are part of a necessary system, whose existence is not resented.

It is all the easier not to resent the existence of the cosmos because the "principle of evil" in the Platonic-Pythagorean tradition is not a positive principle of evil in the Iranian sense. In all forms of Iranian dualism evil is quite ferociously positive and aggressive. It is conflict-dualism[14] of the most pugnacious kind. (Iranian-style conflict-dualism, with a strongly positive concept of evil, seems still to be curiously popular among some Christians, though it is not favoured by the greatest theologians of the classical Christian tradition. I have certainly known respected Christian thinkers and pastors who, though they technically saved their orthodoxy by professing the doctrine of the fall of Lucifer, were to all practical purposes Iranian dualists[15].) In the Pythagorean-Platonie tradition the principle opposed to good is the principle of indefinite multiplicity, essentially negative and vague. In this lower, material world of space-time separation this is thought of as the principle of irrationality and disorder (which are of course evil: evil for this tradition consists in irrational disorder). But it is also a principle which is necessary to the existence of any system of number and any sort of world, even a Platonic World of Forms or a Gnostic Pleroma. And the cases where a Platonist or Pythagorean momentarily thinks that it would be better if there was no sort of world at all, even the highest, if only the Absolute One and Good existed, and considers that anything less good than the Best is bad, are very rare. The real alternative for philosophers of this tradition, even in their most pessimistic and alienated moods, is not that between the sole existence of a perfectly good World of Light and the additional, unnecessary and undesirable existence of this lower world of darkness, which has something arbitrary in its genesis and is unwilled and unwanted by the power of good. The alternative for Pythagoreans and Platonists is between an absolute and impossible acosmism and a necessary system of two universes, in both of which both opposed principles operate as constitutive forces, though it is only in the lower, material, one and not in the higher,

---

[14] I owe this term, and much of the inspiration for what follows, to Wilfred Cantwell Smith's admirable little popular book, The Faiths of Other Men (Mentor, New York 1965).

[15] It would be irrelevant to discuss the reasons for this here, I suspect that one is that persistent element in Christian teaching and preaching which an ancient Hellene would have called *Tragoedia* (in the later derogatory sense) and a modern educated European would describe as "melodrama". Conflict-dualism, of course, makes a splendid foundation for pulpit rhetoric, and is easily adaptable for political purposes. Supporting evidence for these unkind statements can easily be supplied by many of my readers from their own experience. My own (which would include a full account of the views of the late Rev. William Alexander Armstrong on slugs) must be omitted for the sake of brevity.

intelligible one that the principle which causes indefinite multiplicity does not submit itself completely to the principle which causes form and order and becomes the principle of disorderly, irrational evil. This second principle, in fact, does double duty as an explanation both of the multiplicity necessary to any cosmos and the evil of this lower one. We are dealing here with a very strange sort of dualism which is closer to the Yang-Yin dualism of Chinese thought than to Iranian conflict-dualism but is not simply identical with it as, at least in the context of our lower world, the opposed valuations of "good" and "evil" are given to the complementary principles which can be described as limit-unlimited, light-dark, male-female, etc., and this does not seem to be the case in Chinese thought.

The position is further complicated in the Platonic-Pythagorean tradition by the fact that generally (exceptions will be discussed later) the higher regions of the material cosmos above the moon are considered to be exempt from evil. The opposite principle is not in opposition here, any more than in the intelligible world, but is perfectly pliable and docile, submitting fully to the good purposes of the principle of limit and form, so that all in the material as in the spiritual Upper Cosmos is, though of course in an inferior degree because of its corporeality, beauty, light and rational order. This obviously marks a most important distinction between Platonic-Pythagorean philosophers and Gnostics, which may perhaps be used with caution to help to discern possible Gnostic influence on an individual Greek philosopher (this will be discussed later). For a Gnostic the heavens are evil. For most Platonists to say this is serious blasphemy.

But none the less, for Pythagoreans and Platonists there is much evil in this lower material cosmos which we are compelled to occupy in this life, and a very strong sense of alienation from it is possible. The philosopher of this tradition feels very strongly that he personally belongs to those higher regions in which all is light, order, harmony and peace and there is nothing to hinder his contemplative exercise of the intellect which is his true self, and that he is a stranger and an exile here below, however he explains his presence here. The explanations of the presence of human souls on earth (the presence of permanently embodied divine souls in the heavens, the earth herself regarded as a goddess, and the physical universe as a whole does not seem to have worried anybody, for reasons briefly indicated in the last paragraph) vary, within the limits laid down by Plato himself in the Phaedo, Phaedrus, Republic and Timaeus, between the old Pythagorean-Orphic idea of the pre-natal sin and fall into the cycle of birth and death and the idea that souls, with their divine or god-like nature, are sent down by the higher divine powers to help them in their divine work here below: and the two explanations con be com-

bined, as is shown in the early treatise of Plotinus On the Descent of the
Soul into Bodies[16], which well illustrates the perplexity to which
Platonists were reduced by the apparent discrepancies in Plato's statements and the effort which had to be made to reconcile them. The
treatise, incidentally, should be read from beginning to end if we are to
form a just appreciation of the attitude of Plotinus himself when he was
writing it. The beginning, with its remarkable appeal to personal experience and its collection of the most dualistic passages he could find in the
tradition, is gloomy enough to satisfy Numenius or Porphyry. But cheerfulness about the cosmos and our presence in it breaks in vigorously before the end — and we finally discover that our higher selves do not descend at all, a doctrine to which Plotinus always adhered. The later Neoplatonists, of course, did not follow him in this: a clear account of their
developments and precisions of the doctrine of the descent of the soul is
to be found in a passage of the commentary on the Timaeus by Proclus
which to a considerable extent represents the teaching of Iamblichus[17].
A strongly positive view of the descent predominates here; and elsewhere in Proclus[18] we find some souls who might almost be called
"Bodhisattvas", who descend (apparently more often than they need) to
help their fellow-men because they share in and imitate the providential
ἔρως of the gods. This positive insistence on the god-given functions
which souls descend into this world to fulfill accords well with the late
Neoplatonist account of evil here below which my earlier account
may suggest was the natural and inevitable final development of the
Pythagorean-Platonic doctrine. In it the principle of indefinite multiplicity is no longer in any sense a principle of evil, but is on every level down
to the matter of this world an expression of the divine infinity which proceeds from the unknowable Good which transcends the primal opposition of limit and unlimited. Evil in this form of the doctrine is "negative",
not in the sense of proceeding from a negative principle but in the sense
that it has no principle and no real existence at all, only a parasitic quasi-
existence as defect of good. (It was in this form, of course, that the doctrine was accepted by the classical Christian theologians, who unani-
mously rejected the idea of even a negative independent principle of
evil). Platonism moved steadily away from world-alienation from the
third century onwards. But even in its most pessimistic and alienated
forms in the second century its explanations of the evil of this world and,

---

[16] IV 8 [6].

[17] In Tim. III. 277. 31 ff. Diehl.

[18] In Alc. 32. 9 ff. (pp. 14–15 Westerink). This is part of the great passage on the divine
ἔρως which leads higher beings to help and care for those below them, of which Socrates is
the supreme human example.

still more, of the reasons for our exile in it and alienation from it, have little in common with those of the Gnostics. They belong to different worlds of thought.

3. Possible influences of Greek philosophy on the Gnosis

This consideration should govern any discussion of possible influences of Greek philosophy, in its Platonic-Pythagorean or any other form, on alienated Gnosticism. This is not a subject on which I propose to say very much. I am not qualified to do so, and in the present state of Gnostic studies it would be foolish to say anything at all definite. When the Nag-Hammadi literature has been completely published, and critically considered and compared with many other sources of information, old and new, about various sorts of Middle Eastern and Mediterranean religion, by a generation or two of scholars, it may become possible to say something solidly based and convincing about the origins of various sorts of Gnosticism, and to make at least some probable general statement well supported by evidence about the origin of this way of faith as a whole. But I do at present hold to a fairly strong belief which would, I think be widely accepted, that we are dealing here with a distinct way of feeling and thinking about God, man and the world which has little in common with any way of feeling and thinking to be found among Greek philosophers[19].

Gnostics did certainly refer to Greek philosophy and mythology and interpret them in their own way to give authority to their views among people of Hellenic tradition. The most solid piece of evidence which has so far been produced for this is the extraordinary little document contained in the Nag-Hammadi library which has been published as the "Titellose Schrift", which is in fact a garbled version of Plato Republic 588B – 589B[20].

---

[19] This is admirably stated and argued in the introductory section of Jonas's great German book (see n. 3). The question whether Jonas extends the bounds of Gnosticism too far will be explicitly discussed later in the chapter in so far as it concerns Greek philosophers, especially Plotinus (some differences of opinion on this may already have become implicitly apparent). Another excellent statement of the view I am here accepting is to be found in Gilles Quispel, Gnosis als Welt-Religion (Zürich 1951), pp. 26–27.

[20] Facsimile Edition of the Nag-Hammadi Codices, Codex VI (Leiden, E. J. Brill 1972) pp. 48–51: Abhandlungen des Deutschen Archäologischen Instituts Kairo Koptische Reihe Band II, ed. Martin Krause und Pahor Labib (Glückstadt 1971) pp. 166–169. My attention was drawn to this by my colleague, the eminent scholar in the field of Near Eastern religion, Prof. Dr. E. Segelberg and his pupil Mr. Elias Matsagouras. Cp. also the information given about Carpocratian respect for ancient philosophers in Irenaeus Adv. Haer. I. 25. 6 and the remarkable Naassene exegesis of mythology and mystery-cults reported by Hippolytus, Ref. V, 7–9.

But I must here draw attention to a matter of the greatest importance which must be considered whenever there is any question of the "influence" of anything on anybody. This is the sharp distinction which must be drawn between two kinds of relationship which may exist between a person and the religious or philosophical tradition by which he is said to be influenced. One should, in my opinion, only speak of "influence" without very careful and precise restrictions and qualifications when someone's mind has been formed to an important extent by a tradition: when, that is, he has been taught by great thinkers of that tradition and / or has read the writings considered authoritative in that tradition in their original languages (which may or may not be his own) under the guidance of competent inheritors of the tradition. This sort of genuine influence is of course compatible with original and dissident thinking and unprecedented courses of action when the person so influenced matures. And a person may be influenced in this real way by two or more, perhaps ultimately incompatible, traditions. This, as I am now inclined to think, is the normal condition of modern European man, influenced at once by the Judaic and Hellenic traditions: hence many of our present discontents. Of course, when a person is brought up and formed in a tradition which dominates his environment so completely that it never occurs to him consciously to think or act in any way contrary to the tradition, he is not influenced by the tradition: he is part of the tradition. This is true whether a tradition is ancient and deeply rooted, or recent and only transitorily predominant. mere *Zeitgeist:* though a *Zeitgeist* seldom manages to dominate its period or environment completely.

But there is also the very common case where someone uses ideas derived from a tradition to which he remains extraneous to help himself develop, or to commend to others, ideas or projects for action which really derive from the tradition in which he was formed. This can be done at varying levels of depth or superficiality: from the Hindu thinker who is not so "Westernized" that he can be regarded as an example of a person genuinely influenced by two incompatible traditions, but who knows a great deal about Western thought and civilization and uses Christian or non-Christian Western ideas to commend his own tradition to the West or help him develop it for his own people; or the Christian theologian who has spent many years in India and knows Indian sacred writings well in their original languages, who uses, say, the Vedanta to help him in his missionary work or to develop his own theology. At the superficial extreme there are the politicians and pseudo-prophets who use generally misunderstood and garbled ideas and quotations from respected authorities to give spurious authority to ideas and projects derived from different and perhaps despicable sources. There are probably Gnostics to be found who make extraneous use of Greek philosophy at every level of depth and superficiality (though most of them seem to a historian of Greek philosophy to be nearer the superficial end). But the distinction which I have made needs to be carefully applied in many other fields of study. It needs to be applied particularly rigorously when some venerable tradition is being blamed for the disastrous consequences that its alleged "influence" has brought about. Many choice examples of its neglect can be called from the copious modern literature on e.g: the deplorable influence of Biblical thought on Christian conduct (admittedly the Bible is a somewhat ethically ambiguous collection of documents); or the shocking consequences of Plato's political thought (I do not think that Plato was always politically right). In these instances it is extremely important to have a thorough scholarly and historical knowledge, and understanding, both of the tradition alleged to have done the influencing and of the thoughts and actions which it is alleged to have influenced, in their full historical setting, before one begins the attack. The same precautions, of course, need to be observed when dealing with the alleged influences of more modern and less venerated traditions (g.g: the various pernicious influences alleged to have been exerted by Hegel and Hegelianism).

I think, then , in general, that any influence which may have been exerted by any kind of Greek philosophy on Gnosticism was not genuine but extraneous and, for the most part superficial. We are dealing with the use of Greek ideas, often distorted or strangely developed, in a context which is not their own, to commend a different way of faith and feeling, not with a genuine growth of any variety of Gnosticism out of philosophy, whatever some ancient heresiologists may have thought. And I do not believe in a general spirit or characteristic of the thought of late antiquity which expresses itself equally in Gnosticism, orthodox Christianity and late antique philosophy. This is perhaps my main difference with Jonas. It will be discussed shortly in the context of the thought of Plotinus, and it is not of a kind to affect my appreciation of much which he says about Gnosticism. So many of Jonas's, and many other people's, statements to which strong exception has been or could be taken could be made perfectly correct by the simple expedient of narrowing them a little – by saying, instead of "the spirit of late antiquity", "the spirit of Gnosticism" or (in other cases) "the very varied spirits of some small religious groups". To read some accounts of the "other-worldliness" of late antiquity, one would suppose that Alexandria and Rome were full of enormous basilicas packed to the doors with Gnostics and that the School of Plotinus was about the size of the modern University of Rome. This was not in fact the case. And, in speaking of more modern times, it is often better to say something like "the intellectual circles I then frequented" than "the intellectual world of the time". (I was young and interested in ideas in the late 1920's and early 1930's, and I do not recall that anyone in the intellectual circles which *I* frequented, in Britain or the Catholic German-speaking lands which I then visited a good deal, ever mentioned Heidegger). We are all of us, scholars, philosophers and theologians, too much inclined to assume that the part of the world we are interested in is the whole world.

None the less, there is at least some possibility that in one area and in the case of one tradition of Gnosticism the influence of the Platonic-Pythagorean type of Greek philosophy, though still extraneous, may have been more than superficial. (To assess the strength of this possibility accurately would require more knowledge of the possible variations of Iranian and other Eastern dualisms than I possess). This influence may show itself in the tendency, which appears quite early, to reduce the independent principle of evil to something in itself inert and passive, which is only stirred into activity by the entrance into it of some power or powers from the World of Light, which remains the only source of activity[21]. This does not mean, of course, that the originally passive and inert principle of evil in the systems which postulate it is simply a duplicate of the Platonic-Pythagorean principle of indefinite multiplicity: the two ways of thinking remain fundamentally different wholes, in which every part or element is conceived differently and operates in a different way because of the difference of the whole. But there may be some Hellenic influence discernible in the tendency to prefer an originally negative and passive principle of evil to one which is active against good by its own power and its own motion, just as there is quite probably some Iranian influence the other way when Platonic-Pythagorean philosophers stress very strongly the irrational disorderly activity of the principle of indefinite multiplicity acting as principle of evil in this lower world. This will be discussed later: but it may be as well to say at once that "Iranian" in the previous sentence is not intended to mean "Gnostic". As for the Gnostic systems which manage to explain the evil or inferiority of our world without postulating an independent principle of evil at all, such as that of Basilides (who is really in general remarkably cheerful and optimistic for an "alienated" Gnostic[22]) and the great imaginative theology of Valentinus, I should be inclined to postulate a predominant Christian influence rather than one deriving from Greek philosophy to account for this

---

[21] My attention was drawn to this by a paper sent to me by our esteemed editor, Barbara Aland, Synkretismus im Syrisch-Persischen Kulturgebiet in Abhandlungen der Akademie der Wissenschaften in Göttingen, Philologisch-Historische Klasse, III. Reihe, No. 96 (Göttingen 1975). She might, perhaps be a little disconcerted by the idea she has put into my head. The article, as its title suggests, deals with an area in which direct Hellenic influence is unlikely – it is a comparison between the systems of Bardesanes and Mani. But she does point out the relationship between the idea of passive, inert evil mentioned in the text. which appears in the system of Bardesanes, and the "three principle" Gnosticisms of the Sethians and Naassenes, and the (even for a Gnostic) very odd and original Justin with his free use of allegorically interpreted Hellenic mythology (Hippolytus V 26). In none of these is the third power involved in the formation of the universe an active and positive principle of evil (indeed in Justin "Eden" is not wholly evil at all, though her character is decidedly ambiguous). The concept of "restless motion" as an origin of evil, which appears in Bardesanes (art. cit. pp. 127–129) might possibly be worth a little further investigation in connection with Plato Timaeus 52–53, though a non-Hellenic origin for it may be demonstrable.

[22] See Hippolytus Ref. VII. 20–27. Basilides knew, and presumably disapproved of, a full-blooded Iranian conflict-dualism type of Gnosticism. See Hegemonius, Acta Archelai 67. 5, 7–11.

characteristic of their systems (whatever the connections of some aspects of the thought of Valentinus with earlier "three-principle" systems may be). The nonexistence of any sort of independent principle of evil was, after all, seen by the Christians of the early centuries (and thereafter) as one of their cardinal points of difference with the pagans, and they insisted very strongly that evil in the world must be accounted for exclusively by falls of spirits and men and not by any such independent principle (we shall consider later how far the second principle in Neo-Pythagoreanism and later Platonism was genuinely independent, and how far the Christians misunderstood many of their adversaries on this point). I still, however, find the supposition of G. C. Stead[23] attractive, that (probably through Hellenistic Judaism) strangely combined Platonic-Pythagorean conceptions of the fall of the individual soul and the evil soul in matter in one of the forms which that concept took in the second century, played their part in the genesis of the theology of Valentinus, even if that part was a subordinate one.

4. Possible influences of Gnosis on Greek philosophy

a) In the 2nd century

We shall now turn to the other side of our main subject, the possibility of some Gnostic influence on some forms of later Greek philosophy. This is something about which a historian of Greek philosophy may be able to say something less vague, general and tentative than what has been said about possible influence the other way in the preceding pages. I shall deal only with some forms of Platonic-Pythagorean philosophy in the second and third centuries, which are the only ones whose consideration is relevant to the subject-matter of this chapter. An important general point must be made by way of introduction to the examination of the thought of the several particular philosophers to be examined here. This is that in all cases among these very traditionally-minded people we are dealing with Platonic exegesis, and often (perhaps oftener than our evidence permits us to see) with a very well established exegesis, going back in some cases to the Old Academy. Their main object is to give the authentic interpretation of Platonic doctrine (coupled sometimes with traditional accounts of the teaching of Pythagoras) or of particular passages in the Dialogues. When, therefore, we are confronted with an interpreta-

---

[23] See G. C. Stead, The Valentinian Myth of Sophia, in Journal of Theological Studies N. S. XX. 1. 1969. This is a very well documented and careful article, which explores the possibilities of Hellenic influences on the theology of Valentinus far more thoroughly than I can do here.

tion of Plato which is either known to have a long earlier history or is natural-seeming and may go back further than our earliest evidence for it, it seems unnecessary and undesirable to assume any Gnostic or other extraneous influence. This is the case with the idea of the evil soul in matter as the principle of evil in the material universe, which is very easily based on an exegesis of Laws 896E – 897D (combined with Timaeus 52–53) which is natural-seeming (though, as I believe, mistaken)[24]. This being so, if, as I suggested above, we are to see some evidence of the influence of Iranian conflict-dualism on the vigour with which some second-century philosophers emphasize this doctrine, we must find some evidence other than the vigorous assertion of the doctrine for seeing it, and we must remember that we are dealing simply with a question of emphasis, not ot the derivation of new doctrine from an alien source. In Plutarch, the earliest in date of the philosophers to be considered, we can, I think, find such evidence, with other interesting and curious things relevant to our investigation, at least in his most Orientalizing work, the De Iside et Osiride (Plutarch cannot, of course, be relied on to be an entirely consistent thinker). The passage on the evil world-soul, cited by Stead in the article mentioned earlier, from the De Animae Procreatione in Timaeo[25], has nothing to suggest an origin other than Platonic. But in the De Iside et Osiride, though the doctrine is in all essentials the same, Iranian conflict-dualism (about which Plutarch seems quite well informed) is explicitly referred to (along with many other things) to support Plutarch's interpretation of Plato[26], and it may therefore, have helped to lead him to prefer and emphasize this explanation of the problem of evil. A mild and secondary influence of Iranian conflict-dualism does not, of course, bring Plutarch anywhere near the Gnostics. But there are other features in this particular work which may seem to bring him rather closer. One is the acceptance, at one point, of at least a minimum influence of the active principle of evil in the heavens. Typhon-Seth is responsible for what seem to be regarded as irrational disturbances, like eclipses, in the Upper Cosmos[27]. This does not, however, bring Plutarch very close to the Gnostics after all. The heavens themselves are not evil or caused by an evil power for him, even in this

---

[24] I do not propose, here or in what follows, to involve myself in vast and complex questions about what Plato really meant, in disputed passages of the Dialogues or reports of his unwritten doctrines. These are matters in which certainty is difficult (perhaps impossible). It would more than double the length of this chapter to discuss even a selection of them at all adequately, and would be irrelevant to our purpose here.

[25] Chapter 6, 1014 D–1015 C: cp. Stead, art. cit. (n. 23) p. 101.

[26] Chapters 46–47, 369 D–370 C. At the beginning of chapter 46 the antiquity (and therefore the authority) of Zoroaster is stressed.

[27] Chapter 49, 371 B.

passage but only irrational perturbations in them: and there are two
neighbouring passages which express a preference for the normal sort of
late Hellenic cosmic piety, in which the Upper Cosmos is wholly good[28].
The other curious feature of Plutarch's theology in this treatise which
gives his thought a superficial resemblance to some Gnostic systems is
what happens to matter as a result of his unusually sharp separation of it
from the active evil soul. Matter, the passive principle in the formation of
the cosmos, is clearly presented as a female principle submitting lovingly,
with a passionate desire of the good, to the good active principle of form
and order in the cosmos, its demiurge or creator whom the Egyptians call
Osiris. She is, in fact, the goddess Isis[29], good in herself but subject to
continual attack by the evil power. This attractive but melodramatically
imperilled female has a certain resemblance to the Spirit in the (perhaps
rather oversimplified?) account of a Sethian-Ophite (?) system by
Irenaeus[30]. But one must proceed very cautiously here. The resemblance
may be in the picturesque personification rather than the doctrine: and,
as anyone familiar with allegorical painting knows, very similar beautiful
female figures may symbolize a great variety of different things. And,
when one looks closer, there are very fundamental differences of doctrine. No Gnostic did, or could, identify the Spirit as a good female principle with matter. But for Plutarch Isis is matter, and this means that matter is good and divine, the honoured consort[31] of the supreme God, who
in Plutarch and the whole tradition of Platonic exegesis to which he belongs is the Demiurge of the Timaeus – there is no distinction between
First God and Demiurge, as there is in other second-century
philosophers. Perhaps what we have just noticed is not the most Gnostic
but the most anti-Gnostic feature of Plutarch's Isiac theology. In any
case Plutarch's whole view of the cosmos is profoundly opposed to that of
the alienated Gnostics. This is a good world, formed of good matter in
time[32], by the one good God. The evil in it is caused by an independent
principle with limited powers, which never gets the upper hand. We can
confirm the profoundly un-Gnostic character of Plutarch's world-view
by comparing it with that of another Platonist in the same tradition, the
late second-century Atticus. He was another vigorous exponent of a conflict-dualism based on Laws X applied to the explanation of the Timaeus
(we do not know that he cited Iranian authority in support of this, but

---

[28] Chapter 45, 369 D: Chapter 51, 372 A.

[29] Chapter 53.

[30] Adv. Haer. I. 30. The position in the original Gnostic documents describing a similar
system appears a good deal more complicated: cp. the Apocryphon of John. But this is a
matter better left to the judgement of Gnostic specialists.

[31] Chapter 58, 375 A.

[32] De Animae Procreatione in Timaeo Chapter 4, 1013 E–F.

Proclus couples him with Plutarch, and he was probably influenced by the earlier philosopher)[33]: and he does not seem, as far as we know, to have separated the evil soul from matter as sharply as Plutarch. But his world is Plutarch's world, a good world formed in time by the one good God, who watches over and guides every detail in it by his providence, the evil in it being explained by the continuing turbulent irrational activity of the pre-existent, independent evil soul, so that God is not responsible for it. These simple, pious, fundamentalist Platonists who base their religious philosophy on a very literal interpretation of the Timaeus are, precisely because of their adoption of their form of conflict-dualism, able to take a view of this world, in spite of their vivid consciousness of the evil in it, which is in essentials truly Platonic, opposed to that of the alienated Gnostics, and closer than that of any other Platonists to the Judaeo-Christian tradition: orthodox Christians were aware of this, as the preservation of such extensive fragments of Atticus by Eusebius and the affection felt for Plutarch down to the time of John Mavropous show.

We must now turn to consider the very curious and distinctive thought of Numenius. Here there does seem some real possibility of some kind of interaction between the thought of this most original (as far as we can judge) of second-century philosophers and some forms of Gnosticism. It would, of course, be easier here to determine who had influenced whom if we could date with a fair degree of exactitude the actual first appearance (not the first appearance in the original form of any literature known to us directly or indirectly) of important Gnostic ideas, and if we were quite sure where in the second century to place Numenius. The editor of the excellent Budé edition of the fragments, Professor E. Des Places, has now, I believe, joined Beutler and Waszink in supposing him to belong to the first, rather than the second half, of the century[34]. But Numenius, whose interest in and respect for Oriental thought seems rather more lively even than was usual among philosophers of his time, and who was exceptional in knowing something about Judaism (how much, we cannot be certain) and perhaps even a little about early Christianity[35], would be the philosopher, of those about whom we know anything in the second century, most likely to be influenced in some degree

---

[33] Proclus In Tim. I, 381, 26–382, 12 Diehl. For the very simple (as far as our evidence goes) basic doctrines of Atticus, presented in the form of anti-Aristotelian polemic, see Eusebius P. E. XV, 798 C–804 A (III and IV Baudry).

[34] For the earlier opinion of des Places (second half of the century) see Numenius, Fragments (Paris 1973) p. 7. (first page of Notice): for the view of R. Beutler see R.-E. Supp.-Bd. VII, 1940 c. 665, and for Waszink's assent to it J. W. Waszink, Timaeus a Calcidio Translatus (London and Leiden ²1975) p. LXXXVI n. 2.

[35] Frr. 1 a, b, c des Places (9a and b and 32 Leemans), Fr. 8 des Places (17 Leemans), Fr. 10a des Places (19 Leemans).

52

by some form of Gnosticism, and perhaps we can find some evidence in the fragments that he was so influenced. From what has already been said, it is clear that I shall not be looking for evidence of Gnostic influence in his strong assertion of the doctrine of the evil soul in matter[36], even though it is accompanied by a gloomy view of this world and man's lot in it[37]. His distinctive doctrine that there are two souls in man, if it suggests any extraneous influence, suggests an influence of something like the Judaism of the Qumran community rather than of Gnosticism[38]. Nor shall I be tempted to see anything Gnosticizing in his separation of the First God from the Demiurge. The clear distinction of a First, ineffably transcendent, God or Mind above a Second God or Mind is to be found in the first-century Neo-Pythagorean Moderatus and in Alcinous (whose one surviving work was unkindly taken away from him by modern scholars and given to Albinos, but has now been convincingly restored to him by Professor J. Whittaker[39].) Moderatus will be discussed later in a different context, where he will not appear very Gnostic (he may be the principal source of the distinction in Numenius): and only the most frenetic Gnostic-hunter could find anything Gnostic in the prosaic Hellenism of Alcinous (whose doctrine of two divine Minds clearly results from an attempt to combine the theologies of Plato and Aristotle).

But there are other points of doctrine in the fragments which do seem to me to suggest some Gnostic influence. Numenius seems to have asserted that there was evil in the heavens more uncompromisingly and less hesitatingly than Plutarch: and, though in the passage of Calcidius where we find this doctrine attributed to him[40] it appears as a perfectly logical deduction from the fact that the heavenly bodies are material, some Gnostic influence cannot be excluded here. And when we turn to consider closely what Numenius says about the character and activity of his Demiurge, we find a good deal which is even more interesting. The curi-

---

[36] Fr. 52 des Places (Test. 30 Leemans).

[37] Fr. 48 des Places (Test. 40 Leemans).

[38] Fr. 44 des Places (Fest. 36 Leemans): cp. the Qumran Community Rule III–IV, but cp. also E. R. Dodds, Numenius and Ammonius, in Entretiens Hardt V (Vandoeuvres – Genève 1957) p. 7 ff. for other possible Oriental sources, some of them Gnostic.

[39] J. Whittaker, Parisimus Graecus 1962 and the Writings of Albinus, 1–2 in Phoenix 28 (1974) 3 and 4.

[40] Fr. 52, p. 97, 81–98, 92 des Places (Test. 30 Leemans). There is so much dispute about how much, if any, of the long passage in Macrobius Comm. in Somn. Scip. I 10–12, about the descent of the rational soul through the heavens and the increments which it acquires there, comes from Numenius that I have not cited it as supporting evidence here. But des Places has assembled enough evidence to show that at least the celestial geography of the descent comes from Numenius (Frr. 30–35: see his Note Préliminaire, pp. 80–81). And if the whole passage comes from Numenius, as Dodds thinks (loc. cit. n. 38) it would strengthen the case for Gnostic influence here (see the discussion of Dodds's paper in the Hardt volume, pp. 53–54).

ous features of his account have often been noted. I will give my own summary interpretation of what I find in the fragments. Some of it would probably have, rightly, struck any second-century Platonic-Pythagorean reader as original in expression, but not going outside the permissible limits of the tradition. The Demiurge is brought into existence, probably eternally, by the First, perhaps as a kind of reflex of the First's eternal intellective act, and in coming into existence as a thinking mind he "self-makes" his own idea, which is the secondary οὐσία and ἰδέα of the beginning of Fragment 16, of which the First can reasonably be said to be the cause: this is in fact the immanent idea in the Demiurge's mind which he uses in making the cosmos[41]. So far so good, from a second-century Platonic point of view. But elsewhere we discover some strange things about this Second God. He is good (this is repeatedly stressed in the fragments) but none the less has a certain ambiguity and imperfection about him. He is contemplative, and regulates his demiurgic action by his contemplation[42]. He looks to his father the supreme God and Good either continuously or turn and turn about[43]. But, being essentially in motion[44], he is not content to be only contemplative, but has what seems to be regarded by Numenius as a regrettable desire tò go and work in matter, and indeed manages to unite it, give it form, and make a cosmos of it, but is himself "split" by it because it is a dyad, and no longer directs himself towards his own intelligible nature (and its source), but forgets himself in his concern for matter: and it is in this unfortunate state that he becomes the Third God, the part or aspect of himself which is entirely immanent in the cosmos[45]. He "goes through the heavens" and is "sent down through the spheres" and our "journeying" as intelligent beings in this world is in him[46]. This, I think, is as far as we can safely go on the basis of the reliable quotations from Numenius in Eusebius (I suspect some confusion at more than one point in the account of the opinions of Numenius given by Proclus)[47]. And it is enough, on my interpretation of the odder phrases and passages in the fragments, to raise some consider-

---

[41] All this is taken from Fr. 16 des Places (25. Leemans). For earlier discussions and interpretations of each fragment cited which I have taken into account see the headings and footnotes of des Places to each fragment.

[42] Fr. 18 (27. Leemans).

[43] Fr. 18. If one compares the ἔπειτα θεωρητικὸς ὅλως Fr. 16, 12, with the end of Fr. 12 (21 Leemans), where Numenius is clearly trying to get the extraordinary myth of the Politicus (268 D – 274 E) into his Platonic theology (cp. the use of περιωπή in l. 20 of the Numenius fragment which occurs in exactly the same context in Politicus 272 E 4), it seems quite likely that the phrase in Fr. 16 has some kind of temporal sense after all.

[44] Fr. 15 des Places (24. Leemans).

[45] Fr. 11 des Places (20 Leemans).

[46] Fr. 12 des Places (21 Leemans).

[47] See Fr. 21 and 22 des Places (Test. 24 and 25 Leemans).

able suspicion of a degree of Gnostic influence. A "split", distracted Demiurge, desiring matter and forgetful of himself and his Father the Good is not an altogether Platonic figure. A small point of language supports this suspicion. Numenius at least once calls the Demiurge "the lawgiver"[48]. This sound very much as if he was identifying him with the God of the Jews seen from a rather Gnostic point of view. But one should not carry ones suspicions of Gnostic influence on some points of doctrine in the fragments so far as to present Numenius himself as any sort of alienated Gnostic. His Demiurge, whatever his imperfections, remains good[49], contemplative, and in direct continuous or recurrent contemplative contact with the Supreme God or Good in which he receives the Forms on whose model he makes the world: there is no suggestion in the fragments that Numenius had any sort of spirit of revolt or resentment against him, or despised him as a stupid, arrogant and inferior being, or thought it possible for the philosopher to reach a higher stage of contemplation and unity and intimacy with the Good than the Demiurge (at any rate at his best). This is natural, because the material world of Numenius is essentially a Platonic, not a Gnostic world. It is "this beautiful cosmos, beautified by participation in the Beautiful"[50], a world in which good predominates[51], though there is much evil in it, and embodiment for man is always an evil and escape from the body possible and to be desired (as Empedocles, and sometimes Plato, had said with emphasis centuries before). Numenius, for all his "Orientalism" remains a Platonic-Pythagorean philosopher who looks at Gnosticism, as he looks at other Oriental, non-Greek ways of thinking, from the outside, adopting and adapting any ideas from the Gnostics which he thinks will be helpful for his Platonic philosophical purposes.

b) On Plotinus

The Platonism and Neo-Pythagoreanism of the second century A. D. seems to be characterized by the highest degree ever reached in the Platonic-Pythagorean tradition of pessimism about the material world and sense of alienation in it and desire to escape from it. In all Platonism

---

[48] 'ο νομοθέτης Fr. 13 des Places (22 Leemans).

[49] See especially Frr. 19–20 des Places (28–29 Leemans).

[50] Fr. 16 des Places (25 Leemans).

[51] See especially a striking passage in the long report of Calcidius of the teaching of Numenius on evil (Fr. 52 des Places, Test. 30 Leemans, p. 98, 100–120 des Places – from chapters 298–299 of Calcidius). This shows very well how close Numenius, in spite of the ultra-pessimistic, somewhat Gnosticizing streak in his thought, managed to remain to the Timaeus.

a kind of sliding or fluctuation in the valuation of the material world, and a corresponding variability of feeling about our own embodied presence in it, is always inescapably possible. This is because the material universe is not for Platonists the only universe there is, as it is for Stoics and Epicureans and most modern thinkers, which has to be taken as we find it without reference to anything beyond itself, and accepted or condemned, judged bad or good, patterned and meaningful or unpatterned and meaningless, in one way or another, in itself and by itself. For Platonists the material world is always the image of the intelligible, and the best possible image on the level of corporeslity and space-time separateness, because made by the divine goodness doing the best it can on this level. It is therefore possible for them to attend predominantly in their thinking and feeling about this world to the fact that it is the best possible image, a glorious and venerable icon not made with human hands of the intelligible goodness and beauty: or to think of this only occasionally, and advert predominantly to the fact that it is only an image on the lowest possible level of existence, and therefore inauthentic, spectral, inevitably tainted with the imperfections bound up with corporeality and space-time scattering and separation, and so inferior to its intelligible archetype. Not only can different Platonists take up different positions on this scale of valuation, but the same Platonist (and this applies from Plato himself onwards) can fluctuate and slide up and down the scale, varying in his valuation of this world in different moods or contexts, or even adverting almost at the same moment and in the same context to both possible ways of looking at the world as image. The second century Platonists and Platonized Pythagoreans, especially Numenius, seem to be of all Platonists the most inclined to remain near the lower end of the scale of valuation of the material world. In the third century a movement up the scale towards a much more positive and world-accepting attitude begins, and the inaugurator of this movement is Plotinus: it is carried on and developed by the later Neoplatonists, with the exception of Porphyry, who seems to have been inclined to revert to the position of Numenius. This change of attitude had incalculably vast consequences for the future. This at least is the opinion, I think, of most competent contemporary students of late Hellenic thought, an opinion which I share and may perhaps have done a little to help to form[52]. I am aware, of

---

[52] An excellently expressed statement of the view which I am here putting forward (based on a very thorough and detailed knowledge of the whole world of late antiquity) is to be found in Peter Brown, The World of Late Antiquity (London 1971), Chapter VI pp. 70–80. On the far-reaching influence of this last great re-assertion of truly Hellenic Platonism see also in the first instance, the good summary sketches in R. T. Wallis, Neoplatonism (London 1972) Chapter 6, pp. 160–178 (with a good bibliography) and R. A. Markus, Christianity in the Roman World, (London 1974), Chapter 9, pp. 162–184.

course, that the view of Plotinus (with which he would certainly himself have agreed) as the great pagan anti-Gnostic and, with Irenaeus on the Christian side, inaugurator of the movement which led European thought decisively away from any nearness to the world-view of alienated Gnosticism (however persistently ways of thinking and feeling reminiscent of Gnosticism or ultra-pessimistic Platonism may reappear in particular religious or intellectual groups from time to time) is at variance with that of the great scholar whom we are honouring here[53] and a good deal of disagreement with his expressed opinions must necessarily appear in the account of Plotinus with which I shall conclude this chapter: though it is perhaps worth remarking that our variant views are not completely incompatible. It could have been (though I do not think it was) because Plotinus was fighting the Gnostic in himself to the end of his life that he was such an effective anti-Gnostic apologist and so successful in turning Hellenic thought away from any approach to the Gnostic world-view. I shall conclude with Plotinus because I think that it was he who firmly established the main outlines of anti-Gnostic Neoplatonism: his successors only developed and at some points completed his work. Another reason is that to go further would mean discussing the attitudes of Alexander of Lycopolis and of Christian thinkers influenced by Neoplatonism to the Manichees: and this would both extend this chapter beyond all permissible limits and lead me into an area in which I am utterly incompetent. I am even more an alien in the cosmos of Manichaean scholarship than I am in the learned world which devotes itself to the study of earlier Gnostics. In any case, what Alexander of Lycopolis has to

---

[53] In the continuing absence of Band II 2 of Gnosis und Spätantiker Geist I must depend for any detailed statement of Jonas's views on Plotinus on his paper read to the Colloque on Neoplatonism at Royaumont, The Soul in Gnosticism and Plotinus, in Le Néoplatonisme, (Paris 1971) pp. 46–53, reprinted in Philosophical Essays (see n. 1) pp. 324–334: this is unfortunately based on a very narrow selection of texts from the Enneads. I have discussed it very thoroughly in the course of a close study of the text of III 7 [45], on chapter 11 of which Jonas particularly relies, with a friend of his and mine, Dr. Peter Manchester, to whom I owe much in what follows – and much more. Jonas's full study of III 7, Plotin über Ewigkeit und Zeit in Politische Ordnung und Menschliche Existenz (München 1962) pp. 295–319 came to my attention too late for me to give it here the consideration it deserves. In any case, this very important study of the treatise On Time and Eternity would need much more extended discussion than is possible here, including the necessary comparisons with the commentary of Werner Beierwaltes on the same treatise, with the same title, published five years later (Plotin über Ewigkeit und Zeit, Frankfurt am Main 1967). And the views of Jonas on the points at issue here concerning Chapter 11 seem to be substantially the same in this earlier study and in his Royaumont paper. I am also well aware that Jonas's views on the relationship of myth, mysticism and metaphysics really require much more extensive and careful discussion than the summary expressions of disagreement which are all that I have felt there was place for here. It is to be hoped that a paper by Dr. Manchester which does much more justice to the subject may be published before too long.

say against the Manichees adds nothing substantial to the anti-Gnostic
apologetic of Plotinus, and the attitudes to the world of the earlier
Platonists to whom he is in some respects closer, and his thought is in
general not very interesting for our purposes here[54].

A detailed discussion of the explicit anti-Gnosticism of Plotinus and the implicitly Gnostic elements which have been detected in his thought must be pre-
faced by a couple of general statements of opinion which will indicate clearly the
point of view (the bias, if any reader prefers the word) with which I approach the
study of the philosophy of late antiquity, and Neoplatonism in particular. First, I
regard generalizations about the thought of late antiquity which try to get everything and everybody in, about a *Zeitgeist* which in some way determines all
thought in the period, with very great suspicion. My long studies of the period
have led me to recognize in it (as I probably should in any other period which I
studied as closely, and certainly do in our contemporary world) considerable and
irreducible diversities. I am prepared to speak, with caution, restrictions and
qualifications, of a *Zeitgeist* which dominates to a certain extent particular groups
within the period, especially the one which it is easiest to see most clearly, the
small Hellenically educated minority in the Graeco-Roman world: something of
the sort seems to be manifested, for instance in their traditionalism and dislike of
conscious originality and their increasing tendency to some form of monotheistic
piety. Even with this kind of restriction, however, my study of Neoplatonism has
led me to believe that general statements, even about a particular philosophy,
should be regarded, not as definitive statements of the essential truth about their
subject, but as tentative hypotheses requiring criticism and correction which may
eventually lead to their abandonment in favour of a better hypothesis – to be
criticized in its turn. Perhaps, unlike Thaumasius[55], I am not really very interested in general statements. And my view of *Zeitgeister* tends to be pluralistic
or polydaemonistic – if any of my German readers remark pityingly at this point
"How English!" they can do so without offence to me, but I shall note that they
have implicitly conceded my daemonological point. Second, I must say that I do
not (looking at it as an outsider) find Gnostic mythology an example of what
might be called "deep" myth, of a sort which can be assumed to underly unconsciously all the philosophical and religious thinking of the period. Gnostic myths
seem to me examples of secondary myth, of a relatively sophisticated and literary
character, more like Platonic myths than the myths which lie behind Hesiod, or
more like Tolkien than the ancient Norse myths. This does not mean that I do not
regard them as expressing very deep and sincere feelings about the world and
man's nature and condition, or that I do not recognise that they often successfully
use great universal symbols (light for good, darkness for evil etc.) which go very
deep indeed: for some of the great Gnostics had excellent poetic imaginations. I
do not in general deny the possibility of the influence of myth on philosophy (no
pupil of F. M. Cornford's could do so) but I like to proceed with caution, remem-

---

[54] See P. W. Van der Horst and J. Mansfeld, An Alexandrian Platonist Against Dualism
(Leiden 1974).
[55] Porphyry Life of Plotinus, Chapter 13.

bering what I said about "influence" earlier, and considering each particular case separately. And I certainly do not believe that myth generates mystical experience, though myths, theologies and philosophies will determine the language in which mystics (and others) speak of mystical experiences.

That Plotinus was explicitly anti-Gnostic, and that one of his main ground of quarrel with the Gnostics was their valuation of the material cosmos and its maker, no reader of the treatise Against the Gnostics[56] can doubt. But this does not of course exclude the possibility of unconscious Gnostic influence on his thought. My main reason for disbelieving in any degree of such influence which was in any way important during his writing period (we know nothing of the earlier development of his thought) is one which cannot be adequately defended here. This is that, after some forty years of close study of the whole text of the Enneads, I simply do not believe that Plotinus in his later life thought like a Gnostic, or even like Numenius. I could only be convinced of the contrary (if at all) by a Plotinian scholar who knew the text of Plotinus as well as, or better than I do: and those with whom I am acquainted (I think the majority) do not seem at all inclined to think that Plotinus was an unconscious Gnostic. I cannot possibly produce evidence here which will sufficiently demonstrate the grounds for this conviction, especially as it is very largely a question of balance and emphasis, which can only be determined by a study of the whole. I can only say that I have discovered in Plotinus an intense enjoyment of this world in all its horizontal richness and diverse beauty and variety. This does not exclude the continual presence to his mind of the other extreme point of the Platonic scale of valuation of the world as image, and the characteristic Platonic fluctuation and movement up and down the scale, mentioned earlier (p.108). But the lesson, both theoretical and practical, which I and many others have learned from reading Plotinus and later Neoplatonists (and much of Plato himself) is an intense love and appreciation of the beauty of this world which would have disgusted a Gnostic and made him feel us terribly deluded. We must love this world with detachment, without self-centred desire, and with full realisation that it is not the highest, and if our love fails in detachment and becomes tainted with lust for individual self-satisfaction we can become bewitched and entrapped by the world. But we must love the world. Perhaps in our cultural history this kind of Neoplatonic influence has been more often apparent in religious contemplatives, writers, artists, and scientific observers of nature than in professional philosophers, and so may sometimes have escaped the attention of the latter. One of the most beautiful expressions of Plotinus'

---

[56] II 9 [33] – a polemical appendix to the great work quartered by Porphyry, which consists of III 8 [30] V 8 [31] V 5 [32] and II 9 [33].

enjoyment of the endlessly outspreading richness of the diverse beauty of this world is to be found in the first part of the treatise On Providence, which is his most serious consideration of the problem of evil[57]. Nobody could read the second half of the thirteenth chapter and suppose that it was written by someone who hated this world. We should also observe the way cheerfulness keeps breaking in to his most pessimistic (in a second-century Platonic way) accounts of this world. We have already noted this in his early treatise On the Descent Of the Soul (see p. 98) and there are two striking examples in the very late treatise on matter and evil[58]. But the most remarkable and important clue to his real attitude is perhaps the way in which he insists on getting all the living variety of the material cosmos into the intelligible world, sometimes stressing the diverse life of that world to a point which either strains his concept of eternity seriously (it certainly leads to inconsistencies of language) or points the way forward to a very fruitful development of ancient thought about time and eternity – much more work needs to be done here, and is now in progress. This is particularly apparent in the treatise On The Intelligible Beauty, the second part of the great work of which the Ennead treatise Against the Gnostics is the conclusion, and in the great "first movement" (so to speak) of the treatise On How the Multitude of the Forms came into Being and on the Good[59]. The vision which Plotinus has of the intelligible world here is, as Peter Brown says of the art of late antiquity, "innerworldly" rather than "otherworldly"[60].

We should also briefly consider in this context the attitude of Plotinus to his own body. Platonists often feel more hostile and alienated when thinking about their own bodies than when thinking about the material cosmos as a whole, and it is generally assumed that this is true of Plotinus. But there are some qualifications to be made. We have been, perhaps, inclined to pay rather too much attention to the first chapter of Por-

---

[57] III 2 [47] 13, 17–33.

[58] I 8 [51] 14, 36–37, 15, 23–28.

[59] V 8 [31] 3 and 4; VI 7 [38] 1–15.

[60] Op. cit. (n. 52) p. 74 and on the similar quality which he rightly sees in Byzantine art, p. 78. Of course we should not forget that a great deal of the surviving art of late antiquity, and even some surviving Byzantine art, was not "innerworldly" or "otherworldly", but just worldly. Cp. for instance (I mention only works which I have seen) the charming baroque reliefs of Lepcis Magna, and the mosaic pavements of North Africa and Piazza Armerina in Sicily for the third-early-fourth centuries, and for worldly Byzantine art, the fragments of the floor mosaics of the Great Palace at Constantinople (still completely late Hellenistic in style and subjectmatter, though considerably later) and the only surviving Byzantine secular wall mosaics in Palermo (equally worldly, though in a more Persian manner). And much late antique and mediaeval religion was of course equally worldly – the ordinary man in the Mediterranean area (and elsewhere), from peasant to emperor, has usually had a fairly down-to-earth and business-like attitude to the divinity coupled with a deep and genuine instinctive reverence for divine powers operative in his immediate environment.

phyry's Life (which was, after all, written by Porphyry and not by Plotinus) and the many, perfectly sincerely expressed, Phaedo-style Platonic commonplaces in the Enneads which seem to confirm that his attitude was that described by Porphyry, and to neglect somewhat a good deal in the Enneads which suggests a calmer, more benign and tolerant attitude to his own body and to embodiment in general. There are the short discussion of embodiment in The Descent of the Soul and long discussion in his principal work on the soul which show that embodiment is a good and necessary part of the great self-diffusion of the Good through the universes to the last and lowest limits of possible existence, and not necessarily and inevitably an evil for the embodied souls[61]. There is the remarkable passage (which fits its context very well) in which Plotinus shows that the λόγος of man in the intelligible world must include his body as well as his soul, and denies the Platonic commonplace that the soul is the man[62]. Less general and more indicative of his personal attitude to his own body is the noble end of the late treatise On Well-Being where he shows that he thinks he should take leave of his aging and probably by that time repulsively diseased body as a Menuhin might take leave of his favourite violin[63]. And there are two considerations of great importance which should not be forgotten. One is that Plotinus is never in the least worried about the greatest and highest souls known to him being everlastingly embodied, the souls of the heavenly gods and the earth-goddess and the soul of the whole universe. They simply provide him with ideal examples of what our attitude and conduct should be in our own embodiment. And the other is that, of all ancient thinkers, pagan or Christian, he is the least interested in life after death and escape from the body. This is because of his well-known doctrine that the true, higher self, does not descend but remains an eternal inhabitant of the intelligible world, and his assurance, based on experience, that he can live on that higher level in this world and this body, and that without neglecting his earthly duties. Heaven for Plotinus is here and now. To use Gnostic language for a moment, he is sure he has never left the Pleroma, the World of Light, and so needs no saving revealed γνῶσις, complete with escape – plan, to get him back there. This should be very seriously considered when we are trying to determine whether there is any concealed Gnosticism in the thought of Plotinus.

There are one or two points of detail which must be dealt with before we can be completely satisfied that the thought of Plotinus is profoundly un-Gnostic and anti-Gnostic, and will continue to appear so even if we

---

[61] IV 8 [6], 6–7; IV 3 [27], 9–17.

[62] VI 7 [38] 4–6: cp. p. 114 and n. 59 for the context.

[63] I 4 [46] 16, 20–29.

leave the passionate rejection of Gnosticism in his polemical treatise out of account (as I am deliberately doing in this part of the chapter). I shall discuss these as briefly as possible, as there now exists a great deal of exegesis of the passages and points of doctrine concerned which I find satisfactory and to which any reader who wishes to pursue these matters further can be referred. The first question to be dealt with is what Plotinus means when he uses the very Gnostic-sounding word "Τόλμα", "audacity" of his Second and Third Hypostases, Intellect and Soul, or, without using the word, uses language about them which expresses the same idea. These passages[64] (they are few and far between, and cannot be taken as expressing the real thought of Plotinus without balancing them against many others and the impression produced by the Enneads as a whole) have been very thoroughly discussed by Naguib Baladi, who has perhaps penetrated most deeply into the real mind of Plotinus at this point, and by John M. Rist in an outstandingly concise, precise and careful survey of all the evidence[65]. An essential preliminary point has been established by these and previous discussions: this is that Plotinus' use of τόλμα has a clearly demonstrable Hellenic philosophical history history behind ist. Τόλμα was a name given to the Dyad, the principle of indefinite multiplicity which is both essential to the existence of any kind of plurality and so of any kind of universe and, ultimately, the principle of evil (see p. 96), by the strongly Platonized Pythagoreans who held that he Indefinite Dyad (the Platonic name for this principle) was not an independent correlative principle (this was probably the earlier Pythagorean view) but was produced in some way by the primal Monad. This sort of Platonized monistic Pythagoreanism can be traced back at least to the Pythagoreans whom Alexander Polyhistor knew in the first century B. C.[66]. I have little to add to the earlier discussions of this later Pythagoreanism and the use of τόλμα in it, but I would like to point out the relevance here of a Neo-Pythagorean passage which has not, perhaps been sufficiently considered in this context, though it has been much discussed in others. This is the famous report of the doctrine of Moderatus given by Simplicius on the authority of Porphyry, which – in spite of oc-

---

[64] The passages which need to be taken into consideration are for *Nous* VI 9 [9] 5, 24–9 (where τολμήσας is used); III 8 [30] 8, 30–39: for cosmic soul III 7 [45] 11 (the passage on which Jonas mainly relies) and perhaps V 2 [11] 2, 1–4: for individual souls V 1 [10] 1, 1–5 (where τόλμα is used; but I shall give reasons for holding that passages dealing with the falls and faults of individual souls are not very relevant to our present discussion).

[65] See N. Baladi, Origine et signification De l'Audace Chez Plotin, in Le Néoplatonisme (see n. 53) pp. 89–99 and La Pensée de Plotin (Paris 1970) a book entirely devoted to the theme of τόλμα in all its forms in Plotinus: and John M. Rist, Monism: Plotinus and some Predecessors, in Harvard Studies in Classical Philology, Vol. 69 (1965) pp. 329–344.

[66] All the essential Neo-Pythagorean texts are conveniently collected in C. J. de Vogel, Greek Philosophy III (Leiden 1959) VI. 24. 1. (with very useful short elucidations).

casional spasms of doubt whether Zeller might not have been right after all, and Moderatus might not have been thoroughly Neoplatonized by Porphyry – I am on the whole inclined to accept as the genuine teaching of a Neopythagorean of the first century A. D.[67] If we can discover anything relevant to the subject of τόλμα in it, it will be very much to our purpose here, because the passage strikingly anticipates Plotinian Neoplatonism, as has often been pointed out (this is the reason for Zeller's disbelief and my occasional doubts), and Moderatus was probably read by Plotinus, as he certainly was by his contemporary Longinus[68]. The passage does not contain any reference, explicit or implicit, to τόλμα, but it does contain an exceptionally clear account (for a Pythagorean) of how the Dyad is generated from the One. We learn that the primal One, the "Unitary Logos", wishing to produce from himself the origin of beings, by self-privation made room for indefinite formless quantity, which is the Dyad, the principle on which the Demiurge works to produce the world in the Timaeus, the ultimate origin of evil. If we remember the well-established Pythagorean equation of the Dyad with τόλμα, we shall see that the "audacity" which separates the Dyad from the One is something initiated by the One himself, the process by which he, so to speak, makes room for himself to create the universes. Of course in Plotinus there is no question of the One having to make room for himself to create by self-privation. His infinite power overflowing eternally and inevitably in self--diffusive goodness gives him, so to speak, plenty of room. But it does look probable that his reading of the Pythagoreans, from whom he took the name and idea of τόλμα, may have helped him to the conclusion to which I suggested some time ago he should have come if he worked the question out fully, that the ultimate responsibility for τόλμα must lie with the One or Good itself[69]. And if it originates in the Good, it cannot be bad. It is the Good which produces the unformed life which in its contemplative return becomes the best being there can be, the only authentic being which is as like the Good as possible, the One – Many or One-Being of Intellect: but the return must be eternally checked if anything other than the Good is to exist at all; Intellect, the World of creative Forms, cannot ever simply disappear back into the primal unity if the

---

[67] On this passage (Simplicius, In Phys. 230, 34–231, 27 Diels) see Zeller, Phil. III 2 (⁵1923) pp. 130f.; E. R. Dodds, The Parmenides of Plato and the Origin of the Neoplatonic One, in Classical Quarterly XXII (1928) pp. 129–142 and P. Merlan in The Cambridge History of Early Greek and Later mediaeval Philosophy (²Cambridge 1972) Part I, Chapter 5 C, pp. 91–94 (where the passage is fully quoted and translated).

[68] Porphyry, Life, 20, 75.

[69] In the Cambridge History (see n. 67) Part III, Chapter 15, pp. 242–3. My account of Gnosticism in the following pages is perhaps rather over-simplified, and I im not now very enthusiastic about my suggestion that Gnostic ideas may have influenced Plotinus' thought about the One and the World of Forms.

Good is to diffuse himself as he must. It is this checked return, this eternal "standing away", this separation which leaves Intellect as near the One as is compatible with separate existence, which is the primary τόλμα on which any audacities which may be discerned at lower levels ultimately depend. And, in Baladi's phrase, it must be regarded as a "good audacity". There is one passage[70] where Plotinus momentarily regrets the self-separation of Intellect (in Neoplatonic thought every created or derived being is co-responsible for its own creation or derivation) and says it would be better if it had not happened – though the language here (τόλμα – words are not used) suggests a sort of drunken absent-mindedness rather than an audacious rebellion. But this must be balanced against the enormously greater weight and bulk of the passages where the glory and goodness and beauty of Intellect as the primary image and first self-diffusion of the Good are celebrated – there is much to this effect in the same work from the first part of which the passage just referred to is taken[71]. I would suggest that the passage represents a passing emotional intensification of the mystic's sense of the worthlessness of all things in comparison with the Absolute Good[72], which leads him for a moment to say that it would have been better if they had never been. And it certainly well illustrates the point made earlier (p. 96) that for a philosopher in the Pythagorean-Platonic tradition the only dreamable (hardly seriously thinkable) alternative to the present state of things is an impossible acosmism, not the existence of an intelligible or spiritual world of light without the unnecessary and undesirable addition of a material world of darkness and evil.

As has already been said all lower audacities depend on and must to some extent be judged in relation to the primary τόλμα of Intellect. I do not propose to discuss extensively here the τόλμα, fault of fall of individual souls. This is because, as we have already seen, and as should be well known, the sin and fall of individual souls was part of the Pythagorean-Platonic tradition from the beginning. All that needs to be pointed out in considering Plotinus' individual development and adaptation of the ancient common doctrine is that the first descent of souls into bodies cannot for him be regarded as simply a fall resulting from a sin or weakness: it is also part of the divine plan to diffuse goodness, form and order as far as it will go[73]: this was a line of thought elaborated by his suc-

---

[70] III 8 [30] 8, 30–39.

[71] For V [32] 12, in which it seems that the intelligible beauty can distract us from the Good, and an attempted reconciliation of it with the equally remarkable and unusual VI 7 [38] 22 see my Beauty and the Discovery of Divinity in the Thought of Plotinus, in Kephalaion (Assen 1975) pp. 160–162.

[72] Cp. the famous I 6 [1] 7: what follows here to the end of the treatise well brings out that for Plotinus the only way to the Good is through the World of Forms – Intellect.

[73] See p. 115 and n. 61.

cessors[74]. We should also remember that for Plotinus, unlike his predecessors and most of his successors, there is no question of our true self falling at all. The higher individual soul remains a permanent inhabitant of the world of Intellect; it is only its λόγος which enters into the composite of soul and body which can be spoken of as behaving with bad audacity, sinning by moving deeper than it need into the material world in self-forgetful self-centredness, and suffering the consequences[75]. This must be remembered when we come to consider the one passage, on which Jonas greatly relies, in which something like τόλμα and fall of cosmic soul may seem to appear (this is alone relevant to the question of possible Gnostic influence). The passage is the eleventh chapter of the treatise On Time and Eternity[76]. There are some features about the treatise and the chapter which would make me rather unwilling to accept it as representing the true and essential thought about cosmic soul of Plotinus. The treatise is very firmly based on our own experience of time and eternity here below, as is stated in the first chapter, which is one of Plotinus' best accounts of his own philosophical method. To take experience as well as tradition and reason into account is of course characteristic of Plotinus, but in this case it leads to an unusually close assimilation of cosmic soul to individual soul in that some part or power of cosmic soul is said to reason discursively. Now more often than not discursive reason is denied to cosmic soul in its creative and ruling activity: this is characteristic of its normal assimilation to Intellect, whose thought and creative activity are of course totally non-discursive[77]. There are even a couple of passages in the Enneads where Plotinus seems inclined to bypass both Soul and discursive reason and place the material world and our sense-perception of it directly next to the intelligible world and Intellect's immediate self-awareness[78].

---

[74] See p. 98 and nn. 17–18.

[75] Plotinus maintains this doctrine from the beginning to the end of his writing period: it is first mentioned in IV 8 [6] 8 and particulary clearly and forcibly stated in I 1 [53].

[76] II 7 [45] 11.

[77] Jonas is mistaken in supposing that the absence of discursive thought in Φύσις (Nature) in III 8 [30] 1–4 is in itself a sign of weakness. Nature is indeed weak because it is so far removed from the Good, at the penultimate stage of the procession: but its non-discursiveness brings it disconcertingly close to the first stage of the procession, Intellect itself. For the very complex questions arising from Plotinus' various accounts of the relationship of Intellect, Soul and discursive reason see my Elements in the Thought of Plotinus at Variance with Classical Intellectualism, in Journal of Hellenic Studies (XCIII (1973) pp. 16–18 and H. J. Blumenthal, Nous and Soul in Plotinus: Some Problems of Demarcation, in Plotino e il Neoplatonismo in Oriente e in Occidente (Roma 1974) pp. 203–219.

[78] V 8 [31] 7 (where it makes no difference whether one assumes the intermediate ministry of Soul in the production of the material world from the intelligible or not , and there is nothing between the two): VI 7 [38] 7, 29–31 (the startling remark ὥστε εἶναι τὰς αἰσθήσεις ταύτας ἀμυδρὰς νοήσεις, τὰς δὲ ἐκεῖ νοήσεις ἐναργεῖς αἰσθήσεις).

Chapter 11 of the treatise seems to be rather light-hearted to bear so much weight (I believe that Plotinus could be light-hearted, and was not always as wholly serious as Porphyry would have liked him to be and believed him to be). Of course he knew that he must give a philosophically respectable explanation of the obstinate fact of the temporality of this world which was in perfect accordance with the Timaeus. But there is something a little casual about the chapter, in spite of its enormous importance in the history of the philosophy of time, and the suspicion has crossed my mind that perhaps he was not overwhelmingly interested in the philosophy of time (incredible as that must seem to a Heideggerian). But this is rather subjective, and let us consider what the chapter says perfectly seriously, in its context. What we learn from it is that a "power" or "part" of cosmic soul[79] has a fussy independent nature and wants to be on its own and have more by having its mental objects in succession and not all at once, and turns from noetic rest to the successional activity of discursive reasoning, and so "times" itself and what it brings into being, the material world, which it "enslaves" to time[80]. We should note that there is no question of a descent of cosmic soul altogether into discourse and time: it is only a "part" or "power" of it that moves in this way. And cosmic soul must of course in Plotinus be distinguished from the hypostasis Soul, Soul as a whole. The soul of the universe is the greatest of individual souls, the senior member of the soul family[81]. Soul in fact does not "fall" at all in this passage: it simply, so to speak, lets a dianoetic power or λόγος of itself descend to the discursive level, thus generating the temporal world. There is nothing in the chapter to exclude the supposition that cosmic soul continues, as elsewhere in the Enneads, to preside over the world of becoming thus generated in noetic quietness. And this is in perfect accord with what is said elsewhere in the treatise about individual souls. We begin from the fact that we have ideas both of time and eternity: and we find as we go on that we have an idea of eternity because we have the eternal in ourselves and have a share in eternity[82]. As al-

---

[79] lines 49–50.

[80] lines 30–31. Nobody who is accustomed to Plotinus' deliberate and self-conscious use of "mythical" or "story" language (which he explains himself perfectly clearly in VI 7, 35, 27–30 and III 5 [50] 9, 24–29) will take the past tenses here very seriously, or regard the whole account as unconsciously mythical rather than a deliberate use by Plotinus of his "story-telling" manner of exposition.

[81] On this distinction (and many further complications and, at times, inconsistencies in the accounts given of the relationships of the various souls in Soul) see H. J. Blumenthal. Soul, World-Soul and Individual Soul in Plotinus in Le Néoplatonisme (see n. 53) pp. 55–63.

[82] 1, 1–6; 5, 1–11; 7, 1–10, where we are told, in turning our minds from eternity to time to come down "not altogether, but as time came down" (οὐ πάντη καταβάντες, ἀλλ᾽ οὕτως, ὥσπερ κατέβη χρόνος I. 10) – a very significant remark.

ways, neither individual souls nor cosmic soul have really fallen: their authentic, highest part remains in eternity. The function of the discursive-temporalizing part or power which descends is to provide a Platonic explanation, in accordance with the teaching of the Phaedrus and the Laws that soul-movement is always prior to body-movement, of the temporality of this world: it is only when the problem of explaining this arises that it is required. And, though language suggestive of τόλμα is certainly used, and the descent of the part or power of soul which generates time has, perhaps, a somewhat more ambiguous kind of audacity about it than the τόλμα of Intellect because it is further from the Good, what happens is not very dreadful after all, no sort of cosmic disaster. The temporal-material world, as we have seen, though on the lowest level of existence, is generally regardes as a noble and necessary part of the whole, the best possible image of the eternal intelligible. And the view of time taken in the treatise is sometimes very positive. It is not just the destroyer and devourer, as so often in Greek thought, but that which enables generated things to have some kind of fulness of life and perfection[83], even if only an imperfect image of eternal life and perfection. I find in the treatise no concealed Gnostic mythical drama, no real fall of soul and consequent cosmic tragedy, but an exposition (which in chapter 11 takes a selfconsciously and rather cheerfully mythical-picturesque form) of something which seems to be in accord with sound normal Platonic and Plotinian doctrine.

The other subject on which something must be said before concluding is the place which Plotinus occupies in the development of ancient thought about the problem of evil. On this subject so many excellent recent discussions exist that I can be brief[84]. The first point to which I would like to draw attention is the extreme attenuation of the absolute evil which Plotinus identifies with matter as compared with the vigorous, turbulent, principle of evil in the conflict – dualisms of Plutarch, Atticus and Numenius which we have studied (pp. 104/09). It is mainly, I think, on these, the Platonists whom they knew best, that Christians based their conviction that Platonists believed in an independent, uncreated matter

---

[83] 4, 19–29; 6, 38–42.

[84] I would particularly recommend John M. Rist, Plotinus on Matter and Evil, in Phronesis 6. (1961) pp. 154–166: which, besides much else relevant to our present subject, disposes very satisfactorily of the idea of Puech and others that Plotinus changed his doctrine of evil in reaction against the Gnostics, an idea which does not accord with the content and chronological order of the main treatises in which he discusses the subject. See also his Plotinus: the Road to Reality (Cambridge 1967) Chapter 9, pp. 112–129. Cp. also D. O'Brien, Plotinus on Evil, in Le Néoplatonisme (see n. 53) pp. 114–146, with the criticisms of Rist in his Plotinus and Augustine on Evil, in Plotino e il Neoplatonismo (see n. 77) and my own in my paper Tradition, Reason and Experience in the Thought of Plotinus in the same volume, p. 189 n. 30.

and principle of evil (as the early Pythagoreans probably did, and as Plato may have done, though the evidence here, as usual, becomes more difficult to interpret the more closely one looks at it). The evil matter of Plotinus marks the ultimate limit of procession from the Good[85] – he is here in the later, Platonized Pythagorean tradition which we have considered (pp. 95–98). It is the limit, the point at which procession must stop because the last trace of good has been communicated. As such it is absolute absence of good, and so absolute negation of good, so absolute evil. And this total negativity has a strange, phantasmogenic, distorting quality which is (at least sometimes) the main reason for the grave evils and imperfections of that part of the material world in which matter operates (if negativity can be said to operate) as evil: that is, only the Lower Cosmos below the moon (and even here the earth herself is an entirely good goddess)[86]. There is no evil in the heavens for Plotinus as there was for Numenius. This is a rather paradoxical doctrine, a kind of transition stage between the outspoken dualism of the second-century Platonists and the more consistent position of the later Neoplatonists, for whom matter was not evil and there was no principle of evil at all (see p. 98). There is even one (perhaps unguarded) remark in the Enneads which anticipates the later position in one way, though not in another. This is the remark in a very positive passage about the material world that matter is "a sort of ultimate form"[87]. This of course would make it good (there are no evil forms in Plotinus), though it would not make it, as in the later Neoplatonists, the good infinity which is a manifestation of the transcendent formless infinity of the Good.

The other point to which I would draw attention is the complexity and tentativeness of the treatment of the problem of evil as a whole in the great late treatise On Providence[88]. Here Plotinus is trying to evaluate the material universe as a whole, with its mixture of good and evil and overwhelming predominance, though never complete triumph, of good, and not, as in the slightly later treatise On What Are and Whence Come Evils[89] dealing with the specific traditional problem of matter and evil. Every possible explanation of physical and moral evil in this world appears here: the presence of evil matter, the weakness of the forming principle because of its distance from its source, the still greater inferiority of individual souls in earthly embodiment, the "Karma" doctrine according

---

[85] The passages which seem to me and others to indicate this clearly are I 8 [51] 7. 16–23; II 3 [52] 17, 21–25; III 4 [15] 1, 10–17. On the significance of the discussion in IV 8 [6] 6, 18–28 see Rist art. cit. (n. 84).

[86] II 1 [40] 4–5; II 9 [33] 8. For the earth-goddess see IV 4 [28] 22.

[87] V 8 [37] 7, 22–23.

[88] III 2–3 [47–48].

[89] I 8 [51].

to which the apparent injustices suffered by individuals are punishments for (that is to say, inevitable consequences of) their sinful life in previous incarnations. And there are extensive passages, written under strong Cynic-Stoic influence and using various forms of the traditional Cynic commonplace that "all the world's a stage", where there is something like the dualism which I have called "Chinese" (though I might equally well have called it "Indian") in which the light and dark, beautiful and ugly, things and people in this world cannot really be called good and evil in any absolute sense because they all contribute, in their own ways, to the total harmonious pattern of this Heraclitean universe[90]. And none of the explanations seem to satisfy him completely. There is no claim anywhere in the treatise that a complete and final solution to the problem of evil has been reached, though a passionate faith in the goodness of the universal order here below runs through the whole, and the treatise ends with an extremely cryptic metaphor (derived, in my opinion, from watching the pruning of fruit-trees or vines). Perhaps the greatest contribution which Plotinus made to the endless discussion of the problem of evil is the vivid sense of how difficult it all is which this treatise conveys. A comparison of it with any Gnostic revelation will, I think, show clearly the difference between a Gnostic and a Greek philosopher.

5. Conclusion

My conclusions can be summed up very shortly. First, I think that the whole question of the relationship of Gnosis and Greek philosophy should be approached very cautiously, with a clear definition of what is meant by Gnosis and a precise and detailed study of individual systems and thinkers on both sides in their historical context. Second, I do not think the time has yet come for an assessment of the possible influence of Greek philosophy on any form of alienated Gnosis (that is Gnosis other than the kind expressed in the cosmically optimistic treatises of the Hermetica). But I suspect that, when such an assessment can be safely made, it may prove to be in the treatment of the principle and problem of evil by some Gnostics that such an influence may show itself, in competition with Iranian conflict-dualism. Finally, I think that a close examination of the Greek philosophers of the relevant period shows that the Pythagorean-Platonists of the second century came closest to Gnosticism, and that one of them Numenius, may actually show signs of some Gnostic influence, though he remains a Greek philosopher, not a Gnostic. And I hold that in the third century a strong reaction against Gnosti-

---

[90] See especially III 2, 15–17 (cp. Bhagavad Gītā II).

cism becomes clearly apparent, led by Plotinus, whose influence, reinforcing the anti-Gnostic elements in orthodox Christianity, was decisive
in ensuring the ultimate defeat in our culture of the Gnostic way of thinking and feeling about this world. In the first three centuries of our era,
and thereafter, Greek philosophy remained an intellectual force distinct
from alienated Gnosticism, and from the third century onwards (and often before) Platonic philosophy in particular has been a force working,
not only on the comparatively superficial level of polemic, but very deep
down in the thoughts and feelings of men of our tradition, against the
alienated Gnostic attitude to the world, reinforcing elements in traditional Christianity opposed to Gnosticism, and opposing those Gnostic
influences which have persisted in the Christian tradition.

THE ARROGANT ARCHON AND THE LEWD SOPHIA:

Jewish Traditions in Gnostic Revolt

BY

NILS A. DAHL

THE presence of Jewish traditions in gnosticism is generally recognized. Scholars also agree that at least in some branches of gnosticism there is an element of revolt. The question is how to explain this combination of traditional and revolutionary, Jewish and anti-Jewish components. What, exactly, were the early gnostics revolting against? The most impressive answer to such questions is that of Hans Jonas: the target of the gnostic revolt was the world itself. Gnostic anti-Judaism is an aspect of an anticosmic attitude.[1] Jonas is certainly right that the theory of Jewish origins does not in itself explain what made gnosticism gnostic. But against Jonas's own explanation it must be objected that the target of the gnostic revolt is the Creator of the world rather than the world itself. According to widespread gnostic opinion, the world is indeed better than its Creator. The Demiurge thought that he had created the world by his own power but, without knowing it, he had been inspired by his mother, Wisdom; he modelled his work after the pattern of higher realms.

The difference between gnostics and more orthodox Jews and Christians is not to be located in the degree of evil and misery ascribed to human existence in the world so much as in the explanation given for the regrettable state of affairs. According to the orthodox explanation the one God, who is both good and just, subjected the world to futility as a punishment for the transgressions of angelic and human beings. The misery of life on earth is evidence of God's punishment and of his pedagogical discipline. The gnostics, in contrast, traced evils and misery back to the inferiority of the god who created the world, and to his subordinate powers. Both parts in the conflict thought

---

[1] See esp. H. Jonas, "Delimitation of the Gnostic Phenomenon," in *Le Origini dello Gnosticismo: Colloquio de Messina* (ed. U. Bianchi; Supplements to *Numen* 12; Leiden: Brill, 1967) 90-104. This volume contains several contributions to the theme Gnosticism and Judaism. See also the collection *Gnosis und Gnostizismus*, ed. K. Rudolph (WF 262; Darmstadt: Wissenschaftliche Buchgesellschaft, 1975), esp. articles by Kretschmar, van Unnik, Rudolph, Nock, Pokorný, and Drijvers.

their opponents to be guilty of blasphemy. Representatives of biblical orthodoxy thought that the gnostics were guilty of blaspheming the one God, the Creator and Father. Radical gnostics thought that their monotheistic opponents committed blasphemy by attributing passions like jealousy and wrath to the Supreme Being, making his judgement and punishment causes of evil.

The god against whom the radical gnostics revolted was, obviously, the God of exclusivist, biblical monotheism. The radicalism of the revolt presupposes both a close contact and a situation of conflict. We can therefore restate the problem of the Jewish origins of gnosticism by asking: Was the gnostic identification of the inferior Demiurge with the God of "psychic," orthodox Christians preceded by an earlier stage, at which some gnostics revolted against the God of strictly monotheistic Jews?[2] Not only the presence of Jewish components in gnosticism but also some rabbinic texts favor a positive answer to this question.

In his investigation of rabbinic polemics against those who say that "there are two powers in heaven," Alan Segal has made it seem likely that at its earliest stage this polemic was directed against speculations about a secondary divine being, the agent or vice-regent of God. It matters relatively little whether this being was called the Angel, Archangel, Logos, Eikon, *deuteros theos*, "lesser YHWH," or something else. Only at a later stage, "two powers in heaven" became a catchall phrase which included Christians, gnostics, and others who deviated from strict monotheism.[3]

In their defense of monotheism, second-century rabbis appealed to passages like Deut 32:39, "I, even I, am He, and there is no other god beside me." In a number of gnostic texts, similar passages, mostly drawn from Isaiah 44-46, are attributed to the Creator of this world, the Demiurge. Within a gnostic context, the formula of divine self-revelation has become a vain claim made by an Archon ignorant of the powers above himself. The close correspondence between rabbinic and gnostic texts is best explained on the assumption that some "two

---

[2] For the conflict between Valentinian gnostic and orthodox Christians, see esp. Elaine H. Pagels, "'The Demiurge and His Archons'—A Gnostic View of the Bishop and Presbyters?" *HTR* 69 (1976) 301-24. Pagels raises the question "how the doctrine of God actually functions in each type of literature" (303). In cooperation with Alan Segal, I have for some years tried to approach the early stage of the gnostic controversy with a similar question.

[3] See A. E. Segal, *Two Powers in Heaven: Early Rabbinic Reports about Christianity and Gnosticism* (SJLA 25; Leiden: Brill, 1977). The book is a revised version of a Yale dissertation, 1975.

powers heretics" responded to the rabbinic polemic by portraying the god of their intransigent monotheistic opponents as an inferior deity, an ignorant and arrogant Archon. In the situation of conflict, the doctrine of two powers was radicalized. The secondary element in the deity was degraded and no longer simply seen as a manifestation and agent of the supreme God.[4] As a result of the polarization, "two powers heretics" who became gnostics made a separation between the agent of creation and giver of the law on the one hand and the agent of true revelation and redemption on the other. This explanation of the gnostic split in the deity accounts for the presence of Jewish traditions in the gnostic revolt, while at the same time providing reasons for the great ambivalence with which these traditions are used.

The theory set forth by Segal and myself assumes that at least one main branch of radical gnosticism originated in some syncretistic Jewish fringe group, in opposition to the strict monotheism of emerging "normative Judaism." The theory explains a number of data better than any current explanation.[5] The question is whether the theory will stand closer scrutiny. It might be objected that the correspondence between rabbinic polemic and gnostic response is less than complete.[6] But this hardly means more than that both parts in the controversy

---

[4] The most important text occurs in *Mek. R. Ishmael*, Shirta 4 (on Exod 15:3) and Baḥodesh 5 (on Exod 20:2), with a somewhat divergent version in *Mek. R. Shimeon*, Beshallaḥ 15. See Segal, *Two Powers*, 33-57, for text and commentary, and esp. 251-59 for the correlation of rabbinic and gnostic evidence. In his conclusions, p. 265, Segal formulates the hypothesis "that the radicalization of gnosticism was a product of the battle between the rabbis, the Christians and various other two powers sectarians who inhabited the outskirts of Judaism."

[5] I have myself discussed the correlation of rabbinic and gnostic texts in papers presented at a Harvard-Yale New Testament colloquium, spring 1977, and at the SBL Annual Meeting in St. Louis, fall 1977. It is of special interest to observe that *Mek. R. Ishmael*, Baḥodesh 5, contains a comment of R. Nathan which is not found in the parallels (see note 4). This comment seems to presuppose a form of the heresy which considered the "two powers" to be antagonistic, rather than correlated; see Segal, *Two Powers*, 57-59. Arguing that Exod 20:2 could be used to refute the heretics, R. Nathan is reported to have said, "For when the Holy One, Blessed be He, stood up and exclaimed, 'I am the Lord thy God,' was there any one who stood up to protest against him?" A similar argument would seem to be presupposed by gnostic texts which report that the Archon was indeed rebuked for his claim to be the only God; see p. 694 below.

[6] The rabbis mainly draw upon Deut 32:39 or 6:4 and relate these passages to the Sinai revelation, while gnostic exegetes more often use passages from Second Isaiah. Cf. G. W. MacRae, "The Ego-Proclamation in Gnostic Sources," *The Trial of Jesus* (ed. E. Bammel; SBT, 2d ser. 13, London: SCM, 1970), esp. 123-29.

stressed the aspect which was most important to them. The rabbis
were mainly interested in demonstrating that the God of Israel, who
gave the Torah at Mount Sinai, was the only God, beside whom
there is no other. He is both YHWH and Elohim, at the same time
just and full of mercy.[7] It is, therefore, quite natural that early rabbinic
polemic against the two powers heresy is contained in a midrash on
Exod 20:2.[8] The interests of the early gnostics were different. They
placed the claim of the Archon, that he is God and there is no other,
within the context of the creation story, because paraphrase and reinterpretation of the early chapters of Genesis made it possible to argue
that they themselves possessed a higher wisdom than did the creator
of the world and that their inner self was of a higher nature than he.
In practice, this meant that they were not subject to the Creator-Archon
nor to the authority of the interpreters of his law.

The purpose of the present paper is to show that a closer investigation of gnostic sources is likely to support the theory that controversy
with representatives of strict Jewish monotheism is one factor in the
gnostic revolt. I can only make suggestions and shall concentrate my
remarks on three points: (1) the setting of the "vain claim" within
the context of gnostic exegesis—or alteration—of the creation story
in Genesis; (2) the relationship of the gnostic myth to the widespread
theme of a ruler (god, angel, or man), who in his hybris claims to be
God or like God; (3) the interrelations between the arrogant Archon
and his mother, Sophia or Achamoth, who is sometimes called
Prunikos, the Lewd One.

THE VAIN CLAIM AND GNOSTIC GENESIS INTERPRETATION

The idea that the Power who created the world, or some other inter-
mediary being, assumed that he or she existed alone, or claimed to be
divine, occurs in a number of texts, many of which report the claim
in some oblique form.[9] In several texts, including Irenaeus's and Hippo-

---

[7] In addition to Segal, *Two Powers*, 53-57, see N.A. Dahl and A. Segal, "Philo
and the Rabbis on the Names of God," *JSJ* 9 (1978) 1-28.

[8] See the preceding notes, 4-7. *Mek. R. Ishmael*, Baḥodesh 5, however, contains
also prooftexts from Isa 46:4; 44:6; 41:4; and, in the saying of R. Nathan, Isa 45:19,
a passage which the rabbis read as a reference to the revelation at Sinai, where the
Torah was offered to all nations. Other rabbinic texts make it clear that the early
chapters of Genesis were of key importance for "two powers" heretics; see Segal, *Two
Powers*, 74-83, 108-20, 121-34, 135-39, 148-51.

[9] See examples in note 12. Oblique forms of the claim occur also in *Apocry.Jn*,
CG II 12: 4-9 and BG 42: 19-43: 6; *OnOrgWld*, CG II 100: 29-33; *SJC*, CG III 107: 9-12;

lytus's versions of Valentinian cosmogonies, the claim of the Demiurge, that he is the only God, is reported in direct speech and in words which in the Bible are attributed to God himself.[10] I shall here concentrate on a special group of texts which have several features in common : the *Hypostasis of the Archons* (CG II,*4*); the work without title, now called *On the Origin of the World* (CG II,*5*); the *Apocryphon of John* (CG II,*1* and BG,*2*); the *Gospel of the Egyptians* (CG III,*2*); and Irenaeus, *Adversus haereses* 1.29 and 30.[11] From these texts, it is possible to abstract a pattern which in its complete, but nonexistent, form includes the following items:

1. *Setting*, at some point in the story of creation.

2. *Introduction*, several times with introductory comments. E.g., *HypArch* 86: 27-30: "Their chief is blind; [because of his] Power and his ignorance [and his] arrogance, he said, with his [Power]: ..."; *ApocryJn*, BG 44: 9-13: "He looked at the creation that was with him, and the multitude of angels that was with him ... and said to them: ..." See also *HypArch* 94: 19-21; *OnOrgWld* 103: 8-10; *ApocryJn*, BG 11: 18-19; 13: 5-8; *GEgypt* 58: 23-24; Irenaeus, *Haer.* 1.29.4; 30.6.

3. *Vain claim*, in words derived from Isa 45:5, 6, 18, 21; 46:9 (or sim.). E.g., *HypArch* 86: 30-31: "It is I who am God; there is none [apart from me]." Cf. *HypArch* 94: 21f. (95: 5); *OnOrgWld* 103: 11-13 (107: 30f., 112: 28f.); *ApocryJn*, CG II 11: 20f.; Irenaeus, *Haer.* 1.30.6. *ApocryJn*, BG 44: 14f.: "I am a jealous God; apart from me there is none" (Exod 20:5; Isa 46:9, or sim.). Cf. CG II 13: 8f.; *GEgypt* 58: 25f.; Irenaeus, *Haer.* 1.29.4.

4. *Comment*. E.g., *HypArch* 86: 31f., 94: 22f.: "When he said this,

---

BG 118:19-22. I am indebted to Anne McGuire, who has prepared a comprehensive chart of the many variants of the vain claim, checking the Coptic texts. For the purpose of the present paper I have mostly relied upon, and quoted from, *NHLibEng*. I have also made use of translations in W. Foerster, ed., *Gnosis* (tr. R. McL. Wilson; 2 vols.; Cambridge: University Press, 1972). References to Irenaeus, *Adversus haereses*, follow the traditional system of enumeration (Mangey, Stieren, et al.), which is also reproduced in the edition of Harvey.

[10] According to Irenaeus, *Haer.* 1.5.4, it was through the prophets that the Demiurge made his claim, "I am God and there is no other." This could, possibly, be an early form, as argued by H.-M. Schenke, *Der Gott "Mensch" in der Gnosis* (Göttingen: Vandenhoeck & Ruprecht, 1962) 88. More likely, the reference to the prophets is a Valentinian modification of more mythological versions. The parallel passage in Clement, *Excerpta ex Theodoto*, does not mention the "vain claim" but only the ignorance of the Demiurge (49.1, cf. 53.4). See also, however, *Haer.* 2.9.2 and Hippolytus, *Haer.* 6.33.

[11] Some of the same items, but not the claim itself, were already part of the teaching of Satornilos (or Saturninus), as summarized by Irenaeus, *Haer.* 1.24.1-2. Both the claim and related items recur in Epiphanius, *Haer.* 25, on libertine Gnostics.

he sinned against the Entirety." Cf. *OnOrgWld* 103: 13f. Other comments, *ApocryJn*, CG II 11: 21f.; *GEgypt* 58: 26-59.1. *ApocryJn*, BG 44: 15ff.: "Already showing the angels with him that another god existed," etc.; cf. CG II 13: 9-13.

5. *Rebuke*, by a voice from above (from Incorruptibility, from the Mother, or sim.). E.g., *HypArch* 86: 32-87: 4: "You are mistaken, Samael." Cf. *HypArch* 94: 24-26; 95: 5-7; *OnOrgWld* 103: 15-18. Irenaeus, *Haer.* 1.30.6: "Do not lie, Yaldabaoth."

6. *Disclosure*, combined with the rebuke or as an alternative to it. *ApocryJn*, BG 47: 15-18; CG II 14: 13-15: "The Man exists and the son of Man." Cf. *GEgypt* 59: 1-3; Irenaeus, *Haer.* 1.30.6. *OnOrgWld* 103: 19-28: "An enlightened, immortal man [or: an immortal Light-Man] exists before you," etc.

7. *Challenge*; the Archon calls for a revelation. *HypArch* 94: 27f.: "If any other thing exists before me, let it become visible to me!" *OnOrgWld* 107: 36-108: 2: "If someone exists before me, let him appear so that we may see his light."

8. *Appearance* of an image (in the water) and/or of light. *HypArch* 87: 11-16: "As Incorruptibility looked down into the region of the Waters, her Image appeared in the Waters," etc. Cf. *OnOrgWld* 103: 28-31; 107: 18f. (Gen 1:2b?). *HypArch* 94: 28-31: "And immediately Sophia stretched forth her finger and introduced Light into Matter." Cf. *OnOrgWld* 108: 2-14; 111: 29-31; 112: 25f. (Gen 1:3). *ApocryJn*, BG 48: 1-9; CG II 14: 18-34; *GEgypt* 59: 4-9 (Gen 1:2b-3?).

9. *Proposal* to create man, made by the Archon or his Powers (Gen 1:26). *HypArch* 87: 23-26; *OnOrgWld* 112: 32-113: 4; *ApocryJn*, CG II 15: 1-4; BG 48: 10-14; Irenaeus, *Haer.* 1.30.6.

10. *Formation* of man from the earth (Gen 1:27 + 2:7). *HypArch* 87: 27ff.; *OnOrgWld* 113: 9ff.; *ApocryJn*, BG 48: 14ff.; CG II 15: 5ff.; *GEgypt* 59: 9; Irenaeus, *Haer.* 1.30.6.

Only *On the Origin of the World* contains all items in this "pattern," but here the sequence is interrupted by other items, by repeated appearances, and also by back references to the "vain claim." Both in the *Hypostasis of the Archons* and in the long recension of the *Apocryphon of John* elements of the pattern recur several times. The abstract pattern does not pretend to reproduce the literary composition of the texts as we have them, nor did it ever have an independent existence of its own. Differences of outline and in details make it unlikely that the similarities are due to dependence upon any one written source. Yet, it is not only the individual items that recur;

even the order of the items remains remarkably constant wherever key elements of the pattern occur. This indicates that the various writings and reports in which we find traces of the "pattern" all draw upon some common tradition.

The three last items in the pattern are all directly related to the creation story in Genesis, the "appearance" to Gen 1:2b or 1:3, the "proposal" to Gen 1:26, and the "formation" of man to Gen 1:27 and 2:7. Some other texts suggest that it was satisfaction with his work of creation that made the Demiurge think that he was divine.[12] But in the group of texts on which we have concentrated our attention, the "vain claim" always precedes the proposal to create man in Gen 1:26. So do the items which are most closely related to the claim: the introduction, comment, rebuke, and also the disclosure and challenge wherever these elements occur (items 2-5 and 6 and 7). Occasionally, the vain claim is placed right at the beginning of the story of creation: the Archon made his arrogant claim when he opened his eyes and saw a vast quantity of matter without limit (Gen 1:2a; see *HypArch* 94: 19-22).[13] More often, he is reported to have made his claim after he had generated offspring or created powers, angels, etc.[14] But even so the claim is placed before the Spirit moved upon the waters (Gen 1:2b), as well as before there was light (Gen 1:3).[15] The

---

[12] *TriTrac*, CG I 100: 36-101: 5 clearly alludes to the refrain "God saw that it was good" (Gen 1:10, 25, 31, etc.); cf. 100: 19-25 and 101: 20, 25. "Oblique claims" after the creation of the world are also attested by *Ps.-Clem. Rec.* 2.57 (Simon); and by Hippolytus, *Haer.* 5.25.3 (cf. 23.4-5, [Pseudo-] Basilides) and 26.15 (Justin's *Baruch*).

[13] At this point, *OnOrgWld* 100: 29-33 only reports that the Archon, when he only saw water and darkness, thought that he alone existed. A similar illusion is attributed to "Darkness" in *ParaShem*, CG VII 2: 15-16; 3: 3-4, and to the "Pleromas" and the "Powers" in *TriTrac* 79: 12-18 and 84: 3-7.

[14] See *HypArch* 94: 34-95: 5; *ApocryJn*, CG II 11: 18-22 (cf. 12: 4-9; BG 42: 18-43: 4); Irenaeus, *Haer.* 1.29.4. According to *ApocryJn*, CG II 13: 5-9; BG 44: 9-15, and *OnOrgWld* 103: 2-13 the Archon addressed his boasting claim to the angels which he had created. All of these texts presuppose that the angels (or powers) were created on the first day, in accordance with ancient Jewish tradition attested by *Jub.* 2:2; see R. H. Charles, *The Book of Jubilees* (London: Black, 1902) 10-13. Thus also *The Cave of Treasures* 1:3 (C. Bezold, ed., *Die Schatzhöhle* [Leipzig, 1883] 1; P. Riessler, *Altjüdisches Schrifttum* [Augsburg: Filser, 1928] 942). In agreement with *Jub.* 2:3, *OnOrgWld* 103: 5-8 also reports that the angels praised their Creator. The standard rabbinic opinion, that the angels and spirits were not created until the second (or fifth) day, betrays an antiheretical tendency.

[15] Thus also *HypArch* 86: 27-31 and *GEgypt* 58: 23-59: 1. Only Irenaeus, *Haer.* 1.30, allows for a later setting of the claim. Here there is no "appearance," and reminiscences of Gen 1:2-6 occur before the birth of the Archon, within the Sophia myth. But since similar events recur at various stages in gnostic cosmogonies, this does not tell us where the vain claim should be located in Gen 1:1-25. The Valentinian

appearance of the image (or likeness) according to which the Archon
and his powers wanted to create man (item 8) can be associated either
with the Spirit upon the waters or with the light of the first day. As
both the Spirit and the Light (of Wisdom) could be interpreted as
manifestations of the Mother, some texts seem to conflate Gen 1:2b
and 1:3. Only *On the Origin of the World* has retained a clear distinction
between the revelation of "the likeness of her [Pistis's] greatness in
the waters" and the appearance of the light, in which a human likeness
was revealed.[16]

In general, *On the Origin of the World* has incorporated larger
portions of the creation story in Genesis than have the other writings
with which we are concerned. This treatise alludes to all the seven
days of creation, even though the biblical Hexaëmeron (or Heptaë-
meron) has been rearranged into an Octaëmeron which has a different
order of days.[17] The other texts of the group do not follow the whole

cosmogonies in Irenaeus, *Haer.* 1.1-8, and Hippolytus, *Haer.* 6.29-36, do not contain
items 4-8 of the "pattern," but even here the creation of man follows upon the "vain
claim." A setting within the creation story is probably also presupposed in references
to the claim which the Archon once made, in *GrSeth*, CG VII 53: 27-54: 4 and 64:
18-65: 1, and *TriProt*, CG XIII 43: 27-44: 4, as well as in *OnOrgWld* 107: 31-34
and 112: 25-31 and Irenaeus, *Haer.* 1.30.7.

[16] The appearance of the likeness of Pistis in the waters (Gen 1:2b) made the
Archon grieve (*OnOrgWld* 103: 28-34; 107: 18-34; see also 108: 28-32). Then the
coming of the light, in which a human likeness appeared (Gen 1:3), made him
ashamed and made the Authorities laugh at him (*OnOrgWld* 108: 2-24; 111: 29-34;
112: 10-113: 5). Apparent complications are mainly caused by the intervening sections
on Sabaoth (103: 32-106: 18, with another allusion to Gen 1:3 in 104:3-9) and on
Eros (109: 1-25). The long recension of the *Apocryphon of John* ingeniously combines
Gen 1:2b and 1:3: the Image of the Father was, in a human form, revealed in the
waters above, whose underside was illuminated so that the Authorities, through the
light, could see the form of the image in the water (CG II 14: 18-34). Even *ApocryJn*,
BG 48: 1-9 and *GEgypt* 54: 4-9 presuppose a conflation of Gen 1:2b and 3 into one
appearance of the image.

[17] Events of the first day of Genesis (1:1-5) are reported both in *OnOrgWld* 94:
30-101: 2 and in 102: 35-103: 2 and 107: 18-109: 1. The events of the second and third
days (Gen 1:6-10) have been condensed (*OnOrgWld* 101:2-9). The creation of plants
on the third day is combined with the trees of Paradise (Gen 1:11-12; 2:8-9; *OnOrgWld*
109:25-111:24). The creation of the animals on the fifth, and part of the sixth, day
(Gen 1:20-23, 24-25) has been placed before the creation of the luminaries on the
fourth (Gen 1:14-19; *OnOrgWld* 111:24-28; 112:1-10). For the creation of man on
the sixth day (Gen 1:26-31 and 2:7), see 112: 29-113: 13 and 114: 18-115: 3, with an
insertion about how Sophia Zoe anticipated the Authorities and created her man first,
the androgynous "Eve of Life," *OnOrgWld* 113: 13-114: 15 (cf. Gen 1:3; 2:21). For
the rest on the seventh day (Gen 2:1-3), see *OnOrgWld* 115: 23-27. Finally, the third,
earthly Adam, the "man of the law," is said to have appeared on the eighth day (*OnOrgWld*
117: 28-118: 2), apparently a reference to *OnOrgWld* 115: 31-116: 8 (Gen 2:23, cf. 2:7).
The transposition of the fourth and fifth days has obscured the meaning of the

text of Genesis 1 but move directly from Gen 1:1-3 to Gen 1:26-27 and from there to Gen 2:7ff. In the *Hypostasis of the Archons* both the first part (86: 20-93: 2) and the revelation of Eleleth to Norea (93: 2-97: 22) follow this abbreviated outline of Genesis 1-2, and the *Apocryphon of John* and the relevant section of the *Gospel of the Egyptians* do the same. The report of Irenaeus in *Haer.* 1.29 breaks off with the vain claim, but the continuation is likely to have been more or less similar to what we read in the *Apocryphon of John*.

The omission of large portions of Genesis 1 in these texts is all the more remarkable because most of them follow the biblical account more closely from the creation of man onward, in several cases up to the Flood story. The concentration upon Gen 1:1-3, 1:26-27, and 2:7 makes it clear that the origin of mankind, not the origin of the world, is in the focus of interest. The main point of the plot is that human beings, enlightened by revealed wisdom, have a knowledge that the Creator did not have, and therefore realize that they are his superiors. The general theme may have been the origin and preservation of the seed of Seth. In the treatise *On the Origin of the World*, traditions similar to those preserved in the *Hypostasis of the Archons* and the *Apocryphon of John* seem to have been incorporated, together with heterogenous elements, into a more complete retelling of the creation story.[18]

The various texts with which we have dealt have in common both the "vain claim," the surrounding "pattern," and the basis in the biblical story of creation. Yet they differ not only in wording, in details, and in exegesis, but also in the way in which the plot works, exposing the foolishness of the Creator and his associates, with the

---

statement that the Light-Adam, who appeared on the first day, remained upon the earth for two days. It goes back to the Jewish tradition that after the third day the original light of Gen 1:3 was withdrawn and reserved for the age to come, and then the luminaries were created on the fourth day (e.g., *Gen. Rab.* 3.6; *b. Ḥag.* 12a). This has been overlooked both by A. Böhlig in Böhlig and P. Labib, *Die koptisch-gnostische Schrift ohne Titel* (Berlin: Akademie, 1962) 68 f., and by M. Tardieu, *Trois mythes gnostiques* (Paris: Etudes Augustiennes, 1974) 94. Tardieu, pp. 85-139, esp. 131-35, has made a learned and interesting attempt to interpret the eight-day scheme of the present text. His construction, however, would collapse if only two letters (co) are to be restored in the lacuna in CG II 117: 32, as presupposed by the translation "on the sixth day" adopted by Bethge and Wintermute, *NHLibEng.*, 173. Tardieu follows Böhlig in reading "on the fourth day." "Sixth" seems preferable, even though a lacuna in the Coptic text makes both readings possible, as Anne McGuire informs me.

[18] In spite of close parallels between *On the Origin of the World* and the *Hypostasis of the Archons*, it is unlikely that one of these works was a literary source for the other.

result that their plans fail and the divine element in mankind is preserved and eventually redeemed. The differences extend through the stories of Adam and Eve, Paradise and transgression, up to the Flood story. Some disagreements are quite substantial, but even so they are variations of common themes and patterns of thought, as distinct from the surface pattern of items listed above.

In some respects, the differences within our group of gnostic texts are like disagreements between exegetes who belong to the same religious community or the same theological school. They disagree in their exegesis but approach the texts with the same general presuppositions. I am even reminded of the difference between individual rabbis, apparent, e.g., in the early chapters of *Genesis Rabbah*. The gnostics, of course, did not edit their texts as midrashim, recording the opinions of various teachers. But I have the impression that behind our group of texts there is some sort of an esoteric, yet flexible, exegetical school tradition. The gnostics read their own ideas into the texts, but so have exegetes done at all times. Sometimes they interpreted what the biblical authors ought to have said rather than what they actually said. But even that phenomenon is neither exclusively ancient nor exclusively gnostic. But the gnostics went even further. They consciously turned the texts upside down. The illuminated understanding and the esoteric tradition became more normative than the written text. The *Apocryphon of John* can explicitly say that Moses was wrong (BG 45: 8ff.; 58: 16ff.; 59: 17ff.; CG II 13: 18ff.; 22: 21ff.; 23: 3f.).

A conflict between theologies, in which interpretation and reinterpretation of Scripture, and even biblical criticism, provide the weapons, is nothing unusual.[19] But the radical gnostics with whom we are dealing did not merely fight the false theology of their opponents, they maintained that this theology referred to a false God. The character of the gnostic interpretation of the early chapters of Genesis indicates that originally these opponents were Jews and not Christians.

All the gnostic texts which have the "vain claim" and the surrounding pattern include some Christian elements. But in the *Hypostasis of*

---

[19] Thus, there are both major differences and striking analogies between the controversy between the gnostics and their Jewish and Christian opponents and Paul's conflict with non-Christian and Christian Jews. Even in Paul's case, both the under-standing of God and the social identity of his elect ones are at stake. See "The One God of Jews and Gentiles," in my *Studies in Paul* (Minneapolis: Augsburg, 1977), and the unpublished Oslo dissertation (1978) by Halvor Moxnes, "Theology in Conflict: Studies in Paul's understanding of God in Romans" (forthcoming in the series NovTSup).

the Archons the overtly Christian component is minimal, mainly to be found in the introduction (86: 20-27) and in the conclusion (96: 20 ff.). It is considerably stronger in other texts, at least in the *Apocryphon of John*, *On the Origin of the World*, and Irenaeus, *Haer.* 1.30.[20] But the Christian elements in these texts vary a great deal and they are incorporated into the literary compositions at different points. What our texts have in common is due to their basis in the early chapters of Genesis, into which the pattern for the vain claim has been inserted. There is no evidence of Christian influence upon the main elements of this esoteric Genesis interpretation. The New Testament authors and other early Christian writers had an interest in the first chapters of Genesis that centered on christology and eschatology. Christ was the mediator of creation as well as of redemption, the Logos or the Image of God; there was an analogy between the first creation and the new creation in Christ, etc.[21] The points of contact between this Christian use and the early gnostic interpretation of Genesis are few and do not require the assumption of any direct contact one way or the other.[22]

If we turn to Jewish sources, however, it is obvious and generally recognized that the gnostic texts include a number of features which are also known from Jewish exegesis, mostly either from Philo of from targumim and rabbinic midrashim. The clearest example may be the understanding of the creation of Adam, including the theme of the

---

[20] Christian elements are less prominent in the source used by Irenaeus, *Haer.* 1.29, than in the preserved versions of the *Apocryphon of John*. The *Gospel of the Egyptians* raises special problems, since Seth is depicted as a heavenly redeemer who manifested himself in Jesus (e.g., 63: 4-64: 9). The *Apocalypse of Adam* may be a non-Christian gnostic work, but the conjecture that a form of the "vain claim" should be read in CG V 66: 26f. is hardly tenable. Mandaean texts contain some analogies to the boast of the Demiurge, e.g., *Ginza* R III, Petermann 93 (ET, after Rudolph, in Foerster, *Gnosis*, 2, 170 f.). It might be interesting to investigate how far they too reflect a conflict situation.

[21] See, e.g., John 1:1-18; Rom 5:12-19; 8:18-30; 1 Cor 8:6; 11:3-11; 15:21-22, 44-49; 2 Cor 4:6; 5:17; 11:3; Gal 3:27-28; Eph 5:30-32; Col 1:15-20; Heb 1:2-4; 4:3-11; Rev 21:1; 22:1-5. On the correlation of the first and the last things, see my essay "Christ, Creation, and the Church" (1956), reprinted in *Jesus in the Memory of the Early Church* (Minneapolis: Augsburg, 1976) 120-40.

[22] I see no evidence that New Testament authors presuppose or combat a split within the deity or a separation between the mediator of redemption and the agent of creation. Cf., e.g., H. Hegermann, *Die Vorstellung von Schöpfungsmittler im hellenistischen Judentum und Urchristentum* (Berlin: Akademie, 1961). This, however, does not mean that gnostic parallels to the New Testament are irrelevant. The rabbis considered both gnostics and "orthodox" Christians two powers heretics and both groups are likely to have reinterpreted similar traditions, e.g., about the divine Eikon or Logos, each in its own way.

"golem" (Gen 2:7).[23] Other examples include the understanding of the light of the first day as a heavenly light (Gen 1:3) and of the image in Gen 1:26 as an hypostatized manifestation of the supreme God.[24] It even happens that two divergent interpretations of the same verse, e.g., Gen 4:1, are attested both in gnostic and in rabbinic sources.[25]

It is unnecessary to add further details, but some more general features should be mentioned. Hebrew or Aramaic names and etymologies are so common in our gnostic sources that at least some elements of the gnostic Genesis interpretation must go back to exegetes who were more familiar with the original languages of the Jewish Scriptures than was Philo. We also find traces of speculations about the names of God in the Hebrew Bible.[26] The anthropomorphic and anthropopathic language used about God in Genesis 2-3 or 6:6-7 was offensive to the gnostic exegetes. We know that it also caused problems to Philo and, to some extent, to the rabbis, while the early Christians hardly addressed such problems. An influence of Platonic traditions, especially from the *Timaeus*, upon gnostic

---

[23] See esp. Birger A. Pearson, *The Psychikos-Pneumatikos Terminology* (SBLDS 12; Missoula, Montana: Scholars Press, 1973) 17-23, 51-81.

[24] On Jewish traditions about the original light, see S. Aalen, *Die Begriffe "Licht" und "Finsternis" im Alten Testament, im Spätjudentum, und Rabbinismus* (Oslo: Norske Videnskaps-Akademi, 1951) 163-70, 262-69. On the "Image" in Gen. 1:26f., see J. Jervell, *Imago Dei: Gen. 1:26f. im Spätjudentum, in der Gnosis und in den paulinischen Briefen* (FRLANT 76; Göttingen: Vandenhoeck & Ruprecht, 1960), esp. 52-69, 76-86, 96-107, 136-40; H.-M. Schenke, *Der Gott "Mensch"*, esp. 69-71, 120-43.

[25] According to Irenaeus, *Haer.* 1.30.9, Cain and Abel were sons of Adam and Eve, but *HypArch* 89: 28-31; 91: 12 makes Cain the son of the Archons; see B. Layton in *HTR* 70 (1977) 60-61, notes 84 and 85. *GEgypt* 117: 15-18 and *ApocryJn*, CG II 24: 15-25; BG 62: 7-63: 5, have other variants of an exegesis which took Gen 4:1 to mean that an angelic prince, called Yahweh, had seduced Eve and begotten Cain and Abel. Outside gnosticism, this angel was identified with Satan, as already John 8:44; 1 John 3:12; and 2 Cor 11:3, 14. See my article "Der Erstgeborene Satans und der Vater des Teufels," *Apophoreta: Festschrift ... Haenchen* (ed. W. Eltester; BZNW 30; Berlin: Töpelmann, 1964) 70-84.

[26] See, e.g., *ApocryJn*, CG II 24:15-25; IV 38: 1-4; BG 62: 7-63: 5, where "Yave" and "Eloim" are identified with Cain and Abel, or vice versa. One can even wonder if the notion that the angelic agent of creation claimed to be God has something to do with the use of divine names in Genesis 1 ff. To a gnostic, as to a skeptical reader, the YHWH Elohim of Genesis 2-3 could not be the true God, as he was ignorant and envious (see, e.g., *TestimTr*, CG IX 45: 23-48: 15). Yet in Gen 1:1-2:4 the Creator is called Elohim. If the agent of creation was identical with the giver of the Law, he would himself have claimed to be God. Only Justin's book *Baruch* differs from other gnostic texts in considering Elohim, the Creator, to be the second god, who in his vanity thought that he was Kyrios, the Good One (Hippolytus, *Haer.* 5.26.15f.). In several gnostic texts Hebrew names of God reappear as names of some of the seven powers, e.g., Irenaeus, *Haer.* 1.30.5; *ApocryJn*, CG II 11:26-12: 25.

Genesis interpretation is present, e.g., in the notion that earthly realities are imitations of heavenly models. Like Philo, the gnostic exegetes also assimilate elements of hellenistic astronomy, physics, physiology, etc., with the biblical story of creation. Only from the late second century onward did Christian theologians like Theophilus of Antioch begin to incorporate the type of learned Jewish Genesis exegesis which the gnostic texts presuppose and transform.

All of this points to some fringe group of hellenized Judaism, not towards early Christianity, as the original setting for the type of Genesis interpretation which has been preserved in the *Hypostasis of the Archons*, the *Apocryphon of John*, and related writings. Both the variability of gnostic exegesis and its affinity, in points of detail, to diverse Jewish sources indicate that the contact between "proto-gnostic" and more "orthodox" Jewish exegetes extended over some period of time. This is just what we should expect if the assumption is correct that the gnostic portrayal of the biblical Creator-God as an ignorant and arrogant Archon reflects a sharpening of the controversy, on both sides. Under the attack of strict Jewish monotheism, some early form of gnosticism was radicalized, and speculative, probably esoteric, Genesis interpretation was turned into a gnostic myth.[27]

THE MYTH OF THE ARROGANT RULER

What I have here called the "vain claim," i.e., the attribution of proof texts for an exclusive monotheism, e.g., Isa 45:5 or 46:9, to a

---

[27] I must leave open the question when and where this radicalization occurred. The known evidence suggests that the rabbinic polemic against "two powers" sectarians goes back to the period 70-135 C.E. This is also likely to be the time in which adherents of the doctrine of "two powers" revolted and turned radical gnostics. Excluded from the synagogues, some of them found a temporary refuge in the Christian church. It should be added, however, that not all branches of the gnostic movement were equally revolutionary. The "vain claim" and related features are not attested for the earliest Samaritan and Syriac gnostics (Simon Magus, Dositheus, Menander, Saturninus) nor does it occur in writings like *Poimandres*, the *Naassene Sermon*, the *Apophasis Megale*, *Eugnostos the Blessed*, or the *Gospel of Truth*. The interest in esoteric knowledge of cosmological secrets, more or less dependent upon Genesis, must also have continued outside what we call gnosticism, see, e.g., *2 Enoch* 24-33 and *Sefer Yeṣirah*. More syncretistic examples occur in K. Preisendanz, ed., *Papyri Graecae Magicae* 1-2 (2d ed.; Stuttgart: Teubner, 1973-74). The "Leiden Cosmogony" in *PGM* 13, 138-206, with a parallel in 443-564, can even be considered to be gnostic in a wider sense of the term. We hear, e.g., about rivalry between the seven gods who were created when God laughed seven times (177-86, 191-206, and, with additional details, 494-563). But even apart from its magical use, this text is an example of cosmological, perhaps esoteric, gnosis, but not of saving, dualistic, or revolutionary gnosticism.

subordinate Demiurge or Archon, is generally seen as a classical example of gnostic radicalism. Relatively few scholars seem to have discussed the claim in any detail, however. The notion that the world was created by one or several agents or angels[28] does not in itself explain the polarization which makes the agent a counterfeit of the supreme God. H.-M. Schenke has taken the "vain claim" to illustrate the development from allegory to myth.[29] But the attribution of sayings of the God of the Bible to an inferior deity can hardly be considered an example of allegorical interpretation, and the notion of a process of development does not explain the revolutionary character of the gnostic use of Scripture.

As an example of a different approach, I quote R. A. Bullard: "The account of the blasphemy of the Demiurge is probably not so much a creation of Gnostic exegesis as a result of a myth of the haughty Demiurge coming into contact with Jewish monotheism."[30] But Bullard's explanation is not the only alternative to that of Schenke. On the one hand, gnostic interpretation is itself mythopoetic. On the other hand, in religions that recognize sacred scriptures as in some sense normative, interpretation of the scriptures provides the chief means for incorporating scientific knowledge, philosophical insights, or even myths. The outcome of such efforts may well be something that is new, not only in comparison with more traditional interpretations of the sacred texts but also in comparison with the ideas that informed the reading of the texts. That happens even when the reinterpretation is less radical than in gnosticism.

Where the Creator is portrayed as an arrogant Archon, he is indeed cast into a mythical role. But I do not see evidence that the gnostic myth of the haughty Demiurge preceded the contact with biblical monotheism. What happened in this case, as in others, was much more that some gnostics in their mythopoetic exegesis made use of already existing mythological, though not gnostic, motifs. The motif of a god, angel, prince, or man who wanted to be like God, or who in his

---

[28] Cf. G. Quispel, "The Origin of the Gnostic Demiurge," *Gnostic Studies* I (Istanbul: Nederlands Historisch-Archaeologisch Instituut, 1974) 213-20 (reprinted from *Kyriakon: Festschrift J. Quasten* [1970] 271-76). According to Jarl Fossum, who at the Yale Conference read a paper on "The Origin of the Concept of the Demiurge," there is also some Samaritan evidence for the notion that the world was created by an angel.

[29] *Der Gott "Mensch,"* 87-93. Schenke's other examples are much more to the point (pp. 72-84 and 69-71).

[30] *The Hypostasis of the Archons* (PTS 10; Berlin: De Gruyter, 1970) 51.

vanity and hybris claimed that he was himself God, occurs in many variations, both in ancient myths and in fairy tales.[31] For our purpose, it is not necessary to discusses whether we have to do with one myth in several variations or with several myths with a common theme. The Old Testament has preserved two classical variants of the theme, in Isaiah 14 and Ezekiel 28. Perhaps the story of the fall in Genesis 3 should be added as a third, modified variant (see esp. Gen 3:5).

Isaiah 14 is an ironical lamentation for the king of Babylon, the Day Star, son of Dawn, who would ascend above the heights of the clouds and make himself like the Most High but who is brought down to the depths of the Pit (see esp. Isa 14:12-15). The oracle in Ezekiel 28 is directed against the prince (*nāgid*, ἄρχων) of Tyre, who said, "I am a god" (Ezek 28:2, 9) and considered himself wise as a god (Ezek 28:6). Moreover, in Ezek 28:11ff. he is depicted with features of the first man who, full of wisdom, was placed in Eden but later cast away so that he, like the king of Babylon in Isaiah 14, became an object of mockery. The Archon of our gnostic texts has been cast in the role of such haughty rulers. It is possible to detect some allusions to the biblical texts, especially Isaiah 14, and it is quite probable that the designation of the Archon as an "aborted fetus" goes back to an understanding of Isa 14:19 which is attested both by the targum and by Symmachus.[32]

---

[31] See, e.g., J. Morgenstern, "The Mythological Background of Psalm 82," *HUCA* 14 (1939) 29-126, esp. 101-14; M. Pope, *El in the Ugaritic Texts* (*VT*Sup 2, Leiden: Brill, 1955) 27-32, 97-103; A. Yarbro Collins, *The Combat Myth in the Book of Revelation* (HDR 9; Missoula, Montana: Scholars Press, 1976) 81 with notes 130-34 and 162 with note 27. More or less distant analogies to the gnostic myths of the Demiurge have been collected by U. Bianchi, "Le problème des origines du gnosticisme et l'histoire des religions," *Numen* 12 (1965), esp. 166-68 with notes. For the ongoing discussion about the mythological background of Isaiah 14, see also B.S. Childs, *Myth and Reality in the Old Testament* (SBT 27; London: SCM, 1960) 61-71; and articles by P. Grelot, *RHR* 149 (1956) 18-48; V. Oldenburg, *ZAW* 82 (1970) 187-208; J.W. McKay, *VT* 20 (1970) 451-64; P.C. Craigie, *ZAW* 85 (1973) 223-25. On Ezekiel 28 see, e.g., H.G. May, "The King of the Garden of Eden," *Israel's Prophetic Heritage: Essays in Honor of James Muilenburg* (ed. B.W. Anderson and W. Harrelson; London: SCM, 1962) 166-76.

[32] For *kĕnēṣer niṭʿāb* in Isa 14:19 the Septuagint has ὡς νεκρὸς ἐβδελυγμένος, Symmachus ὡς ἔκτρωμα (ἐβδελυγμένος), and targum *kĕyahaṭ ṭĕmir*. See J. Ziegler, ed., *Isaiah* (Göttingen Septuaginta 14; 1939) and L. Lütkemann and A. Rahlfs, "Hexaplarische Randnoten zu Is. 1-16," in *Mitteilungen des Septuaginta-Unternehmens* 2 (*NachrGesGöttingen*, 1915, Beiheft) 328-29. For the Archon as ἔκτρωμα, see *HypArch* 94:15; *ApocryJn* BG 46:9-14 (CG II 13:33-36, "the cover of darkness" [?]); Hippolytus, *Haer.* 6.31.1-5 (Valent.). Cf. *OnOrgWld* 99:1-100:6. The term ἔκτρωμα can

It would require detailed investigations to find out how far the gnostic myth of the arrogant Archon draws upon Isaiah 14 and Ezekiel 28, and how far it is influenced by other variants of the mythical theme. In any case, already the biblical oracles apply ancient mythological motifs to enemies of the people of God. Later on, various adversaries were depicted as haughty rulers who claimed to be divine or were acclaimed as gods: Nebuchadnezzar in Judith (3:8; 6:12); Antiochus Epiphanes in Daniel (11:36f.); Pompey in the *Psalms of Solomon* (2:28f.); Caligula in Philo (*Gaium* 22, 74-80, 93-97, 118, 162); Herod Agrippa in Acts (12:21-23) and Josephus (*Ant.* 19.8.2 § 344-50); Nero in the *Sibylline Oracles* (5.33-35, 137-54, 214-21) and in the *Ascension of Isaiah* (4:6-8). In 2 Thessalonians (2:4) the "man of lawlessness" is said to proclaim himself to be God. Traces of the theme recur in Rev 13:1, 5-6. Later it became part of the Antichrist tradition.[33] Not only the general theme but also allusions to Isaiah 14 are also used in Christian polemic against Simon Magus and, possibly, in Jewish polemic against Jesus.[34]

In some cases, the polemic against political or religious adversaries was clearly occasioned by claims that were actually made by them or on their behalf. Yet there is no clear distinction between historical persons, symbolic representatives, and eschatological figures, but rather

---

also be applied to the lower Sophia: Irenaeus, *Haer.* 1.4.1; 8.2 (with reference to 1 Cor 15:8); Hippolytus, *Haer.* 6.36.3; or to other entities: *OnOrgWld* 99: 8-10 (Envy); Hippolytus, *Haer.* 5.25.6 (the Sonship left without form, according to Ps.-Basilides). For anthropological applications, see Clement, *Exc. Thdot.* 68, and Hippolytus, *Haer.* 5.17.6 (Perates). Tardieu, *Trois mythes*, 59 n. 60, compares with the Harpocrates myth in Plutarch, *Isid.* 19 and 65 (358D-E, 377B-C). A combination of a biblical passage with current hellenistic ideas is just what we should expect. For the connotations of the term ἔκτρωμα, see esp. J. Munck, "Paulus tanquam abortivus (1 Cor. 15:8)," *New Testament Essays: Studies in Memory of T.W. Manson* (ed. A.J.B. Higgins; Manchester: University Press, 1959) 180-94, with references to earlier studies by A. Fridrichsen in *Symbolae Philologicae O.A. Danielsson* (Uppsala, 1932) and G. Björck in *ConNT* 3 (1939).

[33] For the theme in general, see also Sir 36:10 and the midrash on rulers who considered themselves divine in *Mek. R. Ishmael*, Shirta 8 (on Exod 15:11); cf. *b. Ḥul.* 89a; *Tanḥ. B. Wa'era* 7-8 (11b). See further E. Haag, *Studien zum Buche Judith* (Trier Theological Studies 16; Trier: Paulinus, 1963) 22-25, 33-35, 68-78; J.J. Collins, *The Sibylline Oracles of Egyptian Judaism* (SBLDS 13; Missoula, Montana: Scholars Press, 1974) 84-85; Yarbro Collins, *The Combat Myth*, 162-63, 166-68, 178-83; R.A. Aus, "God's Plan and God's Power," *JBL* 96 (1977), esp. 542 on 2 Thess 2:4 and Ezek 28:2.

[34] For legends about Simon, see *A. Petr.* (Verc.) 4, 10, 31f. (= *Mart.* 2-3); *Ps.-Clem. Rec.* 2.9.5-7, cf. 10.2; 3.47; Arnobius, *Adv. nat.* 2.12. For Jewish polemic, possibly against Jesus, *y. Ta'an.* 2.1 (65b, 59f.).

an interplay between history and myth and between claims made and polemical response. We should keep in mind that even the great adversary, the devil, was depicted as the Lucifer of Isaiah 14.[35] The name Samael makes it likely that some features have been transferred from the fallen prince of angels to the arrogant Archon of the gnostics.[36] But the gnostic Archon is not a satanic figure. On the whole, the Lucifer myth and the gnostic myth of the Creator-Archon are most likely to be analogous examples of mythopoetic exegesis and reinterpretations of ancient mythologoumena.[37]

The gnostics followed a fairly common practice in making polemical use of a mythological theme. What is unique is that they cast the Creator of the world himself into the role of the arrogant ruler who claims that he is God and that there is no other. We can say that the theme was remythologized. The mythopoetic polemic is not directed against an earthly ruler, against the symbolic or eschatological adversary of the people of God, or against the religious hero of a heretical

---

[35] E.g., *Life of Adam and Eve* 15; *2 Enoch*, recension A, 29:4f.; (apocryphal) 3 Cor. 3:11; cf. *Asc. Isa.* 10:13. Morgenstern, *HUCA* 14 99-106; K. L. Schmidt, "Lucifer als gefallene Engelmacht," *TZ* 7 (1951) 161-79.

[36] On Sam(m)ael as a name of the devil, see *3 Apoc. Bar.* 4:8; 9:7; *Asc. Isa.* 2:1, etc.; G. Scholem, *EncJud* 14. 719-22. Scholem has explained the obscure name Yaldabaoth as meaning "begetter of *abaoth*," wherein *abaoth* was an equivalent of Sabaoth, as in magical papyri. See Scholem, "Jaldabaoth Reconsidered," in *Mélanges d'histoire des religions offerts à Henri-Charles Puech* (Paris: Presses Universitaires, 1974) 405-21; cf. Layton, *HTR* 70, 72-74 n. 67. Yaldabaoth is indeed depicted both as the father of Sabaoth and as the begetter of the heavenly forces (*ṣabaoth*), identical with the Archigenetor who claimed, "I am God [and I am] your Father and it is I who [begot] you and there is no [other] beside me" (*TriProt*, CG XIII 43: 35-44: 2, cf. Deut 32:6, 18). Explanations offered in *OnOrgWld* 100: 10-14 and, possibly, 103: 23 f. are secondary, but Scholem's explanation hardly excludes the possibility that the name Yaldabaoth was understood as a persiflage of *Yah(weh) 'ēl(ōhē) ṣabaōth*. The differentiation between Yaldabaoth and his son Sabaoth illustrates the ambiguous attitude to the God of the Bible; see esp. *HypArch* 95: 1-96: 14; *OnOrgWld* 103: 2-107: 14. One might guess that this differentiation corresponds to a distinction between the zealous opponents of the gnostics and other Jews or, at a later stage, Christians for whom there was a hope of repentance. See now Francis T. Fallon, *The Enthronement of Sabaoth* (NHS 10; Leiden: Brill, 1978).

[37] It is highly unlikely that the mythical motif was "degnosticized" and transferred from the Demiurge to the devil, as Schenke argued in *Der Gott "Mensch"*, 92f. There is even less reason to assume a gnostic background for the motif in late versions of legends about Yima, the primordial king (or man); see A. Christensen, *Le premier homme et le premier roi dans l'histoire légendaire des Iraniens* 2 (Leiden: Brill, 1934) 69, 103; cf. 86, 91, 116. We have much more to do with variations of a common theme, as recognized by O. Wintermute, "Gnostic Exegesis of the Old Testament," *Interpretation of the Old Testament in the New: Studies in Honor of W.F. Stinespring* (ed. J. M. Efird; Durham, North Carolina: Duke University Press, 1972), esp. 256-60.

group, but against the God of monotheistic opponents. The early
Christians applied the same mythical theme to an Antichrist figure.
But Yaldabaoth, Samael, or whatever he is called, is not an Antichrist
but a counterfeit God. This confirms that, originally, the gnostic revolt
was directed against the jealous God of exclusivist Jewish monotheism
and his zealous representatives on earth. Only later was the polemic
redirected to aim at the God of the Christians and against the
hierarchical authorities who acted as his representatives. But, at least
in Valentinianism, the revolutionary element was modified.[38]

THE LEWD SOPHIA

It is still necessary to add some remarks about the relationship
between the Archon-Creator and his mother, Sophia or Achamoth. In
some texts she is called Prunikos, the Lewd One, and thereby distinguished from a higher Sophia. In many respects, she is a gnosticized
variant of the hypostasized Ḥokmah of Jewish Wisdom literature (e.g.,
Proverbs 8, Job 28, Sirach 24).[39] But to a higher degree than her
Jewish antecedent, the gnostic Sophia has also features of a female
deity. For our purpose, it does not matter whether these features
have been taken over from Isis or from some other goddess. In any
case, the gnostic Sophia is a mother figure, the universal Mother
as well as the mother of the Archon, her aborted fetus. She is identified
with the heavenly Eve, the "mother of the living," and with the
Spirit (rûaḥ), which is female. Thus, she is the Spirit of God that
moved upon the water (Gen 1:2b).[40] In many gnostic texts, the

---

[38] See Pagels, "The Demiurge and his Archons," esp. 323 f., and cf. her *The Gnostic
Paul* (Philadelphia: Fortress, 1975). The opposite trend is clear in the *Second Treatise
of the Great Seth*, where the polemic against the God and the hierarchy of the church
is very sharp. See esp. CG VII 59: 19-61: 14 and 64: 18-65: 17; J. A. Gibbons, "The
Second Logos of the Great Seth: Considerations and Questions," in *SBLSP 1973*
(ed. G. MacRae) 2. 242-61. The data do not allow for the construction of any single
trajectory, whether the line of development is supposed to lead from a strictly dualistic
gnosis toward modified, more monistic systems, or from esoteric knowledge over
pre-gnostic and proto-gnostic ideas toward dualistic "gnosticism." In order to account
for the complex realities, one would have to take account of both trends and to pay
special attention to the relationship between gnostic groups and the larger religious
communities upon which they depend like parasites upon the host.

[39] See G. C. Stead, "The Valentinian Myth of Sophia," *JTS* 20 (1969) 75-104;
G. MacRae, "The Jewish Background of the Gnostic Sophia Myth." *NovT* 12 (1970)
86-101.

[40] See esp. A. Orbe, "Spiritus Domini ferebatur super aquas," *Gregorianum* 44 (1963)
691-731. On Wisdom as the daughter or consort of God and mother of all things, see

Mother not only has many names and aspects, she is also split up into several separate figures.

The distinction between a lower, earthly, and a higher, heavenly, wisdom is ancient, but the gnostic duplication, or multiplication, of "the Mother" cannot simply be understood as a mythologized version of this distinction. Nor is the combination of various components in the gnostic Sophia figure likely to provide a sufficient explanation. The gnostic Sophia myths are highly complex. They may contain reinterpretation of earlier mythologoumena as well as mythopoetic exegesis. Be that as it may, the gnostic Sophia myth, in most of its manifold variants, provides an etiology for the origin of the arrogant Archon and his vanity.[41] This suggests that we may find a clue in the notion of Sophia as the mother of the Logos. Philo attests not only this notion but also a divine triad of God the Father, the Mother, Sophia, and the Logos (or the world).[42] The triad of Father, Mother, and Son (the supreme deity, the female aspect of the deity, and the divine agent) reappears again and again in gnostic texts.[43] But whereas the Philonic Logos was the agent of revelation and salvation as well as the agent of creation, gnostics made a separation between the agent of creation, the Archon, on the one hand, and the divine agent of revelation and redemption on the other. This duality of of agents implied the assumption of two "Son" figures and necessitated a duplication of the Mother, e.g., a distinction between the female

---

B. L. Mack, *Logos und Sophia* (SUNT 10; Göttingen: Vandenhoeck & Ruprecht, 1973) 13 f., 67-70, 155-58, etc. On the Holy Spirit as mother of Jesus, see the *Gospel of the Hebrews*, fragments 2 and 3 in Hennecke-Schneemelcher (E.T. ed. Wilson) 1. 163f. Cf. also the invocations of the Mother Holy Spirit in *A. Thom.* 27 and 50 and the devaluation of Ruha in Mandaic texts.

[41] See *HypArch* 84: 2-19; *OnOrgWld* 98: 11-100: 29; *ApocryJn*, CG II 9: 25-10: 19; BG 26: 15-38: 17; Irenaeus, *Haer.* 1. 29.2-4; 30.1-3. The accounts of the origin and fall of the Mothers contain mythopoetic Genesis exegesis, mostly based upon Gen 1:1-3, 26 f.; 2:7; 3:20. The principle of successive series of models and copies allowed for projections of elements from Genesis 1-5 into the supramundane realms. But because of its premundane setting, the Sophia myth could not be patterned after the narrative sequence in Genesis. That may be one reason why the gnostic Sophia myth is open to much more variation than the myth of the arrogant Archon.

[42] *Fuga* 108-9; *Ebr.* 30-33; *Leg. All.* 2.49. In Philo's doctrine, Logos is much more important than Sophia; see Mack, *Logos und Sophia*. The triad God, Sophia, and Logos is therefore likely to have been current in some branch of hellenized Judaism. Cf. the christianized version of the triad in Theophilus, *Autol.* 1.7; 2.15.

[43] E.g., *ApocryJn*, CG II 2: 13; 9: 9-11; BG 21: 19-20; 35: 18-20; *GEgypt* 41: 7-9; 42: 4, etc.; Irenaeus, *Haer.* 1.29.3; 30.2. Cf. *OnOrgWld* 105: 23-31; *TriProt* 37: 20-22 and passim. See also A. Böhlig's paper in this volume, 617-634.

consort of the Supreme Being, mother of the Redeemer-Son, and
the lower Sophia who produced the arrogant Archon. In most of
our texts, the system of divine emanations or aeons is even more
complicated, as the origin of the lower Sophia is preceded by several
male-female couples.[44]

The function of the gnostic Sophia myth as an etiology of the
origin of the Creator-Archon provides a key factor that explains the
duplication or multiplication of Mother Wisdom. It does not, however,
explain why the lower Sophia in some texts is called Prunikos, the
Lewd One. Antecedents for the idea suggested by this name may
be found in Jewish Wisdom traditions as well as in the character of
female deities. Figurative language in Proverbs 1-9 depicts wisdom
as a lady who, like her counterpart, the seductive "alien woman" (or
"Lady Foolishness"), invites men to her house.[45] Several Jewish texts
use sexual imagery to describe love for wisdom and her pleasures.[46]
Gnostic texts are pervaded with sexual imagery, most often in the
form of references to heavenly syzygies. The term Prunikos is well
attested by the heresiologists,[47] and the *Second Treatise of the Great*

---

[44] Even in this connection, Gen 1:26-27 served either as a point of departure
or as a point of contact or, most likely, as both. The passage not only provided a biblical
warrant for a Platonic doctrine of models and copies but suggested also that, like the
first created man, even the higher "images" were "male and female," i.e., either
androgynous or couples. Already Philo, *Fuga* 51, made the comment that Wisdom,
the daughter of God, could be said to be a father, since her nature is male; see Layton,
HTR 70, 47-48 n. 15.

[45] See Prov 9:1-18; cf. 2:16-19; 4:6-7; 7:1-27; G. Boström, *Proverbia-Studien:
Die Weisheit und das fremde Weib in Spr. 1-9* (LUÅ, N.S. 1, 30/1; Lund: Gleerup, 1935),
esp. 156-74.

[46] See, e.g., Sir 15:2; Wis 6:12, 17f.; 7:7-10, 28; 8:2; and esp. 11QPs[a] 21.11 ff.
(= Sir 51:13-30), ed. J. A. Sanders, *The Dead Sea Psalms Scroll* (Ithaca, N.Y.: Cornell
University, 1967) 113-17; *DJD* 4 (1965) 79-85. For ancient themes and later inter-
pretations, see M. Pope, *The Song of Songs* (AB 7C; New York: Doubleday, 1977),
esp. 110f., 153-79. Cf. also the materials collected by H. Schlier, *Der Brief an die
Epheser* (Düsseldorf: Patmos, 1958) 159-66, 264-76.

[47] The name Προύνικος is attested by Celsus (Origen, *Cels.* 6.34. See further
Irenaeus, *Haer.* 1.29.4; 30.3, 7, 9, 11, 12; Epiphanius, *Haer.* 21.2.4.5 (Simonians), 25.3.2
(libertine Gnostics);(37.3.2;4.2 (Ophites). According to Origen, *Cels.* 6.35, even Valentinians used the name. See also Epiphanius, *Haer.* 31.5.8-9; 6.9, on Valentinian aeons
as androgyne *prunikoi*. Epiphanius also attests the verb προυνικεύω, *Haer.* 25.4.1
and 37.6.2, and the abstract noun προυνικία, 31.5.7. Outside gnostic writings, the
adjective is used with sexual connotations in *Anthologia Palatina* 12.209 (προύνικα
φιλήματα). Elsewhere, the unusual noun προύνικος (from προ-ενεικω?) could designate
a (hired) porter or, as a term of abuse, a low fellow. The semantic development has,
apparently, a partial analogy in that of the English word "lewd," which earlier meant
vulgar, rude, base, etc. In the gnostic usage, προύνικος has clearly sexual connotations
(lewd, unchaste, lascivious, voluptuous or sim.) but it is not a term for a prostitute or a
promiscuous woman.

Seth explicitly speaks of "our sister Sophia who is a whore" (CG VII 50: 25-28). But harlotry is not a prominent feature in the versions of the Sophia myth attested by the writings with which we have mainly been concerned, the *Hypostasis of the Archons, Apocryphon of John,* etc.[48]

The lewdness of the lower Sophia may be suggested by reports that in her libidinous passion she conceived and gave birth, or rather aborted, without a consort, or without the consent of her consort.[49] An enigmatic passage in Irenaeus, *Haer.* 1.30.7, may be especially relevant in this connection. Here we learn that, according to some Ophite gnostics, Prunikos rejoiced because she saw that Yaldabaoth and his powers were overcome by their own creation, since Adam and Eve, after they had eaten from the tree of knowledge, recognized the Power who is above all and separated themselves from their makers. She is said to have exclaimed, once again, that since the Incorruptible Father existed, he who once called himself father (i.e., Yaldabaoth) lied, and since the Father and the First Female existed, even she had sinned by her adultery ("et haec adulterans peccavit"). It is not quite clear whether *haec* refers to Prunikos herself or to the "Female from the Female," who originated from the body which Prunikos put off and who became the mother of Yaldabaoth.[50] There is nothing in the context to suggest adultery in the sense of illicit sexual intercourse.

---

[48] In some other texts, the main female figure is described as promiscuous. The statement "I am the whore and the holy one" is an example of unity in contrasts (*Thund,* CG VI 13: 18; not in the similar words of Eve, "the instructor," as reported in *OnOrgWld* 114: 8-15). In Justin's book *Baruch,* the virgin Israel-Edem is identified with Leda, Danae, and Hosea's harlot wife (Hippolytus, *Haer.* 5.26.34, 35 and 27.4; Hos 1:2). She is the mythological representative of the soul (5.26.8, 25, 36). The *Exegesis on the Soul* (CG II,6) describes the soul as a prostitute, but provides at best a distant parallel to the Sophia myth. The figure of Ennoia-Helena provides a closer analogy to the lewd Sophia; see G. Lüdemann, *Untersuchungen zur simonianischen Gnosis* (Göttinger Theologische Arbeiten 1; Göttingen: Vandenhoeck & Ruprecht, 1975) 55-78. Lüdemann suggests that the story of Simon and the harlot Helena is a Christian counter-legend, but that there was some warrant for it in genuine Simon Magus traditions. According to Epiphanius, *Haer.* 25.2 and 3, some "Gnostics" taught that the Powers were robbed of their "seed" through intercourse with Barbelo or Prunikos, who appeared to them in beauty. Some even reenacted the myth sacramentally, collecting semen and menstrual blood. Apparently, the legend of the seduction of Eve has been transformed into gnostic myth and ritual. See note 25 and, for another gnostic use of the motif, *HypArch* 89: 14-33; *OnOrgWld* 116: 32-117: 15.

[49] See, e.g., Irenaeus, *Haer.* 1.29.4 (without consort); *HypArch* 94: 5-8; *ApocryJn,* CG II 9: 25-32; BG 36: 16-37: 16; *SJC,* CG III 114: 13-18.

[50] Foerster, *Gnosis* (ET) 1. 90, takes *haec* to be the object of *peccavit* and *adulterans* to have the general sense of falsifying, but adds a parenthetical question mark.

The participle *adulterans* may refer either to the fall of Prunikos, who descended into the water and took on a body, or to the action of the Female from the Female which caused the birth of the Archon. In any case, the connotation seems to be the passion and lust of an adventurous woman, in contrast to the integrity of the Incorruptible Father and his consort the First Female. Such an understanding would also fit the description of Prunikos in Irenaeus, *Haer.* 1.29.3, and of Sophia in the *Apocryphon of John* and the *Hypostasis of the Archons.*[51]

The term "a Female from a Female" is also attested in a password to be used by the ascending soul when it arrives at the place of the "detainers" who steal souls: "Achamoth had no father nor male consort, but she is a female from a female. She produced you (pl.) without a male, since she was alone and in ignorance as to what [lives through] her mother because she thought that she alone existed. But [I] shall cry out to her mother" (*1ApocJas*, CG V 35: 10-19, with a close parallel in Irenaeus's report about the Marcosians, *Haer.* 1. 21.5). The double attestation of the formula makes it likely that it is ancient. One part of it has a partial parallel in the *Apocryphon of John*, where the ignorant Archon is said to have thought that there existed no other but his mother alone (CG II 13: 28-30; BG 46: 4f.). I would guess that this is a later variation of the theme that the Mother herself had the illusion that she alone existed. The idea is clearly reminiscent of the words of the virgin daughter of Babylon: "I am, and there is no one besides me" (Isa 47: 8, 10). Since the "vain claim" of the Archon is derived from passages in Isaiah 44-46, there can hardly be any doubt that the analogous claim of his mother goes back to Isaiah 47. If so, the name προύνικος might be an otherwise unattested translation of the equally unusual Hebrew word 'ādînâ, ("you lover of pleasures," RSV), which in Isa 47:8 is used as a designation of the virgin daughter of Babylon.[52]

---

[51] *ApocryJn*, BG 37: 10f., explicitly says that Sophia brought her product forth "because of the lewd element (προύνικος) within her" (CG II 10: 1 has "because of the invisible power that is in her.") According to Irenaeus, *Haer.* 1.29.4, Prunikos looked down into the lower regions in the hope of finding a consort there. In 1.30.3 the agitation of Prunikos is associated with the "moving" of Gen 1:2b. Reports about Valentinian cosmogonies stress the passion of Sophia (Irenaeus, *Haer.* 1.2.2, especially her search for the Father). Another version of the theme occurs in *OnOrgWld* 108: 14-19, where Pronoia, the consort of the Archon, is said to have become enamored of Light-Adam.

[52] For 'ādînâ in Isa 47:8 the targum has *mĕpannaqtā*; LXX has τρυφερά. The text of Symmachus and other later Greek versions does not seem to have been preserved.

As the arrogant Archon was cast into the role of the king of Babylon in Isaiah 14, so his mother would seem to have been cast into the role of Babylon herself. The two analogous examples of mytho-poetic exegesis with a polemical scope are likely to have been inter-related, even if the interconnection is no longer clearly visible in our sources. This suggestion receives some indirect confirmation from the analogy with apocalyptic use of Isaiah 14 and 47. As features from the king of Babylon in Isaiah 14 were transferred to the eschatological adversary, so were features from Isaiah 47 transferred to the great harlot, Babylon/Rome; see esp. Revelation 17-18. A Sibylline oracle announces that Rome shall sit as a widow because she said, "I alone am (μόνη εἰμὶ), and none shall bring ruin on me" (*Sib. Or.* 5.168-77, cf. Isa 47:8-10).[53] Thus, there is some similarity between the gnostic Archon and the eschatological adversary and between the lower wisdom in gnosticism and the world city in apocalyptic. But this similarity does not favor the theory of a development from apocalypticism to gnosticism, once suggested by Robert M. Grant.[54] What happened was, much more, that similar, in part biblical, in part mythological, imagery could be applied to counter-entities, in apocalyptic to the last adversary and to the world city in contrast to the heavenly Jerusalem, in gnosticism to the Creator-Archon and to his mother the lower Sophia in contrast to the higher Wisdom that had been revealed to the gnostics.

Philo can depict Wisdom or Virtue, represented by Sarah, as a heavenly city, whereas Hagar, "sojourning," is a symbol of encyclical education.[55] Some gnostic, mainly Valentinian, texts identify the lower, psychic Wisdom with the heavenly Jerusalem.[56] It might be too bold to suggest that this identification goes back to the same circle of early gnostic exegetes who also depicted the lower Sophia with features of the lewd virgin daughter of Babylon.[57] Even without this conjecture,

---

[53] See J. J. Collins, *Sibylline Oracles*, 79; cf. 66-71 on *Sib. Or.* 3.75-92 and 11.243-60, 271-314. Collins refers to Isa 47:8-9 on p. 67f. but, strangely enough, not on p. 79.

[54] *Gnosticism and Early Christianity* (1959; 2d ed., New York: Harper & Row, 1966).

[55] See, e.g., *Leg. All.* 3.1, 3, 244, and cf. the allusion to Isa 54:1 in *Praem.* 158. For the Hagar-Sarah allegory in general, see, e.g., *Cher.* 3-10; *Mut.* 137-41, 253-62. In Gal 4:21-31 Paul draws upon a variant of the allegory; cf. J. B. Lightfoot, *St Paul's Epistle to the Galatians* (London: Macmillan, 1876) 198-200. The Pauline version suggests that the identification of the Mother (Sarah, Wisdom) with the heavenly city (Jerusalem) may have been more important in the tradition than in Philo's use of it.

[56] See Irenaeus, *Haer.* 1.5.3; Hippolytus, *Haer.* 6.34.3-4; cf. 30.3. The Naassene use of the notion is somewhat different: Hippolytus, *Haer.* 5.8.7.

[57] In the book *Baruch*, Babylon is one of the angels of Israel-Edem and identified with Aphrodite and Omphale; see Hippolytus, *Haer.* 5.26.4, 20, 28. Thus, an identi-

the gnostic Sophia myth, like the myth of the arrogant and ignorant Creator, is an example of Jewish traditions in gnostic revolt.

On the whole, the lewd Sophia comes off much better in the gnostic texts than does her son, the arrogant Archon. This confirms that the real target of the gnostic revolt was not the wisdom of the dissenters' strictly monotheistic opponents, but their god, the God in whose name some early rabbis condemned the forerunners of the gnostics as "two powers heretics" who violated the one basic doctrine of Judaism: the Lord our God, the Lord is one.

---

fication of the heavenly Jerusalem with Babylon, the virgin daughter and the harlot, is quite conceivable as part of the gnostic revolt, but the evidence is slim.

Chapter Seventeen

Use, Authority and Exegesis of Mikra in Gnostic Literature

Birger A. Pearson

Introduction

It used to be thought that one of the chief characteristics of Gnosticism, as 'the acute hellenization of Christianity,[1] was a rejection of the OT.[2] Even before the publication of the new source material for Gnosticism, such as the Nag Hammadi corpus,[3] this view was hardly tenable, for the ancient heresiologists themselves complained not so much that the Gnostic heretics rejected the OT but that they interpreted it incorrectly.[4] The fact is, the Gnostic interpretation of Mikra is a very complicated matter, and there is great variety in the range of attitudes adopted by Gnostics vis-a-vis the Bible. Now that the new source material is available a comprehensive assessment of the use, authority, and exegesis of Mikra in Gnostic literature is possible.

Unfortunately, no such comprehensive assessment exists,[5] and such a project is beyond the purview of the present study. In this article I shall try instead to summarize the present state of scholarship on this issue, and, concentrating chiefly on some of the new sources from Nag Hammadi, attempt some conclusions of my own.[6]

---

[1] So the famous dictum of Harnack, *History of Dogma* 1, 227. Harnack's position still has its defenders; see e.g. Beltz, 'Gnosis und Altes Testament', 355.
[2] Harnack, ibid., and pp. 169-73; Bauer, *Orthodoxy and Heresy*, 195ff. This view is rightly rejected by Von Campenhausen, *Formation*, 75.
[3] See Robinson, *Nag Hammadi Library*. Unless otherwise indicated, all English translations of the Nag Hammadi Coptic texts in this article are taken from that volume. Citations in each case are according to page and line of the MS. Cf. Robinson, *Facsimile Edition*.
[4] Cf. Von Campenhausen, *Formation*, 76.
[5] A number of articles on the problem have been published. See e.g. Tröger, *Altes Testament*, and esp. the articles in that volume by Haardt ('Schöpfer und Schöpfung'), Nagel ('Auslegung'), Weiss ('Gesetz'), Bethge ('Geschichtstraditionen'), Beltz ('Elia redivivus'), Szabó ('Engelvorstellung'), and Schenk ('Textverarbeitung'). See also Beltz, 'Gnosis und Altes Testament'; Krause, 'Aussagen'; Wilson, 'The Gnostics and the Old Testament', Simonetti, 'Note sull' interpretazione'; Filoramo-Gianotto, 'L'interpretazione gnostica'. Additional studies, such as articles on individual Gnostic tractates, are cited below (passim).
[6] This article can be taken as a companion study to my article in *Compendia* II/2, 443-81 ('Jewish Sources').

635

95

Basic Issues

While it is no longer argued by scholars that the Gnostics completely rejected the OT, it is still occasionally stated that they were only concerned with the opening passages of Genesis.[7] Such an assertion is easily refuted. R.M. Wilson has effectively challenged it simply by referring to the index of scripture-citations in the two-volume anthology of Gnostic texts edited by W. Foerster.[8] The statistics he assembles do show a predilection on the part of the Gnostics for the early chapters of Genesis, but most of the other parts of the OT are represented as well, seventeen books in all.[9]

A more complete statistical analysis has recently been put forward by G. Filoramo and C. Gianotto,[10] using a data base that includes all of the heresiological sources as well as the Coptic texts from Nag Hammadi and the other Coptic sources. Around 600 OT references have been assembled. Again, the opening passages of Genesis predominate – 200 of 230 references to Genesis are concentrated on Gen 1-11 – but the other parts of the Bible are represented as well.[11]

More important, of course, is the question as to *how* the OT is utilized and interpreted in the Gnostic literature. It is at this point that the issues become complicated, for there is a bewildering variety of interpretive methods and attitudes displayed in the sources.

Some useful attempts have recently been made to classify the Gnostic use of the OT, with reference to examples drawn from the Gnostic sources. P. Nagel,[12] for example, identifies the following six categories, providing examples for each:[13]

1. Openly disdainful rejection of figures and events from the Old Testament (*NHC* VII, 2: *Treat. Seth*; *NHC* IX, 3: *Testim. Truth*).
2. Exposition in a contrary sense, through changes in roles and functions (*NHC* II, 4: *Hyp. Arch.*; *NHC* II, 5 and XIII, 2: *Orig. World*; *NHC* V, 2: *Apoc. Adam*; the Peratae).
3. Corrective exposition, closely related to group 2 (*NHC* II, 1; III, 1; IV, 1; and *BG*, 2: *Ap. John*; the Ophites).
4. Appropriation of 'neutral' passages by means of allegorical interpretation (Justin, *Baruch*; the Naassenes; *Pistis Sophia*).
5. Eclectic references to individual passages of the OT in support of certain doctrines or cult-practices (the Valentinians; libertine Gnostics).

---

[7] E.g. Betz, 'Am Anfang', 43; Yamauchi, *Pre-Christian Gnosticisim*, 144f.

[8] Wilson, 'The Gnostics and the Old Testament', 165. Cf. Foerster, *Gnosis* 2, 350-52.

[9] Genesis, Exodus, Leviticus, Numbers, Deuteronomy, Joshua, 1 Samuel, 2 Samuel, 1 Kings, Job, Psalms, Proverbs, Isaiah, Jeremiah, Ezekiel, Daniel, and Hosea. See Wilson, ibid.

[10] Filoramo-Gianotto, 'L'interpretazione gnostica'.

[11] Ibid., 55f.

[12] Nagel, 'Auslegung', 51. See also Simonetti, 'Note sull' interpretazione'; and Filoramo-Gianotto, 'L'interpretazione gnostica'.

[13] I use here the standard American sytem of abbreviation of the Nag Hammadi texts.

6. Etiological and typological interpretation of the Old Testament, in part with a soteriological tendency (*NHC* I, 5: *Tri. Trac.*; *NHC* I, 3 and XII, 2: *Gos. Truth*; *NHC* II, 3: *Gos. Phil.*; *NHC* II, 6: *Exeg. Soul*; *Pistis Sophia*).

Nagel points out that there is some overlapping in this classification, and that more than one of these categories can be reflected in a single text. He regards the first three categories as closely related to one another, and sharply distinguishes them from the other three.[14]

It is to be noted that virtually all of the Gnostic texts cited by Nagel as examples of the six categories of OT interpretation, with the arguable exception of the *Apocalypse of Adam*,[15] are Christian Gnostic texts, or at least texts which show Christian influences. The question thus arises as to what role was played by Christian doctrine in the development of Gnostic OT interpretation, as well as the whole issue of the existence of an originally non-Christian *Jewish* Gnosticism.[16] Some of the scholars who have studied the problem of Gnostic OT interpretation have expressed strong scepticism as to the existence of a Jewish Gnosticism and a Gnostic interpretation of the OT unmediated by Christianity. For example, H.-F. Weiss, in his study of the Tora in Gnosticism, suggests that the various Gnostic attitudes adopted toward the Tora all reflect the basic Christian contrast between the Law and the Gospel.[17] H.-G. Bethge, in his study of Gnostic interpretation of the historical traditions in the OT, concludes that Gnostic interpretation of the OT is a feature of Christian Gnosticism, and did not arise in 'heterodox' Judaism.[18]

The strongest stand on this issue has been taken by W. Beltz, in a short article devoted to 'Gnosis and the Old Testament' and the 'question of the Jewish origin of Gnosis'. He states in this article that there are no OT passages used in

---

[14] Nagel, ibid. He goes on in his article to analyze the various Gnostic interpretations of the Paradise narrative in Gen 2-3.

[15] On *Apoc. Adam* as a 'Jewish Gnostic' text see my discussion in 'Jewish Sources', 470-74, and 'Problem', 26-34. *Apoc. Adam* is the only Gnostic text included in the new collection of OT Pseudepigrapha edited by J.H. Charlesworth. See *OTP* 1, 707-19 (translation and introduction by G. MacRae).

[16] For discussion of the problem see e.g. Pearson, 'Jewish Sources', 443-45, 478-80; also 'Problem', 15-19, and Van den Broek, 'Present State', 56-61.

[17] Weiss, 'Gesetz', esp. p. 73. Somewhat anomalously he goes on to acknowledge that Mandaeism, with its negative picture of Moses as the prophet of the wicked *Rūhā*, stands 'outside the scope of early Christian Gnosticism', and cites K. Rudolph's studies on the Jewish origins of Mandaean Gnosticism (ibid., p. 80 and nn. 46-51).

[18] Bethge, 'Geschichtstraditionen', esp. 109. Cf. also Maier, 'Jüdische Faktoren'.

637

the Gnostic texts from Nag Hammadi which are not already found in the NT.[19] He also argues in support of Harnack's view of Gnosticism as the 'acute hellenization of Christianity' on the grounds that the Church was stronger than Judaism, and the 'anti-Jewish' strain in the Gnostic materials can therefore better be attributed to Christians than to disaffected or heretical Jews.[20]

Both of Beltz's assertions are manifestly wrong, as has been pointed out by W. Schenk. As to the first, it suffices simply to say that the key text from the OT used in the Gnostic parody of the foolish Creator ('I am god and there is no other', Isa 45:22 = 46:9) is absent from the NT. Even if it were there, the important question would be *how* the OT is used in the respective cases.[21] As to the second assertion, it is unlikely that the Christian population in the Roman Empire exceeded that of the Jews until well into the fourth century.[22] But even if the Church were numerically stronger than Judaism much earlier, Beltz's statistical argument is irrelevant to the issue of the existence of a Jewish Gnosticism. After all, Christianity itself began as a 'Jewish heresy'![23]

Three Hermeneutical Presuppositions

In exploring further the question as to how the Gnostics used the OT, it will be useful to set forth the 'hermeneutical presuppositions',[24] or attitudes toward the OT, adopted by the Gnostics. There are three main possibilities, and all of them are found in the sources:
1. a wholly negative view of the OT;
2. a wholly positive view; and
3. intermediate positions.[25]
It will be noted that the question of the methods used in interpreting the OT texts is bound up with these presuppositions, especially the presence or absence of allegorical interpretation and the application or non-application of literal interpretation. Referring to Nagel's six categories of interpretation (discussed above), we can provisionally associate the negative stance with category 1, the

---

[19] Beltz, 'Gnosis und Altes Testament' 355, repeated on p. 356 with reference to the index of biblical passages in the Nestle edition of the Greek NT. Beltz's argument is cited with approval by Yamauchi, 'Jewish Gnosticism', 487. Beltz repeats his assertion as to the Christian mediation of 'Jewish elements' in Gnosticism in 'Elia redivivus' (p. 141, citing his earlier study). In that article he makes much of the absence from the Gnostic material of the Jewish eschatological tradition of the appearance of Elijah and Enoch in the end of days (*Apocalypse of Elijah*, etc.). But this tradition is possibly present in the fragmentary tractate, *Melchizedek* (*NHC* IX, 1), p. 13 of the MS. See Pearson, *Nag Hammadi Codices IX and X*, pp. 25, 63-65.
[20] Beltz, 'Gnosis und Altes Testament' 357.
[21] Schenk, 'Textverarbeitung', 301f. On the 'blasphemy of the Demiurge' see below.
[22] So Schenk, 'Textverarbeitung', 304.
[23] Cf. Pearson, 'Jewish Sources', 479f., where I cite the talmudic saying concerning the 'twenty-four sects of heretics' among the Jews (*P.T. Sanhedrin* 10, 29c).
[24] The term is that of Filoramo and Gianotto, 'L'interpretazione gnostica', 56.
[25] Ibid., 56f. Cf. Krause, 'Aussagen'. Krause cites as examples of the three stances the same three texts from Nag Hammadi discussed in what follows.

638

positive stance with category 6, and the intermediate positions with categories 2 to 5 (and partially with 6).

While a detailed account is not possible here, I shall treat first the three basic stances with reference to selected examples from Christian Gnostic texts.

WHOLLY NEGATIVE STANCE: THE SECOND TREATISE OF THE GREAT SETH

The Second Treatise of the Great Seth (*NHC* VII, 2)[26] is a revelatory exhortation purportedly addressed to an embattled group of Gnostic Christians by Jesus Christ in an attempt to bolster their steadfastness in the face of persecution by a more powerful group. Strongly polemical, this text attacks adversaries who are easily identifiable as catholic Christians associated with a growing ecclesiastical establishment.[27] As part of its attack, the document advances a radical dualist doctrine of antagonism and separation between the highest God and the Creator, between Christ and the world, and between the true Christians and those who are attached to the OT. This tractate contains the most violent attack against the OT and its heroes that can be imagined:

> Adam was a laughingstock, since he was made a counterfeit type of man by the Hebdomad (= the Creator), as if he had become stronger than I (Christ) and my brothers . . . Abraham and Isaac and Jacob were a laughingstock, since they, the counterfeit fathers, were given a name by the Hebdomad, as if he had become stronger than I and my brothers . . . David was a laughingstock in that his son was named the Son of Man, having been influenced by the hebdomad . . . . Solomon was a laughingstock, since he thought that he was the Christ, having become vain through the Hebdomad . . . . The 12 prophets were laughingstocks, since they have come forth as imitations of the true prophets . . . Moses, a faithful servant, was a laughingstock, having been named 'the Friend', since they perversely bore witness concerning him who never knew me. Neither he nor those before him, from Adam to Moses and John the Baptist, none of them knew me nor my brothers (62, 27-64, 1).

The text goes on to attack the 'doctrine of angels' (= the Tora)[28] associated with these figures, with its 'dietary laws' and 'bitter slavery'. The climax is reached with a virulent attack on the God of the OT:

> for the Archon was a laughingstock because he said, 'I am God, and there is none greater than I. I alone am the Father, the Lord, and there is no

---

[26] For discussions see Krause, 'Aussagen', 450f.; Bethge, 'Geschichtstraditionen', 104-06; Weiss, 'Gesetz', 78f.; Filoramo-Gianotto, 'L'interpretazione gnostica', 59f. The only critical edition of this tractate so far published is Painchaud, *Grand Seth* (with French translation).

[27] Painchaud suggests that it was written in Alexandria at the beginning of the third century; see *Grand Seth*, 6f.

[28] Cf. Gal 3:19.

639

other beside me. I am a jealous God, who brings the sins of the fathers upon the children for three and four generations'.[29] As if he had become stronger than I and my brothers! But we are innocent with respect to him, in that we have not sinned, since we mastered his teaching. Thus he was in an empty glory. And he does not agree with our Father. And thus through our fellowship we grasped his teaching, since he was vain in an empty glory. And he does not agree with our Father, for he was a laughingstock and judgment and false prophecy (64, 17-65, 2).[30]

Here is a wholesale rejection of the OT: its heroes of faith, its history of salvation, its legal demands, and its God. The text's inclusion of John the Baptist in the list of OT figures serves to strengthen the denial of any suggestion that Christ had any human forerunners at all, much less that he has come in fulfillment of OT prophecy. Yet this text should not be considered necessarily as 'anti-Jewish', for in fact the opponents attacked in it are not Jews but ecclesiastical Christians for whom the OT is still holy scripture.[31]

The closest analogy to this tractate's rejection of the OT in the history of Christian heresy is the attitude adopted by Marcion and his followers.[32] The closest analogy in the history of the Gnostic religion is the Mandaean tradition, for which Moses is the prophet of the evil *Rūhā*, and the Creator of biblical tradition is the chief of the demons.[33] The analogies break down in each case, however. Marcion, though undoubtedly influenced by Gnosticism, was not a Gnostic but a Christian who carried to radical extremes the Pauline doctrine of justification by *faith* (not *gnosis*) apart from the works of the Law.[34] The Mandaeans were both anti-Jewish and anti-Christian, though they probably originated as a splinter-group of Palestinian Judaism,[35] and share a number of traditions with the Gnostics known to us from the Nag Hammadi sources.[36] The community behind *Treat. Seth* was an embattled group of Christian Gnostics (or Gnostic Christians), whose attitude toward the OT was forged out of controversy with other Christians. In their total rejection of the OT they may have been

---

[29] Cf. Isa 45:5, 22; 46:9; Exod 20:5. These passages are part of a Gnostic traditional complex, the 'Blasphemy of the Demiurge'. The author of *Treat. Seth* is probably using the Gnostic tradition, rather than quoting the OT directly, as suggested by Schenk ('Textverarbeitung', 305f.). On the 'Blasphemy of the Demiurge' in Gnostic tradition see below.

[30] For a good commentary on this passage see Painchaud, *Grand Seth*, 128-34.

[31] Bethge, 'Geschichtstraditionen', 106.

[32] On Marcion's rejection of the OT and his role in the development of a NT canon see Von Campenhausen, *Formation*, 148-67.

[33] Weiss, 'Gesetz', 80.

[34] See the classic work of Harnack, *Marcion*, and the recent work by Hoffmann, *Marcion*.

[35] On the Mandaeans see Rudolph, *Gnosis*, 343-66, and literature cited there. For a convenient selection of Mandaean texts in English translation, with valuable discussion by Rudolph, see Foerster, *Gnosis* 2, 121-319.

[36] See e.g. Rudolph, 'Coptica-Mandaica'.

influenced by Marcionites,[37] though, as the Mandaean case shows, their own Gnostic presuppositions could have led them to this stance.

Another Nag Hammadi tractate, *The Testimony of Truth* (*NHC* IX, 3), has been brought into close association with *Treat. Seth* in respect to its aggressive attitude toward the OT.[38] That tractate, too, is a polemical attack on other Christians, in this case not only directed against the ecclesiastical establishment but also against other Gnostics.[39] Its use of the OT is multi-faceted, and while the Law and the OT Creator are vigorously attacked, it is evident that the author looks upon the OT as a source of Gnostic revelation that can be ferreted out by means of allegorical interpretation. *Testim. Truth* is an especially interesting tractate in that it contains two extended 'midrashim', a Gnostic one on the serpent in Paradise (45, 30-46, 2) and one that is not necessarily Gnostic on David and Solomon (69, 32-70, 24). Both midrashim are subjected by the Christian Gnostic author to allegorical interpretation.

I have commented extensively on *Testim. Truth* elsewhere.[40] Suffice it to say here that its use of the OT is not the same as that of *Treat. Seth*.

WHOLLY POSITIVE STANCE: THE EXEGESIS ON THE SOUL

The Exegesis on the Soul (*NHC* II, 6)[41] is devoted to an exposition of the divine origin, fall, and reintegration of the human soul. The doctrine of the descent and ascent of the soul was widespread in the Hellenistic-Roman world, and is part and parcel of the popular Platonism of the period. *Exeg. Soul* presents this doctrine with a Gnostic twist, depicting the (female) soul's descent as a fall into prostitution. Its ascent requires 'repentance' and consists in a restoration of the soul, as a renewed virgin, to her Father's house.

What is of interest to us here is the use made of the OT in this remarkable text. Scriptural passages are cited extensively as 'proof-texts' for the various aspects of the soul's experience, as set forth by the tractate's author.[42] The following examples are taken from the first part of the tractate:

---

[37] Cf. Von Campenhausen, *Formation*, 77.

[38] Nagel, 'Auslegung', 51, and discussion above.

[39] See e.g. Pearson, 'Anti-Heretical Warnings', and Koschorke, *Polemik der Gnostiker*, esp. 91-174.

[40] Pearson, 'Jewish Haggadic Traditions'; *Nag Hammadi Codices IX and X*, esp. 101-203; 'Gnostic Interpretation'; 'Jewish Sources', 457.

[41] For discussion see Krause, 'Aussagen', 452-56; Wilson, 'Old Testament Exegesis'; Kasser, 'Citations'; Nagel, 'Septuaginta-Zitate'; Guillaumont, 'Une citation'. Critical editions of this text so far published are Krause, *Koptische und hermetische Schriften*, 68-87, and Sevrin, *L'Exégèse* (with French translation). See now also the important monograph, with French translation and commentary, by Scopello, *L'Exégèse*.

[42] As Nagel has shown, the LXX text is closely followed in the OT passages quoted in *Exeg. Soul* (Nagel, 'Septuaginta-Zitate'). See also Kasser, 'Citations'. Scopello and Sevrin both argue for the use of an anthology on the part of the author: see Scopello, *L'Exégèse*, 13-44, and Sevrin, *L'Exégèse*, 13.

Now concerning the prostitution of the soul the Holy Spirit prophesies in many places. For he said in the prophet Jeremiah, 'If the husband divorces his wife and she goes and takes another man . . .' (Jer 3:1-4). Again it is written in the prophet Hosea, 'Come, go to law with your (pl.) mother, for she is not to be a wife to me nor I a husband to her . . .' (Hos 2:2-7). Again he said in Ezekiel, 'It came to pass after much depravity, said the Lord . . . You prostituted yourself to the sons of Egypt, those who are your neighbors, men great of flesh' (Ezek 16:23-26) (129, 5-130, 20).

The author is not content simply to cite scriptural proof texts, but he (or she)[43] offers specific interpretive commentary on key words or phrases in the scriptural text, as can be seen in the passage immediately following the material previously quoted:

But what does 'the sons of Egypt, men great of flesh' mean if not the domain of the flesh and the perceptible realm and the affairs of the earth, by which the soul has become defiled here, receiving bread from them, as well as wine, oil, clothing (cf. Hos 2:5), and other external nonsense surrounding the body in the things she thinks she needs (130, 20-28).

The author then proceeds to fortify his argument with references to, and quotations from, the NT, proceeding subsequently with additional teaching, with scriptural proofs from the Old and New Testaments, and in one case with an apocryphal passage from Ps.-Ezekiel.[44] The author's fund of revelatory scripture is larger than usual, however, for he quotes Homer in the same way that he does the Bible:

Therefore it is written in the Poet, 'Odysseus sat on the island weeping . . .' (*Odyssey* 1:48-59) (136, 27-35).

This is followed by two quotations from *Odyssey* 4. Our author evidently regards the Bible and 'the Poet' as equal sources of revelation, specifically as allegories of the soul's fall and restoration. His pagan contemporaries were already treating Homer in this way;[45] so it was simply a matter of adding the Christian scriptures to the fund of revelation concerning the nature and destiny

---

[43] *Exeg. Soul* is one of the Nag Hammadi tractates for which a female author could easily be posited. Cf. Scopello's discussion of the role of the feminine in this and other texts (*L'Exégèse*, 49-55). Scopello, however, does not argue for a female author, referring to the author as 'il' (ibid., p. 55). For convenience I also use the masculine gender in what follows, while leaving the question as to the sex of the author completely open.

[44] 135, 31-136, 4. This passage, formerly associated with *1 Clem.* 8:3, was first identified as Ps.-Ezekiel by Guillaumont, 'Une citation'. On Pseudo-Ezekiel see now Schürer, *History* (Rev.ed.) III/2, 793-96.

[45] See esp. Porphyry, *De antro nympharum*, a commentary on *Odyssey* 13:102-12; and Plotinus' interpretation of the flight of Odysseus from Circe and Calypso, *Enn.* 1:6, 8. On the allegorical interpretation of Homer in Hellenistic antiquity see esp. Buffière, *Les mythes d'Homer*.

642

of the human soul. In the process some new (Gnostic) features were added to the doctrine, including material related to the Valentinian myth of Sophia.

Exeg. Soul is clearly a 'late' product of Christian Gnosticism, as is particularly evident from its eclecticism. Its affinities with Valentinian Gnosticism have been noted.[46] Its affinities with the Naassene Gnostic system are also noteworthy.[47] The Naassenes interpreted Homer in much the same way as the author of *Exeg. Soul*.[48] The OT is also treated in a notably positive way in the Naassene material, with the application of allegorical interpretation.[49] Indeed the Naassene use of the OT is exceedingly sophisticated,[50] ranging from the use of 'proof texts' – for example, Isa 53:8 is quoted with reference to the Divine Man, Adamas[51] – to the poetical elaboration of an OT psalm as an allegory of the soul's salvation as a result of the descent of Jesus the Saviour.

The last-named example deserves further comment, involving as it does one of the most beautiful examples of Gnostic poetry preserved from antiquity. I refer, of course, to the so-called 'Naassene Psalm' (Hippolytus, *Refutatio* 5:10, 2), in which the soul is presented as a 'hind', weeping in her wanderings in the cosmic labyrinth until Jesus asks his Father to send him down to help the soul 'escape the bitter chaos', by transmitting 'the secrets of the holy way . . . Gnosis'.[52] As M. Elze has brilliantly demonstrated, this beautiful poem is a Gnostic interpretation of Psalm 41 (LXX): 'As a hind longs for the springs of the waters, so longs my soul for you, O God . . .'[53]

OT psalms are included among the scriptural passages utilized in *Exeg. Soul*. Psalm 45:10-11 (LXX 44:11-12) is quoted to show the Father's desire for the soul's repentance (133, 15-20). Psalm 103 (102):1-5 is quoted with reference to the ascent of the soul to the Father (134, 16-25). Psalm 6:6-9 (7-10) is quoted at the end of the tractate as part of a final exhortation to repentance (137, 15-22).

---

[46] According to Krause ('Aussagen', 456) it is a Valentinian product; according to Sevrin (*L'Exégèse*, 58-60) it is pre-Valentinian; according to Scopello (*L'Exégèse*, 48) it relies on Valentinian traditions and much else besides (passim).

[47] Noted by W. Robinson, 'The Exegesis', 116f. For the Naassene material see esp. Foerster, *Gnosis* 1, 261-82, providing a translation of Hippolytus *Refutatio* 5:6, 3-11, 1. See also the important work by Frickel, *Hellenistische Erlösung*. Another Gnostic work preserved by Hippolytus, *Baruch* by the Gnostic Justin, presents an interesting contrast to *Exeg. Soul* in its interpretation of the prophet Hosea, citing Hos 1:2 as referring to the 'mystery' of the ascent of 'Elohim' to 'the Good' (= Priapus!) and his divorce from 'Eden' (*Ref.* 5:27, 4). For a translation of *Baruch*, with discussion by E. Haenchen, see Foerster, *Gnosis* 1, 48-58. Cf. also Batey, 'Jewish Gnosticism', and Kvideland, 'Elohims Himmelfahrt'.

[48] Hippolytus, *Refutatio* 5:7, 30-39 (*Odyssey* 24:1-12); 5:8, 35 (*Odyssey* 4:384f.); 5:7, 36 (*Iliad* 4:350); 5:8, 3 (*Iliad* 15:189).

[49] Cf. Nagel, 'Auslegung', 51, and discussion above.

[50] Unfortunately no extended analysis of the Naassene use of the OT exists, and space does not allow for such an analysis here.

[51] Hippolytus, *Refutatio* 5:7, 2. The passage is introduced with the formula, 'it is written'.

[52] The best edition of the Greek text, with ET and commentary, is Marcovich, 'The Naassene Psalm'. I have used his translation here.

[53] My translation of v. 1. See Elze, 'Häresie und Einheit', 402f.

643

A similar use of the OT psalms, with the same positive stance toward the scriptural text, is found in *Pistis Sophia*, one of the Coptic Gnostic writings known before the discovery of the Nag Hammadi corpus.[54] In that text the heroine, 'Pistis Sophia', whose mythic fall and restoration are paradigmatic of the fall and restoration of the Gnostic soul, cries out in 'repentance' to the world of light and is ultimately restored by Jesus. There are thirteen such 'repentances', accompanied by extended quotations from the Psalms[55] and the *Odes of Solomon*[56] as 'proof texts' of the experience of salvation. G. Widengren, in an important article, has analysed the use of the OT in *Pistis Sophia*,[57] and I shall therefore forego any further comment here, except to say that the affinities between that text and *Exeg. Soul* are manifest.[58]

INTERMEDIATE POSITIONS: PTOLEMAEUS' LETTER TO FLORA AND OTHER TEXTS

The *Letter to Flora* by the Gnostic teacher Ptolemaeus, a disciple of the famous Valentinus, is one of the few precious Gnostic texts coming down to us from antiquity in its original Greek form (as quoted by Epiphanius).[59] In this letter Ptolemaeus addresses a certain lady, presumably an uninitiated seeker, on the subject of the Law of Moses and the extent of its continuing relevance to the (Gnostic) Christian life. Ptolemaeus' starting point is 'the words of the Saviour' (Jesus), from which it is concluded that the Law is divisible into three parts: a part attributable to God and his legislative activity, a part attributed to Moses himself, and a part added by 'the elders of the people' (4.1-14). The Law of God, in turn, is divided into three parts: The Decalogue, fulfilled by the Saviour, an imperfect part abolished by the Saviour, and a third (cultic) part that must be interpreted 'spiritually', i.e. allegorically (5.1-7.1). Ptolemaeus finally reveals his Gnostic stance by identifying the 'God' who gave the Law as the Demiurge, the Creator of the world, who is actually inferior to the perfect God, the Father (7.2-7). The import of his previous discussion, however, is that the Law is still to some extent authoritative, as defined by 'the words of the Saviour'. Even its cultic legislation contains revelation of value when it is subjected to allegorical interpretation.

---

[54] For the latest edition, with English translation, see MacDermot, *Pistis Sophia*.

[55] Ps 102 (LXX):1-5 is quoted in *Pistis Sophia* 2:75; the same passage is quoted in *Exeg. Soul* (as noted above).

[56] The Coptic translation of parts of Odes 1, 5, 6, 22, and 25 in *Pistis Sophia* was the only version of the *Odes of Solomon* known until the discovery of the Syriac version and then a Greek MS. of Ode 11. The *Odes* are not a Gnostic composition, contrary to the opinion of some scholars. For an English translation, with introduction and bibliography, see Charlesworth, *OTP* 2, 725-71.

[57] Widengren, 'Hymnen'. Cf. also Kragerud, *Hymnen*, and Trautman, 'La citation'.

[58] See esp. Krause, 'Aussagen', 450, 452; Filoramo-Gianotto, 'L'interpretazione gnostica', 65-69.

[59] Epiphanius *Adversus Haereses* 32:3, 1-7, 10. The standard edition is Quispel, *Ptolémée*. For a good English translation, with introduction, see Foerster, *Gnosis*, 1, 154-61. For an important discussion see Von Campenhausen, *Formation* 82-87; cf. also Weiss, 'Gesetz', 82f.

644

This important text of the Valentinian school, though dealing especially with the Law (i.e. the Pentateuch), can be seen to express the typical Valentinian Gnostic position vis-a-vis the OT as a whole: Even though it is inspired by an inferior deity, the OT contains valuable truth which 'the Saviour' fulfills, or which, when subjected to allegorical interpretation, reveals *gnosis*. The Valentinian use of the OT thus derives not only from Gnostic religious presuppositions (the inferior Creator, etc.) but also from general, non-heretical Christian tradition.

One of the Valentinian texts from Nag Hammadi,[60] *The Tripartite Tractate* (*NHC* I, 5),[61] presents a discussion of the OT prophets comparable to that on the Law in Ptolemaeus' letter. In the framework of a general discussion of various philosophies and theologies existing in the world (108, 13-114,30),[62] the author discusses the various 'heresies' that existed among the Jews as a result of their differing interpretations of scripture (112, 14-113, 1)[63] and offers the following assessment of the prophets:

> The prophets, however, did not say anything of their own accord, but each one of them (spoke) of the things which he had seen and heard through the proclamation of the Saviour. This is what he proclaimed, with the main subject of their proclamation being that which each said concerning the coming of the Saviour, which is this coming. Sometimes the prophets speak about it as if it will be. Sometimes (it is) as if the Saviour speaks from their mouths, saying that the Saviour will come and show favour to those who have not known him. They (the prophets) have not all joined with one another in confessing anything, but each one thinks on the basis of the activity from which he received power to speak about him . . . Not one of them knew whence he would come nor by whom he would be begotten, but he alone is the one of whom it is worthy to speak, the one who will be begotten and who will suffer (113, 5-34).

This passage sounds perfectly 'orthodox', until we realize that, in the context, the 'race of the Hebrews', including the prophets, are 'psychic' people attached to the inferior Creator, who himself is only an 'image of the Father's image' (110, 22-36).

The Valentinians were by no means the only Gnostics who developed this 'intermediate' position vis-a-vis the OT. Another of the Nag Hammadi texts,

---

[60] The other Valentinian texts are: *Pr. Paul* (I, 1); *Gos. Truth* (I, 3 and XII, 2); *Treat. Res.* (I, 4); *Gos. Phil.* (II, 3); *Interp. Know.* (XI, 1); and *Val. Exp.* (XI, 2). Still other Nag Hammadi texts betray Valentinian influences.

[61] There are two critical editions: Kasser et al., *Tractatus Tripartitus*; and Attridge, *Nag Hammadi Codex I* 1, 159-337 + 2, 217-497. For a discussion of its use of the OT see Zandee, 'Alte Testament'.

[62] For an important discussion and commentary see Attridge, ibid., 1, 185f. and 2, 417-35.

[63] On this passage in relation to rabbinic discussions of 'heresy' see Logan, 'Jealousy', 199-200.

645

The Concept of Our Great Power (*NHC* VI, 4),[64] not a Valentinian text but perhaps influenced by Valentinian Gnosticism, adopts such a stance in presenting a Gnostic-apocalyptic presentation of world history. In this interesting text, which has been referred to as an 'epitome of a Christian Gnostic history of the world,'[65] history is divided into three epochs or 'aeons': the 'aeon of the flesh' (38, 13; 41, 2), brought to an end by the Flood; the 'psychic aeon' (39, 16f.; 40, 24f.), during which the Saviour appears and which will end in a conflagration (46, 29f.), and a future 'aeon of beauty' (47, 15f.), which is an 'unchangeable aeon' (48, 13). The Creator is referred to as 'the father of the flesh', who 'avenged himself' by means of the water of the Flood (38, 19-32). Yet, in contrast to most Gnostic treatments, Noah is presented as 'pious and worthy', and a preacher of 'piety' (*eusebeia*, 38, 26).[66]

Many more examples could be cited here, but we can conclude this part of our discussion with the observation that an 'intermediate' stance vis-a-vis the OT is the most characteristic attitude toward the scriptures displayed in the Gnostic sources in general. Scripture is viewed largely as the product of a lower power (or lower powers), but it is nevertheless capable of revealing gnosis so long as the proper exegetical method is adopted. In the case of the Christian Gnostic documents, the proper method involves allegorical exegesis and/or a Christo-centric approach according to which Christ perfects or fulfills the OT or parts thereof.

There remains another set of questions to consider: Does the Christian Gnostic material exhaust our available evidence? That is to say, is there a Gnostic use of Mikra which is not at the same time 'Christian' in some recognizable sense? The Mandaean material already briefly cited[67] suggest that there is.

---

[64] There are two critical editions: Parrott, *Nag Hammadi Codices V, 2-5 and VI*, 291-326; and Cherix, *Le Concept*. For discussions of its use of the Old Testament see Krause, 'Aussagen', 451; Bethge, 'Geschichtstraditionen', 97f.; Filoramo-Gianotto, L'interpretazione gnostica', 60.

[65] Bethge, 'Geschichtstraditionen', 97, crediting H.-M. Schenke.

[66] Cf. Bethge's discussion of the various Gnostic interpretations of Noah and the Flood, 'Geschichtstraditionen', 94-98.

[67] See our discussion of *Treat. Seth*, above.

646

'Rewritten Scripture'

THE APOCRYPHON OF JOHN AND RELATED LITERATURE

The Apocryphon of John (NHC II, 1; III, 1; IV, 1; *BG*, 2)[68] is, in its present form, a Gnostic apocalypse[69] in which the risen Christ transmits revelation of 'mysteries' to his disciple John concerning 'what is and what was and what will come to pass' (II 2, 16-18; cf. 1, 1-2). It is one of the most important of the Gnostic texts that have come down to us, for it contains a Gnostic myth which probably served as the basis for the myth developed by the great Gnostic teacher, Valentinus, and further elaborated by his disciples, especially Ptolemaeus.[70]

Not long after the publication of the Berlin Gnostic Codex in 1955, S. Giversen published a valuable article on the use of the OT (especially Genesis 1-7) in *Ap. John.*[71] Using the *BG* version, Giversen first distinguishes the forms that use of the OT take in the text:

1) actual quotations, with introductory formula (e.g. 'the prophet said');
2) quotations without introductory formula;
3) expressions and phrases clearly derived from the OT text, or sentences recounting events described in the scripture; and
4) use of key words that call for special (allegorical) interpretation.

Instances of the first category also include direct refutation of what 'Moses said'. Among the examples cited by Giversen, the following also illustrates the fourth category, i.e. use of key words:

> 'The Mother (Sophia) now began to be agitated *(epipheresthai)*, knowing her deficiency, since her consort had not concurred with her when she was degraded from her perfection'. But I (John) said, 'Christ, what does "be agitated" *(epipheresthai,* cf. Gen 1:2 LXX) mean?' He smiled and said: 'Do you think that it is as Moses said, "over the waters"?' (Gen 1:2).

---

[68] The following critical editions have been published: of the BG version, Till-Schenke, *Gnostische Schriften*; of the version in NHC II, Giversen, *Apocryphon Johannis*; of all three Nag Hammadi versions, Krause, *Drei Versionen*. The English translation in Robinson, *Nag Hammadi Library* (by F. Wisse) renders the 'long recension' in *NHC* II. For ET of the *BG* version ('short recension'), together with the parallel material in Irenaeus, *Adversus Haereses* 1:29, see Foerster, *Gnosis* 1, 105-20. For discussions of the use of the OT in *Ap. John* see Giversen, 'Apocryphon of John', and Pearson, 'Biblical Exegesis'. See also my analysis of *Ap. John* in 'Jewish Sources', 458-64, 453f.; and 'Problem', 19-26.

[69] For a genre-study of Gnostic apocalypses see Fallon, 'Gnostic Apocalypses', esp. 130f. (on *Ap. John*).

[70] See esp. Quispel, 'Valentinian Gnosis'; Perkins, 'Ireneus', 199-200; and *Gnostic Dialogue*. 79; Jonas, *Gnostic Religion*, 199.

[71] Giversen, 'Apocryphon of John', published originally in Danish in 1957. For a valuable analysis of *Orig. World (NHC* II, 5 and XIII, 2) along the same lines see Wintermute, 'Gnostic Exegesis'.

No, but she saw the wickedness and the apostasy which would attach to her son (the Creator). She repented . . .[72]

In discussing the question as to *how* the author of *Ap. John* interprets Genesis, Giversen states that the interpretation is 'largely – but not exclusively – allegorical'.[73] He rightly qualifies this with reference to the basic Gnostic doctrines: phenomena in this world are only likenesses of realities in the world of light; the Creator and his world are evil and inferior to the highest God and the world of light; etc. The attitude taken toward the biblical text is mixed: What 'Moses said' is sometimes flatly rejected, but sometimes the counter interpretation is bolstered by referring to another biblical passage (e.g. the citation of 'the prophet' Isaiah at 59, 1-5). In general, the use of Genesis often involves a 'reverse' interpretation. What is presented in *Ap. John*, finally, does not involve a rejection of Genesis, or a revision of its text, but 'secret doctrine', i.e. 'true knowledge'.[74]

Giversen's discussion is quite sound as far as it goes, i.e. insofar as it takes account of *Ap. John* in its present form as a post-resurrection revelation transmitted by Christ to John and by extension to Christian Gnostic readers. However, formal analysis of the text reveals that it is a composite product, and contains editorial expansions of an earlier stratum of material. The effect of this redactional activity was to create a specifically Christian Gnostic text out of an earlier non-Christian Gnostic revelation. This was done by adding a framework according to which 'Christ' is providing revelation to John, by opening up the text at ten different points so as to create a dialogue between 'Christ' and his

---

[72] *BG* 44, 19-45, 13; ET in Foerster, *Gnosis* 1, 113. See Giversen's discussion (64f.). Giversen (66f.) provides the following table of Genesis passages used in one way or another in *Ap. John*:

Genesis	Ap. John (BG)
1:2	45, 1.7.10.19
1:26	48, 10-14
2:9	57, 8-11
2:15-16; 3:23-24	56, 1-10
2:17	57, 12-13
2:21	58, 17-18
2:21-22	59, 18-19
2:24	60, 7-11
3:16	61, 11-12
3:23	61, 19-62,1
4:25	63, 12-14
6:1-4	74, 1-5
6:6	72, 12-14
6:17	72, 14-17
7:7	73, 5-6

Other passages in Genesis could be added to this list. See e.g. my discussion of the 'Blasphemy of the Demiurge' (below); also my discussion of the use of Gen 2:7 in *Ap. John*, in 'Biblical Exegesis'.
[73] Giversen, 'Apocryphon of John', 67.
[74] Ibid., 75f.

interlocutor, John, and by adding a few easily recognizable glosses.[75] That such a procedure was actually carried out with Gnostic texts is indisputably proven in the case of two other Nag Hammadi writings, *Eugnostos* (III, 3 and V, 1) and *the Sophia of Jesus Christ* (III, 4 and *BG*, 3).[76]

The putative Urtext underlying *Ap. John* consists of theosophical revelation (the unknown highest God and the world of light), cosmogony (fall of Sophia, the lower world, and the blasphemy of the Demiurge), and soteriology, in which the primal history in Genesis is retold with the use of other biblical and extra-biblical materials in such a way as to emphasize the saving role of Sophia in behalf of the Gnostic elect, the 'race of Seth'.[77] Such a text can appropriately be labelled 'rewritten scripture'.

The closest analogies to this kind of text are the Jewish pseudepigraphical literature, specifically those writings which fall into the category of 'rewritten scripture', such as portions of *1 Enoch*, *Jubilees*, the *Genesis Apocryphon* from Qumran, the Books of Adam and Eve, and the like.[78] The putative Urtext of *Ap. John* is only one of a number of Gnostic texts that can be classified as 'rewritten scripture'.[79] Such texts, in my opinion, represent the earliest stage of Gnostic literary production, and can be seen as a bi-product of the history of Jewish literature. They are comparable in their method of composition and in their use of biblical texts and extra-biblical traditions to the Jewish pseudepigrapha. The difference, of course, is in what is conveyed in the respective literatures. If, for example, the *Book of Jubilees* is a rewriting of Genesis 1 – Exodus 14 for the purpose of presenting an alternative sectarian halakha,[80] the Urtext of *Ap. John* is a rewriting and expansion of Genesis 1-7 for the purpose of presenting an alternative, sectarian *myth*, a myth which will serve to reveal saving *gnosis*.[81] The use made of the biblical text in the respective cases are quite comparable both in terms of method and in terms of attitude. That is to say, the biblical text is not rejected out of hand; it is corrected and amplified by the composition of a superior version of the truth.

---

[75] See my discussion in 'Jewish Sources', 458-61, and 'Problem', 19-26, and literature cited there.

[76] *Soph. Jes. Chr.* is a Christian Gnostic 'revelation dialogue' that has been constructed as such using *Eugnostos*, a non-Christian text, as its basic source. See esp. Krause, 'Literarische Verhältnis'; Parrot, 'Religious Syncretism'; and Perkins, *Gnostic Dialogue*, 94-98.

[77] *Ap. John* has rightly been included in the group of texts which belong to 'Sethian' Gnosticism. On the Sethian form of Gnosticism see esp. Schenke, 'Gnostic Sethianism'; Pearson, 'Figure of Seth'; and the other essays in Layton, *Rediscovery* 2. Cf. also Stroumsa, *Another Seed*.

[78] See esp. Nickelsburg, 'Bible Rewritten'.

[79] Cf. Filoramo-Gianotto, 'L'interpretazione gnostica', 69-73, a valuable discussion with the heading, 'Reinterpretazione o rescrittura del racconto biblico'. The following texts attributed to the 'gruppo Sethiano' are discussed under that heading: *Ap. John; Hyp. Arch.* (*NHC* II, 4); and *Orig. World* (*NHC* II, 5 and XIII, 2). Cf. also the extensive discussion by Simonetti of Gnostic reinterpretation of the opening passages in Genesis ('Note sull' interpretazione', 9, 347-59 + 10, 103-26).

[80] Nickelsburg, 'Bible Rewritten', 97-104.

[81] On Gnosticism as a 'mythological phenomenon', see e.g. Stroumsa, *Another Seed*, 1-14; Jonas, 'Gnostic Syndrome', esp. 266-73.

To be sure, there is an observable difference between the Gnostic texts and the Jewish pseudepigrapha, even the most 'non-conformist' or 'sectarian' of them. This difference is so basic that it finally marks Gnosticism off as a new religion altogether, one that has broken through even the widest definable boundaries of what constitutes 'Judaism'. The following passage from *Ap. John* exemplifies this breach:

> And when he saw the creation which surrounds him and the multitude of angels around him which had come forth from him, he said to them, 'I am a jealous God and there is no other God beside me'. But by announcing this he indicated to his angels who attended to him that there exists another God, for if there were no other one, of whom would he be jealous? (*NHC* II, 13, 5-13).

This passage, containing the 'blasphemy of the Demiurge', is found in a number of Gnostic texts, and reflects the Gnostic end product of a discussion in Jewish circles concerning 'two powers in heaven'. The Gnostic conclusion to the debate effectively marks a 'revolution' on the part of Jewish Gnostics against the biblical Creator and a radical alienation from his created order.[82] The text itself is artfully constructed as a rewriting (and re-ordering) of the biblical material in Genesis 1. The Gnostic author indicates that he knows that the 'creation' (Gen 1:1) 'seen' (Gen 1:4, 10, 12, 18, 21, 25) by the Creator is nothing 'good'; rather it is darkness and chaos (Gen 1:2), and the Creator himself is not only arrogant but foolish,[83] not understanding the import of his own vain pronouncements (Isa 45:21; 46:9; Exod 20:5).

The blasphemy of the Demiurge is immediately followed in *Ap. John* by the statement (quoted above) concerning the 'moving to and fro' (= 'repentance') of 'the mother' (= Sophia), a reinterpretation of Genesis 1:2. Following Sophia's repentance a *bat qôl* comes from heaven with the announcement 'Man exists and the son of Man' (14, 14f.). With this revelation we come to know the identity of the highest God whose existence (together with that of his 'son', primal Adam) has been blasphemously denied by the Creator. The highest God is 'Man' (cf. Gen 1:26f.).[84]

The material that follows in the text deals with the creation of earthly man, a composite being whose inner self is akin to 'Man', the highest God. The Gnostic account of the creation of Adam was constructed with the use and reinterpretation of a number of Jewish exegetical traditions, some of which reflect the influence of contemporary Platonism.[85] The import of this Gnostic 'rewritten scripture' is that the knowledge of God requisite to salvation is really

---

[82] See esp. Dahl, 'Arrogant Archon', and Culianu, 'Angels'.
[83] One of the three names given to the Creator in *Ap. John* is 'Saklas' (Aramaic for 'fool'). The other names are 'Samael', and 'Yaldabaoth'; all three occur together in the text at II 11, 16-18. On these names see Pearson, 'Jewish Haggadic Traditions', 466-68; Barc, 'Samaèl-Saklas-Yaldabaôth'.
[84] See Schenke, *Der Gott 'Mensch'*.
[85] See Pearson, 'Biblical Exegesis', and now esp. Van den Broek, 'Adam's Physic Body'.

knowledge of the awakened self within, a 'man' whose kinship with 'Man' makes him superior to the world and its Creator.

That such a doctrine, so self-evidently alien to the biblical tradition (both Old and New Testaments), was read out of the Bible and given expression in the form of 'rewritten scripture' is one of the fascinating curiosities of ancient Jewish history, indeed, of the history of Hellenistic-Roman religion in general.

While *Ap. John* is arguably the most important Gnostic text for the purposes of this discussion, there are others, too, that fit the category of 'rewritten scripture'. Some of these are closely related to *Ap. John* in terms of structure and content: *The Hypostasis of the Archons (NHC* II, 4);[86] *On the Origin of the World (NHC* II, 5 and XIII, 2);[87] and the system described by Irenaeus in *Adversus Haereses* 1:30.[88] Like *Ap. John*, these texts have undergone Christianizing redaction. *The Apocalypse of Adam (NHC* V, 5) is an especially interesting example of rewritten scripture because of its relation to the Jewish Adam literature.[89] There is no discernible Christian content in *Apoc. Adam*. *The Paraphrase of Shem (NHC* VII, 1),[90] another non-Christian text, should probably be included in the category of rewritten scripture, though the divergences from the biblical text are greater in that writing. In addition, the Mandaean anthropogonic myths are clearly related to that of *Ap. John* and other Gnostic texts.[91] Unfortunately, limitations of space prevent us from taking up these materials for discussion here.

Conclusions

The earliest Gnostic literature was heavily indebted to the text of Mikra and biblical exegetical traditions. Though the Gnostics denigrated the biblical Creator by relegating him to an inferior position below a transcendent Deity, they did not reject the Bible itself. On the contrary, they came to their radical theology and worldview in the very process of *interpreting* the scriptural text, the authoritative ('canonical') status of which was self-evident. Their earliest literature took the form of 'rewritten scripture' and resembled in that respect some of the pseudepigraphical literature produced in sectarian Jewish circles.

---

[86] For the most recent editions see Layton, 'Hypostasis', and Barc, *L'Hypostase*. The latter posits several redactional stages in the text's composition, the most primitive of which is a product of Jewish Gnosticism.

[87] The basic edition is still Böhlig, *Schrift ohne Titel*. See Wintermute, 'Gnostic Exegesis', for an analysis of that text's use of the OT.

[88] That system is not labelled by Irenaeus, but scholarly tradition refers to it as 'Ophite'. For ET and discussion see Foerster, *Gnosis* 1, 84-94. For a good discussion of that text's correlation of the biblical prophets with the various archontic powers (1:30, 10-11) see Fallon, 'Prophets'. On the problem of 'Ophite' Gnosticism in general see Kaestli, 'L'interprétation du serpent'.

[89] See my discussion in 'Jewish Sources', 470-74, and 'Problem', 26-34, and literature cited there.

[90] See my discussion in 'Jewish Sources', 475f., and literature cited there, to which should be added Roberge, 'Le rôle du Noûs'.

[91] See esp. Rudolph, 'Grundtyp', and discussion above.

The Gnostic writings were mythological in character, and relied heavily on the primal history of Genesis and current Jewish interpretations thereof. Indeed, there is every reason to believe that the authors of the early Gnostic texts were disaffected Jewish intellectuals open to the various religious and philosophical currents of Hellenistic syncretism.

Early in the history of the Gnostic religion, the Christian mission exerted a profound influence on Gnostic thinking. And, vice-versa, Gnosticism came to play a prominent role in the early development of the Christian religion, particularly as Christianity moved away from its ethnic Jewish matrix and assumed a separate identity as a Hellenistic religion. The coalescence of Gnosticism and Christianity was expressed particularly in making Jesus Christ a Gnostic 'saviour' figure, i.e. a revealer of *gnosis*. The literary manifestation of this trend first takes the form of editorial Christianization of originally non-Christian texts. This was accomplished by attributing the Gnostic myth to Jesus Christ and/or by making him the paradigm of Gnostic salvation. Eventually a new Gnostic Christian literature was created.

The Bible ('Old Testament') was part of the Christian heritage, as it was of the Gnostic heritage. But there was considerable variety in the way in which Gnostic Christians looked upon it. Three basic attitudes emerged:
1) open rejection of the OT; 2) whole-hearted acceptance of it; and 3) an intermediate position according to which the biblical text was inspired by the lower Creator or lesser powers, but nevertheless contained 'spiritual truth' to be ferreted out by means of a spiritual (allegorical) exegesis.

Authorization for this procedure was found in revelation attributed to the Saviour, Jesus Christ, and various of his apostles.

As we have seen, the use and interpretation of Mikra among the various Gnostic groups in antiquity is characterized by a great deal of variety and complexity, thanks to the creative inventiveness of the different Gnostic teachers in their elaboration of Gnostic mythological consciousness. The full story of this process has by no means been told in the present study. It is to be hoped that someone will take up this challenging task in the future.

Bibliography

The standard bibliography on Gnosticism (except Manichaeism and Mandaeism) is SCHOLER, *Nag Hammadi Bibliography*. The best monographic treatments of Gnosticism are JONAS, *Gnostic Religion*; RUDOLPH, *Gnosis*; and FILORAMO, *L'attesa della fine*. The Nag Hammadi texts are available in English translation in a single volume: ROBINSON, *Nag Hammadi Library* (including also the tractates in the Berlin Gnostic Codex). The standard anthology of other Gnostic materials in English translation is FOERSTER, *Gnosis* (2 vols.).

No monograph on the use of Mikra in Gnostic literature exists. A collection of articles on the problem has been published (TRÖGER, *Altes Testament*) as well as individual articles in various journals, Festschriften, etc. (see above, n. 5).

652

Simon and Gnostic Origins

Simon Magus, according to Irenaeus, was the father of all heretics, *ex quo universae haereses substiterunt* [1]. Unfortunately, although he often refers to one gnostic or another as a disciple of Simon, the good bishop does not really provide us with any family tree, or any real demonstration of connections and relationships. His account of Simon's teaching takes up less than five pages in Harvey's edition, and that includes the Greek extracts preserved by Hippolytus and Harvey's own notes as well. The report begins with the narrative of Acts and goes on to mention the statue set up by Claudius, and Simon's trinitarian claims. Then comes the myth of Helen, with the account of the creation of the world by angels [2], and the assertion that because of the misgovernment of these angels he himself had descended to put things right.

This system, such as it is, may be regarded as fairly primitive, in that as with other early Christian-gnostic groups there is as yet no Demiurge [3]. The syncretism with Greek mythology might suggest a fairly advanced stage in the fusion of Christianity with classical culture, but that presupposes the traditional view of the origins of Gnosticism. We have no means of knowing the extent to which a Samaritan, as distinct from a Jew of Judaea, might have been familiar with Greek ideas, and ought not to rule out the possibility without more ado. Christian elements play a relatively small part, and could be regarded as merely grafted on to a fundamentally pagan system: the trinitarian claims, the docetic statement *passum autem in Judaea putatum, cum non esset passus,* the identification of Helen as the lost sheep of the parable. According to Foerster [4], Simon " shows no relationship with Christianity ", and reports which present him in such a light are to be received with caution.

---

1. Adv. Haer. III Praef.; ib. I 16.2 Harvey.

2. There is a slight discrepancy here, in that in the main report Helen is said *generare angelos et potestates, a quibus et mundum hunc factum dixit* (p. 192 Harvey), whereas at II. 8.2 (p. 272) we read *mundum ab angelis eius factum.*

3. Cf. FOERSTER, *Die Gnosis,* Zürich/Stuttgart 1969, i. 47: one of the elements common to the first Christian gnostics is " dass sie als Weltschöpfer nicht den Gott des Alten Testamentes *ausdrücklich* nennen ".

4. *Ib.* 41.

Irenaeus' report, however, already raises many questions. In speaking of „ the father of all heretics ", does he mean to imply a genetic relationship, or merely that Simon was the first to take this line? How much of this report can be traced back to the historical Simon, and how much was fathered on him by later members of the sect? Was Simon himself a gnostic, and in what sense? Can we really identify Simon the heresiarch with the Simon of Acts, or has some development taken place in the interval between? Jonas for example writes „ the terms in which Simon is said to have spoken of himself are testified by the pagan writer Celsus to have been current with the pseudo-messiahs still swarming in Phoenicia and Palestine at his time about the middle of the second century " [5]. Was Simon then a gnostic *Offenbarungsgott,* downgraded by Luke to the status of a mere travelling magician, or was he a magician exalted by later generations, or another of the false prophets and false messiahs described by Celsus?

Before going on to consider some modern responses to these questions, it may be well to give a brief survey of some of the other ancient source-material. Irenaeus' reference to the statue may recall the story in Justin's First Apology [6], but it should be noted that Justin merely dates Simon to the reign of Claudius, and does not say the statue was erected by Claudius. Nor does Irenaeus appear to mention Simon's birthplace Gitta. Irenaeus may, as Harvey says [7], be following Justin, but we have no means of determining what additions or modifications he may have made. It is a mistake to assume too readily that everything in a later writer was already in a source he is known, or may be suspected, to have used.

The statue appears again in the Acts of Peter [8], although here it is said to have been set up by the senator Marcellus (c. 10). The interesting thing is that in this document, roughly contemporary with Irenaeus, there is little or nothing of Simonian Gnosticism. As Schneemelcher puts it [9], the purpose of these Acts is not to conduct a heresy hunt; it is " to demonstrate, in the persons of Simon and his constantly victorious adversary, that God is stronger than Satan, whose service Simon has entered ". " We are dealing, not with the doctrines of Simonian Gnosticism, but with the contest between God and the devil ". Indeed, " the picture of Simon given in the Acts of Peter clearly illustrates its difference from the anti-heretical literature. The doctrine of this arch-heretic is

---

5. *The Gnostic Religion,* Boston 1958, 103.

6. Justin Martyr, 1 Apol. 26.

7. *Sancti Irenaei libri quinque adversus haereses,* ed. W. W. HARVEY (Cambridge 1857), i. 191 n. 1.

8. See HENNECKE-SCHNEEMELCHER, *NT Apocrypha* ii, London 1965, 1974, 259ff.

9. *Op. cit.* 273 (the following quotations are all from this page).

suppressed, and instead of it anti-Christian objections of a general character are attributed to him ". Simon, as in the Acts of the Apostles, is nothing more than a magician. This shows that by the end of the second century there were at least two traditions, the heresiological which regarded Simon as the father of all heresies, and this other tradition deriving from Acts, that he was a mere magician [10]. It could of course be argued that this second tradition is due to Christian propaganda [11], a deliberate playing down of Simon's role and significance, but we should also consider whether it is not possible to reconcile these two traditions, whether there may not be truth in both.

With the pseudo-Clementines we enter into debated territory, and encounter problems which cannot possibly be discussed in the time at our disposal; questions of sources and redaction, of underlying older documents, of the relation (if any) to the earlier Acts of Peter, and so on. Lucien Cerfaux long ago declared himself profoundly sceptical of the value of this material [12], and more recently Karlmann Beyschlag has pronounced it almost completely worthless [13]. One of the few points which Beyschlag singles out as noteworthy is the legend of Simon and Dositheus, which introduces yet further ramifications [14]. Simon of course appears in Acts in Samaria, according to Justin he was a native of a Samaritan village, and the most recent discussion of the Dositheans regards them as a Samaritan sect. It is not surprising that attempts have been made to link Simon with a pre-Christian Samaritan gnosis, but here as so often we are faced with the problem of a lack of adequate documentary sources for the period with which we are concerned.

---

10. Cf. B. ALAND (see n. 16) 65 n. 114: Dass die Petrusakten ihre Nachrichten über Simon dennoch nicht nur aus Apg. 8, 4ff. beziehen, zeigt die Tatsache, dass sie auch von Simons Anspruch, der Christus zu sein, wissen (4). Es muss also eine von der Simonianischen Gnosis unabhängige Überlieferung gegeben haben, die sich wie diese ebenfalls auf Simon berief und den Charakter Simons als göttlicher Zauberer aus Apg. 8, 4ff. weiter ausschmückte. Gegen sie wenden sich die Petrusakten.

11. Cf. LÜDEMANN, *Untersuchungen zur simonianischen Gnosis*, Göttingen 1975, 41: Den Christengegner als Magier abzustempeln, ist eine in der frühchristlichen Polemik oft gehandhabte Methode. But were Elymas and the sons of Sceva also gnostics?

12. *Recueil L. Cerfaux*, Gembloux 1954, 248 n. 1 (from an article originally published in 1925).

13. *Simon Magus und die christliche Gnosis*, WUNT 16, Tübingen 1974, 67.

14. Particularly in regard to Samaritan associations. For Dositheanism see now ISSER, *The Dositheans. A Samaritan Sect in late Antiquity*, Leiden 1976. K. RUDOLPH, *ThR* 37 (1972) 338 considers the attempt „ die samaritanischen Traditionen auszuwerten " as more successful than other investigations of Simonian gnosticism. See his discussion of the literature, 338-347.

Finally there is the report of Hippolytus, which in part reproduces that of Irenaeus but also includes an ostensibly Simonian document, the Megale Apophasis. As Beyschlag notes [15], none of the earlier reports about Simon shows any knowledge of this document, and Hippolytus himself appears to have come across it only at a fairly late date. The general opinion has been that while it may derive from the Simonian *school* it represents a late stage of development, and is not to be connected with Simon himself [16]. Nevertheless „ bis heute sind die Stimmen nicht verstummt, die den Anspruch der Apophasis, eine Werk jenes Urvater der Häresien zu sein, als rechtens anerkennen " [17].

Precisely at this point there have been two recent and almost simultaneous attempts to re-open the question of gnostic origins, by claiming the document as early and the work of Simon himself. One of these attempts, by J. M. A. Salles-Dabadie, has on the whole met with a rather cool reception [18]. He claims that the document presents a gnosis so archaic that we should not even consider it a gnosis if we did not know that several later gnostic systems drew their inspiration from it. Kurt Rudolph, however, observes that this theory of the use of the Apophasis in reports of other gnostic systems could just as easily be inverted, as showing the development of the Simonian system, a development *culminating* in the Apophasis. As Rudolph remarks, the Nag Hammadi library affords examples of the growth of just such Offenbarungsschriften [19].

The other study, by Josef Frickel [20], takes a different line of approach, although Salles-Dabadie claims that despite differences of detail they are agreed on an essential point: that the Apophasis bears witness to an archaic and not a late form of gnosis [21]. This, however, is not entirely correct. Frickel's argument is that what we have in Hippolytus

---

15. *Beyschlag* 39.

16. See the references in Beyschlag, 40 n. 66: Abgesehen von den in der vorigen Anm. genannten Stimmen ist das wissenschaftliche Urteil über den simonianischen Quellenwert der Apophasis seit eh und je eindeutig negativ.

17. B. ALAND, *Proceedings of the International Colloquium on Gnosticism, Stockholm 1973* (Kungl. Vitterhetsakademiens Handlingen. Filologisk-Filosofiska Serien 17, Stockholm 1977) 35. Dr. Aland holds „ dass die Apophasis... eine verhältnismässig späte Schrift der Gnosis ist, an der sich das Verhältnis von Gnosis und Philosophie beispielhaft studieren lässt ".

18. J. M. A. SALLES-DABADIE, *Recherches sur Simon le Mage, I. L'Apophasis megale* (Cahiers de la Revue biblique), Paris 1969. Cf. RUDOLPH 331ff.; BEYSCHLAG 92f.; LÜDEMANN 26ff.; ALAND 37.

19. RUDOLPH 337.

20. FRICKEL, *Die „ Apophasis Megale " in Hippolyt's Refutatio* (Orientalia Christiana Analecta 192), Rome 1968. Cf. RUDOLPH 325ff.; BEYSCHLAG 91f.; LÜDEMANN 26.

21. SALLES-DABADIE 9 n. 2 (foot of p. 10).

is not the Apophasis itself, but a pharaphrase or commentary upon it, and that it is the original Apophasis which goes back to Simon. As Lüdemann observes, the two parts of this theory can be separated [22], and while the first has commanded a wide measure of recognition and acceptance, the second — the identification of Simon as author — remains in doubt. The problem here is that we have no means of proving for this period that the alleged author of a book ever actually wrote it. In an age when the traditional ascriptions of the books of the New Testament are widely disputed, it is no longer possible to accept without more ado the statements of early Fathers about works attributed to heretical leaders.

Reference has already been made to two further studies, by Karlmann Beyschlag and Gerd Lüdemann [23]. Published almost at the same time, they represent rather divergent positions. Beyschlag's work constitutes a challenge to the *religionsgeschichtlich* approach which has so long been dominant in New Testament studies, and in particular to the thesis of Ernst Haenchen, which he says " zumindest in Deutschland so gut wie keinen Widerspruch, vielmehr allerwärts gläubige Anerkennung und Nachfolge gefunden hat " [24]. For Beyschlag, Simon was " bereits eine Grösse der Vergangenheit, als man ihn zum Inbegriff aller Gnosis, ja des Christentums überhaupt, erhob " [25]. So far from being a pre-Christian form of Gnosticism, Simonianism is secondary. Indeed, the widely held assumption of a pre-Christian Gnosticism is much less firmly based than is generally assumed : " Indem Simon Magus aufhört zu sein, was er nicht war, nämlich ein vorchristlicher (oder " frühgnosti-scher ") Offenbarungsgott, bricht die einzige angeblich historich gesicherte Stütze für den Frühansatz des übrigen christlichen Gnostizismus zusam-men, und damit ein gutes Stück jenes Faszination, die das gnostische Problem auf das Boden des NTs lange Zeit besessen hat " [26]. This is in line with the views advanced by Hermann Langerbeck [27] and others, who as Beyschlag himself observes represent " eine ausgesprochene Min-derheit ", but are not for that reason to be discounted. The merit of this general position is that it focusses upon the classic Christian gnostic systems of the second century, and breaks with the habit, long too pre-

22. LÜDEMANN 26. Cf. also ALAND 37.

23. See above, notes 10 and 12. For a critique of Beyschlag, based on an earlier article, see RUDOLPH 330 n. 1.

24. BEYSCHLAG 90, referring to HAENCHEN, *ZThK* 49 (1952) 316-349 (= *Gott und Mensch*, Tübingen 1965, 265-298). Against Haenchen see also BERGMEIER, Quellen vorschristlicher Gnosis? *Festschrift K. G. Kuhn*, Göttingen 1972, 200ff. (BEYSCHLAG 98 n. 43 ; LÜDEMANN 28f.).

25. *Ib.* 217.

26. *Ib.* 218.

27. *Aufsätze zur Gnosis*, ed. H. DÖRRIES, Göttingen 1967.

valent, of interpreting first-century material in the light of them, reading first-century material with second-century spectacles. Its weakness is that it does not allow enough for the trends and tendencies which were undoubtedly already present in the first century, for the development which finally culminated in the classical gnosticism. Long ago Cerfaux wrote " Dans son fond, la religion de Simon n'avait pas été, à ses débuts, du " gnosticisme ". C'était une gnose à base de mythes païens et de magie. Un jour arriva cependant où ... la doctrine s'incorpora un nouvel élément. Les thèmes *gnostiques* apparurent " [28].

This distinction appears to be a valid and useful one, in that it affords a basis for the reconciliation of two contrasting positions [29]. It should not, however, be taken as an *Auseinanderreissen* [30] of what belongs together: there is continuity and development from the vague and rather nebulous gnosis to the developed systems of gnosticism. On the other hand we ought not to assume too readily a smooth unbroken process — Hans Jonas for one has objected to " the view of a smooth 'transition' instead of a decisive break, a mere mutation in the same genus " [31]. We have to recognise both continuity and discontinuity. The problem is that as we probe further back it becomes more and more difficult to be certain. Was Simon already a gnostic, as Haenchen tried to show, and in what sense? A gnostic in the wider sense of gnosis, which might be applied to Philo and many others, or in the specific sense of the classical second-century systems? Many scholars might accept the first alternative, but the second is simply not proven. All attempts so far made have failed to bridge the gap between the Simon of Acts and the Simon of the heresiologists. It cannot be shown that the historical Simon already held the developed gnostic doctrines later attributed to him.

In a footnote [32] Beyschlag remarks that recent studies are marked off from the earlier ones by their very length. Instead of major articles we now have monographs, like his own. This has made this sub-division of gnostic study into a field in which only specialists can find their way. It may also afford some excuse for the cursory treatment given to these studies in this paper, and the neglect of some others. From Lüdemann's study a few points only may be mentioned: first, that we cannot get back behind the recognition that alien doctrines have been fathered on Simon by the heresiologists (p. 29); and second that the description of him as the father of all heresies was born in the struggle with Gnosis

---

28. *Recueil Cerfaux* I, 256.
29. See WILSON, *From Gnosis to Gnosticism, Mélanges Puech*, Paris 1974, 423-9.
30. See RUDOLPH, *ThR* 36 (1971) 18ff.
31. *The Bible in Modern Scholarship*, ed. J. P. HYATT, Nashville 1965, 291.
32. BEYSCHLAG 89 n. 28.

(p. 37). Irenaeus or his predecessors turned the gnostic principle of tradition against them, and traced everything back to Simon. Attempts to identify Simon as magician, prophet or gnostic are incapable of proof (p. 54), and he prefers to leave the question of the historical Simon open (p. 81).

Where then does all this leave us with regard to the Simon of Acts? It is clear that we cannot trace back to him the doctrines of the later Simonian sect, whether these doctrines were attributed to him by his own followers or, as Lüdemann suggests, by the heresiologists. In terms of the wider and vaguer sense of gnosis he may be called " gnostic ", but we have to recognise the development which took place within the Simonian school, in particular the possibility of development from a non-Christian into a Christian-gnostic sect [33]. For Simon himself the prophets of Celsus, or such figures as Apollonius of Tyana and Alexander of Abounoteichus, still seem to provide the closest parallels. It is true that early Fathers sometimes dismissed their opponents as mere magicians, and that Luke may have degraded Simon from some higher status [34] — but other heretics are alleged to have been disappointed candidates for the episcopate. It cannot be assumed that such allegations are *always* merely propagandist. The usage must have started somewhere, and for some reason, presumably because in some case it actually did happen, and was later thought to be a useful method of disposing of an opponent. Could Simon in Acts have provided the example that was later to be followed?

By Luke's time gnosticism was beginning to be a problem for the Church. It has even been suggested that his work was written as a defence against gnosticism [35]. It may be that he pillories gnostic leaders in the person of Simon [36]. What is certain is that there is a gap still to be bridged between the Simon of Acts and the Simon of the heresiologists [37].

St. Mary's College   R. McL. WILSON
St. Andrews, Fife
KY16 9JU.

---

33. RUDOLPH, *ThR* 37 (1972) 332-3 note.

34. „ Dass Lk harmonisiert und bagatellisiert (eben auch Simon degradiert!) ... ist heute gesichertes Wissen der nt-lichen Wissenschaft " (RUDOLPH, *ThR* 37, 332 note).

35. C. H. TALBERT, *Luke and the Gnostics*, Nashville 1966.

36. C. K. BARRETT, *Luke the Historian in Recent Study*, London 1961, 62.

37. Only after this paper was complete was my attention drawn to an article in *Religious Studies Review III*, 1977, by WAYNE MEEKS: *Simon Magus in Recent Research*. I am happy to find our conclusions are largely in agreement.

Numen, Vol. XXII, Fasc. 2

GNOSIS AND GNOSTICISM:
A STUDY IN METHODOLOGY

BY

HENRY A. GREEN

St. Andrews University, Scotland

Introduction

There has been a noticeable absence in the study of Gnosis and Gnosticism of a sociological perspective. With the exception of E. Michael Mendelson's paper "Some Notes on a Sociological Approach to Gnosticism" presented at the Messina Colloquium in 1966 [1]) and Hans Kippenberg's article, "Versuch einer soziologischen Verortung des antiken Gnostizismus" in *Numen* in 1970 [2]), sociological studies are absent [3]). Mendelson, a professional social anthropologist, suggested for consideration a number of sociological questions but unfortunately left them unanswered. Instead he proceeded to present us with examples from his own field of research, Buddhism, as an analogous situation. His sociological analysis of Gnosticism, therefore, is severely limited and neither substantive nor theoretical. At most, we can only pay attention to his suggestion that an analysis of Gnosticism move from the ideological level of analysis to that of sectarian conflict with special consideration given to "patterns of social relations" [4]). On the other hand, Kippenberg, a theologian with sociological interests, argues from a Sociology of Knowledge and Sociology of

---

1) E. Michael Mendelson, "Some Notes on a Sociological Approach to Gnosticism" in *Le Origini dello Gnosticismo*, (ed.) U. Bianchi, Supplement to *Numen*, Vol. 12, (1967) pp. 668-676. (Hereinafter *Le Origini*).

2) Hans Kippenberg, "Versuch einer soziologischen Verortung des antiken Gnostizismus" in *Numen*, Vol. 17, (1970) pp. 211-232.

3) I have recently become aware of a third sociological study entitled, *Gnostische Gemeinschaften*, a Ph. D. dissertation by Hans Kraft, University of Heidelberg in 1950 (Abstract: *Theologische Literaturzeitung*, Vol. 75, (1950) p. 628) but unfortunately have not been able to obtain it. Given its early date and the nature of the abstract, I am inclined to think that its sociological content may be less than rewarding.

4) E. M. Mendelson, *op. cit.*, pp. 669-670 and 673-674.

Religion conceptual perspective and attempts to demonstrate that the ideological elements of Gnosticism are a reflection of a socio-political reality in which the Gnostics felt repressed and alienated. His thesis is that the sects of the Gnostic movement bred among the impotent Hellenized intellectual elite of the eastern fringes of the Roman Empire.

Kippenberg's argument is based on Topitsch's neo-positivist approach to ideological analysis which emphasized the ideological roots of philosphical systems [5]). We can view Topitsch's model as a continuation of one school of German Sociology which posits that structural similarities exist between metaphysical doctrines and everyday experience and as such the former can be conceived as analogous and arising out of the latter. Kippenberg also ventures to use Eric Fromm's model which posits that every image of God is a projection of political authority [6]). By integrating a psychological model with Topitsch's portrait of ideology, Kippenberg attempts to provide us with evidence of the ways in which ancient Gnosticism interpreted the social reality of Imperial Rome and transformed it into a new world-view for their own interpretations of God, man and the world.

Kippenberg's novel interpretation has been criticized by Peter Munz on a number of points [7]). Methodologically Munz considers the framework of the Sociology of Knowledge to be itself ideological, and suggests as an alternative, that instead of looking from either end of the continuum, metaphysical-religious beliefs or political social experience, we explore for a missing link between social forms and thought forms [8]). Second, Munz criticizes Kippenberg's choice of what he perceives to be the central theme of Gnosticism. Munz believes that Kippenberg's choice of the Evil Demiurge as analogous to Roman Imperial tyranny is mandatory because Kippenberg's theory posits

---

5) H. Kippenberg, *op. cit.*, pp. 213-214. For E. Topitsch's view see his *Sozialphilosophie zwischen Ideologie und Wissenschaft*, (Luchterhand 1961), especially pp. 261-296.

6) H. Kippenberg, *op. cit.*, pp. 230-231. For E. Fromm's ideas see his *Das Christusdogma und andere Essays*, (München 1965), especially pp. 9-91.

7) Peter Munz, "The Problem of *'Die Soziologische Verortung des antiken Gnostizismus'*" in *Numen*, Vol. 19, (1972) pp. 41-51.

8) Munz's suggestion is closely alligned with that of Mary Douglas' in her book *Natural Symbols* (London 1970). Munz favours Douglas' suggestion that the human body might be that missing link, the vehicle through which social forms and religious beliefs are connected. Munz, *op. cit.*, pp. 49-51.

that ideologies are constructed from human experience. On the contrary, we would argue that Munz has misinterpreted Kippenberg. It is not the Evil Demiurge that is central for the Gnostics; it is their passion for freedom through *gnosis* [9]).

Kippenberg's attempt at delimiting sociological concepts to be considered in a sociological analysis of Gnosticism must be seen in the context of an experimenter probing for new chemicals. It is due to the fact that it is pioneer work that there will be negative reactions. But this need not detract from Kippenberg's approach despite Munz's comments [10]). Munz could well take heed of the recommendations of Gnostic scholars regarding the need for sociological investigations notwithstanding Kippenberg's shortcomings [11]). It is unfortunate that Kippenberg's study is the only sociological study in spite of these recommendations. Nevertheless, the frequency of their occurrence in literature about Gnosticism over the last decade indicates the increasing awareness of this deficiency on the part of Gnostic scholars. And, of course, this development has been further enhanced by 'Proposal Six' of the Messina Colloquium, a colloquium specifically focussed on Gnosticism, which stated: "the Colloquium expresses the hope that further study will deepen the... sociological aspects of the movements of Gnosticism" [12]).

Although, given the above, individuals such as Robert Haardt have

---

9) H. Kippenberg, *op. cit.*, p. 225. The intention of the Gnostics is "... ein herrschaftsfreies Seinsverhältnis" and "sich durch Rekurs auf seine Vernunft ausserhalb des irrationalen Machtsystems zu begeben".

10) P. Munz, *op. cit.*, p. 50.

11) For example, as early as 1963 Kurt Rudolph called for a sociological analysis with special emphasis placed on the socio-economic causes of Gnosticism ("Stand und Aufgaben in der Erforschung des Gnostizismus" in the Tagung für allgemeine Religionsgeschichte, in *Sonderheft der Wissenschaftlichen Zeitschrift der Friedrich-Schiller-Universität*, (Jena 1963) pp. 89-102). Th. P.van Baaren in a Messina paper mentioned the "... almost complete ignorance of sociological aspects of Gnostic communities" and advocated research into the consequences of Gnostic belief systems on everyday life ("Towards a Definition of Gnosticism" in *Le Origini* pp. 174-180). For a synopsis of those at Messina who individually encouraged a sociological study of the Gnostic movements, see George MacRae, "Gnosis in Messina" in *The Catholic Biblical Quarterly*, Vol. 28, (1966) pp. 329-330. And as recently as 1973 Petr Pokorný has recommended an examination of the social background and environment of the Gnostics ("Der Soziale Hintergrund der Gnosis" in *Gnosis und Neues Testament*, (ed.) Karl-Wolfgang Tröger, (Berlin 1973) pp. 77-88, hereinafter Tröger, *Gnosis)*.

12) *Le Origini*, p. xxix.

7

commented with reference to those who entertain the possibility of a
sociological analysis that "in der Gnosisforschung ist die Quellenlage
nach wie vor so prekär, dass ein soziologischer Aufweis von Real-
gründen äusserst schwierig ist" [13]), this observation need not be a
deterrent. For example, the absence of a sociological perspective does
not deny the fact numerous scholars have attempted to take social
and economic factors into account. However, instead of employing this
evidence from a sociological *Weltanschauung* either theoretically or
methodologically, these factors are applied only as secondary
evidence [14]).

Given the above 'call' for a sociological analysis it seems quite
apposite that a review of methodological approaches in the study of
Gnosis and Gnosticism be undertaken in order to assess whether a
particular or distinct sociological method or theoretical perspective has
indeed been attempted. This descriptive analysis will be conducted
in the following manner. First a descriptive review of previous methodological studies in the analysis of Gnosis and Gnosticism will be
pursued. Second, the fundamental methodological approaches of Gnostic scholars will be discussed. This section will also demonstrate that
there are no intrinsic differences in the methodological approaches of
students of Gnosticism. Third, the defects and limitations of this
methodological approach will be analysed.

Robert Haardt and his Methodological Studies

In Gnostic research there has been no systematic attempt at describing and analysing the various methods through which scholars
conduct their research, with the exception of Robert Haardt. Dr.
Haardt within the last decade has presented two articles on methodology, common the second, an updated and expanded version of his
original [15]). Both these articles can be considered on the one hand as an

---

13) R. Haardt, *Die Gnosis: Wesen und Zeugnisse*, (Salzburg 1967) p. 25.

14) For examples of scholars who use these factors as secondary evidence,
see R. M. Grant, *Gnosticism and Early Christianity*, revised edition, (New York
1966) and G. Quispel, *Gnosis als Weltreligion*, (Zurich 1951).

15) R. Haardt, "Bemerkungen zu den Methoden der Ursprungsbestimmung
von Gnossi" in *Le Origini*, pp. 161-174 and "Zur Methodologie der Gnosisforschung" in Tröger, *Gnosis*, pp. 183-202. Because the second article, "Zur Methodologie der Gnosisforschung" is both more recent and exhaustive, I shall only
refer to the Messina paper in passing or in footnotes. Also Dr. Haardt has a
short section on methodology in the introduction of his book, *Die Gnosis: Wesen*

apology for the limitations of Gnostic research, and on the other, as a call for new methods.

Dr. Haardt begins his analysis by noting the complementary nature of the definition of Gnosis and the definition of its origin. Because of this and the fact that in Gnostic research there is no uniform conception of Gnosis, Haardt's working premise is that only through interpreting each author's definition of Gnosis and his particular development of its origin, is it possible to understand the individual methods employed [16]). Schematically he divides the attempts at the derivation of Gnosis and its origin into three major categories according to their function: those which argue predominately from the 'History of Motifs' and which tend towards a *regressus ad infinitum*; derivations which are 'Reductive' either in the sence of a sociological or a pyschological explanation and can be considered as a special subdivision with the context of 'History of Motifs'; and finally, those which are indebted to Philosophy and especially the 'existential-ontological' interpretation [17]).

Dr. Haardt describes the function of the 'History of Motifs' as follows: "Die auf motivgeschichtlicher Basis arbeitende religionsgeschichtliche Methode versucht durch Aufweis historischer Affiliationen ein religiöses Phänomen zu fundieren" [18]). This method can be further described as the affiliation of motifs in literary texts with historical phenomena of the same culture from within which they supposedly originated. Frequently, according to Haardt, History of Religions and *Religionsgeschichtliche Schule* researchers employ this method of 'History of Motifs' in their investigations when isolating themes or motifs and tracing their development. From Dr. Haardt's viewpoint, these motifs or derivations of Gnosis are intrinsically linked to "ebenfalls typisierten zeitlichen Antezedentien" such as Greek-Hellenistic, Oriental, Jewish-Orthodox, Jewish-Heterodox, Christian or combinations thereof [19]). In the course of his subsequent

---

und Zeugnisse, op. cit., pp. 17-29, which is similar to the paper he presented at the Messina Colloquim.

16) Tröger, *Gnosis*, p. 183.

17) *Le Origini*, pp. 161-162; Tröger, *Gnosis*, pp. 184-185. In his Messina paper Haardt considers the 'existential-ontological' method to be subsumed by the second.

18) Tröger, *Gnosis*, p. 191.

19) *Le Origini*, p. 161; Tröger, *Gnosis*, p. 184.

discussion he makes reference to scholars who argue for 'Pre-Gnosticism', 'Proto-Gnosticism' and 'classical' Gnosticism. Haardt provides numerous examples of the above temporal antecedents in conjunction with these positions: A. Harnack, F. C. Burkitt, H. A. Wolfson, C. Schneider, H. Leisegang, R. McL. Wilson and S. Pétrement under the Greek-Hellenistic category [20]); W. Anz, W. Bousset and R. Reitzenstein under the Oriental [21]); and G. Quispel and B. K. Stürmer from Jewish-Orthodox [22]). Dr. Haardt readily admits that these subdivisions within the 'History of Motifs' are neither exclusive nor exhaustive, but rather are gleaned from the implicit or explicit evidence as stated by each author who believes his data has established a particular preponderance of influences. Haardt also draws our attention to the fact that many 'History of Motifs' researchers attempt to identify Gnostic motifs such as the Heavenly Redeemer in pre-Gnostic literary texts. This identification, according to Haardt, leads these researchers to claim the respective cultural backgrounds as the 'real' origin of Gnosis. Dr. Haardt again provides examples and discusses this usage of motifs, especially those of Widengren, Schmithals and Schoeps [23]).

The second category of Dr. Haardt's schematization is the 'Reductive'. He describes the function of the 'Reductive' category as follows:

> ...unterscheiden wir gegenüber motivgeschichtlichen Rückfragen reduktiv argumentierende Ableitungen, welche den Ursprung der Gnosis durch ein Phänomen zu erklären suchen, welches selber nicht mehr der Ebene des von ihm Begründeten angehört. Der Konstitutionsprozess, der die Gnosis begründet hat, wird hier psychologisch oder soziologisch erklärt. [24]

This description is further clarified when he discusses the 'Reductive' category's relationship to that of the 'History of Motifs':

> Dabei ist es aber keineswegs so, dass die neuen Methoden die motivgeschichtlichen Methoden ausschlössen, nur kommt ihnen innerhalb der Motivgeschichte eine reduktive Funktion zu. [25]

More simply, researchers in order to further document historical affiliations within literary contexts seek material foundations which

---

20) *Le Origini*, pp. 162-163; Tröger, *Gnosis*, pp. 185-187.
21) *Le Origini*, pp. 163-164; Tröger, *Gnosis*, pp. 187-189.
22) *Le Origini*, pp. 164-165; Tröger, *Gnosis*, pp. 189-190.
23) *Le Origini*, p. 166; Tröger, *Gnosis*, pp. 190-191.
24) *Le Origini*, p. 162; Tröger, *Gnosis*, p. 184. As mentioned previously Haardt has included the 'existential-ontological' method within this second category in his Messina paper, n. 17.
25) Tröger, *Gnosis*, p. 191.

have sociological or psychological overtones. According to Haardt, these overtones are

> ... entweder im Sinne einer wiederum gegenständlich gedachten Bedingung des Zustandekommens einer Verbindung von Motiven vorstellen (Grant, Burkitt) oder aber diesen Grund als Formprinzip auffassen, etwa im Sinne einer gnostischen Selbsterfahrung, wobei diese psychologisch verstanden ist (Puech, Quispel). [26]

For example, from Haardt's perspective, Robert Grant combines sociological and psychological elements when he relates the collapse of Jewish apocalyptic hopes to the material conditions of Jerusalem in 70 A. D. as evidence for the origin of Gnosis [27]). Or, for example, Quispel employs psychological evidence by integrating the fragmentation of culture in late antiquity with man's change of psyche [28]). But despite the form of analysis, be it psychological or sociological, Dr. Haardt affirms in conclusion that "In allen diesen Fällen von psychologischer [oder von soziologischer] Reduktion ist das Grundanliegen die Synthese der Vielfalt motivlicher Gestaltungen der Zeugnisschicht" [29]).

The final classification of Haardt's investigation of the various methodological approaches to Gnosis is that taken from Philosophy. Dr. Haardt labels this approach the 'existential-ontological' and considers Hans Jonas to be its primary spokesman. According to Haardt, the 'existential-ontological' method is not to be viewed as contributing towards a causal analysis either in the sense of the 'History of Motifs' or the 'Reductive' methods; rather it is to be considered as a tool with which an understanding of the unique character of the state of Gnostic existence can be established. For example, whereas Bousset argues from 'History of Motifs' hypothesizing that Gnostic dualism arose from a fusion of Persian and Platonic dualism, Jonas' hypothesis would be that the Gnostic experience of self can only be interpreted by going beyond the material historical conception of Gnosis and as such, a causal analysis would be inapplicable [30]). According to Haardt, Jonas' primary concern is to uncover the parallel intrinsic ontological structures between two chronologically removed spiritual horizons,

---

26) Tröger, *Gnosis*, p. 192.
27) *Le Origini*, p. 168; Tröger, Gnosis, p. 192.
28) *Le Origini*, pp. 167-168; Tröger, *Gnosis*, pp. 193-194.
29) Tröger, *Gnosis*, p. 194.
30) *Le Origini*, p. 168; Tröger, *Gnosis*, pp. 194-195.

that of to-day and that of the Gnostic epoch [31]). From Haardt's viewpoint, that which contributes towards causing Gnosis in the two methods discussed above becomes for Jonas only interesting supplements arising from the Gnostic 'existential-ontological' foundation. Haardt sums up Jonas' position by stating, "Die existenzial-ontologische Analytik der Gnosis diente ihm nicht zur Kausalanalyse des Ursprungs von Gnosis" [32]), and Jonas' purpose as an attempt to explain the metamorphosis from 'mythological' to 'philosophical' Gnosis [33]).

After describing Jonas' 'existential-ontological' approach, Dr. Haardt considers several others within this category such as S. Arai, R. Bultmann, H. M. Schenke, W. Schmithals and C. Colpe [34]). For example, Haardt considers Bultmann within this category because he has described his own method as one which "will also nicht *historische Forschung* in dem Sinne sein, dass sie neues religionsgeschichtliches Material bringt.... Die Aufgabe ist vielmehr die der *Interpretation.* Gefragt wird nach dem Existenzverständnis...." [35]). But Robert Haardt also points out that Bultmann's findings are complementary to the method of 'History of Motifs' [36]). In fact, Haardt asserts that many of those listed above as primarily concerned with the 'existential-ontological' mode of procedure frequently combine complementary traits as a matter of course from either the 'History of Motifs' or the 'Reductive' methods [37]).

Dr. Haardt in his articles also criticizes each of the above methods for what he considers to be imperfections or limitations. According to Haardt the primary limitation of the 'History of Motifs' is that it tends towards a *regressus ad infinitum* [38]). The researcher continually looks for the 'first' cause, the 'magic' historical moment, the 'perfect' link. In addition, this process of retracing and backdating of motifs can lead to extrapolations from different and often chronologically

---

31) Tröger, *Gnosis,* p. 194.
32) *Le Origini,* p. 168; Tröger, *Gnosis,* p. 194.
33) Tröger, *Gnosis,* p. 195.
34) *Le Origini,* pp. 169-170; Tröger, *Gnosis,* pp. 195-198.
35) *Le Origini,* p. 169; Tröger, *Gnosis,* p. 196; R. Bultmann, *Das Urchristentum im Rahmen der antiken Religionen* (Zurich 1949) p. 8.
36) Tröger, *Gnosis,* p. 196.
37) *Le Origini,* pp. 170-172; Tröger, *Gnosis,* pp. 198-200.
38) *Le Origini,* p. 164; Tröger, Gnosis, p. 191.

mixed texts that at best can only hint at a doubtful source. The result is that it is extremely difficult to make any definitive predictions with regard to Gnostic origins [39]. The 'Reductive' approach is criticized by Haardt for being tautological. Rather than applying complementary data as evidence for the origin of Gnosis, from Haardt's perspective, the criteria employed are itself a synthesis of similar data but cloaked with psychological or sociological traits [40]. And given the fact that this method has only a reductive function within the method of 'History of Motifs' as previously described [41]), the criticisms for the 'History of Motifs' approach equally apply to this method. Finally, Dr. Haardt criticizes the 'existential-ontological' method for never explicity clarifying the structures and traits of the Gnostic's unique conception of existence [42]. Furthermore, according to Haardt, the 'existential-ontological' approach's claim that it can in no way be derived from the 'History of Motifs' is exaggerated given its simultaneous utilization of modes of analysis from the 'History of Motifs' [43]).

The discussion of methodology by Robert Haardt has revealed serious limitations in the methods through which Gnosis and Gnosticism are analysed. The 'History of Motifs' is the most dominant method and the method most often criticized. Because of this fact and because the 'History of Motifs' is the basis for all the methods discussed by Haardt we wish to propose that there is at present one central method of analysis in the study of Gnosis and Gnosticism, that is, the method of 'Motif Methodology'.

Motif Methodology

'Motif Methodology' can be defined as 'a scheme of classification based on dominant ideas, themes, or motifs which are rooted in the meaning of words in literary contexts, and attached by speculative thematic affiliations to cultural backgrounds'. In the study of Gnosis and Gnosticism this method is nearly exclusively employed within the following isolated contexts or combinations: '*Religionswissenschaft*', 'Religio-historical' or 'Phenomenological'. The analysis of these motifs is rooted not in notions of empirical historical human experience;

---

39) Tröger, *Gnosis*, p. 191.
40) Tröger, *Gnosis*, pp. 193-194.
41) See above p. 100 and n. 25.
42) Tröger, *Gnosis*, p. 199.
43) See above p. 102 and n. 37.

on the contrary, the 'motif methodologist' bases his analysis on abstractions of meanings taken from literary sources and their concomitant traditions, without addressing himself, for the most part, to the relationship between these non-empirical concepts and concepts of human action. The 'motif methodologist' can be distinguished by his philological, mythological or philosophical concerns, be they with or without religious overtones.

Dr. Haardt's analysis of the methodological approaches in the study of Gnosis primarily revolves around a single theme: the employment of the 'History of Motifs'. It is to this method that both his 'Reductive' and 'Philosophical' approaches are indebted for their existence. The lack of definition with regard to the particular nature of the three typological methods and the criteria with which we are to distinguish them as separate, unique methods in part contributes to our conclusion that they are essentially one and the same: that is, they all deal with the delineation and development of motifs. In addition, this lack of definition produces not only ambiguity and confusion in our appreciation of the different methods he discusses, but also prompts us to question the logical criteria on which his analysis is grounded.

Our divisions of *'Religionswissenschaft'*, 'Religio-historical' and 'Phenomenological' in 'Motif Methodology' are based on epistemological and methodological criteria. The basic criteria to differentiate these three divisions are metaphysical assumptions. Ideal *'Religionswissenschaft'* as defined by Dr. Pummer does not presuppose a religious faith, is an empirical science and as such is subject to the rules of the scientific method which begin with empirical documentation [44]).

---

44) *'Religionswissenschaft'* is a German term that can denote Science(s) of Religion(s), Comparative (Study of) Religion(s), History of Religions, Religion, Religious Studies and Religiology. Because of the lack of consensus among *'Religionswissenschaft'* researchers with regard to definition, aim and epistemological foundation of their discipline, and the fact that philologists, philosophers, phenomenologists and historians, as well as social scientists and theologians, at one time or another have considered themselves to be encompassed by the discipline of *'Religionswissenschaft'*, for purposes of clarification we shall distinguish those who argue theologically from *'Religionswissenschaft'* as well as those who argue phenomenologically rather than historically. Our primary criteria for this differentiation are epistemological. Nevertheless, it will become apparent in the subsequent discussion that these epistemological distinctions can not be made mutually exclusive as authors do combine complementary epistemological assumptions; rather than attempt such a comprehensive fabrication we have chosen as indicators for differentiation the fundamental metaphysical assumptions of

The 'Religio-historical' method, on the other hand, because of its theological assumptions differs from *'Religionswissenschaft'* [45]). The 'Religio-historical' method is dependent on certain metaphysical as-

these researchers. For the purpose of my argument I have accepted Reinhard Pummer's definition. *'Religionswissenschaft'* is identical to the History of Religions and can be conceived as an "umbrella term for a discipline whose two intrinsic branches are: the History of Religions, in the narrow sense, that is the historical development of specific religions by the method of a horizontal cross-section or *'längsschnittmässig'*, and in the broad sense, the systematic or thematic study of religious phenomena tending towards a vertical cross-section or *'Querschnitt'* " (R. Pummer, *"Religionswissenschaft* or Religiology" in *Numen*, Vol. 19, (1972) pp. 91-128, and especially pp. 102-109). Dr. Pummer's subsequent elaboration of the sub-disciplines of ideal *'Religionswissenschaft'* — Phenomenology of Religion, Geography of Religion, Psychology of Religion, Sociology of Religion, Ethnology and Anthropology (p. 109f.) makes us question the viability of such a comprehensive discipline. Dr. Pummer describes these auxiliary disciplines as follows: "no matter under which category of sciences these various auxiliary disciplines of *'Religionswissenschaft'* are subsumed, one thing is generally agreed upon, the empirical character of the study undertaken by them" (p. 110). But, in addition, we would add that although all these sub-disciplines appeal to scientific empiricism neither are the individual methods identical nor are the historically conditioned traditions always complementary. Pummer, on the other hand, is aware that ideal *'Religionswissenschaft'* as an autonomous discipline may not exist given the fact that, at present, *'Religionswissenschaft'* has "no common vocabulary, *Problematik*, and methodology" (pp. 108-109). It is rather an eclectic interpretation of all fields of study — philosophical, scientific or non-scientific — with reference to religion. His article, therefore, can be viewed as a 'call' on his behalf for the empirical scientific discipline of ideal *'Religionswissenschaft'*. My present task in this section is not to argue for or against the viability of such an 'open' definition of ideal *'Religionswissenschaft'* or the likelihood of such an empirical autonomous discipline; rather it is only to demonstrate how scholars of Gnosticism, among many of whom identify themselves as 'historians of religions', employ the discipline of *'Religionswissenschaft'* as defined by Pummer. (See below, n. 56). It is our intention to draw attention to their historical and philological concerns which are primarily dependent on their application of motifs and by so doing bring to light the shortcomings of *'Religionswissenschaft's'* metaphysic of positivism as described by Pummer, and simultaneously substantiate our earlier claims that a Sociology of Religion *Weltanschauung* has not been exercised.

45) Although I have defined this method as 'Religio-historical' I am not concerned with New Testament scholarship that is identified by this denotation. Nor am I concerned with the *Religionsgeschichtliche Schule* in this context. The *Religionsgeschichtliche Schule* is encompassed by *'Religionswissenschaft'* unless the findings have been applied as evidence for theological positions. If this has occurred these findings would be classified under the 'Religio-historical' approach according to our criteria of epistemological differentation as explained above (n. 44). For an example of an application of evidence for theological positions see Marcel Simon, "The *Religionsgeschichtliche Schule*, Fifty Years Later" in *Religious Studies*, Vol. 11, (1975) pp. 135-144.

sumptions and beliefs that are radically different from those of *'Religionswissenschaft'* as defined above. The results of this method, therefore, are of a different nature than the results of an investigation which does not presuppose such a religious faith. Frequently those who utilize this method are inclined towards implicit theological claims. This is not to deny that these studies contain a great deal of valuable insights which can be empirically documented; it is rather that they make use of certain concepts which are empirically unverifiable and filled with with unarguable *a priori* assumptions which have purposely been left tacit [46]). And finally our third division, the 'Phenomenological', although considered by some to be analogous to the systematic branch of *'Religionswissenschaft'* [47]), cannot be included if *'Religionswissenschaft'* is within the hermeneutic tradition [48]). 'Phenomenology' is considered to be a neutral description of phenomena as they are self-manifested with the aid of the epoché (i.e. suspension of judgment) as opposed to a pre-structured manifestation of phenomena as determined by various interpretative schemes [49]). According to C. J. Bleeker the 'Phenomenological' method "uncovers the hidden structure [of phenomena] by showing that they [i.e. the phenomena] are built up according to strict inner laws" [50]). Elsewhere he describes it as "assisting the student by giving him insight into the essence and the structure of religious phenomena" [51]). It is also described as "the

---

46) Many who employ a 'Religio-historical' approach have very close affinities with *'Religionswissenschaft'*. It could be said that they are related and interdependent. The crucial criteria for differentiation are that of empirical indicators and scientific assumptions, (R. Pummer, *op. cit.*, pp. 99-102). "Theology is therefore never a 'pure' science" (R. Zwi Werblowsky, "Marburg — and After?" in *Numen*, Vol. 7, (1960) p. 220).

47) For example, see K. Rudolph, "Die Problematik der Religionswissenschaft als akademisches Lehrfach" in *Kairos*, Vol. 9, (1967) p. 30.

48) This should pose serious problems for Kurt Rudolph who advocates incorporating philosophical and historical hermeneutics into *'Religionswissenschaft'*. It is paradoxical for him to advocate an hermeneutic whose primary concern is 'interpretation' and on the other hand, conduct phenomenological studies which affirm a suspension of judgment and practise both phenomenological and eidetic reduction. See *Ibid.* pp. 22-42 and "Zur Problematik der Religionswissenschaft" in *Kairos*, Vol. 10, (1968) p. 290f.

49) A. Frazier, "Models for a Methodology of Religious Meaning" in *Bucknell Review*, Vol. 18, (1970) p. 24. See also R. Pummer, *op. cit.* and C. J. Bleeker, *The Sacred Bridge*, Supplement to *Numen*, Vol. 7, (1963).

50) C. J. Bleeker, *Ibid.* pp. 14 and 17.

51) C. J. Bleeker, "The Contribution of the Phenomenology of Religion" in

search for basic motifs or ideas" [52]) or the "hinting intuitively at 'meaning' " [53]). The 'Phenomenological' method, therefore, can be conceived as a non-interpretative intuitionism of essences that has close affinities to a transcendental philosophy [54]). In conclusion, our three divisions of 'Motif Methodology' can be summarized as follows: Ideal *'Religionswissenschaft'* appeals to scientific empiricism, 'Religio-historical' to faith and 'Phenomenological' to empathy (i.e. *verstehen*). Or put differently, ideal *'Religionswissenschaft'* appeals to the metaphysics of positivism, 'Religio-historical' to the metaphysics of theology and 'Phenomenological' to the metaphysics of idealistic philosophy.

Dr. Haardt's typological categories are neither individually unique nor epistemologically distinct. In addition, he does not consider his own methodic operation and interpretation which is dependent not only on intellectual and religious climates and his own professional training, but also on the hermeneutic situation itself as the source of assumptions for his methodological conventions. In contrast to Robert Haardt's descriptive analysis of the methodological approaches to the study of Gnosis and Gnosticism the following sections will proceed to provide evidence of the employment of 'Motif Methodology' within the three contexts outlined above.

(a) *'Religionswissenschaft'*

'Religionswissenschaft' is identical to the History of Religions and can be conceived as an eclectic integration of all disciplines that study religion [55]). One only need examine the content of the papers delivered

---

Problems and Methods of the History of Religions, Supplement to *Numen,* Vol. 19, (1972) p. 44.

52) J. Waardenburg, "Religion between Reality and Idea" in *Numen,* Vol. 19, (1972) p. 200.

53) U. Bianchi, "The Definition of Religion. On the Methodology of Historical-Comparative Research" in *Problems and Methods of the History of Religions, op. cit.,* p. 29.

54) It would seem that those who employ this method stand in a much closer relationship to Husserl than they are willing to admit. For example, see C. J. Bleeker, "The Relation of the History of Religions to Kindred Religious Sciences" in *Numen,* Vol. I, (1954) pp. 147-150. In our context 'Phenomenology' is frequently employed in conjunction with themes from Heideggerian philosophy and described as 'existential-phenomenology'. For a notable application see Hans Jonas, *The Gnostic Religion,* revised second edition, (Boston 1963). See below pp. 118-129.

55) See above n. 44.

at the Messina Colloquium to endorse the prevalence of this approach [56]). But it will become apparent from the subsequent discussion of this method that the application of 'Religionswissenschaft' is not identical to our definition of ideal 'Religionswissenschaft'. The discord, in part, can be explained by the chaotic state of the discipline and the fact that 'motif methodologists', regardless of their respective approach, support their conclusions with motifs rooted in the meaning of words in literary contexts [57]). Our analysis is not to discredit the value of 'Religionswissenschaft' but rather only to bring to light the way in which Gnostic scholars make use of this approach.

One approach of 'Religionswissenschaft' can be represented by the *Religionsgeschichtliche Schule* or History of Religions School [58]). The *Religionsgeschichichtliche* formulation of myth is essentially a literary category. It applies a particular narrative which when bound together with an historical hypothesis is understood to be at the root of the phenomena. Wilhelm Bousset's *Hauptprobleme der Gnosis* [59]) and Richard Reitzenstein's *Poimandres* and *Die Hellenistischen Mysterienreligionen* [60]) were among the earliest to utilize 'Motif

56) In fact the Colloquim was planned by the International Association for the History of Religions and was described by its primary organizer, U. Bianchi, as follows: "En effect, le Colloque de Messine a été un Colloque d'historiens des religions...." („Le Problème des Origines du Gnosticisme" in *Le Origini*, p. 1).

57) Reinhard Pummer describes the problem as follows:

... while there is virtually general agreement as to what constitutes sound scientific study of religious traditions, the area of theories and category formation in the science of religion is far from being sufficiently developed. From the questions around a definition of religion... to that of validity... and the problem of understanding and explanation in the science of religion, there is much that needs continuous rethinking.

See his "Recent Publications on the Methodology of the Science of Religion" in *Numen*, Vol. 22, (1975) pp. 162-163. Elsewhere in the same article he quotes N. Smart's comment that "for various reasons, the science of religion has heavily concentrated on literary studies" (p. 176). Also see above n. 44.

58) As mentioned previously it is important to note that Marcel Simon has recognized that the *Religionsgeschichtliche Schule* and its findings have been applied as evidence for one or more theological positions. See above n. 45 and his "Histoire des Religions, Histoire du Christianisme, Histoire de l'Église: Réflexions méthodologiques" in *Liber Amicorum: Studies in Honour of Professor C. Bleeker*, Supplement to *Numen*, Vol. 17, (1969) p. 195.

59) Wilhelm Bousset, *Hauptprobleme der Gnosis*, (Göttingen 1907).

60) Richard Reitzenstein, *Poimandres*, (Leipzig 1904) and *Die Hellenistischen Mysterienreligionen*, 3rd edition, (Leipzig 1927).

Methodology'. Both scholars employed primarily philological methods in their analysis to arrive at their conclusion that Gnosis was derived from Oriental dualistic influences and pre-Christian. For example, Reitzenstein followed the classical tradition which advanced the hypothesis that Zoroaster influenced Greek thought, emphasizing the Gnostic Redeemer motif in which the *Anthropos* or Primal Man functions as a Redeemer. And by 1921 in his *Das Iranische Erlösungsmysterium* [61]), Reitzenstein had developed the variant forms which this Primal Man myth had presupposed and the connections which bound the later Hellenic forms of the myth together with the original Iranian source [62]). G. Widengren to-day is the chief exponent of this theory of an Iranian genesis and his Messina paper can be viewed as a direct attempt to validitate Reitzenstein's perspective from a History of Religions mode of analysis. Widengren concludes his paper by asserting that "les problèmes auxquels l'École de l'Histoire des Religions a travaillé se sont montrés d'une richesse qui n'est pas épuisé". [63]) Unfortunately, the question of chronology frequently arises with the History of Religions School as they utilize late literary sources, especially Mandean, as evidence for Proto-Gnosticism [64]).

Th. P. van Baaren, on the other hand, differentiates between 'Gnosis' as "a certain conception of knowledge" and 'Gnosticism' as "a historic form of religion" and emphasizes the latter in any analysis. He describes his method as the following: "the method of addition and subtraction does not work in the History of Religions.... the only way

---

61) R. Reitzenstein, *Das Iranische Erlösungsterium*, (Bonn 1921).

62) See below pp. 29-30 for a brief outline of some of the arguments for and against the much debated Redeemer motif.

63) G. Widengren, "Les Origines du Gnosticisme et l'Histoire des Religions" in *Le Origini*, p. 60.

64) See E. Yamauchi, *Pre-Christian Gnosticism*, (London 1973), Chapter 8, pp. 117-142 for the leading arguments that the Mandaeans had their origin in pre-Christian Palestine, especially those of K. Rudolph, *Die Mandäer I: Das Mandäerproblem*, (Göttingen 1960) and "Problems of a History of the Development of the Mandaean Religion" in *History of Religions*, Vol. 8, (1969) pp. 210-235 and R. Macuch, "Der gegenwärtige Stand der Mandäerforschung und ihre Aufgaben" in *Orientalistische Literaturzeitung*, Vol. 63, (1968) pp. 5-14 and "Anfänge der Mandäer" in *Die Araber in der Alten Welt II*, (eds.) F. Altheim and R. Stiehl, (Berlin 1965) pp. 76-190. In contrast to those who argue for their origin being pre-Christian see E. Yamauchi, *Gnostic Ethics and Mandaean Origins*, (London 1970). Also see K. Rudolph's review of Yamauchi's thesis in *Theologische Literaturzeitung*, Vol. 97, (1972) pp. 733-737.

[to consider] Gnosticism [is] as a historic complex belonging to a certain age and a certain place and forming a certain part of a certain culture" 65). In other words, van Baaren chooses the 'horizontal' method of History of Religions and de-emphasizes the role of dominant motifs in exchange for a positivistic metaphysic whose statements can be verified scientifically through the examination of Gnostic behavioural patterns. Unfortunately van Baaren has not implemented his own suggestions.

Another approach of 'motif methodologists' within the context of *'Religionswissenschaft'* is that forwarded by R. M. Grant and G. Quispel 66). As explained previously, Dr. Haardt has designated these studies as psychological and/or sociological 67). Although we observe psychological or sociological elements, there is no evidence of a psychological or a sociological *Weltanschauung*, either theoretical or methodological, to support Haardt's contention. Quispel, for example, claims a debt to Jungian analysis and proceeds to search for thematic religious motifs in Gnosis which to Quispel are archetypal manifestations of the 'spiritual' structure in mankind 68). The conclusion of this exploration is the definition of Gnosis as being "the mythical projection of practical experience" 69). But Quispel does not differentiate 'natural' from 'cultural' symbols and his reliance on the 'unconscious' to explain empirical phenomena brings more new questions to bear on his argument than those he has already answered. Jung's vocation was dedicated to elucidating the psychological structures of the 'unconscious'. Quispel's analysis, on the other hand, although a direct application of Jung's psychological structures to Gnosis, lacks the necessary scientific refinements from psychology to be considered positivistic. At best, Quispel's insights into the nature of the Gnostic experience must stand as only conjectural conclusions, suppositions, unsupported by empirical evidence 70).

---

65) Th. P. van Baaren, *op. cit.*, p. 174.
66) See above n. 14.
67) See above, pp. 100-101.
68) H. E. W. Turner in *The Pattern of Christian Truth,* (London 1954) has similarly observed Quispel's application of Jungian psychology to the problems of Gnosticism (pp. 114-117).
69) G. Quispel, *op. cit.,* p. 17.
70) In general, Quispel provides a great deal of historical evidence that Gnosticism is of Jewish origin; however it is his analysis of Gnosis as man's unconscious spirit which is related to the ground of "Being" that we are question-

In contrast to Quispel, Grant's analysis is more social-psychological than psychological. His thesis is that the roots of Gnosticism originated in the "debris of apocalyptic-eschatological hopes which resulted from the falls of Jerusalem" [71]). But as with Quispel there is neither a social-scientific framework nor historical evidence. Grant's closest application of social-psychological criteria occurs when he compares the Plains Indians of nineteenth century United States to the Gnostics of the second century A. D. His conclusion from this comparison is that "when their [Jewish] warfare failed, the traditional culture became inadequate . . . . [resulting in the concomitant consequences of] social maladjustment . . ., questioning of custom, social unrest, increased non-conformity, breakdown of social control and personality maladjustment" [72]). Unfortunately his following analysis considers motifs rather than empirical social evidence which will verify his conclusion.

The role of 'Motif Methodology' in Grant's works is much more observable in his Messina paper entitled, "Les êtres intermédiaires dans le judaisme tardif" [73]). Here Grant focussed on the possibility of Jewish-apocalyptic elements being transformed into anti-cosmic dualist Gnostic motifs within heterodox Judaism. His examination included the role of angels, demons and other such intermediaries between late Judaism and Gnosticism. But as in the cases described above, his analysis considers motifs rather than employing these ideas as indicators of social consciousness or behaviour.

The last spokesman of '*Religionswissenschaft*' we shall examine is Petr Pokorný. In a recent article, "Der soziale Hintergrund der Gnosis", Pokorný argues for a non-Christian origin of Gnosis in the Hellenized Jewish Diaspora [74]). Like W. Schmithals [75]) Pokorný takes the position that Paul's opponents at Corinth were Gnostics and

---

ing. Phenomenologically or with the aid of Jungian archetypes this is possible; but empirically verifiable it is not. Nevertheless, Quispel's application of motifs in conjunction with historical evidence is most illuminating. For recent examples, see "The Origins of the Gnosis Demiurge" (1970) and "The Birth of the Child. Some Gnostic and Jewish Aspects" (1973) republished in G. Quispel, *Gnostic Studies,* Vol. I, (Leiden 1974).

71) R. M. Grant, *op. cit.,* p. viii.

72) *Ibid.,* pp. 34-35.

73) R. M. Grant, "Les êtres intermédiaires dans le judaisme tardif" in *Le Origini,* pp. 141-161.

74) Petr. Pokorný, *op. cit.*

75) W. Schmithals, *Gnosticism in Corinth,* translated by J. E. Steely, (New York 1971).

suggests that the *Corpus Hermeticum* is reliable as evidence. He then attributes the origin of Gnosis to heterodox Jews who were opposed both to orthodox Judaism and to the Greek polis. Finally he combines all these divergent assumptions in an attempt to associate the libertine and mystical sects of Sabazios and Hypsistos to the libertine and mystical traits of Gnosis [76]). Like Quispel and Grant, Pokorný bases his thesis on the ideological characteristics of Gnosis rather than behavioural concepts. His analysis of trade, class and culture is superficial and his assessment of the Jewish population in Alexandria is highly conjectural to say the least [77]). Furthermore, his reconstruction of the Gnostic mystery meal can be considered as no more than the product of his fertile imagination [78]). Pokorný, we would argue, is more concerned with hypothesizing what might have been than with what did in fact occur.

We would suggest that since Quispel, Grant and Pokorný are not professionally trained pyschologists or sociologists, we abstain from designating these studies as Psychological or Sociological, given the fact they do not apply normative positivistic methods or 'accepted' theories from either Sociology or Psychology, but only consider socio-cultural indicators as secondary to their 'Motif Methodology' [79]).

It is obvious from the above discussion of our representative examples that the application of the History of Religions is not identical to our definition of ideal *'Religionswissenschaft'*. We observed that the primary concern of these studies emphasized motifs in literary contexts rather than social relationships or social structures. In other words, we understand these studies to be philological and historical, not positivistic and humanistic. Our analysis attempted only to discuss the way in which Gnostic scholars make use of this approach. Nevertheless, it strongly confirms Dr. R. Pummer's 'call' that *'Religionswissenschaft'* become an empirical scientific discipline [80]).

---

76) Petr Pokorný, *op. cit.*, pp. 80-81.

77) *Ibid.*, p. 86.

78) *Ibid.*, pp. 84-85.

79) Dr. Pummer also maintains that theological statements or philosophical statements that make use of psychological or sociological terminology cannot be called Psychology of Religion or Sociology of Religion *'Religionswissenschaft'* or Religiology, *op. cit.* (p. 110). With reference to Quispel we are more tolerant, given the fact that Jungian analysis even if 'mystical' is also considered acceptable in some circles of Psychology.

80) See above n. 44.

(b) *'Religio-historical'*

As explained previously, many of the scholars who study Gnosis and Gnosticism have implicit theological assumptions although they employ similar methods to those of *'Religionswissenschaft'* [81]). For example, R. P. Casey in an article entitled, "Gnosis, Gnosticism and the New Testament" argues that Gnosticism is a second century Christian heresy by evoking the 'true' message of the New Testament [82]). In this section we shall examine three proponents of this approach, Cardinal Jean Daniélou, Professor R. McL. Wilson and Professor R. Bultmann and elucidate their methodology.

Cardinal Daniélou's thesis is that Gnosis had its *Sitz im Leben* in a Christian setting inspired by Jewish-Christian apocalyptic motifs. In order to understand this conclusion, Daniélou's position must be viewed in the light of his most important work, *The Theology of Jewish Christianity* [83]). In this study Daniélou postulates that historically there existed a particular Jewish-Christian thought system expressed in the motifs of late Judaism which became the sub-structure of early Christianity. His thesis on Gnosis, therefore, is a sub-theme of his *magnum opus*. Daniélou's conclusion rests on doctrinal criteria, the examination of the New Testament, Patristic, Apocryphal and Gnostic literary genres which exhibit Jewish-Christian content.

In opposition to Daniélou's thesis, R. A. Kraft has commented, "Daniélou's theology of Jewish-Christianity seems to be an idealistic abstraction . . . without special regard for the question of whether any actual person or group of persons ever consciously adhered to such a 'theology' " [84]). And A. F. J. Klijn, while crediting Daniélou for his documentation and analysis of early Jewish influence on nascent Christianity, emphatically states, "that it is impossible to define the term Jewish-Christian because it proved to be a name that can readily be replaced by 'Christian' " [85]). Furthermore, Daniélou's acceptance at

---

81) See above n. 46.

82) R. P. Casey, "Gnosis, Gnosticism and the New Testament" in *The Background of the New Testament and its Eschatology*, (eds.) W. D. Davies and D. Daube, (Cambridge 1956) pp. 52-81.

83) J. Daniélou, *The Theology of Jewish-Christianity*, translated by J. H. Baker, Vol. I, (London 1964).

84) R. A. Kraft, "In Search of 'Jewish-Christianity' and its Theology" in *Judéo-Christianisme*, (Paris 1972) p. 86.

85) A. F. J. Klijn, "The Study of Jewish-Christianity" in *New Testament Studies*, Vol. 20, (1974) p. 426.

8

face value or apologetically of Patristic literature with regard to the Gnostics and his implicit theological status provide us with evidence of his metaphysics of theology [86]).

Professor R. McL. Wilson's book, *Gnosis and the New Testament* can be appreciated as an unparalleled example of the application of 'Motif Methodology' [87]). Within the first several pages he immediately begins to discuss several key problems in the study of Gnosis and Gnosticism and writes, "Gnosticism is fundamentally syncretistic.... It would be more accurate to recognize the various 'spheres of influence' mentioned as the *ultimate* sources of particular ideas, and proceed to the attempt to trace the channels by which they passed into the developed Gnostic systems" [88]). Elsewhere he states his procedure as thinking " ... in terms of growth and development... [of] the combination of ideas, the way in which they are blended together, the associations which they come to have..." [89]) Wilson's compact, lucid monograph provides the reader with numerous examples of some of the motifs which have been claimed as Gnostic in the New Testament, and on the other hand, Gnostic use of New Testament motifs. For example, when discussing the classic motif of the pearl he cites *The Gospel of Philip*, "Logion 48", Irenaeus' account of the system of Ptolemy and Plotinus [90]). He then comments on this motif's affinity to *"Logion 29"* of *The Gospel of Thomas* and 2 Corinthians 4:7 and asks:

> ...are all these to be grouped together and classified as 'Gnostic'? Or should we not rather recognize the occurrence of a common motif, which may or may not have passed from one tradition to another, and proceed to examine the use that is made of it in different contexts [91]).

R. McL. Wilson's premise is that one must begin one's investigation with the historical movement of 'classical' Gnosticism of the second century A. D. and, avoid the reading back into first century terminology

---

86) For example, in his discussion of the relevance of the message of Jewish-Christianity for to-day (*op. cit.*, p. 408) or in his definition of Gnosis as "The saving knowledge of what the divine action proclaimed in the Gospel message..." (p. 405).
87) R. McL. Wilson, *Gnosis and the New Testament*, (Oxford 1968).
88) *Ibid.*, p. 6.
89) *Ibid.*, p. 10.
90) *Ibid.*, pp. 19-20.
91) *Ibid.*, p. 20.

...associations and connotations which that terminology does have in the second century A.D., and at the same time to recognize, already in the first century, the points of growth for second century theories [92]).

His corpus of studies affirms the validity of this position.

Similar to Daniélou, affirmations of faith are influential in his analysis. For example, in his conclusion to his chapter on Gnostic use of the New Testament he describes the difference between the Church's legitimation and that of the Gnostics as one of control—

> such a writer as Irenaeus is governed by the Church's Rule of Faith, whereas the Gnostics endeavour to mould the Scriptures to their own theories... There is all the difference in the world between an interpretation that is brought to the text from without and one which emerges from the text itself [93]).

Surely the Gnostics had their own controlling structures within their various schools. And what is the correct interpretation given the historical evidence that conceptual similarities between various early Christian writings and movements are tainted by later theological judgments regarding Orthodoxy, heterodoxy and heresy? In addition, an orthodox Jew can similarly inquire about "interpretations from within or without" [94]). Although Professor Wilson's application of 'Motif Methodology' has very close affinities with the method of *'Religionswissenschaft'* his results are of a different nature than those who employ the History of Religions method.

The third and last theologian we shall examine is Rudolph Bultmann. Unlike Daniélou who postulates motifs within a Jewish-Christian context or Wilson who emphasizes the social movements of Gnosticism and their particular application of Gnostic and New Testament motifs, we consider Bultmann's studies as an attempt to validate the German view of Gnosis. This position assumes that Gnosis is essentially a non-Christian movement which manifested itself in numerous geographical locations and which both preceeded and influenced Christianity. Bultmann, for example, in his book, *The Theology of the New Testament*, adopts this view and devotes an entire section to an analy-

---

92) *Ibid.*, p. 23.

93) *Ibid.*, p. 84.

94) Elsewhere R. McL. Wilson comments that although "the Gnostics often adhere to the literal words of Scripture.... the Gnostic theories [are] not the plain meaning of the Biblical text" (*Ibid.*, p. 76). Again a Jew can well ask, 'are the Christian theories the plain meaning of the Old Testament texts'?

sis of Gnostic motifs, attempting to provide evidence of Gnostic
influence on the early Church and of Gnostic motifs in the New
Testament [95]).

As we have already seen to be the case with our discussion of
Daniélou, Bultmann's analysis of Gnosis can only be understood within
the context of his faith and methodology, but unlike the former's
historical context, Bultmann's is philosophical. Bultmann perceives his
task as that of producing an existentialist interpretation of the New
Testament, of demythologizing it, and of providing an hermeneutic
that is grounded within an universal human anthropology [96]). Because
demythologizing employs the existential meaning of myth and not the
Religionsgeschichtliche formulation it is necessary that first we clarify
his debt to the *Religionsgeschichtliche Schule*. According to R. Johnson,
"through Reitzenstein, Bultmann had learned to understand myth as
a soteriological narrative; that is, the story of Primal Man or Heavenly
Redeemer as this originated in the dualistic religion of Iran and was
then appropriated by a variety of Hellenistic religions ... including
Christianity" [97]). Thus Bultmann could argue that the myth of the
Redeemer was pre-Christian and simultaneously denoted the form
through which the faith of the early Christian movement first came to
expression [98]). He therefore can write, "of all the mythological influences on the New Testament, the strongest is the oriental-gnostic
salvation myth which, so far as we can see, goes back to the Iranian
myth of the Primal Man" [99]). But with the adoption of Heidegger's
anthropological categories Bultmann began to move toward an existentialist interpretation of Hellenistic myths as an expression of existence
and away from the *Religionsgeschichtliche* narrative. Heidegger's

---

95) Rudolph Bultmann, *The Theology of the New Testament,* translated by
K. Grobel, Vol. I, (London 1952) pp. 164-183. The primary motifs he discusses
are those of *pneuma,* eschatology, the cosmic drama, Primal Man and redemption.

96) This interpretation of Bultmann's task is from 1941 onwards. For a
detailed discussion of the various stages of Bultmann's fundamental philosophical-
theological position and his historical situation see Roger A. Johnson, *The Origins
of Demythologizing,* Supplement to *Numen,* Vol. 28, (1974).

97 *Ibid.,* p. 89.

98) For Bultmann's analysis see "Urchristliche Religion (1915-1925)" in *Archiv
für Religionswissenschaft,* Vol. 24 (1926) pp. 83-164, and especially pp. 100-102.

99) As quoted in R. Johnson, *op. cit.,* p. 102. For Bultmann's original see
"Mythus und Mythologie im Neuen Testament" in *Die Religion in Geschichte
und Gegenwart,* 2nd edition, (Tübingen 1930) col. 393.

existential analysis of the ontological structures of "Being" allowed Bultmann the opportunity to address himself to the question of the unique anthropological character of the Christian understanding of human existence. And, soon after, Jonas' idealistic schema of history in conjunction with Heidegger's *Daseinanalytik* provided the historical application of the existentialist hermeneutic with regard to Gnosticism and the ordering of the data of the Hellenistic world. This indebtedness to Jonas can be no more clearly observed than in the preface to Jonas' *Gnosis und spätantiker Geist*, Volume I, where Bultmann writes, "the method of the author, that of apprehending the authentic meaning of an historical phenomenon through the principle of existential analysis, appears to me to have proven its fruitfulness here" [100]). And this statement is immediately followed by Bultmann's theological concern that "this work will fructify the *geistesgeschichtliche* research .... in the sphere of New Testament interpretation" [101]).

On the other hand, Bultmann never abandons Reitzenstein's reconstructed Iranian prototype myth in his analysis of the origins of New Testament mythological motifs. On the contrary, Bultmann implicitly presupposes the substance of the *Religionsgeschichtliche* view of myth and acknowledges the Primal Man of Iran as the pre-Christian Gnostic myth of the Heavenly Redeemer [102]). The emphasis has transferred from Reitzenstein's reconstructed Iranian prototype to Jonas' *Geist* of Gnosticism. The unique character of the Christian understanding of existence has come to mean faith as the authentic resolution to the human condition.

According to Johnson, Bultmann's interpretation of the Hellenistic age necessitates the decisive role of Gnosticism in establishing the fundamental structure of New Testament self-understanding in the history of *Dasein's* self-understanding. Although Gnosticism shares an ontological continuity with the ontic Christianity differentiation be-

---

100) As quoted in R. Johnson, *op. cit.*, p. 116. For Bultmann's original see "Vorwort" in *Gnosis und spätantiker Geist* by Hans Jonas, 2nd edition, Vol. I, (Göttingen 1954) p. vii.

101) *Ibid.* This hope is later manifested by Bultmann himself. See *Kerygma Myth*, edited and translated by R. H. Fuller, 2 Volumes, (London 1957-1962). He specifically states his task as follows: "to produce an existential interpretation of the dualistic mythology of the New Testament along similar lines to that of Hans Jonas' existentialist interpretation of Gnosticism". p. 16.

102) R. Johnson, *op. cit.*, p. 125.

tween them radically separates them. Gnosticism neither apprehended the dialectical nature of this new relationship of *Dasein* to its world nor realized in faith the eschatological existence. The results of these misinterpretations were speculative knowledge or mystical experience. Christianity, on the other hand, actualized in Christian faith the new understanding of self and world, grounded in the believer's "being known by God" 103). Demythologizing as understood by Johnson has come to mean "a systematic extension... of the doctrine of justification of faith.... and justification of faith means literally a new form of self-understanding" 104). From the above discussion it is obvious that Bultmann both has employed motifs and has argued from a metaphysic of theology.

(c) *'Phenomenological'*

The 'Phenomenological' method in our context attempts to identify and associate religious movements together on the basis of their common elements in the hope that structural universal laws can be postulated. This approach is inclined towards an existential analysis or has certain similarities to that of the systematic branch of *'Religionswissenschaft'* 105). There are numerous Gnostic scholars who adopt this position including Hans Jonas, U. Bianchi, C. J. Bleeker and K. Rudolph. In this final section we shall describe Jonas' contribution as representative because of the influence that has been generated by his 'existential-phenomenological' analysis.

As previously alluded to Jonas was extremely important in the development of Bultmann's existential hermeneutic. He was a student of Bultmann and Heidegger at Marburg and came to know the world of Hellenistic religions and myths through the former and the nature of *Dasein* through the latter. As early as 1930 Jonas had begun to analyse the relation of the objectivation of myth to the existentialist root of myth in Gnosis 106) and by 1934 had published the first volume

---

103) *Ibid.*, pp. 242-243.
104) *Ibid.*, pp. 197 and 201.
105) For not including 'Phenomenology' within 'Religionswissenschaft' see above, pp. 103-106, especially n. 44 and n. 48 and our contention that the metaphysics of *'Religionswissenschaft'* are materialistic and are objectively orientated whereas those of 'Phenomenology' are idealistic and subjectively orientated.
106) H. Jonas, "Einleitung: Zum Problem der Objektivation und ihres Formwandels" in *Gnosis und spätantiker Geist, op. cit.* Vol. 2, p. 1-23. Originally this was published as *Der Begriff der Gnosis*, (Göttingen 1930).

of his revolutionary epic on Gnosticism [107]). Philosophically Jonas' aim was to relate Heideggerian existentialism in conjunction with the historical idealism of Hegel to Gnosticism in order to explain the objectivation of *Geist*. Existentially, his aim was "to understand the spirit speaking through these [philosophical] voices and in its light to restore an intelligible unity to the baffling multiplicity of its [i.e. Gnostic] expressions" [108]). Jonas' concern therefore was not the 'origins' of Gnosis in the sense of a genealogical line of descent; rather it was with the 'essence' of Gnosis [109]). His method also involved the delineation of motifs, not in an historical context, but supported by a comparative-phenomenological foundation [110]).

Accepting Hegel's interpretation of history as the history of *Geist* expressed dialectically, Jonas proposed that the Hellenistic period was crucial in the dialectical development of *Geist*. According to Jonas, although Hellenistic literature dramatizes the fundamental new self-understanding of *Geist* in history this new self-understanding appears in a form antithetical with its own intention. It is only due to the fact that Jonas presupposes a continuity between the original existential phenomena and his own existence because of their mutual participation in a common history of *Geist* that we are able to interpret this new self-understanding of *Dasein*. Furthermore, not only does Jonas perceive a relationship of existential continuity, mediated through a common history of *Geist*, he also assumes that we are better able to interpret what the author of Hellenistic texts meant than the author himself could because we are situated in a more fully developed moment of *Geist*. Thus it is not the texts themselves or the data of history that are important to Jonas — "now this we understand not as some kind of empirical subject . . . .", rather it is "a transcendent constitutive which, however, is rooted in a factual historical apprehension of *Dasein*" [111]). The texts of the Hellenistic age initiate a new epoch

---

107) H. Jonas, *Gnosis und spätantiker Geist, op. cit.*, Vol. I.

108) H. Jonas, *The Gnostic Religion, op. cit.* p. xvii.

109) Colpe proposes the concepts of 'origins' and 'essence' as descriptive of the distinction between the '*Religionsgeschichtliche*' approach to Gnosticism and that of Jonas' existential. See C. Colpe, *Die Religionsgeschichtliche Schule: Darstellung und Kritik ihres Bildes von gnostischen Erlösermythus*, (Göttingen 1961) p. 201.

110) Hans Jonas, "Delimitation of the Gnostic Phenomenon — typological and historical" in *Le Origini*, pp. 92-109.

111) As quoted in R. Johnson, *op. cit.*, pp. 227-228. For Jonas' original see *Gnosis und spätantiker Geist, op. cit.*, Vol. I, pp. 12-13.

of *Dasein* which stand in contrast to the previous Hellenic and Hebrew forms of self-understanding 112).

Although Jonas' method provides valuable insights into Gnostic forms of existence we question his imposition of twentieth century conceptual formulations on thought patterns of two thousand years ago. Does twentieth century nihilism have the same meaning to Gnosticism as twentieth century nihilism to twentieth century Existentialism? Is Jonas' hypothesis that "the 'existentialist' reading of Gnosticism . . . invites as its natural complement the trial of a 'gnostic' reading of Existentialism" possible? 113). Can 'anthropological acosmism arise' 114) from any cosmic nihilism because of man's alienation from nature? Does every cosmic nihilism beget the characteristics through which Existentialism might evolve? Does his use of historical idealism with reference to the history of *Geist* really give us a superiority over the original author in interpreting the text? And finally, can anyone intuit these 'essences' through the application of his 'existential-phenomenological' method because we also mutually participate in a common history of *Geist*?

Although we are sympathetic to Jonas' contention that man's perception of his ontological foundation was radically transformed two thousand years ago, the question that must be posed is, 'can semantic structures be found for historical events that evolve within different locations, at different times and in different ways'? It is worthwhile before passing judgment to keep in mind R. McL. Wilson's comment that

> from a phenomenological point of view it may be perfectly legimate to group religious [and philosophical] movements together on the basis of their common elements; but this does not necessarily mean that these movements stand in any genetic relationship or that there is any direct connection between the earlier and the later 155).

(d) *Gnosis and Gnosticism*

In the above three contexts of 'Motif Methodology' we have observed that Gnostic scholars whatever their approach might be — pre-Chris-

---

112) The above analysis of Jonas' interpretation of history as the history of *Geist* has been borrowed from R. Johnson, *op. cit.*, pp. 207-231.

113) Hans Jonas, *The Gnostic Religion*, *op. cit.*, p. 321.

114) *Ibid.* See Epilogue, "Gnosticism, Existentialism and Nihilism", pp. 320-340.

115) R. McL. Wilson, *Gnosis and the New Testament*, *op. cit.*, p. 7.

tian Gnosticism, Gnosticism as a second century heresy, or the simultaneous development of Gnosticism and Christianity without dependence on the other for origin — employ this general methodology. Frequently individual methods overlap and it is not uncommon for a Gnostic researcher to employ two of the methods discussed above simultaneously. For example, Bultmann uses both the 'Religio-historical' and 'Phenomenological' methods. Our classification has chosen the more dominant traits of an author's method and has categorized him accordingly. It is our opinion that the primary characteristic of differentiation is metaphysics which distinguishes one author from another and one method from another where a particular author employs both. Given the nature of our study it is impossible to eliminate all combinations of the above methods; rather we feel that it is more legitimate and beneficial to be aware of the different shades in the modes of analysis, and not offer a methodological panacea. Our classification has attempted only to make the reader aware of the dominance of 'Motif Methodology' and to inaugurate a 'call' for established criteria in Gnostic analysis. The combination of methods within 'Motif Methodology' will continue to exist as long as the central concern of each method is the development of motifs in literary contexts.

Part of the ambiguity and confusion generated by 'Motif Methodology' in the study of Gnosis and Gnosisticism can be alleviated through explicit definitions such as those proposed and agreed upon at the Messina Colloquium for Gnosis, Gnosticism, Pre-Gnosticism and Proto-Gnosticism [116]). In addition, Wilson's differentiation between motifs employed 'descriptively' or 'derivatively' can further aid us in our conceptual clarification [117]). Nevertheless, innumerable unquestioned historical answers will remain alongside, with further methodological enigmas. It is our belief that if we are to modify the present state of Gnostic research as described by Dr. Haardt—"in der historischen Erforschung der Gnosis nimmt die Motivgeschichte den breitesten Raum ein" [118]) — we must proceed towards the implementation of alternative methodologies. It is time that we begin to pay more attention to Wilson's cue that "we must continually ask whether

---

116) *Le Origini*, pp. xxvi-xxviii.
117) R. McL. Wilson, *Gnosis and the New Testament, op. cit.*, p. 24.
118) R. Haardt, *Die Gnosis: Wesen und Zeugnisse, op. cit.*, p. 17.

we are in fact asking the proper questions or drawing the correct conclusions from our data . . . ." " [119]). To this we should add whether
we are in fact using all methodologies available and applicable.

Defects of 'Motif Methodology' [120])

In the above section on 'Motif Methodology' we have described
the application of *'Religionswissenschaft'*, 'Religio-historical' and
'Phenomenological' methods in several contexts. Also we have accounted for the approaches of numerous Gnostic scholars and commented on their particular mode of analysis. The purpose of this
section will be to consider the limitations and short-comings of 'Motif
Methodology'.

Dr. Haardt has criticized the 'History of Motifs' methods for
objectifying types of evidence identifiable in terms of literary-histor-
ical attitudes. According to Haardt, this procedure involves the assumption of causal connections between these imaginative fabrications
without the necessary evidence of how the original objectivations
occurred [121]). In sociological terminology this means that the motifs,
which were originally abstracted from reality as constructs for descriptive purposes, have become *reified* and are taken as objective, con-
crete aspects of reality although historically or empirically non-
existent [122]). The particular danger of *reification* is that the motif
or construct readily becomes hypostatized into an entity and the
investigator duly sets out in quest of the motif or idea he has fabri-
cated [123]). The result of this approach yields a form of non-history

---

119) R. McL. Wilson, *Gnosis and the New Testament, op. cit.*, p. 30.

120) For a general critique of the history of ideas to which I am indebted
for numerous arguments, see Quentin Skinner, "Meaning and Understanding
in the History of Ideas" in *History and Theory*, Vol. 8 (1969) pp. 3-53. For a
critique of Skinner's position see Bhikhu Parekh and P. N. Berki, "The History
of Political Ideas: A Critique of Q. Skinner's Methodology" in *Journal of the
History of Ideas*, Vol. 34 (1973) pp. 163-184.

121) R. Haardt, *Die Gnosis: Wesen und Zeugnisse, op. cit.*, p. 17.

122) *Reification* can be defined as 'the converting of an abstract concept into
a materialized, empirical object'. It also has the connotation in Sociology of
'assuming that the concept is something other than the product of human activity'.
See Peter Berger and Thomas Luckmann, *The Social Construction of Reality*,
(New York 1967) pp. 89-92.

123) R. McL. Wilson in *Gnosis and the New Testament, op. cit.*, addresses
himself more generally to the problem when discussing the comments of A.

which is almost entirely given over to pointing out earlier 'anticipations' from subsequent evidence. In our analysis, *refication* not only applies to Haardt's 'History of Motifs' but also to 'Motif Methodology' in general.

C. Colpe, for example, in his enlightening criticism of the *Religionsgeschichtliche Schule* demonstrates how Reitzenstein and Bultmann, among others, have *reified* the Gnostic Redeemer myth [124]. Colpe describes how there never was any textual evidence to support the existence of a pre-Christian, archetypal Redeemer myth and that there were also unresolved problems in the dating and origins of the texts cited as evidence for this hypothesis. His conclusion is that the so-called pre-Christian Iranian myth of the Heavenly Redeemer is actually a post-Christian creation. In other words, the motif has been *reified* by particular researchers without acknowledgement that it is in reality non-existent.

For example, Bultmann originally argued that the Gospel of John presupposes this Redeemer myth by postulating that the Mandaeans originated as a group of adherents of John the Baptist and suggested textual parallels from Mandaean and Manichaean literature, the Odes of Solomon and the Apocryphal Acts of the Apostles as evidence [125]. And later, after the adoption of his existential hermeneutic, he no longer speaks of several sources but nevertheless, does not desert Reitzenstein's basic historical hypothesis. Agreeing with Colpe, we would argue that Bultmann's hypothesis rests on highly conjectural references from literary pieces of evidence that are of considerably late origin and therefore is no more than a hypostatization of his own

---

Richardson with reference to the hypostatization of a pre-Christian Gnosticism. Wilson quotes Richardson's conclusion: "we are in danger of hypostatizing certain rather ill-defined tendencies of thought and then speaking as if there were a religion or religious philosophy called Gnosticism, which could be contrasted with Judaism or Christianity. There was of course no such thing". (pp. 9 and 34).

124) C. Colpe, *op. cit.*

125) R. Bultmann, "Die Bedeutung der neuerschlossenen mandäischen und manichäischen Quellen für das Verständnis des Johannesevangeliums" in *Zeitschrift für die neutestamentliche Wissenschaft und die Kunde der der älteren Kirche*, Vol. 24 (1925) pp. 100-146. Also see his commentary on *The Gospel of John*, translated by G. R. Beasley-Murray et al., (Oxford 1971) where he assumes the Gnostic myth as the background of the Gospel. With regard to Mandaean arguments see above, n. 64.

invention. Colpe describes this process of *reification* in the following
way:

> Das Modell 'gnostischer Erlöser-mythus' ist insofern richtig, als sich alle
> Vorstellungen, die in das Modell integriert sind, aus Systemen, wie wir sie
> uns eben vergegenwärtigt haben, auch wirklich belegen lassen. Und als eine
> moderne Konstruktion aus Mosaiksteinchen verschiedenster Herkunft braucht
> man es deshalb nicht abtun, weil es sich im grossen und ganzen, abgesehen
> vom Erdenwandel und der Weihestiftung des 'Urmensch-Erlösers', mit dem
> manichäischen System deckt. Problematisch an diesem Modell ist, dass
> in seinem 'Mythus'-Begriff alle Bedeutungen mitschwingen, die dieses Wort
> im Verlauf der Religions- und Philosophiegeschichte gewonnen hat und
> die die Religionsphänomenologie ausbreitet. Direkt falsch an diesem Modell
> scheint mir zu sein, dass es de facto mit dem ganzen Anspruch archäischen
> Gewichtes belastet ist, als sei der gnostische Erlösermythus irgendwann in
> grauer Vorzeit entstanden, irgendwo im fernen weiten Orient, den man
> sich nur wenig genauer als 'Iran' vorzustellen hat, dann durch Raum und
> Zeit gewandert, um bald in diesem, bald in jenem Überlieferungskreise,
> z.B. in der Weisheitsdichtung, bei Philo, in den Adams-spekulationen und
> in der Apokalyptik, einige Mosaiksteinchen zu hinterlassen, dann in Ma-
> nichäismus noch einmal zu grandioser Einheit zusammengewachsen und bei
> den Mandäern endgültig in seine Bestandteile zerfallen [126]).

Bultmann is not alone in hypostatizing a pre-Christian Gnostic
Redeemer myth. Kurt Rudolph is also of the opinion that the Gnostic
Redeemer myth is of pre-Christian origin and adduces Mandaean
literature as proof [127]). And W. Schmithals, a Bultmannian disciple,
admits that the Gnostic Redeemer myth is the result of a combination
of two pre-Christian different myths but does not pause to ask when,
where and by whom did this combination occur [128]).

In order to avoid this problem the student of Gnosticism must
continually be aware that the particular idea he is discovering is only
a construct — that is, a heuristic device, a tool for analysis which at
best can only describe, not explain. Furthermore, the application of a
construct in research, if to prove profitable, must be developed not
only in relation to the cultural backgrounds from which it is hypothesized, but also in accordance with strict methodological rules [129]).

---

126) C. Colpe, *op. cit.*, p. 191.

127) See above n. 64.

128) W. Schmithals, *op. cit.* Also see *The Office of Apostle in the Early
Church,* translated by J. E. Steely, (New York 1969). R. McL. Wilson has made
a similar observation in *Gnosis and the New Testament, op. cit.*, pp. 27-28.

129) For a discussion of these methodological rules see C. G. Hempel, "Typological Methods in the Social Sciences" in *Philosophy of the Social Sciences:
A Reader*, (ed.) M. Natanson, (New York 1963) pp. 210-231.

Only then the possibility of postulating causal connections through the use of *reified* constructs, and at the expense of historical data, becomes feasible, even if still highly tenuous [130]).

Second, many researchers search for the motif they expect to find. When analysing New Testament, Patristic, Apocryphal and Gnostic literature, Bultmann, in the above example, looked for the myth of the Redeemer. Others such as R. M. Grant search for eschatological-apocalyptic hopes in late Judaism, and W. Schmithals looks for motifs of *"gnosis"* in the New Testament [131]). The result is that there is the danger of converting ambiguous, vague or allegorical remarks by a Gnostic into the investigator's Gnostic motif.

Bultmann, for example, attempts to demonstrate that Paul had used Gnostic terminology and to "some extent the vocabulary and approach of the Gnostics" [132]). He assumes that the terminology of Colossians (eg. 2:3) and Ephesians (eg. 3:19) was fashioned in opposition to Gnosticism and that I Corinthians 1:17f., 6:12f., and 8:1f. prove that Paul's opponents at Corinth had been a movement of

---

130) For arguments against a pre-Christian Gnostic Redeemer myth see H. M. Schenke, *Der Gott 'Mensch' in der Gnosis*, (Göttingen 1962) who argues that there was no Redeemer myth as a totality until Manicheism, the final integration being a result from a long process of growth and development. Recently Schenke has re-examined his position and his conclusions stand in sharp contrast to his earlier position focussing on the fact that there is no Gnosis without a Redeemer. And Schenke's conclusion is still antithetical to that of Bultmann's. See "Die neutestamentliche Christologie und der gnostische Erlöser" in Tröger, *Gnosis*, pp. 205-231. Also see Petr Pokorný, *Die Epheserbrief und die Gnosis: Die Bedeutung des Haupt-Glieder-Gedankens in der entstehenden Kirche*, (Berlin 1965) who develops the theme of an *Anthropos* myth which is rooted to Jewish speculation. Quispel, likewise, emphasizes the Jewish roots of the Redeemer myth. In an article entitled, "Der gnostische Anthropos und die jüdische Tradition" in *Gnostic Studies*, *op. cit.*, pp. 173-195 Quispel concluded his argument as follows: "Und vollends hat die Gnosis, soweit wir sie bisher kennengelernt haben, keine Erlösergestalt gekannt.... Wenn es auch vielleicht eine vorchristliche Gnosis gab, so doch nimmermehr einen vorchristlichen gnostischen Erlöser" (p. 195). Others such as R. P. Casey, *op. cit.*, and C. H. Dodd, *The Interpretation of the Fourth Gospel*, (Cambridge 1953), specifically attack Bultmann's thesis. For a general review of the arguments and the literature see C. Colpe, *op. cit.* and E. Yamauchi, *Pre-Christian Gnosticism*, *op. cit.*, pp. 23-35, 29-34 and 163-169.

131) For Grant see above, p. 112; for Schmithals, see *Gnosticism in Gorinth*, *op. cit.*

132) See the article by Bultmann in *Theological Dictionary of the New Testament*, (ed.) G. Kittel, translated by G. W. Bromiley, (Grand Rapids, Michigan 1964), Vol. I, p. 709.

Gnostic *"pneumatics"* [133]). Similarly, Schmithals views the opponents of Paul at Corinth as Gnostic and considers certain motifs of Philippians, Galatians, I and II Thessalonians as evidence that Paul was combatting Gnosticism [134]). Although one cannot discount this argument outright, the historical evidence does not warrant such a conclusion [135]).

There are also authors who interpret the history of the period under consideration according to the particular historical motif they expect to discover. In the analysis of events that coincided with the rise of Christianity and Gnosticism, Tacitus' remarks about Nero's persecution of Christians [136]) for example, have led G. E. M. de Ste. Croix to postulate that the sole reason Christians were persecuted as early as 64 A. D. was for their name [137]). Alternatively, these remarks by Tacitus are more frequently interpreted only as indicating that Christians were persecuttd by Romans as scapegoats for Nero's domestic and international failures [138]). Frend even goes one step further than G. E. M. de Ste. Croix and postulates that the persecutions of Christians from Nero onwards in the Roman Empire failed because the Church provided country folk with "social justice and freedom . . . [and] gave direction to an otherwise confused mass of economic, social and religious discontents" [139]). In this example, history, rather than providing empirical evidence for feasible casual connections as to why the Christians were persecuted, is employed as a tool for polemics and as a medium for social Christian theology.

On the other hand, rather than crediting a Gnostic or New Testament writer with a meaning he could not have intended to convey, the Gnostic researcher might read into the motif more than what is stated or implied. Van Groningen's study of first century Gnosticism

---

133) *Ibid.*, p. 709.

134) W. Schmithals, *Gnosticism in Corinth, op. cit.*, and *Paulus und die Gnostiker: Untersuchungen zu den kleinen Paulusbriefen*, (Hamburg 1965).

135) C. Colpe, *op. cit.*, pp. 140 and 147.

136) Tacitus, *The Annals of Imperial Rome*, Bk. 15: 44.

137) G. E. M. de Ste. Croix, "Why were the Early Christians Persecuted" in *Past and Present*, No. 26, (1963) pp. 6-39.

138) For views expressing the contrary to Ste. Croix's perspective see, for example, A. N. Sherwin-White's article, "Why were the Early Christians Persecuted: An Amendment" in *Past and Present*, No. 27, (1964) pp. 23-27.

139) W. H. C. Frend, "The Failure of the Persecutions in the Roman Empire" in *Past and Present*, No. 16, (1959) p. 24.

reads into Hellenism "a scientific impulse" and states that "the very nature of Gnosticism itself suggests a very strong prevailing spirit of scientism" [140]). Jonas reads twentieth century nihilism into second century Gnosticism and Bultmann, accepting Reitzenstein's analysis, accounts for Gnostic dualism through Oriental influence [141]).

Conceptual clarification and the ability of the investigator to differentiate between a Gnostic motif that is being 'descriptively' employed and one that is a 'derivation' from a pre-Christian Gnosis would be most useful in rectifying this shortcoming. Reading more into the data than is empirically observable is as serious a fault as discovering a pre-conceived motif that is expected to appear, regardless of the fact of its spuriousness.

The third limitation of 'Motif Methodology' is closely affiliated to scholars' exploration for their 'expected' motifs discussed directly above. Discussion of motifs frequently degenerates into a debate about whether the given motif in question 'really emerged' at a given time or whether it is 'really there' at all in any form in the New Testament, Patristic, Apocryphal, Pseudepigraphic, Qumran or Gnostic literature. This pursuit for a given motif has affinities with what Dr. Haardt has designated as a *regressus ad infinitum* [142]). The search for the 'first' cause is no more or less than attempting to discover the 'real' moment a particular motif emerged in a particular text or at a particular time, *ad infinitum*. For example, Van Groningen's 'first' motif is 'scientism', Bousset's and that of many of his disciples in the *Religionsgeschichtliche Schule* 'dualism' and Grant's 'apocalypticism'. Reductive hypotheses may be necessary given the nature of our data but are not sufficient for a study of Gnosis and Gnosticism. We must remind ourselves of Van Baaren's comment at the Messina Colloquium with regard to reductive hypotheses: "Gnosticism is only partly determined by the elements [i.e. motifs] it contains, but mostly by the way in which they function together forming an integrated whole" [143]).

Fourth, most Gnostic writers were themselves inconsistent in their description of their religion or in the use of their ideas. For example

---

140) G. Van Groningen, *First Century Gnosticism*, (Leiden 1967) p. 18.

141) See the discussions above: for Jonas, pp. 119-120 and for Bultmann, pp. 116-119.

142) See above p. 102 and n. 38.

143) Th. P. van Baaren, *op. cit.*, p. 175.

four extant copies of the *Apocryphon of John* have allowed us to observe and enumerate the deviations both in descriptions and motif between the four versions of the *Apocryphon of John* itself and Irenaeus' account in *Adversus Haereses* [144]). The fact is that since we have so many varied Gnostic systems and schools of thought there will always be exceptions or supplemental appendages no matter how desperately we try to hunt for common denominators between systems, or throughout the literary sources of that epoch, regardless of the fact that similar motifs appears in so many distinct systems. Our only other alternative is to accept Jonas' phenomenological conclusion that the crudity of the myths and their inconsistency are really examples of the new epoch of *Dasein* in the dialectical movement of the history of *Geist,* and therefore expected.

A corollary to the above is that "the very structure of language itself seems to impede our understanding" [145]). Professor Wilson has commented that

> ... the problem of determining to what extent the same words, the same concepts, even the same statements preserve their meaning in continuity right through the history of a tradition, and to what extent they may be modified and reinterpreted in course of time... is the more difficult when it is a case not merely of one linguistic tradition, but several [146]).

It would seem much more helpful if, rather than attempt to explain away these inconsistencies, we accept them as relevant and examine them within their own historical contexts. To explain away apparent contradictions between various motifs — for example, within the four versions of the *Apocryphon of John,* or between such distinct systems with one, two or three principles [147]) — is to deny the fact that there are legitimate differences. We should seek these differences and pose questions of why they should occur not only from the perspectives of the 'motif methodologist' or the sociologist, but from the perspective of the Gnostic.

---

144) W. Foerster, *Gnosis,* English translation edited by R. McL. Wilson, Vol. I, (Oxford 1972) pp. 100-120.

145) E. Benz, "On Understanding Non-Christian Religions" in *The History of Religions: Essays in Methodology,* (eds.) J. Kitagawa and M. Eliade, (Chicago 1959) p. 117.

146) R. McL. Wilson, *Gnosis and the New Testament, op. cit.,* p. 18.

147) W. Foerster, *op. cit.,* in his introductory discussion describes these distinct systems in detail, pp. 9-19.

Fifth, a 'Phenomenological' method which aids us in finding the 'essence' of religious phenomena but is independent of time and space and of attachments to a given cultural environment must be approached with a high degree of caution. Without history where is man? Can we accept the hypothesis that "il a existé une humanité archétypique antérieure à un homme historique"? [148]). Can Phenomenology ignore history and at the same time make inquires into so-called 'essences'? Can semantic structures be 'transcendental'? Is Eliade's *a priori* assumption that religious symbols express a 'transcendental' meaning acceptable and does our acceptance then grant him a license to hypothesize that "one is justified in supposing that this meaning might have been already grasped dimly in an earlier epoch"? [149]). Can everyone *verstehen*, have empathy or as Jonas writes "a musical ear" to hear the sounds of a Gnostic genus? [150]).

M. Eliade's assumption, which is representative of the 'phenomenological' position, that "spiritual creation is irreducible to a pre-existent system of human values" [151]) is comparable to saying that spiritual 'essences' are normative, history is subordinate and that causation is non-existent. In addition, J. Waardenburg has commented that the 'Phenomenological' method of the epoché can be understood for many "as an indirect introduction to theology; [that] Phenomenology of Religion in actual fact functioned as *ancilla Theologiae*" [152]). In the light of this, Van Baaren's comment that "phenomenology underestimates the extent to which all religious complexes are culturally determined and as such [are] not open to a phenomenological approach" needs to be given greater attention [153]).

Sixth, questions of chronology need to be raised. Haardt's criticism of the 'History of Motifs' for retracing and backdating motifs to earlier motifs leading to extrapolations from different and often

---

148) G. Widengren, "La Méthode Comparative: Entre Philologie et *Phenoménologie*" in *Numen*, Vol. 18 (1971) p. 168, quoting R. Pettazzoni's critique of Phenomenology, *Studi e Materiali de Storia delle Religioni*, Vol. 31, (1960) p. 35.

149) E. Eliade, "Methodological Remarks on the Study of Religious symbolism" in *The History of Religions: Essays in Methodology, op. cit.*, p. 107.

150) H. Jonas, in *Le Origini, op. cit.*, p. 104.

151) M. Eliade, *The Quest: History and Meaning in Religion, op. cit.*, p. 173. This is especially directed to J. P. Sartre who has been the polar model for his concept of religious man.

152) J. Waardenburg, *op. cit.*, p. 198.

153) Th. P. van Baaren, *op. cit.*, p. 175.

9

chronologically mixed texts equally applies in our opinion to all methods in 'Motif Methodology' [154]). The primary question, of course, is the dating of the literature. The Apocryphal, Psuedepigraphic and Qumran literary discoveries are of utmost importance because of their historical relationship to Gnosticism. But over and above these related primary sources are the original Gnostic texts of the Nag Hammadi Library. The present consensus is that the Nag Hammadi Library was the library of a Gnostic group and according to Doresse, "the place of discovery and the age of the manuscripts both lead us to believe that this library was hidden at the latest, about the beginning of the fifth century [A.D.], at the time when the Pachomian monasteries... finally extended their influence over the region" [155]). Recently this approximation has been narrowed further to mid fourth century because of the dating of Codex II to 339 A.D., *terminus a quo* [156]). On the other hand, comparatively speaking, the enigma of dating the Library is easier than the dating of the individual documents and each individual *logion*.

We must also be careful not to impose twentieth century conceptual formulations on the thinking of 1900 years ago. J. Munck has critized scholars like Bultmann, and more generally those who argue for a pre-Christian Gnosticism, for using twentieth century concepts and assumptions and then discovering these same assumptions and concepts prevalent in antiquity [157]). We would suggest that R. A. Kraft's comments with reference to Cardinal Daniélou's Jewish-Christianity can equally be relevant for those who conduct research in the field of Gnosis and Gnosticism. Rather than think in terms of Daniélou's Jewish-Christians, we recommend substituting the world of the Gnostics when asking the following questions:

Should not the descriptive categories for our study of men and movements

---

154) See above pp. 102 and 103.

155) J. Doresse, *The Secret Books of the Egyptian Gnostics*, translated by P. Mairet, (London 1960) p. 135. For an alternative explanation of the Library's origin see T. Säve-Söderbergh, "Gnostic and Canonical Gospel Traditions" in *Le Origini*, pp. 552-562, who suggests that the Library could have been created for haeresiological purposes.

156) *Introduction to the Facsimile Edition of the Nag Hammadi Codices*, (Leiden 1972) p. 4.

157) J. Munck, "The New Testament and Gnosticism" in *Current Issues in New Testament Interpretation*, (eds.) W. Klassen and G. Snyder, (London 1962) p. 225.

in history derive from the historical situations themselves — from the self consciousness of the participant? How can [twentieth century] abstraction[s] ... help me to understand what was happening among early [Gnostics] [158]).

In order for an analysis to proceed from the second century A.D. to proof for pre-Christian Gnosticism, and simultaneously not become tainted by twentieth century terminology, the following questions need to be asked. 1) Is there a genuine similarity between writer A (pre-second century A.D.) and writer B (second century A. D.)? 2) Could writer B not have found the motif in another writer than A? 3) What is the probability of the similarity being random? 4) Could writer B not have developed the motif independently? We would suggest that it would be more beneficial if we were willing to adapt ourselves to different orientations and abandon our excess baggage when it has become apparent that our analysis had depended upon a series of conjectures. We must consciously and continually ask what the Gnostics meant to convey to their own kind 1900 years ago. Our account of what writer B meant must make use of the range of descriptions which the writer himself could at least in principle have applied to describe what he was saying or doing. We cannot correctly appraise a writer's action by saying that he failed to do or say something according to twentieth century criteria unless it is first clear that he did have, and could have had, the intention of saying or acting in the manner that we have imputed to him [159]). We must also remember that twentieth century thinking is culturally bound and limited by the empirical historical evidence that is available.

Seventh, we agree with Dr. Haardt's criticism of the 'Reductive' approach as being tautological but we would advocate that this criticism by Haardt should equally apply to certain cases of 'Motif Methodology' in general [160]). Again we refer to A. A. Kraft's comments about Daniélou's Jewish-Christianity as relevant for us if we consider the context as Gnostic rather than Jewish-Christian:

Is there any way of breaking through the circularity of arguments whereby

---

158) R. A. Kraft, *op. cit.*, p. 89.

159) Arguments from silence are one of the many ways Gnostic scholars utilize Patristic evidence either for or against pre-Christian Gnosticism. For criticisms of the *argumentum e silentio*, see R. McL. Wilson, "From Gnosis to Gnosticism" in *Mélanges d'Histoire des Religions*, offerts à Henri-Charles Puech, (Paris 1974) p. 426.

160) See above, p. 103.

the reconstructed 'theology' [or systems] provides the primary evidence for
the existence of [Gnosis or Gnosticism] as an entity, while the supposed
evidence of [Gnosis or Gnosticism] as an entity is the rationale for recon-
structing [Gnostic] 'theology' [or systems] [161]).

Finally, we would argue that any commitment to the hermeneutical
principle of unifying contemporary phenomena under a common principle of interpretation such as those of Bultmann and Jonas excludes
the opportunity of pluralistic methods or pluralistic perspectives.

The above shortcomings of 'Motif Methodology' illustrate that it is
not the existence of motifs in the study of Gnostic literature that is
in question, but the conceptual propriety of treating such a method as
self-sufficient. More generally, we are questioning the underlying
assumption of this whole methodological approach of focusing on the
texts themselves without due attention to the contexts of other social
phenomena which impinge on, and help to explain them.

The study of an idea, a theme, a concept, a motif, from one century
to another inevitably leads to problems. Besides the obvious danger of
engendering empirically false claims resulting in spurious conclusions,
there is the peril of exposure to what Lovejoy has called the 'great
chain of being' [162]). It may be just as valid to speak of an age of
submission (political, rather than faith) or an age of confidence (trust
in oneself) as to speak of an age of 'eschatological-apocalypticism'
(Grant). Even if we restrict the study of a motif to a given historical
period in order that we can 'possibly' rule out changed connotation,
there still remains underlying conceptual confusion in attempting to
focus on a single motif or a collection of motifs as an appropriate
unit of historical investigation. In addition, placing emphasis on only
philological concerns is narrow and creates obvious limitations. The
words denoting the motif may vary dramatically and with incompatible
intentions. And the study of motifs based on syntax frequently fails
to distinguish between the occurrence of the words which denote the
given idea and the use of the relevant sentence by a particular agent
on a particular occassion with a particular intention to make a particular
assertion. Both James Barr [163]) and C. H. Dodd [164]) have demonstrated that there is a great deal of complexity in understanding a word

---

161) R. A. Kraft, *op. cit.*, p. 87.
162) A. O. Lovejoy, *The Great Chain of Being*, (New York 1960).
163) J. Barr, *The Semantics of Biblical Language*, (Oxford 1961).
164) C. H. Dodd, *The Bible and the Greeks*, (London 1935).

or motif of 1900 years ago and that precedents are more fiction than fact in Gnostic antiquity. Furthermore, concentration on motifs is almost by definition atomistic, presenting concepts isolated from the total schemes in which alone they have meaning. Given all the above it appears, in our opinion, that we have only a variety of statements made with words by a variety of different writers with a variety of intentions and as such, *there is no history of an idea to be written, but only a history of various people who used the idea and of their varying social situations* [165]). The question that needs to be posed if a sociological perspective is to be inaugurated is to which particular audience and in which particular socio-economic period did the Gnostic author wish to address himself [166]).

Edwin Yamauchi has also presented criticisms of methodology in his book *Pre-Christian Gnosticism* [167]). These criticisms are not critical of 'Motif Methodology' in the above sense of our discussion, but rather are comments on methodological fallacies that have been involved in the advocacy of the thesis of pre-Christian Gnosticism. Yamauchi distinguishes five such faults: the use of late sources; the assumption that Gnosticism was an unified phenomenon through the centuries whose influence can be detected by its Gnostic motifs; the use of the New Testament itself as evidence; the use of 'parallels and dependencies', such as those cited from Mandaean texts; and the appeal to authority, that is, the uncritical acceptance of statements by previous scholars who have written about Gnosticism. Yamauchi's primary concern in discussing these criticisms of methodology is to

---

165) This final conclusion should in no way be interpreted as a reproach of those who apply 'Motif Methodology'. It is only couched in this manner to bring to light the need to balance the scales. The history of an idea or a motif is both necessary and appreciated in the study of Gnosis and Gnosticism. We are only suggesting that studies of motifs should not exclude other methodologies and hope that this brief critique will encourage others to follow suit.

166) For an example of the dangers of not asking this question see Dr. R. M. Grant's comment on the Valentinian exegesis of the New Testament in *The Gospel of Philip* with reference to paragraph 125. According to Grant, this passage "is significant for the study of exegesis in general, for it shows the dangers of allegorization without the controls provided either by common sense or some dogmatic system with roots on earth" (p. 8). Grant can be criticized for applying New Testament standards of allegorization and Christian precedent to a text that was written for a different audience. See *Journal of Biblical Literature*, Vol. 79 (1960).

167) E. Yamauchi, *Pre-Christian Gnosticism, op. cit.*, pp. 170-186.

place doubt on a pre-Christian Gnosticism as represented by the *Religionsgeschichtliche Schule*.

We have attempted in this section to outline some of the general shortcomings of 'Motif Methodology'. The result has led us to question the conceptual propriety of treating such a method as self-sufficient. 'Motif Methodology', it would appear in our opinion, can only be one methodology among many in the study of Gnosis and Gnosticism. Given that every religious experience is expressed and transmitted in a particular historical context, we would advocate that communication be initiated between social scientists and Gnostic scholars [168]. For "communication is not only a matter of 'to' but of 'between' and in this respect understanding involves not only language forms but social structures" [169].

---

168) More generally, the inauguration of such a meeting, jointly sponsored by the American Academy of Religion and the Society of Biblical Literature, has taken place recently (1975). The title of the study group's mandate is "The Social World of Early Christianity".

169) As quoted in A. N. Wilder, "New Testament Hermeneutics To-day" in *Current Issues in New Testament Interpretation, op. cit.*, p. 51 from H. Kraemer, *The Communication of Christian Faith*, (Philadelphia 1956).

Flee Femininity: Antifemininity in Gnostic Texts and the Question of Social Milieu

1. INTRODUCTION

The gnostic tractate *Zostrianos* exhorts its readers to "flee from the madness and bondage of femininity" (NHC VIII 131,5f.). Similar statements are found in other Nag Hammadi texts, and the sentiment they express is not uncommon in late antiquity. This essay will analyze the meaning of the various expressions of antifemininity in the Nag Hammadi tractates. Further, it will consider whether antifemininity is an integral aspect of Gnosticism and whether it implies a special social milieu for the texts in which it occurs.

The word "femininity" which will be used in this study is an awkward term, but it has the advantage that it is appropriately abstract and that it is indefinite in meaning. More established synonyms, such as femaleness, feminineness, and womanhood, which are normally used to translate γυναικεία, or ΜΝΤΟϨΙΜΕ, have the problem that they bring along connotations that may be misleading. Femininity can more easily take on a new meaning if the context requires this.

For the modern reader, antifemininity has a range of at least four possible meanings. On the one end of the spectrum is misogyny, though if this meaning were intended in our texts, one would expect a warning against women rather than against femininity. Moving to increasing abstraction, one expects on the other end of the spectrum the devaluation of or aversion to anything of the feminine gender or associated with it. To the educated Greek, this category would include even a larger group of nouns. The author of the *Exegesis on the Soul* (NHC II,6) appeals to the feminine gender of the word *psychē* in order to portray it as a woman.[1] A striking example of this in some gnostic as well as nongnostic texts is the tendency to hypostatize divine attributes of the feminine gender as divine female beings.[2] There is no evidence, however, that negative connotations were attached to femininity in this broadest sense of the word.

Between these two possible meanings of femininity, there are more restricted usages which refer to something normally associated with women but which can be distinguished from them. One such meaning is effeminacy which, to be sure, most ancients felt was something men should avoid. Greek has special words for effeminacy,[3] however, and thus it can be ruled out as a possible meaning of femininity. But other restricted meanings are possible of "evils" which in late antiquity were associated with women but which might also hold men in "bondage." A modern analogy of this would be "machoism" which is more specific than masculinity but not of the essence of being male. Thus it is quite possible for a man to be "antimachoistic" or for a woman to act in a "macho" fashion. It would seem that we must look for such a meaning of antifemininity that potentially could apply to both men and women.

The point of studying the various occurrences of antifemininity in the Nag Hammadi texts is not simply to elucidate these passages but, if possible, to draw some conclusions concerning the relationship between antifemininity and Gnosticism. Since the reason for limiting the examples to Nag Hammadi tractates is mainly practical, it becomes questionable whether it is legitimate to draw general conclusions on the basis of these occurrences. There is, first, the possibility that the Coptic owner or owners of the Nag Hammadi Codices selected tractates for inclusion on the basis of their antifemininity stance. If this was the case, then there must also have been other selection principles, for most tractates do not speak to the issue, though none contradict it.

In defense of the limited group of texts on which conclusions will be based, it can be said that there is no secure basis available to draw general conclusions for Gnosticism.[4] The contours of Gnosticism are too

1. *Exeg. Soul* 127,20f.; also Origen refers metaphorically to the soul as a woman (*Comm. in Matt.* 12.4).
2. E.g., Sophia, Ennoia, Epinoia, and Pronoia in the *Apocryphon of John* (NHC II,1; III,1; IV,1; BG 8502,2).
3. Γυναικοειδής, γυναικικός, γυναικοτραφής, etc.
4. I have argued that for normal purposes the gnostic tractates in the Nag Hammadi Codices can be considered representative for Gnosticism (F. Wisse, "The 'Opponents' in the New Testament in Light of the Nag Hammadi Writings," in *Colloque international sur les textes de Nag Hammadi* [ed. B. Barc], 103f.).

blurred, and while it can be said that gnostic texts share a certain world view, there appears to be no consistency in the way this is expressed. Thus, finding a number of texts associated with Gnosticism that differ greatly in character and content but agree more or less in their view of femininity is a remarkable and significant fact that would permit one to speak of a trend or tendency. As with all generalizations pertaining to Gnosticism, conclusions will need to be modest and open to qualification.

To draw inferences from gnostic texts concerning their social milieu is even more hazardous than to draw general conclusions relevant to Gnosticism. The topics are often so far removed from the normal concerns of daily life that they give no solid clues for the *Sitz im Leben* ("life situation"). The assumption made already by the ancient heresiologists that these texts expressed the official teachings and practices of various sects appears to be mistaken.[5] Only in a strictly orthodox setting would one expect a text to stay within the confines of the official teaching and practices of the sect in question.[6] There can be little doubt that gnostic tractates were written within an uncontrolled, heterodox milieu. Thus they more likely reflect the idiosyncratic visions and opinions of an individual than those of a group or sect. This in itself has social implications, though not very definite ones. It suggests a situation that left room for heterodox speculative thought which could count on at least a limited appreciative readership.

There is, however, a factor that may make it possible to be more definite about social milieu. Antifemininity has obvious implications for self-understanding and life style. The reader of these texts is expected to be able to escape the bondage of femininity. We must see whether this suggests a particular social setting.

2. ZOSTRIANOS (NHC VIII,1)

Perhaps the most striking occurrence of antifemininity is found in *Zostrianos*, a long and poorly preserved tractate, which is mainly concerned with obscure speculations about the heavenly world but which

5. See F. Wisse, "The Nag Hammadi Library and the Heresiologists," *VC* 25 (1971), 205–23; and idem, "Prolegomena to the Study of the New Testament and Gnosis," in *The New Testament and Gnosis: Essays in Honour of Robert McL. Wilson* (ed. A. H. B. Logan and A. J. M. Wedderburn), 139–42.
6. See F. Wisse, "The Use of Early Christian Literature as Evidence for Inner Diversity and Conflict," in *Nag Hammadi, Gnosticism, and Early Christianity* (ed. Hedrick and Hodgson), 41.

has a fascinating parenetic section at the end. It is presented as the preaching of Zostrianos to the holy seed of Seth after his return to earth and reentry into the body. I shall quote the main part of the preaching of Zostrianos:

> Strengthen the innocent, [elect] soul, and [observe] the (state of) change here and seek the unchangeable unborn state. [The] Father of all of these invites you. [Though they] wait for you and do you harm, he will not forsake you.
>
> Do not baptize yourselves in death, nor entrust yourselves to those inferior to you instead of those who are superior. Flee from the madness and bondage of femininity, and choose for yourselves the salvation of masculinity. It is not to suffer that you came, but you came to dissolve your bonds. Release yourselves and that which binds you will be dissolved. Save yourselves, in order that that one (fem.) may be saved. (130,20—131,14)[7]

There is also a reference to femininity near the beginning of the tractate just before Zostrianos leaves his body and the perceptible world to receive the divine revelations. It reads:

> After I separated from the bodily ($\sigma\omega\mu\alpha\tau\iota\kappa\acute{o}\nu$) darkness which is in me, and the natural ($\psi\upsilon\chi\iota\kappa\acute{o}\nu$) chaos in mind, and the femininity of lust ($\grave{\epsilon}\pi\iota\theta\upsilon\mu\acute{\iota}\alpha$) [that is] in darkness, I did no longer make use of it. (1,10–15)

Antifemininity is not incidental to the tractate. It forms the center of the preaching to the "straying multitude" and it figures prominently in the author's self-understanding. The context is that of metaphysical and anthropological dualism common in late antiquity. The innocent soul needs to be saved from the perceptible world of change which is hostile to it, and from the bondage of femininity which is connected with lust and darkness. Salvation is found in the unchangeable state of unbornness which appears to be linked with masculinity, that is, the state of being released from the bondage of femininity.

The passage at the beginning of the tractate makes clear that it is possible to separate from femininity already in this life, though it is closely associated with bodily existence. The passage does not describe Zostrianos's separation from the body—that happens in 4,20–25—but his preparation for the revelation experience. It probably meant that he was no longer governed by "bodily darkness," "natural mental chaos," and "the femininity of lust."

---

7. The translation of this and the following passages is my own. Significant differences with text editions will be noted. As yet there is no text edition for *Zostrianos*. My translation differs considerably from the one published in *Nag Hammadi Library* (ed. Robinson), 393.

The preaching of Zostrianos is for "a living generation and to save those who are worthy and to strengthen the elect" (4,15–17). Though this, no doubt, excludes much of humankind, there is no hint that it excludes women. Femininity in the meaning of sexuality and procreation is something that can enslave everyone, and its opposite, masculinity, does not appear to be a natural quality of males but a state that all must seek in order to be saved.

It should be noted that the antifemininity in *Zostrianos* is found together with a description of a heavenly world in which hypostatized female beings play an important and positive role. Further, mythologoumena link the tractate to so-called Sethian Gnosticism as represented in the *Apocryphon of John*, and vocabulary and the title link it to early Neoplatonic circles.[8]

3. THE DIALOGUE OF THE SAVIOR (NHC III,5)

In sharp contrast with *Zostrianos*, the *Dialogue of the Savior* is a heterodox Christian writing which stands in an unclear relationship to Gnosticism. The passage relevant to antifemininity reads:

> The Lord said, "Pray in the place where there is no woman." Matthew said, "Pray in the place where there is [no woman]," he tells us, meaning, "Destroy the works of femininity," not because there is any other (manner of) [birth], but because they will cease [giving birth]. Mary said, "They will never be obliterated." (144,15–23)

The dialogue about the obliteration of the works of femininity continues in the tractate, but unfortunately lacunae obscure the meaning. Helmut Koester and Elaine Pagels, who wrote the introduction to the text edition of the *Dialogue of the Savior*, believe that this passage "does not suggest a metaphysically motivated sexual asceticism."[9] Their reason for this remains unclear. It is hard to deny that the passage has strong ascetic overtones. Prayer and the presence of women are claimed to be incompatible. In the tractate this saying is interpreted by Matthew to mean the same as the saying, "Destroy the works of femininity," which we know also from the *Gospel of the Egyptians*.[10] The works of femininity are specified as procreation. The *Dialogue of the Savior* goes well beyond

---

8. See J. H. Sieber, "An Introduction to the Tractate *Zostrianos* from Nag Hammadi," *NovT* 15 (1973) 237f.
9. S. Emmel, ed., *Nag Hammadi Codex III,5: The Dialogue of the Savior*, 15.
10. As quoted by Clement of Alexandria in *Stromateis* 3.63.

1 Cor. 7:5 which indicates that sexual abstinence is appropriate during a time of prayer.

There is a striking parallel to the obliteration of the works of femininity in the sectarian, encratic treatise *Testimony of Truth* (NHC IX 30,18—31,5). It portrays the descent of the Son of man upon the Jordan as the end of *the dominion of carnal procreation.* This supports the interpretation that antifemininity in the *Dialogue of the Savior* is an encratic rejection of the sexual process of procreation.

4. THE *FIRST APOCALYPSE OF JAMES* (NHC V,3)

The *First Apocalypse of James* is a heterodox Christian treatise that makes use of Valentinian traditions. Two passages refer to femininity:

> Since you have [asked] concerning femininity, femininity existed, but femininity was not [first]. And [it] prepared for itself powers and gods. (24,25–29)

> The perishable has [gone up] to the imperishable, and the work of the femininity has arrived up to the work of this masculinity. (41,15–19)

Though the fragmentary state of the *First Apocalypse of James* makes interpretation difficult, something can be said about the meaning of femininity. The first passage refers most likely to the fall of Sophia and the evil archons who came into being through her. The second passage echoes 1 Cor. 15:53. It is likely that the work of femininity is not just parallel to what is perishable but identical with it, and the same can be said for masculinity and imperishability. This would link the passage to *Zostrianos*, though the antithetical tone of the latter has been replaced by more moderate transformational language. The two passages in the *First Apocalypse of James* are linked by the identification of femininity with the perishable, created order. While one cannot speak of antifemininity in these two passages in the *First Apocalypse of James*, they do share with *Zostrianos* a radical devaluation of femininity rooted in classical metaphysical dualism.

5. THE *TRIPARTITE TRACTATE* (NHC I,5)

This lengthy and very complex Valentinian treatise contains one curious reference to femininity. The relevant part of the passage reads:

> . . . the faces, which are forms of masculinity, since they are not from the illness which is the femininity, but are from this one who already has left behind the illness. (94,16–20)

In a learned note, Harold W. Attridge and Elaine Pagels tried to elucidate the passage.[11] They understand the illness of femininity to refer to the offspring that Sophia begot without the help of her male partner, the Savior. They suggest further that the imagery derives from patriarchal marriage law. In spite of all kinds of background material drawn from other Valentinian sources, the passage in the *Tripartite Tractate* remains impenetrable, as do many other ones in this treatise.

The little that is clear is that femininity is something negative and masculinity is positive. Is leaving behind the illness of femininity similar to fleeing the bondage of femininity? Even if there is a distant relationship, it should be noted that the *Tripartite Tractate* does not draw from its negative view of femininity practical applications for the life of the believer.

6. THE *BOOK OF THOMAS THE CONTENDER* (NHC II,7)

This ascetic, Christian treatise includes one reference to femininity. It reads:

> Woe to you who love the practice (συνήδεια) of femininity and her polluted intercourse. (144,8–10)[12]

In this case it is clear that femininity is identical to sexuality. The message is similar to the one in the parenetic section in *Zostrianos*.

7. THE *GOSPEL OF THOMAS* (NHC II,2)

Logion 114 of the *Gospel of Thomas* does not use the term "femininity," but it deserves to be treated in the context of antifemininity. It reads:

> Simon Peter said to them, "Let Mary leave us, for women are not worthy of the life." Jesus said, "Behold, I shall lead her in order that I may make her male, that she too may become a living spirit which resembles[13] you males. For every woman who will make herself male will enter the Kingdom of Heaven." (51,18–26)

It is not surprising that this saying has received much comment. Recently it has received a full treatment in an article by Jorunn Jacobsen

11. H. W. Attridge, ed., *Nag Hammadi Codex I (The Jung Codex)*, 369f.
12. J. D. Turner translates "the intimacy with womankind and polluted intercourse with it" (*The Book of Thomas the Contender*, 33 and 179). It is difficult to support this meaning on the basis of the Coptic.
13. The translation "resembling you males" wrongly suggests that the antecedent is Mary rather than a living spirit.

Buckley which includes a summary of previous interpretations as well as her own attempt at finding the saving *hermēneia*.[14]

Before commenting on the meaning of any of the logia, the opening words of the *Gospel of Thomas* need to be considered, for they present the modern reader with a serious predicament. The author of these words claims that the logia he has collected are the hidden sayings of Jesus. In other words, he believes that they are mysterious by their very nature. This means that as far as he is concerned, *their meaning is not known!* Great value is put on seeking and finding the meaning; those who find it "will not taste death" (32,10–14).

It would appear that modern commentators of the *Gospel of Thomas* do not really believe the author's claim that the meaning of the logia is a mystery. To be sure, they admit that the sayings are difficult to understand, but they take for granted that the author had a definite meaning in mind and that one can discover this meaning if one sees it against the background of Gnosticism as known from other sources.

Before we make such far-going assumptions, however, the claim of the author deserves to be taken more seriously. It can hardly be denied that all the sayings would appear "hidden" to the normal reader. We should not be deceived by the fact that as scholars we know that a number of them were not meant to be mysterious in their original setting. This does not make them less enigmatic to the author of the *Gospel of Thomas* and his intended readers.

The *Gospel of Thomas* does not give us any reasons to assume that the logia are only enigmatic on the surface and have a sensible meaning if one can break the gnostic code. Neither would it have made sense for the author to give some of the hidden sayings he found in the tradition an openly gnostic slant after telling the readers that the meaning is mysterious. The predicament of the modern interpreter is now clear. The author's "theology" is limited to the opening words. He believed that an esoteric, and most likely mystical, interpretation of enigmatic sayings would lead to salvation. The author may have followed his own advice and may have had certain meanings in mind for the sayings, but we do not know what they were, and it is useless to speculate on them. We cannot even be sure that he was a Gnostic. We know, for example, that mystical interpretation of enigmatic speech was practiced in early Pachomian monasticism.[15]

14. Buckley, "An Interpretation of Logion 114 in the *Gospel of Thomas*," *NovT* 27 (1985) 245–72.
15. See H. Quecke, *Die Briefe Pachoms*, chap. 2.

The modern interpreter can only hope to find the meaning of a certain logion if there is reason to believe that it was not enigmatic in its original setting. This appears to be the case for many of the sayings. But this nonmysterious meaning should not be attributed to the 'author' of the *Gospel of Thomas*. Some sayings may have come from a gnostic or encratic or early catholic environment, but this need not have been the same as that of the 'author.' The sayings as a group have only one factor in common: their apparent enigmatic nature. To attribute a coherent gnostic theology to them can be done only through eisegesis.

For logion 114 this means that it was either enigmatic from the start, and thus without a recoverable meaning, or was assumed to be enigmatic by the 'author' of the *Gospel of Thomas*, but clear in its original setting. The conflict between logia 114 and 22, which has puzzled modern interpreters, is no longer a problem, for it is to be expected in a collection of mystery sayings from different backgrounds. There is also no justification to look for clues in logion 61 and others to unravel the hidden meaning of logion 114.[16]

If logion 114 was not originally 'hidden,' then it means what it says. Taken that way, the logion shows remarkable similarities to the anti-femininity passages in the other Nag Hammadi texts. Peter's words should not simply be dismissed as a misogynic remark which is corrected by Jesus.[17] The need for Mary to leave the company of disciples is not far removed from the dominical injunction in the *Dialogue of the Savior* 'to pray in the place where there is no woman.' The words of Jesus in logion 114 do not contradict Peter, for they affirm that Mary cannot enter the kingdom if she remains a woman. The work of femininity must be destroyed, but there is salvation in masculinity which is the state of being a living spirit.[18]

8. ANTIFEMININITY

The meaning of femininity in the passages under discussion appears to focus on sexuality and birth. To the pre-Freudian, male mind which was ignorant of the male libido, sexuality appeared to be located in the female and thus was identical with femininity.[19] Masculinity, on the

16. This is the procedure followed by J. J. Buckley in her article.
17. Buckley, 'An Interpretation of Logion 114 in the *Gospel of Thomas*,' 246.
18. For a list of similar statements in late antiquity, see *RAC*, 8:242f.
19. This is the understanding reflected in the quotation from the *Gospel of the Egyptians* in *Stromateis* 3.63. Clement, who represents a moderate position on marriage,

other hand, was thought to be free from sexuality and birth. Men and women must flee the bondage of femininity and seek the salvation of masculinity. The message and context of antifemininity is basically encratic.

9. GNOSTICISM

Antifemininity is at home in gnostic texts but is certainly not limited to them. It appears weakest in Valentinian types of speculation and strongest in encratic Christian writings. Antifemininity is readily combined with speculations of the "Sethian" type, which tend to see sexuality as an evil invention of the forces of darkness to prevent living spirits from returning to the pleroma.[20] There is also a connection between antifemininity and Neoplatonism as *Zostrianos* and the writings of Plotinus and Porphyry indicate.[21] The obvious link between antifemininity and gnostic literature should caution interpreters against drawing inferences concerning the role of women in Gnosticism from the positive role of hypostatized female beings in the pleroma.

10. SOCIAL MILIEU

To flee femininity, that is, the "works" of birth and sexuality and corruptibility, does not only necessitate an ascetic life style but naturally leads to a form of monasticism. For men this meant avoiding the company of women entirely, as was the rule in Egyptian monasticism[22] and as is still enforced on Mount Athos in Greece. The visions of comely maidens, which continued to trouble hermits and monks, were explained as temptations from the devil.[23]

It is likely that the gnostic writings that espouse antifemininity presuppose such an encratic setting of which there are many examples in the late second and the third centuries C.E. Gnostic writings need not have given rise to encratism, but they would have found a sympathetic environment in encratic circles. This is supported by the fact that the

is in agreement with it but rejects the need for encratism, since he believed that begetting children can be, and should be, an act of the will rather than of desire (*Stromateis* 3.57).

20. E.g., the *Apocryphon of John* (NHC II 24,26–31) and *On the Origin of the World* (NHC II 109,1–29).

21. Cf. Plotinus *Ennead* 3.5.1 and Porphyry *De abstentia* 2.34.45; 4.20.

22. See *RAC*, 8:260 and K. Heussi, *Der Ursprung des Mönchtums*, 226f.

23. See *RAC*, 8:259.

Christian heresiologists did not draw a clear distinction between Encratites and Gnostics. Already the first patristic reference to encratism, Irenaeus's treatment of Tatian, includes gnostic traits.[24] A certain Severus, who according to Eusebius[25] became the head of the Encratite sect following Tatian, is portrayed by Epiphanius as a full-blown Gnostic.[26] Encratism lies at the heart of Marcionism and Manicheism, and even if Montanism and Valentinianism were not encratic in the technical sense of the word, both movements incorporated a profound form of asceticism.

The Nag Hammadi Codices as a collection witness to the close connection between Gnosticism and encratism. Not only are gnostic and encratic tractates found in the same codex, but not a few of the texts combine gnostic and encratic themes. A good example of this is the *Testimony of Truth* (NHC IX,3) which can be described equally well as an encratic document which makes use of gnostic material or as a gnostic treatise on the necessity of celibacy.

This overlap between Gnosticism and encratism appears to extend even to the original setting of the Nag Hammadi Codices. Evidence from the bindings strongly suggests that they were copied and used by Pachomian monks around the middle of the fourth century C.E.[27] Apparently the early cenobitic movement drew on a wide variety of heterodox ascetics who brought along the books they cherished. Gnosticism lost its home in the Christian ascetic movement when the orthodox church hierarchy brought the monastic movement under its control during the second half of the fourth century C.E.[28] Apart from Manicheism, this appears to have eliminated Gnosticism from the bounds of the Roman Empire.

24. Irenaeus *Adv. haer.* 1.28.2.
25. Eusebius *Historia ecclesiastica* 4.29.4f.
26. Epiphanius *Haer.* 45.
27. See the discussion in F. Wisse, "Gnosticism and Early Monasticism in Egypt," *Gnosis: Festschrift für Hans Jonas*, 433–40.
28. This also involved the purging of heretical books in the possession of monks; it provides us with a likely reason for the burial of the Nag Hammadi Codices at some distance from the Pachomian monastery. (See Wisse, "Gnosticism and Early Monasticism," 436f.)

HOW MANY GNOSTICS?

Our sense of the evolution of religion from the Hellenistic
cults to Christianity at a time when "philosophy became more
religious and religion more philosophic," as has been quipped, has
prepared us to accept the phenomenon of Gnosticism as a widespread
development which represented a significant threat as a Christian
heresy, and had "pagan" and Jewish counterparts which if not
"Gnostic" by definition showed some strong affinities to communities which we would admit to being Gnostic. I first discussed
Gnosticism with William Willis, and although he warned me I might
not find the contents of the Nag Hammadi texts congenial, I persisted, and welcome this opportunity to present him with this
produce of my stubbornness.[1]

Modern explanation of the ideas called Gnostic had developed
through the interpretation of remarks by the church fathers, examination of such Hermetic texts as that known as "Poimandres,"
study of new discoveries such as the seventeenth-century finds,
the Bruce and Askew codices and the Berlin Gnostic papyrus, until
the massive collection from Nag Hammadi burst upon the world just
after mid-century. Now, characteristically, scholars are able to
present an extensive theology and mythology as Gnostic, drawing
heavily on the Nag Hammadi texts to supplement what can be said
about the belief from Christian attacks, from pagan writings, from
remarks by neoplatonists and even from the Manichaean and Mandaean
texts. Despite the spanking administered by Morton Smith in 1978,[2]
we persist in treating Gnosticism as a "stance" which, if not a
single religion, is found in a large number of cults and systems
from the end of the pre-Christian era on into the early centuries
of the Christian era, perhaps because we mean by "Gnostic" any
system which exhibits dualism or reliance on nonratiocinative
knowledge. That would make Gnosticism a modern construct, of

---

1 I should like to thank my colleague, T. D. Barnes, for
generous and very helpful advice as I was preparing this material
for publication.

2 "History of the Term Gnosticos," *The Rediscovery of Gnosticism*. Proceedings of the International Conference on Gnosticism
at Yale: New Haven, Connecticut, March 28-31, 1978, Bentley Layton,
ed., Vol. 2 (Leiden 1981) 796-807.

297

course, rather than an ancient phenomenon created by the reasoning
which Smith so winningly describes as Platonic circularity.

I use the modern construct to answer a question implied by
Smith, but not directly asked. Among the important questions he
posed were: "2. What Christians, individually or in groups, claimed
to be *gnostikoi*, and when, and why?" and, "3. What, if any, non-
Christians made the same claim, and when, and why?" Precious few
would call themselves Gnostics, on Smith's argument, based on use
of the actual term, perhaps not even the neoplatonic Gnostics of
Porphyry's title "Against the Gnostics" for Plotinus' *Ennead* 2.9;
nor, if we follow Smith's argument strictly, can we confidently
call the writers--or collectors--of the Nag Hammadi texts "Gnostic."
But this restriction of the term does not help me to answer the
question which comes to my mind when I read the Nag Hammadi texts
and others similar to them: who, in the first three or four centuries of our era, believed, or found religious or philosophical
validity, in this?

By this I do not seek to identify those who merely felt confidence in a personal perception of truth, in a way like the
Quakers of today, but those whose personal perception led them to
the construction of elaborate cosmologies and hierarchies of
divinity. And even here, I do not mean those like Philo or
Plotinus who thought they were building in rational fashion even
though they used such traditional Greek arguments that things must
be what they are because it would not be "right" for the opposite
to obtain. Their arguments were structured, whereas the proposi-
tions of the Nag Hammadi texts come full-blown in revelation. But
even eliminating what we can, at first glance there seem to be
quite a lot of people who "knew" these cosmologies and dualistic
concepts. Earlier than the fourth-century Nag-Hammadi texts we
find the most notable to include: the persons responsible for the
Greek fragments of the Gospel of Thomas found at Oxyrhynchus;
Valentinus and his followers, of whom we particularly note their
greatest systematizer Ptolemaeus, who worked in the latter part of
the second century, as well as people like Marcus and Heracleon of
whom we know primarily from the heresy-hunters; Basilides, described contradictorily by Irenaeus and Hippolytus, and of whom we
have a few fragments outside the texts of his opponents; Carpocrates, his son Epiphanius and their followers; Naassenes, Sethians
and Ophites, whose existence and concepts can be reconstructed from
the comments of heresiologues as well as from Nag Hammadi and other

tractates; perhaps Marcion, say some moderns; Clement of Alexandria, with a secret gospel of Mark, includes himself, as Smith
argues. The list would seem to be impressive, and if taken to
represent a sizable number of people would justify the common view
that these ideas held great currency in the first century of our
era. Such evidence as can be brought to bear on the matter, however, suggests the opposite, and although I acknowledge the impossibility of proving a negative, I hope the following comments
will at least induce caution about the extent of "Gnostic" ideas.
The evidence which I think may be of significance in this matter
can be grouped under three headings. First, because of Christianity's concern with heretical ideas of this type and with the
opposition of groups which may be termed Gnostics, we should look
in summary manner at the actual body of the church before the mid-
third century, as well as the organizational relationship it took
in relation to ideas we can find in the writings I have mentioned.
Second, we should consider the extent to which these ideas might
belong to a Hellenic heritage. And finally, it will be worth
considering the actual remains as evidence of interest in their
contents.

Christians and the Church to the Death of Origen

It is now almost a commonplace to remark that early Christianity was an urban phenomenon, striking roots first into communities of prosperous and educated Greeks, rather than among the
lowly poor, slaves and women. The evidence from the papyri shows
quite convincingly that for some part of the third century, at
least, when Christians were a small element in the society,[3] they

---

3 I cannot here deal in much detail with the much-discussed
question of the timing of the great Christian expansion, a place-
ment which in significant measure depends on whether the statements
of Origen (esp. *Contra Cels.* 8.44; other relevant passages quoted
by A. Harnack, *Expansion of Christianity in the First Three Centuries*, trans. Moffat [N.Y. 1905] 2.158-62), suggesting small numbers, refer to the earlier part of Origen's life or relate to the
period closer to the middle of the century. The figures of R.
Bagnall, "Religious Conversion and Onomastic Change in Early Byzantine Egypt," *BASP* 19 (1982) 105-23, which indicate a very small
number of Christian *names* in the Egyptian population even in the
latter part of the third century, may seriously understate the
Christian element in depending on identification of Christians by
nomenclature, but they might support a later reference for Origen's
statement. I have no doubt that circumstances varied in Egypt and
throughout the empire, so that we need not reject the testimony of
Pliny, *Ep.* 10.96.9-10, that in the early second century they came

came from the members of the urban class with money.[4] The nature
of the Christian texts and reading matter also suggests that the
Christian community was educated and financially well-off.[5] And
in these early Christian texts, much of the ethical and social
thought reflects the ideas of the moneyed class rather than that
of the poor whom Christians were urged to pity[6] or to aid in
charity.[7] While restraint may be urged in treatment of slaves,[8]
there is no hint of any sentiment for abolition of the institution,
nor is Ignatius unusual among Christian writers in urging docility
on the enslaved.[9] "Pie in the sky when you die," cynics called
this attitude in the nineteen-thirties, particularly when it was
expressed by preachers with no experience of unemployment, the
dole, or selling apples to eat. The Christian writers of the
first two centuries were no different in consoling the unfortunate
with hope of the next world.

It would be remarkable if this had not been the case. With
so many of the early Christians and their leaders coming from the

---

"from every age, every rank, and from both sexes..." that "the
contagion of this superstition has reached not only the cities but
the villages and even the fields," with the result that temples
had become deserted, sacrifices abandoned and it was even hard to
find a buyer for sacrificial meat. There is, however, probably
exaggeration in claims like that of Tertullian, *Apology* 1.7 and
To Scapula 3, that the Christians are everywhere, of every age,
sex and rank, and are nearly the majority in every city.

4 E. A. Judge and S. R. Pickering, "Papyrus Documentation of
Church and Community in Egypt to the Mid-fourth Century," *Jb.Ant.
u.Chr.* 20 (1977) 47-71 and J. van Haelst, "Les sources papyrolo-
giques concernant l'église en Egypte à l'époque de Constantin,"
Proceedings of the Twelfth International Congress of Papyrology
(Toronto 1970) 501.

5 Very few of these texts predate 250, and their quality
indicates that they derive from a community not impoverished, and
one which owned and used a wide variety of scriptural and non-
biblical religious texts. See C. H. Roberts, *Manuscript, Society
and Belief in Early Christian Egypt*, Schweich Lectures of the
British Academy 1977 (London 1979) 22, 63.

6 E.g. Clement *Ep.* 1.59.4.

7 Mandate 8 of the popular *Shepherd of Hermas* is typical:
"Serve widows, attend orphans and those in want, ransom from their
miseries the slaves of God."

8 *Didache* 4.10-11.

9 Ignatius *To Polycarp* 4.3.

prosperous urban classes,[10] their texts could be expected to reflect the sense of the ordered world as that class saw it. Although there were those like Tertullian or the even more extreme
Tatian who rejected the world of the urban rich in favor of an
ascetic interpretation of the words of Jesus and the apostles,
the values of self-deprivation always remained a minority position,

---

10 Marcion, for example, is said to have been a shipowner,
and prosperous. Even the early martyrs came from the better
classes, as one of the best known, Perpetua, who at twenty-two
years of age and nursing her infant, was imprisoned with a pregnant slave who feared that she could not share her mistress' death
for Christ because the Romans did not execute pregnant women. Perpetua's father appealed again and again to his daughter to recant,
but to no avail, and--specifically said to have been a member of
the nobility--she went to the beasts. Another, the soldier Marinus, is said to have been "honorable for rank in the army and outstanding in birth and wealth" (*Hist. Eccl.* 7.15), and educated men
and bishops like St. Ignatius and St. Polycarp could hardly have
come from the lower ranks of society. In Gaul, the martyr Vettius
Epagathus was described by Eusebius (*Hist. Eccl.* 5.1.10) as "distinguished." Eusebius' account of the many killed in Lyons and
Vienne at the time included many Roman citizens whom the governor
beheaded (*Hist. Eccl.* 5.1.47), as was their right as against being
thrown to the beasts like non-citizen Christians. In Rome itself
where Eusebius says perhaps tendentiously that many who were outstanding for wealth and family were turning to Christianity by the
reign of Commodus at the end of the second century, the martyrdom
of one Apollonius--by beheading--took off a man reputed among the
faithful for his education and philosophy, at least as Eusebius
tells the tale (*Hist. Eccl.* 5.21). Elsewhere, we have evidence
that Christians had penetrated the army by the third century, such
as the Roman soldier Marinus, who was to have been advanced to
centurion when the proposed promotion brought his denunciation.
We also have evidence of a significant number of Christians in
military service with no apparent action being taken to restrict
them at Dura, where we can see the coexistent worship of Christians,
Jews, followers of Mithra and devotees of Roman official religion
and traditional Greek gods. Here, as the study of the history of
the Christian building as well as that of the Roman garrison and
the city as a whole shows (C. H. Kraeling, *The Christian Building,
The Excavations at Dura Europus*, Final Report VIII, Part II [New
Haven 1967], esp. 107-11), the growth of the space needed for
Christian worship should probably be associated with the growth of
the garrison, bringing to this remote border city Christians whose
conversions had taken place in the more active centers of missionary
activity. Finally, outside the army but in the families of Roman
bureaucrats, there were Christians as early as the third century
even among people of senatorial rank, for a senator named Asturias
arranged for the burial of the martyr Marinus with great magnifi-
cence (Eusebius, *Hist. Eccl.* 7.16, cited, with others who are
either certainly or probably both Christian and members of the
senatorial class, by W. Eck, "Das Eindringen des Christentums in
den Senatorenstand bis zu Konstantin der Grosse," *Chiron* 1 (1971)
381-406). These are but a few of the items which have led many
students of the history of the church to revise the earlier idea
of the poverty and low status of the people who were Christians
during the centuries before Constantine.

with support which might fluctuate in extent but which never even
approached endorsement for all by orthodox leaders. Still less
was there any sense that the upper class ought to give up its
position to any extent for the liberation or improvement of the
material condition of the oppressed. Much more characteristic
was the reasoning of Clement of Alexandria, who twisted Jesus'
rejection of the rich into a more comfortable justification of
riches if used with discretion and charity.[11]

An important reason for this orientation of Christian thought
goes beyond the class from which it originated. The issues with
which Christian writers dealt related inevitably to what I call
the "curriculum" of the times, an orientation which goes beyond
matters of schooling and study and reaches to the heart of what is
understood to affect and even control human life. Here the fundamentally declarative nature of almost all Hellenic religion and
most philosophic cosmology came into play. In a world in which
magic, astrology, dream-interpretation, omen-reading and the like
were the norm, a statement about reality constructed out of a
series of arguments seemed like a much more advanced intellectual
achievement, even though the arguments might be based in the final
analysis merely on untested and unjustified assertions. So Christian writers consistently attacked the magicians and the sooth-
sayers on the grounds that only Christian ideas held the truth,
that the divine was reached through Christ and adherence to his
words, and that any apparent successes in magic, astrology or the
like were the wicked works of demons who still plagued the world
in opposition to God. Christian thinkers, particularly in view of
their Greek philosophical tradition, felt the need to determine
and then demonstrate the "truth" of the passion of Christ, to establish precisely what had happened and what its significance was
for human life. This was the more critical to the extent that
there was diversity of interpretation, and that Christian ideas
came under attack from intelligent and virtuous thinkers and not
just from crude persecutors.

It was, in fact, the crude and excruciating maltreatment of
Christians in the persecutions which attracted some non-Christians
to investigate the new religion. The well-educated Tertullian, at
the beginning of the third century, portrayed himself as

---

11 That is the import of his *Who is the Rich Man Who is to
be Saved?*

exceedingly impressed when he saw how cheerfully condemned Christians faced the prospect of death and bore its painful imposition.[12]
Their confidence brought his conversion to a truth which eliminated
or offset the two human misfortunes which had most occupied the
minds of philosophers--death and pain. And, as he tried to guide
others to the fulfilment of his own perception of the life in
Christ, the intensity of his vision and his personality brought
out the urgency with which he sought the true interpretation and
condemned the false and heretical. He found enough of the latter,
for Christian thinkers had long differed on the nature of Jesus
as man or God, on His relation to God the Father and the Holy
Spirit, as well as on issues relating to the governance of the
Christian churches and their relation to the parent Judaism.

As early as the end of the first century, these matters occupied Christian writing. In the *First Letter of Clement*, the
writer calls on the Corinthians to submit to their elders and to
abandon their dissension and schism. Around that time, or soon
after, Ignatius, in his letters written in the course of his journey to martyrdom in Rome, returns again and again to two themes,
the authority of bishops over their churches, and attacks on docetism. The heresy was a long-lasting one and appeared in many
guises among early Christians, and Ignatius met it in many ways,
including citations of scripture.[13] And the union of Jesus with
the Father is made paradigm for the congregation with its leaders,
for as He did nothing without God, so Christians are to do nothing
without the bishop or the elders.[14] Ignatius writes to the
Trallians (II) of their subordination to the bishop as to Christ,
to the Philadelphians (IV) to use only one Eucharist as there is
"one flesh of Christ, one cup of his blood of union, one altar,
one bishop." He attacks those who do not accept the Eucharist as
Christ's flesh.[15] He goes on to demand (VIII) that all follow the
bishop and the elders, that no act relating to the church be done
without the bishop, and insists that the Eucharist is valid only
when celebrated by a bishop or his appointee, while a baptism or a

---

12 Cf. *Apologet.* 15, *To Scapula* 5; what he saw is, as he says
in *Apologet.* 50.13, "the attraction to our religion."

13 *Letter to the Smyrnaeans* 3.

14 *Ep. to the Magnesians* 7.

15 *Smyrnaeans* 7.

religious meal without the bishop is unlawful. The foundation of
the disciplined church is clear, along with some of the basic
theological and liturgical positions of the later Church. It is
in the context of this developing orthodoxy and against the background of theological and organizational controversy that we see
the emergence of the Christians whose texts came from the sands of
Nag Hammadi. Indeed, it is often said that the ideas and popularity of these "Gnostic" heresies provided the catalyst for the
formulation of orthodox doctrine and organization, much as Marcion's manipulation of Christological and Pauline texts motivated
the creation of the NT canon.

Some of the basic patterns for the development of Christianity
can be seen here, established long before Christianity had won a
large following in the Greek or Roman world. There was nothing in
mainstream Christianity which could not find acceptance by some
Greeks, even those deeply imbued with Hellenism, and by the middle
of the second century Justin Martyr, in Rome, was attempting to
present in apologies addressed to the emperors a harmonization of
Christian thought with Hellenic intellectualization. Before he
himself suffered martyrdom, he had won over a well-trained intellectual, a Syrian Greek who was studying philosophy in Rome.
Tatian's career exemplified a number of the tendencies and tensions
of the early church, as he rejected Justin's accommodation with
Greek learning and thought and denied the value of the Hellenic
tradition. His *Oration to the Greeks* gives some idea of his
thought, presenting views of Christianity which deviate quite
strikingly from what we read elsewhere. Although there are observations typical of those which early Christians addressed to
the Greeks, like the claim of the antiquity of the Judaeo-Christian
tradition, with Moses asserted as predating the Trojan war,[16]
Tatian's attack on acting, dancing, gladiatorial shows, dramatic
presentations and other spectacles[17] belongs to an ascetic trend
in Christianity which, as in Tatian's case, would verge on or even
cross the line to heresy. Tatian's theology held God as a timeless
being without beginning, invisible, impalpable, the creator of
whatever is visible and material.[18] He embraced a concept of the

---

16 *Oration to the Greeks* 36, ed. Whittaker.

17 *Ibid.* 22.

18 *Ibid.* 4.2.

logos as the beginning of the universe, the "firstborn" work of
God. He embraced the notion of the resurrection of the flesh, an
essential Christian concept, but took the view that before birth
humans do not exist, but are simply latent in matter, and that in
the same way, after death revert to the earlier state of nonexistence. There is in his theology an aversion to the world and
to matter--"for the cosmos still pulls us, and through debility I
turn to matter"[19]--which can find parallel in some Greek thought
and in Christian mysticism. But the abstention from flesh, from
sexual activity and other precepts of self-denial which Tatian set
out for the community which he established in the East deviated
too strikingly from mainline Christianity to become accepted as
the disciplined churches established the parameters of what was
permissible teaching. Nor was it characteristic of Hellenism.
Philo's admiration for the Therapeutae of Egypt was not an expression of his Greek upbringing.

Too little remains of Tatian's writings to determine all he
taught. To the asceticism he seems to have added the Christian
endorsement of poverty, and more, acceptance of the worth even of
women, even old ones, and children to be taught;[20] and to the Greek
complaint that Christians talk absurdities among women and virgin
boys he makes no denial, riposting only with a list of Greek customs
he calls absurd themselves. There are enough similarities in his
writings to have made some moderns think that Tatian ought to be
grouped with the Gnostics or with those Christians of Gnostic persuasion, but he differs enough from the Gnostics whose ideas have
come to light recently that even to those with the most comprehensive sense of Gnosticism, his discipline and his group represent
another separate version of second-century Christianity.

It would be nice to know something about the social background
of the followers of Valentinus or other Gnostics of the second century, or even the users of the fourth-century Nag Hammadi texts,
but in view of the exiguous nature of evidence about the class of
the Christians in general it is hardly surprising that we have lost
trace of the members of the suppressed sect. We have the evidence
of the quality of the texts from Nag Hammadi to go on, but these,
according to Robinson, range from productions suggesting low cost

---

19 *Oration to the Greeks* 20.1.

20 *Ibid.* 32.1.

to others showing some elegance and craftsmanship.[21] Whoever they
were, however, it is clear today that their philosophical stance,
whatever its relation to Hellenism as it had evolved over a mil-
lennium, called them into opposition to the Christianity of the
fathers.

The authorities had good reason to repress people with these
ideas, and to suppress their teachings. The driving command to
obey the bishops and elders which we read in the letters of Ignatius
and Clement encountered a stubborn and argued resistance among
them, and the idea of a disciplined church which would protect and
propound the "truth" was completely alien to the idea of the *gnosis*.
In the churches and assemblies, either in their own or as part of
other groups, they operated along an understanding of Jesus' message which was very different from that of the writers of the texts
which are now orthodox, and even their manner of service struck
"regular" bishops as outrageous. In contrast to Ignatius' restriction to the bishop or his appointee of the celebration of the
Eucharist for it to be valid, the people called Gnostics recognized
no such authority, and preachers or readers at services were selected by lot on each occasion.[22] No one member of a congregation
had more authority than another, and even women could participate
fully and with as much authority as any male. Furthermore, the
belief that each person had the capability of achieving that mystic
"*gnosis*" or knowledge of the divine and the cosmos meant that the
official interpretation of God's actions and will or the meaning
of Jesus' words and deeds could be overridden or ignored in favor
of knowledge which was more direct. It is, in a way, a mystic's
version of the Socratic demand for the "therapy of the soul," at-
tending to one's spiritual state to ensure that the soul is as
good as it can be. As in the Socratic prescription, a life of
this sort is open to anyone--rich or poor, male or female, slave
or freeman--and with its achievement also possible for any, a
Christian community with Gnostic leanings could look to any member
for insight and leadership to the mystic knowledge.

To Christians who did not share this attitude, however, the
whole collection of Gnostics, their doctrines and ideas like them,
were anathema, because they propounded ideas of personal revelation

---

21   J. M. Robinson, ed., *The Nag Hammadi Library in English*
(Leiden 1977; New York 1981) 14-17 (= *NagHamLibEng*).

22   E. Pagels, *The Gnostic Gospels* (New York 1979) esp. 49-52.

which ran counter to the developing consensus endorsing episcopal
authority deriving ultimately from those who had known Jesus.
Furthermore, the elaborate cosmologies and the complex relationships between the true father and the various powers, emanations
and archons which we find in texts like those from Nag Hammadi
bear no connection with the Christological traditions which were
circulating by the end of the first century in the name of Matthew,
Mark, Luke and even John, while Marcion himself, although profes-
sedly cleaning up the act, presented nothing like that in his corrected *Luke*. Even Paul at his most pneumatic was a far cry from
Nag Hammadi. Once the response to the Marcionite text had created
the canon around 200, there was not only scriptural exclusion of
all these writings of Nag Hammadi type, but scriptural authority
for the rejection of their ideas. Within Christianity, the Nag
Hammadi mentality had to fight against the obstacles of office-
holders and an accepted tradition in order to win its way. What
would it encounter among the Greeks who had not yet accepted the
word?

Hellenism and the Nag Hammadi Mind

The texts which Mohammed Ali found in 1945 made a good deal
of our knowledge of Gnosticism "flesh," as it were, giving us books
through which to interpret these beliefs and with which to evaluate
the complaints of the orthodox, who for the most part had been the
only source of our knowledge of these groups and beliefs. Over the
centuries, what the church and others knew of the Gnostics had been
limited to what could be read in extracts--usually quite short--
quoted by the orthodox incident to their attacks, or, in some instances, longer summaries of Gnostic doctrines by Irenaeus and
others, although much of that, as we can now see from the Nag Hammadi texts, was not a misrepresentation of Gnostic doctrines and
ideas. The authorities had done their job well: there were no
texts, until the eighteenth-century finds of Bruce and Askew codices
and the 1896 acquisition of the Berlin Gnostic papyrus, with publication of this last completed only in 1955. In the light of the
apparent concern over Gnosticism in the early church, and in the
absence of texts, the Hermetic corpus assumed a disproportionate
relevance to Gnosticism, although at best only one text, the
Poimandres, could be said to have any clearly Gnostic ideas.

The general resemblance between the Hermetica and some aspects
of Gnostic ideas provided Greek texts which were believed to cast

light on Gnosticism, and justified connecting it with Hellenism,
so that, for example, Harnack could see it as the extreme Hellenization of Christianity. But increasing acquaintance with the British and Berlin texts showed the differences more clearly, so that
writers were forced to admit the Hermetica were "illuminated by a
clear and tranquil Hellenic philosophy quite unlike the doctrines
of our heretics,"[23] but still wanted to find the Hermetica related
to Gnosticism.[24] However, beyond a general participation in the
same kind of speculation which was not foreign to Philo and Plotinus, the Greek texts in the Hermetic Corpus are not Gnostic, for
they lack some of the most striking and particular aspects of
Gnostic texts, such as, for example, the emphasis on dualism. On
the other hand, some whose sense of "Gnosticism" goes beyond the
characteristics of the Nag Hammadi mentality will still include
the Hermetica as Gnostic, as they will also the Odes of Solomon
and the other hymns which contain some themes with resemblances
to Gnostic texts.

In any case, the Nag Hammadi texts provide a clear connection
between the Nag Hammadi mentality and Hellenism, for they were
translated from Greek texts, many or all of which are thought to
have been tracts originally composed in Greek, some of which are
still preserved in early papyrus fragments. We are still in the
first stages of evaluating their significance, for the political
and scholarly disputes over ownership and publication rights have
meant that it has been some thirty years before they could join
the community of knowledge. Translated and copied over the years
until they were hidden by their burial sometime around 400, they
are not all Christian and they need not be completely representative of a single system of belief, but there are enough connections
between the expressions of faith and doctrine in these texts to
show clear affinities between some doctrines attacked by mainstream
Christian writers and the ideas of the texts treasured by this
community in upper Egypt. But they are varied, and include a
translation of a short passage from Plato's *Republic*, two clearly

---

23 J. Doresse, *The Secret Books of the Egyptian Gnostics*
[trans. of *Les livres secrets des Gnostiques d'Egypte*, 1958]
(London 1960) 99.

24 *Ibid.*; "Semi-Gnostic," R. McL. Wilson, *Gnosis and the New
Testament* (Oxford 1968) 22. Hans Jonas, *The Gnostic Religion*, 2nd
ed. (Boston 1963) 147, cites especially Poimandres as Gnostic
cosmogony and anthropogony independent of the Christian Gnostics.

Hermetic tractates, *The Discourse on the Eighth and Ninth* and
Asclepius 21-29, as well as a number of treatises which do not
contain specifically Gnostic notions.

After a first glance at some of them, one might be prompted
to remark that Christianity could have offered more if some of
these ideas, rather than orthodoxy, had prevailed. The denial of
episcopal authority over doctrine and organization would have
militated against some of the worst excesses of Church discipline
over the centuries, and the endorsement of private belief and the
private conscience is certainly attractive today. Furthermore,
some of the specific assertions, particularly those attributed to
Jesus himself, strike a sympathetic chord in many. For example,
one tractate known as *The Gospel of Thomas*, not a gospel in the
style of those of the New Testament, assembles along with sayings
of Jesus which appear in the canonical gospels some that add
different dimensions to Jesus' message, as, for example,

> Jesus said, "If those who lead you say to you, 'See,
> the Kingdom is in the sky,' then the birds of the sky
> will precede you. If they say to you, 'It is in the
> sea,' then the fish will precede you. Rather, the
> Kingdom is inside of you, and it is outside of you. When
> you come to know yourselves, then you will become known,
> and you will realize that it is you who are the sons of
> the living Father. But if you will not know yourselves,
> you dwell in poverty and it is you who are that
> poverty.[25]

We should not be misled into seeing this as a survival of the old
Greek prescription to "know thyself," or a form of Socratic advice,
for it is clear here and elsewhere that knowing relates to the
understanding of oneself in terms of cosmology, knowing not only
the nature of humankind but knowing the Son, the Father, the "root
of all things," and these in Gnostic terms.[26] There is, however,
a pantheistic sense to this passage in *The Gospel of Thomas*, which
in fact has other sayings of this nature, as that in which Jesus
says not only that he is the light and the All, but: "Split a piece
of wood, and I am there. Lift up the stone, and you will find Me
there."[27]

----

25 Translation, T. O. Lambdin, in *NagHamLibEng* p. 118.

26 Cf. for examples, *The Dialogue of the Savior*, trans. H.
Koester and E. H. Pagels, *NagHamLibEng* p. 234, and *The Testimony
of Truth*, trans. B. A. Pearson, *NagHamLibEng* p. 411.

27 §77, *NagHamLibEng*, p. 126.

There are, however, other themes which some may not find so
attractive. There is the sense of hostility to mankind on the
part of the Powers or of God--weaker in power than the Father but
no less real or effective. This aspect of belief turns up in many
texts, and is particularly notable in the interpretation of the
fall from paradise, when the serpent persuaded Eve to eat of the
fruit of the Tree of Knowledge. Of God's command and retribution
the text asks:

> But of what sort is this God? First [he] envied Adam
> that he should eat from the tree of knowledge...after-
> wards he said, "Let us cast him [out] of this place,
> lest he eat of the tree of life and live for ever."
> Surely he has shown himself to be a malicious envier.[28]

As *The Hypostasis of the Archons* tells the tale, the Serpent is
imbued with the "Female Spiritual Principle," and tells Eve that
the chief of the Rulers forbade the eating of the fruit out of
jealousy; and the Gnostic interpretation of the expulsion from
Eden is judgment on the condition of man in the world, as the
Rulers

> threw Mankind into great distraction and into a life of
> toil, so that their Mankind might be occupied by worldly
> affairs and might not have the opportunity of being
> devoted to the Holy Spirit.[29]

The world in which we live is the work of malevolent spirits,
who impede the knowledge of the ultimate, the Father, the Holy
Spirit who can be reached by a transcendent knowledge which Jesus
both is and brings. The knowledge--*gnosis*--is in fact a hidden
truth which comes through Jesus:

> He reveals what is hidden of him--what is hidden of him
> is his Son--so that through the mercies of the Father
> the aeons may know him and cease laboring in search of
> the Father, resting there in him, knowing that this is
> rest. Having filled the deficiency, he abolished the
> form--the form of it is the world, that in which he
> served. For the place where there is envy and strife
> is a deficiency, but the place where (there is) Unity
> is a perfection. Since the deficiency came into being
> because the Father is known, from that moment on the
> deficiency will no longer exist.[30]

---

28 Trans. S. Giversen, B. A. Pearson, *NagHamLibEng* p. 412.

29 Trans. R. A. Bullard, *NagHamLibEng* p. 156.

30 *The Gospel of Truth*, trans. G. W. MacRae, *NagHamLibEng*
p. 41.

This interpretation of Christianity is preoccupied with this perception of the Father through and in the Son, focusing a religious
life on a revelation of the nature of reality through Jesus, expressed, as in *The Gospel of Thomas* 17-18:

> And Jesus said, "I shall give you what no eye has
> seen and what no ear has heard and what no hand has
> touched and what has never occurred to the human mind."
>   The disciples said to Jesus, "Tell us how our end
> will be."
>   Jesus said, "Have you discovered, then, the begin-
> ning, that you look for the end? For where the begin-
> ning is, there will the end be. Blessed is he who will
> take his place in the beginning; he will know the end
> and will not experience death."[31]

This preoccupation with knowledge--self-knowledge of humanity and
of the Father--is inextricably linked with the conception of the
direct perception of each individual and rejection of ecclesiastical authority. And the emphasis on salvation achieved only through
knowledge--mystical *gnosis*--eliminates any serious concern with the
kind of ethical issues which emerge in at least some mainstream
Christian writing, undoubtedly the reason that ethics assumes so
unimportant a position in these works of the Nag Hammadi library.

However much the emphasis on *gnosis* and the therapy of the
soul may bear similarity to or have roots in Platonism or neoplatonism, so that Gnostics could find themselves--if not their
colleagues--comfortable in the circle around Plotinus, the
notion of the world as the arena of conflict between malevolent
powers and a good deity is fundamentally alien to Hellenism. In
the thousand years between Homer and Plotinus, that idea hardly
appealed as an explanation for the existence of evil in the world.
Whether the cosmic order was screened from man, as in Homeric
thought and Sophoclean writings, whether the rules of the gods
could be known as Aeschylus asserted, or didn't exist, according
to Euripides, Greeks did not adopt anything like Persian dualism.[32]
Even if Gnostic "evil" was, as Pagels suggests, emotional harm like
that treated by the Stoics and Epicureans, rather than the traditional Greek evils of pain, misfortune, death and the like,[33] it
emerged out of the dualism of conflict between opposing forces, an
explanation which would have occurred neither to Epicurus nor the

---

31   *NagHamLibEng* p. 120.

32   The *Prometheus*, Aeschylean or not, is the major work that
comes closest to this theme of conflict between good and evil divinities, but is hardly an exemplar of dualism.

33   Pagels, *op. cit.* (n. 22) 172.

Stoic masters. One direct example of response to the dualism in
question on the part of the Hellenic tradition comes from an
attack on Manicheeism penned in the latter part of the third century by Alexander of Lycopolis.[34] Alexander treated the Manichaeans as Christian, and while he did not find Christianity in itself
uncongenial, he took the Manichaeans to task, *inter alia*, as examples of philosophical failure. Christian philosophy, he says in
chapter 1, is chiefly devoted to ethical instruction, but it is
ethical exhortation without establishing principles. While ordinary people may make great progress in virtue, later adherents
split into sects and thus the leaders of sects and ordinary people
are inclined to internal strife in the absence of norms to decide
issues; there is a striving for novelty, a conversion of philosophy
into a hopelessly complex thing. Alexander himself, however, uses
not uncomplex Platonist cosmology, but of the middle, non-Plotinian
tradition, in his refutation of the dualism he attacks, and his
arguments against aspects of the doctrine come from the Greek tradition. For example, in attacking the notion that the moon takes
divine power in its first half, new to full moon, and then in the
second half transmits it to the sun which sends it on to God,
Alexander draws on Greek astronomy, and in allowing reasonableness
to Christ's crucifixion as a means of remission of sins, on analogy
to sacrifice for a city's safety, he denies its validity as a means
of teaching, when words would serve.

To those imbued with the traditions of Hellenism, the expressions of dualism ran counter to all the assumptions with which
Greek philosophy and literature dyed their intellects. Furthermore, the modes of thought, the absence of verbal argument, the
apocalyptic character and the revelatory cosmologies of so much of
the Nag Hammadi style of communication made it fundamentally uncongenial to those reared in the traditions of Hellenism. That we
find some of these characteristics exhibited to an extent in
Plotinus may help explain the limited extent of that philosopher's
influence and audience, which was almost non-existent in the century after his death.[35] Alexander's reaction to the doctrine of

---

34 *An Alexandrian Platonist Against Dualism. Alexander of
Lycopolis' Treatise 'Critique of the Doctrines of Manichaeus,'*
trans. and comm. P. W. Van der Horst and J. Mansfield (Leiden 1974).

35 J. M. Rist, "Basil's Neoplatonism: Its Background and
Nature," *Basil of Caesarea: Christian, Humanist, Ascetic. A Six-
teen-Hundredth Anniversary Symposium*, Pontifical Institute of
Mediaeval Studies (Toronto 1981) 137-220.

crucifixion as pedagogy illustrates the Hellenic reaction to
transcendent *gnosis* in contrast to the use of argument. The
revelatory nature of the Nag Hammadi texts, illustrated by even
so non-cosmological a tractate as the *Gospel of Thomas* with Jesus'
promise of what eye has not seen, ear has not heard, mind has
never met, are in direct opposition to the manner of achieving
knowledge on which the long tradition of Hellenism depended.

While we are too late in the history of Greek philosophy to
find much more than Alexander's Hellenism in response to this tradition outside of Christian writers, we need little more than the
most casual perusal of the Nag Hammadi texts to remind us how
fundamentally alien they are to anything we have read in the Greek
tradition. In the generation before Alexander, Celsus' attack on
Christianity depended in some significant measure on an attack on
doctrines like these as Christian. Not only did Celsus the
Hellene attack Cainites, Ophites, Simon Magus, and doctrines of
multiple heavens and the like, all part of or similar to the
traditions which produced the Nag Hammadi texts, the good Greek
Origen would have no part of them either and excluded them from
the Christian community.[36] Earlier than this, the Greek tradition
was for the most part happily innocent of this kind of writing.
Nothing in Plutarch suggests he ever heard of any of it, and the
absence of citation of this polymath in the mountain of citations
produced by the students of Gnosticism is a silence which surely
must be given some weight. And Lucian's satire, even if it can be
pressed to allude to contemporary philosophical speculation at all,
can at best be made out to refer to revelatory ideas only in the
vaguest way, and then, of course, as an attack.[37]

So there is an argument from silence, and though it naturally
would not be convincing in itself, it reinforces what we conclude
from the work of Alexander and Celsus and from a comparison between
Hellenism and the Nag Hammadi tradition. The two had very little

---

36 *Contra Celsum* 3.13; 5.62; 6.21, 24-26; 7.40.

37 C. Robinson, *Lucian* (London 1979) 48-52, representing the
second century as "an age of compulsive emotional communication
with the supernatural" (p. 48) and noting that Lucian reflects the
prevailing mood "in many ways not at all," finds nothing stronger
than a statement in the *Menippus* that the content of the revelation from the eastern magician is no better than a commonplace.
If Lucian knew about the elaborate dualisms, complex cosmologies,
multiple heavens and the like which characterize the third century
traditions, he certainly chose to make no allusion to them.

common ground, and those who occupied Hellenic terrain took few
steps toward the other. By and large, any of those educated in
the Greek tradition who show familiarity with the other are hostile and denunciatory. The texts of the Hermetic Corpus and those
like the *Odes of Solomon* illustrate affinities to Gnosticism, but
they are as close to the speculations of neo- and middle Platonists.
They represent a mind-set in later Hellenism which developed out of
the early tradition, but for the most part they originate out of
philosophical rather than religious traditions. The Greeks who
wrote most of the originals of the Nag Hammadi translations, on
the other hand, cannot have been very representative of the
Hellenic tradition. Insofar as they are Hellenic, they represent
a very exceptional tradition.

The Corpus of "Gnostic" Texts

        A summary description of the Nag Hammadi library is impres-
sive: 12 codices, 8 leaves from a thirteenth, over a thousand pages
carrying 52 tractates in all. Even allowing for duplication and
excluding the fragment of translation of Plato's *Republic*, there
are 45 separate works which exhibit, in one way or another, characteristics of the tradition we have been discussing. The discovery multiplied many times our corpus of texts in this tradition,
and it is small wonder that they have inspired such an outpouring
of discussion and scholarship over the last forty years. But we
should not be misled by the number of library shelves now given
over to "Gnosticism." Translations of the Nag Hammadi library,
with introductions and indices, can be fitted into a book of under
500 nicely printed pages. It is a much smaller book than the one
Porphyry made out of the work of Plotinus, or the volumes which
make up, to cite pointedly, Philo Judaeus.

        Besides related material like the Hermetic Corpus, the *Odes*,
The Sentences of Sextus and other similar material which has turned
up in manuscript forms, a number of texts besides the Nag Hammadi
tractates have become known through attestation by papyrus fragments. It will be helpful to list briefly all the works in the
tradition which are attested by surviving manuscripts[38] of the

---

        38 But not including Gnostic works alluded to or reported by
Christian writers and others. The *Allogenes* and *Zostrianos* referred
to in Porphyry's *Life of Plotinus* do, in fact, seem to have turned
up among the Nag Hammadi texts, of which a number have been equated
with varying measures of certainty to tracts mentioned by Christian
writers.

first four centuries, incident to an assessment of its quantity in comparison to texts in other traditions, Christian, both Coptic and Greek, and Hellenism in general. In dealing with the Gnostic material, I take my time-frame liberally, and include such important texts as those in the fifth-century Berlin Gnostic Papyrus (BG, see below). In the list below, titles not specifically attested in the mss. are enclosed in quotation marks, works designated by the asterisk are conceded by modern commentators to contain no specifically "Gnostic" themes, and items in the Nag Hammadi list marked § are also attested in other mss.

Nag Hammadi Codices

(BG = Berlin Gnostic Codex 8502; BM = British Museum; NHC = Nag Hammadi Codex; NHS = Nag Hammadi Studies)

The Prayer of the Apostle Paul, NHC I 1

"The Apocryphon of James," NHC I 2

The Gospel of Truth, NHC I 3; XII 2

The Treatise on the Resurrection, NHC I 4

"The Tripartite Tractate," NHC I 5

§ The Apocryphon of John, NHC II 1; III 1; IV 1; BG 8502.2

§ The Gospel of Thomas, NHC II 2; *P. Oxy.* I 654; 655

The Gospel of Philip, NHC II 3

The Hypostasis of the Archons, NHC II 4

"On the Origin of the World," NHC II 5; XIII 2

The Exegesis on the Soul, NHC II 6

The Book of Thomas the Contender, NHC II 7

The Gospel of the Egyptians, NHC III 2; IV 2

Eugnostos the Blessed, NHC III 3; V 1

§ The Sophia of Jesus Christ, NHC III 4; BG 8502.3; *P. Oxy.* VIII 1081

The Dialogue of the Savior, NHC III 5

The Apocalypse of Paul, NHC V 2

The "First" Apocalypse of James, NHC V 3

The "Second" Apocalypse of James, NHC V 4

The Apocalypse of Adam, NHC V 5

* The Acts of Peter and the Twelve Apostles, NHC VI 1

* The Thunder, Perfect Mind, NHC VI 2

Authoritative Teaching, NHC VI 3

The Concept of Our Great Power, NHC VI 4

"The Discourse on the Eighth and Ninth," NHC VI 6

§*"The Prayer of Thanksgiving," NHC VI 7[39]

§ Asclepius: "21-29," NHC VI 8[40]

  The Paraphrase of Shem, NHC VII 1

  The Second Treatise of the Great Seth, NHC VII 2

  The Apocalypse of Peter, NHC VII 3

 *The Teachings of Silvanus, NHC VII 4

  The Three Steles of Seth, NHC VII 5

  Zostrianos, NHC VIII 1

  The Letter of Peter to Philip, NHC VIII 2

  Melchizedek, NHC IX 1

  "Norea," NHC IX 2

  "The Testimony of Truth," NHC IX 3

  Marsanes, NHC X 1

  The Interpretation of Knowledge, NHC XI 1

  "A Valentinian Exposition," with "On the Anointing," "On Baptism A" and "B," "On the Eucharist A" and "B," NHC XI 2

  Allogenes, NHC XI 3

  Hypsiphrone, NHC XI 4

§*The Sentences of Sextus, NHC XII 1[41]

  Trimorphic Protennoia, NHC XIII 1

  "Fragments," NHC XII 3

Texts Not Attested at Nag Hammadi

  The Gospel of Mary, BG 8502.1; *P. Ryl.* III 463

*The Acts of Peter, BG 8502.4[42]

  The Acts of Thomas, Lipsius-Bonnet, *Acta Apostolorum Apocrypha* II 2

  "The First Book of Jeu" (= The Great Logos Corresponding to Mysteries), Bruce Codex[43]

---

39   A Hermetic prayer known also from mss. in Greek and Latin versions.

40   A Hermetic text earlier attested in Latin, with some Greek quotations.

41   Attested also in Latin (Rufinus), Greek, Syriac, Armenian, and with seven sentences in Ethiopian. Only the Latin and Coptic represent the bulk of the original collection; cf. P.-H. Poirier, *Les sentences de Sextus (NH XII 1)*, Bibl. Copte de Nag Ham., Section Textes 11 (Quebec 1983) 12-17.

42   I cite this non-Gnostic text only because it is found with the three Gnostic works in the Berlin Gnostic papyrus.

43   C. Schmidt, V. MacDermot, *The Books of Jeu and the Untitled Text in the Bruce Codex*, Nag Hammadi Studies 13 (Leiden 1978); the texts incorporated fragments of two hymns and a fragment on the passage of the soul, which I do not enumerate as separate texts.

"The Second Book of Jeu," Bruce Codex

"Untitled Text," or "Setheus," Bruce Codex

Pistis Sophia, Askew Codex[44]

Hymn of Poimandres, (with other liturgical prayers) *BKT* VI 6.1

"Naassene Psalm," *P. Fay.* 2 (cf. *P. Lond. Lit.* 240)

"Invocation to Divinity," *P. Oxy.* XII 1566

"Fragment of a Tractate," Kahle, *Bala'izah* 52

"Gnostic Text," *Miscellanea Giovanni Galbiati* 2 (Milan 1951) 182-188

"Gnostic Text," *Miscellanea Giovanni Galbiati* 2 (Milan 1951) 182-188 verso

"Gnostic Fragment," *P. Oxy.* I 4

(Apocryphon) of Moses, *P. Leid.* II W

"Gnostic," BM 522[45]

"Gnostic Amulet," *P. Oxy.* VI 924

"Gnostic Amulet," *P. Oxy.* VII 1060

"Gnostic Amulet," *P. Princ.* II 107; a later example: *P. Oxy.* XVI 2063: sixth century

The number of Gnostic works listed, in Greek or Coptic, comes to 64, in at least 78 texts when duplicates of the same works (apart from later mss.) are added in. I have not included the fragment of the *Republic*, of course, and both figures should probably be reduced by 6 to deduct the texts which have no specifically Gnostic material. It is still apparently not a bad tally until it is compared with the numbers of identified Christian texts listed by Kahle[46] for Coptic and Van Haelst[47] for Greek, on the Christian side, or for Hellenism, with the statistics in the tables drawn up almost twenty years ago by Willis.[48] The vast preponderance of

---

44 *Koptisch-Gnostische Schriften I, Die Pistis Sophia, Die beiden Bücher des Jeu, Unbekanntes Altgnostisches Werk. Griech. Christ. Schriftst.* 13 (Berlin 1905) trans. C. Schmidt; 3 aufl. W. Till. *Griech. Christ. Schriftst.* 45 (Berlin 1959).

45 I have not seen this text. It is listed by P. E. Kahle, *Bala'izah. Coptic Texts from Deir el-Bala'izah in Upper Egypt* (London 1954) 1.273.

46 *Ibid.*, Appendix I: A List of Early Coptic Manuscripts, 1.269-78.

47 J. van Haelst, *Catalogue des Papyrus Littéraires Juifs et Chrétiens*, Université de Paris IV Paris-Sorbonne, Série Papyrologie 1 (Paris 1976). Greek texts listed below are identified by Van Haelst's numbers.

48 "A Census of the Literary Papyri From Egypt," *GRBS* 9 (1968) (1968) 205-41.

the Gnostic material is Coptic, but even comparing the whole body
of material with the testimonia of Coptic documentation, we find
the Nag Hammadi and other Gnostic texts outweighed by conventional
Christian Coptic texts predating the fifth century. The evidence
on the Coptic side only begins with the few third-century texts
emerging from the then very small community of native (as against
Greek) Christians in Egypt. From that century Kahle found nothing
but 1 text of the OT representing 2 works (Amos and Hosea) in the
form of a Greek-Coptic glossary, and he classified as third- or
fourth-century 2 more OT mss. (one of Ecclesiastes, the other
containing Song of Songs, Lamentations and Ecclesiastes in an Old
Fayumic translation, along with Greek versions of other works).[49]
Other early Coptic texts attest the existence in Coptic by the
fourth century of: all the gospels but Mark, Acts, the Pauline
and Catholic epistles--21 letters, and Revelations, to the total
of 26; of at least 25 OT works, including the 12 minor prophets;
apocryphal, patristic and miscellaneous, 12 works; (plus 3 works
not specifically Christian in content). There were, in summary,
at least 63 works translated into Coptic known by Kahle in 1954,
and, omitting Gnostic texts and uncertain fragments, his tallies
of individual manuscripts found, including the scanty third-
century material, may be summarized by the following figures:
NT - 17; OT (including Ps. and LXX apocrypha) - 21; Apocrypha,
Patristic, Miscellaneous - 12. To his totals may be added 8 more
fourth-century Coptic mss. of which I know, without having engaged
in a thorough search, which attest 6 OT works and 3 NT works.[50]

The picture on the Greek side is, naturally, one of much
greater domination by orthodox Christian works. For the second
and third centuries alone (and adopting the most conservative
dates), almost the entire NT canon is represented: 4 gospels, Acts,
9 letters of Paul (Rom., Heb., I, II Cor., Eph., Gal., Phil., Col.,
I Thess.); Titus, James, II John, and Revelations, to a total of 18
works.[51] To these 18 NT works we must add 8 identified patristic

---

49   See below, van Haelst no. 263.

50   *P. Bodmer* III, John; VI, Proverbs; XVI, Exodus; XVIII,
Deuteronomy; XXI, Joshua; XXIII, Isaiah; P. Mich. inv. 3521, John
(E. Husselman, *The Gospel of John in Fayumic Coptic*, Univ. Mich.
Kelsey Mus. Studies 2, 1962); P. Mich. inv. 3520 ined., Ecclesias-
tes, I John, II Peter (Husselman, *op. cit.* p. 43 n. 18).

51   371, 497, 534, 547, 555, 565.

papyri dated to the second or third centuries.[52] Then there are
4 OT works which can be identified with complete confidence as
Christian: Eccles. in a ms. with Coptic OT works and the text of
Acts of Paul,[53] an Isaiah with Old Fayumic glosses,[54] and Chester
Beatty VI with Numbers and Deuteronomy in a lot made up of Christian works, and showing the Alexandrinus and Vaticanus recension
in addition to being a codex. Then there are 4 Christian apocrypha
of the third century,[55] and a miscellany of some 10 or more liturgical or theological items which are called Christian.[56] This
brings us to a total of 44 works attested in Christian use before
the end of the third century. When we include in the Christian
corpus 27 OT works in codex form dated before the end of the third
century, we have almost the whole of Scripture, in the Christian
corpus, representing 25 works more to bring the Christian "library"
to a total of 69. And a tally of separate New and Old Testament,
apocrypha, and patristic papyri, yields another 54 texts of this
material copied before the end of the third century, making up,
with the works cited, 84 individual mss. Thus at least 69 separate
works and at least 84 individual texts in Christian hands survived
the disruptions of the Diocletianic persecutions at the end of the
third century, a figure obtained without considering any of the
texts dated third to fourth century,[57] and predating the growth
of the Christian community after Constantine which brought the

---

52   Clement of Alexandria?, *On Prophecy?*, 636; *Shepherd of
Hermas*, 657; Irenaeus, *Adv. Haer.* 671; Julius Africanus, *Kestoi*,
674; Origen, 3 or 2 + 1 misattributed texts, 688, 691; Tatian,
Diatessaron, 699; Theonas?, *Ep. vs. Manich.*, 700.

53   263.

54   293.

55   An unknown gospel of Johannine Type, 586; Acts of Paul
605; a gospel episode relating to Peter's denial of Christ, 589;
and a gospel close to that of Peter, 592.

56   I use the conservative figure of 10 for the works which
may be culled from 850, 962, 1036, 1108, 1121, 1122, 1130, 1133,
1137, 1145, 1151, 1152, 1156.

57   NT papyri dated either III/IV or variously III and IV by
different editors: 21; OT papyri so dated: 9; NT apocrypha: 4;
OT apocrypha: 1; patristic: 5; liturgical and unidentified Christian texts: 5; total: 45.

wealth of material of the fourth century[58]--a century which, it
should be noted, produced much of our Gnostic material--and which,
when added in, would bring the total to at least 237 pieces. Even
allowing for some of this material having come from Gnostic readers,
the preponderance of canonical and "main-line" Christian materials
over that which could be considered Gnostic is so great as to show
that even in Egypt, Gnostic interests accounted for only a small
proportion of Christian reading.

The relation of the Gnostic materials to the wider world of
Hellenism is much easier to see, thanks to Professor Willis' yeo-
man work in categorizing the texts in Pack[2]. As his table III
reveals, there are 1881[59] Greek literary papyri which can be dated
to the first three centuries, a figure to be contrasted to the 84
Christian papyri which represent less than five percent of that
number. While I do not suggest that the proportions represent
the proportions of Christians among the literate, it is interesting
that the figure will not be far off that of the percentage of
Christians in the population adduced by Bagnall. It is perhaps
more significant to contrast the figure for Christian texts dated
III/IV or IV, 153, with the total for Greek literary texts of the
fourth century, 187.[60] Even allowing for the inexact match between Willis' slotting texts as either III or IV in his tables,
and my own procedure of including those of III/IV as IV for classification purposes, it is obvious that the proportion of Christian
materials rises dramatically from the end of the third century on,
as would be expected. But Gnostic materials bulk very small
against the total of non-religious texts, and if all non-Greek
texts were excluded, would dwindle almost to nil. Gnostic texts
not only are negligible in comparison to the corpus of Greek
literary papyri, they represent a relatively small ratio against
the total of Christian texts and, although the corpus of Christian
in Greek vastly outweighs that in Coptic in our period, it is Coptic which produces most of the Gnostic material, and there is very
little at all on the Greek side.

---

58 Accepting as fourth-century all texts for which dates as
late as that century have been suggested, and excluding all those
for which later (i.e. IV/V or after) have been suggested by any
editor, the minimum numbers are: NT: 22; OT 36; NT apocrypha: 6;
OT apocrypha: 5; patristic: 12; liturgical and miscellaneous: 37;
total: 108.

59 1896, less 15 Patristic texts of the period revealed by
Table VII.

60 Subtracting 17 Patristic texts from Willis' figure of
204 in Table III.

The Importance of the Gnostics

While it is. as I have said, impossible to prove a negative,
I think that the evidence relating to Gnosticism now shifts the
burden of proof onto those who would argue that the movement occupied a very large place in the Christian community or had any
significant impact among the Greeks. As I have shown, what I call
the "Nag Hammadi" mentality is out of place, and indeed ran counter to most of what we find in early Christian writing. It is
certainly out of step with most of Hellenism. On these grounds
alone we ought to be suspicious of any portrayal of the Gnosticism
of the Nag Hammadi mentality as having any important influence on
the development of later Hellenism, whether Christian or otherwise.
When we take that suspicion and check it against the realia, which
are the actual texts left to us, we find the suspicion more than
justified. "Gnostic" writing constitutes a negligible proportion
of the Greek texts we have, and even such papyri as the Oxyrhynchus
fragments of the Gospel of Thomas exhibit the less extreme characteristics of the Nag Hammadi texts. In the body of religious
writing attested in texts of the first four centuries of our era,
Greek or Coptic, the Nag Hammadi materials and texts like them are
no more than about a quarter of the quantity of more regular
Christian papyri.

In the small numbers which the Christians made up until the
church's growth in the third or fourth century, the Gnostics even
in such number still probably represented an uncomfortably large
group. At a time when the leadership, men like Irenaeus, Ignatius
and Origen were trying desperately to impose order on this group
so prone to disagreement, doctrinal dispute and schism, members who
could look to a distinguished leader like Valentinus and whose
ideas were related to those of a significant enough group like the
followers of Marcion could hardly be ignored. So the early fathers
who were concerned to establish an orthodoxy were constrained to
devote a significant amount of their writing to attacks on Gnostic
doctrines, and by this perhaps disproportionate attention have
left us the exaggerated picture of the importance of the Gnostics.
Insofar as they were important or offered any conceivable threat
by their numbers, they did so at a time when the numbers of Christians overall still made up a small portion of the overall population. Once the church grew and spread through a large proportion
of the population, the Gnostic group failed to keep pace, re-
strained, I have no doubt, by all those factors militating against

acceptance of their ideology which I have already adduced in the
first part of this paper. They were easily suppressed in the
fourth century, and the group which buried its texts at Nag
Hammadi did so, in all probability, because they could find no
safe place to put them nor enough reliable people to protect them.

UNIVERSITY OF TORONTO   ALAN E. SAMUEL

IN SEARCH OF VALENTINUS

BY

G. C. STEAD

THE researches of the past thirty years have yielded some valuable new insights into the theology of the Valentinians, but have done little to relieve the obscurity which surrounds Valentinus himself. The outlines of the problem are familiar enough. We possess only a few fragments of Valentinus's own writings, transmitted by Clement of Alexandria, Hippolytus, and Marcellus of Ancyra,[1] together with a few biographical details. On the other hand there are complex and circumstantial accounts of the Valentinian system, provided by Irenaeus, Hippolytus, and others, which agree in broad outline despite many differences of detail. To these can be added a collection of fragments ascribed to Theodotus, made and annotated by Clement, and the fragments of Heracleon, mostly drawn from Origen's *Commentary on St. John*, collected by A. E. Brooke in 1891.

The problem is that the fragments of Valentinus, taken by themselves, would give no ground for supposing anything but a Platonizing[2] biblical theologian of some originality, whose work hardly strayed beyond the still undefined limits of Christian orthodoxy; and this squares with the report[3] that Valentinus had hopes of being made Bishop of Rome, but was passed over, despite his acknowledged talents, not, we are told, on the ground of unorthodoxy, but in favour of a candidate who obtained the post *ex martyrii praerogativa*, in recognition of his status as a confessor. On the other hand Irenaeus and Hippolytus present us with a highly complex and manifestly heretical mythology, in which an elaborate system of heavenly powers is propounded and the Jesus of the Gospels is fragmented and displaced. Half a century ago E. de Faye[4] could argue that the contrast between

---

[1] The short work *De sancta ecclesia* long attributed to Anthimus of Nicomedia is now assigned to Marcellus; see M. Richard, *MScRel* 6 (1949) 5-28. M. Simonetti (*RSLR* 9 [1973] 313ff.), who is critical of other attributions to Marcellus, accepts this.

[2] Cf. Tertullian, *Carn.* 20; *Praescr.* 30.

[3] Tertullian, *Adv. Val.* 4; cf. A. Hilgenfeld, *Die Ketzergeschichte des Urchristentums Urkundlich Dargestellt* (Leipzig, 1884) 284-87.

[4] *Gnostiques et Gnosticisme* (Paris, 1913).

these two modes of thought is so extreme that the developed
Valentinian system must be sharply distinguished from the teaching
of Valentinus himself, and that reliable information about this latter
can only be gathered from the fragments. More recently critical opinion
has tended to follow F. Sagnard, who showed that the various reports
of Valentinian teaching, though daunting in their complexity, do
manifest a very large measure of overall agreement; and clearly the
simplest way of explaining this agreement is to postulate that at least
the main elements in the system can be traced back to Valentinus
himself.

Very shortly after the publication of two important works by
Sagnard[5] the contents of the Nag Hammadi library became available
in some degree to specialists, and reports of them began to reach
the general public. Some of the newly found works were quickly
recognized as Valentinian;[6] and this recognition encouraged scholars
to compare them with the accounts of the fully developed Valentinian
system preserved by the ecclesiastical writers; at this point they were
influenced partly by a perfectly proper desire for economy in hypotheses,
partly by the then prevailing trend of scholarship—in which of course
the distinguished French scholar I have mentioned was joined by
other notable authorities. This development, as it seems to me, has
led to an overconfident assimilation of the new sources to the old,
in which points of agreement have been emphasized and elaborated,
while inconsistencies and omissions in the evidence have been, not
indeed ignored, but underrated. Thus the magnificent edition of the
Tripartite Tractate devotes a great deal of space in the notes to quoting
Irenaeus and Hippolytus on various details of the Valentinian system;
it does not stress the possibility that this particular author may be
using a different and possibly simpler set of ideas. And in other
documents the literary character of the work is invoked, perhaps
rightly, to explain why no detailed agreement can be expected.

Two other complicating factors may be mentioned. First, there are
problems of dating, often discussed in the context of the question
whether there was a pre-Christian gnosticism. It might seem that a
highly elaborate system, such as that which Irenaeus ascribes to
Ptolemaeus, could not be in any way convincing unless large elements

---

[5] *La Gnose Valentinienne et le témoinage de Saint Irénée* (Paris, 1947); *Clément
d'Alexandrie : Extraits de Theodote* (SC 23; Paris, 1948).

[6] Especially the *Gospel of Truth*, the *Treatise on Resurrection*, and the *Gospel of
Philip*; possibly others; see R. Kasser et al. (ed.), *Tractatus Tripartitus* (Bern, 1973) 1. 311.

of it were already familiar; and more generally, that the complex gnostic mythologies presuppose a process of development extending over several generations. But the time interval between Valentinus and Ptolemaeus seems too short to accommodate such a development, unless one postulates some further factor; thus the Valentinian system may have borrowed some elements from an already complicated mythology such as that found in the *Apocryphon of John*. But if Valentinus adopted this material, why does it leave so little trace in the fragments? If some later writer, how did it come to influence so many different exponents of Valentinian ideas?

Secondly, it is of course oversimple to picture the history of gnostic thought as a one-way process of complication and accretion. This has to some extent been recognized; thus in some of the newly discovered works, where details of the fully developed Valentinian system seem to be presupposed but are not elaborated, and at the same time ideas characteristic of orthodox Christianity are introduced which the fully developed systems either ignore or preclude, such cases have been sometimes explained as representing a 'primitive' or 'original' phase of gnosticism, and so as antedating the full development, sometimes in terms of 'rechristianization',[7] as if a writer who makes rather slight and incidental allusions to gnostic ideas must himself at some time have accepted the developed system in all its complexity, and later have partly discarded it in the light of a growing sympathy with orthodox churchmen. Such a process is of course perfectly possible; but to assume it may be a sign of undue reliance on genetic explanations. It seems to me that there is very little necessary connexion between complexity and date, and that more allowance needs to be made for differences in education, background, and temperament between different writers. Those writers who had an uninhibited liking for complex and pretentious mythology could construct a very elaborate system in a few years at most, given that the fashion was established; the longer version of the *Apocryphon of John* might serve as an example. Others, of a somewhat more critical turn of mind, may have formulated complex systems as a result of a scholastic attempt to remove contradictions by a synthesizing process; Ptolemaeus, for instance, in the system reported by Irenaeus, shows such traits, as I have suggested elsewhere.[8] Once again, a writer may be prepared to

---

[7] See M. L. Peel (ed.), *The Epistle to Rheginos* [= *Treatise on Resurrection*] (London, 1969) 179-80, and Kasser, *Tractatus Tripartitus*, 314.

[8] 'The Valentinian Myth of Sophia', *JTS* N.S. 20 (1969) 89-90.

profess allegiance to a system in a particular work for a particular
purpose without committing himself to it as a permanence; the writings
of Philo and Plutarch abound with such cases, and it is more than
possible that Valentinus adopted a similar attitude towards gnostic
mythology; he may have both promoted and stood aloof from a
complex theology which was already in being.

Failing some totally unforeseen further discovery, there will be no
quick solution to these problems; but we may try to throw light on
them by enquiry from two directions. First, can anything fresh be
said about the Valentinus fragments in the light of our increased
understanding of the philosophy, and especially the Platonism, of the
second century A.D.? Secondly, what light do the new sources provide
if we are open to the possibility that the Valentinian movement may
have been a good deal less homogeneous and more flexible than some
recent critics have suggested? Is it possible to close the gap between
Valentinus and the developed systems in the light of our new discoveries?

Our best information about Valentinus comes from the six fragments
quoted by Clement, together with his introductory and supplementary
comments. In fragments 1, 2, and 4-6[9] he professes to quote
Valentinus's exact words; and it seems not improbable that he is
using two written sources. Nos. 1-3 are each drawn from a letter,
though only no. 3 gives the lemma, 'Letter to Agathopus'; nos. 4
and 6 specify a homily, and no. 5 follows so closely after no. 4 in
Clement's text that despite a certain change of subject it may well
come from the same source.

Such scanty material, of course, can easily be overworked and
suggest ill-founded conclusions; but some facts about Valentinus seem
reasonably well established. I have called him a biblical Platonist. The
use of a Greek Genesis in fr. 1 is obvious enough, though of course this
text was used by gnostics of many different schools. But St. Matthew's
Gospel seems to appear in fr. 2; there is a suggestion of 19:17 in
εἷς δέ ἐστιν ὁ ἀγαθός, of 5:8 in the concluding declaration that the
pure in heart shall see God, and of 12:45 in the image of the human
heart invaded by many devils. These parallels have been duly noted
by Stählin and Völker. More tentatively we might suggest that the
'docetic' description of Jesus absorbing all his food without remainder

---

[9] I follow W. Völker's numeration (*Quellen zur Geschichte der christlichen Gnosis*;
Tübingen, 1932). Hilgenfeld's is the same for nos. 1-4, usefully includes Clement's
comments in no. 5, gives the same no. 6 but a different 7, from Eulogius, which
Völker omits; thus V. 7, 8, = H. 8, 9, while V. 9 is not in H.

could be based on an eccentric reading of Matt 7:19, or perhaps on a derived text in which this phrase was taken out of context, καθαρίζων πάντα τὰ βρώματα. Jesus did not simply declare that all food was clean (a literal-minded exegete could draw bizarre conclusions from this interpretation, since any educated Greek would know about omnivorous tribesmen, and about philosophical apologists for cannibalism!);[10] Jesus purified and so digested all that he ate, and formed an exception to the rule stated in Matt 7:19a. Presumably also fr. 6 intends some allusion to a written collection of scriptures current in the Church, though the immediate contrast is that between secular writings and the law which is metaphorically inscribed on the heart; there may be faint echoes here of Rom 2:15 and of Hos 2:25, which is quoted at Rom 9:25.

As for Valentinus's Platonism, we must of course note the comparative depreciation of the visible world, which is contrasted with the 'living aeon' in fr. 5, and which the 'children of life' must annul or dissolve (fr. 4); this general notion is once again hardly distinctive, and it is pointed up by the biblically based suggestion that the creation or moulding (πλάσις) even of the first man was in itself defective and had to be supplemented by the power of the divine Name (fr. 5). A much more definite indication of Platonic influence would appear if we could trust the reference to 'appendages' (προσαρτήματα) in Clement's introduction to fr. 2 as indicating that Valentinus actually used this word; for it is clearly a term of philosophic stamp, having close parallels in Marcus Aurelius (τὰ προσηρτημένα, 12.3.4) and Plotinus (σώματι προσηρτημένῳ, Enn. 1.4.4; cf. συνηρτημένα, Enn. 1.1.9; and προσφῦναι in Albinus 16 [p. 172.9, 15], cf. Plato R. 10, 611d), and seems to look back to Plato's description of the soul as like the sea god Glaucus whom 'the clinging overgrowth of weed and rock and shell has made more like a monster than his natural self (loc. cit., cf. 519ab).[11] Unfortunately this deduction is unreliable, since a reference to προσαρτήματα is first made in connexion with the school of Basilides, and indeed a fragment attributed to his son Isidore argues that such a theory of wrongdoing may diminish man's sense of responsibility by allowing him to claim that compulsive temptations come from an outside source. The passage which Clement

---

[10] SVF 1. 254, 3. 746-50.

[11] Cf. also Phdr. 250c, which explains the sudden introduction of the phrase ὀστρεῶδη σώματα in Iamblichus, De Anima, in Stobaeus, 1.378 W.; see A. J. Festugière, La Révélation d'Hermès Trismégiste (EBib; Paris, 1953) 3. 218 n. 2.

then quotes from Valentinus deals with the subject of temptations
and impurities in the soul, but in distinctly different terms and with
a different objective; he speaks of evil spirits invading the heart, as
Jesus speaks in the New Testament, rather than of accretions or
incrustations; and his main theme is not the need for responsible
self-direction, but rather the impossibility of man's unaided effort to
expel the demons; purity can only be achieved through the providence or visitation of the one good Father 'whose outspoken word
(*parrhêsia*) is the manifestation through the Son'. This suggests that
some caution is needed in accepting Clement's accusation that Valentinus
teaches that there is a race of men who are 'saved by nature'; he puts
forward this charge, in *Str.* 2.115, only by asking the unanswerable
question why God's providence does not operate continuously to
prevent all wrongdoing.

What impression do the fragments convey of the heavenly hierarchy?
The most important sources here are frr. 1, 2, and 5, while something
may also be learnt from the explanation which Hippolytus attaches
to fr. 8. Certain features can be seen at once. The highest place is
occupied by the One who is good, the only good Father, 'whose
declaration is the manifestation through the Son', to give a simpler
rendering of *parrhêsia*. It is not at once clear whether the Son is to be
identified with the divine Logos, unless we trust fr. 9 (Ps.-Anthimus =
Marcellus) more literally than I am inclined to do; the reference might
be simply to the divine power in Jesus (fr. 3). At a lower level we
have the divine Sophia, according to Clement's explanation of fr. 5;
and the Demiurge, although he is 'the image of the true God' (ibid.),
and is called God and Father, no doubt ranks below her, since he is
her *plasma*, is 'moulded' by her (*Str.* 4.90.2). This of course agrees with
numerous accounts of Valentinian doctrine, including Hippolytus's
explanation of fr. 8 (*Haer.* 6.37), which compares the Valentinian psalm
he quotes with the three orders of beings set out in the second Platonic
Epistle (312e), though Valentinus, says Hippolytus, begins from below.
Even so, the psalm itself hardly confirms the triadic pattern which
Hippolytus professes to find in it; its order is flesh, soul, air, ether,
and the fruits which proceed from the abyss (*bythos*), followed by a
puzzling reference to an infant (*brephos*). Hippolytus equates 'flesh'
with matter, 'soul' with the Demiurge, 'air' with 'the spirit which is
outside the Pleroma', and this again with 'the external (or excluded?)
Sophia', and 'ether' with 'Sophia within the Limit (*Horos*) and all
the Pleroma', which is presumably identical with 'the whole emission

of the Aeons from the Father', while the concluding reference to the infant remains obscure; it is of course tempting to connect it with fr. 7, also from Hippolytus, where Valentinus is said to have claimed a vision of an infant child (*paida nêpion*) who declared himself to be the Logos—which could suggest that Valentinus placed the Logos next to the Father, and above the other 'fruits' or Aeons. The mention of two Wisdoms has no parallel in the fragments transmitted by Clement, though it is commonplace in the developed system; but Hippolytus does not suggest that the higher Sophia is also involved in error and confusion, as with Ptolemaeus. He knows this doctrine, of course, in view of his earlier account; but in 6.37 he is clearly adding matter derived from a separate source.

For what it is worth, then, Hippolytus does claim that Valentinus distinguished three levels of reality; and not, in this case, the usual triad of spirit, soul, and matter. I think that in 6.37.5 the emendation Σιγήν (for MS πᾶσι γῆν) must be wrong, since it leaves the following genitive unexplained; I prefer Hilgenfeld's πηγήν; we then have a triad of the Father, the Aeons, and the cosmos, which is roughly comparable to the familiar middle-Platonic triad of God, the Ideas, and matter.

But perhaps a little more may be deduced from frr. 1, 2, and 5. Fr. 1 clearly depends on well-known extrabiblical traditions about the creation of Adam, set going no doubt by attempts to account for the plural verb 'let us make', Gen 1:26, in the light of Plato's assistant creators in the *Timaeus* (41a-c, 42de;[12] cf. Philo, *Op.* 72ff., *Conf.* 168ff., *Fuga* 68ff.), and introducing angels (and often a lower Demiurge) as responsible for his moulding (see, e.g., Irenaeus, *Haer.* 1.24 = Hippolytus, *Haer.* 7.28 [Saturninus], Hippolytus, *Haer.* 5.7.6 [Naassenes], and among the new texts *ApocryJn* BG 48: 10 = CG II 15: 1, *ApocAd* CG V 64: 15). In Valentinus fr. 1 the angels are afraid 'when he spoke too boldly for a moulded creature' (or perhaps 'uttered loftier words than' such a being, ὅτε μείζονα ἐφθέγξατο τῆς πλάσεως) 'on account of Him who had given in him (Adam) a seed of the heavenly being and spoken boldly'. Adam's lofty speech is a puzzle which I do not remember having seen explained; I would be inclined to refer it to Gen 2:19, noting the importance which Philo attaches to the giving of names in the tradition of Plato's *Cratylus* (*Op.* 148-50; *Leg. All.* 2.15, *Mut.* 63, *Quaes. Gen.* 1.20-21); a gnostic

---

[12] See *inter alia* P. Boyancé, 'Dieu cosmique et dualisme: les archontes de Platon', *Le Origini dello Gnosticismo* (ed. U. Bianchi; Leiden, 1967) 340-56.

writer would no doubt assume that the Demiurge did not know the right
names, an interpretation which Philo mentions and rejects at *Op.* 149,
Quaes. Gen. 1.21.[13]

Who then is the preexistent man? Hilgenfeld (*Ketzergeschichte*, 294)
and Förster (*Von Valentin zu Herakleon*, 92) assume that he is the
Father, referring us to Irenaeus, *Haer.* 1.30, where the Sethians are
said to give the name Man to 'the God of all', the 'first God'. This
may perhaps be right; there are indeed other gnostic sects which make
the same equation, for instance the Naassenes (Hippolytus, *Haer.* 5.6.4-5,
cf. 10.9.1), Monoimus (ibid. 8.12.2, etc.) and some Valentinians
(Irenaeus, *Haer.* 1.12.4); and the word 'preexistent' (προόντος)—if this
reading is sound—also occurs in Hippolytus's account of the Naassenes
as a designation of the supreme being (5.7.9; 9.1, cf. Epiphanius,
Haer. 31.5.6). But I think there is something to be said for the view
that Valentinus, like Philo, interpreted the creation account of Genesis 1
as referring to the ideal man and equated him with the divine Logos.
For the implanting of a heavenly seed—presumably a parallel to the
biblical in-breathing of the breath of life, Gen 2:7—is accompanied
by 'bold speaking', παρρησιαζόμενον, on the part of the invisible
'seed-giver' also; and this naturally suggests the παρρησία predicated
of the Son in fr. 2. In Clement, *Exc. Thdot.* 2.1 it is certainly the Logos
who implants a male seed in the sleeping soul. Further, it would be
natural within a Platonic framework to think of the ideal man as
'established' (καθεστῶτος) within the natural man; but would the
supreme God be so described? And is παρρησιάζω a natural word
to use of the Almighty, who has no one even theoretically capable
of opposing or threatening him?[14] I am not sure whether these are
points of substance; but if accepted, they would show that Valentinus
gave a prominence to the Logos which is obscured in the developed
systems, and would help to explain fr. 7 (his alleged vision of the
Logos), and even fr. 9, his alleged Trinity of three natures or
hypostases.

There is, moreover, an allusion to the creation—though an oblique
one—in fr. 5. We may render: 'Concerning this God (viz., the world-
creating God who is responsible for death) he intimates (αἰνίττεται)
the following—I quote verbatim—: "Just as the image is something

---

[13] Cf. *On the Origin of the World*, CG II 120: 17-26, where Adam's naming of the
animals is given some prominence.

[14] Cf. however Ps 11:6 (12:5) quoted at *1 Clem.* 15.7, which W. Bauer's Lexicon
notes as unique.

less than the living face, so equally the cosmos is something less than the living Aeon. What then is the reason for the image? The greatness of that face which has provided the likeness for the painter, so that he may be honoured through his name; for the form (of God?) was not found in full reality, but the name filled up what was lacking in the moulded creature. And the invisible (nature) of God worked with it (Him?) to produce faith in (?) the moulded being." ' This recalls fr. 1 in its suggestion that the creature had limited capacities which were supplemented by a higher power. And the continuation, obscure though it is, implies that there are two beings who cooperate (*synergein*), one being the Name, and the other 'the invisible', *to aoraton*, of God. But 'the Name' is now widely recognized as a christological title, following (e.g.) Quispel's discussion of its use in the *Gospel of Truth*.[15]

Hilgenfeld (299-300) interpreted this phrase quite differently; following Grabe, he took 'the Name' as part of the metaphor, as meaning the title under a portrait, which reveals an identity which the picture does not fully disclose. Hilgenfeld also assumed that Clement, though better informed than we are, made a gross error in identifying the portrait-painter as Sophia. Sagnard, on the other hand, maintains that the passage alludes to numerous details of the fully developed 'Ptolemaean' system; but he offers no opinion as to whether Clement is right in understanding Valentinus to see Sophia as the portrait-painter, and if so, what his meaning might be. Here, it seems to me, there is scope for further investigation.

Plato, as is well known, makes numerous attempts to explain the relationship between the ideal world and the ordinary world; at some stage he perhaps came to see that it can only be expressed in metaphorical terms, since it is bound to be *sui generis* (so, perhaps, *Prm.* 131). But he often speaks of an imitation and the reality corresponding to it; and quite often of a *visible* likeness, a drawing or painting. The word Ζωγράφος and its cognates occur about forty times in Plato's dialogues, sometimes without any great philosophical resonance, as in *R.* 2, 373c, where paintings are mentioned simply as an example of luxurious furniture; sometimes in the context of a theory of names or theory of knowledge, as in *Cra.* 430b; sometimes in that of psychology, as *Phlb.* 39b; or of ethics, as *R.* 6, 500e; and sometimes of the theory of Ideas, as *R.* 10, 596eff. I would pick out

---

[15] See esp. 37: 37ff., translated and discussed in F. L. Cross (ed.), *The Jung Codex* (London, 1955) 69-76; cf. 'J. Daniélou, *Theology of Jewish Christianity* (London, Chicago: 1964) 147-63; Clement, *Exc. Thdot.* 86.2; 26.1, discussed ibid. 153.

eight passages as especially significant, namely, *Cra.* 430b ff.; *Sph.* 236b; *Phlb.* 39b; *Phdr.* 275d; *R.* 5, 472d; ibid. 6, 500e ff.; ibid. 10, 596a ff.; and *Ep.* 7, 342. It should be noted that several of these passages would be known to ancient readers who depended on anthologies which, as so often in the postclassical period, emphasized the ethical and theological sides of Plato's thought while neglecting the epistemological and the political. Thus *R.* 6, 500cd, is (with *Tht.* 176b) a *locus classicus* for the thought that likeness to God is the goal of human endeavour; *Phlb.* 39, as we shall see, speaks of 'the good man loved by the gods'; and *R.* 10, 597b is the sole proof text for the important doctrine that God makes the Ideas. It would be easy to suppose that the fragment of the *Republic* which is found in a Coptic version in Nag Hammadi Codex VI, i.e., 588b-589b, derives from a translation which originally continued to this point.

Moreover, although the word Ζωγράφος itself has proved enigmatic to some interpreters of gnosticism, it is used by Plato in association with other terms which reappear either in postclassical summaries of Platonism, or in gnostic documents, or in both. The painter is a craftsman, *dêmiourgos* (*Phlb.* 39b, *R.* 10, 596e). He is, or is compared to, a maker or poet, *poiêtês*, *R.* 596d, 597d. His productions are imitations or images, *mimêmata*, *eikones*, *eidôla*, *phantasmata*, *Cra.* 430b,e, 431c; *Sph.* 236b,c; *Phlb.* 39b,c, 40a; *Phdr.* 276a; *R.* 598b. A significant passage in the *Phaedrus* (275e-276d) compares paintings to 'dumb' (i.e., written) words who need their 'father' to defend them, and contrasts these with another 'word' which is 'written with intelligence in the mind of the hearer, and is powerful in its own defence'; this may well form part of the tradition underlying Heb 4:12. In *Phlb.* 39b ff. we find a discussion of memory and imagination, memory being compared to a clerk (*grammatistês*) who records and repeats the facts, whereas there is in our souls 'another *dêmiourgos*', a painter, who makes images, both memories of the past and hopes for the future (39e); the good man loved by the gods has pleasures and hopes that are true. For the Platonist, of course, the memory of our heavenly origin is equivalent to a knowledge of heavenly realities (see, e.g., *Phd.* 72e ff., esp. 75c, 76de); and knowledge of our origin is one of the basic ideas of gnosticism (see esp. Clement, *Exc. Thdot.* 78.2). In a rather different vein, we find Sophia creating κατὰ τὴν μνήμην τῶν κρειττόνων (Irenaeus 1.11.1, *lect. pot.*).

In *R.* 10, 596 ff., Plato discusses the relation of common objects to the ideal forms; the craftsman who makes those objects has the form before his eyes, but does not make it; however there is a kind of craftsman who makes imitations or representations of things, namely, the painter. Plato then suggests that common objects are related to their ideal forms in much the same way as paintings to the objects they represent; thus there are three orders of things, forms, objects, and their imitations, and three kinds of craftsmen, named at 597b as 'painter, bedstead-maker and god'. This text, we have noted, was important to later Platonists as their authority for the doctrine that God makes the forms. But by the first century A.D. we already see the beginnings of a movement to emphasize the transcendence of the source of all being by attributing the making of the world to a secondary power, the divine Logos. Philo, though understandably cautious in this respect, is already willing to refer to the Logos as 'second cause' (*Quaes. Gen.* 3.34) and 'second God' (in Eusebius, *P.E.* 7.13.1), and as the God of the unenlightened (*Leg. All.* 3.207, *Somn.* 1.238), though he commonly also pictures him in impersonal terms as the instrument *by which* God made the world. But by the second century the word τεχνίτης has become appropriated to this power in Platonist circles, and δημιουργός can be used of the Logos by the Christian apologist Tatian (*Orat.* 7); while among the gnostics, quite apart from its well-known pejorative application to the God of the Old Testament, we find the title '*First* Demiurge' assigned to the Saviour in Clement, *Exc. Thdot.* 47.1.

It is therefore a perfectly natural extension of this usage to the next member of Plato's hierarchy if 'the painter' stands for the divine Wisdom, understood as a cosmic power junior to the Logos, and as responsible for the perceptible world, a representation of the ideal world whose beauty it dimly reflects. This latter notion is certainly found in Valentinian texts (*GTr* 17: 19-20, *TriTrac* 79: 10, which may be compared with Philo, *Op.* 139, Albinus 10.3 (p. 165.3) and Numenius fr. 16. A triad of God, Craftsman and Painter could easily be developed in connexion with the well-known triad of God, the Ideas, and Matter, which we have already noted in connexion with Hippolytus, *Haer.* 6.37.

Of course we do not find the Logos named as a bedstead-maker! But the word is not essential to Plato's argument; even in the *Republic* passage it alternates with τέκτων; but in either case motives of reverence would discourage its use in theology. Philo mentions carpentry as a banausic occupation (*Leg. All.* 1.57), though he does use the more dignified word ἀρχιτέκτων in connexion with the making

of the ideal world (*Op.* 24), and at *Mut.* 29-31 it is linked with
ποιητής, δημιουργός and τεχνίτης. Philo reserves these terms for the
Father, we should note; but besides these, the only common-life
occupations which he applies by metaphor to God are (by Leisegang's
index) ἡνίοχος (Platonic) and κυβερνήτης (cf. *Plt.* 273e), together
with δᾳδοῦχος and φυτουργός, once each.

Does Valentinus, like his followers, give the name Demiurge to an
inferior deity, the offspring or product of Sophia? Clement certainly
tells us, when introducing fr. 5, that death is to be destroyed, and
that it is the work of the being who created the world; and this is
reasonably well confirmed by the quotation, where the 'image' is said
to be 'inferior to the living face' and its existence needs to be
explained; clearly the term 'image' has been reapplied, in a manner
comparable to Clement, *Exc. Thdot.* 7.5.

The gnostic conception presumably has its main roots outside
Platonism, in an adverse judgement on the Old Testament creator-god,
and cannot easily be fitted into the scheme which we earlier outlined.
Nevertheless an ingenious Platonist might appeal to *R.* 598bc, where
the painter is said to paint other workmen, and a good painter could
depict a carpenter (γράψας ἂν τέκτονα) whom children and simple-
minded people would take for a (or 'the'?) real carpenter. This offers
a possible parallel to Clement's comment on fr. 5, where he says that the
Demiurge is the image of the true God, according to Valentinus, and is
the moulded work (*plasma*) of the painter, Sophia; and we may again
compare the *Excerpta*, 47.1-2, where the Saviour is said to be the
first and universal *dêmiourgos*, and Sophia the second; her first work
is the putting-forth (προβάλλεται) of an image of the Father, a god
through whom she (*sic*) made heaven and earth. And I may perhaps
be forgiven for adding one further reference to the *Cratylus*, 431de,
where Socrates is arguing that some images, i.e., names, are good and
some are not; his inference is, 'Perhaps, then, one craftsman of names
will be good, and the other bad?'—and continues with a sentence
which could easily be rendered, 'And so the name *of the latter* was the
Lawgiver'!

I have spent a good deal of time on a possibly speculative pursuit
of Platonic parallels; but before we leave this field, there are two
other points at which I think Plato's influence can be certified. The
first concerns the use of the term 'image', *eikon*. In the great majority
of cases this implies something derived or copied from a corresponding
reality, and thus necessarily inferior to it (see esp. *Cra.* 432d). But

in *Sph.* 236b the contrast is drawn between the *eikon*, as the true image, which genuinely resembles the reality, and the *phantasma*, which merely appears to do so. This shows us the term *eikon* closely approaching the sense of 'genuine reality' itself; and this approach seems to be completed in Philo's usage. Sometimes, of course, the common Platonic sense of 'imitation' is to the fore; but in *Leg. All.* 1.43 the 'man' of Gen 2:8 is interpreted to mean heavenly Wisdom, which Moses called 'the beginning and the image and the vision of God' (ἀρχὴν καὶ εἰκόνα καὶ ὅρασιν θεοῦ); this clearly indicates at least a genuine image. But further, in *Somn.* 1.79 'incorporeal images' appear to be the same as 'most holy Ideas', and these are undoubtedly to be understood in a realist, Platonic sense, as transcendent *realities*, even if their function is also to reproduce 'the form of God' (Gen 32:31, cited in the text). Once again, in *Spec. Leg.* 1.171 Philo interprets the smoke of the sacrificial incense as a thank-offering for 'the rational spirit within us, which was shaped according to the original Idea of the divine image' (πρὸς ἀρχέτυπον ἰδέαν εἰκόνος θείας). Clearly 'image' here is equivalent to 'idea', or at least not inferior to it; and the passage connects with others in which the divine Logos is identified with the Man κατ' εἰκόνα, at the 'iconic' or ideal level, as contrasted with the man καθ' ὁμοίωσιν.[16]

This usage of *eikon* no doubt helps to explain the contrast between 'image' and 'shadow' in Heb 10:1; but further, I believe it provides the clue to a most puzzling passage in the *Gospel of Thomas*, 84: 'Jesus said: When you see your likeness, you rejoice. But when you see your images (εἰκών) which came into existence before you, which neither die nor are manifested, how much will you bear!' The contrast of image and likeness suggests Gen 1:26, but in this case the images are superior to the likeness, in contrast to Irenaeus, *Haer.* 1.5.5; Clement, *Exc. Thdot.* 50.1; 54.2.[17] Such preexistent immortal images can be explained as our true selves, or as the guardian angels which the Valentinians pictured as our heavenly bridegrooms; but the term εἰκών becomes easier to understand if one notes that it is a possible term for the

---

[16] This use of εἰκών reappears in some philosophical texts, e.g., Timaeus Locrus 99d (cited in *LSJ*) and Alexander of Aphrodisias, *Commentary on Aristotle's Metaphysics*, pp. 83.16 and 771.24-772.7 Hayduck. In the first passage εἰκών and παράδειγμα are used as synonyms, although clearly distinguished in the preceding lines. The second passage shows that εἰκών was used as an equivalent of παράδειγμα by Pythagoreans.

[17] The exposition of Gen 1:26 cited in Hippolytus, *Haer.* 6.14.5-6 from the *Apophasis Megale* perhaps takes a high view of the 'image', though the 'likeness' is not explained.

211

Platonic Idea, and that some Platonists at least taught that there were Ideas corresponding to individual human selves.

Suppose that Valentinus was a Platonist, as we have argued hitherto; and that he did indeed accept a complex myth akin to that of the *Apocryphon of John*; and that we discard forced explanations, such as that of a sudden change of mind: we then have to ask ourselves whether a Platonist could have accepted a hierarchy of Aeons as a possible representation of the Platonic theory of Ideas. It is clearly impossible that anyone could have retained both systems, regarding them as simply unconnected; for both alike profess to disclose the structure of the unseen world and its relation to the source of all being. We have therefore to look for trends of opinion within the Platonic schools which saw the Ideas as comparable to living and personal beings, including but not limited to the individual beings who live human lives.

For this purpose the definition of Platonism need not be too narrowly restricted. A philosopher such as Plutarch, who was clearly recognized as belonging within the school tradition, could make sympathetic use of Eastern mythology in his work *On Isis and Osiris*. In another direction, Platonists could extend their range by borrowing from the Stoics; a syncretism of this kind can be detected in Philo; again, a little later than Valentinus, the *Chaldaean Oracles* show what inventive complexity of cosmological teaching can be constructed on a broadly Platonic basis. In fr. 37 Ideas 'whizz out' and 'leap out' from the Father's mind and burst like waves upon the rocks of the material world; while a Stoic motif appears in the use of fire imagery for their source (lines 4, 14). Stoic influence may also help to explain the fact that the Valentinians on the whole prefer the more Stoic and biblical-sounding term πνεῦμα to the Platonic νοῦς to express the highest element in human life, the element which unites some men at least to the celestial world.

A well-known sentence in Tertullian[18] relates that Valentinus himself conceived the Aeons simply as attributes of the Father, and that it was Ptolemaeus who distinguished them as *personales substantias*. Of course the contrast may be too sharply drawn; it might be better to think of a difference in emphasis.[19] Certainly in the Church Fathers' reports their status seems to be ambiguous; and this with some good

---

[18] *Adv. Val.* 4.

[19] Cf. my paper 'The Valentinian Myth of Sophia', *JTS* N.S. 20 (1969) 87-88.

reason, for one should not assume that human language and human imagery does justice to the highest realities either by stating a series of predicates or by picturing a chain of genetic descent. The formation of the Aeons is commonly described as 'emission', προβολή; the verb προβάλλεσθαι can suggest either physical growth and extension[20] or the exercise of mental powers;[21] but this function is often performed by Aeons acting in pairs, as if it were the begetting of a human offspring. It is commonly felt, and indeed Irenaeus observed,[22] that something akin to individual human existence is first clearly demanded when we reach the figure of the erring Sophia; indeed it is part of the tradition that her error was prompted by the desire to act independently and to assert her individual being.[23]

How would a second-century Platonist approach this position? Most probably, with two complexes of problems in mind: first, the generation of numbers from the One; and secondly, the notion of the Ideas as thoughts of God, the two problems being linked by the enigmatic doctrines attributed to Xenocrates, that the soul is a self-moving number, and that the Ideas themselves are numbers. Some light may be thrown on these dark sayings if we remember that Pythagorean and Platonic tradition associated numbers with geometrical figures, and that Plato himself had connected the series of extensions (point, line, plane, solid) with the cognitive processes, mind, knowledge, opinion, sensation; noticing also that the development of spatial dimensions is associated with a decline towards less perfect forms of cognition.[24] Aristotle also reports what is probably Xenocrates' view, that the numbers *desire* unity[25]—perhaps because it is the ideal form of the order which they impose on indefinite quantities?—from which von Arnim and Krämer[26] conclude that Xenocrates thought of the numbers as living beings.

Considering the Ideas as thoughts of God, a Platonist who was even mildly pessimistic about the material world would not represent it as an original and primary purpose of the ultimate power, any more than

---

[20] See e.g., Irenaeus, *Haer.* 2.17, discussed in my *Divine Substance* (Oxford, 1977) 195-9.

[21] See, e.g., Porphyry, *Sent.* 29, p. 13.10 M.; Iamblichus, *De Anima*, in Stobaeus, 1.370 W.

[22] Irenaeus, *Haer.* 2.12.2; 2.17.10.

[23] Irenaeus, *Haer.* 1.2.2; Hippolytus, *Haer.* 6.30.7.

[24] Aristotle, *De An.* 1.2, 404b22-24.

[25] Aristotle, *EE* 1.8, 1218a24-26.

[26] H. J. Krämer, *Ursprung der Geistmetaphysik* (Amsterdam, 1964) 62-63, 162.

the Christian Origen did. He would not therefore think of the Ideas as archetypes (παραδείγματα) of species or objects in this world, as they are often represented by Philo; they would rather be archetypes of ideal existence in the intelligible world; they would be characters or roles which the Father in some way assumes or projects and so brings into distinct existence. Since he is the source of all these, no one of them singly could represent or comprehend his mysterious being. Platonic Ideas of virtues would approximate to this picture; it would be easy to reflect that an ideal form of virtue can only exist in a context which allows of life and decision; and traditional personifications of virtues would make this transition seem natural. But the Platonic tradition did in fact develop a concept of the Ideas as being not only intelligible but themselves intelligent. Plotinus is the best-known exponent of this tradition,[27] but it is clearly represented in the *Chaldaean Oracles*, especially in fr. 37 mentioned above, where dynamic physical imagery is used to convey the vigour of what are more properly described as mental acts:

> Νοῦς πατρὸς ἐρροίζησε νοήσας ἀκμάδι βουλῇ
> παμμόρφους ἰδέας, πηγῆς δὲ μιᾶς ἄπο πᾶσαι
> ἐξέθορον· πατρόθεν γὰρ ἔην βούλη τε τέλος τε.
> Ἀλλ' ἐμερίσθησαν νοερῷ πυρὶ μοιραθεῖσαι
> εἰς ἄλλας νοεράς· κόσμῳ γὰρ ἄναξ πολυμόρφῳ
> προὔθηκεν νοερὸν τύπον ἄφθιτον...
> Ἔννοιαι νοεραὶ πηγῆς πατρικῆς ἄπο...

It should not be thought that νοερός is used here simply as a substitute for νοητός, *metri gratia*; this may be shown from fr. 81, which has the same combination of physical and psychological imagery:

> τοῖς δὲ πυρὸς νοεροῦ νοεροῖς πρηστῆσιν ἅπαντα
> εἴκαθε δουλεύοντα πατρὸς πειθηνίδι βουλῇ.

We may think the author's use of philosophical and religious tradition irresponsible; but he is surely right on one major point, that analogies drawn from human experience cannot provide any really adequate description of the highest realities.

The *Tripartite Tractate* enables us to see how the same problem is handled by the Valentinian school, in an imperfectly translated text, it is true, but one which is not fogged by the insensitive reporting of the Church Fathers. In this document the Aeons are infinite in

---

[27] See P. Hadot, 'Etre, Vie, Pensée chez Plotin et avant Plotin', *Les Sources de Plotin* (Fondation Hardt, Entretiens 5; Vandœuvres-Geneva, 1960) 107-41.

number (59: 7-8, 28; 67: 20, 23) and except for a primary and Christian-sounding triad of Father, Son and Ecclesia they are not named. They are exhibited initially as God's thoughts (60: 3), and do not serve as paradigms for the physical world, but are representations of his own nature (61: 37). They are beings *sui generis*, and normal language has to be strained to describe them; note for example the conjunction 'seeds (?), thoughts, roots, offspring, minds' at 64: 1-6, which compares closely with the Αἰῶνας καὶ λόγους καὶ ῥίζας καὶ σπέρματα καὶ πληρώματα καὶ καρπούς attributed to Marcus in Irenaeus, *Haer.* 1.14.2. The author clearly pictures an evolution or creation by stages, which is not unambiguously either a progress or a decline,[28] but from which independent personalities result. Whence then do these originate? The question is not quite easy to answer because of the, possibly intrusive, presence of Ecclesia (57: 34-59: 16), which suggests a company of preexistent personalities; otherwise one might think simply of the Father's thoughts or designs. Initially they were hidden in the mysterious being of the Father, known indeed to him but unknown to themselves (60: 16-29); but the Father gave them existence for themselves (61: 4-7, 33) and knowledge of Himself (61: 12; 62: 2; 63: 10-11). Initially unconscious like unborn children (61: 18-24) they receive knowledge and virtue (62: 12-14) and praise Him (63: 27); thus they become minds (64: 6), able to wish and think and speak (64: 15-17) and to gain knowledge of the Father through the divine Logos (65: 6-31); lastly they obtain free will (69: 28). The author lays some stress on the successive stages of this development, explaining more than once that it has to wait for a suitable moment (62: 18-22, 30; 64: 33-65: 1; 67: 34-35); not of course because the Father is ungenerous (a well-known Platonic theme appearing also in *GTr* 18: 36-40), but to discourage premature confidence (62: 21-25), to avoid the annihilating effect of a sudden revelation (64: 33-37) and to discourage one-sided presentations (68: 17-28), since it is only in mutual agreement and cooperation that they are able to comprehend their source (ibid.). Their free will, however, has the result that these wise provisions are in some measure frustrated, a theme which we need not now pursue in detail.

---

[28] It has to be remembered that Platonists tended to associate multiplication and growth with a loss of purity and concentration; Speusippus occupies a somewhat isolated position in holding that evolution is productive of good, though admittedly there are traces of his influence in our period, e.g., Philo, *Op.* 67-68, cf. *Sacr.* 14-16.

This author thinks of the heavenly powers as infinite in number. The Valentinian systems reported by the Church Fathers appear to fix the number of Aeons at thirty or some other prescribed limit,[29] which makes it difficult to understand another feature of their doctrine, namely that the elect not only have heavenly counterparts or bridegrooms but will themselves be united with these and enter the *pleroma* 'becoming themselves intelligible Aeons', *Exc. Thdot.* 64.1, cf. Irenaeus, *Haer.* 1.7.1. How does this doctrine of a common nature and common destiny for the spirituals and the Aeons themselves appear in relation to the Platonic tradition?

Some Platonists, as we have observed, taught that there are Ideas, and thus eternal existences, of individuals. This doctrine sometimes takes the markedly optimistic form of asserting the affinity of *souls* as such with the ideas. The main authority for this view will have been the *Phaedo*, especially 79c-80b, noting that it is possible to infer from this passage that the soul is not only *like* the highest realities but belongs to their number, being συγγενής (79d). Again, both Speusippus and Posidonius appear to have defined the soul as 'the Form of universal extension', ἰδέα τοῦ πάντῃ διαστατοῦ;[30] and whatever this phrase may originally have meant, it is clear that some Platonists took it to mean that the soul is an Idea, an opinion which Plutarch understandably disowns. We may notice also the view of Numenius[31] that the soul contains all the higher realities, 'the intelligible world, gods, demons, and the good', which might possibly be compared with the Valentinian picture of the Aeons as interpenetrating each other.

A better-known strand in the Platonic tradition teaches that only the rational element, and not the soul as such, is akin to the intelligible world; it also distinguishes three classes of men such that only the highest and best is dominated by the reason, and sometimes represents the soul as intermediate between heavenly and earthly things.[32] This provides an obvious point of departure for the doctrine that the intermediate class of men are those dominated by the soul, i.e., the psychics; and generally this opinion is closer to the Valentinian position, where indeed the Platonic term νοῦς sometimes takes the place of the more familiar πνεῦμα to denote the highest element. But

---

[29] E.g., Epiphanius, *Haer.* 31.6.
[30] Plutarch *An. procr.* 22; Iamblichus in Stobaeus, 1.364 W.
[31] Fr. 41 des Places = Test. 33 Leemans.
[32] Plutarch, *An. procr.* 22.

it may still be useful to review some varieties of Platonic teaching on the relationship between the soul and the ideal world as a possible setting for the Valentinian conceptions of the Aeons and the spiritual men.

Calvisius Taurus, if we can trust Iamblichus's report of him (in Stobaeus 1.378 W.) seems to have taken a markedly optimistic view: 'the souls are sent by the gods to earth either... in order that there may be as many living beings in the cosmos as there are in the intelligible realm; or... to present a manifestation of the divine life... for the gods become evident and manifest themselves through the pure and unsullied life of the souls'. The first alternative suggests that the souls have their counterparts in the ideal world, like the Valentinian 'bridegrooms'; and presumably as *individual* ideas; for if 'as many living beings' were taken to mean 'as many *kinds* of living beings' only one human soul would be needed.[33]

The gnostic Basilides also presents a radically optimistic view. He takes over a Platonic myth of a choice of lives by three classes of rational beings, which can also be found in Philo. In the usual form of the myth, the three classes are distinguished by the varying degrees in which they yield to the attractions of the body and of earthly things, and the lowest class is represented as entirely given over to bodily concerns, like the *hylikoi* in Valentinian anthropology. In Basilides' version, however, the highest class of the three reverts immediately to the heavenly world (Hippolytus, *Haer.* 7.22.8) and the second follows with some difficulty, aided by the Holy Spirit (ibid. 9-16); it is only the third class that remains within the germinating lower world, and even this apparently has the respectable motive of 'conferring and receiving benefits' (ibid. 16, cf. 10-11). All these classes indeed share the dignity of 'sonship', υἱότης, which is withheld even from the Holy Spirit (ibid. 12-13).

Philo reproduces the same myth in a less optimistic and more typical form. The version given in *Gig.* 12-15 has some features in common with Basilides. All three classes share the common denominator of souls, but those of the first class refuse all dealings with the earth, and are appointed to wait upon their creator. A second group emerge with difficulty from the whirlpool of bodily passions and return to their source; these are the souls of genuine philosophers who follow

---

[33] Cf. Aristotle, *Metaph.* 12.3, 1070a18: if Aristotle's ὁπόσα φύσει means 'as many *kinds* of natural being', this interpretation could easily be missed.

Plato's advice by meditating upon death (*Phd.* 64a, 67e, 81a, often quoted by Philo and the Fathers). The third class are completely overwhelmed by the body and worldly concerns. Philo remarks in conclusion that souls, demons, and angels are one and the same. Some features of this account reappear in *Plant.* 14, though here Philo begins with two classes of souls, some of which enter into bodies at certain appojnted times, but others remain aloft, while the purest of these inhabit the ether, and are called heroes by the Greeks but angels by Moses. This version resembles Basilides in entirely disregarding unworthy motives for incarnation. In *Somn.* 1.138 the picture is slightly more complex: the lowest class of souls become bound to mortal bodies, but a higher class leave them and ascend; some then return to mortal life, but others disdain it and are raised to the etherial region. Others again, the purest and best, have no desire for earthly things, but attend the great king; and these are called demons by the philosophers, but angels by the sacred Word. In all these passages, therefore, angels are identified with virtuous souls in a Platonic context; but in other places the angels are identified with λόγοι and δυνάμεις, and these again with ἰδέαι. There is in fact a complex overlapping of the terms ἄγγελοι, δυνάμεις, ψυχαί, λόγοι, ἀρεταί, ἰδέαι, and εἰκόνες, together with σφραγῖδες and παραδείγματα; and this seems to me to show that Philo had access to a Platonic tradition in which the Ideas were regarded as personal beings, possibly even with varying moral destinies; since if he had merely wished to find a philosophical justification for the Hebrew doctrine of angels, the ἥρωες and the δαίμονες would have satisfied his needs.

Another school of gnostics having several features in common with the Valentinians, and also indebted to Platonism, regarded souls as a debased form of the Ideas. These are the Docetists reported by Hippolytus. For them the Ideas appear to correspond to the 'characters' in which the self-knowledge of the Aeons expresses itself; they compose a νοητὴ φύσις but have also a cosmic function (*Haer.* 8.9.3); but on 'cooling down' and losing the heavenly light they turn into souls (ψυχαὶ γὰρ αἱ ἰδέαι καλοῦνται, ὅτι ἀποψυγεῖσαι τῶν ἄνω ἐν σκότει διατελοῦσι, ibid. 10.1), and enter into successive bodies, until at the coming of the Saviour their *metensomatosis* comes to an end. Another passage, 8.10.9, brings out the contrast between the celestial origin of the Ideas and their limited existence as souls on earth.

In the light of these Platonic parallels it becomes at last possible to understand a feature of Valentinianism which the *Tripartite Tractate* has brought into prominence; namely, that there is no sharp line to be drawn between the divine imagination projecting new forms of its own perfection and the divine creativity producing perfect offspring who may live a human life but are destined for incorporation into the *pleroma*, the grand consummation of the divine self-realization and self-giving.

3

SETHIAN GNOSTICISM:
A LITERARY HISTORY

John D. Turner

John D. Turner is both Professor of Religious Studies and Professor of Classics and History at the University of Nebraska—Lincoln, having taught at that institution since 1976. Professor Turner has devoted much of his academic career to Nag Hammadi studies both in terms of writing and service.

He has served on the Society of Biblical Literature Nag Hammadi Seminar as well as on the Steering Committee of the Nag Hammadi Section of that society. From 1971–72 he was an associate of the Technical Subcommittee for the International Committee for the Nag Hammadi Codices of UNESCO and the ARE.

Written contributions to Nag Hammadi studies have included numerous articles on the relationship of Gnosticism to Platonic philosophy and the *editio princeps* of the *Book of Thomas the Contender*.

Preface

The following analysis of the literary dependencies and redactional history of the Sethian gnostic texts from Nag Hammadi and elsewhere allows one to assign them to various periods during the first four centuries of the Christian era. The texts thus dated seem to reflect a coherent tradition of mythologumena that includes: (a) a sacred history of Seth's seed, derived from a peculiar exegesis of Genesis 1–6; (b) a doctrine of the divine wisdom in its primordial, fallen, and restored aspects; (c) a baptismal rite, often called the Five Seals, involving a removal from the fleshly world and transportation into the realm of light through the invocation of certain divine personages; (d) certain Christological speculations relating Christ to prominent Sethian primordial figures such as Adam and Seth; and (e) a fund of Platonic metaphysical concepts relating to the structure of the divine world and a self-actuated visionary means of assimilating with it.

55

221

The result of the study suggests that Sethianism interacted with Christianity in five phases: (1) Sethianism as a non-Christian baptismal sect of the first centuries B.C.E. and C.E. which considered itself primordially enlightened by the divine wisdom revealed to Adam and Seth, yet expected a final visitation of Seth marked by his conferral of a saving baptism; (2) Sethianism as gradually Christianized in the later first century onward through an identification of the pre-existent Christ with Seth, or Adam, that emerged through contact with Christian baptismal groups; (3) Sethianism as increasingly estranged from a Christianity becoming more orthodox toward the end of the second century and beyond; (4) Sethianism as rejected by the Great Church but meanwhile increasingly attracted to the individualistic contemplative practices of third-century Platonism; and (5) Sethianism as estranged from the orthodox Platonists of the late third century and increasingly fragmented into various derivative and other sectarian gnostic groups, some surviving into the Middle Ages.

I. The Sethian Literature

Mainly following the lead of Hans-Martin Schenke of the *Berliner* (DDR) *Arbeitskreis für koptisch-gnostische Schriften*,[1] current scholarship considers the following literature to be representative of Sethian Gnosticism: The Barbeloite report of Irenaeus (*Haer.* I.29); the reports on the Sethians (and Archontics) by Epiphanius (*Pan.* 26 and 39–40), Pseudo-Tertullian (*Haer.* 2) and Filastrius (*Haer.* 3); the untitled text from the Bruce Codex (Bruce); and the following treatises from the Nag Hammadi Codices and BG8502: four versions of the *Apocryphon of John* (*Ap. John* BG8502, 2 and NHC III,1 [short version]; NHC II, 1 and IV, 1 [long version]); the *Hypostasis of the Archons*; the *Gospel of the Egyptians*; the *Apocalypse of Adam*; the *Three Steles of Seth*; *Zostrianos*; *Melchizedek*; the *Thought of Norea*; *Marsanes*; *Allogenes*, and *Trimorphic Protennoia*.

II. The Sethian Themes

So far as I can see, most of the Sethian documents cited above originated in the period 100–250 C.E. They seem to derive their content from five basic complexes of doctrines: (1) a fund of Hellenistic-Jewish specu-

---

[1] H.-M. Schenke, "System" and "Sethianism."

lation on the figure of Sophia, the divine wisdom; (2) midrashic interpretation of Genesis 1-6 together with other assorted motifs from Jewish scripture and exegesis; (3) a doctrine and practice of baptism; (4) the developing Christology of the early church; and (5) a religiously oriented Neopythagorean and Middle-Platonic philosophical tradition of ontological and theological speculation.

A. Sophia Speculation

As appropriated by Sethianism and the Gnostics in general, Sophia is a hypostatized form of Ḥokmah (i.e., the divine Wisdom of Proverbs 8, Job 28, Sirach 24) and is regarded as a female deity, perhaps also connected with the Spirit that moved over the water in Gen 1:2-3. In the gnostic texts, Sophia functions at many levels under various names in a highly complex way. She functions as a creator and savior figure on a higher level as the divine Thought, which increasingly distinguishes itself from the high deity through various modalities, and gives rise to the divine image in which man is made. But she also functions on a lower level as the mother of the ignorant demiurge and the enlightener and savior of the divine image captured by the demiurge in human form. N. A. Dahl, in this regard, stresses the role played by the thought of Philo in this complex of ideas, particularly the notion of Sophia as Mother of the Logos and as the Mother figure in a divine triad of God the Father, Sophia the Mother, and Logos the Son.[2]

B. Interpretation of Genesis 2-6

Given the existence of an upper (either undeclined or restored) and lower Sophia, conceived as Mother, and her upper and lower sons, the Logos and the Archon, the peculiar Sethian reinterpretation of Genesis 2-6 easily follows: the anthropogony; the inbreathing of the divine Spirit; the sending of Eve or her extraction from Adam; the eating from the tree of knowledge; expulsion from paradise; the birth of Cain, Abel, Norea, and Seth and his seed; the flood and intercourse between women and the angels, with the addition of the story of Sodom and Gomorrah; and a final judgment and salvation. These episodes are interpreted in terms of a series of moves and countermoves between the upper Mother and Son and the lower Son in a contest over the control of the divine Spirit in mankind. In a very early period, still within the context of a disaffected and heterodox Judaism (and working with Jewish materials and gnosticizing Hellenistic-Jewish principles of interpretation), the peculiar Sethian doctrines concerning the origin, incar-

[2] Dahl, "Archon," 2. 689-712; see in particular pp. 707-8, and n. 44 (p. 708).

nation, subsequent history, and salvation of these Gnostics were worked out in terms of the upper and lower Adam, Seth, and seed of Seth. In particular this involved the doctrines of heavenly dwellings (the four Lights) for the exalted counterparts of the "historical" Sethians, and the tripartitioning of history into four basic epochs of salvation. These epochs could be delineated by events in the lower world, such as the flood, the conflagration, and the final overthrow of the Archons (as in the *Apocalypse of Adam* and the *Gospel of the Egyptians*). Or these epochs could be marked by the three descents from the upper world of a Savior (as Father, Mother and Son) involving (1) the inbreathing of the divine Spirit into Adam, (2) the arrival of the luminous Epinoia (a Sophia figure) in the form of Eve, and (3) the final appearance of Seth as the Logos (or Christ; cf. the *Apocryphon of John*, and the *Trimorphic Protennoia*). Other schemes or combinations of these episodes were also worked out. If there is anything peculiarly Sethian in the tractates under discussion, it would show itself here, since these speculations in fact constitute the sacred history of the Sethian Gnostics.

C. The Baptismal Rite

In addition, it is clear that some form of baptismal ritual is peculiar to the Sethians. In whatever baptismal tradition the Sethians stood, it is clear that it was spiritualized as part of a general trend that shows itself throughout the first century in both Christian and probably non-Christian baptizing circles. In particular, the Sethian baptismal water was understood to be of a celestial nature, a Living Water identical with light or enlightenment, and the rite itself must have been understood as a ritual of cultic ascent involving enlightenment and therefore salvation. This could also involve polemic against ordinary water baptism, as in the *Apocalypse of Adam*.

D. Christianization

Gradually, but especially during the second century, Sethianism was Christianized, particularly by the identification of the Logos (the last member of the Father-Mother-Son triad) with Christ. This process could move in a positive direction by adding explanatory Christological glosses as in the *Gospel of the Egyptians*, or even casting Sethian materials into the framework of a revelation dialogue between Christ the revealer and a revered disciple as in the *Apocryphon of John*. Or it could move in a more polemical direction, as in *Trimorphic Protennoia*. So also the reverse movement could occur, in which Sethian materials were built into originally Christian materials circulating among Sethians, as could be the case with *Melchizedek*.

E. The Platonic Contribution

Finally, during the late first and throughout the second and third centuries, Neopythagorean and Platonic metaphysics made a strong impact on Sethianism. They served to structure its world of transcendent beings by means of ontological distinctions, and to explain how the plenitude of the divine world might emerge from a sole high deity by emanation, radiation, unfolding, and mental self-reflection. Neopythagorean arithmology helped to flesh out the various triadic, tetradic, pentadic, and ogdoadic groupings of the transcendental beings. Besides metaphysics, there was also at home in Platonism a by-now-traditional technique of self-performable contemplative mystical ascent toward and beyond the realm of pure being, which had its roots in Plato's *Symposium* (cf. 210A–212A). Interest in this technique shows itself in such figures as Philo, Numenius, the author(s) of the *Chaldean Oracles*, and in Plotinus. This technique not only supplemented earlier apocalyptic notions of ecstatic visionary ascent (perhaps associated with the spiritualized Sethian baptismal ritual as in *Trimorphic Protennoia, Gospel of the Egyptians, Zostrianos,* and perhaps in *Marsanes*), but it also created new forms apparently independent of such a baptismal context as in *Allogenes* and *Three Steles of Seth.* Most importantly, though, the older pattern of enlightenment through gnōsis "knowledge," conferred by a descending redeemer figure, could be replaced by a self-performable act of enlightenment through contemplative or visionary ascent, whether for individuals (*Allogenes* and *Marsanes*) or for a community (*Three Steles of Seth*).

III. Chronology and Redaction

On the background of these basic complexes of ideas, the following reconstruction of the composition and redaction of the Sethian treatises is suggested, although it is impossible to know which version of a particular document may have been available at each stage to the composers of the various treatises. Thus one ought perhaps to speak more generally of the redaction and incorporation of doctrines and traditions rather than of the particular extant documents that today serve as their exponents or instances.

A. Before 100 C.E.

One might begin with the (already Christianized) Ophite system of Irenaeus (cf. *Haer.* I.30), where one finds the triad of beings Man, Son of Man, and Third Male, the first two of whom, as suggested above, may

have been conceived as androgynous. There is also a lower mother
figure, the Spirit, who emits Sophia-Prunicos, who by gravity descends
to and agitates the waters below, taking on a material body. When she is
empowered from above to escape this body and ascend to the height,
she becomes the father of the Archon Yaldabaoth. The Archon produces
seven sons named as in the *Apocryphon of John*, and boasts that he
alone is God, to which his mother responds that "Man and the Son of
Man" are above him. Then follows the making of the man and the
woman both of whom are specially enlightened by Sophia, and the
stories of the tree of *gnōsis*, the expulsion from paradise, the birth of
Cain, Abel, Seth and Norea, the flood, and finally the incognito descent
of Christ, the Third Male, through the seven heavens. He puts on Sophia
and rescues the crucified Jesus. Many of these motifs are at home in the
Sethian treatises, but especially in *Ap. John* BG8502,2:44,19ff.; NHC
II,1:13,3ff. (similarly in other versions), which is not paralleled by the
Barbeloite system of Iren. *Haer.* I.29. Much of this material common to
the *Apocryphon of John* and the Ophites is connected with the interpretation of Genesis 2–6, and one also finds versions of this material in
the *Apocalypse of Adam, Hypostasis of the Archons*, and summarized in
the *Gospel of the Egyptians*. The Ophite system describes repeated
salvific acts of Sophia: providing the divine model for the protoplast,
enlightening of Eve, protecting her light-trace from conception through
the Archon, aiding the conception through the Archon, revealing the
significance of Adam and Eve's bodies, and aiding the conception of
Seth and Norea and the birth of the wise Jesus. The final salvific act is
the deliverance of Sophia and Jesus by Christ.

   1. *Early Sethian Eschatology.* The Sethian versions of this activity
structure it into four distinct epochs of saving history marked by the
flood, the conflagration and the judgment of the powers as in the
Apocalypse of Adam and *Gospel of the Egyptians*. Or the epochs are
marked by three distinct manifestations of a being more exalted than
Sophia who descends first in a male mode, then in a female mode as
Epinoia, and finally as the Logos (as in the *Apocryphon of John,
Trimorphic Protennoia* and *Gospel of the Egyptians*). What makes the
Sethian versions' adoption of this history of deliverance distinctive is
their stress on Seth and their self-identification with Seth's seed, "the
unshakeable race," who since the flood and conflagration live simultaneously on earth and in the aeons of the four Lights until the judgment
of the Archons by a dramatic eschatological manifestation of Seth as the
Logos. Between the conflagration and the final judgment of the Archons,
the Sethians keep in contact with their heavenly counterparts by means
of: (a) revelations Seth left behind inscribed on steles of brick and clay,

or on wooden tablets, or in certain books, all preserved on a special mountain, as well as by means of (b) a ritual of celestial ascent conceived in baptismal imagery, which Seth conferred upon his seed for their enlightenment.

2. *Sethian Tripartitions.* In accord with their tripartition of the history of salvation and of the modes in which the redeemer appears throughout this history, the Sethians structured their transcendent world into Father-Mother-Son triads as a more distinctive way of conceiving the saving work of the transcendent (aspect of) Sophia than was the (more biblical) triad of Man (the high deity), Son of Man (the androgynous heavenly Adam), and a Son of the Son of Man (Seth; cf. the terminology of the non-Sethian *Eugnostos* and *Sophia of Jesus Christ*). The androgynous image of God could be conceived either as the heavenly Adam (Adamas, Geradamas) or, stressing its female aspect, as the Thought (Ennoia) of the high deity who could be conceived as the Mother of the Son of Man. Thus her voice reveals to the Archon the existence of her higher consort, Man or the Father, and of her offspring, the Son of Man. Of course, conceiving the second member of the triad as female, a transcendent Sophia-figure distinguished from the Sophia who worked below, meant a transformation of the second member into a Mother (still androgynous) figure distinguished from Adamas the Son of Man (who now takes third place). This duplication is reflected in the alternate but equivalent designations of the Mother as, for instance, male virgin, womb, Father of the All, first Man, and thrice-male. Note, for example, how the second part of the *Apocryphon of John* in NHC II prefers the designation Mother-Father (II,1:5,7; 19,17; 20,9; 27,33) instead of the designation "merciful Father" or "merciful Mother" as in BG8502,2 (but cf. 77,11 which has "Mother-Father"). While this might account for the identification of the Father and Mother portion of the triad, the identification of the Son is a more complex problem. Given the tripartite Sethian history of salvation, the Son would be involved in the third and finally decisive salvific manifestation of the divine into the world. He could be the third manifestation of the Illuminator (*Apocalypse of Adam*) or the Logos which puts on Jesus, which in *Gospel of the Egyptians* is identified with Seth or in *Trimorphic Protennoia* with Christ. Or he could be viewed as the Christ who has appeared to John the son of Zebedee after the resurrection (*Apocryphon of John*). Or he could be simply conceived as the third and finally effective saving manifestation of the divine as in the Pronoia-hymn at the end of the *Apocryphon of John* II,1 (not even distinguished as Son).

This divine triad could be conceived in two fundamental ways: as a vertically schematized ontological hierarchy that gives rise to and structures the transcendent world, or else as a horizontally schematized succession of three divine manifestations. In the latter case, the three manifestations might be conceived as three manifestations of a single being in three modes such as the Father-Voice, Mother-Speech, Son-Logos (*Trimorphic Protennoia*), or as three separate beings in some sense identical with but mythologically distinguished from a higher being, such as the Autogenes, the Epinoia of Light, and Christ, all sent by the (Mother-)Father in the *Apocryphon of John*. The vertical scheme is illustrated in the Invisible Spirit, Barbelo, and the Autogenes in *Allogenes, Zostrianos, Three Steles of Seth* and *Marsanes*. In the Christianized Sethian theogonies, the third level is called either Christ (Iren. *Haer.* I.29, *Apocryphon of John* and the first part of *Trimorphic Protennoia*) or the Thrice-Male Child of the Great Christ (*Gospel of the Egyptians*).

3. *Hymnic Accounts of the Savior's Descent.* A careful reading of the *Apocryphon of John* (longer version) reveals that *Trimorphic Protennoia* is, in part, an expansion of the concluding Pronoia hymn (*Ap. John* II,1:30,12–31,25). The hymn contains a brief aretalogical self-predication of the divine Pronoia speaking in the first person singular (31,12–16) followed by the narration of her three descents into Chaos or Hades taking on the form of the seed to save them (30,16–21; 30,21–31; 30,31–31,25). In the third stanza there is a sudden shift from a third person plural to a third person singular designation for her seed, introduced by a gloss in 31,4 identifying the prison of Hades as the prison of the body. This seems to introduce material originally foreign to the hymn (reflected once earlier in *Ap. John* II,1:23,30–31) employing the *topos* of awakening sleepers (cf. Eph 5:14) ensnared in the bonds of oblivion by reminding them of their predicament (31,4–10 and 31,14–22). It seems likely that the third stanza of the original hymn must have concluded:

> And I entered into the middle of their prison and I said: "I am the Pronoia of the pure light; I am the thinking of the virginal Spirit, he who raised you (plural) up to the honored place." And I raised them up and sealed them in the light of the water with Five Seals in order that death might not have power over them from this time on.

One finds a very close equivalent of this hymn in the second half of the Naasene Psalm (Hipp. *Ref.* 5.10.2), where Jesus says:

> Look Father: this prey (the fallen soul) to evils is wandering away to earth, far from thy Spirit, and she seeks to escape the bitter Chaos but knows not how to win through. For that reason send me, Father. Bearing Seals I shall descend; I will pass through all the Aeons; I shall reveal all the mysteries and I shall deliver the secrets of the holy way, calling them Gnosis.[3]

[3] See Marcovich, "Naasene Psalm," whose translation I adopt.

Clearly these two hymns have been influenced by the same complex of ideas: the descent of a revealer bearing seals into Chaos, and its bitterness, to rescue the soul below. While the Naasene Psalm also tells of the descent of the soul and displays the male Jesus as savior, the Pronoia hymn tells only of the threefold descent of the feminine Pronoia (or remembrance thereof), the last of which succeeds in raising up Pronoia's members, who are viewed as consubstantial with her.

4. *A Descent Hymn Elaborated: Trimorphic Protennoia.* The Pronoia hymn, or something much like it, then underwent expansion in its first stage as an aretalogy of Protennoia as Father-Voice, Mother-Speech, and Son-Word now found in *Trimorphic Protennoia*. Furthermore, another stage of composition was devoted to spelling out the "mysteries" communicated by the revealer as well as the nature of the (Five) "Seals" brought by him or her. A final stage saw to its Christianization.

Assuming that *Trimorphic Protennoia* finds its basis in the hymnic ending of the longer version of the *Apocryphon of John,* a closer analysis shows the following approximate compositional history for *Trimorphic Protennoia.* The underlying basis of the tractate can be seen in the consistent *egō eimi* "I am" self-predications of Protennoia which are structured into an introductory aretalogy (XIII,1:35,1–32) identifying Protennoia as the divine Thought (35,1–32) followed by three *egō eimi* aretalogies of about forty lines each in the same style. The second and third of these aretalogies form separate subtractates in *Trimorphic Protennoia* (Protennoia is the Voice of the Thought who descends first as light into darkness and gives shape to her fallen members [35,32–36,27; 40,29–41,1]; Protennoia is the Speech of the Thought's Voice who descends second to empower her fallen members by giving them spirit or breath [42,4–27; 45,2–12; 45,21–46,3]; and Protennoia is the Word of the Speech of the Thought's Voice who descends a third time in the likeness of the powers, proclaims the Five Seals, and restores her seed [members] into the Light [46,5–7; 47,5–23; 49,6–23; 50,9–20]). If this, or something like it, is what the author started with, it can be seen that he has expanded this tripartite aretalogy with six doctrinal insertions (36,27–40,29; 41,1–42,2; 42,27–45,2; 46,7–47,top; 47,24–49,top and 49,22–50,9). Three of these insertions are "mysteries" which Protennoia is said to have communicated to her sons. The first and longest insertion (36,27–40,29) narrates the story of the Autogenes Christ and his four Lights. The last of these Lights (Eleleth) emits Sophia (his Epinoia) to produce the demon Yaldabaoth who steals the Epinoia's power to create the lower aeons and man. It concludes with the restoration of Epinoia-Sophia who is regarded as completely innocent of fault. It is constructed in third person narrative.

The first of the "mysteries" (41,1–42,2) narrates the loosening of the bonds of flesh by which the underworld powers enslave Protennoia's fallen members. This mystery is announced in direct discourse to a second person plural audience. The second mystery (42,27–45,2), called the "mystery of the (end of) this age" (42,28), is addressed to a similar group in the second person plural. It narrates an apocalyptic announcement of the end of the old age and the dawn of the new age with the judgment of the authorities of chaos, the celestial powers, and their Archigenetor. The third mystery (47,24–49,top), called "the mystery of Gnosis" (48,33–34) is again addressed to a second person plural audience, now called the "brethren." It narrates the descent of Protennoia as the Word who descends incognito through the various levels of the powers and strips away the corporeal and psychic thought from her brethren and raises them up to the Light by means of a baptismal-celestial ascent ritual identified as the Five Seals.

It is clear that *Trimorphic Protennoia* has been secondarily Christianized. Three glosses identifying the Autogenes Son with Christ in the first subtractate (37,[31]; 38,22; 39,6–7) probably derive from the traditional theogonical materials common to the *Apocryphon of John* and Iren., *Haer.* I.29, upon which the author has drawn. But in the third subtractate the situation is much different, and seems to suggest that *Trimorphic Protennoia* has undergone three stages of composition. First, there was the triad of aretalogical *egō eimi* self-predications of Protennoia as Voice, Speech, and Word. Second, this was supplemented by doctrinal insertions based upon traditional Sethian cosmological materials similar to those of *Apocryphon of John* and Iren. *Haer.* I.29, as well as upon (apparently non-Sethian) traditional materials treating the harrowing of hell and the eschatological overthrow of the celestial powers, and again upon Sethian traditions about the baptismal ascent ritual of the Five Seals. After circulation as a Sethian tractate in this form, the third stage of composition seems to have been the incorporation of Christian materials into the aretalogical portion of the third subtractate.

Specifically, the narrative of the incognito descent of Protennoia as Word, hidden in the form of the Sovereignties, Powers, and Angels, culminating in the final revelation of herself in her members below, seems to have undergone a Christological interpretation. In 47,14–15, it is said that as Logos, Protennoia revealed herself to "them" (i.e., humans?) "in their tents" as the Word (cf. John 1:14). In 49,7–8 it is said that the Archons thought Protennoia-Logos was "their Christ," while actually she is the Father of everyone. In 49,11–15, Protennoia identifies herself as the "beloved" (of the Archons), since she clothed herself as

Son of the Archigenetor until the end of his ignorant decree. In 49,18–20 Protennoia reveals herself as a Son of Man among the Sons of Man even though she is the Father of everyone. In 50,6–9, Protennoia will reveal herself to her "brethren" and gather them into her "eternal kingdom." In 50,12–16, Protennoia has put on Jesus and borne him aloft from the cross into his Father's dwelling places (cf. John 14:2–3). In this way traditional Christological titles such as Christ, Beloved, Son of God ("Son of the Archigenetor") and Son of Man are polemically interpreted in a consciously docetic fashion. By implication, the "orthodox" Christ is shown to be the Christ of the "Sethian" Archons; the "orthodox" Beloved is the beloved of the Archons; the "orthodox" Son of God is the "Sethian" son of the ignorant Archigenetor; and the "orthodox" Son of Man is only a human among the sons of men, while for the Sethians, the true Son of Man is Adamas, the Son of the supreme deity Man (the human form in which the deity revealed himself as in *Ap. John* II,1:14,14–24 and *Gos. Eg.* III,2:59,1–9), or perhaps he is Seth, the Son of Adamas as in *Ap. John* II,1:24,32–25,7. Therefore, the Protennoia-Logos is in reality the Father of everyone, the Father of the All who only *appears* as the Logos "in their tents" (*skēnē*; a gloss on "the likeness of their shape" in *Trim. Prot.* XIII,1:47,16 in what seems to be conscious opposition to John 1:14). That is, he *appeared* in the "likeness of their shape" but did not become flesh as the "orthodox" believe. In only disguising himself as the "orthodox" Christ, the Logos indeed had to rescue Jesus from the "cursed" (not redemptive!) cross and restore him to the "dwelling places of his Father." In what seems a conscious reference to John 14:2–3, Jesus did not prepare a place for his followers; instead, the Logos, invisible to the celestial powers who watch over the aeonic dwellings (i.e., the four Lights?), installs Jesus into his Father's dwelling place (*Trim. Prot.* XIII,1:50,12–16; perhaps in the Light Oroiael as in *Gos. Eg.* III,2:65,16–17).

Most of these polemical Sethian reinterpretations of "orthodox" Christology in *Trimorphic Protennoia* seem to depend on key texts from the Gospel of John in order to score their point in any acute fashion, although this has been a matter of scholarly dispute.[4] It seems that the

---

[4] Cf. the discussions of G. Schenke, "Protennoia"; Helderman, "Zelten"; H.-M. Schenke, "Sethianism," 607–12; and summarizing the debate, Robinson, "Sethians." My own position is that *Trimorphic Protennoia* underwent superficial Christianization in its second stage of redaction, but specific and polemical Christianization in its third stage of redaction. The superficial resemblances to the Johannine prologue scattered throughout *Trimorphic Protennoia* are to be explained by the emergence of both texts from gnosticizing oriental sapiental traditions at home in first-century Syria and Palestine, as suggested by Colpe, "Überlieferung," 122–24. The Christological glosses in the first sub-tractate are to be explained by the influence of the theogonical section of the *Apoc-*

key to the resolution of this dispute lies in the recognition that *Tri-morphic Protennoia*, in its first two stages of composition, was a product of non-Christian Sethianism, drawing its Logos-theology from a fund of oriental speculation on the divine Word and Wisdom as did the pro-logue to the Gospel of John in a similar but independent way. But both the prologue and *Trimorphic Protennoia* later underwent Christianiza-tion in a later stage of redaction; the prologue in Johannine Christian circles, and *Trimorphic Protennoia* in Christianized Sethian circles. Indeed, *Trimorphic Protennoia* may have undergone Christianizing redaction in the environment of the debate over the interpretation of the Gospel of John during the early second century. This debate is reflected in the Johannine letters, and a bit later in western Valentinian circles is concerned with the interpretation of the Logos (e.g., The *Tripartite Tractate* of NHC I) and of the Gospel of John (e.g., Ptolemaeus in Iren. *Haer.* I.8.5 and the Fragments of Heracleon).

5. *The Early Sethian Baptismal Rite.* The spiritualized conception of baptism as a saving ritual of enlightenment reflected in the Sethian texts must also have been current in the first century, to judge from the complex of ideas in Col 2:8–15, where circumcision (regarded as a stripping off of the body of flesh) is connected with a baptism conceived as a dying and rising, and Christ's death is interpreted as a disarming of the principalities and powers. To judge from the Sethian baptismal mythologumena, the Sethians, wherever they derived their original rite, must have developed it in close rapprochement with Christianity. They must have sustained their initial encounter with Christianity as fellow practitioners of baptism, indeed a baptism interpreted in a very sym-bolic and spiritual direction. For example, the Sethian name for their Living Water, itself a conception found also in Johannine Christianity (John 4:7–15), is Yesseus Mazareus Yessedekeus, which seems very much like a version of the name of Jesus into which Christians were baptized, perhaps in a threefold way. Yet to adopt this name did not necessarily mean understanding oneself principally as a Christian, as the rather cryptic and concealed form of this name suggests. Indeed it was adopted by the redactor of the (apparently in all other respects) non-Christian *Apocalypse of Adam.*

In many respects, the baptismal rite seems to have provided the

ryphon *of John.* But the more striking parallels to the Gospel of John discussed here, as well as the explicit application of apparent Christological titles to Protennoia-Logos, seem to me to constitute deliberate "Christianization," although in a strictly polemical vein. Whether the redactor of the third compositional stage hypothesized by me is really Sethian or heterodox Christian is impossible to tell; in any case he is certainly not an "orthodox" or "apostolic" Christian, though perhaps he might be a "super Johannine" (heretic) of the sort suggested by Brown, "Sheep."

context or occasion for many of the principal Sethian themes to coalesce in various combinations. This is quite obvious in the case of the Sethian rite of cultic or individual ascent, and also in the theme of the descent of the redeemer bearing the Five Seals. Yet the web of interlocking themes could be even more complex, as in the case of *Apocalypse of Adam*, part of which seems to draw on an old mythical pattern to illustrate thirteen versions of the descent of the Illuminator. It exhibits a myth which could be developed in various ways to portray the origin of mankind, the origin of the Savior, and perhaps the origin of both water baptism and celestial baptism as well.

In a very illuminating article, J. M. Robinson[5] drew attention to a series of striking parallels between the structure and motifs of the thirteen kingdoms, i.e., thirteen opinions concerning the coming of the Illuminator "to the water," and a similar mythical structure to be found in the NT Apocalypse of john (Rev 12:1–17) and reflected in the baptism and "temptation" stories of Mark 1:9–13, and in some fragments from the *Gospel of the Hebrews*. As can be seen from Robinson's study, there underlies Mark 1, Revelation 12 and *Apoc. Adam* V,5:77,26–82,19 a basic mythical structure concerning a divine child and his divine mother who are threatened by an evil power, but who are rescued and find safety in the wilderness until the evil power is destroyed. This general pattern could be made to apply not only to Adam and his divine mother or to Seth and his mother Eve, but also to the birth of Jesus, to Mary and their flight to Egypt from Herod, and perhaps more remotely to certain aspects of the Isis-Osiris-Horus cycle.

For our immediate purposes, however, it is important to see that facets of such a myth were applied to baptism not only in Mark (where wilderness is also ultimately a place of safety) and in the fragments of *Gospel of the Hebrews* but also in *Apocalypse of Adam*. In Mark the Savior is baptized in the (ordinary) water to which he comes, after which the Spirit descends to the Savior together with a Voice that pronounces him Son of God. The parallel in Matthew agrees, but has reservations about the baptism in water by John. Luke omits explicit mention of Jesus' baptism by John, and has the Spirit descend on Jesus during his post-baptismal prayer. The Fourth Gospel suppresses Jesus' explicit baptism by John in mere water, demoting John to the Voice of one crying in the wilderness, whose only subsequent function is to witness to the descent of the Spirit upon Jesus. Instead, the Fourth Gospel (John 4:7–15) understands Jesus as the source of Living Water, which to drink means eternal life, and as the one who will baptize with the Holy Spirit,

---

[5] Robinson, *"Gattung of Mark,"* 119–29.

which the author identifies with the Living Water (John 7:37–39). Like-wise, the second compositional stage of *Trimorphic Protennoia* regards the Logos, who descends with the Five Seals at the conclusion of the first-stage aretalogy, as the Logos-Son. He pours forth Living Water upon the Spirit below out of its source, which is the Father-Voice aspect of Protennoia, called the unpolluted spring of Living Water. So also *Gospel of the Egyptians* understands the descent of Seth as Logos to be the bestowal of a holy baptism, probably in Living Water. These baptismal descents of the Logos or Seth are initiated by Barbelo, the Father-Mother, an exalted Sophia figure, who communicates to those who love her by Voice or Word (the Johannine prologue, *Trimorphic Protennoia*). Jewish wisdom texts portray the exalted Sophia as the fountain or spring (cf. Sirach 24; Philo, *Fug.* 195) from which comes the Word like a river (Philo, *Somn.* 2.242; cf. *Fug.* 97), the Mother of the Word through whom the universe came to be (*Fug.* 109; cf. *Trimorphic Protennoia* and the Johannine prologue). To be baptized in her water is to receive true *gnōsis*. Thus her Voice (*bath qol*) is the revelation of the truth: e.g., "Man exists and the Son of Man" in the *Apocryphon of John* or the *Gospel of the Egyptians*; "This is my beloved Son" in Mark 1:11 (cf. 9:7), where the heavenly Voice comes down to water; similarly the Voices in *Trim. Prot.* XIII,1:40,8–9; 44,29–32 and *Apoc. Adam* V,5:84,4. Indeed it is likely that *Trimorphic Protennoia* derived its scheme of Voice, Speech, and Logos from such a complex of notions.

The conclusion to be drawn from these clusters of ideas is that the Sethian soteriology involving the saving descent of Barbelo, or of her Voice, or of Seth or of the Logos was most likely worked out in a baptismal environment characterized by speculation on the significance of words spoken and waters involved (cf. *Zost.* VIII,1:15) during the first century.[6] In this environment it rubbed shoulders with Christianity, but

---

[6] Gnostic Sethianism must have originated among the numerous baptismal sects that populated Syria and Palestine, especially along the Jordan valley, in the period 200 B.C.E.–300 C.E.: the Essenes/Dead Sea sect, the pre-Christian Nasareans of Epiphanius, John the Baptist and his followers, the Jewish-Christian Nazorenes, the Ebionites, Pauline and Johannine Christians, Naasenes, Valentinians/Marcosians, Elkasaites, Sabeans, Dositheans, Masbotheans, Gorothenians, Hemero-baptists, Mandeans, and the groups behind the *Odes of Solomon, Acts of Thomas, Pseudo-Clementines,* Justin's *Baruch,* etc. (cf. Thomas, *Mouvement baptiste*). These baptismal rites, often representing a spiritualizing protest against a failing or extinct sacrificial temple cultus (so Thomas), are mostly descendants of ancient Mesopotamian New Year enthronement rituals in which the king, stripped of his regalia, symbolically undergoes a struggle with the dark waters of chaos, cries for aid, is raised up and nourished by water or food, absolved and strengthened by a divine oracle, enthroned, enrobed, and acclaimed as king, acquiring radiance and authority (e.g., tablets III and IV of "I will praise the Lord of Wisdom," ANET 434–36). Similar imagery of struggle and exaltation can be found in Psalms 18, 30, 69, 80, 89, 110, 114 and 146 (cf. 1 Kgs 1:38–47; it may be that suffering in the water and baptism [or drink]

probably did not fully take the step of identifying their savior with Christ or Jesus, which it would soon do, but in a rather polemical fashion.

are two aspects of the function of water in these rites). In 2 Esdr 13:1-6 the rising of the Son of Man is accompanied by the issuance of his cosmic voice. In 2 Enoch 22, Enoch is raised up before God by Michael, stripped of his earthly garments, anointed and enrobed in glory so that he shines. In the Maccabean period, T. Levi 8:2-10 portrays the priest Levi as "a priest forever" (cf. Melchizedek); he is commanded to put on priestly garments (including the garment of truth), but then is invested as a royal figure (anointed, given a staff, washed, fed bread and wine, clad with a glorious robe, linen vestment, purple girdle and crowned). In T. Levi 18:6-7 at the advent of the eschatological priest, a star arises, emitting the light of knowledge; the Father's voice issues from the heavenly temple; the spirit of understanding rests on him in the water; the priest will open the gates of paradise, feed the saints from the tree of life and bind Beliar.

Baptismal and ascensional motifs occur frequently in patristic heresiological reports: the Sethians (Hipp. Ref. 5.19.21: washing in and drinking from living water, celestial enrobing); Justin's Baruch (Hipp. Ref. 5.27.2-3: drinking from and baptism in living water as opposed to earthly water); the Naasenes (Hipp., Ref. 5.7.19: washing in living water, anointing; 5.8.14-18: issuance of the divine voice over the flood, passing through water and fire, lifting up of gates; 5.9.18-20: drink of living water) and the Marcosians (Iren. Haer. I.21.3-5 baptism in the name of Achamoth, anointing in the name of Jao, anointing for heavenly ascent). Valentinian baptism is reflected in the baptismal appendices to A Valentinian Exposition and in the Gospel of Philip. Baptismal motifs occur in the Odes of Solomon, especially Ode 11:7-16 (drinking living water, stripping away of folly, enrobing with radiance and enlightenment) and Ode 24:1-5 (the voice of the Dove above the Messiah and the opening of the abysses; cf. Ode 17:1-16 and its parallels with Trim. Prot. XIII,1:41,4-42,2 which is interpreted as a baptism). The sequence of acts in the Five Seals of Trim. Prot. XIII,1:48,15-35 is very much like the sequence of acts in the Mandaean Masbūtā as summarized by Rudolph, Mandäer, 2.88-89: entrance into the "Jordan," triple self-immersion, triple immersion by the priest, triple sign with water, triple drink, crowning, invocation of divine names, ritual handshake, and ascent from the "Jordan"). In Trimorphic Protennoia, the one baptized is enrobed before baptism as seems to be the case among the Qumran sectaries, the Mandaeans, and later Christian rites (apparently only Elchasaites were baptized naked).

It is quite likely that the early Sethian baptismal milieu was the setting for the baptismal mythologumena in the Sethian treatises, and especially for the hymnic materials in Gos. Eg. III,2, pp.66-67, Apoc. Adam V,5, pp.78-82, Melch. XI,1, pp.5-6 and 16-18, and in the baptismal material of Trimorphic Protennoia. These materials seem to envision the descent of the savior into the world, corresponding to the descent of the king or of the one baptized into water or world of chaos, but also the spiritual visionary ascent of the one baptized out of the water, or world, into the light, corresponding to the enthronement and exaltation of the king, priest, or priest-king. Allogenes, Three Steles of Seth, and especially Zostrianos with its celestial baptism reflect in their visionary ascent scheme only the enthronement-exaltation-glorification aspect of the baptismal rite. There seems to be a close correspondence of the pattern of baptismal immersion and emergence with the humiliation and exaltation pattern of the ancient enthronement rituals. On such grounds certain of the NT Christological hymns employing a similar pattern may also be seen against a baptismal environment, especially the Johannine prologue, Phil 2:6-11, Col 2:9-15, 1 Tim 3:16, and 1 Pet 3:18-22. The portrayal of the deliverer or his forerunner as a light dawning (anatellein or anatolē) or entering the world is associated with the advent of the priest-king of T. Levi 18 and of John the Baptist (of priestly descent) in Luke 1:76-79 (and perhaps in the Johannine prologue if it once applied to the Baptist). Such texts may in part reflect the eschatological advent of the star and scepter of Num 24:17 (often interpreted as referring to a royal and a priestly messiah by the Dead

6. *The Earliest Sethian Compositions.*   Thus I would suggest that by
the end of the first century, Sethians possessed at least the following
sacred texts. First, several versions of a possibly hymnic narrative of the
threefold descent of the divine Mother like the one contained at the end
of the longer version of *Apocryphon of John* according to which the
third descent was finally effective and was understood to be the mythical origin of a Sethian baptismal rite called the Five Seals. This might
also have existed in the form now embedded as source B in C. W.
Hedrick's redactional theory of the *Apocalypse of Adam*,[7] in which three
men (!) appear to Adam in a dream to awaken him from the sleep of
death (V,5:65,24–66,12; 67,12–21). They speak of the third descent of the
Illuminator who performs acts that disturb the God of the powers. He
cannot recognize the power of this "man" and punishes his flesh only
after he has caused his elect to shine and he has withdrawn to the holy
houses (the four Lights?) in the great aeon from which he had come
(V,5:76,8–11; 76,14–82,17; 82,19–83,4). Indeed, the redactor leads us to
believe that prior to his withdrawal, he imparted to his elect a secret
gnōsis which is "the holy baptism of those who know the eternal

Sea sect; cf. 1 QM 11,6; 1 QSb 5,20–25; 4 QTestim 9–13; CD 7,9–21; also *T. Judah* 24 and
Rev 22:16).
     The judgment upon the sons of Seth reflected in Num 24:17, as interpreted in the
Damascus Document (CD 7,9–21) and the Samaritan tradition (*Asatir* II,3), that Seth
founded Damascus have been used to show that the Samaritans of Damascus claimed to
be the true generation of Seth (the people of the Northern Kingdom) whom the scepter,
the prince of the Qumran community, was coming to destroy (Beltz, "Samaritanertum").
Since no orthodox Samaritan traditions reflect this Qumran tradition, Beltz suggests it
was a Samaritan sectarian tradition, and that it was the Dositheans who thought of
themselves as sons of Seth, an identification perhaps reflected in the mention of
Dositheus in *Steles Seth* VII,5:118,10–19. While a connection between the Sethians and
Dositheans is only a suggestion, certain Dositheans apparently constituted a baptizing
sect of the first and second centuries C.E. (Vilmar, *Abulfathi annales*, 151–59; *Ps. Clem.
Rec.* 2.8 and *Hom.* 2.24; Origen, *Cels.* 1.57; 6.11; Euseb. *Eccl. Hist.* 4.22; cf. Montgomery,
Samaritans, 253–63). The Pseudo-Clementines link Dositheus with Simon Magus and
John the Baptist (*Rec.* 1:54–63; 2.8; *Hom.* 2.15–24; 3.22); these accounts are of doubtful
historical value, but they may reflect an original association of John or Simon or
Dositheus with Samaria. A possible connection between John (and Jesus!) and Samaria
occurs in the first four chapters of the Fourth Gospel, especially if his baptismal activity
at Ainon near Salim is to be located in Samaria as Scobie thinks (*John the Baptist*, 163–
77; 187–202; perhaps this Ainon=spring has to do with "ainon" in *Gos. Eg.* IV,2:44,25 and
"ainos" in *Trim. Prot.* XIII,1:39,1). These possible links between the Baptist, heterodox
Samaritanism, the Fourth Gospel and early Sethianism deserve further investigation. In
any case, both John the Baptist and Seth are portrayed as eschatological figures who
introduce a baptismal rite, as Jesus also is portrayed insofar as he is identified with Seth
in the Sethian literature. The introduction of this rite is connected with a cosmic
judgment, involves a passing through water and, in the synoptics, a pending baptism with
fire (or the Holy Spirit). These are complexes of ideas which in an early Sethian
baptismal environment might have been linked to the Sethian tripartite eschatology
marked by flood, fire and final judgment.
     [7] Hedrick, "Adam," and more fully, *Apocalypse*.

knowledge through those born of the word and the imperishable illuminators (the four Lights?) who came from the holy seed (of the celestial Sethians): Yesseus, Mazareus, Yessedekeus, [the Living] Water" (V,5:85,22–31). Furthermore, the tripartite narrative attributed above to the first redactional stage of *Trimorphic Protennoia* would belong here.

B. 100–125 C.E.

The first quarter of the second century must have seen the development of a theogonical account of the successive begettings of the triad Father-Mother-Son conceived as the Invisible Spirit, Barbelo, and their Son. Such an account underlies the Barbeloite system in Iren. *Haer.* I.29. By now, the basic triad has been embellished by the addition of an elementary set of hypostatized divine attributes, which themselves could form pairs so as to produce further beings, such as the four Lights which were probably objects of vision in the spiritualized Sethian baptismal rite of the Five Seals. The first quarter of the second century seems to have been a period of vigorous arithmological speculation on the first ten numbers, but especially the first four numbers, comprising the Pythagorean *tetraktys* "the sum of the first four numbers." This was carried on by such Pythagoreanizing Platonists as Theon of Smyrna and Nicomachus of Gerasa, who in turn depend in part on similar arithmological and mathematical theories produced by such early first-century Platonist figures as Dercyllides, Adrastos of Aphrodisias (a Peripatetic commentator on Plato's *Timaeus*) and Thrasyllos, a court philosopher under the Emperor Tiberius. The harmonic ratios produced by these first four numbers and the geometric entities of point, line, surface, and solid had been applied to the structure and the creation of the world soul long before by Plato and his successors in the old Academy, especially Speusippus and Xenocrates. Thus it is not necessary to assume that the Barbeloite system of Iren. *Haer.* I.29 is dependent upon Valentinus or his successors, Polemy and Heracleon, or vice versa, since this arithmological lore was by now readily available in the handbooks employed in the dense network of urban schools where anyone who wished to become literate might study them alongside the *Timaeus* itself. Although this Sethian "Barbeloite" theogonical material exists in a number of treatises each of which adds its own special touches (e.g., Iren. *Haer.* I.29, *Apocryphon of John, Gospel of the Egyptians, Allogenes, Zostrianos, Three Steles of Seth, Marsanes* and *Trimorphic Protennoia*), it seems that the material common to the *Apocryphon of John* and Iren. *Haer.* I.29 represents the earliest form.

In the early second century the principal emphasis of gnostic speculation on the beyond seems to be the explanation of how the current

world came to be and how and whence the savior originated and
descended with enlightening gnōsis. This speculation seemed to require
a Father and Mother who produced and sent the Son. The peculiar
exegesis of Genesis 1–6 with its emphasis on the primordial origins of
the heavenly and earthly Sethians was the only obvious aetiology by
which the Sethians could maintain any sense of separate identity as the
elect ones. This mythology, presented in narrative as a temporal succession of successive human generations, required to be matched by a
similar but less temporally conceived succession of the unfolding hypostases and offspring of the high deity.

    1. *The Apocryphon of John.* To judge from Iren. *Haer* I.29 and the
four versions of the *Apocryphon of John* (which represent already
Christianized versions of the Sethian myth of Barbelo the Mother and
the sender of both the primordial saviors, Autogenes and Epinoia
[Sophia, Eve] and also the eschatological savior, the Autogenes [Chris-
tianized as Christ], the *Apocryphon of John* first exhibited the following
profile. The Father, the invisible virginal Spirit, emitted his female
aspect conceived as his Thought (Ennoia) which took shape as his First
Thought (or Forethought) named Barbelo, who in Jewish tradition was
probably a manifestation of the divine Name. Since (as her name
suggests) God is in four, she requests the Invisible Spirit to realize four
of her attributes as separate hypostases: Foreknowledge, Incorruptibility, Eternal Life and Self-begotten or Autogenes. The last of these is
later identified with her Son Adamas, or Christ. Since Barbelo is the
self-begotten divine Mind and wisdom of God, her Son should likewise
possess similar powers and so his own attributes (Mind, Will, Logos and
Truth) are manifested. At this point, there remains to be explained the
origin of the four Lights, the celestial dwellings of Adamas, Seth, the
celestial seed of Seth, and the future home of the historical Sethians.
They are a traditional part of the Sethian's baptismal lore as shown in
Gos. Eg. III,2:64,9–65,26 and in the baptismal prayer in *Melch.* IX,1:16,
16–18,7. The four Lights are explained by forming a tetrad of pairs
composed of the hypostatized attributes of both Barbelo and her Son so
that the "Autogenes" attribute of the Son and the Incorruptibility aspect
of Barbelo produced the four Lights: Harmozel, Oroiael, Davithe, and
Eleleth. At that point, to judge from the current versions of the
Apocryphon of John and the *Gospel of the Egyptians*, Barbelo caused a
further pairing of her attribute of Eternal Life and her Son's attribute of
Will (Thelēma). They give rise to four further feminine attributes, Grace,
Will (Thelēsis), Understanding, and Wisdom (the upper Sophia, perhaps
called Phronesis; cf. *Hyp. Arch.* II,4:93,18–19 and 94,2–4). This sets the
stage for the fall of Sophia, a lower aspect of the Mother. After giving

rise to the Archon, she projects the image of the Son, Adamas. Later still, she causes the conception of Seth and his seed, whom she also rescues, either by herself or, as in the *Apocalypse of Adam*, by angelic beings, perhaps the servants of the Lights. In order to provide even more primordial spiritual prototypes of these beings, a further pairing of attributes, the Mother's Foreknowledge and the Son's Mind, must have produced the archetypal patterns for Adam, Seth, and his seed. They are then placed in the first three of the four Lights, leaving the fourth as a dwelling for the restored lower Sophia.

The systems of Irenaeus and the *Apocryphon of John* each contain subtle departures from this hypothetical arrangement, either by way of simplification, confusion, or more likely, in the case of the *Apocryphon of John*, to enhance the position of Christ instead of Adamas as the Son in the wake of Christianization. As van den Broek has pointed out,[8] the birth of Autogenes from Ennoia and Logos found in Irenaeus is suppressed in the *Apocryphon of John* because Autogenes is identified with the Christ who has, in the extant versions of the Barbeloite system, become identified as the Son of the Father and Barbelo. He points out that while in the *Apocryphon of John* Christ the Son is identified with his Autogenes aspect, in Iren. *Haer.* I.29, this Autogenes and his son Adamas are lower beings produced by Ennoia and Logos. They receive, however, great honor in a way that would suit a much higher being. He shows convincingly that, since Irenaeus says all things were subjected to Autogenes, the Barbeloite system originally considered him little less than God, crowned with glory and honor and given dominion over all things, an application of Ps 8:4–6. Originally, therefore, Autogenes had a higher rank. This would be the rank that Christ the Son now holds in the Christianized system, although this presupposes a stage still prior to the Father-Mother-Son triad in which there was Man and the Son of Man, little less than God. Thus the development of the bisexual nature of the Son of Man into Mother and Son demoted the Son, the Autogenes Adam, one notch. The Barbeloite system preserved the rank of Autogenes by identifying him with Christ (*Ap. John* BG8502,2:30,6; but not in NHC II,1) but demoted Adamas. On the other hand, Irenaeus' version demoted both Autogenes and Adamas, leaving only Christ as the supreme Son.

The *Apocryphon of John* results from a combination of this theogony with the Sethian story of Yaldabaoth's creation of the protoplasts and the subsequent struggle between him and the Mother depicted in terms of Genesis 2–6. The entire work is then construed as the final revelation

---

[8] "Autogenes."

of the Mother who in the form of Christ reveals the whole thing to his disciple John. The source upon which the longer and shorter versions seem to depend may possibly have been produced during the first quarter of the second century. The long negative theology of the Invisible Spirit at the beginning seems quite in keeping with the interests of such thinkers of this period as Basilides, the Neopythagorean Moderatus and, farther afield, of Albinus. As E. R. Dodds showed in 1928,[9] this negative theology is only a natural development of Plato's doctrine of the Good "beyond being in power and dignity" in the *Republic*, 509B and of the speculations about the non-being of the One in the *Parmenides*, 137Cff.

Perhaps by the end of the first quarter of the second century, the shorter recension (BG8502,2 and NHC III,1), supplemented by the short excursus on the soul (BG8502,2:64,9–71,2) came into existence in the form of a dialogue between the resurrected Christ and his disciple John, son of Zebedee, together with the appropriate Christian glosses substituting Christ for the Autogenes Adam (cf. the similar phenomenon in the case of *Eugnostos* and the *Sophia of Jesus Christ*).

2. *Trimorphic Protennoia.*   Perhaps at this time the second compositional stage of the *Trimorphic Protennoia* was also achieved by the addition of the four mysteries to the triple descent aretalogical narrative, as discussed above. The first of these mysteries indeed seems dependent on the already Christianized system common to the *Apocryphon of John* and Iren. *Haer.* I.29, and the fourth draws on the Sethian baptismal tradition of the Five Seals.

C. 125–150 C.E.

Toward the end of the first half of the second century, *Trimorphic Protennoia* may have reached its present (polemically) Christianized form. This period may also have seen the redaction of the longer version of the *Apocryphon of John* in Codices II and IV by the addition of a long section on the many angels that contributed parts to the body of the protoplastic Adam, claimed to be derived from a "book of Zoroaster" (II,1:15,29–19,11) and the inclusion of the Pronoia hymn at the end (II,1:30,11–31,25; discussed above).

1. *The Apocalypse of Adam* (Source B).   The redactional combination of a triple descent narrative culminating in the Sethian rite of baptismal enlightenment with a major version of the Sethian history of salvation derived from an exegesis of Genesis 1–6 in the case of the *Apocryphon of John* may have occurred at about the same time that part

---

[9] "The *Parmenides* of Plato," esp. 132–33.

of a similar triple descent narrative (fleshed out with the opinions on the thirteen kingdoms) in source B of the *Apocalypse of Adam* was connected by its redactor with the Genesis-inspired Sethian salvation history of source A. At the same time he also incorporated Sethian baptismal tradition, but in a polemical way. Although the *Apocalypse of Adam* was not Christianized in an obvious way by the redactor, it is at least arguable that Source B contained concepts that originated in close contact with Christianity such as the punishing of the flesh of the man upon whom the spirit has come (V,5:77,16–18) and the (unsatisfactory) speculations on the origin of the Illuminator as the son of a prophet, or son of a virgin or son of Solomon attributed to the second, third, and fourth kingdoms (V,5:78,7–79,19). Just as is the case with the Christological motifs in the third subtractate of *Trimorphic Protennoia*, such concepts seem to be introduced in a polemical vein, suggesting that the triple-descent motif may have been developed in connection with an attempt to distinguish Sethianism from Christianity with its increasing stress on the once-for-all nature of Christ's redeeming activity. For Christianity, the period of Israel was one only of preparation for the advent of salvation in Christ, while for the Sethians, salvation had been in principle already achieved in primordial times, with the raising of Seth and his seed into the Aeon. Thus the first and second descents of the redeemer had actually already performed the fundamental work of salvation in primordial times and left witnesses to it on inscribed steles and in books. The third descent of the redeemer is therefore only to remind the earthly Sethians of what had been accomplished for them in the past, and to grant them a means of realizing this in the present through the baptismal ascent ritual.

That this third descent of the redeemer is identified with the pre-existent Christ who brings salvation as *gnōsis* rather than salvation through his death on the cross should occasion no surprise. There were tendencies toward such views in Johannine Christian circles as well. One should bear in mind that also during this period (140–160 C.E.) Valentinus likewise developed the notion of a pneumatic Christ coming to waken the sleeping spirit in humankind, a notion which lies at the core of his system. Valentinus and his successors made Christ the focus of their system and thus were allied principally with Christianity. The Sethians, however, seemed to find their sense of uniqueness in opposition to the Church on the grounds just mentioned. Since various groups were not isolated from one another but freely made use of texts and ideas borrowed from other groups, the adoption of Christ into their system was only natural, but did not fundamentally change its basically non-Christian nature and inner cohesion.

2. *The Hypostasis of the Archons.*   Finally, it is also probable that in
the mid-second century or slightly later, *Hypostasis of the Archons*
reached its present Christianized form, perhaps derived from a hypothetical "Apocalypse of Norea," posited by H.-M. Schenke[10] as the
source common to *Hypostasis of the Archons* (II,4) and *On the Origin of
the World* (II,5). The prominence in this work of Norea as sister of Seth
and offspring and earthly manifestation of Sophia through Eve may
have inspired the short treatise *Norea*, which conceives Norea in two
levels. She is the upper Sophia who cried out to the Father of the All
(i.e., Adamas conceived as Ennoia) and was restored to her place in the
ineffable Epinoia (perhaps the Light Eleleth to whom she cries in
Hypostasis of the Archons) and thus in the divine Autogenes. Yet she is
also the lower Sophia manifested as daughter of Eve and wife-sister of
Seth who is also yet to be delivered from her deficiency, which will
surely be accomplished by the intercession of the four Lights, or their
ministers. It is interesting that here Adamas is himself the Father of the
All, yet is also called Nous and Ennoia as well as Father of Nous, a set of
identifications which recalls the bisexual nature of Adamas as both
Father and Mother, or Man and Son of Man (which are perhaps the two
names that make the "single name" Man).

In this presentation, I have urged an early dating (125–150 C.E.) for the
*Apocalypse of Adam, Hypostasis of the Archons, Norea, Trimorphic
Protennoia,* and the longer recension of the *Apocryphon of John;* earlier
yet (100–125 C.E.) for the shorter recension, the first two compositional
stages of *Trimorphic Protennoia* prior to its Christianization, and source
B of the *Apocalypse of Adam;* and a still earlier date (prior to 100 C.E.) for
the traditional materials they include: the Sophia myth, the exegesis of
Genesis 1–6 and other OT traditions, and an already spiritualized Sethian baptismal rite. Christian influence was at work in all these periods
and explicitly so in the last two, while Neopythagorean speculation becomes influential around 100–125 C.E. On the other hand, the polemical
use of Christological motifs appears in the last period, 125–150 C.E.,
when explicit heresiological summaries and refutations of the gnostic
systems begin to appear, e.g., Justin's lost *Syntagma.* All these documents stress the movement of salvation from above to below by means
of descending redeemer revealers appearing at certain special points in
primordial and recent history, bearing *gnōsis* and not infrequently
conferring a baptismal rite (not in *Norea* or *Hypostasis of the Archons*).

---

[10] "Sethianism," 596–97.

D. *150–200 C.E.*

Aside from *Allogenes, Zostrianos, Marsanes,* and *Three Steles of Seth,* there are two of the Sethian works which I have not placed in this period: *Melchizedek* and *Gospel of the Egyptians.* The latter seems to me to have taken shape a bit later, somewhere in the second half of the second century, since it seems to presuppose the existence of the extant versions of the *Apocryphon of John, Trimorphic Protennoia,* and the baptismal nomenclature (especially Yesseus Mazareus Yessedekeus) known to the redactor of *Apocalypse of Adam. Melch.* IX,1:16,16–18,7 and 5,17–6,10 also seem to presuppose, especially in its baptismal doxology, the five doxologies in *Gos. Eg.* IV,2:59,13–29; III,2:49,22–50,17; 53,12–54,11; 55,16–56,3; 61,23–62,13. The key element is the mention of Doxomedon as first-born of the Aeons, a name apparently unattested elsewhere except in *Gospel of the Egyptians* and *Zostrianos.*

1. *The Gospel of the Egyptians.* As H.-M. Schenke has suggested, the emphasis of *Gospel of the Egyptians* seems to lie upon baptismal traditions and prayers which conclude it (cf. III,2:64,9–68,1), while the preceding sections seem to function as a mythological justification for them. Indeed the first part of the *Gospel of the Egyptians* seems to be built almost entirely on these five doxologies or presentations of praise which enumerate the origins of the principal transcendent beings of this treatise. These are the great Invisible Spirit, the male virgin Barbelo, the Thrice-Male Child, the male virgin Youel (a double of Barbelo), Esephech the Child of the Child (a double of the Triple Male Child), the great Doxomedon Aeon (containing the last three beings; cf. *Zost.* VIII,1:61,15–21 and *Gos. Eg.* III,2:43,15–16: the great aeon, where the Triple Male Child is), and various other pleromas and aeons. Apparently *Gospel of the Egyptians* understands the Invisible Spirit, Barbelo and the three beings (Thrice-Male Child, Youel and Esephech) contained in the Doxomedon aeon to constitute the Five Seals. This suggests a baptismal context for these doxologies, perhaps also suggesting Schenke's[11] notion of a divine pentad (cf. *Ap. John* II,1:6,2 and *Steles Seth* VII,5,120,20) of names (cf. *Trim. Prot.* XIII,1:49,28–32; "the Five Seals of these particular names") which are invoked in the course of the baptismal ascent (in five stages: robing, baptizing, enthroning, glorifying, rapture into the light, XIII,1:48,15–35). Thus the Son figure of the Father-Mother-Son triad of the *Apocryphon of John* has been subdivided into another Father-Mother-Son triad, leaving the Autogenes Logos dangling in this system, although still produced by the (Invisible) Spirit and

---

[11] H.-M. Schenke, "Sethianism," 603–4.

Barbelo ("Pronoia") and still establishing the four Lights by his Word. It would appear that the *Gospel of the Egyptians* has combined two traditions. They are the Invisible Spirit-Barbelo-Autogenes triad from the system of the *Apocryphon of John* and *Trimorphic Protennoia*, and another tradition of a pentad, derived from the Sethian baptismal tradition. Strikingly, *Gospel of the Egyptians* also seems to move towards the postulation of another triad (which is possibly developed, for example, by *Allogenes* into the Triple Power) between the Invisible Spirit and Barbelo, namely "the living Silence," an unspecified Father and a Thought (Ennoia, which in turn becomes the Father in the triad, Father/Ennoia, Mother/Barbelo, and Son/Thrice-Male Child). Finally, Adamas seems to occupy a still lower rank, as in the *Apocryphon of John* (where he is produced by Foreknowledge and Mind): Adamas follows and is separated from the Autogenes Logos, and is produced by "Man" (perhaps the Invisible Spirit) and a lower double of Barbelo, Mirothoe. In turn Adam conjoins with Prophania to produce the four Lights and Seth, who conjoins with Plesithea to produce his seed.

Gospel of the Egyptians seems also to know the myth of Sophia from the version found in *Trimorphic Protennoia* according to which a voice from the fourth Light Eleleth urges the production of a ruler for Chaos, initiating the descent of the hylic Sophia cloud, who produces the chief archon Sakla and his partner Nebruel, the makers of twelve aeons and angels and of man. After Sakla's boast and the traditional voice from on high about the Man and Son of Man, a double of Sophia (Metanoia) is introduced to make up for the deficiency in the Aeon of Eleleth due to Sophia's descent. She descends to the world which is called the image of the night, perhaps reflecting an etymology of Eleleth's name, perhaps Lilith or *lēylā* "night," and suggesting that Eleleth is ultimately responsible for the created order.

Gospel of the Egyptians also mentions the three parousias of flood, conflagration and judgment through which Seth passes, which seems to show awareness of the scheme of *Apocalypse of Adam* in its presently redacted form. Again this tradition is set in a baptismal context, since the third descent of Seth serves to establish a baptism through a Logos-begotten body prepared by the virgin (Barbelo?). And indeed this Logos-begotten body turns out to be Jesus, whom Seth puts on, as in *Trim. Prot.* XIII,1:50,12–15 (cf. the Ophite version of this theme in Iren. *Haer.* I.30.12–13).

Finally there is the lengthy list of the various baptismal figures (*Gos. Eg.* III,2:64,9–65,26) and the two concluding hymnic sections (*Gos. Eg.* III,2:66,8–22, and 66,22–68,1) which Böhlig-Wisse have adroitly reconstructed in the form of two separate hymns of five strophes each, perhaps again reflecting the tradition of the Five Seals. In this regard, the Five Seals tradition may even have given rise to the fivefold repetition of the doxologies (enumerated above) constituting the basis of the theogony in the first part of *Gospel of the Egyptians.* The concluding baptismal hymns are strongly Christian in flavor, especially the first one, mentioning Yesseus Mazareus Yessedekeus and, very frequently, Jesus. The list of baptismal figures preceding the prayers reveals a multitude of new figures (most of which show up in the baptismal sections of *Zostrianos*) alongside the more traditional ones, such as Micheus, Michar, Mnesinous, Gamaliel and Samblo (in *Apocalypse of Adam* and *Trimorphic Protennoia*), and Abrasax and Yesseus Mazareus Yesse-dekeus (in *Apocalypse of Adam*). Also included are Adamas, Seth and his seed, and Jesus residing in the four Lights Harmozel, Oroiael, Davithe, and Eleleth (as in *Apocryphon of John* and *Trimorphic Protennoia*).

Before passing on to the *Allogenes* group of treatises, one should also note the occurrence of Kalyptos in *Gos. Eg.* IV,2:57,16, a name which may be present in translated form also in *Trim. Prot.* XIII,1:38,10 as a cognomen for Barbelo. Likewise in *Gos. Eg.* IV, 2:55,25 there seems to occur the phrase "the First One who appeared," likely a translation of Protophanes (here apparently a cognomen for the Thrice-Male Child), a term occurring also in *Ap. John* II,1:8,32 as a cognomen for Geradamas, further suggesting an original connection between Adamas and the Triple Male Child. Perhaps also Prophania, who in *Gospel of the Egyptians* functions as Adamas' consort in the production of Seth and the four Lights, is a feminine variant of Protophanes, again suggesting the bisexual Adamas, the Son of Man, as the first to appear, doing so in Sethian terms as both female (Mother, Barbelo, the Ennoia of the First Man) and male (the Autogenes Son).

2. *Allogenes and Zostrianos.* *Zostrianos* is heavily indebted to the Sethian *dramatis personae* especially as they occur in *Gospel of the Egyptians*, and collects these into three rather distinct blocks (*Zost.* VIII,1:6; also pp. 29–32 and 47). But the bulk of *Zostrianos* is cast in a truly new scheme and conceptuality, which seems to have been developed independently by the author of *Allogenes* and adopted by *Zostrianos* in a somewhat confused way. This new scheme is the Sethian practice of visionary ascent to the highest levels of the divine world, which seems to be worked out for the first time by the author of *Allogenes* utilizing a large fund of philosophical conceptuality derived from contemporary Platonism, with no traces of Christian content. *Zostrianos* appears to be based on the scheme of visionary ascent and the philosophical conceptuality of *Allogenes*, but it makes a definite

attempt to interpret this ascent in terms of the older tradition of
baptismal ascent and its own peculiar *dramatis personae*, especially as
they occur in *Gospel of the Egyptians*.

The metaphysical structure of both *Allogenes* and *Zostrianos*, as well
as *Three Steles of Seth*, appears to be centered on the triad Father-
Mother-Son as is the case with the *Gospel of the Egyptians*, *Apocryphon
of John*, and *Trimorphic Protennoia*. In *Zostrianos* this triad is conceived as a vertical hierarchy of beings. The Father at the metaphysical
summit (perhaps himself beyond being) is the Invisible Spirit and is
accompanied by his Triple Powered One. Below him, the Mother
member of the triad is named Barbelo, who herself subsumes a triad of
hypostases. The highest of these is Kalyptos, the Hidden One. The next
lowest is Protophanes, the First-Appearing One, who has associated
with him another being called the Triple Male (Child). The third of the
triad is the Son called the divine Autogenes.

So also the various levels of the Aeon of Barbelo, the divine Mind
(Nous), are described in terms of their content, again expressed in terms
of the Platonic metaphysics of the divine intelligence ("noology"). As the
contemplated Mind, Kalyptos contains the paradigmatic ideas or authentic existents; Protophanes, the contemplating Mind, contains a
subdivision of the ideas ("those who exist together"), i.e., universal ideas,
perhaps "mathematicals," distinguished from the authentic existents by
having "many of the same" and being combinable with each other
(unlike the authentic existents; cf. Plato, according to Aristot. *Metaph.* I.
6 and XIII. 6), and also distinguished from the ideas of particular things
("the perfect individuals"). The particular ideas ("the [perfect] individuals") are contained in Autogenes, a sort of demiurgic mind (the
Logos) who shapes the realm of Nature (*physis*) below. Since the
distinction between the "individuals" in Autogenes and "those who exist
together" in Protophanes is rather slight for the author of *Allogenes*, the
Triple Male Child fits nicely as a sort of mediator between them. This
mediating function of the Triple Male also qualifies him for the title of
Savior (*Allogenes* XI,3:58,13–15).

The doctrine of the Triple Powered One found in *Allogenes* also
occurs in *Three Steles of Seth*, *Marsanes*, and *Zostrianos*. It is clearly
the most intriguing feature of these treatises and perhaps the crucial
feature by which they can be placed at a definite point in time (and in
the Platonic metaphysical tradition). In *Allogenes*, *Three Steles of Seth*,
and *Zostrianos*, the Triple Powered One of the Invisible Spirit consists
of three modalities: Existence, Vitality or Life, and Mentality or Knowledge (or Blessedness). In its Existence modality, the Triple Powered One
is continuous with (i.e., potentially contained within) and indistinguish-

able from the Invisible Spirit. In its Vitality modality, the Triple Powered One is the boundlessness of the Invisible Spirit proceeding forth in an act of emanation both continuous and discontinuous with the Invisible Spirit and its final product, Barbelo, the self-knowledge of the Invisible Spirit. In its Mentality modality, the Triple Powered One has become bounded as Barbelo, the self-knowledge of the Invisible Spirit. It has taken on form and definition as perceiving subject with the Invisible Spirit as its object of perception.

This is the same doctrine as is found in the anonymous Parmenides commentary (Fragment XIV) ascribed by Hadot to Porphyry,[12] where the Neoplatonic hypostasis Intellect unfolds from the absolute being (to einai) of the pre-existent One in three phases. In each phase the three modalities of the Intellect (namely Existence, Life, and Intelligence) predominate in turn. First as Existence (hyparxis), Intellect is purely potential, resident in and identical with its ideas, the absolute being of the One. In its third phase, Intellect has become identical with the derived being (to on) of Intellect proper (the second Neoplatonic hypostasis) as the hypostatic exemplification of its paradigmatic idea, the absolute being of the One. The transitional phase between the first and third phase of Intellect is called Life and constitutes the median modality of Intellect (boundless thinking). The same idea is also found in Plot. Enn. 6.7. 17,13–26:

> Life, not the life of the One, but a trace of it, looking toward the One was boundless, but once having looked was bounded (without bounding its source). Life looks to the One, and determined by it, takes on bound, limit, form . . . it must then have been determined as (the Life of) a Unity including multiplicity. Each element of multiplicity is determined multiplicity because of Life, but also is a Unity because of limit . . . so Intellect is bounded Life.

What is really original in Allogenes, besides the importation of Platonic metaphysics into Sethianism, is the scheme of visionary ascent experienced by Allogenes. Certainly Sethianism was familiar with accounts of the ecstatic visionary ascents of Enoch, Elijah, Abraham, Jacob, Paul and others contained in Jewish and Christian apocalyptic. Allogenes, however, is distinguished by a Platonically inspired visionary ascent of the individual intellect in which it assimilates itself to the hierarchy of metaphysical levels with which it was aboriginally consubstantial but from which it had become separated.[13] In Allogenes, one undergoes the ascent according to a prescribed sequence of mental states: earthbound vision; ecstatic extraction from body and soul involving a transcending of traditional gnōsis; a silent but unstable seeking of

---

[12] Hadot, Porphyre.
[13] See my "Threefold Path," 341–46 and Williams, "Stability."

oneself; firm standing; and sudden ultimate vision characterized as an ignorant knowledge devoid of any content that might distinguish between subject and contemplated object. Each stage is characterized by increasing self-unification, stability and mental abstraction, a movement away from motion and multiplicity to stability and solitariness.

The prototype of such an experience is found already in Plato's *Symposium* 210A–212A, where Socrates recounts his path to the vision of absolute beauty into which he had been initiated by Diotima. In such mysteries, ultimate vision or *epopteia* was the supreme goal, also expressed as assimilating oneself to God insofar as possible (Plato, *Theatetus*, 176B). This was a traditional quest of religious Platonism not only in Plato, but also later in such figures as Philo (who, however, shunned the notion of total assimilation to God), Numenius, Valentinus, perhaps Albinus, Clement of Alexandria, Origen, and many others besides. In the period under discussion, this tradition culminates in Plotinus.

In such a way, Allogenes achieves a vision of the Aeon of Barbelo and the beings comprising it (*Allogenes* XI,3:57,29–58,26), then transcends his earthly garment and even his own knowledge by means of a vacant ignorance and sees the Mentality, Vitality, and Existence aspects of the Triple Powered One of the Invisible Spirit (XI,3:58,27–60,37). At this point, Allogenes is suddenly filled by a primary revelation of the Unknowable One and his Triple Power (*Allogenes* XI,3:60,37–61,22). The rest of the treatise is mostly devoted to an interpretation of his visionary experience in terms of a negative theology (*Allogenes* XI,3:61, 32–62,13; supplemented by a more positive theology, XI,3:62,14–67,20). This negative theology contains a nearly word-for-word parallel with the one found in the beginning of the *Apocryphon of John*: *Allogenes* XI,3:62,28–63,23=*Ap. John* II,1:3,18–35=BG8502,2:23,3–26,13. *Allogenes* is thus likely to have borrowed from the *Apocryphon of John*.

E. 200–300 C.E.

When one realizes that *Allogenes* and *Zostrianos* are probably to be included in the "apocalypses of Zoroaster and Zostrianos and Nicotheus and Allogenes and Messos and those of other such figures" (Porph. *Vit. Plot.* 16) whose stance was attacked by Plotinus and whose doctrines were refuted at great length by Amelius and Porphyry himself in the period 244–269 C.E., one may date *Allogenes* around 200 C.E., with *Zostrianos* coming a bit later around 225 C.E. (Porphyry certainly recognized it as a spurious and recent work). *Allogenes* is also to be included among the various Sethian works under the name of Allogenes mentioned by Epiphanius around 375 C.E. (*Pan.* 39.5.1; 40.2.2). Furthermore, Plotinus, in his antignostic polemic (*Enn.* 3.8; 5.8; 5.5 and 2.9, tractates

30–33 in chronological order, which constitute the original complete antignostic tractate recognized by Harder, "Schrift Plotins"), probably has these tractates in view.

1. *Zostrianos*. While *Allogenes* (like *Three Steles of Seth*) takes no interest at all in the realm of Nature below Autogenes (mentioned only once at *Allogenes* XI,3:51,28–32 as containing failures rectified by Autogenes), *Zostrianos* and *Marsanes* do treat this realm. They seem to enumerate six levels of being below Autogenes, called the thirteen cosmic aeons (i.e., the world), the airy earth, the copies (*antitypoi* made by the Archon) of the Aeons, the Transmigration (*paroikēsis*); the Repentance (*metanoia*) and the "self-begotten ones" (plural). Although it is unclear in *Zostrianos* as it now stands, the Untitled Text of the Bruce Codex (Schmidt-MacDermot, *Bruce Codex*, 263,11–264,6) allows us to conjecture that "the self-begotten ones" constitute the level at which Zostrianos is baptized in the name of Autogenes. It contains the Living Water (Yesseus Mazareus Yessedekeus), the baptizers Micheus, Michar (and Mnesinous), the purifier Barpharanges, a figure called Zogenethlos and, besides these, the four Lights Harmozel, Oroiael, Davithe, and Eleleth, together with Sophia. In *Zostrianos*, Adamas is found in Harmozel; Seth, Emmacha Seth and Esephech the Child of the Child, in Oroiael; and the seed of Seth, in Davithe. In addition, certain triads of beings are either residents in or cognomens of the four Lights (*Zost.* VIII,1:127,16–128,7). It is unclear whether the repentant souls (of the historical Sethians?) are contained in Eleleth, as would be expected, or in the level of Metanoia immediately below the self-begotten ones. It appears also that the figures of Meirothea (*Zost.* VIII,1:30,14–15) and Plesithea (*Zost.*VIII,1:51,12) and Prophania (*Zost.*VIII,1:6,31) also belong to the self-begotten ones. It seems that in comparison to *Allogenes*, *Zostrianos* really is guilty of multiplying hypostases, but these are no doubt derived from the Sethian baptismal tradition, not only from free invention. It seems fair, then, to see *Zostrianos* as a derivative from *Allogenes* and *Gospel of the Egyptians*.

2. *The Three Steles of Seth*. The *Three Steles of Seth* clearly represents the same system as *Allogenes*; yet it is constructed as a triptych of presentations of praise and blessing to Autogenes, Barbelo, and the pre-existent One in connection with a communal practice of a three-stage ascent and descent. After an initial revelation and various blessings rendered by Seth (*Steles Seth* VII,5:118:25–120,28) who praises the bisexual Geradamas as Mirothea (his mother) and Mirotheos (his father), the rest of the treatise uses the first person plural for ascribing praise to (1) the Triple Male, (2) to Barbelo who arose from the Triple Powered One (characterized by being, living and knowing, and is also called Kalyptos and Protophanes), and (3) to the pre-existent One who is

characterized by the existence-life-mind triad. The whole concludes with a rubric (*Steles Seth* VII,5:126,32–127,22) that explains the use of the steles in the practice of descent from the third to the second to the first; likewise, the way of ascent is the way of descent. The fact that the method of descent is mentioned first is strange (one notes that the Jewish Merkabah mystics called themselves *Yordē Merkabah*, "descenders to the Merkabah"). Another instance of the interdependence of these texts is a common prayer tradition: *Steles Seth* VII,5:125,23–126,17, *Allogenes* XI,3:54,11–37 and *Zost.* VIII,1:51,24–52,24; 86,13–88,bottom.

3. *Marsanes.* Last of all, *Marsanes* and the Untitled Text of the Bruce Codex should be mentioned as probably the latest of the Sethian treatises that we possess. Like *Zostrianos* and *Allogenes*, *Marsanes* records the visionary experience of a singular individual, probably to be regarded as one of the many manifestations of Seth. B. A. Pearson in his fine introduction to this tractate,[14] suggests that the name Marsanes, mentioned in the Untitled Text of the Bruce Codex (Schmidt-Mac-Dermot, *Bruce Codex*, 235,13–23) in connection with Nicotheos (and Marsianos by Epiphanius [*Pan.* 40.7.6] in his account of the Archontics), reflects a Syrian background for its author, and dates *Marsanes* in the early third century. But one might argue for dating it to the last quarter of the third century since it indeed posits an unknown Silent One above even the Invisible Spirit, in much the same way as Iamblichus during the same period posited an "Ineffable" beyond even the One of Plotinus.

As mentioned previously, the first ten pages of *Marsanes* present a visionary ascent to, and descent from, the highest level of the divine world. They depict the same basic structure as *Allogenes*, but with the omission of the Triple Male and the addition of at least the Repentance (perhaps in unrecoverable parts of the text one would find mention of the Transmigration and Antitypes) and the "cosmic" and "material" levels. From page 55 onward one notes the occurrence of a few baptismal terms, such as "wash," "seal," and perhaps "[Living] Water" (*Marsanes* X,1:65,22). Indeed the entire perceptible and intelligible universe is structured according to a hierarchy of thirteen seals. Aside from the narrative of the unfolding of Barbelo from the Triple Powered One (of the unknown Silent One, or of the Invisible Spirit?) and the plentiful occurrence of Platonic metaphysical terms such as "being," "non-being," "truly existing," "partial," "whole," "sameness," "difference" (esp. *Marsanes* X,1:4,24–5,5), one learns that Marsanes has not only come to know the intelligible world, but also that "the sense-perceptible world is [worthy] of being saved entirely" (X,1:5,22–26), an idea quite in line with *Allogenes* as well. These texts, *Allogenes*, *Zostrianos*, *Three*

---

[14] Pearson, *Codices IX and X*, 229–50.

Steles of Seth, and *Marsanes*, which I call the *"Allogenes* group," all exhibit a tendency not only toward an ontological monism, but also, save perhaps in the case of *Zostrianos* with its Sophia myth, a rather positive attitude toward the sense-perceptible world, the realm of Nature. Even *Zostrianos*, which affirms the existence of the demiurgic work of the Archon, its artificiality and its death-threatening bondage, concludes: "Release yourselves, and that which has bound you will be dissolved. Save yourselves, in order that it may be saved" (VIII,1:131,10–12).

4. *The Untitled Text of the Bruce Codex.* Finally, as previously mentioned, the Untitled Text of the Bruce Codex also belongs among the Sethian treatises, and seems to have affinity mostly with *Zostrianos* and *Gospel of the Egyptians*. It is almost entirely devoted to an elaborate cosmology involving the transcendent Sethian *dramatis personae* arranged into various levels and groups called "fatherhoods" and "deeps" consisting of myriads of powers. It narrates the descent of the light-spark and Christ through Setheus, bearing a salvation which seems to be effected by the baptismal rite already discussed. It is by all standards a most complex work defying any simple analysis. I can do no more than state that Schmidt[15] has dated it to the end of the second century, although I would be inclined to put it a bit later, around 350 C.E., but for no reason other than its extraordinary prolixity in comparison with the other Sethian treatises.

IV. Conclusion

It may be that the Sethians' gradual shift away from their original communal baptismal context, interpreted by means of a rich history of their primordial origins and salvation, towards the more ethereal and individualistic practice of visionary ascent contributed to the eventual decay and diffusion of those who identified with the Sethian traditions. Around 375 C.E., Epiphanius has difficulty recalling where he had encountered Sethians, and says that they are not to be found everywhere, but now only in Egypt and Palestine, although fifty years before they had spread as far as Greater Armenia (*Pan.* 39.1.1–2; 40.1). Perhaps the burgeoning pressure of officially sanctioned Christianity after Constantine drove them away from their former community centers. Their initial rapprochement with Christian ideas, alternating between positive in the case of *Apocryphon of John, Hypostasis of the Archons* and *Melchizedek*, and more negative and polemical in the case of *Trimorphic Protennoia, Gospel of the Egyptians*, and the *Apocalypse of Adam*, may have proved a liability. While Christological concepts could

---

[15] Schmidt, *Schriften*, 664.

clearly depict the eschatological advent of Seth in their own era, to adopt these meant also to reinterpret them in a Sethian way and thus challenge a more "orthodox" Christological interpretation. Although this preserved for a time their separate conscious identity as an elect body, in the long run it must have earned the hostility of the increasingly better organized, institutional, "orthodox" church. Certainly influential church fathers holding powerful positions in the church singled out the Sethians along with many others for attack. At first, this attack was perhaps rather pedantic, sarcastic, and theoretical, but in the case of a Tertullian or later an Epiphanius, it could become brutal and libelous. Though thrust away by the church, many Sethians no doubt held on to their own version of Christianized salvation history, but concentrated more and more on spiritualizing it along a vertical, transcendent axis. Such an emphasis on vertical transcendence at the expense of a sense of primordial history must have weakened their sense of traditional historical grounding and communal solidarity.

The final stage seems achieved in the *Allogenes* group, where the Sethians, if they thus identified themselves any longer, moved into rapprochement with pagan Platonism. Epiphanius tells us that the Archontic branch of Sethianism had rejected baptism and the sacraments associated with the church. This happened possibly around the inauguration of the Sassanide era, the time of the vision and mission of Mani, who also rejected baptism. Without some cultic or communal form of this rite, individual Sethians were left to their own devices. An increasing emphasis on self-performable techniques of spiritual ascent with its attendant possibilities for individualism possibly entailed a further weakening of communal awareness traditionally grounded in ritual and primordial history. While initially welcomed into Platonic circles, their insistence on enumerating and praising their traditional divine beings with hymns, glossalalia, and other forms of ecstatic incantation must have irritated more sober Platonists such as Plotinus, Porphyry and Amelius. Although the Platonists initially regarded the Sethians as friends, soon they too, like the heresiologists of the church, began writing pointed and lengthy attacks upon them for distorting the teaching of Plato which they adapted to depict their own spiritual world and the path toward assimilation with it. This rejection, coupled with the official sanction of Christianity under Constantine and the attendant pressure against the very paganism the Sethians had turned to, may have contributed to the fragmentation of the Sethian community into a multitude of sectarian groups (e.g., Audians, Borborites, Archontics; perhaps Phibionites, Stratiotici, and Secundians), some of which survived into the Middle Ages—a true scattering of the seed of Seth!

George W. MacRae, SJ

THE EGO-PROCLAMATION IN GNOSTIC SOURCES

A NUMBER of modern interpreters propose that the crucial moment in the Jewish trial of Jesus according to Mark is reached with Jesus' use of the absolute form of the ἐγώ εἰμι proclamation (14.62). Against a background of Old Testament usage this formula is taken to be a divine self-revelation which constitutes the blasphemy for which Jesus is condemned (14.64).[1] It is not the purpose of this paper to determine whether such an acknowledgement in Mark of what is undeniably a common Johannine usage provides a correct exegesis of the trial scene.[2] Instead, we wish to investigate the extent to which Gnostic sources made use of the ἐγώ-formulas and to inquire both about the origin of the Gnostic usage and its relationship to the New Testament. Although this study is only marginally related to the main theme of this volume, its author does not hesitate to offer it in gratitude to the eminent scholar whom we honour in these pages, for it will reflect still another facet of his broad interests in the New Testament and its world.

In his study of the ἐγώ-proclamation in the New Testament, Stauffer has drawn attention to the way in which Mark 14.62 serves as a model for a scene in the life of the Gnostic leader Simon Magus in the Pseudo-Clementine *Homilies*. To the words of Dositheus, εἰ σὺ εἶ ὁ ἐστώς, καὶ προσκυνῶ σε, Simon replies simply, ἐγὼ εἰμι, and thus wins the adoration of his rival.[3] In reality, the

---

[1] See, e.g., E. Stauffer, *Jesus and His Story*, ET London 1960, pp. 100, 150ff.; H. Zimmermann, 'Das absolute "Ich bin" in der Redeweise Jesu', *Trierer Theologische Zeitschrift* 69, 1960, pp. 1–20.

[2] It is noteworthy that Stauffer in his *TWNT* article on ἐγώ had at first regarded Mark 14.62 as an 'ordinary' use of ἐγώ εἰμι in contrast with Mark 13.6 or John 8.28: *TDNT* II, p. 352.

[3] *Hom.* II.24.6, ed. B. Rehm, *Die Pseudoklementinen I* (GCS), 1953, p. 45;

Pseudo-Clementine passage is as ambiguous as its Marcan model: in both cases it makes good sense to see in the use of ἐγώ εἰμι more than a mere affirmative response, 'I am', but in neither case is one compelled to do so.[4] It is therefore of interest to inquire whether Gnostic sources in general recognized and used either an absolute or a predicative form of ἐγώ εἰμι as a claim to divine or transcendent identity. The following investigation is based in particular on some of the Coptic Gnostic sources from the Nag Hammadi library. It will study first the 'I am God' formula and secondly the use of 'I am' with a variety of predicates in the manner of the Fourth Gospel.

I

To begin with, we do not find any other instances in the Gnostic sources of the absolute ἐγώ εἰμι to parallel the Marcan and Johannine ones. Instead, there is an extremely common Gnostic parallel which also alludes to the Deutero-Isaian background from which the New Testament ἐγώ εἰμι very probably springs. This usage is the boast of the Demiurge in the Gnostic creation myths, 'I am God and there is no other.' The saying of the creator-God in Second Isaiah so fascinated the Gnostic mind that it is almost endlessly repeated in the sources as an empty boast of the inferior Jewish creator. And it is easy to see why, for it was precisely the heart of the Gnostic revelation to show that this statement was wrong. The God of Israel was deluded; worse, he was a deceiver. There *is* another God, the ineffable, unnamable Deity of the Pleroma whose light is shared by the immortal spark dwelling in pneumatic (i.e. Gnostic) man. And the ultimate Gnostic refutation of the exclusive claims of Judaism lay in the persuasion that the boast of the Demiurge Yahweh was an empty lie.[5] It is paradoxical, part of the very paradox of Gnosticism itself, that whereas the

---

cf. Stauffer, article ἐγώ, p. 354. In *Jesus and His Story*, p. 153, the same author suggests that Simon adopted this usage as a result of hearing Jesus use it in Samaria, but this suggestion involves a series of historical judgements about both the Fourth Gospel and the Pseudo-Clementines that are difficult to maintain. A similar reserve must be mentioned, it seems to me, about Stauffer's main point, that the use of ἐγώ εἰμι goes back to Jesus himself.

[4] In his famous classification of the I-sayings, R. Bultmann, *Das Evangelium des Johannes* (KEKNT, 19th [= 10th] ed.), 1968, pp. 167–8, regards *Hom.* 2.24.6 as a genuine revelation-formula of the *Rekognitionsformel* type.

[5] Cf. Irenaeus, *haer.* II.9.2 (ed. Harvey, vol. I, p. 272).

Deutero-Isaian 'I am God' formula was primarily a polemic against polytheism, the Gnostics should have borrowed this very formula in the service of a cosmic dualism.

The context in which the boast occurs is very similar in all the Gnostic works in which the statement occurs. As a typical example it will be enough to cite merely one instance, from the Apocryphon of John, in which the allusion to Isa. 45.5 (etc.) is combined with a reference to Ex. 20.5 or Deut. 5.9 (θεὸς ζηλωτής):

> But when [Ialdabaoth] saw the creation that surrounded him and the crowd of angels who were about him, who had come into being from him, he said to them, 'I, I am a jealous God and there is no other God but me.' But in uttering this he indicated to the angels who were beside him that there was another God, for if there were no other, of whom would he be jealous?[6]

H.-M. Schenke has assembled some of the Gnostic instances of this boast of the Demiurge for the purpose of distinguishing between Gnostic allegorical exegesis and Gnostic myth.[7] Several additional passages can now be added to his list, but what is primarily intended here is to make a few observations on the Gnostic use of the Old Testament citations as well as of the ἐγώ-proclamation.

The possible Old Testament passages alluded to, in addition to Ex. 20.5 and/or Deut. 5.5–9, are the following: Deut. 4.35 and 32.39; Hos. 13.4; Joel 2.27; and especially Second Isaiah 43.10–11; 44.6; 45.5–6, 18, 21–2; 46.9.[8] Apart from the specific allusions to the 'jealous God', it is very difficult to assert categorically which other passages are being cited in the Gnostic documents. It is true that some citations are closer in form to one passage than to another, but we cannot be sure that we have accurate citations in any case. It is most unlikely, as the variations between different

---

[6] Codex II, 13.5–13; M. Krause and P. Labib, *Die drei Versionen des Apokryphon des Johannes*, Wiesbaden 1962, p. 145.

[7] *Der Gott 'Mensch' in der Gnosis*, Göttingen 1962, pp. 87–93; see also A. Orbe, 'El pecado de los Arcontes', *Estudios Eclesiásticos* 43, 1968, pp. 354–7.

[8] I would regard it as unlikely (against Stauffer, *Jesus and His Story*, p. 145) that the presence of the formula in Deut. 32.39–40 is due to Deutero-Isaian influence. The Song of Moses is certainly pre-exilic and doubtless very ancient; cf. G. E. Wright 'The Lawsuit of God: a Form-critical Study of Deuteronomy 32', in *Israel's Prophetic Heritage*: Essays in honor of James Muilenburg, ed. B. W. Anderson and W. Harrelson, London 1962, pp. 26–67. Similarly, it is not clear that Hos. 13.4 is a post-exilic interpolation. Though typically exploited by Second Isaiah, the formula may be much older.

versions of the same work, e.g. the Apocryphon of John, would suggest. There is at least one reason, however, to think that the Gnostic citations are derived from Second Isaiah, and that is the fact that the boast of the Demiurge regularly occurs in a creation context. Very often it is precisely at some critical stage of his creative work that the archon asserts his pretended divinity, and the Gnostic cosmogonies have woven the claim into their midrashic treatment of the Genesis creation story.

Most authors who have commented on the Gnostic sources point out the allusions to Isa. 45.5 or 46.9, but the fact that Deutero-Isaiah itself may have enjoyed some special prominence in the circles in which Gnosticism arose has for the most part gone unnoticed. For one thing, it is widely held that certain aspects of Deutero-Isaiah exercised a special influence on the development of Jewish apocalyptic thought.[9] Its insistence on universalism and its open conflict with the claims of polytheistic paganism made it especially welcome to both apocalyptic and Hellenistic Judaism.[10] The Servant Songs themselves may have been influential in the development of the apocalyptic Son of Man concept as well as in the self-consciousness of the Qumran sectarians.[11] Thus if Gnosticism is particularly indebted to Jewish apocalyptic, as a detailed study of its imagery and attitudes would lead one to believe, some preference for Second Isaiah, along with the much more obvious dependence on Genesis, is only to be expected.

But is there anything more or less peculiar to Second Isaiah

[9] It is not, of course, presumed that the book of Isaiah was divided in antiquity in the manner in which modern commentators treat it, but because of the radical change of tone and subject, ancient readers would naturally have recognized some distinction. Such elements as the theology of creation, the polemical insistence on monotheism, the role of the servant, etc., belong to one part of the book only.

[10] Cf. W. Bousset, *Die Religion des Judentums im späthellenistischen Zeitalter*, 3rd ed., by H. Gressmann, Berlin 1926, pp. 243, 304–7. The influence of Second Isaiah on the wisdom literature, especially the Wisdom of Solomon, has been pointed out by D. Georgi in *Zeit und Geschichte*: Dankesgabe am Rudolf Bultmann, ed. E. Dinkler, Tübingen 1964, p. 266. It may be argued that the wisdom tradition played a significant role in the development of Gnostic mythology (e.g. the Sophia myth), and thus we may have another link between Second Isaiah and the Gnostics. The wisdom literature is also interested in the theology of creation.

[11] For a summary of the arguments alleged, see D. S. Russell, *The Method and Message of Jewish Apocalyptic*, London 1964, pp. 338–40. Stauffer, *Jesus and His Story*, p. 145, remarks that Isaiah seems to have enjoyed special favour at Qumran.

that would appear attractive to the Gnostic mentality itself? Here we may mention the theology of creation, the explicit insistence on monotheism (which the Gnostic would wish to 'correct'), certain references to the role of wisdom and knowledge (e.g. in Isa. 53.11), and the use of Sabaoth as a proper name, in the LXX virtually confined to Isaiah.[12] The fact that Second Isaiah actually did influence Gnostic sources in a special manner would have to be brought out by a number of detailed references in the Coptic Gnostic works such as the Untitled Work of Nag Hammadi Codex II and the Gospel of Truth, and in the patristic sources, such as Hippolytus's account of the Naassenes, which contains many citations from Isaiah.[13] Finally, there seems to be very definite influence of the Servant Songs and of the whole context of Second Isaiah on the portrayal of the redeemer or revealer figure in the Coptic Gnostic Apocalypse of Adam.[14]

In particular the context of some of the Deutero-Isaian monotheistic claims would prove especially suggestive for the irreverent setting into which the Gnostics place the citation. For example, Isa. 45.18–19:

I am the Lord, and there is no other. I did not speak in secret, in a land of darkness; I did not say to the offspring of Jacob, 'Seek me in chaos',

or in a different vein, Isa. 47.10:

You felt secure in your wickedness, you said, 'No one sees me'; your wisdom and your knowledge led you astray, and you said in your heart, 'I am, and there is no one besides me.'

In both these cases one would have to suppose a Gnostic exegesis at work, but it is significant to note that both contexts would be less suggestive for the Gnostic mind in their LXX form than in their Hebrew form: e.g. μάταιον ζητήσατε instead of תֹהוּ בַקְּשׁוּנִי in

[12] Cf. C. H. Dodd, *The Bible and the Greeks*, London 1935, pp. 16–17.
[13] See, e.g., the indexes of the various editions.
[14] Cf. A. Böhlig and P. Labib, *Koptisch-gnostische Apokalypsen aus Codex V von Nag Hammadi*, Berlin 1963, pp. 86–117; G. W. MacRae, 'The Coptic Gnostic Apocalypse of Adam', *The Heythrop Journal* 6, 1965, pp. 33–4. Is there an allusion to the prominence of Isaiah in Jewish apocalyptic and/or in Gnosticism in John's statement that Isaiah 'saw his glory' (12.41)? R. M. Grant, 'Gnostic Origins and the Basilidians of Irenaeus', *VC* 13, 1959, p. 123, suggests that in their use of the Caulacau formula from Isa. 28.10 some Gnostics may have taken this statement literally.

45.19, whereas it is precisely out of the primordial chaos that the Demiurge utters his boast. Thus if passages such as this did influence the Gnostic usage, it must not readily be assumed that they were known to the early Gnostic myth-makers in Greek, but rather in the Hebrew or perhaps in a Targumic version.

But even though the likelihood of a special Gnostic predilection for Second Isaiah is established, perhaps we must avoid overstating the case with regard to Gnostic use of the 'I am God' formulas, for there is some reason to think that this statement had become almost a commonplace in some late Jewish circles.[15] Moreover, there are non-Gnostic examples in which it is used specifically in a pejorative setting, such as the idle boast of Babylon in Isa. 47.10 cited above. In Ecclus. 33.1 (36.10) God is called upon to avenge his people: 'Crush the heads of the rulers of the enemy, who say, "There is no one but ourselves" ' ($o\dot{v}\kappa$ $\check{\epsilon}\sigma\tau\iota$ $\pi\lambda\dot{\eta}\nu$ $\dot{\eta}\mu\tilde{\omega}\nu$), but in this instance the main part of the formula is merely implied. A Gnostic reading of such a passage is easy to imagine, however. Finally, two passages from the Christian sections of the Ethiopic Ascension of Isaiah attribute the same boast to the evil angel Beliar (referring to Nero) and to the 'princes of this world';

> And all that he hath desired he will do in the world: he will do and speak like the Beloved and he will say: 'I am God and before me there has been none.' And all the people in the world will believe in him. And they will sacrifice to him and they will serve him saying: 'This is God and beside him there is no other.'
>
> For they have denied Me and said: 'We alone are and there is none beside us.'[16]

In discussing the significance of the first of these passages, Stauffer draws attention to the support it gives for the use of the 'I am' formula by Jesus, 'the Beloved' whose speech Nero emulates.[17] But since neither the canonical sources nor any other early Christian works ever attribute to Jesus the words of Isa. 43.10 or of any similar Old Testament passage, except the absolute use of

---

[15] See, for example, the use of אני הוא ולא אחד in the Passover Haggadah in explanation of 'I am Yahweh' in Ex. 12.12, pointed out by D. Daube, *The New Testament and Rabbinic Judaism*, London 1956, pp. 325–9; Stauffer, *Jesus and His Story*, p. 147.

[16] Trans. R. H. Charles, *The Ascension of Isaiah*, London 1900, pp. 27 (4.6–8), 71 (10.13). Schenke, *op. cit.*, p. 93, notes these passages also.

[17] *Jesus and His Story*, pp. 150–1.

ἐγώ εἰμι, Stauffer is forced to conclude that the Ascension of Isaiah draws upon an independent tradition. Whether or not there was such a tradition must remain a matter for conjecture, but for Jesus ever to have applied to himself explicitly any of the Isaiah statements such as 'I am God and there is no other besides me' would be incongruous both with the indirect nature of his self-revelation in Mark and John and with the exigencies of his mission among the Jews in general. On the other hand, the author of this section of the Ascension of Isaiah may be drawing simply on a familiarity with the canonical tradition of Jesus' absolute use of ἐγώ εἰμι and on an apocalyptic familiarity with the Deutero-Isaian statement repeated in other contexts. At any rate, there is some witness to the currency of the statement as a blasphemous expression of arrogance in Jewish sources. But merely because the Coptic and other Gnostic works use the citation in a parallel sense, we are not obliged to conclude that they owe it to apocalyptic sources rather than to Isaiah itself, since Gnostic exegesis of the Old Testament is generally perverse in any case, arising from an anti-Jewish bias. And the creation context of the Gnostic cosmogonic myths still seems to favour direct use of Deutero-Isaiah.

The ἐγώ εἰμι statement is spoken by the inferior creator-God in a wide variety of Gnostic sources,[18] and always with the same intention on the part of the writer: to demonstrate that gross

[18] Valentinians: Irenaeus, *haer.* I.5.4 (Harvey I, pp. 46–7); Hippolytus, *ref.* VI.33 (W. Völker, *Quellen zur Geschichte der christlichen Gnosis*, Tübingen 1932, p. 132); see also *haer.* II.9.2 (Harvey I, p. 272). Basilides: *ref.* VII.25.3 (Völker, p. 52). Justin's *Baruch: ref.* V.26.15 (Völker, p. 29). Barbelognostics: *haer.* I.29.4 (Harvey I, p. 226). Ophites: *haer.* I.30.6 (Harvey I, p. 232). Apocryphon of John: Codex II: 11.20–1; 12.8–9; 13.8–9 (Krause-Labib, pp. 140–5); BG 43.2–3; 44.14–15 (W. Till, *Die gnostischen Schriften des koptischen Papyrus Berolinensis 8502*, Berlin 1955, pp. 126–8). Hypostasis of the Archons: 134.30–1; 142.21–2; 143.5 (P. Labib, *Coptic Gnostic Papyri in the Coptic Museum at Old Cairo*, Cairo 1956). Untitled Work of Codex II: 148.32–3; 151.11–13; 155.30–1; 160.28–9 (A. Böhlig and P. Labib, *Die koptisch-gnostische Schrift ohne Titel aus Codex II von Nag Hammadi*, Berlin 1962, pp. 42, 48, 58, 70). Apocalypse of James II: 56.26–57.1 (fragmentary and conjectural; Böhlig-Labib, *Apokalypsen*, p. 78). Apocalypse of Adam: 66.28–9 (conjectural; *ibid.*, p. 98). Egyptian Gospel: 58.24–6 (J. Doresse, 'Le livre sacré du grand Esprit invisible', *Journal Asiatique* 254, 1966, pp. 386–7). Also the unpublished Paraphrase of Shem (Codex VII, Tractate 1; cf. J. Doresse, *The Secret Books of the Egyptian Gnostics*, ET London 1960, p. 149). Other examples of the theme may be found in: C. S. C. Williams, 'Eznik's Résumé of Marcionite Doctrine', *JTS* 45, 1944, pp. 65–73; and in the Cathar work republished by R. Reitzenstein, *Die Vorgeschichte der christlichen Taufe*, Leipzig and Berlin, 1929, p. 309.

ignorance which the creator-archon possesses and transmits to his followers. Generally the author points out how mistaken the claim is, sometimes by merely calling it a lie or ignorance,[19] sometimes by the logical argument in the Apocryphon of John passage quoted above, and sometimes by a rebuke from Sophia or from a voice out of the pleromatic region, reminding the Demiurge that a higher God exists.[20] With rare exceptions, the Gnostic writers do not themselves refer to the Demiurge as 'God', but only represent him as making this false claim for himself.[21]

To sum up, the boast of the Demiurge in the form 'I am God and there is no other' is a fixed element of the Gnostic creation myth which recurs in numerous Gnostic sources. It provides an excellent example of the use of ἐγώ in divine self-proclamations and is rooted in the usage of Deutero-Isaiah or at least in the Jewish apocalyptic application of the Old Testament monotheistic utterance. There is no positive indication in this Gnostic mythologoumenon that the Gnostics were aware of the absolute use of ἐγώ εἰμι as a claim to divinity, nor is there any reason to suggest that this Gnostic usage is indebted to the Christian use of Deutero-Isaiah or to the claims of Jesus.

II

A second form of the ἐγώ-proclamation in Gnostic sources as well as in the New Testament is the use of 'I am' with a variety of predicates. In this instance, the comparison to be drawn is with the Fourth Gospel. In the Coptic Gnostic library there are several important instances of this usage which may be briefly described here.

The first is found in Tractate 2 of Codex VI, a codex which contains several Hermetic works. Tractate 2 is entitled 'The Thunder: Perfect Mind' (*TEBPONTH: NOYΣ N̄TEΛIOΣ*). This work is a proclamation entirely in the first person, spoken by an apparently female figure who is probably meant to be the figure

---

[19] E.g. *Apocryphon of John*, Codex II, 11.20–1 (Krause-Labib, p. 140).

[20] E.g. Irenaeus, *haer.* I.30.6 (Harvey I, p. 232).

[21] The Apocalypse of Adam is a notable exception to this general rule, when Adam refers to the lower deity as 'the God who made us'; cf. Codex V, 64.17, etc. The Sophia Jesu Christi (BG 104.4–7; Till, p. 248) apparently refers to the boast of the Demiurge and his assumption of the name God: 'on account of the pride and the blindness and the ignorance [of the Demiurge], for a name was given to him.'

named in the title. In fact, the word 'thunder' does not recur in the work (apparently, for there are lacunae), and νοῦς τέλειος recurs only once and only if a probable reconstruction is correct. In the latter case the speaker specifically says, 'I am the [perfect] mind.' The name 'thunder' suggests a divine or quasi-divine voice and reminds us of a usage very frequent in many ancient literatures: e.g. the *Juppiter tonans* of classical literature, the magical papyri, the God of the Old Testament, John 12.29, Rev. 10.3–4, etc. In particular one may call attention to the epithet of Isis, in the Kyme aretalogy, 42: 'I am the mistress of the thunder.'[22]

In its content the tractate consists of three types of statement, more or less intermingled throughout: self-proclamations in the first person singular ('I am the first and the last', etc.), exhortations to heed the speaker ('Look upon me . . ., hear me,' etc.), and reproaches ('Why have you hated me . . .?' etc.). These are addressed to 'hearers' (ἀκροατής), 'you who know me', etc., and to 'Greeks' as opposed to 'barbarians': 'For I am the wisdom (σοφία) of the Greeks and the knowledge (γνῶσις) of the barbarians.' This may, however, be a purely conventional designation; compare Kyme aretalogy 31: 'I appointed languages for Greeks and barbarians.'[23] Perhaps a similar caution has to be made with regard to the possible mention (the reading is uncertain) of Egypt.

What is particularly distinctive about this document is the fact that the numerous 'I am' proclamations contained in it are for the most part either sharp antitheses, e.g. 'I am the mother and the daughter', or outright paradoxes, e.g. 'I am the mother of my father and the sister of my husband, and he is my offspring', or 'I am knowledge and ignorance; I am shame and boldness'.

Any attempt to classify this work in terms of the types of literature represented in the Nag Hammadi collection may be premature until it can be studied in detail and compared with the entire corpus. There is nothing at all specifically Christian in it and very little that is Jewish, although the style is occasionally reminiscent of the wisdom hymns. On the other hand, the work does not appear to be especially 'Gnostic' either. One recognizes such passages as the following:

What is within you is what is outside you, and the one who fashioned

[22] J. Bergman, *Ich bin Isis. Studien zum memphitischen Hintergrund der griechischen Isisaretalogien*, Uppsala 1968, p. 302.
[23] *Ibid.*

the outside of you shaped the inside of you. And what you see outside of you you see inside of you; it is revealed and it is your garment.[24]

But it is not clear that even such a popular Gnostic image is originally Gnostic. Nor does The Thunder appear to be related to the Hermetic works in the same codex.

The closest analogies are to the Isis hymns which have been studied most recently by J. Bergman, who traces the origin of the aretalogy hymns to Egyptian soil.[25] It seems highly likely that The Thunder owes its use of the first-person style to the aretalogy form, which, of course, had spread far beyond Egypt. But except for occasional indirect allusions such as those mentioned above, this work does not have the same predications as the aretalogies do. Notably, the aretalogies predicate a wide variety of things about Isis, but they do not use the forms of antithesis and paradox found in The Thunder. We shall return momentarily to what may be a possible significance of this difference.

M. Krause has pointed out a parallel to this work in a short, probably hymnic passage attributed to Eve, the first virgin, in the Untitled Work (Tractate 5) of Codex II which reads as follows:[26]

> I am the part of my mother, and I am the mother; I am the woman, I am the virgin; I am she who is pregnant; I am the physician; I am the comforter of birth-pangs. It is my husband who begot me, and I am his mother and he is my father and my lord; he is my power; whatever he wishes he says. I come into being reasonably (εὐλόγως). But I have begotten a lordly man.[27]

In its setting in the Untitled Work this passage has all the marks of a citation of traditional material, and though it is not a direct quotation, we doubtless have a more ample witness to the same tradition in The Thunder.

We find what is a somewhat different use of the predicative ἐγώ εἰμι proclamation in two other works from the Nag Hammadi collection, which can be dealt with only very briefly here. The

---

[24] Cf. Gospel of Thomas, logion 22 (A. Guillaumont et al., *The Gospel according to Thomas*, Leiden 1959, p. 16); Gospel of Philip 116.4–6 (J.-E. Ménard, *L'Evangile selon Philippe*, Paris 1967, p. 80 and references, p. 188).

[25] See n. 22 above.

[26] Cf. *Le origini dello gnosticismo*, ed. U. Bianchi (Supplements to *Numen*, 12), Leiden 1967, p. 82.

[27] 162.7–15 (Böhlig and Labib, *Schrift ohne Titel*, p. 74).

first is the main work of Codex XIII, 'The Triple Protennoia',[28] a narrative composition in three parts, told in the first person by the revealer figure. Besides containing the classic account of creation and the pre-creation drama familiar from many of the Nag Hammadi works, it describes the triple descent of the revealer into the world to save the divine spark in mankind. The work is filled with proclamations in the I-style, some of which are antithetical, but not in the paradoxical style of The Thunder. It may be noted that this work contains the name Christ and a few other Christian allusions, but it is at best only very superficially Christianized.

There is a close parallel to this work in the longer ending of the Codex II version of the Apocryphon of John.[29] This is also a first-person narrative of the triple descent of the Pronoia into the world to awaken the dormant gnosis in men. The parallel here also extends to the frequent use of the first-person style of proclamation: 'I am the perfect Pronoia of the all . . .; I am the richness of the light, I am the remembrance of the Pleroma.'[30] In a study of this passage I have suggested that this ending was a hymnic, probably cultic summary of a narrative recital of the Gnostic 'salvation history'.[31] It is now apparent from Codex XIII that we have an extended narrative of the same material with which to compare the hymnic summary.

Finally, in surveying the use of the ἐγώ-proclamation in Gnostic sources, we should call attention briefly to two sayings of the Gospel of Thomas which also contain 'I am' proclamations attributed to Jesus: 'I am the one who exists out of that which is the same' and 'I am the light which is above them all; I am the all'.[32] It is easy to recognize the Gnostic colouring of the Thomas saying 'I am the light *which is above*' as opposed to the Johannine 'I am the light *of the world*'. If it is not actually independent of the New Testament usage – and I think that it is – the Thomas use of the 'I am' style is different, and it may be another instance of an already traditional form.

To conclude this brief survey of the predicative use of ἐγώ-proclamations in the Gnostic sources, I should like to suggest

[28] Cf. J. M. Robinson, 'The Coptic Gnostic Library Today', *NTS* 14, 1967–8, p. 401.
[29] 30.11–31.25 (Krause-Labib, pp. 195–8).
[30] 30.11–12, 15–16.
[31] *Le origini dello gnosticismo*, p. 502.
[32] Logia 61 and 77 (Guillaumont, pp. 34, 42).

possible lines for comparison with the Fourth Gospel. Two observations will be made without detailed development; they are intended merely as suggestions for further research.

First, it has often been objected to Bultmann's commentary on the Fourth Gospel that his derivation of the Johannine use of the 'I am' style from Mandaean sources is questionable, not least because of the doubtful antiquity of the Mandaean materials. Sometimes a compromise is reached in the proposal that both John and the Mandaean writings shared a common source in this respect.[33] With such abundant evidence of the Gnostic use of predicative $\dot{\epsilon}\gamma\dot{\omega}$ $\epsilon\dot{\iota}\mu\iota$ proclamations, one can shift the focus of the discussion away from Mandaeism, and it may be found that the Gnostic sources – whose antiquity is still, of course, uncertain – offer an even closer parallel.

Secondly, it has already been observed that the predicative 'I am' proclamations found in these Gnostic sources may have originated in the syncretistic form of the Isis aretalogies, but that The Thunder adds a new element in its use of antithesis and paradox. I would suggest the following brief analysis of this difference. In the Isis hymns the purpose of the many 'I am' sayings is to state the *universality* of the goddess Isis: she is known by many names, she is the source and origin of the manifold religious aspirations of men. In a word, Isis corresponds to all that men worship and think and long for. But the paradoxical form of the 'I am' sayings in The Thunder seems to me to have as its goal a statement of the *transcendence*, not merely the universality, of the revealer, perfect mind. She is not simply the truth or reality of all men's aspirations, but she is of a higher order than the moral, conventional and rational standards of the world. She is both the saint and the prostitute, both peace and war, both innocence and sin, both law and lawlessness, both master and slave, both silence and word, both hidden and revealed, both wise and foolish. In the face of divine revelation no human values are adequate.

Now, of course, the Fourth Gospel does not use this paradoxical form in the $\dot{\epsilon}\gamma\dot{\omega}$-proclamations of Jesus. Nevertheless, it may be that the Fourth Gospel, taking into consideration its over-all structure and its techniques, uses the form of $\dot{\epsilon}\gamma\dot{\omega}$-proclamation not merely to assert that Jesus must be recognized as or identified

---

[33] See, e.g., E. Schweizer, *EGO EIMI . . .* (FRLANT 56), 1939.

with[34] the variety of human religious symbolism: bread, light, shepherd, life, etc.,[35] but that Jesus in his truest reality *transcends* all of this and is revealed only in the moment of his return to the Father, through death and resurrection, as the love of the Father for men. This suggestion is based on the view that the Fourth Gospel means to pass a negative judgement, as ch. 12 explicitly does, on the success of Jesus' self-revelation through sign and symbol. In effect it would suppose that the evangelist is not merely influenced by a complex and syncretistic religious background, but that he deliberately makes use of such a background for his interpretation of the meaning of Jesus.[36] This view cannot be substantiated in detail here, nor has it been the intention of this paper to do so, but if it is tenable, it points to a parallel between some of the Gnostic sources in which the ἐγώ-proclamation appears and the Fourth Gospel – a parallel not so much in words or explicit allusions, as in religious outlook and religious discourse.

[34] Using the classification of Bultmann, *Das Evangelium des Johannes*, p. 168.
[35] Compare the remarks of Stauffer, article ἐγώ, *TDNT* II, p. 350; Schweizer, *op. cit.*, p. 122.
[36] Cf. e.g., E. Fascher, 'Platon und Johannes in ihren Verhältnis zu Sokrates und Christus', *Das Altertum* 14, 1968, p. 83; Schweizer, *op. cit.*, p. 167.

Ethics and the Gnostics

by R. McL. Wilson

(St. Mary's College, St. Andrews, Fife Ky 16 9JU (Schottland))

Several years ago, when the study of the Nag Hammadi texts was still in its infancy, it was asserted that these new documents showed the gnostics to have been 'even blacker' than they were painted by the early Fathers. At the time, at least one reader wondered how the author knew. The texts were not then readily accessible — in fact they were locked away in the Coptic Museum in Cairo, pending settlement of questions of ownership. Only one codex had been smuggled out of Egypt, and the process of editing and translating its contents extended over a period of some twenty years[1]. The first direct access to the texts, as distinct from the various reports and inventories published by J. Doresse, H. C. Puech and others, came with the appearance of the *editio princeps* of the Gospel of Truth and Pahor Labib's photographic edition containing a number of pages belonging to the Codex Jung and the greater part of five treatises from Codex II[2]. There was nothing here to support the assertion. In contrast, Jean

---

[1] The Gospel of Truth from the Codex Jung was published in 1956, the final part of the Tractatus Tripartitus in 1975. The delay was occasioned at least in part by the problems of co-ordinating translations of the Coptic into three different modern languages, which entailed circulation and discussion of the material by correspondence among a group of eventually seven scholars in several different countries. In the event, complete co-ordination proved to be impossible, and the translations accordingly differ, sometimes quite appreciably. James M. Robinson is not altogether fair in speaking of a monopoly (*Religious Studies Review* 3, 1977, 17–29), since the group was expanded at least twice, first by the inclusion of Wilson and Zandee and then by the addition of Kasser and Vycichl. Prior to their publication, the texts in this codex were admittedly not available to other scholars, but that was to prevent premature release — and the editors were themselves bound by contract not to publish articles of their own on a given text for a period of some months after its publication. In retrospect it might have been better to have adopted a simpler and more basic form of publication, as suggested at the time by W. C. Till, but that is another matter. Incidentally, the draft English translation circulated by the Claremont Coptic Gnostic Library project in preparation for *The Nag Hammadi Library in English* carried on every page a notice restricting its use to authorised persons.

For bibliography relating to the Nag Hammadi library, see D. M. Scholer, *Nag Hammadi Bibliography 1948–1969* (NHS 1, Leiden 1971), supplemented annually, apart from 1976, in *Novum Testamentum*.

[2] *Coptic Gnostic Papyri in the Coptic Museum at Old Cairo*, Cairo 1956. Plates 1–46 contain pages belonging to the Codex Jung, and plates 47–158 the first four treatises of Cod-

Doresse, in the first full-scale survey of the library[3], says bluntly: 'Nothing in these documents leads us to suppose that the Gnostics in question were addicted to licentious rites: one finds oneself almost disappointed in this, so freely had the heresiologists given us to understand that mysteries of that description were common practice in the principal sects!'

Scholars had long been accustomed to noting the curious phenomenon that asceticism and lubricity could both spring from the self-same root, the gnostic denigration of this present world and its Creator, and explanations lay readily to hand. On the one side, the gnostic did not belong to this world and should have nothing to do with it. His mind was set on higher things, and the daily concerns of the ordinary citizen in this life had no relevance for him; they were to be avoided so far as possible. On the other side, it was alleged, the gnostic was 'saved by nature'. Nothing that he did could affect that fact, and he was therefore at liberty to do whatsoever he chose. Indeed, hostility to the Demiurge could be construed to mean that the gnostic had a positive duty to disobey his commands, and hence to transgress against the laws imposed by the God of the Old Testament. On the one side the road led straight to asceticism, on the other to practices of a libertinarian character.

More recent studies have placed the whole matter in a different perspective, particularly in the light of the Nag Hammadi texts. As K. Rudolph notes[4], 'Gnosis is not a "theology of salvation by nature," as the heresiologists caricature it; it is rather thoroughly conscious of the provisional situation of the redeemed up to the realisation of redemption after death. Otherwise the extant literature which relates to existential and ethical behaviour is inexplicable. Naturally the fact remains that the pneumatic element cannot perish and its entry into the Pleroma is preordained, but the why and the how are not independent of the right conduct of its bearer'. In point of fact, the gnostics were wrestling with problems which have perplexed adherents of more orthodox traditions, in particular the reconciliation of divine grace and human freedom. The Westminster Confession of Faith for example affirms effectual calling, by which the elect are regenerated and renewed, and determined to that which is good (ch. X); but the last sentence of the preceding chapter declares 'The will of man is made perfectly and immutably free to do good alone in the state of glory only'. A later chapter (XX: Of Christian Liberty) is quite specific: 'They who, upon pretence of Christian liberty, do practise any sin, or cherish any lust, do thereby destroy the end of Christian liberty; which is, that,

---

ex II with some twelve pages of the anonymous treatise which was given the title On the origin of the World. This was just under half the text of the latter work.

[3] *The Secret Books of the Egyptian Gnostics*, London 1960, 251 (ET of *Les livres secrets des gnostiques d'Egypte*, Paris 1958).

[4] *Gnosis*, Edinburgh 1983, 117 (ET of *Gnosis*, Leipzig 1977, 135).

being delivered out of the hands of our enemies, we might serve the Lord without fear, in holiness and righteousness before him, all the days of our life'. In Pauline terms, it is by grace that we are saved, and not of works; yet conduct and good works are not irrelevant to Christian living.

At a later point[5], Rudolph echoes Doresse's comment: 'It is at any rate striking that thus far no libertine writings have appeared even among the plentiful Nag Hammadi texts. The witnesses for the libertine tendency are restricted to the Church Fathers and even here the evidence is uneven and in particular not easy to put into chronological sequence. At times it looks as if libertinism appeared rather late ... and as if individual sects (for example, the Simonians, the Basilidians and the Valentinians) first arrived at these conclusions in the course of their further development'.

Here a number of points call for attention. In the first place, the Fathers were engaged in polemic, concerned to refute and denounce what they regarded as a dangerous heresy; and it is not uncommon for polemic to degenerate into vilification. 'Une fois l'aversion contre une classe d'hommes créée et enracinée par un motif quelconque, dans l'objet haï tout devient haïssable: l'opinion préconçue donne naissance ou crédit à des fables, à des calomnies, qui contribuent, à leur tour, à la généraliser et à la fortifier, quelquefois même survivent à ses véritables causes'[6]. These words were written with reference to the slanders against the Jews which appear in Greek and Roman authors, but this 'loi fatale' is capable of wider application. We may recall the slanders directed against early Christians, the accusations of atheism, Thyestian banquets, promiscuity. In the light of this, the patristic statements must be viewed with some reserve. It is possible that some groups, or some individual gnostics, were guilty of the practices alleged, but we have no ground for assuming that all were guilty or that these practices were characteristic.

A second point is that the allegations vary from one Father to another: it may be not that libertinism appeared rather late, as Rudolph suggests, but that later Fathers were more inclined to bring such charges, with or without foundation. Certainly the most extreme cases are recorded by Epiphanius, and Epiphanius is notoriously not the most reliable of witnesses. Irenaeus is severe in his condemnation of Carpocrates (I 25. 1–6) and the Cainites (I 31. 1–2), but these are groups for whom we have no direct evidence, and may have been quite exceptional. Moreover we can see in the case of Jews and Christians how some of the allegations might have arisen through misunderstanding or misrepresentation, and the same may hold for the gnostics. One need only consider what a rite called 'the bridal chamber' might suggest to an outsider who had no knowledge of its real nature, the more especially if he knew of the sacred prostitution asso-

---

[5] Op. cit. 254 (German ed., 260).

[6] T. Reinach, *Textes d'auteurs grecs et romains relatifs au judaisme*, Paris 1895, xvi.

ciated with some other cults. In the Gospel of Philip however it is the highest of the sacraments, symbolised by the Holy of Holies in the Temple at Jerusalem, and as 'the marriage undefiled' is expressly contrasted with earthly marriage. As Rudolph notes[7], Irenaeus provides us with the necessary background: at the consummation, according to the Valentinians, the gnostic is to be re-united with his celestial counterpart in the Pleroma (the bridal chamber). Since the human predicament originates in a disruption of the primal unity, symbolised by the separation of Adam and Eve (cf. Gospel of Philip 68.22−26; 70.10−22), 'the return of the soul to the arms of her partner or ideal prototype, prefigured in that of Sophia herself, is the decisive event at the end of time'. It is of course possible that some groups sought to symbolise this consummation by some form of ritual intercourse, but we have no proof that they did. The emphasis on continence even within the bonds of marriage in such works as the Acts of Thomas suggests otherwise.

Irenaeus at one point (I 6.3 f.) speaks of some who 'secretly seduce women', or even openly parade their shameless conduct, and others who 'initially made an impressive pretence of living with (women) as sisters' but 'were convicted in course of time when the "sister" became pregnant by the "brother"'[8]. This passage, in his report on the Valentinians, is det-

---

[7] Op. cit. 245 (German ed., 251); see his discussion, 245−247. Following H. G. Gaffron, he regards it as 'probably even a kind of sacrament for the dying'. Irenaeus says nothing of any sexual act in this connection; 'it would be contrary to the "spiritual" interpretation of this "marriage"'.

[8] The passage recalls one interpretation of the 'famous crux' (Chadwick, NTS 1, 1954−5, 267) of I Cor. 7: 36−38, which some scholars have understood to refer to "the elementary, early relationship which soon afterwards developed into the *virgines subintroductae* of the later Church" (Moffatt, *First Corinthians*, London 1938 (repr. 1947), 99. So too NEB: "partner in celibacy"; but the footnotes suggest another interpretation: "virgin daughter"). As the NEB margin indicates, reference to a "spiritual" marriage is only one of several possible interpretations of the Corinthians passage (cf. Barrett, *First Corinthians*, London 1968, 182−185; Conzelmann, *Der erste Brief an die Korinther*, Göttingen 1969, 160−161. Like Chadwick and Prof. Greeven (NTS 15, 1968−69, 375), they understand it of an engaged couple; cf. RSV "betrothed"). That there were "libertine" trends in Corinth is evidenced by 1 Cor. 5:1 ff., 6:12 ff., but it should be noted a) that the first of these passages refers to a single case, and b) in the second instance the preceding verses (9−11) are a reminder that "some" of the Corinthians had formerly not led irreproachable lives − but they were washed, sanctified, justified, and are therefore under an obligation to glorify God in their bodies (6:20). In neither case is there ground for thinking that Paul's censure applies to all the Corinthian Christians, or even to a large number. Their fault was that they tolerated the offender of 5:1 ff., and were in danger of being misled by the claims of the (possibly quite small) group in view at 6:12 ff. It may be added that it is by no means certain that Paul's opponents in Corinth were fully "gnostic" in the second-century sense of that term, and that there were also tendencies in the direction of asceticism.

ached from its context in Werner Foerster's anthology and adduced separately, on the ground that it does not correspond with the rest of the account of Valentinian gnosis. 'Nor can any libertinism be recognised in the letter of Ptolemaeus to Flora, in the central section of the *Excerpta ex Theodoto*, or in the fragments of Heracleon's Commentary on John'[9]. Foerster deduces that Irenaeus is not referring to the common doctrines of ordinary Valentinians, but to 'a mere group'. Frederik Wisse, in a cogent presentation of the case for the 'ascetic' view[10], observes 'Dies muß im Licht des valentinianischen Mysteriums vom Brautgemach gesehen werden, dem offenbar in bestimmten Fällen ein enthaltsames Zusammenleben eines Bruders und einer Schwester folgte. Es ist kein Wunder, daß die Gegner für diese Praxis nur Zynismus und Spott übrig hatten. Doch war dieses asketische Ideal auch bei den Orthodoxen weitverbreitet, und daß dahinter ernster religiöser Eifer stand, läßt sich nicht bezweifeln, auch wenn es nicht immer erfolgreich verwirklicht wurde'. Comparing the similar situation in the Acts of Thomas, he suggests that wives converted to the gnostic faith might have abandoned their husbands to devote themselves to a life of *encrateia*. The husbands evidently complained to Irenaeus that the gnostics had stolen away their wives; and finally, when the wives returned in penitence they would portray their gnostic teachers in the darkest colours, in order to present themselves as the innocent victims of wicked deceivers. This certainly has the ring of truth about it, and would provide another indication of the way in which these aspersions grew and developed.

In this context, reference should be made to some characteristics of polemic. In the first place, in Reinach's words, 'dans l'objet haï, tout devient haïssable'. Therefore even what might otherwise be accounted good must be taken *in malam partem*. Thus Irenaeus writes of Saturnilus (I 24.2) that 'many of his followers abstain also from animal food, and through this feigned continence they lead many astray'. Similarly Epiphanus writes (XL 2.4) that some Archontics 'pretend to an affected abstinence and deceive the simpler sort of men by making a show of withdrawal from the world in imitation of the monks'. Gnostic abstinence, in the eyes of the Fathers, is thus not genuine but a sham and a pretence, intended to deceive the unwary into thinking them other than they really are. On the other hand Irenaeus in the same context notes that for Saturnilus marriage and procreation 'are of Satan', and even Epiphanius writes of the followers of Severus that they 'abstain completely from wine', because of the evils which it produces, and say that those who consort in

---

[9] *Gnosis* i, Oxford 1972, 313 (ET of Die *Gnosis* i, Zürich and Stuttgart 1969, 400).

[10] 'Die Sextus-Sprüche und das Problem der gnostischen Ethik', in Böhlig-Wisse, *Zum Hellenismus in den Schriften von Nag Hammadi*, Göttinger Orientforschungen VI. Reihe, Bd. 2, Wiesbaden 1975, 70.

marriage 'fulfil the work of Satan' (XLV 1.8; 2.1). In neither case in there any suggestion of hypocrisy or deceit.

A second feature of polemic is a tendency to generalise from particular cases: a practice known or alleged to be indulged in by some is simply assumed to be characteristic of all. It is possible, as already noted, that some groups, or some individual gnostics, were guilty of such practices, but that is no justification for the assumption that all were tarred with the selfsame brush. We have to look for the general trend, the dominant tendency, and from all that we know of the period that seems more likely to have been ascetic in character rather than libertine. As Wisse writes (p. 72): 'Zum mindesten ist klar, daß solche Exzesse bei den Gnostikern Ausnahmen waren: sie sind kein Kriterium, nach dem man die ganze Bewegung beurteilen kann. Die jetzt zahlreich bekannt gewordenen gnostischen Originalwerke zeigen, daß das ethische Interesse der Gnostiker entschieden asketisch war'.

Wisse takes as his starting-point the presence in the Nag Hammadi library of a Coptic version of the Sentences of Sextus, which he describes as a typical example of hellenistic religious ethics. The popularity of this work is shown by its translation into Latin and Syriac, and in part into Armenian and Georgian. Introducing his translation in *The Nag Hammadi Library in English*[11], Wisse calls it a collection of maximes with a strongly ethical and ascetic tone, and adds 'Although the tractate itself cannot really be considered a Gnostic treatise, its esoteric, moral asceticism seems to make it quite compatible with the other tractates from the Nag Hammadi collection . . . the evidence indicates that the library was the property of a group which placed a strong emphasis upon sexual asceticism'. The presence of non-gnostic works in a largely gnostic collection was initially the cause of some perplexity, but is probably to be explained on the assumption that these works were congenial to the owners, if they were gnostics, or at least were thought to be of the same general character as more strictly gnostic works. Several years ago, Wisse noted that if there is a unity in the library, it is to be found not in doctrine but in the ethical stance of the tractates[12], and in a recent study G. Sfameni Gasparro writes: 'La conclusione più prudente è quella di riconoscere come, nella complessità e varietà delle tendenze dottrinali espresse nei trattati copti di Nag Hammadi, l'elemento unificante sia costituito − nello sfondo sostanzialmente gnostico − da un interesse peculiare per tematiche di astensionismo, sessuale sopratutto ma talora anche alimentare che, a titolo diverso, emerge dalla maggior parte di essi'.[13]

---

[11] *The Nag Hammadi Library in English* (General Editor: James M. Robinson), New York, London, Leiden 1977, 454 (abbreviated NHLE).

[12] 'The Nag Hammadi Library and the Heresiologists', *Vigiliae Christianae* 25, 1971, 220.

[13] *Enkrateia e Antropologia:* Le motivazioni protologiche della continenza e della verginità

The Coptic version of Sextus is unfortunately extant only in part, and the missing 'sentences' include most of those which Wisse (p. 75) adduces as evidence for the ascetic tendency. However, there are two blocks more or less complete (157–180, 307–397), and in Wisse's view 'es ist so gut wie sicher, daß die dazwischenliegenden Maximen 181–306 ursprünglich nicht gefehlt haben, und dasselbe kann für die ersten 156 der Sammlung angenommen werden'. In that case practically all of the relevant 'sentences' would have been included, and moreover in a text showing a remarkable agreement with the Greek version edited by Chadwick (Wisse 74). Even the extant Coptic however contains pointers to an ascetic morality: 'It is better to die [than] to darken the soul because of [the] immoderation of the belly' (345); 'Say with [your] mind that the body [is] the garment of your soul; keep it, therefore, pure since it is innocent' (346); 'Unclean demons do lay claim to a polluted soul; ⟨the⟩ evil demons will not be able to lay hold of a soul which is faithful and good in the way of God' (348–9; perhaps one might compare 'saying' 61 in the Gospel of Philip (65.1–27). Here too there is an ascetic element: he who comes out of the world is above desire and fear, master over nature (lines 28–30)).

The second work adduced by Wisse is the Teachings of Silvanus, 'a rare example of an early Christian Wisdom text' (NHLE 346) showing Platonic and Stoic as well as Biblical influences. Here again we read: 'The soul which is a member of God's household is one which is kept pure, and the soul which has put on Christ is one which is pure' (109.4–8). The opening lines speak of 'the struggle against every folly of the passions of love and base wickedness, and love of praise, and fondness of contention, and tiresome jealousy and wrath, and anger and the desire of avarice' (84.20–26). The soul is bidden to bring in mind as its guide, and reason as its teacher (85.24–26). Later we find 'Turn toward the rational nature and cast from yourself the earth-begotten nature' (94.16–18), and towards the end 'My son, first purify yourself toward the outward life in order that you may be able to purify the inward' (117.25–28). The admonition 'Be sober and shake off your drunkenness, which is the work of ignorance' (94.20–22) recalls the New Testament use of this metaphor, but at the same time the reference to 'ignorance', like the mention of 'robbers' at 85.2; 113.33, may indicate how these works could be interpreted in ways congenial to gnostics. Silvanus also refers to the bridal chamber (94.28), in which according to Wisse the mind is illuminated (p. 78). That would provide a link with such works as the Gospel of Philip, but possibly some reserve is called for here: the preceding words refer to

nel cristianesimo dei primi secoli e nello gnosticismo, Rome 1984, 148. The chapter relating to Gnosticism extends over pages 115–166. Reference may also be made to the papers delivered at the colloquium on 'La tradizione dell' *enkrateia*: motivazioni ontologiche e protologiche' held in Milan in 1982 (ed. U. Bianchi). Rome: Edizioni dell' Alenes 1985.

natural birth, and slight modification of the translation could convey a different impression: 'When you entered into a bodily birth, you were begotten. You came into being inside the bridal chamber. You were illuminated in mind'. A gnostic, of course, would understand the phrase of the celestial bridal chamber, but if originally it went with the preceding sentence it would have referred to natural birth. This is just one case, and there are others, in which it may be that we have not yet completely resolved the problems of understanding and interpretation.

Wisse's third text, the Authoritative Teaching, is described as 'weniger deutlich christlich als Sılvanus und gleichzeitig ausgeprägter gnostisch' (p. 78 f.). The gnostic character of this text has however been disputed (cf. Gasparro 158), and Wisse himself elsewhere calls it 'not obviously heretical'[14]. In that respect it is like another tractate which shows some similarities in theme and content, the Exegesis on the Soul, which Ménard calls 'bel et bien un traité gnostique'[15], whereas Wisse considers it merely heterodox and questions whether the use of certain concepts in the text is really gnostic. More important for present purposes is an earlier comment: 'Only celibacy would be consistent with the teaching of the tractate (i. e. ExSoul). Repentance remains, of course, the dominant theme, but an ascetic way of life appears to be a part of it'[16]. If Krause's reconstruction is correct, incidentally, the Exegesis offers a clear statement of salvation by grace alone: 'So wird die Seele durch die Wiedergeburt gerettet werden. Das aber kommt nicht durch asketische Worte, auch nicht durch Künste, auch nicht durch geschriebene Lehren (= Lehrbriefe), sondern es ist die Gna[de Gott]es, vielmehr ist es das Geschenk Got[tes für den Men]schen'[17]. H. M. Schenke however offers a different restoration of the lacunae, while *The Nag Hammadi Library in English* makes no attempt to fill them[18]. Here again we are confronted by problems of translation and interpretation, in this case complicated by lacunae in the manuscript. Edi-

---

[14] 'On exegeting "The Exegesis on the Soul"', *Les Textes de Nag Hammadi* (ed. J. E. Ménard), Leiden 1975, 69.
[15] 'L'"évangile selon Philippe" et l'"exégèse de l'âme"', *Les Textes de Nag Hammadi* 67.
[16] Art. cit. 78. For the questioning of the concepts mentioned, see p. 79.
[17] *Die Gnosis* ii, Zürich and Stuttgart 1971, 133 (ET Oxford 1974, 108); cf. also Krause-Labib, *Gnostische und hermetische Schriften aus Codex II und Codex VI*, Glückstadt 1971, 81f. for the Coptic text (134.28–33).
[18] 'Sprachliche und exegetische Probleme in den beiden letzten Schriften des Codex II von Nag Hammadi', OLZ 70, 1975, 8 and 12; NHLE 185 reads: 'Thus it is by being born again that the soul will be saved. And this is due not to rote phrases or to professional skills or to book learning. Rather it is the grace of the [. . ., it is] the gift of the [. . .].' See also Wisse, art. cit. 76, who says 'the lacunae resist reconstruction in places', but adds 'The fact that salvation comes only through grace is used by the author as a further ground for the soul to repent and call upon God for mercy (135.4–15)'. The Greek word ἄσκησις of course does not necessarily carry the connotation of asceticism.

torial reconstruction, however well-meant and however plausible, may be misleading.

According to G. W. MacRae[19], the Authoritative Teaching contains no typical gnostic cosmogonic myth but appears to presuppose 'a generally gnostic, i. e. anticosmic dualist, understanding of the fate of the soul in the material world'. Reference to the Pleroma (22.19) and to 'her bridegroom' (22.23) naturally suggests the Valentinian concept of the bridal chamber; but at least one Christian hymn from a later age salutes Jesus as 'Shepherd, Husband, Friend', and a footnote in the edition runs: 'The imagery is common in the Bible, the Fathers, Gnosticism (especially Valentinian)'. A later reference to 'her true shepherd' (33.2) evokes the comment 'The precise expression is not Johannine but invites comparison with Jn 10:11 and the Johannine use of ἀληθινός in other contexts'.[20] Curiously, there is no reference to the Johannine passage at 32.10f., where it would seem to be equally apt: here the soul 'runs into her fold, while her shepherd stands at the door'. Rev. 3:20 is however cited. In the light of the references now available in the edition, the Christian influence may perhaps be considered slightly stronger than Wisse originally allowed.

Wisse's final example, the Testimony of Truth, is also now available in edited form, with an extensive introduction and notes by B. A. Pearson[21]. Right at the outset, the 'old leaven' of the scribes and Pharisees is identified with 'the errant desire of the angels and the demons and the stars' (29.15−18). The Pharisees and scribes are 'those who belong to the archons', and 'no one who is under the law will be able to look up to the truth, for they will not be able to serve two masters' (29.18−24). The law in fact is rejected − because it commands one to take a wife or husband, and to multiply like the sand of the sea (29.26−30.5). When John the Baptist saw the power which came down upon the Jordan river, he knew 'that the dominion of carnal procreation had come to an end' (30.25−30). A later section (38.27−41.4) urges the necessity for radical rejection of all that pertains to carnal generation. 'No one knows the God of truth except solely the man who will forsake all of the things of the world' (41.4−8).

It could be argued that some of this material is not particularly ascetic, but simply represents fairly conventional morality. The point is however that it is definitely not libertinarian in character. The gnostics were people of their time, and shared with other groups the attitude and outlook of the period. The evidence of the Nag Hammadi texts, like that of the extracts quoted by the Fathers from the Valentinians (see above), suggests a moral standard at least as high as that of other contemporary groups, and on occasion even stricter. The tendency was in the direction of asceticism

---

[19] *Nag Hammadi Codices V, 2−5 and VI*, Leiden 1979, 258.
[20] Op. cit. 282−3.
[21] *Nag Hammadi Codices IX and X*, Leiden 1981, 101−203.

and encratism, rather than towards libertinism. Gasparro, after reviewing the documents mentioned and some others, speaks of 'le decisive tendenze encratite che percorrono sia gli scritti di più evidente ispirazione diteista e di impostazione "mitica" sia quelli a carattere didattico-parenetico, poco o nulla interessati a speculazioni teo-cosmologiche'[22].

In a recent book G. A. G. Stroumsa writes 'At the root of the Gnostic rejection of the material world and its creator lies an obsessive preoccupation with the problem of evil'[23]. Whatever its form, the 'gnostic myth' is intended to provide an explanation for the human predicament, for the trials and tribulations of the human race in the world as we know it. Gnostic ethics is dominated by a concern for purity, for the restoration of a lost ideal, for the recovery of a primal innocence, and is therefore in the main of an ascetic or encratite character. Some groups, or some individuals, may have drawn conclusions leading to libertinism, but all the evidence suggests that they were exceptional. Two points deserve some mention in conclusion: in the first place, if the gnostics were predominantly encratite, this does not mean that all encratites were gnostic; nor does it justify attaching the label 'gnostic' to any document showing encratite features. We need to refine our categories and definitions, as indeed the discussion of some of the texts above has shown, for example by restricting the use of the label to those cases in which there is reasonably clear evidence of gnostic mythology in the text. The Nag Hammadi library has made it abundantly clear that if its owners were gnostics they were perfectly prepared to make use of hermetic or other literature which was congenial to their own ideas, or could be interpreted in conformity with them. If they were not gnostics, of course, it shows that the kind of confusion which has beset modern investigation was already prevalent in the ancient world: the people who brought these texts together presumably thought they belonged together. And secondly we need to reconsider some of the implications. In the past the view that asceticism and lubricity could both spring from the same root has led to the designation of both encratite and libertinarian texts as 'gnostic', which in turn has fostered the kind of *Pangnostizismus* that by ignoring important differences has found gnostics under every stone and behind every bush. A case in point is the ethical section in Galatians, which has sometimes been regarded as directed against antinomian 'gnostics'. To the contrary, the evidence of the Nag Hammadi texts would suggest that gnostics would have welcomed Paul's injunctions. They too could speak in terms of bondage to the flesh and freedom in the Spirit.

---

[22] *Enkrateia e Antropologia* 165.
[23] *Another Seed:* Studies in Gnostic Mythology, Leiden 1984, 17.

ROBERT McL. WILSON

ALIMENTARY AND SEXUAL ENCRATISM
IN THE NAG HAMMADI TRACTATES

It was for a long time not uncommon for scholars, writing about the gnostics, to comment on the curious phenomenon that in their systems asceticism and lubricity could both spring from the self-same root. This root was of course the gnostic disparagement of the world and all that belonged to it. On the one hand the conclusion was drawn that the gnostic would have nothing to do with the world. Procreation, for example, meant only the subjection of yet more souls to the sway of the Demiurge. At a later stage we read, with reference to Manicheism, « Since the ruin of the Hyle is decreed by God, one should abstain from all ensouled things and eat only vegetables and whatever else is non-sentient, and abstain from marriage, the delights of love and the begetting of children, so that the divine Power may not through the succession of generations remain longer in the Hyle » [1]. As Jonas notes, however, « the full rigorism of the Manichean ethics is reserved for a particular group, the "Elect" or "True", who must have led a monastic life of extraordinary asceticism », whereas the great mass of believers lived under less rigorous rules [2]. In the strictly gnostic texts known to us, not much is actually said about abstinence from foods, but the occurrence of such taboos in ascetic traditions from Pythagoreanism onwards would seem to suggest that the same would hold for the gnostics.

On the other hand the conclusion was that as a spark of the divine the gnostic was « saved by nature ». Whatever he might do, whatever might befall, he could not lose his spiritual nature. « Just as gold, when placed in mud, does not lose its beauty but

---

[1] Alexander of Lycopolis, as quoted by Jonas, *The Gnostic Religion*, Boston 1958, p. 231; cfr. also Rudolph, *Die Gnosis*, Leipzig 1977, 364 f., who notes that the Manichean Electi were required to fast for 100 days in the year.

[2] Jonas, 232.

retains its own nature, since the mud is unable to harm the gold, so they say that they themselves cannot suffer any injury or lose their spiritual substance, whatever material actions they may engage in » [3]. A similar analogy, that of a pearl in mud, appears in the Gospel of Philip [4]: « when the pearl is cast down into the mud it does not become greatly despised, nor if it is anointed with balsam oil will it become more precious. But it always has value in the eyes of its owner. So with the sons of God wherever they may be. They still have value in the eyes of their Father ». Here again, however, the analogy is not exclusively gnostic: there is something very similar in the Enneads of Plotinus [5]. Moreover, it does not always carry libertinarian associations.

More recently, the idea that the gnostics claimed to be « saved by nature » has been called in question [6]. From the new texts « wird nämlich deutlich, dass die "Pneuma-Natur" des Gnostikers einerseits durchaus auch als Gnade Gottes verstanden werden kann, andererseits das Heil nicht automatisch sicher ist, sondern von einem entsprechenden Lebenswandel begleitet sein muss, der dem erlangten Zustand eines "Erlösten" auch entspricht... Die Gnosis ist keine "substanzhafte Heilstheologie"... Natürlich bleibt es dabei, dass das "Pneumatische" nich zugrunde gehen kann und sein Eingang ins Pleroma vorbestimmt ist, aber das Warum und Wie ist vom rechten Verhalten des Trägers nicht unabhängig » [7]. In similar vein F. Wisse has argued that Plotinus' attacks upon the ethics of the gnostics are due to his own conclusions from gnostic teaching, and not necessarily grounded in fact. So too with the heresiologists—gnostic libertinism was the exception rather that the rule As evidence he adduces from the Nag Hammadi library the Sentences of Sextus, the Teachings of Silvanus, the Authentikos Logos

---

[3] Iren. adv. haer. I 6.2 (translation from Foerster, *Gnosis* (ET 1972), vol. 1, p. 139; cfr. Foerster's Introduction, *op. cit.*, 2 ff.

[4] Codex II 62.17-26 (translations from the Nag Hammadi texts are from *The Nag Hammadi Library in English*, Leiden 1977. In this case line 23 is slightly modified, cfr. Wilson, *The Gospel of Philip*, London 1962, 109).

[5] Cfr. Enn. i. 6.5 ad fin. in Mackenna's translation.

[6] See Rudolph 134 f., referring to L. Schottroff, « Anima naturaliter salvanda », in W. Eltester (ed.), *Christentum und Gnosis* (BZNW 37, Berlin 1969), pp. 65-97.

[7] Rudolph, loc. cit., cfr. also pp. 258 ff.

and the Testimonium Veritatis [8]. The first two of these documents are not specifically gnostic compositions [9], but their presence in the collection does at least indicate that their contents were congenial to the owners, and there is ample other evidence in the library to support this position. It may be that some gnostic groups did adopt libertinarian views and practices, but the evidence of the Nag Hammadi library points the other way. As Rudolph writes, « die Zeugnisse für die libertinistische Richtung sind uns nur durch die Kirchenväter bekannt und auch hier nicht gleichmässig, vor allem chronologisch nicht leicht anzuordnen. Verschiedentlich sieht es so aus als ob der Libertinismus erst eine spätere Erscheinung ist... und als ob einzelne Sekten (zum Beispiel die Simonianer, die Basilidianer und die Valentinianer) erst im Laufe ihrer Fortentwicklung zu diesen Konsequenzen gelangt sind » [10]. The fact of the matter is that we have no single gnostic document of a libertinarian character. Evidence for gnostic libertinism is due almost entirely to the writtings of opponents, and we cannot always assume that these are reports at first hand. « Bei den meisten handelt es sich um eine Verbreitung von Gerüchten, die die Kirchenväter nur zu gerne von ihrer Gegnern zu glauben bereit waren » [11].

As already noted, not much is said in the extant gnostic texts about abstinence from foods, but the one clear reference also affords a clear example of patristic bias. Writing of Saturninus, Irenaeus says « many of his followers abstain also from animal food, and through this feigned continence they lead many astray » [12]. The first part of this statement may well be historical fact, since Irenaeus does not say they *professed* to abstain; the second, however, with its implication of hypocrisy, of a feigned continence, is

---

[8] « Die Sextus-Sprüche und das Problem der gnostischen Ethik », in Böhlig-Wisse, *Zum Hellenismus in den Schriften von Nag Hammadi* (Göttingen Orientforschungen, VI Reihe: Hellenistica, Band 2, Wiesbaden 1975), pp. 55-86.

[9] Cfr. the relevant introductions in *The Nag Hammadi Library in English*.

[10] *Op. cit.*, p. 260.

[11] Wisse 65. At a later point (71 f). Wisse observes that not all the reports need regarded as exaggerated or false; but excess was the exception, not the rule.

[12] Adv. haer. I 24.2 (translation from Foerster, vol. 1, 41).

at least open to question. Such a bias is more obvious in Epiphanius' account of the Archontics [13], but Epiphanius is notoriously not
the most reliable of witnesses: « Some of them have polluted their
bodies by licentiousness, but others pretend to an affected abstinence and deceive the simpler sort of men by making a show of
withdrawal from the world in imitation of the monks ». Epiphanius here goes beyond what Irenaeus says of the followers of
Saturninus by alleging that the Archontics *pretend* to an affected
abstinence.

The gnostic attitude to fasting, as represented in the Gospel
of Thomas, might at first sight appear ambiguous, even self-contra-
dictory. In logion 6, in response to a question from the disciples
about fasting, prayer, alms and diet, Jesus replies « Do not tell lies,
and do not do what you hate ». In logion 14 he says « If you fast,
you will give rise to sin for yourselves; and if you pray, you will be
condemned; and if you give alms, you will do harm to your spirits ».
In logion 104 the disciples say « Come, let us pray today and fast »,
and Jesus answers « What is the sin that I have committed, or
wherein have I been defeated? But when the bridegroom leaves
the bridal chamber, then let them fast and pray » (cfr. Mark 2. 20
and par.). All of this would seem to imply a repudiation of fasting,
but some other texts put a somewhat different complexion on the
matter. In logion 27 Jesus says « If you do not fast as regards the
world, you will not find the Kingdom. If you do not observe the
Sabbath as a Sabbath. you will not see the Father ». If we take
these passages in association with one from the Epistle of Ptolemy
to Flora [14], another picture emerges: « As to fasting, he wants us to
be engaged not in physical fasting but in spiritual fasting, which
amounts to abstinence from all that is evil. External, physical fasting
is observed even among our followers, for it can be of some benefit
to the soul, if it is engaged on reasonably, whenever it is done
neither by way of imitating others, nor out of habit, nor because
of the day, as if it had been specially appointed for that purpose ».
We may recall the words of the Didache: « Let not your fastings
be with the hypocrites, for they fast on the second and the fifth

[13] Epiph. Pan. XL 2.4 (Foerster, 297).
[14] Ap. Epiph. Pan XXXIII 5.13 (Foerster 159); cfr. G. Quispel's notes
(SC 24 bis, Paris 1966, 97 f).

day of the week; but do ye keep your fast on the fourth and on the preparation (the sixth) day » [15] — which may not in fact be so superficial as appears at first sight [16]. It is not the outward act of fasting that is important, the observance of fasting on appointed days, but the attitude of heart and mind of which it is the outward symbol. Also relevant in this context are the words of Josephus concerning John the Baptist, that baptism was acceptable to him « if they used it not for the begging off (*paraitesis*) of certain sins, but for the purification of the body, inasmuch as the soul had already been cleansed by righteousness » [17]. As these non-gnostic references show, this is not something specifically gnostic, but part of an older and wider tradition reaching back on the Biblical side at least to the prophecies of Isaiah:

> « Is such the fast that I choose,
> a day for a man to humble himself?
> Is it to bow down his head like a rush,
> and to spread sackcloth and ashes under him?
> Will you call this a fast,
> and a day acceptable to the Lord?
>
> Is not this the fast that I choose:
> to loose the bonds of wickedness,
> to undo the thongs of the yoke,
> to let the oppressed go free,
> and to break every yoke?

[15] Didache VIII. 1, tr. J. B. Lightfoot, *The Apostolic Fathers*, London 1891, p. 232.

[16] For possible explanations cfr. e.g. Jeremias, JTS 10 (1959), p. 133.

[17] Ant. XVIII. 117. Cfr. also the Qumran Community Rule: « When his flesh is sprinkled with purifying and sanctified by cleansing water, it shall be made clean by the humble submission of his soul to all the precepts of God » (Vermes, *The Dead Sea Scrolls in English*, Harmondsworth 1962, p. 75). The preceding lines refer to cleansing from all sins « by the spirit of holiness uniting him to His truth » (cfr. perhaps the Gospel of Truth 26.30 - 27.4?). The Teachings of Silvanus (Cod. VII 117.25 ff.) contains the injunction « first purify yourself toward the outward life in order that you may be able to purify the inward » (NHLE 361). On « baptist » sects cfr. most recently K. Rudolph, *Antike Baptisten*, SB Sächs. Akad. Leipzig, Phil. - hist. Klasse 121.4 (1981).

Is it not to share your bread with the hungry,
and bring the homeless poor into your house;
when you see the naked, to cover him,
and not to hide yourself from your own flesh? » [18].

True religion, for the gnostic as in other traditions, is not
just a matter of outward observance. It is a concentration upon
external formalism that is deprecated.

To complete the picture, reference may be made to some
passages in the apocryphal Acts. The service of the belly, according
to the Acts of Thomas [19], « plunges the soul into cares and anxieties
and sorrows ». In another passage we read « How much more
must those who believe in my God serve him with great holiness
and purity and <chastity>, free from all bodily pleasures, adultery
and prodigality, theft and drunkenness and service of the belly
and (other) shameful deeds? » [20]. It is pertinent to note that the
Acts of Thomas is generally recognised to be the most gnostic in
character of the major Acts. In the second of these passages the
« service of the belly » might be understood of the lower passions generally, but it may be assumed that abstinence from bodily
pleasures would include abstinence in matters of food. Certainly
Thomas is presented as a man of extremely ascetic habits: right at
the beginning, at the wedding feast, « while they ate and drank,
the apostle tasted nothing » [21]. Twice it is said of him « He eats
only bread with salt, and his drink is water », and in one of these
contexts there is reference to continual fasting and prayer [22]. In
the Acts of John (93) it is said « if ever he (i. e. Jesus) was invited
by one of the Pharisees and went (where) he was invited, we
went with him; and one loaf was laid before each one of us by
those who had invited (us), and so he also would take one; but
he would bless his and divide it among us; and every man was
satisfied by that little (piece), and our own loaves were kept intact,
so that those who invited him were amazed ». Here there is ob-

[18] Isaiah 58.5-7 (RSV).
[19] Ch. 28 (Hennecke-Schneemelcher, NT Apocrypha ii (ET London 1965),
p. 457).
[20] Ch. 126 (NT Apo. ii. 510).
[21] Ch. 5 (NT Apo. ii. 444).
[22] Ch. 20 and 104 (NT Apo. ii. 453, 496).

vious reminiscence of the feeding miracles in the gospels (Mark 6:35 ff. and par.), but there may also be reference to the breaking of bread in the Eucharist. At all events the ideal presented in these texts is one of ascetic abstinence and poverty. According to the Nag Hammadi Authoritative Teaching, « we go about in hunger and in thirst, looking toward our dwelling place, the place which our conduct and our conscience look toward, not clinging to the things which have come into being, but withdrawing from them » [23]

Rather more common are references to abstinence from wine, although here we have to take into account the metaphorical sense of intoxication as well as the literal. According to the Authoritative Teaching [24], « wine is the debaucher ». Severus, according to Epiphanius [25], held that wine « confuses the mind of man... Hence such people abstain completely from wine ». The Nag Hammadi treatise On the Origin of the World says « After Eros, the grapevine sprouted up from the blood which was poured upon the earth. Therefore those who drink it (the vine) acquire for themselves the desire for intercourse » [26]. Here it is clearly the associations of intoxication and sexual debauchery that are in view. The Teachings of Silvanus contains the injunction « O soul, persistent one, be sober and shake off your drunkenness, which is the work of ignorance » [27]. This could be intended literally, but there is at least the latent suggestion of the metaphorical sense as well, and this emerges more clearly in a later passage: « Give yourself gladness from the true vine of Christ. Satisfy yourself with the true wine in which there is no drunkenness or error » [28]. Drunkenness, stupor, the sleep of intoxication, are common metaphors for the state of the unredeemed. Towards the end of Poimandres we find: « I began to

[23] Codex VI 27.14-21 (NHLE 280).

[24] *Ibid.* 24.16-17 (NHLE 279). The passage relates to the prostitution of the soul, with which we may compare the Exegesis on the Soul in Codex II.

[25] Pan. XLV 1.8 (Foerster 46).

[26] Codex II 109.25 ff. (NHLE). The blood appears to be identified with the light poured out on the earth by Pronoia following her vain attempt to embrace the angel who appeared to the powers of darkness. Eros himself comes « out of the first blood », and is responsible for the introduction of sexual intercourse.

[27] Codex VII 94.19-22 (NHLE 351).

[28] *Ibid.* 107.26-30 (NHLE 356).

proclaim to men the beauty of piety and knowledge: You peoples, earth-born men, who have given yourselves up to drunkenness and sleep and to ignorance of God, sober up, stop being drunk, bewitched by unreasoning sleep » [29]. In the Gospel of Thomas (log. 28) Jesus says: « I took my place in the midst of the world, and I appeared to them in flesh. I found all of them intoxicated; I found none of them thirsty. And my soul became afflicted for the sons of men, because they are blind in their hearts and do not have sight: for empty they came into the world, and empty too they seek to leave the world. But for the moment they are intoxicated. When they shake off their wine, then they will repent ». In the Gospel of Truth the state of the « ignorant » is described in terms of a nightmare; of the man who possesses *gnosis* it is said « He knows as one who having become drunk has turned away from his drunkenness, (and) having returned to himself, has set right what are his own » [30]. In the Apocryphon of James the Saviour says to the disciples « Your heart is drunken; do you not, then, desire to be sober? » [31].

Another passage in the Gospel of Thomas however (log. 13) presents a different metaphor. In a scene reminiscent of Peter's confession at Caesarea Philippi (Mark 8:27 ff. and par.) it is Thomas who makes the most satisfactory answer, and Jesus replies « I am not your Master. Because you have drunk, you have become intoxicated from the bubbling spring which I have measured out ». To this we may perhaps add log. 108, « He who will drink from my mouth will become like me ». We may recall such passages in the Fourth Gospel as John 4:14 and perhaps 7:37 ff., and also the idea in Philo, sometimes thought to be his own invention, of a « sober intoxication », an inspiration of the Spirit manifested in prophecy and in other ways [32]. The negative metaphors, for the state of the ignorant, « the stupor of the demons » [33], would however appear to be the more prominent.

Once again such abstinence is not peculiar to the gnostics,

[29] Poim. 27 (Foerster 334).
[30] Codex I 29.2 - 30.4; 22.16 (NHLE 43, 40).
[31] *Ibid.* 3.9-10 (NHLE 30).
[32] Cfr. Lewy, *Sobria Ebrietas* (BZNW 9, Giessen 1929).
[33] On Org Wld 110.25 f. (NHLE 169).

but part of a tradition of long standing, at least as far back as the Rechabites (Jer. 35:5-9). If the Old Testament can refer to « wine which cheers gods and men » (Judg. 9:13, cfr. Ps. 105:15, Eccl. 10:19), there are also repeated warnings against its intemperate use. « Wine is a mocker, strong drink a brawler » (Prov. 20:1). Isaiah proclaims woe upon those who « rise early in the morning, that they may run after strong drink, who tarry late into the evening, until wine inflames them » (5:11), while Hosea bluntly says that « wine and new wine take away the understanding » (4:11). The tradition is carried on into the New Testament (e. g. Rom. 14:21; Eph. 5:18; 1 Pet. 4:3). In view of the known and manifest effects of intemperance, it is not surprising that ascetic groups should advocate and practise abstinence.

The clearest evidence for gnostic encratism, and the most frequently mentioned, lies in the realm of sex. For Saturninus, marriage and procreation are of Satan[34]. To Severus, woman also is of Satan. « Hence those who consort in marriage fulfil the work of Satan »[35]. This may seem at first sight incongruous in view of the place given to some women (e. g. Mary Magdalene) in some gnostic texts, but here we must look more closely. There may be differences between the different sects, or within the same group at different stages of its development. Again, the main thrust of such passages is directed against sexual intercourse, so that the criticism may relate to woman in her capacity as temptress, and not simply to the female sex as such. Finally it has to be borne in mind that the aeon responsible for the origin of the lower creation is in many systems female (Sophia), even if the Demiurge himself is commonly male. The position of Sophia in gnostic systems is frequently ambiguous: on the one hand it is her lapse which brings about the creation of this world: on the other the redeemed Sophia is active to rescue the spiritual from the world. At all events, the Gospel of Philip goes some way towards redressing the balance: « As for the unclean [spirits], there are males among them and there are females. The males are they which unite with the souls which inhabit a female form, but the females are they which are mingled with those in a male form, through one who was diso-

[34] Iren. Adv. haer. I 24.2 (Foerester 41).
[35] Epiph. Pan. XLV 2.1 (Foerster 46).

bedient. And none shall be able to escape them, since they detain him if he does not receive a male power or a female power — the bridegroom and the bride » [36].

Reference has already been made to a passage in OnOrgWld which associates intoxication with sexual debauchery. Immediately before it we find the lines: « Just as Eros appeared out of the mid-point between light and darkness, (and) in the midst of the angels and men the intercourse of Eros was consummated, so too the first sensual pleasure sprouted upon the earth.

> <The man followed> the earth,
> The woman followed <the man>,
> And marriage followed the woman,
> And reproduction followed marriage,
> And death followed reproduction » [37].

The Book of Thomas the Contender, a document « consistently and intensely ascetic in doctrine » [38], speaks of the body as derived from intercourse like that of the beasts, and therefore doomed to perish [39]; also of « the bitterness of the fire that burns in the bodies of men... making their minds drunk », or again of its blinding them « with insatiable lust » [40]. An extended series of woes includes the words « Woe to you who love intimacy with womankind and polluted intercourse with it! » [41]. It is in keeping with this that in his final prayer in the Acts of John (113) the apostle should speak of having been kept pure to that hour, « untouched by union with a woman », and indeed of « the repugnance of even looking closely at a woman » [42]. Similarly the Acts of Thomas (12 f.) expands upon the theme of abstinence from intercourse, even within the bonds of marriage. This however is a common theme not only in the Acts of Thomas but in the Acts of

---

[36] Codex II 65.1-11 (cfr. the whole passage to line 26; NHLE 139).

[37] Codex II 109.16-25 (NHLE 168).

[38] J. D. Turner, introduction in NHLE 188.

[39] Codex II 139.2-12 (NHLE 189).

[40] *Ibid.* 139.33 ff.; 140.25. Cfr. also « the bitter bond of lust »; *ibid.* 140.32 (NHLE 190-191).

[41] *Ibid.* 144.8-10 (NHLE 193; the whole page is relevant in this context).

[42] *NT Apo.* ii. 257.

Paul and Thecla, and is developed at length in the Epistle of Pseudo-Titus [43]

In the circumstances, it is at first sight surprising that the Gospel of Philip should give such prominence to a rite described as « the bridal chamber », and indeed even rank it as the highest of the gnostic sacraments — baptism, chrism, eucharist, redemption, bridal chamber [44]. Here however two things must be borne in mind, the Valentinian myth and the clear contrast which this gospel presents between ordinary human marriage and this sacrament of the bridal chamber. « If there is a hidden quality to the marriage of defilement, how much more is the undefiled marriage a true mystery! It is not fleshly but pure. It belongs not to desire but to the will. It belongs not to the darkness or the night but to the day and the light » [45]. The following lines have something of a parallel in the Hermetic Asclepius: « the mystery of intercourse is performed in secret, in order that the two sexes might not disgrace themselves in front of many who do not experience that reality » [46]. Ordinary human marriage is thus viewed in these texts with a certain repugnance. Sexual intercourse, according to the Apocryphon of John, is due to the chief archon, who « planted sexual desire in her who belongs to Adam » [47]. A similar attitude appears in a passage already mentioned in the Acts of Thomas, where the apostle is led against his will to the bridal chamber, to pray for the king's newly-married daughter and her husband [48]. When the « bridal companions » have departed, Jesus in the guise of Thomas urges the young couple to abstain from « this sordid intercourse ». « If you obey, and keep your souls holy for God, then living children will belong to you, whom these hurts do not touch, you will be free from care, leading an untroubled life

[43] See NT Apo. ii. 141 ff.

[44] Codex II 67.27-31 (NHLE 140). On the whole question of sacraments in the Gospel of Philip, see H. G. Gaffron, Studien zum koptischen Philippusevangelium, Bonn 1969 (for the « bridal chamber », see esp. 191 ff.).

[45] Ibid. 82.4-10 (NHLE 149).

[46] Codex VI 65.26-31 (NHLE 300).

[47] Codex II 24.26-29 (NHLE 112; in the Berlin codex (63.2-9, Till 167) the desire of seed is planted in Adam, but intercourse is still the work of the first archon; cfr. Foerster 117).

[48] Acts of Thomas 9-13 (NT Apo. ii. 447-9; Foerster 346-9).

without sorrow and care, expecting to enjoy that uncorrupt and true wedding, and at it you will enter together as bridal companions into that bride-chamber full of immortality and light » [49].

Whether the Valentinian myth should be invoked for the interpretation of this passage in the Acts of Thomas may be open to discussion. In the light of similar attitudes expressed in other documents, perhaps it should not — although it does indicate how a Valentinian could have understood the passage. With the Gospel of Philip it is another matter, since this text is « generally Valentinian in character » [50] and has affinities with the teaching of the Marcosians and the Excerpta ex Theodoto. In the system of Ptolemy, as reported by Irenaeus [51], « When the whole seed is perfected, then, they say, will the Mother, Achamoth, leave the place of the Middle, enter into the Pleroma, and receive her bridgroom, the Saviour, who came into being from all (the aeons), with the result that the Saviour and Sophia, who is Achamoth, form a pair (syzygy). These then are said to be bridegroom and bride, but the bridal chamber is the entire Pleroma. The spiritual beings will divest themselves of their souls and become intelligent spirits, and, without being hindered or seen, they will enter into the Pleroma, and will be bestowed as brides on the angels around the Saviour ». The sacrament of the bridal chamber, whatever its form (of which we are not told), was thus some kind of anticipation of the final consummation. Gaffron argues for the view that it was celebrated as a *Sterbesakrament* or last rites [52]. At all events such an understanding of this sacrament would provide a further incentive to sexual abstinence, since intercourse in this world could be construed as fornication or adultery: the gnostic's true marriage partner is waiting in the Pleroma, and the gnostic must remain pure for that final union. In this connection reference should be made to two passages (§ 71, 78) which trace the origin of death to the separation of the sexes: « If the woman had not separated from the man, she would not die with the man. His separation became the

---

[49] Translation from Foerster 348.
[50] W. W. Isenberg, introduction in NHLE 131; cfr. Wilson, *The Gospel of Philip*, 23.
[51] Adv. haer. I 7.1 (Foerster 139).
[52] *Op. cit.*, p. 218.

beginning of death » [53]. It is this primordial unity that is to be restored in the bridal chamber.

Hippolytus reports of the Naassenes that « they attend the so-called mysteries of the Great Mother, thinking that through those (sacred) actions they will best understand the universal mystery. For these men have nothing (to offer) beyond what is done there, except that they are not castrated, they only perform the functions of those who are castrated. For they urge most severely and carefully that one should abstain, as those men do, from intercourse with women » [54]. This reference to the cult of the Great Mother provides a reminder that there were other groups outside of Christianity which practised asceticism, sometimes in an extreme form. We may recall also the « eunuch » saying in the gospels (Matt. 19:12), which is presented as Jesus' response to a remark by his disciples « If that is the position with husband and wife, it is better not to marry » (NEB). It should be noted that the eunuch saying is introduced by the comment that this is something which not everyone can accept. It is thus here an ideal for some, but not an obligation for all as in some other texts. The Acts of John contains a story about a young man who castrated himself, and was reproved by the apostle for so doing: « you should not have destroyed the place (of your temptation), but the thought which showed its temper through those members; for it is not those organs which are harmful to man, but the unseen springs through which every shameful emotion is stirred up and comes to light » [55].

According to the Testimony of Truth, « the defilement of the Law is manifest; but undefilement belongs to the light. The Law commands (one) to take a husband (or) to take a wife, and to beget, to multiply like the sand of the sea. But passion which is a delight to them constrains the souls of those who are begotten in this place, those who defile and those who are defiled, in order that the Law might be fulfilled through them. And they show that they are assisting the world... » [56]. The following lines present an

---

[53] See Codex II 70.9-22, also 69.22-26 (NHLE 142, 141).

[54] Ref. V 9.10-11 (Foerster 280).

[55] Acts of John 53-54 (NT Apo. ii. 241).

[56] Codex IX 29.26 - 30.13 (NHLE 407). Cfr. K. Koschorke, *Die Polemik der Gnostiker gegen das kirchliche Christentum* (NHS XII, Leiden 1978),

interesting synthesis of Old and New Testament material: « The Son of Man [came] forth from Imperishability, [being] alien to defilement. He came [to the world] by the Jordan river, and immediately the Jordan [turned] back (cfr. Ps. 114. 3; Joshua 3). And John bore witness to the [descent] of Jesus. For he is the one who saw the [power] which came down upon the Jordan river; for he knew that the dominion of carnal procreation had come to an end. The Jordan river is the power of the body, that is, the senses of pleasures. The water of the Jordan is the desire for sexual intercourse. John is the archon of the womb ».

As Pearson notes, this treatise « relentlessly espouses the ideal of strict celibacy » [57]. It also repudiates water baptism: « the fathers of baptism were defiled. But the baptism of truth is something else; it is by renunciation of the world that it is found » [58]. This is obviously directed against the baptismal practice of orthodox Christianity, perhaps also of the Valentinians, but fits very well with the tradition referred to earlier, according to which it is not the outward form or ritual but the inward reality that is important. What is striking in this context is the identification of the water of Jordan as the desire for sexual intercourse, since a passage in the Mishna declares the waters of the Jordan unsuitable for rites of purification because they are « mixed waters » [59]. There may of course be no connection, and at best it must be considered fairly remote, but the coincidence is remarkable. The same attitude, castigating the hypocrisy « which sought through scrupulously careful observance of the ritual of cleanliness to delude men as to the abominable nature of what was within them » [60], appears also in the fragment of an unknown gospel found at Oxyrhynchus (POx. 840).

According to Irenaeus, the Valentinians claimed that conti-

---

esp. 110-116, also his index s.v. Askese. Coptic text with introduction, translation and notes in Pearson, *Nag Hammadi Codices IX and X* (NHS XV, Leiden 1981).

[57] *Op. cit.*, p. 120.

[58] 69.7-24 (quotation of lines 20-24). See Pearson's notes ad loc., also the fragmentary passage 55.4-8.

[59] See Rudolph, *Antike Baptisten* 35 (note 60).

[60] Jeremias in *NT Apo.* i. 93 (tr. G. Ogg), who refers to Mark 7:1 ff., Matt. 15:1 ff. and Matt. 23:27 f.

nence and good works were necessary for the psychics, but not for themselves [61]. This statement however comes at the end of a section which Foerster transfers to a separate chapter under the heading of « Libertine Gnostics », on the ground that it does not conform with the rest of Irenaeus' account of Valentinianism [62]. Reference has already been made to Rudolph's suggestion that it was only in the later stages of the development that libertinarian conclusions were drawn, while it is also possible that such practices were indulged in only by a few. Certainly it is in the main in the later sources that such allegations are found. The main thrust of the original gnostic texts themselves is entirely in the direction of asceticism. Again and again we find admonitions and injunctions to self-denial and repentance, and against conformity with the flesh or love for the world. « Let each one of us dig down after the root of evil which is within one, and let one pluck it out of one's heart from the root » [63]. « Woe to you who hope in the flesh and in the prison that will perish! » [64]. Such statements could be multiplied several times over. Moreover, the emphasis is not upon outward ritual observance but on the attitude of heart and mind. Since the allegations of libertinism are confined to the patristic sources, and may be based on gossip and false report, they must be treated with reserve. When we recall pagan slanders against Christianity, together with the ritual prostitution which was part of some ancient religion, it is not difficult to imagine what reporters without any real or first-hand knowledge might have made of a rite called « the bridal chamber ».

Unfortunately, it is a known fact that practice does not always match profession, and the ascetic standards of our original documents may not have been reflected in the actual lives and conduct of the gnostics. Nor can we assume that these standards were supposed to apply to all. Reference has been made to the Manichean *electi*, who had to endure a rather more rigorous existence than ordinary believers. Something of the same may be true of the Essenes, if there were some who lived ordinary lives in their villages,

---

[61] Adv. haer. I 6.4 (Foerster 139).
[62] *Ibid.* I 6.3 f. (Foerster 313-4).
[63] Gospel of Philip 83.18-21 (NHLE 149).
[64] Thomas the Contender 143-10-12 (NHLE 193).

without having to undergo the rigours of the communal life at Qumran. It was certainly true at a much later date in the Franciscan movement, in which the order of the Tertiaries catered for those in sympathy with the Franciscan rule who by reason of family ties or for other causes were unable to profess obedience to the rule in all its strictness. All such ascetic movements in any case presuppose the existence of a wider group, in sympathy with the movement but living ordinary lives in the world, who may acquire merit by providing for the needs of the ascetics. Finally, the references above to other ascetic traditions make it clear that the gnostics were neither alone nor exceptional in the ancient world.

What Became of God the Mother?
Conflicting Images of God in
Early Christianity

Elaine H. Pagels

Unlike many of his contemporaries among the deities of the ancient Near East, the God of Israel shares his power with no female divinity, nor is he the divine Husband or Lover of any.[1] He scarcely can be characterized in any but masculine epithets: King, Lord, Master, Judge, and Father.[2] Indeed, the absence of feminine symbolism of God marks Judaism, Christianity, and Islam in striking contrast to the world's other religious traditions, whether in Egypt, Babylonia, Greece, and Rome or Africa, Polynesia, India, and North America. Jewish, Christian, and Islamic theologians, however, are quick to point out that God is not to be considered in sexual terms at all. Yet the actual language they use daily in worship and prayer conveys a different message and gives the distinct impression that God is thought of in exclusively *masculine* terms. And while it is true that Catholics revere Mary as the mother of Jesus, she cannot be identified as divine in her own right: if she is "mother of God," she is not "God the Mother" on an equal footing with God the Father.

Christianity, of course, added the trinitarian terms to the Jewish description of God. And yet of the three divine "Persons," two—the Father and Son—are described in masculine terms, and the third—the

This inquiry began as a short talk delivered at the Conference on Women at Bryn Mawr College, initiated by Clare Wofford; it was developed for delivery at "The Scholar and the Feminist III: The Search for Origins," a conference sponsored by the Barnard Women's Center and organized by Jane Gould, Hester Eisenstein, and Emily Kofron. I am grateful for their invitations and for criticism and suggestions offered by many colleagues, especially Cyril Richardson, Wayne Meeks, Nelle Morton, and Rayna R. Reiter.

1. Where the God of Israel is characterized as husband and lover in the Old Testament (OT), his spouse is described as the community of Israel (i.e., Isa. 50:1, 54:1–8; Jer. 2:2–3, 20–25, 3:1–20; Hos. 1–4, 14) or as the land of Israel (cf. Isa. 62:1–5).

2. One may note several exceptions to this rule: Deut. 32:11; Hos. 11:1; Isa. 66:12 ff; Num. 11:12.

[Signs: Journal of Women in Culture and Society 1976, vol. 2, no. 2]

Spirit—suggests the sexlessness of the Greek neuter term *pneuma*. This is not merely a subjective impression. Whoever investigates the early development of Christianity—the field called "patristics," that is, study of "the fathers of the church"—may not be surprised by the passage that concludes the recently discovered, secret *Gospel of Thomas:* "Simon Peter said to them [the disciples]: Let Mary be excluded from among us, for she is a woman, and not worthy of Life. Jesus said: Behold I will take Mary, and make her a male, so that she may become a living spirit, resembling you males. For I tell you truly, that every female who makes herself male will enter the Kingdom of Heaven."[3] Strange as it sounds, this only states explicitly what religious rhetoric often assumes: that the men form the legitimate body of the community, while women will be allowed to participate only insofar as their own identity is denied and assimilated to that of the men.

Further exploration of the texts which include this *Gospel*—written on papyrus, hidden in large clay jars nearly 1,600 years ago—has identified them as Jewish and Christian gnostic works which were attacked and condemned as "heretical" as early as A.D. 100–150. What distinguishes these "heterodox" texts from those that are called "orthodox" is at least partially clear: they abound in feminine symbolism that is applied, in particular, to God. Although one might expect, then, that they would recall the archaic pagan traditions of the Mother Goddess, their language is to the contrary specifically Christian, unmistakably related to a Jewish heritage. Thus we can see that certain gnostic Christians diverged even more radically from the Jewish tradition than the early Christians who described God as the "three Persons" or the Trinity. For instead of a monistic and masculine God, certain of these texts describe God as a dyadic being, who consists of *both* masculine and feminine elements. One such group of texts, for example, claims to have received a secret tradition from Jesus through James, and significantly, through Mary Magdalene.[4] Members of this group offer prayer to *both* the divine Father and Mother: "From Thee, Father, and through Thee, Mother, the two immortal names, Parents of the divine being, and thou, dweller in heaven, mankind of the mighty name. . . ."[5] Other texts indicate that their authors had pondered the nature of the beings to whom a single, masculine God proposed, "Let us make mankind in our image, after our likeness" (Gen. 1:26). Since the Genesis account goes on to say that mankind was created "male and female" (1:27), some concluded, apparently, that the God in whose image we are created likewise must be both masculine and feminine—both Father and Mother.

3. *The Gospel according to Thomas* (hereafter cited as *ET*), ed. A. Guillaumount, H. Ch. Puech, G. Quispel, W. Till, Yassah 'Abd-al-Masih (London: Collins, 1959), logion 113–114.

4. Hippolytus, *Refutationis Omnium Haeresium* (hereafter cited as *Ref*), ed. L. Dunker, F. Schneidewin (Göttingen, 1859), 5.7.

5. *Ref*, 5.6.

The characterization of the divine Mother in these sources is not simple since the texts themselves are extraordinarily diverse. Nevertheless, three primary characterizations merge. First, a certain poet and teacher, Valentinus, begins with the premise that God is essentially indescribable. And yet he suggests that the divine can be imagined as a Dyad consisting of two elements: one he calls the Ineffable, the Source, the Primal Father; the other, the Silence, the Mother of all things.[6] Although we might question Valentinus's reasoning that Silence is the appropriate complement of what is Ineffable, his equation of the former with the feminine and the latter with the masculine may be traced to the grammatical gender of the Greek words. Followers of Valentinus invoke this feminine power, whom they also call "Grace" (in Greek, the feminine term *charis*), in their own private celebration of the Christian eucharist: they call her "divine, eternal Grace, She who is before all things."[7] At other times they pray to her for protection as the Mother, "Thou enthroned with God, eternal, mystical Silence."[8] Marcus, a disciple of Valentinus, contends that "when Moses began his account of creation, he mentioned the Mother of all things at the very beginning, when he said, 'In the beginning God created the heavens and the earth,' "[9] for the word "beginning" (in Greek, the feminine *arche*) refers to the divine Mother, the source of the cosmic elements. When they describe God in this way different gnostic writers have different interpretations. Some maintain that the divine is to be considered masculo-feminine—the "great male-female power." Others insist that the terms are meant only as metaphors—for, in reality, the divine is *neither* masculine nor feminine. A third group suggests that one can describe the Source of all things in *either* masculine or feminine terms, depending on which aspect one intends to stress.[10] Proponents of these diverse views agree, however, that the divine is to be understood as consisting of a harmonious, dynamic relationship of opposites—a concept that may be akin to the eastern view of *yin* and *yang* but remains antithetical to orthodox Judaism and Christianity.

A second characterization of the divine Mother describes her as Holy Spirit. One source, the *Secret Book of John*, for example, relates how John, the brother of James, went out after the crucifixion with "great grief," and had a mystical vision of the Trinity: "As I was grieving . . . the heavens were opened, and the whole creation shone with an unearthly light, and the universe was shaken. I was afraid . . . and behold . . . a unity in three forms appeared to me, and I marvelled: how

6. Irenaeus, *Adversus Haereses* (hereafter cited as *AH*), ed. W. W. Harvey (Cambridge, 1857), 1.11.1.
7. Ibid., 1.13.2.
8. Ibid., 1.13.6.
9. Ibid., 1.18.2.
10. Ibid., 1.11.5.—21.1, 3; *Ref*, 6.29.

can a unity have three forms?" To John's question the vision answers: "It said to me, 'John, John, why do you doubt, or why do you fear? . . . I am the One who is with you always: I am the Father; I am the Mother; I am the Son.' "[11] John's interpretation of the Trinity—as Father, Mother, and Son—may not at first seem shocking but is perhaps the more natural and spontaneous interpretation. Where the Greek terminology for the Trinity, which includes the neuter term for spirit *(pneuma)*, virtually requires that the third "Person" of the Trinity be asexual, the author of the *Secret Book* looks to the Hebrew term for spirit, *ruah*—a feminine word. He thus concludes, logically enough, that the feminine "Person" conjoined with Father and Son must be the Mother! Indeed, the text goes on to describe the Spirit as Mother: ". . . the image of the invisible virginal perfect spirit. . . . She became the mother of the all, for she existed before them all, the mother-father [matropater]."[12] This same author, therefore, alters Genesis 1:2 ("the Spirit of God moved upon the face of the deep") to say "the Mother then was moved. . . ."[13] The secret *Gospel to the Hebrews* likewise has Jesus speak of "my Mother, the Spirit."[14] And in the *Gospel of Thomas*, Jesus contrasts his earthly parents, Mary and Joseph, with his divine Father—the Father of Truth—and his divine Mother, the Holy Spirit. The author interprets a puzzling saying of Jesus in the New Testament ("whoever does not hate his father and mother is not worthy of me") by adding: "Whoever does not love his father and his mother in my way cannot be my disciple; for my [earthly] mother gave me death but my true Mother gave me the Life."[15] Another secret gnostic gospel, the *Gospel of Phillip*, declares that whoever becomes a Christian "gains both a father and a mother."[16] The author refers explicitly to the feminine Hebrew term to describe the Spirit as "Mother of many."[17]

If these sources suggest that the Spirit constitutes the maternal element of the Trinity, the *Gospel of Phillip* makes an equally radical suggestion concerning the doctrine that later developed as the virgin birth. Here again the Spirit is praised as both Mother and Virgin, the counterpart—and consort—of the Heavenly Father: "If I may utter a mystery, the Father of the all united with the Virgin who came down,"[18] that is, with the Holy Spirit. Yet because this process is to be understood

11. *Apocryphon Johannis* (hereafter cited as *AJ*), ed. S. Giversen (Copenhagen: Prostant Apud Munksgaard, 1963), 47.20–48.14.

12. *AJ*, 52.34–53.6.

13. Ibid., 61.13–14.

14. Origen, *Commentary on John*, 2.12; *Hom. On Jeremiah*, 15.4.

15. *ET*, 101. The text of this passage is badly damaged; I follow here the reconstruction of G. MacRae of the Harvard Divinity School.

16. *L'Evangile selon Phillipe* (hereafter cited as *EP*), ed. J. E. Ménard (Leiden: Brill, 1967), logion 6.

17. *EP*, logion 36.

18. Ibid., logion 82.

symbolically, and not literally, the Spirit remains a virgin! The author explains that "for this reason, Christ was 'born of a virgin' "—that is, of the Spirit, his divine Mother. But the author ridicules those "literal-minded" Christians who mistakenly refer the virgin birth to Mary, Jesus' earthly mother, as if she conceived apart from Joseph: "Such persons do not know what they are saying; for when did a female ever impregnate a female?"[19] Instead, he argues, virgin birth refers to the mysterious union of the two divine powers, the Father of the All with the Holy Spirit.

Besides the eternal, mystical Silence, and besides the Holy Spirit, certain gnostics suggest a third characterization of the divine Mother as Wisdom. Here again the Greek feminine term for wisdom, *sophia*, like the term for spirit, *ruah*, translates a Hebrew feminine term, *hokhmah*. Early interpreters had pondered the meaning of certain biblical passages, for example, Proverbs: "God made the world in Wisdom." And they wondered if Wisdom could be the feminine power in which God's creation is "conceived"? In such passages, at any rate, Wisdom bears two connotations: first, she bestows the Spirit that makes mankind wise; second, she is a creative power. One gnostic source calls her the "first universal creator";[20] another says that God the Father was speaking to her when he proposed to "make mankind in our image."[21] The *Great Announcement*, a mystical writing, explains the Genesis account in the following terms: ". . . One Power that is above and below, self-generating, self-discovering, its own mother; its own father; its own sister; its own son: Father, Mother, unity, Root of all things."[22] The same author explains the mystical meaning of the Garden of Eden as a symbol of the womb: "Scripture teaches us that this is what is meant when Isaiah says, 'I am he that formed thee in thy mother's womb' [Isaiah 44:2]. The Garden of Eden, then, is Moses' symbolic term for the womb, and Eden the placenta, and the river which comes out of Eden the navel, which nourishes the fetus. . . ."[23] This teacher claims that the Exodus, consequently, symbolizes the exodus from the womb, "and the crossing of the Red Sea, they say, refers to the blood." Evidence for this view, he adds, comes directly from "the cry of the newborn," a spontaneous cry of praise for "the glory of the primal being, in which all the powers above are in harmonious embrace."[24]

The introduction of such symbolism in gnostic texts clearly bears implications for the understanding of human nature. The *Great An-*

19. Ibid., logion 17.
20. *Extraits de Théodote* (hereafter cited as *Exc*), ed. F. Sagnard, Sources chrétiennes 23 (Paris: Sources chrétiennes, 1948).
21. *AH*, 1.30.6.
22. *Ref*, 6.17.
23. Ibid., 6.14.
24. *AH*, 1.14.7–8.

nouncement for example, having described the Source as a masculo-feminine being, a "bisexual Power," goes on to say that "what came into being from that Power, that is, humanity, being one, is found to be two: a male-female being that bears the female within it."[25] This refers to the story of Eve's "birth" out of Adam's side (so that Adam, being one, is "discovered to be two," an androgyne who "bears the female within him"). Yet this reference to the creation story of Genesis 2—an account which inverts the biological birth process, and so effectively denies the creative function of the female—proves to be unusual in gnostic sources. More often, such sources refer instead to the first creation account in Genesis 1:26–27. ("And God said, let us make mankind in Our image, after Our image and likeness . . . in the image of God he created him: male and female he created them"). Rabbis in Talmudic times knew a Greek version of the passage, one that suggested to Rabbi Samuel bar Nahman that "when the Holy One . . . first created mankind, he created him with two faces, two sets of genitals, four arms, and legs, back to back: Then he split Adam in two, and made two backs, one on each side."[26] Some Jewish teachers (perhaps influenced by the story in Plato's *Symposium*) had suggested that Genesis 1:26–27 narrates an androgynous creation—an idea that gnostics adopted and developed. Marcus (whose prayer to the Mother is given above) not only concludes from this account that God is dyadic ("Let *us* make mankind"), but also that "mankind, which was formed according to the image and likeness of God [Father and Mother] was masculo-feminine."[27] And his contemporary, Theodotus, explains: "the saying that Adam was created 'male and female' means that the male and female elements together constitute the finest production of the Mother, Wisdom."[28] We can see, then, that the gnostic sources which describe God in both masculine and feminine terms often give a similar description of human nature as a dyadic entity, consisting of two equal male and female components.

All the texts cited above—secret "gospels," revelations, mystical teachings—are among those rejected from the select list of twenty-six that comprise the "New Testament" collection. As these and other writings were sorted and judged by various Christian communities, every one of these texts which gnostic groups revered and shared was rejected from the canonical collection as "heterodox" by those who called themselves "orthodox" (literally, straight-thinking) Christians. By the time this process was concluded, probably as late as the year A.D. 200, virtually all the feminine imagery for God (along with any suggestion of an an-

25. *Ref*, 6.18.
26. Genesis Rabba 8.1, also 17.6; cf. Levitius Rabba 14. For an excellent discussion of androgyny, see W. Meeks, "The Image of the Androgyne: Some Uses of a Symbol in Earliest Christianity," *History of Religions* 13 (1974): 165–208.
27. *AH*, 1.18.2.
28. *Exc*, 21.1.

drogynous human creation) had disappeared from "orthodox" Christian tradition.

What is the reason for this wholesale rejection? The gnostics themselves asked this question of their "orthodox" attackers and pondered it among themselves. Some concluded that the God of Israel himself initiated the polemics against gnostic teaching which his followers carried out in his name. They argued that he was a derivative, merely instrumental power, whom the divine Mother had created to administer the universe, but who remained ignorant of the power of Wisdom, his own Mother: "They say that the creator believed that he created everything by himself, but that, in reality, he had made them because his Mother, Wisdom, infused him with energy, and had given him her ideas. But he was unaware that the ideas he used came from her: He was even ignorant of his own Mother."[29] Folllowers of Valentinus suggested that the Mother herself encouraged the God of Israel to think that he was acting autonomously in creating the world; but, as one teacher adds, "It was because he was foolish and ignorant of his Mother that he said, 'I am God; there is none beside me.' "[30] Others attribute to him the more sinister motive of jealousy, among them the *Secret Book of John:* "He said, 'I am a jealous God, and you shall have no other God before me,' already indicating that another god does exist. For if there were no other god, of whom would he be jealous? Then the Mother began to be distressed. . . ."[31] A third gnostic teacher describes the Lord's shock, terror, and anxiety "when he discovered that he was not the God of the universe." Gradually his shock and fear gave way to wonder, and finally he came to welcome the teaching of Wisdom. The gnostic teacher concluded: "This is the meaning of the saying, 'The fear of the Lord is the beginning of wisdom.' "[32]

All of these are, of course, mythical explanations. To look for the actual, historical reasons why these gnostic writings were suppressed is an extremely difficult proposition, for it raises the much larger question of how (i.e., by what means and what criteria) certain ideas, including those expressed in the texts cited above, came to be classified as heretical and others as orthodox by the beginning of the third century. Although the research is still in its early stages, and this question is far from being solved, we may find one clue if we ask whether these secret groups derived any practical, social consequences from their conception of God—and of mankind—that included the feminine element? Here again, the answer is yes and can be found in the orthodox texts themselves. Irenaeus, an orthodox bishop, for example, notes with dismay that women in particular are attracted to heretical groups—especially to

29. *Ref,* 6.33.
30. *AH,* 1.5.4; *Ref,* 6.33.
31. *AJ,* 61.8–14.
32. *Ref,* 7.26.

Marcus's circle, in which prayers are offered to the Mother in her aspects as Silence, Grace, and Wisdom; women priests serve the eucharist together with men; and women also speak as prophets, uttering to the whole community what "the Spirit" reveals to them.[33] Professing himself to be at a loss to understand the attraction that Marcus's group holds, he offers only one explanation: that Marcus himself is a diabolically successful seducer, a magician who compounds special aphrodisiacs to "deceive, victimize, and defile" these "many foolish women!" Whether his accusation has any factual basis is difficult, probably impossible, to ascertain. Nevertheless, the historian notes that accusations of sexual license are a stock-in-trade of polemical arguments.[34] The bishop refuses to admit the possibility that the group might attract Christians—especially women—for sound and comprehensible reasons. While expressing his own moral outrage, Tertullian, another "father of the church," reveals his fundamental desire to keep women out of religion: "These heretical women—how audacious they are! They have no modesty: they are bold enough to teach, to engage in argument, to enact exorcisms, to undertake cures, and, it may be, even to baptize!"[35] Tertullian directs yet another attack against "that viper"—a woman teacher who led a congregation in North Africa.[36] Marcion had, in fact, scandalized his "orthodox" contemporaries by appointing women on an equal basis with men as priests and bishops among his congregations.[37] The teacher Marcillina also traveled to Rome to represent the Carpocratian group, an esoteric circle that claimed to have received secret teaching from Mary, Salome, and Martha.[38] And among the Montanists, a radical prophetic circle, the prophet Philumene was reputed to have hired a male secretary to transcribe her inspired oracles.[39]

Other secret texts, such as the *Gospel of Mary Magdalene* and the *Wisdom of Faith*, suggest that the activity of such women leaders challenged and therefore was challenged by the orthodox communities who regarded Peter as their spokesman. The *Gospel of Mary* relates that Mary tried to encourage the disciples after the crucifixion and to tell them what the Lord had told her privately. Peter, furious at the suggestion, asks, "Did he then talk secretly with a woman, instead of to us? Are we to go and learn from *her* now? Did he love her more than us?" Distressed at his rage, Mary then asks Peter: "What do you think? Do you think I made this up in my heart? Do you think I am lying about the Lord?" Levi

33. *AH*, 1.13.7.

34. Ibid., 1.13.2–5.

35. Tertullian, *De Praescriptione Haereticorum* (hereafter cited as *DP*), ed. E. Oehler (Lipsius, 1853–54), p. 41.

36. *De Baptismo* 1. I am grateful to Cyril Richardson for calling my attention to this passage and to the three subsequent ones.

37. Epiphanes, *De Baptismo*, 42.5.

38. *AH*, 1.25.6.

39. *DP*, 6.30.

breaks in at this point to mediate the dispute: "Peter, you are always irascible. You object to the woman as our enemies do. Surely the Lord knew her very well, and indeed, he loved her more than us. . . ." Then he and the others invite Mary to teach them what she knows.[40] Another argument between Peter and Mary occurs in *Wisdom of Faith*. Peter complains that Mary is dominating the conversation, even to the point of displacing the rightful priority of Peter himself and his brethren; he urges Jesus to silence her—and is quickly rebuked. Later, however, Mary admits to Jesus that she hardly dares to speak freely with him, because "Peter makes me hesitate: I am afraid of him, because he hates the female race." Jesus replies, that whoever receives inspiration from the Spirit is divinely ordained to speak, whether man or woman.[41]

As these texts suggest, then, women were considered equal to men, they were revered as prophets, and they acted as teachers, traveling evangelists, healers, priests, and even bishops. In some of these groups they played leading roles and were *excluded* from them in the orthodox churches, at least by A.D. 150–200. Is it possible, then, that the recognition of the feminine element in God and the recognition of mankind as a male and female entity bore within it the explosive social possibility of women acting on an equal basis with men in positions of authority and leadership? If this were true it might lead to the conclusion that these gnostic groups, together with their conception of God and human nature, were suppressed only because of their positive attitude toward women. But such a conclusion would be a mistake—a hasty and simplistic reading of the evidence. In the first place, orthodox Christian doctrine is far from wholly negative in its attitude toward women. Second, many other elements of the gnostic sources diverge in fundamental ways from what came to be accepted as orthodox Christian teaching. To examine this process in detail would require a much more extensive discussion than is possible here. Nevertheless the evidence does indicate that two very different patterns of sexual attitudes emerged in orthodox and gnostic circles. In simplest form, gnostic theologians correlate their description of God in both masculine and feminine terms with a complementary description of human nature. Most often they refer to the creation account of Genesis 1, which suggests an equal (or even androgynous) creation of mankind. This conception carries the principle of equality between men and women into the practical social and political structures of gnostic communities. The orthodox pattern is strikingly different: it describes God in exclusively masculine terms, and often uses Genesis 2 to describe how Eve was created from Adam and for his fulfillment. Like the gnostic view, the orthodox also translates into sociological practice: by the late second century, orthodox Christians

40. *The Gospel according to Mary,* Codex Berolinensis, *BG,* 8502,1.7.1–1.19.5, ed., intro., and trans. G. MacRae, unpublished manuscript.

41. *Pistis Sophia,* ed. Carl Schmidt (Berlin: Academie-Verlag, 1925), 36 (57), 71 (161).

came to accept the domination of men over women as the proper, God-given order—not only for the human race, but also for the Christian churches. This correlation between theology, anthropology, and sociology is not lost on the apostle Paul. In his letter to the disorderly Corinthian community, he reminds them of a divinely ordained chain of authority: as God has authority over Christ, so the man has authority over the woman, argues Paul citing Genesis 2: "The man is the image and glory of God, but the woman is the glory of man. For man is not from woman, but woman from man; and besides, the man was not created for the woman's sake, but the woman for the sake of the man."[42] Here the three elements of the orthodox pattern are welded into one simple argument: the description of God corresponds to a description of human nature which authorizes the social pattern of male domination.

A striking exception to this orthodox pattern occurs in the writings of one revered "father of the church," Clement of Alexandria. Clement identifies himself as orthodox, although he knows members of gnostic groups and their writings well; some scholars suggest that he was himself a gnostic initiate. Yet his own works demonstrate how all three elements of what we have called the "gnostic pattern" could be worked into fully "orthodox" teaching. First, Clement characterizes God not only in masculine but also in feminine terms: "The Word is everything to the child, both father and mother, teacher and nurse. ... The nutriment is the milk of the Father ... and the Word alone supplies us children with the milk of love, and only those who suck at this breast are truly happy. ... For this reason seeking is called sucking; to those infants who seek the Word, the Father's loving breasts supply milk."[43] Second, in describing human nature, he insists that "men and women share equally in perfection, and are to receive the same instruction and discipline. For the name 'humanity' is common to both men and women; and for us 'in Christ there is neither male nor female.' "[44] Even in considering the active participation of women with men in the Christian community Clement offers a list—unique in orthodox tradition—of women whose achievements he admires. They range from ancient examples, like Judith, the assassin who destroyed Israel's enemy, to Queen Esther, who rescued her people from genocide, as well as others who took radical political stands. He speaks of Arignote the historian, of Themisto the Epicurean philosopher, and of many other women philosophers including two who studied with Plato and one trained by Socrates. Indeed, he cannot con-

42. 1 Cor. 11:7–9. For discussion, see R. Scroggs, "Paul and the Eschatological Woman," *Journal of the American Academy of Religion* 40 (1972): 283–303; R. Scroggs, "Paul and the Eschatological Woman: Revisited," *Journal of the American Academy of Religion* 42 (1974): 532–37; and E. Pagels, "Paul and Women: A Response to Recent Discussion," *Journal of the American Academy of Religion* 42 (1972): 538–49.

43. Clement Alexandrinus, *Paidegogos*, ed. O. Stählin (Leipzig, 1905), 1.6.

44. Ibid., 1.4.

tain his praise: "What shall I say? Did not Theano the Pythagoran make such progress in philosophy than when a man, staring at her, said, 'Your arm is beautiful,' she replied, 'Yes, but it is not on public display.' "[45] Clement concludes his list with famous women poets and painters.

If the work of Clement, who taught in Egypt before the lines of orthodoxy and heresy were rigidly drawn (ca. A.D. 160–80) demonstrates how gnostic principles could be incorporated even into orthodox Christian teaching, the majority of communities in the western empire headed by Rome did not follow his example. By the year A.D. 200, Roman Christians endorsed as "canonical" the pseudo-Pauline letter to Timothy, which interpreted Paul's views: "Let a woman learn in silence with full submissiveness. I do not allow any woman to teach or to exercise authority over a man; she is to remain silent, *for* [note Gen. 2!] Adam was formed first, then Eve and furthermore, Adam was not deceived, but the woman was utterly seduced and came into sin. . . ."[46] How are we to account for this irreversible development? The question deserves investigation which this discussion can only initiate. For example, one would need to examine how (and for what reasons) the zealously patriarchal traditions of Israel were adopted by the Roman (and other) Christian communities. Further research might disclose how social and cultural forces converged to suppress feminine symbolism—and women's participation—from western Christian tradition. Given such research, the history of Christianity never could be told in the same way again.

Department of Religion
Barnard College

45. Ibid., 1.19.
46. 2 Tim. 2:11–14.

8

PHEME PERKINS

Sophia and the Mother-Father: The Gnostic Goddess

The nature of the Gnostic movement complicates any quest for the function of its mythic figures. Gnosticism did not develop as an indigenous religious movement, closely tied to a particular people whose life, dreams, and customs shaped and were shaped by Gnosticism. Instead, Gnosticism appeared out of the radical syncretism and disruption of religious consciousness that accompanied the ecumenic imperialism of the Greco-Roman age.

Many scholars argue that Gnosticism is better defined as a particular hermeneutic, a radical reversal and revaluation of traditional symbols. They warn us that one cannot expect to find some single Gnostic Urmythos out of which all the variations may be said to have evolved. Though some Gnostic traditions appear to have developed a complex structure of female entities out of a triadic Father-Mother-Son, that triad is usually only an ideal type. Frequently, it appears to have been imposed on other dyadic patterns. Gnostic systems as we find them in the Nag Hammadi codices and the church fathers flourished on amalgamation and complexity.

Though the Gnostics allude to other mythic traditions, they have a special involvement with Jewish traditions. In many cases Gnostic writings deliberately exploit Jewish Midrashic traditions contrary to their original intent. Such reversals appear in the Gnostic Sophia figure, which combines the search of divine wisdom for reception in the world (as in *1 Enoch* 42: 1 f.) with the story of Eve. Sophia often appears farther from divinity in her alienation from the heavenly world. She often receives the epithet *prunikos* (lewd). Eve, on the other hand, frequently appears as a source of divine wisdom and revelation.

Another structural peculiarity of Gnostic speculation is the great distance between the divine world, especially God at the origin of

307

numerous aeons, and this one. This vast system serves to mask the instability that ignorance of God introduces into the heavenly world, an instability that is only manifest in Sophia, the youngest aeon. Sophia's marginality to both the heavenly world and this one suggests that Gnosticism exploits that sense of religious transcendence often found in "liminal" situations. At the same time, the whole system drives toward recovery of the primal androgynous unity. The world fractured by imperialism is recovered in the overwhelming monism of the Gnostic pleroma.[1]

Though we may not be able to speak of a single originating Gnostic myth, the Sophia myth appears in many contexts. It cuts across the fundamental distinction in the Nag Hammadi corpus of Sethian and Valentinian systems.[2] One also finds examples of the later rationalizing interpretation of the Sophia story to bring it into line with philosophical and theological requirements of a particular system. Anthropologists have shown that all idiosyncratic, syncretistic religious symbols go through such processes in order to solidify their claim to belong to the greater religious tradition. Such innovations usually express some instability or shift in the social situation. Consequently, some scholars think that Gnostic mythology reflects the alienation of the growing class of educated tradespeople who had no access to the "educated aristocracy" that governed the cities. Others postulate the struggle of Gnostic Christians against the hierarchical developments of orthodoxy as the foundation for the Gnostic revolt and claims of hidden superiority over the god of this world. Whichever sociological hypothesis one adopts, Sophia's liminal situation reflects the tensions and ambiguities of the Gnostic, who was both caught in this world and superior to its authorities.

The Feminine Side of God

The highest God often appears with a female (or androgynous) counterpart. Both mythic and philosophical reflection contributes to this symbol. The pair of Elohim and Eden in *Baruch* (Hipp *Ref* V 26,1–27,5) comes close to the mythic sky-god/earth-mother. Humans mediate between the two. Mythic origins might also be suggested for the generation of heavenly aeons from the divine pair, Father-Barbelo, in *Adv. Haer.* I 29,1. But most examples of the divine pair evidence modification from the philosophical tradition. "Self-generation" and the Gnostic concern for the androgynous nature of divine being belong together: "in the beginning the eternal self-engendered aeon, male-female" (Epiph. *Pan.* 31,5,3). Gnosticism takes over and develops "self-engendered" terminology from the philosophical tradition. It serves to permit the development of lower beings from the primordial divine being without destroying divine unity.

While some triadic formulations, especially those with the feminine Spirit in the third position (e.g., *Adv. Haer.* I 30,1), seek to accommodate biblical traditions, most also show evidence of influence from philosophical speculation. The philosophic tradition is presupposed when the female principle is related to matter or to creation of the material world. *ApocryJn* has developed an original pair, a highest-god-father and virginal female (Barbelo), into a triad of Father-Mother-Son.[3] The long version of *ApocryJn* represented by CG II, *1* shows more evidence of philosophic interest than the short version represented by the Berlin Codex. The description of Barbelo makes her cosmogonic role clear:

> *This is the First Thought, His image.*
> *She was the Mother of the All, because she was before*
> *   them all,*
> *Mother-Father, First Man, Holy Spirit, triple male,*
> *   triple power, triple male-female name, and eternal*
> *   aeon of the invisible ones, and first to come forth.*
> *   (CG II 5,4−11)*

"First to come forth" belongs to the philosophic tradition of the divine as self-engendered. It typically explains the origin of the demiurgic power in the universe. "Mother of the All" belongs to a strand of Platonism that had taken over Stoic gynecological images to describe the origins of the material world. The long version calls Barbelo Mother-Father (CG II 14,19; cp., BG 48,1) and attributes dealings with the lower world to her where the short version simply has "Father." These alterations are philosophically more correct, since the highest divine principle would not take on demiurgic functions (CG II 19,17 f.//BG 51,5 f.; II 20,9 f.//BG 52, 18 f.). However, the short version is not consistent. The Mother-Father's permission for the "opposing spirit" to exist in the universe (II 27,33 f.) is attributed to the Mother (BG 71,6).

Perhaps, the preference for Father in the short version represents an attempt to adapt its picture of divine activity to the divine triad, Father-Mother-Son, which the introductory story equates with Jesus (CG II 2,12−15). The divine triad seems to be a regular feature of Sethian traditions, though its location may vary. *GEgypt* overcomes the implication of divine pair as the initiators. The supreme God evolves the Father-Mother-Son triad (CG III 41,7−12; 41,23−42,4). Both Father and Mother are androgynous (III 42,10 f.//IV 52,2−5). The Mother's cosmological functions are evident in her epithets. She "comes forth from herself" and "presides over the heavens" (III 42,12−21//IV 52,2−14).

A similar pattern appears in *TriProt*, a revelation discourse by each member of the triad. The Father is the image of the invisible spirit and father of all aeons; Mother, the one from whom the all received his image, and the Son, the manifestation of the aeons which come from him. The Mother's revelation is associated with the tree of knowledge. It reveals the ignorance of the lower god (XIII 44,20–29). Her call to gnosis reveals that she is active in shaping and sustaining order in the universe that stems from her, the androgynous Mother-Father (CG XIII 44,29–45,31). The section concludes with a colophon, "On Fate," that indicates that she is associated with the ordering of the world. This function is frequently fulfilled by the Mother or Sophia.

Stead has pointed out that Valentinian traditions have several pictures of Sophia. While Sophia is most commonly the young, "fallen" aeon who must be restored to the pleroma, or Achamoth, the lower Sophia, who will be restored to the aeon along with the Gnostics, there are traditions in which she appears as the perfect consort of God.[4] Tri-Prot suggests that the Mother's involvement with the created world and its order can be maintained along with the image of Sophia as divine consort (Epiph. Pan. 36,2; Clem. Alex. Strom. IV 90,2). Ptolemy, an independent teacher in the Valentinian tradition,[5] modifies a triadic formulation so as to obtain the first Tetrad of an Ogdoad. The triad consists of the Father, the feminine Ennoia, and Nous. The equality between the Nous and the Father provides the possibility for knowledge of God, since only Nous can comprehend him (Adv. Haer. I 1,1).

The divine triad is also associated with knowledge of God in a collection of writings that stem from Gnostic circles known to Plotinus. In this tradition, the divine One-Beyond-Existence is "known" by joining in praise of the divine triad. Zostr has Barbelo as the one who makes knowledge of God possible. Thus, she is similar to Nous in philosophical triads, the basis for knowledge of the One (CG VIII 83,19–21; 118,10–12; 125,11–16). The goal of the mystic quest is to join in the divine praise (VIII 129,8–16). Similar patterns of joining praise and blessing of the divine triad appear in the other writings of this group, Mar (X 8,1–9,25), Allog (XI 45,6–49,38; 50,20 f.; 51,12–16; 52,13–15), and 3StSeth, which gives the praise offered each member of the triad (VII 123,15–124,1; 125,11–14). Unlike their Platonist counterparts, the Gnostic traditions regularly have a female figure as the second member of the divine triad.

Philosophic Origins of the Female Divine Principle

The Gnostics are not entirely without philosophic support in their presentation of the female second principle. A tradition of philosophical interpretation of mythology combined with the Sophia of Jewish wisdom speculation probably provided the fundamental emphasis on the self-engendered divine Mother and her role in the cosmogonic process. This line of interpretation seems to have played a major role in Valentinian tradition.[6] The Sethian traditions, some of which were used by Valentinian teachers, are more indebted to Jewish Midrashic exegesis. They combine the Sophia figure with Eve traditions.

A tradition of Platonic exegesis, influenced by Pythagorean speculation about the Dyad, used the "feminine principle" to interpret *The Timeus*'s speculations on matter and disorder in the universe. Philo's occasional and somewhat inconsistent use of such traditions suggests that while he knew them, they did not play a major role in his thought. He does not associate these traditions with Eve. She represents "sense perception," the faculty necessary to Mind (cf., *LegAll* II 24, Adam equals Mind) to bring it out of the darkness. Without enlightenment from contact with the material world, Mind would not have any knowledge. This context leads Philo to present the newly awakened mind as arrogant. It thinks that all things belong to it instead of to God, despite its own instability (*Cher* 58–64). This epistemological tradition appears frequently in Gnostic stories of the creation of the lower world by the demiurge. When he sees all the creation, the lower powers and archons, which stem from him, he becomes boastful and arrogant. That boast usually provokes his mother, Sophia, to repentance and initiates the cosmogonic foundations for salvation in the creation of Adam, revelation of gnosis to him, and generation of the Gnostic seed.

The tradition of the Dyad is usually identified with the divine Logos in Philo. Sometimes it appears as matter (*SpecLeg* III 180; *Somn* II 70). Sophia apears with the *Timeus* epithets for matter, "foster mother" and "mother of all things" (*Det* 115f). In that passage, she is presented as an "earth mother" figure nourishing all things with milk from her breasts.[7] The closest one comes to the Gnostic Father-Mother-Son triad is the presentation of the Logos as son of God, Father of All, and Sophia, through whom all things come into being (*Fug* 109). A hint of cosmogonic self-generation appears in the use of the epithet applied to Athene, "motherless," for Sophia (*Ebr* 61) and the Logos (*Opif* 100). That tradition is more directly linked with self-generation by Plutarch a century later. Isis is identified with Athene and the express qualification "I came of myself" makes her self-generation clear. The same passage in Philo attributes to Sophia another attribute that will appear in mythic form in the Gnostic story. She is said to "rise above the material cosmos illuminated by the joy residing in God." The cosmological function of the divine female principle necessarily involves her in the lower world, but her divinity necessitates some form of ascent above that world. *LegAll* II 82 attributes the demiurgic function of "ruling all things" to Sophia. In *Ebr* 30–32, the world perceived by the senses is the beloved son of the union between God the Father and Sophia, his knowledge. A Gnostic cosmology would never have the sensible world so closely linked to the divine. Instead, the divine world of the pleroma emerges from the primary pair or the primary triad. Even Philo usually has the world of ideas as the direct product of God. The rather extraneous and unsystematized character of the references to the feminine as the second principle in Philo suggests that he has not integrated such speculations into his own cosmological reflection.

Plutarch's second-century Platonism is closer both in time and development to that in Gnostic systems. He uses the Dyad/Mother-of-All to exegete the Isis myth (*IsOsir* 372-82). He may also have known a tradition, similar to the development of Jewish Sophia speculation, in which Isis equals Wisdom. *IsOsir* 351 E ff. presents her as *eidesis/phronesis*.[8] Though Isis represents the material vessel of the *Timeus*, imperfect and in need of the ordering Logos, she is not a malevolent principle—just as Sophia and the demiurge are not in many Valentinian systems. The duality inherent in Isis's cosmogonic role is repeated in the Gnostic Sophia figure. She is divided between Eros and a longing for divine order, which can only be brought about through the Logos. Similarly, the ordering activity of the Mother in *TriProt* (XIII 40, 4–42,2) requires completion with the final coming of the son, Logos. All of her activity in the world is aimed at that descent.[9] Gnosticism is not simply a tradition of philosophic interpretation. Its figures take on a mythic tonality that the allegorical interpretations of Philo and Plutarch avoid. But their peculiar shape could never be accounted for simply as the development of mythic stories. Philosophic reflection has already shifted the Gnostic perception of the world and its relationship to the divine.

Sophia and the Origins of the World

The vast reaches of the pleroma reflect a peculiarly Gnostic concern with separating the divine from the material world and often from its anthropological correlate, the passions of the human soul. This gulf creates difficulties for the role of the divine feminine in creation. Frequently, the mother, who is responsible for the engendering of the divine aeons, appears to have little relationship to the Sophia, who is responsible for the lower world that we know. Some accounts even have more than one Sophia figure. A weak aeon, whose passion or desire for knowledge becomes the source of the god and substance for this world, she may nevertheless return above to the divine world. However, a lower Sophia may remain bound to this world until all of the divine spirit embodied in it returns to its heavenly place. Sophia continues to play an ordering and providential role over against the cosmos, though the various accounts of her responsibility for its devolution from the heavenly world vary in the negative imagery they associate with that act.

One type of flaw is sexual in its overtones. Even in systems that give a different account, it sometimes appears in the epithet *prunikos* (lewd). Sophia wants to conceive without her consort. Since such conception can only produce a material substance without form, the latter being derived from the male, an ugly, abortionlike mass results. It does not even have the image of its mother (cf. *ApocryJn* CG II 9, 25–10,19; *NatArc* II 94, 4–33; *SJC* III 117, 1–119, 7; *PetPhil* VIII 135, 8–136,15). Other less explicit references of this type speak about an "overflow" from Sophia (*OrigWld* II 98, 13–100,29). *Adv. Haer.* I 30,2–4 attributes the overflow to a double impregnation by the Father and the Son of Man.

A second type of flaw is the desire to imitate the Father. Sometimes Sophia is said to seek to create a pleroma like the one created by the Father (*Zostr* VIII 9, 16–11,9). Or, her desire to create without a consort may be a desire to generate as though she were "unbegotten" (Hipp. *Ref.* VI 30,6–8).

Ptolemy has an epistemological interpretation of the Sophia story. God is unknowable by all the aeons except the Mind. This ignorance of God introduces a certain longing into the pleroma which is manifested in the youngest aeon, Sophia. She makes a brash attempt to know the Father. Such a desire would lead to her dissolution. It must be separated from the heavenly world by the Limit (*Adv. Haer.* I 2, 2–4).

Similar diversity appears in the accounts of Sophia's restoration to the divine world and the healing of whatever passion is embodied in the origins of the god/substance out of which the cosmos will come into being. Sophia's divided nature means that she will require divine assistance—often from the consort whose consent she had failed to gain in the first instance. As the "type" of the Gnostic soul caught in a world to which it does not belong, she must remain tied to this world until all have returned to the pleroma. The Sophia story in *ApocryJn* is typical, though once again the long and short versions diverge in important detail. Sophia's repentance is motivated by the arrogant claim to divinity of her offspring. Prayer from the pleroma to the Father brings divine aid. In the short version, Sophia's consort comes to her assistance (BG 47, 4–7; 60, 12–16). In the long version, the Holy Spirit comes from above to elevate her to the Nineth, above her son (CG II 13,8–14,13; cp., *TriProt* XIII 39, 20–40,4). The long version agrees that the deficiency of Sophia must be corrected (by "epinoia," BG 53,20–54,4; CG II 20,27 f.), but it appears to conceive Sophia as identified with the Mother of the highest triad and consequently not possessed of a consort.[10] In Valentinian systems which stress the "passions" of the lower Sophia as the source of the cosmogonic elements, the Savior must rectify the passion of Sophia. Incorporeal matter is often the product of the process (cf., *Adv. Haer.* I 4,5; *ExcTheod.* 44,1–2; 45,1–2; Hipp. *Ref.* VI 32,5–6.

The rest of the story of origins includes both creative soteriological roles for Sophia. She may be assisted by her consort, by a higher Sophia, by the pleroma in general, or by the Spirit. Such divine intervention in the ordering of the cosmos goes undetected by its rulers (e.g., *Adv. Haer.* I 5,3–6; 17,1). Her most important creative/soteriological activity is to provide Spirit to the human, which the lower god has created after an image of the heavenly archetype that had been revealed to silence his boasting. That hidden Spirit makes humanity superior to its creator (e.g., *TriProt* CG XIII 40, 4–42,2; *NatArc* II 87,20–88,15). Sophia, herself, is sometimes the image according to which Adam is created (*GrSeth* CG VII 50,25–51,20; 68,28–31; *ApocryJn* II 19,15–22,9; *ValExpo* XI 33, 35–39,35; *Adv. Haer.* I 5,5–6; *ExcTheod.* 53,1–5; *Adv. Haer.* I 30,6, where the Mother gives Ialdabaoth the "thought of Man" and has the Father breathe in the trace of light). In *GEgypt* (CG III 56,4–60,18), the heavenly seed of Seth is created by a mother-goddess figure with four breasts. It must be transported from the heavens to the vessels waiting in this world, which are the result of the *metanoia* of the hylic Sophia. *OrigWld* gives an even more complex story of the origins of humanity. The Adam story is repeated on each of the three levels–pneumatic, psychic, and hylic. In the middle of the process, Sophia-Life creates Eve, an androgynous instructor for Adam (CG II 107,18–118,6). This heavenly Eve is identified with Sophia (Isis) by the paradoxical "I am" aretalogy, which she proclaims after she comes forth.

The esoteric and elitist side of Gnostic praxis requires that only a small number of humans have the Spirit. In *NatArc* (CG II 96,19–35) the ancestress of the Gnostics is Norea, Seth's sister. She and the Gnostic race have souls from the Father. The Spirit of truth within makes them immortal. They are referred to as the "sown element," which suggests that a process of heavenly creation and divine sowing such as we saw in *GEgypt* might be envisaged. *ApocryJn*, on the other hand, has the Mother intervene in the creation of the Sethians with a special sending of her Spirit (CG II 24,35–25,16). Similarly, the Valentinians associate Sophia with the pneumatics in a special way. She sends seed into them through the angels. Psychics, on the other hand, simply have the "breathed-in likeness" from the demiurge. The pneumatics will enter the pleroma with Sophia; the psychics be exalted to the Ogdoad with the demiurge. Those with only earthly, animal souls will, of course, perish along with the rest of material creation (*Adv. Haer.* I 7,1; *ExcTheod.* 53,5).

Redemptive Activity by the Mother

The continuation of the stories of the "time of origins" usually establishes a pattern of redemptive intervention by the Mother or Sophia. She must protect her seed/light from destruction by the hostile powers who do not want the truth about their inferiority, ugliness, lack of real divinity to become known among humans. Sophia may rescue her seed from some Old Testament peril (the Sodomites, *Adv. Haer.* 31,1). The flood is particularly common as a hostile incident from which the Gnostic race is saved by some divine agency. *Adv. Haer.* I

30,9–12 has Sophia Prunikos constantly rescuing her light. She saves Noah. She gets around the malicious covenant between the creator and Abraham by having the prophets reveal the future coming of Christ to destroy that covenant. However, she has to enlist the aid of the Mother, the first woman, to prepare a vessel for the coming Christ. Another common time for revelation, as with the Instructor-Eve in *OrigWld,* is at the tree of knowledge. *ApocAd* (CG V 64,5–65,24) has an androgynous Eve-Adam. Eve reveals to Adam the true glory they enjoy and gives him knowledge of the true God. The creator retaliates by dividing them into two sexes. At that point knowledge withdraws.[11] Usually gnosis comes through the tree of knowledge. The Instructor of *OrigWld* (II 118,7–123,31) moves Adam and Eve to disobey the hostile creator and so receive gnosis (cp., *Adv. Haer.* I 30,7). The two versions of *ApocryJn* disagree over who is responsible for the awakening of Adam and rescue from the flood. The short version has Sophia herself. The long version has the heavenly Epinoia, who represents the activity of the highest Mother-Father (CG II 22,19–24,31; 27,31–30,11).[12]

Another type of redemptive activity has the Mother or Sophia responsible for reordering or controlling Fate (another parallel with Isis). The whole revelation of the Mother's activity in *TriProt* dealt with reordering fate (XIII 42,4–45,20). In other places, one finds general assertions about Sophia's providential ordering of the lower world (e.g., *NatArc* II 87,4–10).

A peculiar development of Jewish Midrashic traditions gave rise to a variant on the reordering theme. Instead of a repentance—lifting-up of Sophia, her rejection of Ialdabaoth's boast leads one of his sons, Sabaoth, to repent (*NatArc* CG II 94,34–96,14; *OrigWld* II 103,3–106,35). He worships the heavenly Sophia, is exalted in his own heavens above his father, and is given Sophia-Life as a consort to instruct him. The Valentinian tradition has a general version of the instruction of the lower god. Sophia teaches the demiurge that he is not the only god, but he does not reveal the "mystery of the Father and the aeons" to anyone (Hipp. *Ref.* VI 36,2).

With Sophia's activity confined to "holding actions" against the lower god and ordering of the cosmos until the coming of the revealer of gnosis, one might not consider her much of a savior goddess. Yet we have seen that the Instructor-Eve speaks in Isis-like tones to proclaim her identity. The Marcosian ritual attests that one might pray to the Mother in order to defeat the archons, who wish to hinder the soul's ascent into the pleroma (*Adv. Haer.* I 21,5 and the parallel in *I ApocJas* CG V 35, 19 f.). The Mother, who orders fate, in *TriProt* (XIII 45,2–20) issues a call to awakening and Gnostic baptism.

Both proclamations allude to the functions of the female divine figure in the story of salvation. The long version of *ApocryJn,* which has consistently focused on the Mother-Father as source of salvation, concludes with a proclamation of the threefold coming of the divine Epinoia to aid humanity. The first appears to refer to the awakening of Adam; the second to her activity in ordering fate (the concern with *oikonomia*), and the last to the revealer of gnosis:

> I, the perfect Pronoia of the pleroma, turned myself into my seed, for I existed first, going along every road, for *I am the kingdom of light, I am the remembrance of the pleroma.*
> And I went into the greatness of darkness; I went on until I came to the middle of the prison. And the foundations of chaos shook. I hid myself from them because of their wickedness. And they did not know me. Again, I returned a second time. I went. I came from the light. *I am the remembrance of the pronoia.*
> I came to the middle of the darkness and the inside of Hades seeking my government [*oikonomia*]. And the foundations of chaos shook so that they were about to fall on those in chaos and destroy them. Again I ran up to my root of light, so that they would not be destroyed before the time.
> Yet a third time I went—
> *I am the light which is in the light. I am the remembrance of the pronoia*— so that I came to the middle of the darkness and the inside of Hades. I filled my face with the light of the consummation of their aeon and came to the middle of their prison, that is, the prison of the body, and said, "Let the person who hears arise from the deep sleep." He wept and cried. He wiped away bitter tears and said, "Who is calling my name? Whence comes this hope to me, since I am in the chains of their prison?" I said, "*I am the pronoia of the pure light. I am the thought of the virgin spirit,* who raised you up to the honored place. Arise! Remember that you are the one who has heard and follow your root! *I am the merciful one.* And guard yourself aginst the angels of poverty and the demons of chaos and all who entrap you. And watch out for the deep sleep and the enclosure within Hades." And I raised him and sealed him with the light water of five seals so that death might not have power over him from that time.
>
> (CG II 30,11–31,25)

Here the "I am" predications punctuate a summary of the saving effect of gnosis. The summary would appear to function as a baptismal call to gnosis. But the exhortation to beware of being entrapped also provides a link to another use of the "I am" revelation formula by a female figure. *Thund* uses the paradoxical "I AM" style of the Instructor-Eve as part of a Gnostic wisdom sermon. The hearer is being summoned to follow this Wisdom despite the fact that she is dishonored in the world. Like Isis, this female figure claims to be behind all of human wisdom:

> Why have you hated me in your counsels? For I shall be silent among the silent, and I shall appear and speak. Why then have you hated me, you Greeks? Because I am a barbarian among the barbarians? For I am the wisdom of the Greeks and the knowledge of the barbarians. I am the judgment of the Greeks and the barbarians. I am the one whose image is great in Egypt, and who had no image among the barbarians. I am the one who has been hated everywhere and who has been loved everywhere...I am she

who does not keep festival, and I am she whose festivals are numerous. I am godless, and I am the one whose god is great.
(CG VI 15,31–15,11; 15,23–25)

As so often happens, Gnostic rhetoric has intensified the paradox inherent in the situation of a universal wisdom goddess who goes unrecognized by most of humanity. Yet she is clearly the source of salvation for the person who heeds her call.

Conclusion

This evidence of liturgical acclamation of the Mother, Sophia, Instructor-Eve, Epinoia as source of gnosis should caution us against identifying Sophia's fate in the mythic narrative with her place in Gnostic cult. Further caution is demanded by the fact that most stories do not attach blame to the devolution of the lower world in which she plays such a key role. The theological categories of Christianity often lead interpreters to speak of Sophia's fall and to attribute to it the same negative evaluations tradition has attached to the fall of Eve/Adam.[13] Instead, the structure of Gnostic cosmology does not need to explain fall and alienation from God in terms of sinful disobedience. It needs to explain the distance between the divine world and this one. That cosmological structure makes it necessary that some special process of revelation bring humanity knowledge of that divine world.

The mythic summary of Sophia's wandering fits within the cultic proclamation of saving gnosis. That gnosis overcomes the ambiguities and tensions inherent in the Gnostic's experience of the world. *Thund*'s paradoxes intensify those experiences so as to overcome the disvaluing effect that they might have on the believer. Though the Mother/Sophia is not the highest Father or the only revealer of gnosis, she often appears as the crucial link between the human in this world and that divinity which constitutes his/her truest identity. The peculiar amalgamation of mythic and philosophic discourse suggests that her wisdom also provides a challenge to the claims of human reason advanced through philosophy. The ultimate image of salvation is neither male nor female but the restored unity of an androgynous Mother-Father, who has passed through diversity.

Abbreviations

GNOSTIC WRITINGS

Allog	*Allogenes*	CG XI,3*
ApocAd	*Apocalypse of Adam*	CG V,5
ApocryJn	*Apocryphon of John*	CG II,1
		(long version)
		BG 8502,2
		(short version)

1 ApocJas	First Apocalypse of James	CG V,*3*
GEgypt	Gospel of the Egyptians	CG III,*2*; IV,*2*
GrSeth	Second Treatise of the Great Seth	CG VIII,*2*
Mar	Marsanes	CG X,*1*
NatArc	Nature of the Archons	CG II,*4*
OrigWld	On the Origin of the World	CG II,*5*
PetPhil	Letter of Peter to Philip	CG VIII,*2*
SJC	Sophia of Jesus Christ	CG III,*4*; BG 8502,*3*
3StSeth	Three Steles of Seth	CG VII,*5*
Thund	Thunder, Perfect Mind	CG VI,*2*
TriPot	Trimorphic Protennoia	CG XIII,*1*
Val Expo	Valentinian Exposition	CG XI,*2*
Zostr	Zostrianos	CG XIII,*1*

PHILO OF ALEXANDRIA

Cher	De Cherubim
Det	Quod Deterius Potiori insidiari soleat
Ebr	De Ebrietate
Fug	De Fuga et Inventione
LegAll	Legum Allegoriarum
Somn	De Somniis
SpecLeg	De Specialibus Legibus

OTHER

Adv. Haer.	Irenaeus, *Adversus Haeresus*
Pan.	Epiphanius, *Panarion*
Strom.	Clement of Alexandria, *Stromata*
ExcTheod.	_____, *Excerpta e Theodoto*
Ref.	Hippolytus, *Refutatio omnium haeresium*
IsOsir.	Plutarch, *De Iside et Qsiride*

*Italic number refers to the treatise in the codex.

NOTES

1. E. Voeglin, *Order in History*, IV: *The Ecumenic Age* (Baton Rouge: Louisiana State University Press, 1974), p. 251. On the importance of the element of primordial fusion in Gnostic myth, see M. Tardieu, *Trois Mythes Gnostiques* (Paris: Etudes Augustiniennes, 1974), p. 278.

2. The two main collections of Gnostic writings are the Berlin Codex (referred to by the abbreviation BG) and the thirteen codices found at Nag Hammadi in Egypt, which are in the Coptic Museum in Cairo (referred to by the abbreviation CG). Passages in a Gnostic writing are located by identifying the collection, BG or CG, the codex number (for CG) in roman numerals, and the page and line numbers in arabic numerals.

3. See the discussion of the problem of the dyadic and triadic references to God in Y. Janssens, "L'Apocryphon de Jean," *Museon* 84 (1971):43–48.

4. See G.C. Stead, "The Valentinian Myth of Sophia," *Journal of Theological Studies* 20 (1969):93–95.

5. Ptolemy was an independent Gnostic teacher whose career overlapped with that of Valentinus. Patristic authors present him as Valentinus's successor because they seek to make the Gnostic movement fit into a single chain of traditions; see G. Ludemann, "Zur Geschichte des Eltesten Christentums in Rom. I Valentin und Marcion II Ptolemaus and Justin," *Zeitschrift fur Neutestamentliche Wissenschaft* 70 (1979):102ff.

6. J. Dillon, *Middle Platonism* (London: Dickworth, 1977), pp. 386–89, points out that Valentinians are much closer to Platonic speculation on the imperfection in the material world than they are to any Jewish or Christian speculation on the origin of evil in human sinfulness. The Valentinian system is interpreting the irrational world soul of the *Timeus*. What makes the Valentinian system unusual is the depth of ignorance involved. According to their account the Demiurge cannot see the heavenly forms.

7. Ibid., p. 164, though the language of Sophia's nurturing creation makes her almost an earth mother, she remains a transcendent deity.

8. See G. Quispel, "Jewish Gnosis and Mandean Gnosticism," *Les Textes de Nag Hammadi* (NHS VII; ed. J.E. Menard; Leiden: E.J. Brill, 1975), pp. 80–89.

9. Cp. *GrSeth* CG VII 50, 25–51, 20, Sophia Prunikos prepares monads and places for sons of light; *ExcTheod* 53, 1–5.

10. L. Schottroff, *Der Glaubenden und die feinliche Welt* (Neukirchen-Vluyn: Neukirchner, 1970), pp. 57f., points out the contradictory statement in ApocryJn CG II 14, 7–9.

11. *ApocAd* parodies Jewish salvation history. Though Sophia is not directly responsible, that pattern of salvation history is a series of angelic rescue missions for the Sethians; see my "Apocalypse of Adam: Genre and Function of a Gnostic Apocalypse," *Catholic Biblical Quarterly* 39 (1977):382–95, and, for an alternative reading of the pattern of that salvation history, C. Hedrick, *The Apocalypse of Adam* (Missoula, Mont.: Scholars Press, 1980), pp. 59–84.

12. The short version concludes with a formulaic assertion that the Mother has been active on behalf of her seed despite the fact that the mythic accounts in the short version do not make that activity explicit (BG 75, 10–15, has Mother-Father; 76, 1–6), see Schottroff, pp. 59–66.

13. Schottroff, pp. 42–59. Schottroff observes that the only culpable failure in gnosticism is the failure to respond to the call of revelation (p. 48).

'Gnostic Worship':
the State of the Question

by

David H. Tripp

I. Ten Years

This must be a personal report, rather than simply a *catalogue raisonné* of the researches of recent years, for it springs from a decade of preoccupation with the problem – it appeared at first to be a single problem – of Gnostics worship. The aim of the quest was threefold: 1) to ask what the 'Gnostics' did in their liturgy; 2) to ask what they thought they were doing in their liturgy; and 3) to ask what effect these phenomena had on the developing liturgical life of the Great Church.

A number of widely entertained suggestions (it would be unfair to call them 'generally held assumptions') are inherited by an investigator in this field: that 'Gnosticism' is essentially a unitive body of thought and spirituality, perhaps almost a distinguishable religion; that there is a body of 'Gnostic' religious practice that patient research may identify; that this religion and its cult were a medium through which non-Christian notions, values and practices entered into the growing Christian movement and adapted it. The ulterior motives for such research would be various: chiefly, to seek such historical truth as may be pinned down – but also, perhaps, to check out issues debated among Christians in later days: the battlelines of Catholic-and-Protestant, pro-sacramentalist/anti-sacramentalist, institutional/anti-institutional may be traced beneath the arguments of Hatch and, after him, Harnack, of Reitzenstein and his populariser Bultmann. The topic is therefore one of considerable potential interest!

Examination of the sources led to a major puzzle: there seemed to be an irreconcilable inconsistency between the poetic flights of a Valentinus or a Basilides and the jiggery-pokery of a Marcus or Justin the author of *Baruch*. Even the skilful exegesis of Sagnard, for example, could not make Marcus' invocation of Charis fit into the Sophia-theology of Valentinus and Ptolemaeus. The assumption of an essentially unitive religious movement proved to be a hindrance to satisfactory investigation: it falsified interpretation by creating an expectation that any given source must fit somehow into the thought-world of all other 'Gnostic' sources. As to method: the 'history of ideas' approach was unhelpful; what was needed was to identify specific

210

groups – specific individuals, when possible – and to describe what they *did*, and only then to ask why they did as they did. If it proved then to be possible to group together various schools or their leaders, and to trace common themes, well and good – but that was to be shown *a fortiori*, not assumed *a priori*. This entailed a fresh look at the sources, and a reappraisal of the identification of the people whose ritual life was under examination. Rather than speak glibly of 'Gnosticism', it seemed wiser to speak of 'some early Christian minorities'.

II. The Sources: a rapid Overview

The sectarian sources, known from the 'Catholic' hereseologists hitherto only in quotation (and in quotation of untestable accuracy), became vastly more numerous with the appearance of the Nag Hammadi papyri. The editing, translation and interpretation of their contents has a long way to go, but for our purposes much is already clear. Whatever the purposes of the collection, its sources are diverse: some texts come from the Great Church, some from the Hermetica, some from Jewish mysticism, some from Plato, some from Valentinianism, but most from the Peratae-Naassene-Ophite complex of sects. Very few can be called directly 'liturgical' – perhaps *The Three Steles of Seth* (which seems to be a sort of solo liturgy for the Merkabah devotion), perhaps also *The Apocalypse of Adam* (Naassene), conceivably *Melchizedek* (in which an initiation rite has been traced, and which I should tentatively ascribe to the mysterious and idiosyncratic school of Theodotus mentioned in *Refutation of All Heresies* VII. 35f, and *Panarion* 54f.), and certainly in the *Valentinian Fragments*. (In the now conventional system of reference, these documents are CG VII/5, V/5, IX/1 and XI/2-2e). The remainder of the Nag Hammadi works, like the 'Gnostic' writings already known – from the Askew Codex *(Pistis Sophia)*, the Bruce Codex *('Setheus'*, I-II *Jeu)*, the Berlin Coptic Codex 8502 *(Apocryphon of John, Gospel of Mary)*, Oxyrhynchus Papyri 1, 655, 656 *(Gospel of Thomas)*, Ptolemaeus' Letter to Flora, and other quotations in the hereseologists, are substantial, though indirect, evidence of the life and thought of these worshipping communities.

The testimony of the hereseologists – including, in a sense, *Acts, I John* and *Jude*, as well as the Pastoral Epistles, the letters of Ignatius of Antioch, and most obviously the inferentially traceable *Syntagma* of Justin Martyr, the *Adversus Haereses* (AH) of Irenaeus of Lyons, the *Refutation of All Heresies (Ref.)* usually attributed to Hippolytus of Rome, the same author's *contra Noetum,* the *Panarion* of Epiphanius of Salamis *(Pan.)*, and (to a lesser degree) the later work of Philastrius of Brescia – has had its evidential value confirmed, rather than diminished, by the Nag Hammadi material.

One matter of detail as to the text of Irenaeus may be mentioned here. The already noted difficulty of setting the rites of Marcus the Gnostic and his followers into the framework of Valentinian/Ptolemaean theology made it necessary to question the transmission of the text of AH I. Comparison with the summary of AH I given in the preamble to AH II (I.249-50 Harvey) leads to the idea that the *original* sequence of AH I (although the present sequence of the book is attested as early as Tertullian in *Adv. Valentinianos* iv) was as follows:

(a) the Valentinian/Ptolemaean system described and condemned (I.i.-vi – using chapter-divisions as in Harvey);

(b) the background of the Valentinians in the earlier history of heresies, starting from Simon Magus (I.vii-ix.2) and going on to

(c) Marcus (I.vii-ix.2) as a major item in this list and a pressing concern for Irenaeus and his circle;

(d) the common characteristics of all these heresies, the defiance of the Creator in doctrine and cultic usage, described (I.x.3-xiii), and then

(e) challenged (I.xiv-xv).

The immediate implication of this re-ordering is that Marcus ceases to be a Valentinian, and Valentinus to be responsible for Marcus – and that a new classification of the 'Gnostic' sects, which does not assume their fundamental unity, must be sought.

III. Classification of early Christian Minorities

Some sense of the diverse materials could be made by grouping the early Christian dissidents into three categories – rough and ready, but not unreasonable:

1. 'Cults of Power' – Simon Magus, Menander, Satornil, Cerdo (?), Carpocrates, Marcus and Elchasai;

2. Groups originating from the Separation of Christianity from Judaism – 'Peratae', 'Naassenes', 'Ophites', the Phibionites of Epiphanius, Archontics, various sub-groups without known names either of their own choice or imposed by opponents;

3. 'The Gentile Counter-Churches' – Basilides and Isidore, Valentinus and Ptolemaeus and Herakleon, Marcion, and Tatian – and also Montanus, although he and his Church cannot usefully be

212

pushed into the same theological classification with the others as a 'Gnostic' phenomenon.

Having ordered the material (and the questions to be asked) by this method, it was necessary to ask what these groups *did* when they met to say their prayers, and (if possible) what they *thought* they were doing. It might then be possible to enquire how these bodies of practice related to the life of what was to survive as the Great Church – the 'Catholic' or 'Common-or-Garden' Church, as distinct from the select church(es) of the *Gnostikoi* or 'men of insight'. But this further question should not be allowed to dominate the scene: the ritual life of a community yields its most valuable insights only when examined for its own sake, and with all the sympathy the observer can command.

IV. The 'Gentile Counter-Churches'

These comparatively sophisticated associations have occupied the centre of the stage too much, misleadingly: they have created the mistaken impression that the early Christian minorities were articulate coteries of subtle thinkers (an impression which they would gladly have fostered!) – whereas in fact a major, perhaps the most determinative, feature of their corporate life was their distinctive *practice*, often typical of the conservative or innovative or synthetical conservative behaviour of deprived and isolated sub-cultures.

In any case, the anti-Jewishness of Basilides, Valentinus, and especially Marcion, and their obsession with the very features of the (Jewish-) Christian tradition which they most wished to abandon suggest that they are historically secondary to the cruder 'Naassene'/'Ophite' sects, and even adopted, albeit transformingly, the myths and themes which the latter treasured. It was therefore necessary to leave the 'Gentile Counter-Churches' until the other strands had been thoroughly examined. In the event, as it turned out, it was the ritual life of these groups that remained most mysterious.

Of the Basilidians, a fair amount has been written on their theology, virtually nothing on their liturgy. Their preference for Luke's Gospel (which we must take to include a preference for its liturgical use) has been argued. They had some role in the early history of the Feast of the Epiphany, even if it is hard to believe that the Great Church could have actually followed them in this matter.

The Valentinians, even when we have removed the incantations of

213

Marcus from their repertoire, are less of a puzzle than the Basilidians. If, as seems likely, the Nag Hammadi *Gospel of Philip* is Valentinian (although it has derived its title in CG II/3 from the Naassene 'Gospel of Philip' of which only fragments survive – including an allusion in this book) – then it depicts the Valentinian church as observing an initiation-system consisting of water-baptism, chrismation and eucharist (the last being portrayed as a marriage-feast). The book challenges the initiates to grow spiritually along the lines suggested by the successively increasing importance of the ritual acts, so as to bear fruit in effective missionary work in the world. The Valentinian fragments in CG XI/2-2e, usually called *A Valentinian Exposition + On the Anointing + On Baptism A + On Baptism B + On the Eucharist A + On the Eucharist B*, have been studied as to their doctrinal content by Dr Pagels in *Harvard Theological Review* 65 (1972), but further work is called for from a liturgical point of view. The sequence of water-baptism and chrismation *may* differ from that in GPhilip (and if IX/2-2e is indeed Herakleonite, we may see here a liturgical *differentia* of that Valentinian sub-school); but of greater interest is the possibility (and it is at present no more than a suggestion of the present writer) that we have here an initiation-rite which, chrismation apart, reproduces the pattern in the *Didache*. In the view of Professor Segelberg, the Nag Hammadi *Gospel of Truth* (CG I/3, XII/2) is a confirmation homily.

A number of verses of Valentinian origin – and some others possibly of the same provenance – are extant: fragment 8 in Völker's numbering of Valentinus' own works; if Dr Harzhoff is right, the Naassene hymn from *Ref.* V.10.2 is also by him; Papyrus Berlin 8299 contains a post-initiation hymn which, when contrasted with the equivalent hymn in the Amherst Papyrus 2, has a Valentinian air; and Papyrus Oxyrhynchus 2074, a hymn to Sophia, is very apt for the visitation of the dying. Both the latter make such of the Good Shepherd image, in a fashion reminiscent of the epitaph of Flavia Sophe, which Dr Gilles Quispel has given us strong reason to see as Valentinian.

Lastly, M. Massaux *(New Testament Studies* 5/3, April 1959) has detected in P. Bodmer III an edition of *Genesis* and *John* delicately adapted for Valentinian use.

The materials are not negligible; but their composite character is not yet by any means clear.

Of the liturgy of the Marcionite church – except that it was, in total defiance of logic, virtually identical with that of the Great Church (itself for this period largely unknown!) – little can be said. Tatian is hardly less obscure; but when more results are forthcoming from the investigations

214

instigated by Professor Drijvers into the place of Tatian, Bar Daisan and the *Act of Thomas* in the earliest history of East Syrian Christianity, we shall be much wiser.

Before leaving the 'Gentile Counter-Churches' a word must be said of the Mandaeans and the Hermetica. Both, while of great interest to the history-of-ideas methodology, seem to belong quite outside the Christian thought-world, and are not therefore considered here.

V. The 'Cults of Power'

Simon Magus, familiar from *Acts* 8, has a significance which leaves his historical career far behind: he created a convention – one might almost say a 'myth' – of the cult-leader who is also a cult-object, who invades the growing Christian Church for occultist purposes. History-of-ideas specialists look for a philosophy behind such figures; sociologists of religion, and experienced pastors, recognize a familiar problem: the dominant figure who gathers disciples for the sake of gathering and ruling disciples, and whose cultic practices are directed to the exercise of power over them. There may be truly religious dimensions to this as well – concern for esoteric knowledge, pursuit of theurgic healing or social reconstruction; but power, its acquisition, possession and use, are constant preoccupations in such associations. Modern examples are not far to seek – Aleister Crowley, Alex Sanders, some phases of Mormonism, some kinds of 'house churches'.... Among recurrent features of this type of group are secrecy and syncretism; both have overtones of potency.

Simon, on close examination, turns out to be a comparatively innocuous example, as do Menander, Cerdo and Satornil. In any case, we can discover virtually nothing about their ritual behaviour. Menander's 'baptism into incorruptibility' was forgotten in his own city of Antioch by the time of Ignatius, who shared both his longing for incorruptibility and his intense sense of sacramental realism.

With the Carpocratians we come into a different situation. Their theories are fairly well known, and something is at least conjecturable about their rites. To set people free from the restraints of guilt-feelings, they initiated them into secret mysteries by a version of Christian baptism. The rite included branding. If Professor Morton Smith's discovery of an esoteric edition of *Mark* is anything to go by, they used a purloined copy of this, tricked out of the presbyters of Alexandria, and amplified by them with at least hints of homo-erotic magic. (The story of the theft is so humiliating to the main-stream Church that it has the ring of truth). The initiation led into

215

participation in a 'Love-Feast', at which social distinctions (and moral restraints?) were defied. We go cautiously here, for there is a substantial danger that the Catholic authors exaggerate discreditable features; but the usually reliable and tolerant Clement may be trusted when he says that these serious statements come from Carpocratians themselves (*Stromata* III. ii.198 Stählin).

Carpocrates belongs to the first half of the century. Less than twenty years later there appears the figure of Marcus, of whom Irenaeus has much to say. His description of a parody of the Christian Eucharist, at which Marcus invokes Charis, Grace, to pour her blood out into the cup he holds (whereupon its contents, mixed – white? – wine turns red), and then persuades female congregants to follow his act by filling a big cup to overflowing from a smaller cup, and then convinces them that they can prophesy, so that they may have the privilege of union with him, is derived from eye-witness accounts. The ritual texts, given *in extenso*, are a fascinating mixture of pagan magic and Christian invocation. There can be little doubt that Marcus is plagiarizing traditions of Christian eucharistic worship which already include something like a consecratory epiclesis. This may seem unlikely; but, before the suggestion is dismissed, comparison should be made with the prayer of St. Polycarp in the text of his Martyrdom (ch.xiv.); the vivid sacramental realism of the language of participation in Christ, in the first paragraph, is poised, as it were, to move into the oblation petition of the second paragraph – there is no doubt that this prayer put on the lips of the martyr bishop echoes the style of the eucharistic prayer familiar in Asia c.155 C.E.; and Justin Martyr's account of eucharistic theology in I *Apol.*65-67, from the same period and general area, suggests that the eucharistic elements *being* Christ's body and blood is due to their being 'eucharistized' or 'thanked-over'.

Marcus' disciples are then described as using prayers not composed by their master, at the commendation of the dying. These are more Jewish in tone, and also compatible with the theology of Ptolemaeus. It appears that these are based on prayers used by the Jewish-Christian Naassenes, perhaps already adopted and adapted by Valentinians of Ptolemaeus' school: we see the Christian dissidents influencing one another. Whether they were adapting main-stream Christian usage, or that usage in its later forms was itself influenced by them, is unclear. The latest revision of the Roman Catholic commendation prayers, by its scrupulous avoidance of the language of death as the Great Journey, reflects the suspicion that this terminology, common to Marcosian and Naassene usage and to later Catholic euchology,

216

is of 'Gnostic' origin and therefore suspect. (We note how liturgical research is of more than antiquarian interest!)

The *Book of Elchasai*, 'the Power of God', is clearly related to a Cult of Power of some sort – but not of a Christian sort. Even if it was used by Alcibiades of Apamea in Rome during the episcopate of Callistus as part of a cheap salvation-package, its seeming baptismal rite is not an adaptation of Christian initiation but a pagan Syrian lustral apotropaic act, oddly (and briefly) transplanted. It tells us little more than that Christians are easily fascinated by rites of power.

Most of what is to be discovered of the Cults of Power reveals that they are marginal to Christian liturgical history – although they are a perennial and dangerous phenomenon. Except in some disputed areas, they do more than reflect, usually in misapplied forms, the worship of the conventional Christian congregations. The chief value of a thorough study of them is that they are detached from consideration of the other early Christian minority movements, which are thereby left alone for a more realistic investigation.

VI. Groups left in Isolation by the Separation of Christianity from Judaism

This, the topic most richly illustrated by the Nag Hammadi finds, is appallingly complicated. What is offered here is an over-simplified reading of the mass of material.

At three points, a diverse but basically single tradition of Jewish Christianity that has had its Jewish roots poisoned, comes to light: in the fifth book of the *Refutation*, in the so-called 'heresy of Prodicus' and the 'Gnostics' encountered by the neo-Platonist Plotinus and his circle, and in the 'Phibionites' who tried to capture the soul of Epiphanius. In these cases, we come near (in Epiphanius' case, right-up to) eye-witness testimony.

Ref. V, when closely examined, reveals a bulky library of tractates, from distinct but related sects, which have been edited by a single hand before the Refutator picked them up. The editorial hand is that of one Justin, who added to the collection his own book *Baruch*. He has welded into one this library of mystifying books, which are designed to swamp the reader with torrents of disturbing suggestions until he or she is ready to take on Justin's extreme dualism and to be initiated into it both didactically and ritually. Justin himself knows that his sources are from differing groups: Peratae, Naassenes, and 'Sithians' (who turn out to be simply Naassenes, or 'Ophites', 'Snake-People', who have a lot to say about Seth, the second progenitor of the human race – but they are not really a distinct sect or school).

217

The same people turn up again, using the same library (but without Justin's editing), and in a more sophisticated guise, seeking *entrée* into philosophical circles, as the alleged followers of Prodicus (I take to this to be a false claim to be heirs of Prodicus of Keos and his undeserved reputation for denying the value of prayer) – this phase was known to Clement of Alexandria (*Stromata* I,xv, III.iv, II.31, VII.41) – and, without this transparent pretention, as advocates of Oriental apocalyptic, in Porphyry's *Life of Plotinus* (ch.16).

Epiphanius' encounter with the Phibionites, whom he knew to be a subtype of the Naassenes (one of the groups that *did* call themselves 'Gnostics'), gives a fascinating account of what they *said* of their eucharist, which they called by the Jewish Christian name of 'the true Passover': it included the offering of semen and menstrual blood or sometimes pounded-up foetus, and promiscuous intercourse (*Pan.* 26). His account contains its own correction: he denounced these people – but the resultant police investigation led only to banishment, not to the capital punishment that would have ensued if these univocally goetic practices had been provable. Nonetheless, there remains a solid account of a sect with Jewish-Christian roots, and using several books mentioned in *Ref.* V and in connection with the would-be philosophers.

When all this is put together, and used to order the suitable Nag Hammadi material, a pattern emerges. A group of isolated Christians of Jewish antecedents, the Peratae (from Peraea?), combine in their interest astrological speculation, devotion to the saving Mother (derived from where?), baptism, and a version of the Merkabah mysticism. They gave us the book *Setheus,* and either created or inherited the *Gospel according to Thomas* – an odd book which contrives to disparage prayer and retain sacraments. This tradition developed and divided – the process cannot yet be traced – and some of the lines of tradition became bitterly anti-Jewish, world-denying and Creator-hostile.

In ways too diverse to attempt to unravel here, these traditions combined baptism (and perhaps repeated baptisms into successive mystical states), an ascent-of-the-soul mysticism derived from Jewish models (and conceivably related in some way to the main-stream Christian use of the *Sanctus* as the apogee of eucharistic rapture, with the *Benedictus qui venit* as the welcome by the angels of their kindred spirits into the heavenly presence), and rites for preparing the soul for ascent after death through the threatening heavens into its true home.

The interpretation of the documents is fraught with uncertainty, for the introspective character of world-denying sects is inclined to transfer the true

218

locus of ritual action into the inner mind, where it becomes impossible to say (e.g.) whether repeated baptisms are successive applications of water or renewed immersions of the consciousness in sacred themes.

One major issue is the source of the persistent denial, claiming to come from Jesus himself, of the need or rightness of prayer. Does this go back to a vague misreading of Jesus' non-performance of the Passover at the Last Supper?

VII. Conclusions

This brief sketch indicates, if nothing else, the great gaps remaining in our knowledge of the ritual life of the early Christian minorities. We can have no confidence in asserting that they influenced the Great Church, except in making greater precision in formulae, clearer emphasis on creation and incarnation, assertion of the accessibility of salvation to all, and the openness of the Gospel tradition, inescapably necessary in main-stream Christian worship. There can be no doubt, on the other hand, that their vagaries attest troublesome longings which conventional worship could not – and cannot – satisfy.

BIBLIOGRAPHICAL NOTE

The work on which this article is based is largely set out in the unpublished Ph.D. dissertation, *Worship in Second Century Gnosticism: Studies in the Ritual Life of some early Christian Minorities*, University of Leeds 1984.
Surveys of Gnosticism in general: the older works retain much of their value – Bousset's *Hauptprobleme der Gnosis* (1907) and Koffmanne's *Die Gnosis in ihrer Tendenz und Organisation* (1881) deserve special mention. Best general introductions of recent years R. McL. Wilson, *The Gnostic Problem* (London 1958) and K. Rudolph, *Die Gnosis* (Göttingen 1977). The Nag Hammadi material is excellently presented in English in J.M. Robinson et al., *The Nag Hammadi Library in English* (Leiden 1977). Best guide to bibliography on individual tractates is given by D.M. Scholer, *Nag Hammadi Bibliography* (Leiden 1977, and continued in *Novum Testamentum* in subsequent years).
On Valentinian worship: Tripp, 'The "Sacramental System" of the Gospel of Philip' in *Studia Patristica* XVII (Oxford 1982), with references.
On Marcus: J. Reiling, 'Marcus Gnosticus and the New Testament' in Baarda, Klijn, van Unnik, edd., *Miscellanea Neotestamentica* 1 (= Suppl. to Novum Testamentum XLVII, Leiden 1978). Comparison with the magical papyri (e.g. as ed. by Preisendanz, Leipzig and Berlin 1928, 1931, 1941) is essential.
On Naassens, etc. see the great mass of work on *Gospel of Thomas*- bibliography in Tripp, 'The Aim of the Gospel of Thomas' in *Expository Times* 92/2 (November 1980). Also P. Perkins' studies of christology in *Vigiliae Christianae* 35 (1981) and *Catholic Biblical Quarterly* 43 (1981); Funk, *Die 2. Apokalypse des Jakobus*, diss. theol. Berlin 1971, and published as *Texte und Untersuchungen* 119, Berlin 1976.
Honoured reference must be made to the contributions of E. Segelberg: on Evangelium Veritatis in *Orientalia Suecana* VIII (1959); on Gospel of Philip in *Numen* VII (1960); and 'The

219

Baptismal Rite according to some of the Coptic-Gnostic Texts of Nag Hammadi' in *Studia Patristica* V (= *Texte und Untersuchungen* 80, Berlin, 1962); and 'Prayer among the Gnostics?' in *Gnosis and Gnosticism* (+NHS VIII, Leiden 1977).

These notes should afford a total newcomer to this area an introduction to the literature.

220

JBL 101/1 (1982) 5–37

JESUS
FROM EASTER TO VALENTINUS
(OR TO THE APOSTLES' CREED)*

JAMES M. ROBINSON
CLAREMONT GRADUATE SCHOOL, CLAREMONT, CA 91711

I

THE first hundred years of Christianity—A.D. 30 to 130, more or less—is the period from Easter to Valentinus, or if you prefer, until the Apostles' Creed. That hundred years is also the time in which the NT was written. It is also the time in which oral traditions about Jesus were in circulation. It is this period, largely for these reasons, that occupies us here.

The present paper will not seek to argue for or presuppose a solution to the perennial debate between the traditional (and still largely British) view of Gnosticism as a second-century inner-Christian heresy and the *religionsgeschichtlich* (and Continental) view of Gnosticism as a broad syncretistic phenomenon surfacing at least as early as Christianity in various religions of the day, of which Christianity was only one. While the Nag Hammadi texts seem to have come out on the side of the latter alternative, in that several texts document non-Christian Gnosticism of various traditions (Jewish, Hermetic, Neo-Platonic), pre-Christian Gnosticism as such is hardly attested in a way to settle the debate once and for all. As a matter of fact the dating of the composition of most Nag Hammadi tractates, much less of their sources, has hardly begun, and so can claim nothing like the degree of relative certainty characteristic of the dating of NT books.

Yet the main reason for not approaching the issue of this paper in terms of that perennial debate is that such an approach tends to obscure rather than clarify the situation. For such a clear-cut polarized choice as that debate tends to call upon us to make could blunt our sensitivity to the actual shade of development a text may represent somewhere in the no-person's-land between those crisp options: If Gnosticism could be safely kept out of the first century A.D., then it could be ignored in interpreting Paul's opponents in Corinth, the world of Colossians and Ephesians, the Prologue of John, and the like, with the result that a traditional and misleading

*The Presidential Address delivered 21 December 1981, at the annual meeting of the Society of Biblical Literature, held at the San Francisco Hilton, San Francisco, CA.

exegesis would result. Conversely, the presupposition of pre-Christian Gnosticism invites the anachronism of reading into the situation behind such texts concepts of the second century, from which our knowledge of Gnosticism primarily comes.

To assume a mediating position may thus not be the weakness of indecision and vacillation, but rather an approximation of the historical reality more useful than is either horn of the dilemma: One may assume that second-century Gnosticism did not first emerge then in the full-blown form of the Valentinian and Basilidean systems. For such historical developments call for lead-time, just as, at the next stage, Clement and Origen of Alexandria on the one hand and Irenaeus and Tertullian on the other are inconceivable apart from the century leading up to their systems. Thus even if it were true that Gnosticism as known in the second-century systems did not exist in the Pauline and Johannine schools going back to the first century, the left-wing trajectory out of which second-century Gnosticism emerged must have been contemporary with the Pauline and Johannine schools and could well be a major factor in influencing them. To erect a periodizing barrier between pre-Gnostic apostolic Christianity and second-century Gnosticism would be to falsify history by denying the existence of that trajectory until it reached its outcome in second-century Gnosticism. This would produce the exegetical error of failing to interpret those NT texts in terms of their time as the lead-time for second-century Gnosticism.

The methodological situation is similar when one envisages moving forward from A.D. 30. The apocalyptic radicalism that lead John the Baptist to lose his head, Jesus to be hung up, and Paul to become a habitué of forty lashes lest one (2 Cor 11:24) could hardly have failed to have left-wing successors down through the first hundred years, as main-line Christianity, in part following the lead of Judaism at Jamnia, standardized, solidified, domesticated itself and moved, as sects are wont to do in the second and third generations, toward the mainstream of the cultural environment. Thus the lead-time for Gnosticism coincides with the follow-up time for primitive Christian radicalism. Sometimes that radicalism would have expressed itself in sufficient continuity with the original forms it had taken for the radical fringe (charismatics, martyrs, prophets) to have had the support of the more conventional mainstream. But even within such acceptable limits there occur texts such as Colossians, Ephesians and Ignatius where new thought patterns and language worlds become unmistakably audible. Ultimately at least some of apocalyptic radicalism modulated into gnostic radicalism.

The bulk of the NT, written in the second half of the first century A.D., the middle segment of the first hundred years of Christianity, is thus strung on trajectories that lead not only from the pre-Pauline confession of 1 Cor 15:3-5 to the Apostles' Creed of the second century, but also from Easter "enthusiasm" to second-century Gnosticism. It is on currents such as these, rather than on the traditional assumption of a straight-line development through the "apostolic age" with its unwavering faith once for all delivered to the saints, that we are to discuss the topic before us.

It is indeed in terms of such currents that the polarization of early Christianity into orthodoxy and heresy is to be understood. Heresy is so tenacious and unbending not because of the hardening of its heart, but because of its relatively valid claim to be rooted in an original Christian point. Thus the outcome of the first hundred years of Christianity in orthodoxy vs. heresy does not imply the divine protection of an original revelation from the wiles of the devil, but rather two alternative adjustments of the original position made necessary by the changing circumstances with the passage of time. Hence the theological assessment of such diverging trajectories, though it begins with the historical given that the winner in this competition has been known as orthodox, the loser heretical, has as its first task to acknowledge the historical process leading to this outcome and then to rethink critically what theological validity was gained and lost along each of the diverging trajectories, perhaps with the outcome that values from both trajectories should in fact be affirmed in some formulation for today, which would hence depart from both formulations of yesteryear.

II

The conceptualization or, more literally, the visualization of the appearances of the resurrected Christ are themselves such an instance of a bifurcating morphology. The earliest accessible documentation as a point of departure is Paul. He conceives of the resurrection as bodily, but emphasizes change within the continuity of corporeality (1 Cor 15:40, 43, 48, 54):

There are celestial bodies and there are terrestrial bodies.

It is sown in dishonor, it is raised in glory.

As was the man of dust, so are those who are of the dust; and as is the man of heaven, so are those who are of heaven.

When the perishable puts on the imperishable, and the mortal puts on immortality, . . .

When he comes, the Lord "will change our lowly body to be like his glorious body" (Phil 3:21). Thus it is clear that Paul visualized the resurrected Christ as a heavenly body, luminous. Though the letters of Paul do not narrate the Damascus road experience with its blinding light, this visualization repeatedly narrated in Acts (9:1–19; 22:4–16; 26:9–18) does seem to reflect accurately Paul's own visualization of his experience.

Yet with regard to the significance of Paul's experience, Luke does not reflect Paul's position. Luke demotes the Damascus road experience into Paul's *conversion*, as the church, following Luke rather than Paul, tends to refer to what Paul himself would have us refer to as the resurrected Christ's *appearance* to him. In Luke's hands this event falls outside the period of forty days to which Luke restricts the normative resurrection appearances (Acts 1:3). Paul himself alluded to the appearance of the resurrected Christ to him in order to validate his claim to be an apostle "not from men nor through man, but through Jesus Christ and God the Father who raised him from the dead" (Gal 1:1). That is to say, Paul was not just a delegate, missionary or emissary from a local church, which is the common meaning of the Greek word we all too readily translate (or unthinkingly transliterate) with the very specific designation apostle. But it is the common meaning of delegate which is the only sense in which Luke concedes Paul to be an apostle. For when the church of Antioch sent Barnabas and Saul as its delegates to evangelize Cyprus (Acts 13:3): "Then after fasting and praying they laid their hands on them and *sent them off.*" The latter verb is the verb whose stem is the same as that of the noun *apostolos,* though here it clearly means the church "delegated" them. It is in this sense that Acts 14:4, 14 refers to "the apostles," "the apostles Barnabas and Paul," that is to say, *delegates* of the Antioch church during the "first missionary journey." Luke goes so far as to present Paul preaching about the resurrection in such a way as to exclude himself from being a witness to the resurrection (Acts 13:30–31): "But God raised him from the dead; and for many days he appeared to those who came up with him from Galilee to Jerusalem, who are now his witnesses to the people." After that "first missionary journey" Luke reports (Acts 15:2) that "Paul and Barnabas and some of the others were appointed to go up to Jerusalem to the apostles and the elders," a usage that limits the apostles to those in Jerusalem, conformable to Luke's limitation of the appearances to the original disciples (Acts 1:22).

And yet Paul is the hero of the book of Acts! Scholars have long since recognized what Luke does to Paul, but have thus far been baffled to provide an adequate explanation. For to understand why Paul is here damned with such faint praise one must place Acts in terms of the trajectory from Easter to Valentinus.

There is relatively strong attestation to the fact that the first appearance to a male was to Peter (1 Cor 15:5; Luke 24:34). (Matthew's appending of the appearance to "Mary Magdalene and the other Mary" to the Marcan story of the empty tomb in 28:9–10 and the parallel narration of the appearance to Mary Magdalene in John 20:14–18 actually make her the first to see the risen Christ in these Gospels.) Yet, just as Luke does not narrate the tradition of the appearance to Paul within the limits he imposes on appearances (it is not narrated in Luke 24 or Acts 1), just so the story of the appearance to Peter is not among the resurrection appearances narrated in their proper place at the end of the gospels (Matt 28, Luke 24 and John 20–21).

2 Pet 1:16–17 seems to narrate that resurrection appearance, to judge by its use of a luminous story to accredit Peter in the way a resurrection appearance normally would one as an apostle: "We were eyewitnesses of his majesty. For when he received honor and glory from God the Father. . . ."

This seems a striking parallel to the opening words of the Great Commission by the resurrected Christ (Matt 28:18): "All authority in heaven and on earth has been given to me." 2 Peter would thus seem to describe a resurrection appearance . . . were it not for the fact that what follows is similar to a Marcan narration that occurs in the middle of the public ministry, and hence known not as a resurrection appearance but as the transfiguration: "(For when he received honor and glory from God the Father) and the voice was borne to him by the Majestic Glory, 'This is my beloved Son, with whom I am well pleased,' we heard this voice borne from heaven, for we were with him on the holy mountain." It is indeed probable that Mark has "historicized" what was originally the resurrection appearance to Peter, tying it down to an unambiguous bodiliness by putting it well before the crucifixion, in spite of its luminousness (Mark 9:3): "His garments became glistening, intensely white, as no fuller on earth could bleach them." Matthew compares this luminousness with the sun: "his face shone like the sun" (17:2), language used elsewhere of the resurrected Christ, "his face was like the sun shining in full strength" (Rev 1:16, see below), "brighter than the sun" (Acts 26:13). The original association of the "transfiguration" with Easter may be betrayed in the comment appended to it (Mark 9:9): "And as they were coming down the mountain, he charged them to tell no one what they had seen, until the Son of man should have risen from the dead."

Of course in the Marcan text Peter is accompanied by James and John; but this may well be only an aspect of Marcan historicizing, in that he usually presents these three as admitted to intimate scenes (5:37, 14:33; with Andrew as well 1:29; 13:3). Furthermore Jesus is accompanied by two figures, Elijah with Moses. But far from this fact serving to distance the transfiguration from a resurrection appearance, it associates it specifically with the resurrection appearance in . . . the second-century apocryphal *Gospel of Peter*:

> They saw the heavens opened and two men come down from there in a great brightness and draw nigh to the sepulchre. . . . and both the young men entered in. . . . They saw again three men come out from the sepulchre, and two of them sustaining the other, and a cross following them, and the heads of the two reached to heaven, but that of him who was led of them by the hand overpassing the heavens.

Of course in the Marcan version they are not such mythological heavenly "men," but rather the biblical characters Moses and Elijah, who had nonetheless according to Jewish tradition ascended to heaven. Furthermore they in their way reaffirm the association with resurrection, at least in a Valentinian interpretation of Mark (NH I, 48:6–11): "For if you remember reading in the Gospel that Elijah appeared and Moses with him, do not think the resurrection is an illusion." Thus, just as Luke transferred the luminous appearance to Paul outside the normative period by restricting normative resurrection appearances to forty days, Mark would seem to have transferred the luminous appearance to Peter outside the normative post-crucifixion period back into the public ministry. Mark in fact provides no resurrection appearances, perhaps because those available were so luminous as to seem disembodied. Thus, if Paul had tended to emphasize the difference of the resurrection body, so as to make it possible to affirm the bodiliness of a luminous appearance, the narrations of the empty tomb in the gospels tend to emphasize the continuity of the same body, lest the luminousness of the appearances suggest it was just a ghost, just religious experience.

The only resurrection appearance in the NT that is described in any detail, though it is usually overlooked due to not being placed at the end of a gospel, is in Rev 1:13-16:

> . . . one like a son of man, clothed with a long robe and with a golden girdle round his breast; his head and his hair were white as white wool, white as snow; his eyes were like a flame of fire, his feet were like burnished bronze, refined as in a furnace. and his voice was like the sound of many waters; in his right hand he held seven stars, from his mouth issued a sharp two-edged sword, and his face was like the sun shining in full strength.

Although this appearance took place in the 90s (quite uninhibited by the Lucan doctrine that appearances ended with forty days), it has in common with Paul's much earlier but equally uninhibited luminous visualization of the resurrection in the 30s the fact that these are the only two resurrection appearances recorded by persons who themselves received the appearances, Paul and John of Patmos—and both these authenticated visualizations of a resurrection appearance were of the luminous kind! Thus one may conclude that the original visualizations of resurrection appearances had been luminous, the experiencing of a blinding light, a heavenly body such as Luke reports Stephen saw (Acts 7:55-56): "He, full of the Holy Spirit, gazed into heaven and saw the glory of God, and Jesus standing at the right hand of God; and he said, 'Behold, I see the heavens opened, and the Son of man standing at the right hand of God.'"

Why then would this original visualization have been deprived of its appropriate position at the conclusion of the gospels? Perhaps because these luminous appearances continued, as Stephen, Paul and John of Patmos attest, down through the first century A.D., and, as gnostic sources attest, their increasingly dubious interpretation continued down through the second. And here one can see what they came to mean.

The Letter of Peter to Philip presents a luminous resurrection appearance (NH VIII, 134:9-13)[1]: "Then a great light appeared so that the mountain shone from the sight of him who had appeared." This took place "upon the mountain which is called 'the (Mount) of Olives,' the place where they used to gather with the blessed Christ *when he was in the body*" (133:13-17). From

---

[1] Marvin W. Meyer, *The Letter of Peter to Philip: Text, Translation and Commentary* (SBL DS 53; Chico: Scholars, 1981) 105-12 interprets this text in this broader context.

this language it is clear that the resurrected, luminous Christ is no longer in the body; bodily existence is restricted to Jesus prior to Easter. Thus the Pauline ability to retain both bodiliness and luminousness in his doctrine of the resurrection has given way to a bifurcation: if it is luminous, it is not bodily.

From a gnostic point of view this incorporeality is all to the good. For bodily existence is deficient, stupefied with fatigue, passion, drunkenness, sleepiness, a prison from which the spirit is liberated by its ecstatic trip at conversion and the sloughing off of this mortal coil at death. Thus the gnostics had every reason to retain the original luminous visualization of resurrection appearances, not just because they thereby retained the original Christian perception, but because it was a theological asset in terms of gnostic spiritualism.

In *The Gospel of Mary* (not from Nag Hammadi but from the closely related Coptic Gnostic P. Berol. 8502), Mary not only makes no claim that such a gnostic appearance is bodily; she frankly calls it a vision (10:10–23):

I saw the Lord in a *vision* and I said to him, "Lord, I saw you today in a *vision*." He answered and said to me, "Blessed are you, that you did not waver at the sight of me. For where the mind is, there is the treasure." I said to him, "Lord, now does he who sees the *vision* see it through the soul or through the spirit?" The Savior answered and said, "He does not see through the soul nor through the spirit, but the mind which is between the two—that is what sees the *vision*."

The luminous visualization of resurrection appearances may be the kind of experience that in that day would have been considered a vision. For when it is not a matter of Christ's resurrection, such a luminous appearance can readily be so classified even within the canon. The "two men . . . in dazzling apparel" (Luke 24:4) can be summarized by Luke as "a *vision* of angels" (Luke 24:23). Indeed Paul himself can speak of "*visions* and revelations of the Lord" (2 Cor 12:1). This openness of the luminous visualization to such a visionary interpretation may be what made that visualization increasingly unacceptable when applied to Jesus on the trajectory from Easter to the Apostles' Creed, especially when the disembodied overtones of such visions were exploited in a Gnosticizing way on the trajectory from Easter to Valentinus.

It is just this reduction of resurrection appearances to religious experience that is the foil against which the non-luminous resurrection appearances at the ends of the gospels of Matthew, Luke and John are composed (Luke 24:37–43):

But they were startled and frightened, and supposed that they saw a *spirit*. And he said to them, "Why are you troubled, and why do questionings rise in your hearts? See my hands and my feet, that it is I myself; handle me, and see; for a *spirit* has not *flesh and bones* as you see that I have." And when he had said this he showed them his hands and his feet. And while they still disbelieved for joy, and wondered, he said to them, "Have you anything here to eat?" They gave him a piece of broiled fish, and he took it and ate before them.

This apologetic against a ghostlike experience has pushed Luke to emphasize the "flesh and bones" of the resurrection, which is clearly one step nearer "orthodoxy" than was Paul (1 Cor 15:50): "I tell you this, brethren: *flesh and blood* cannot inherit the kingdom of God, nor does the perishable inherit the imperishable." It is probably such an apologetic against this spiritualizing the resurrection away, as the orthodox would sense it, that is also intended when that conclusion of Luke is summarized at the opening of Acts (1:3–4): "To them he presented himself alive after his passion by many proofs, appearing to them during forty days, and speaking of the kingdom of God. And while staying (literally: sharing salt, eating) with them." Similarly Acts 10:41: "us who were chosen by God as witnesses, who ate and drank with him after he rose from the dead." Similarly in the traditions used by John (John 20:20, 25, 27–28):

> He showed them his hands and his side.
>
> "Unless I see in his hands the print of the nails, and place my finger in the mark of the nails, and place my hands in his side, I will not believe."
>
> "Put your finger here, and see my hands; and put out your hand, and place it in my side; do not be faithless, but believing." Thomas answered him, "My Lord and my God."

This was a bit too materialistic for the "spiritual gospel" that transmitted it, and hence the Fourth Evangelist appended a corrective moving gently in the . . . gnostic direction (John 20:29): "Have you believed because you have seen me? Blessed are those who have not seen and yet believe." Matthew also reports (28:17) that "some doubted." But he has a somewhat different apologetic against an accusation that the resurrection was not real (28:13, 15): "'Tell people, "His disciples came by night and stole him away while we were asleep."' . . . And this story has been spread among the Jews to this day." But an apologetic for the physicality of the resurrection similar to that of Luke-Acts and the Johannine tradition may be implicit in Matthew as well (28:9): "And they came up and took hold of his feet. . . ."

It may be this same apologetic that is responsible for Mark's use of the story of the empty tomb rather than of resurrection appearances. For the emptiness of the tomb makes it clear that it was the same body that was buried which rose from the dead. It must be to underline this point that one finds the otherwise irrelevant details in Luke 24:12: "he saw the linen cloths by themselves," and in John 20:5–7: "He saw the linen cloths lying there . . . ; he saw the linen cloths lying, and the napkin, which had been on his head, not lying with the linen cloths but rolled up in a place by itself." Thus the apologetic interest evident in each of the canonical gospels reflects a secondary stage in the transmission of resurrection appearances, a defense against a (mis)interpretation of a more original stage.

Lest it seem that such a spiritualization of the luminously resurrected Christ as is here presupposed would be limited to a specifically gnostic tendency that could hardly be called primary, one may note that the two instances where the NT contains reports by an eyewitness to the (in each case luminous) appearance of the resurrected Christ, the identification of that appearance as the Spirit seems near at hand. For Paul the resurrection body is *"spiritual"* (1 Cor 15:44), "the last Adam" "a life-giving *spirit*" (1 Cor 15:45). When he comes to speak of the gloriousness of Christ, he calls him the Spirit (2 Cor 3:17–18): "Now the Lord is the *Spirit*, and where the *Spirit* of the Lord is, there is freedom. And we all, with unveiled face, beholding the *glory* of the Lord, are being changed into his likeness from one degree of *glory* to another; for this comes from the Lord who is the *Spirit*." Similarly John on Patmos sees the resurrected Christ, who dictates the letters to the seven churches, as is indicated by the self-identifications (1:17–18; 2:8): "'I am the first and the last, the living one: I died, and behold I am alive for evermore. . . .' The words of the first and the last, who died and came to life." Yet this takes place while John is "in the *Spirit*" (1:10), and the hermeneutical exhortation familiar at the conclusion of parables recurs at the end of each letter in the remarkable formulation (2:7, 11, 17, 29; 3:6, 13, 22): "He who has an ear, let him hear what the *Spirit* says to the churches."

This identification of the luminously resurrected Christ as the Spirit is then in substance what Luke rejects as the false assumption that they had seen a ghost. But it is in fact a way in which the luminous visualization would continue to be described in Gnosticism. In *The Sophia of Jesus Christ* the resurrected Christ appeared on a Galilean mountain (NH III, 91:10–13) "not in his first form, but in the invisible *spirit*. And his form was like a great angel of light. And his likeness I must not describe. No mortal flesh can endure it."

This gnostic spiritualization also comes to expression in a somewhat different conceptualization in an *Apocalypse of Peter*, where Jesus' death and resurrection are replaced with the idea of his bifurcation at the time of the passion into "the living Jesus" (NH VII, 81:19) that did not suffer and "his fleshly part" (81:20), "the body" (83:5) that was crucified. This "living Jesus" appeared however like the resurrected Christ (72:23–26): "I saw a new light greater than the light of day. Then it came down upon the Savior." "The body of his radiance" (71:30), "my incorporeal body" (83:7–8), is actually the Spirit (83:4–15): "So then the one susceptible to suffering shall come, since the body is the substitute. But what they released was my *incorporeal body*. But I am the intellectual *Spirit* filled with radiant *light*. He whom you saw coming to me is our intellectual Pleroma, which united the perfect *light* with my *Holy Spirit*." Luke on the other hand clearly distinguishes the appearances of the resurrected Christ, which terminate after forty days with the ascension, from the gift of the Holy Spirit at Pentecost, ten days later. The resurrected Christ is no ghost!

The primary stage of luminous appearances, in comparison with which the resurrection appearances at the ends of the canonical gospels are secondary, can be identified from vestiges in the non-luminous resurrection stories at the ends of the canonical gospels themselves as well as from the misplaced luminous resurrection stories in the NT, the identification of the resurrected Christ with the Spirit in Paul and Revelation, and the outcome of these trajectories in second-century Gnosticism.

In the resurrection appearances at the end of the canonical gospels the luminous glory of the resurrected Christ has indeed disappeared, though vestiges of that visualization do survive: The apocryphal *Gospel of Peter*, in which the luminous visualization of the resurrected Christ had been presented, had also included "a young man sitting in the midst of the sepulchre, comely and clothed with a brightly shining robe." (This may well be intended to be one of the two men "in a great brightness" who had previously entered the sepulchre and led the resurrected Christ to heaven, since that exaltation scene is followed by the comment that "the heavens were again seen to open, and a man descended and entered into the sepulchre"—a detail that otherwise would have no function.) In the canonical gospels this luminous apparition of the attendant is all that is left of the luminous visualization of the resurrected Christ: "a young man sitting on the right side, dressed in a white robe" (Mark 16:5); "an angel of the Lord," whose "appearance was like lightning, and his raiment white as snow" (Matt 28:2–3); "two men . . . in dazzling apparel" (Luke 24:4; see also Acts 1:10: "two men . . . in white robes"); "two angels in white" (John 20:12).

This vacillation as to whether the apparition is human or angelic is itself revealing. Even when designated human, the apparition is not human in the ordinary sense of an early Christian witness to the resurrection, such as an apostle or the like. For example, Elaine Pagels completely overlooks this "young *man*" in the authentic ending of Mark in favor of the canonicity of the *woman* in the inauthentic long ending of Mark:[2]

> One can dispute [von] Campenhausen's claim on the basis of New Testament evidence: the gospels of Mark and John both name Mary Magdalene, not Peter, as the first witness of the resurrection. [Footnote 22: Mark 16:9; John 20:11–17.]

> This gnostic gospel [*The Gospel of Mary*] recalls traditions recorded in Mark and John, that Mary Magdalene was the first to see the risen Christ. [Footnote 40: Mark 16:9].

The church has indeed tended to classify this youth in Mark as part of the heavenly realm, not the human, in that (s)he reveals divine truth and makes a luminous appearance, as the other gospels clarify the "white robe." Indeed the other gospels initiate the ecclesiastical exegesis to the effect that the youth is an angel, in that Matthew and John use the word angel, whereas

---

[2] Elaine Pagels, *The Gnostic Gospels* (New York: Random House, 1979) 8 and 11; pp. 9 and 13 of the paperback edition, Vantage Books, 1981.

Luke, who had spoken of two *men*, has a flashback in which the scene is recalled as "a vision of *angels*" (Luke 24:23). The apologetic that apparently caused the resurrected Christ's luminosity to fade into the solidity of a physical body did not affect the luminosity of the accompanying figure(s).

There are other vestiges of the luminous non-human visualization of the resurrected Christ in the otherwise very human appearances at the end of the canonical gospels. Even the *interpretatio christiana* of the OT at Easter retains the original emphasis on glory (Lk 24:26): "Was it not necessary that the Christ should suffer these things and enter into his *glory?*" In quite docetic style Jesus passes through locked doors (John 20:19, 26):

> On the evening of that day, the first day of the week, the doors being shut where the disciples were, for fear of the Jews, Jesus came and stood among them and said to them, "Peace be with you."

> The doors were shut, but Jesus came and stood among them, and said, "Peace be with you."

This docetic overtone may also be implicit in the abrupt entry of the resurrected Christ in Luke that leads to the thoroughly refuted assumption that they were looking at a spirit (24:36): "As they were saying this, Jesus himself stood among them, and said to them, 'Peace to you.'" The motif is more obvious in his abrupt departures (Luke 24:31, 51; Acts 1:9): ". . . and he vanished out of their sight." "While he blessed them, he parted from them and was carried up into heaven." "As they were looking on, he was lifted up, and a cloud took him out of their sight."

The failure to recognize the resurrected Christ may also derive ultimately from the luminous visualization. It is quite understandable that one would not recognize a blinding light (Acts 9:5; 22:8; 26:15): "Who are you, Lord?" But it is less obvious in the case of Jesus returning in the very same human body. The motif of non-recognition recurs in the story of the Emmaus road, where it is explained as divine intervention (Luke 24:16, 31): "But their eyes were kept from recognizing him." "And their eyes were opened and they recognized him." Mary Magdalene did not recognize him, but took him for a gardener (John 20:14–15): "She did not know that it was Jesus. Supposing him to be the gardener. . . ." This motif also occurs in the redactional chapter added to John (21:4): "Yet the disciples did not know that it was Jesus." This motif thus retains the tradition that it is not a matter of normal vision, catching sight of a recognizable human companion, but rather that (John 21:1) "Jesus revealed himself." Yet it is no longer a matter of a completely different form, such as a blinding light, but a very human form, mistakable for a tourist on the way to Emmaus, a gardener, or a fisherman standing on the shore. But the lack of recognition and then the sudden recognition is now no longer intelligible in terms of this all-too-human visualization, as it had been and continued to be in the luminous visualization. Thus the non-recognition of Jesus, like the luminous apparition of angels and the sudden appearance and disappearance of Jesus, may be motifs originally developed in connection with luminous visualizations of the resurrected Christ.

Our prevalent view that the church was launched by Easter experiences such as we find at the end of the canonical gospels must as a result be replaced by a recognition that they are secondary to an original luminous visualization of Christ's appearances, replaced as that original Christian experience played more and more into the hands of the trajectory from Easter to Valentinus. Over against that option, emerging orthodoxy, on the trajectory from Easter to the Apostles' Creed, expressed the reality of the bodily resurrection by emphasizing, in spite of supranatural vestiges, the human-like-us appearance of the resurrected Christ: the resurrection of the *flesh*.

To be sure, just as the emerging orthodox alternative retained vestiges of the luminous visualization, the emerging gnostic alternative could on occasion make use of human categories more at home in the orthodox trajectory. For example *The Apocryphon of John* presents the luminous visualization in a kind of fluctuating trinitarian form (NH II, 1:30–2:15):

> Straightway, while I was contemplating these things, behold the heavens opened and the whole creation which is under heaven *shone* and the world was shaken. And I was afraid, and behold I saw in the *light* a *youth* who stood by me. While I looked at him he became like an *old man*. And he changed his form (again), becoming like a *servant*. There was not a plurality before me, but there was a likeness with multiple forms in the *light*, and the forms appeared through each other, and the likeness had three forms. He said to me, "John, John, why do you doubt, and why are you afraid? You are not unfamiliar with this likeness, are you? That is to say, be not timid! I am the one who is with you (pl.) for ever. I am the *Father*, I am the *Mother*, I am the *Son*. I am the unpolluted and incorruptible one."

This threefoldness of the apparition, though described as like three human forms, does not eliminate the overarching luminosity, as may be further illustrated from a parallel text where the three forms are more explicitly luminous (*Pistis Sophia* 4):

> For he gave more *light* than in the hour that he went up to heaven, so that the men in the world were not able to speak of the *light* which was his, and it cast forth very many rays of *light*, and there was no measure to its rays. And his *light* was not equal throughout, but it was of different kinds, and it was of different types, so that some were many times superior to others, and the whole *light* together was in three forms, and the one was many times superior to the other; the second which was in the middle was superior to the first which was below; and the third which was above them all was superior to the second which was below. And the first ray which was below them all was similar to the *light* which had come down upon Jesus before he went up to heaven, and it was quite equal to it in its *light*. And the three *light*-forms were of different kinds of *light* and they were of different types. And some were many times superior to others.

But on the other hand the Valentinian *Gospel of Philip* could use the orthodox visualization for its purposes by stressing, as had Paul, the otherness of the body, but, with orthodoxy, moving beyond Paul (1 Cor 15:50) to speak of the resurrection of the flesh, though emphasizing the Pauline, and now gnostic, emphasis upon otherness (NH II, 68:31–37): "The Lord rose from the dead. He became as he used to be, but now his *body* was perfect. He did indeed possess *flesh*, but this flesh is *true flesh*. *Our flesh* is nothing, but we possess only an image of the true." This is as far as Gnosticism could reach out toward orthodoxy without forsaking its basic position of contrast (which it shared with Paul), expressed in *The Apocryphon of James* (NH I, 14:35–36): "From this moment on I shall strip myself that I may clothe myself." Thus although orthodoxy and heresy could on occasion accommodate themselves to language actually developed to implement the emphasis of the other alternative, by and large they divided the Pauline doctrine of luminous bodiliness between them: Orthodoxy defended the bodiliness by replacing luminousness with fleshliness, heresy exploited the luminousness by replacing bodiliness with spiritualness.

III

A still further bifurcation into heresy/orthodoxy from Easter to Valentinus or to the Apostles' Creed also has to do with the resurrection, but in this case the believer's resurrection—whether it has taken place *already*, presumably at baptism, or whether it has *not yet* taken place but is awaited at the end of time. Apparently this was being debated as early as the 50s in 1 Corinthians. For Paul contrasts the posture of the Corinthians with his own (4:8–9): "*Already* you are filled! *Already* you have become rich! Without us you have become kings! And would that you did reign, so that we might share the rule with you! For I think that God has exhibited us apostles as last of all. . . ." Apparently this is why baptism is so important to the Corinthians but is played down by Paul (1:12–17): "What I mean is that each one of you says, 'I belong to Paul,' or 'I belong to Apollos,' or 'I belong to Cephas,' or 'I belong to Christ.' Is Christ divided? Was Paul crucified for you? Or were you baptized in the name of Paul? I am thankful that I baptized none of you except Crispus and Gaius; lest any one should say that you were baptized in my name. (I did baptize also the household of Stephanas. Beyond that, I do not know whether I baptized any one else.) For Christ did not send me to baptize but to preach the gospel. . . ." Apparently the experience called today (baptismal) *regeneration*, a term that is not yet attested in Paul's time, was at that time designated by some Corinthians as (baptismal) *resurrection*. Thus the ultimate outcome of personal salvation was attained at initiation and need not be reserved for the end time, whose relevance—and even its reality—would tend to disappear. This is apparently the intent of the view Paul criticizes (15:12): "Some of you say that there is no resurrection of the dead." Rather than this being the view of rationalists, who do not believe in resurrection, as used to be assumed, it has been the scholarly assumption for the past half century that this is the view of fanatics who have already attained spiritual resurrection. Paul's own divergent view is expressed in Philippians (3:10–14, 20–21):

> ... that I may know him and the power of his resurrection, and may share his sufferings, becoming like him in his death, that if possible I *may attain* the resurrection from the dead. Not that I have *already* obtained this or am *already* perfect; but I *press on* to make it my own, because Christ Jesus has made me his own. Brethren, I do not consider that I have made it my own; but one thing I do, forgetting what lies behind and *straining forward* to what lies ahead, I *press on* toward the goal for the prize of the upward call of God in Christ Jesus. ... But our commonwealth is in heaven, and from it we await a Savior, the Lord Jesus Christ, who *will* change our lowly body to be like his glorious body, by the power which enables him even to subject all things to himself.

Hardly a generation before Valentinus in the early Second Century this view still was being strongly opposed in the Pauline School (2 Tim 2:16–18): "Avoid such godless chatter, for it will lead people into more and more ungodliness, and their talk will eat its way like gangrene. Among them are Hymenaeus and Philetus, who have swerved from the truth by holding that the resurrection is past *already*." Although Hymenaeus and Philetus are not mentioned by name in Gnostic sources, their view of the resurrection having taken place already is clearly attested in a Valentinian *Treatise on Resurrection* (NH I, 48:30–49:25):

> But the resurrection does not have this aforesaid character [of an illusion]; for it is the truth which stands firm. It is the revelation of what is, and the transformation of things, and a transition into newness. For imperishability descends upon the perishable; the light [!] flows down upon the darkness, swallowing it up; and the Pleroma fills up the deficiency. These are the symbols and the images of the resurrection. This is what makes the good. Therefore, do not think in part, O Rheginos, nor live in conformity with this flesh for the sake of unanimity, but flee from the divisions and the fetters, and *already* you have the resurrection. If he who will die knows about himself that he will die—even if he spends many years in this life he is brought to this—why not consider yourself as risen and (already) brought to this?

But this view opposed by Paul and in the Pauline School is here presented by *appeal* to Paul, that is to say, it is a doctrine of the left wing of the bifurcated Pauline School (45:14–46:2):

> The Savior swallowed up death—(of this) you are not reckoned as being ignorant—for he put aside the world which is perishing. He transformed himself into an imperishable Aeon and raised himself up, having swallowed the visible by the invisible, and he gave us the way of our immortality. Then, indeed, as the *Apostle* said, "We suffered with him, and we *arose* with him, and we went to heaven with him." Now if we are manifest in this world wearing him, we are that one's beams, and we are embraced by him until our setting, that is to say, our death in this life. We are drawn to heaven by him, like beams by the sun, not being restrained by anything. This is the *spiritual resurrection* which swallows up the psychic in the same way as the fleshly.

Here it is made clear that a future physical resurrection has become superfluous, having been replaced by the spiritual resurrection. The doctrine of

body emerged as orthodoxy. But Easter was itself a hermeneutical event, on any account making sense of Jesus in view of his abrupt end. Hence these trajectories of Easter and resurrection experience inevitably influenced the trajectories through which Jesus' sayings and texts witnessing to them would move. The first two instances of post-Easter trajectories may in fact clarify the directionalities at work on the third.

The gloriousness of the resurrected Christ not only vindicated the ignominiously crucified Jesus; it could also, by way of contrast, put Jesus in the shade. Though Paul did not go so far as to repudiate Jesus, as some spiritualists may have done (1 Cor 12:3: "Jesus be cursed!"), nonetheless an invidious contrast is already reflected in Paul: Jesus was sent "in the likeness of sinful flesh" (Rom 8:3), but arose in "his glorious body" (Phil 3:21); "he was crucified in weakness, but lives by the power of God" (2 Cor 13:4). Thus the original disciples and Jesus' family, those who knew him when he was on earth, do not in any way outrank Paul, who never laid eyes on nor was even known to this Jesus (1 Cor 9:1–5):

> Am I not free? Am I not an apostle? Have I not seen [on the Damascus road] Jesus our Lord? Are not you my workmanship in the Lord? If to others I am not an apostle [Acts], at least I am to you; for you are the seal of my apostleship in the Lord. This is my defense to those who would examine me. Do we not have the right to our food and drink? Do we not have the right to be accompanied by a wife, as the other apostles and the brothers of the Lord and Cephas?

This de-evaluation of pre-Easter traditions about Jesus on the part of Paul could, when coordinated with the luminously glorious resurrected Christ of the first trajectory from Easter to Valentinus, ultimately replace the normative role of the sayings of Jesus for primitive Christianity with the much more current and spiritual séances and sayings of the still appearing Lord.

Although Paul would not conceptualize his conversion as already his resurrection, since as an apocalypticist he reserved the resurrection of believers for the future, his conversion was nonetheless for him a comparably dramatic transformation into the spiritual realm, granting him a completely superhuman knowledge of Jesus (2 Cor 5:16): "From now on, therefore, we regard no one from a human point of view; even though we once regarded Christ from a human point of view, we regard him thus no longer." This de-evaluation of pre-Easter interpretations of Jesus on the part of Paul could, when coordinated with the experience of resurrection already on the second trajectory from Easter to Valentinus, ultimately replace the normative role of traditional interpretations for primitive Christianity with much more current and spiritual understandings of traditional sayings of Jesus.

Over against such spiritualistic trajectories the trajectory from Easter to the Apostles' Creed would have to find some way to revalidate the traditional sayings of Jesus and reaffirm their conventional interpretation. The way that was ultimately found was the canonical Gospel *genre*, whose derivation can

347

to a considerable extent be explained in terms of these bifurcating trajectories.

The two largest and best-known collections of Jesus' sayings, Q and *The Gospel of Thomas*, do not seem to have become involved in such an apologetic to maintain that the higher level of meaning inheres in the life of Jesus prior to Easter. In fact it is characteristic of such early sayings collections that they contain no thematic discussion of the turning point of death and resurrection about which the subsequent hermeneutical debate revolved, even though in a sense they straddle that turning point. For the authors of such collections stand within the post-Easter period, whereas much of their material goes back to the pre-Easter period. Thus they contain things said by Jesus prior to his crucifixion and also things said by the resurrected Christ; and they imply interpretations inherent in the tradition as well as interpretations recently granted to them by the resurrected Christ.

This ambivalence of the sayings tradition and hence of early sayings collections was not fully satisfactory to either side in the emerging polarization. If the orthodox manage to use and lose Q and to block the canonization of *The Gospel of Thomas*, opting for the biographical pre-Easter cast provided by the canonical Gospels, the Gnostics, while accepting *The Gospel of Thomas*, really prefer another *genre* of gospel, the dialogue of the resurrected Christ with his disciples. It is this trajectory from the sayings collection to the Gnostic dialogues, as well as its *pendant* in the orthodox trajectory from Q to the canonical Gospels, that is now to be sketched.

Q for its part had no clear bearing in terms of time and space. To be sure, the story of the temptation between the sayings of John the Baptist and the Sermon on the Mount/Plain seems to be moving toward a biographical cast such as Mark 1 offers. But the temptation is generally regarded as a late addition to Q reflecting early Christian exegetical interests; without it, there had been more nearly just a succession of John's, then Jesus' sayings, brought together as a collection of Wisdom's sayings. At the other end of Q the conclusion is so disappointing, from the more biographical point of view of a canonical Gospel, as to have been used as an argument against the existence of Q: "It 'peters out in miscellaneous oracles.'"[3] Since Q, like *The Gospel of Thomas*, refers neither to cross nor to resurrection, it is a moot question whether the author thought of them as spoken before or after Easter.

One may illustrate the problem by comparing the empowering of the resurrected Christ at the opening of the "Great Commission" (Matt 28:18) and the empowering of the Son in the "Johannine Pericope" of Q (Matt 11:27; Luke 10:22): "All authority in heaven and on earth has been given to

---

[3] Edward C. Hobbs, "A Quarter-Century Without 'Q'," *Perkins School of Theology Journal* 33 (1980) 13, quoting Austin M. Farrer, "On Dispensing With Q," *Studies in the Gospels: Essays in Memory of R. H. Lightfoot* (ed. Dennis E. Nineham; Oxford: Basil Blackwell, 1955) 60.

me." "All things have been delivered to me by my Father." If in the case of Matt 28:18 this authorization presupposes the enthronement of Christ as Cosmocrator at the exaltation of Easter (Phil 2:9–11; Acts 2:36), why not in the case of Q? But such a reminiscence of the authorization of Easter in the middle of Q neither implies that Easter falls in the middle of the text, as in the case of Luke-Acts, nor that the "Easter" authorization has been transferred back into the public ministry, as would seem to be the case with the "transfiguration" in Mark, and as the position of the Q text in Matt 11 and Luke 10 might suggest. For Easter does not fall here, or at the beginning or end of Q, or anywhere in Q. Q has the timelessness of eternal truth, or at least of wisdom literature.

The perennial debate about the meaning of the term "the living Jesus" at the opening of *The Gospel of Thomas* also illustrates the problem: Does this expression mean the resurrected Christ, somewhat as, for example, the *Apocalypse of Peter* uses this term to designate the spiritual part of Jesus that ascended to observe from above the crucifixion of "his earthly part" (NH VII, 81:18, 20)? "Living" is indeed tantamount to "resurrected" in Rev 1:17–18: "Fear not, I am the first and the last, and the *living* one; I died, and behold I am *alive* for evermore, and I have the keys of Death and Hades." Or does "the living Jesus" simply identify Jesus as part of the eternal divine realm, as would be suggested by comparison with the expressions "living Father" (Sayings 3, 50), "living One" (Sayings 35, 59, 111), or, of the redeemed, "living spirit" (Saying 114)?

We have been accustomed to think that probably Q had in mind Jesus prior to Easter. But to what extent is such a view really objective, to what extent due to our knowing Q only within the Marcan outline of Matthew and Luke? Similarly we naturally incline to think of "the living Jesus" of *The Gospel of Thomas* as the resurrected Christ. But to what extent is this view really objective, to what extent the result of our knowing *The Gospel of Thomas* only within the context of the Coptic Gnostic codices? Since, like Q, *The Gospel of Thomas* refers neither to cross nor to resurrection, it is a moot question whether the author thought of sayings as spoken before or after Easter. This seems not to have been relevant to the author. *The Gospel of Thomas* certainly has many sayings that the canonical Gospels place prior to Easter—as do modern scholars, in regarding a good number of the sayings in *The Gospel of Thomas* as "authentic" sayings of Jesus. But such sayings are not distinguished by *The Gospel of Thomas* from those that are clearly "inauthentic."

The lack of concern in primitive Christianity and in the sayings collections as to whether the sayings were spoken by Jesus before or after Easter, that is to say, by Jesus of Nazareth or the resurrected Christ, runs parallel with Paul's considering the authority of Jesus represented by the sayings tradition as more or less interchangeable with the guidance of the Spirit given at Easter. For Paul did in fact relativize traditions of Jesus' sayings to a status hardly superior to the guidance of the Spirit (1 Cor 7:10–12, 25, 40):

> To the married I give charge, not I but the Lord, that the wife should not separate from her husband . . . and that the husband should not divorce his wife. To the rest I say, not the Lord . . .
>
> Now concerning the unmarried, I have no command of the Lord, but give my opinion as one who by the Lord's mercy is trustworthy . . .
>
> And I think that I have the Spirit of God.

Indeed a priority of the Holy Spirit after Easter to Jesus prior to Easter may already be suggested in Q (Matt 12:32; Luke 12:10): "And every one who speaks a word against the Son of man will be forgiven; but he who blasphemes against the Holy Spirit will not be forgiven." To be sure, this usual interpretation of an otherwise obscure saying[4] does pose the problem that Jesus prior to Easter here has the honorific title of the coming judge, the Son of man, whereas the "resurrected Christ" is actually represented (replaced?) by the Holy Spirit. Mark heard this saying in a much more orthodox way, in that the Holy Spirit is the Spirit in Jesus prior to Easter (3:28–30), without any contrast to the Son of man. But Q apparently lacks the Marcan (1:12) view of the Spirit entering Jesus at baptism; at best Jesus will bestow the Spirit (Matt 3:11; Luke 3:16).

Rudolf Bultmann's famous *dictum*, that Jesus rose into the kerygma (with its neo-orthodox overtone: the social gospel rose into the old-fashioned gospel, which leaves Q out) could perhaps be reformulated from the point of view of Q to the effect that Jesus rose, as the revalidation of his word, into the Holy Spirit. Thus, rather than narrating a resurrection story, Q demonstrates its reality by presenting Jesus' sayings in their revalidated state as the guidance of the Holy Spirit. Easter is then not a point in time in Q, but rather permeates Q as the reality of Jesus' word being valid now. Or at least so it might seem especially for those who understood the resurrected Christ as Spirit. One may in this regard compare a couplet from one of the enthusiastic kerygmatic hymns (1 Tim 3:16): "He was manifested in the flesh, vindicated [or: justified] in the Spirit," with the saying in Q that names the higher power shared by John and Jesus (Matt 11:19; Luke 7:35): "Yet Wisdom is justified [or: vindicated] by (all) her deeds/children." It is as Spirit or Wisdom that Jesus (and John) lives on in the sayings tradition.

The Fourth Gospel brings to expression this spiritual significance of Easter within the canonical gospel *genre*. The Holy Spirit is breathed on the disciples at Easter (John 20:22) as the Counselor who will in effect continue the sayings of Jesus until the disciples reach the ultimate truth not attained prior to Easter (John 14:46; 15:26; 16:13–15):

> The Counselor, the Holy Spirit, whom the Father will send in my name, he will teach you all things, and bring to your remembrance all that I have said to you.

---

[4] Wolfgang Schenk, *Synopse zur Redenquelle der Evangelien: Q-Synopse und Rekonstruktion in deutscher Übersetzung mit kurzen Erläuterungen* (Düsseldorf: Patmos, 1981) 88.

But when the Counselor comes, whom I shall send to you from the Father, even the Spirit of truth, who proceeds from the Father, he will bear witness to me.

I have yet many things to say to you, but you cannot bear them now. When the Spirit of truth comes, he will guide you into all the truth; for he will not speak on his own authority, but whatever he hears he will speak, and he will declare to you the things that are to come. He will glorify me, for he will take what is mine and declare it to you. All that the Father has is mine; therefore I said that he will take what is mine and declare it to you.

Of course the most obvious thing for which the disciples had not been adequately prepared was Jesus' death. Hence their Easter experiences primarily made up for this deficiency. Thus it is not surprising when individual sayings explicitly said to have been clarified at Easter are references to his death (John 2:22): "When therefore he was raised from the dead, his disciples remembered that he had said this ['Destroy this temple, and in three days I will raise it up,' 2:19], and they believed the scripture and the word which Jesus had spoken." But sometimes there is no such specific reference, but rather Easter has in general become the time when the light dawns (John 12:16): "His disciples did not understand this [Zech 9:9 and the triumphal entry] at first; but when Jesus was glorified, then they remembered that this had been written of him and had been done to him." Even though a specific time reference is not given in John 13:7, the same may be implied: "What I am doing [washing Peter's feet] you do not know now, but afterward you will understand."

Yet it must be said that the sayings ascribed in the Gospel of John to Jesus prior to Easter have already been so updated in terms of Easter as to leave little remaining to be done when one reaches the actual resurrection at the end of this gospel. Such a saying as John 3:13 obviously must be ascribed to the resurrected Christ: "No one *has ascended* into heaven but he who descended from heaven, the Son of Man." One need only compare a statement of the resurrected Christ in *Pistis Sophia* 6 (see below): "I *have been* to the places from whence I came forth." Thus there is an odd tension in John between the doctrine of a shift to a higher hermeneutical level first with the gift of the Spirit at Easter and the presence of that higher level actually at almost every turn prior to Easter. Jesus prior to Easter has authority in the Gospel of John precisely because of the guidance of the Spirit of truth since Easter. That is to say, the highly interpreted sayings of Jesus in the Gospel of John stand in some tension to the canonical gospel *genre* in which they occur, but might seem quite natural in a sayings collection where the question of before or after Easter does not arise.

In this Easter hermeneutic of the Gospel of John the traditions of Jesus are associated with scripture (John 2:22; 12:16, both just cited): "the scripture and the word which Jesus had spoken;" "this had been written of him and had been done to him." Here too the hermeneutical pathos at Easter is motivated by the fact that especially cross and resurrection were to be scripturally supported. But it is nonetheless significant that such hermeneutic is considered distinctive of the period after the resurrection, in that the disciples had not been prepared in advance, as was the case in the Gospel of Mark with its repeated predictions of the passion (John 20:9): "For as yet they did not know the scriptures, that he must rise from the dead."

Luke also seems aware of Easter as the distinctive time of this *interpretatio christiana* of scripture (24:25–26, 32, 44–47):

> "O foolish men, and slow of heart to believe all that the prophets have spoken! Was it not necessary that the Christ should suffer these things and enter into his glory?"

> "Did not our hearts burn within us while he talked to us on the road, while he opened to us the scriptures?"

> "Everything written about me in the law of Moses and the prophets and the psalms must be fulfilled." Then he opened their minds to understand the scriptures, and said to them, "Thus it is written, that the Christ should suffer and on the third day rise from the dead, and that repentance and forgiveness of sins should be preached in his name to all nations, beginning from Jerusalem."

Yet the emphasis on the *interpretatio christiana* of scripture at Easter is not explainable as due merely to its following immediately upon the crucifixion, whose offense could be alleviated through the reassurance that it was predicted. Luke seems to consider Easter to be a distinctive time of hermeneutical revelation. For though not called the Holy Spirit (since Luke reserves that for Pentecost), nonetheless a special divine intervention is intended in the contrasts: "foolish men and slow of heart to believe;" whereupon "he opened to us the scriptures," "he opened their minds." The idea that Easter is on principle the time of a new hermeneutic as the time of the Spirit seems to be established with regard to scripture as well as Jesus' sayings.

The apologetic view of Easter as the time for interpreting scripture as well as Jesus' sayings so as to find in them the cross and resurrection recurs in Justin Martyr (*Apology* 1.50; *Dialogue with Trypho* 106):

> Afterwards, when He had risen from the dead and appeared to them, and had taught them to read the prophecies in which all these things were foretold as coming to pass. . . .

> [The apostles] who repented of their flight from Him when He was crucified, after He rose from the dead, and after they were persuaded by Himself that, before His passion He had mentioned to them that He must suffer these things, and that they were announced beforehand by the prophets. . . .

Once the sayings of Jesus are associated with scripture in terms of authoritative texts to be interpreted, they could hardly fail to have been associated with it in terms of obscurity. For if the Jewish scriptures are not explicitly a Christian book, the sayings of Jesus are not explicitly like the Easter gospel. But the hermeneutical methods already available for providing an *interpretatio christiana* to scripture could be carried over to the sayings of Jesus as well. These hermeneutical methods for updating outmoded but authoritative texts had begun with the Alexandrian interpretation of Homer, and had been adapted within Judaism as the Platonizing interpretation by Philo, the Essene interpretation at Qumran, the gnostic interpretation by Sethians and the Christian interpretation by the early Church.

The theological presupposition of such interpretation can be illustrated from the comment to Hab 2:2 in the Qumran *Commentary on the Book of Habakkuk* (1QpHab):[5]

> God told Habakkuk to write the things that are coming upon the last generation; but the fulness of that time He did not make known to him.
>
> As for that which He said, "for the sake of him who reads it" (or, "that he who reads it may run [may divulge])," its interpretation concerns the Righteous Teacher to whom God has made known all the mysteries of the words of His servants the prophets.

The appropriation of this hermeneutic by primitive Christianity is documented by 1 Pet 1:10–12:

> The prophets who prophesied of the grace that was to be yours searched and inquired about this salvation; they inquired what person or time was indicated by the Spirit of Christ within them when predicting the sufferings of Christ and the subsequent glory. It was revealed to them that they were serving not themselves but you, in the things which have now been announced to you by those who preached the good news to you through the Holy Spirit sent from heaven, things into which angels long to look.

That is to say, the modern heirs of scripture have a special revelation providing them with the key to its meaning. This is why average persons do not accept the sectarian interpretation—they are unenlightened. For though the text seems to mean only the superficial statement any reader sees (the literal meaning), God has revealed to the sectarians his real, esoteric meaning (the higher, deeper, fuller, spiritual meaning).

Technical terminology for such a two-level interpretation of scripture occurs, for example, in Justin's effort to convince Trypho the Jew of the validity of the *interpretatio christiana* (Dialogue 52.1; 68.6):

> The Holy Spirit had uttered these truths in a *parable*, and obscurely.

> There were many sayings written obscurely, or *parabolically*, or mysteriously, and symbolic actions, which the prophets who lived after the persons who said or did them expounded.

---

[5] William H. Brownlee, *The Midrash Pesher of Habakkuk* (SBLMS 24; Missoula: Scholars, 1979) 107. See also his exposition, pp. 110–11: "The prophets did not know all that the messianic age would contain. According to the Babylonian Talmud (Yalk. ii, 368, Eccl. Rabbah i,8) only part of the future glory was shown to the prophets. According to Midr. Shoher Tob to Ps. 90:1, 'With the exception of Moses and Isaiah, none of the prophets knew the content of their prophecies.' Cf. also I Peter 1:10–12. Philo went even further. In Special Laws I, 65, he asserted that the prophets were so completely under the control of God that they did not even know what they were speaking."

Similarly in *Pistis Sophia* (18): "Now concerning this word, my Lord, the power within the prophet Isaiah has spoken thus and has related once in a spiritual *parable*, speaking about the vision of Egypt" [Isa 19:3, 12]. The term "parable" and its synonyms really mean riddle, coded authoritative text.

But the term "parable" can also be used in *Pistis Sophia* to introduce a saying of Jesus that the canonical Gospels placed before the crucifixion, but a saying that is no more than is the Old Testament what one would normally consider a parable; the saying is designated "parable" only in the technical sense of a coded authoritative message subject to a higher interpretation (*Pistis Sophia* 50, 104, 105, 107):

> "O Lord, concerning this, thou didst once say to us in a *parable* [Luke 22:28–30]."

> "I answered, I spake to you in a *parable*, saying [Matt 18:22]."

> "For concerning the souls of men such as these I spoke to you once in a *parable*, saying [Matt 18:15–17; Luke 17:3]."

> "Now concerning such men, I spoke to you once in a *parable*, saying [Matt 10:12–13 parr.]."

This technical use of the term "parable" is clearly intended to set the saying or text in question off from a higher and clearer level "without parable" characteristic of the resurrected Christ's teaching in *Pistis Sophia* (88, 90, 100, 114). That higher level can be designated in its own right as Jesus teaching "openly" (*parrhēsia*: *Pistis Sophia* 17, 18, 19, 24, 25, 43, 65, 67, 69, 71, 74, 80, etc.). Thus the two technical terms come to be juxtaposed as a contrasting pair (*Pistis Sophia* 128; similarly 107, 110): "The Savior answered and said to Maria: 'Question everything which thou dost wish to question, and I will reveal them *openly* without *parable*.'"

To be sure, just as a series of synonyms can occur for the term "in parables," such as "sayings written obscurely, or parabolically, or mysteriously, and symbolic actions" quoted above from Justin, just so there are synonyms for "openly," for example in *Pistis Sophia*: "with assurance and certainty" (88, 90); "face to face" (100); "more and more, openly without parable, and with certainty" (107); "face to face without parable" (114).

Irenaeus accuses the Valentinians of this two-level interpretation of Jesus' sayings, making use of this fluid but technical terminology (1.1.5): "They tell us, however, that this knowledge has not been *openly* [*phaneros*] divulged, because all are not capable of receiving it, but has been mystically revealed by the Savior through means of *parables* to those qualified for understanding it." Thus when Morton Smith[6] sees a "libertine" implication in an excerpt from the Valentinian Theodotus quoted by Clement of Alexandria and ascribed by Smith to a pre-Marcan Aramaic gospel, a much less exciting, indeed pedantic but methodologically more reliable interpretation would be to the effect that again one has (here divided into three progressive levels)

---

* Morton Smith, *The Secret Gospel* (San Francisco: Harper and Row, 1973) 142.

the same contrasting hermeneutic pair expressed in a series of synonyms:[7] "The Savior taught the Apostles at first figuratively and mystically, later in parables and riddles, and thirdly clearly and *openly* [as R. P. Casey freely but accurately translates *gymnos*, in this context meant as a synonym for *parrhēsia*, but which Smith translates literally but tendentiously as 'nakedly'] when they were *alone* [also a hermeneutical cliché—see below—rather than documentation for something 'libertine']."

The frequent use of the term "parable" to designate a coded authoritative text would readily attract to it instances in the sayings tradition of the same term "parable" occurring in the more normal meaning of a simple sermon illustration. Thus in the pre-Marcan collection of three parables imbedded in Mark 4 (vss 2–10, 13–20, 26–29, 30–34: the Parables of the Sower, of the Seed Growing Secretly, and of the Mustard Seed) the first parable is accompanied by its interpretation, introduced by the comment (vs 10): "And when he was *alone*, those who were about him . . . asked him concerning the *parable(s)*." Thereupon followed the higher allegorical interpretation. The pre-Marcan collection also concluded with a specific reference to the two-level procedure (vss 33, 34b): "With many such parables he spoke the word to them, as they were able to hear it; . . . but privately to his own disciples he explained everything."

The Gospel of Mark only heightens the esoteric hermeneutic of this pre-Marcan collection by interpolating a still more exclusivistic characterization of those to whom the higher meaning is granted (vss 11–12): "To you has been given the *secret* (*mystērion*) of the kingdom of God, but for those outside everthing is in *parables*; so that they may indeed see but not perceive, and may indeed hear but not understand; lest they should turn again, and be forgiven." This heightening of the esoteric language is also reflected in the sayings Mark adds to the collection of parables (vss 21–25, especially vss 22 and 25): "For there is nothing *hid* (*krypton*), except to be made *manifest* (*phanerōthē*); nor is anything *secret* (*apokryphon*), except to come to light (*phaneron*)." "For to him who has will more be given; and from him who has not, even what he has will be taken away."

Much of the same esoteric concept recurs as the introductory saying in a cluster of parables imbedded in *The Gospel of Thomas* that Helmut Koester has suggested may be a source antedating that gospel (Sayings 62–66):[8] "It is to those who are worthy of My *mysteries* that I tell My *mysteries*. Do not let your left hand know what your right hand is doing." In this context (in distinction from that of almsgiving in Matt 6:3) the latter part must mean

R. P. Casey, *The Excerpta ex Theodoto of Clement of Alexandria* (London: Christophers, 1934) 82–83.

Helmut Koester, "Introduction" to *The Gospel of Thomas*, in *Nag Hammadi Tractates II, 2–II,7*, (ed. Bentley Layton; The Coptic Gnostic Library; Nag Hammadi Studies; Leiden: Brill, forthcoming).

something to the effect that common people (the "left hand") should not have access to the higher meaning of the "mysteries" known to the inner circle (the "right hand").

The esoteric, not to say eerie, context of a resurrection appearance would almost by definition be such a private setting for higher meaning, especially in view of the hermeneutical importance of Easter. Thus it is not surprising that the technical contrasting terms for designating the literal and spiritual levels of meaning, especially "in parables" and "openly," are used to distinguish the sayings of Jesus before and after Easter. In *The Apocryphon of James* the resurrected Christ says (NH I, 7:1-6): "At first I spoke to you *in parables* and you did not understand; now I speak to you *openly*, and you (still) do not perceive."

In gnostic perspective the resurrected Christ would also have the higher spiritual status of speaking from heaven and being free of the body. This Easter setting for the higher esoteric interpretation would also have the advantage of being able tacitly to concede to emerging orthodoxy the traditions of Jesus prior to Easter, as being only at the lower level, without those traditions being able to challenge the validity of a private séance with the resurrected Christ to which the orthodox were by definition not invited.

Indeed gnostics could shift their higher illumination from the first Easter Sunday forward down into the future beyond the limit of the physical appearances to which the orthodox had come to appeal, in that such physical transactions would in gnostic perspective be no better than the earthbound sayings prior to Easter. This may be the significance of the gnostic motif of Jesus' appearance for gnostic instruction long after the first Easter, since it is only at this later time then that he achieves the true knowledge. Irenaeus (1.28.7) reports the gnostic view: "But after his resurrection he tarried [on earth] *eighteen months*; and knowledge descending into him from above, he taught what was clear. He instructed a few of his disciples, whom he knew to be capable of understanding so great *mysteries*, in these things, and was then received up into heaven."

Similarly *Pistis Sophia* 1-6 actually deferred the normative resurrection appearance eleven years, since it is clear that only after that lapse of time does the luminous status and higher instruction emerge:

> But it happened that after Jesus had risen from the dead he spent *eleven years* speaking with his disciples. And he taught them only as far as the places of the first ordinance and as far as the places of the First Mystery which is within the veil. . . . And the disciples did not know and understand that there was anything within that mystery. . . . But he had only spoken to them in general, teaching them that they existed. But he had not told them the extent and the rank of their places according to how they exist. Because of this they also did not know that other places existed within that mystery. . . .
>
> Now it happened when the light-power had come down upon Jesus, it gradually surrounded him completely. Then Jesus rose or ascended to the height, giving light exceedingly, with a light to which there was no measure. And the disciples gazed after

him, and not one of them spoke until he had reached heaven, but they all kept a great silence. . . . As they were saying these things and were weeping to one another, on the ninth hour of the following day the heavens opened, and they saw Jesus coming down, giving light exceedingly, and there was no measure to the light in which he was.

Then Jesus, the compassionate, said to them: "Rejoice and be glad from this hour because I have been to the places from whence I came forth. From today onwards now I speak with you *openly* from the beginning of the truth until its completion. And I will speak with you face to face, without *parable*. I will not conceal from you, from this hour onwards, anything of the things of the height and of the place of the truth."

This same concept of the deferment of the gnostic teaching of the resurrected Christ is attested as 550 days in *The Apocryphon of James* itself (NH I:2, 19–20). There may have even been a reference to eighteen months, if one may take its reference to eighteen *days* as a textual corruption. Here the related concept of decoding the parabolic level is associated with the tradition of Jesus' parables in the normal sense of the term, in what seems to be a reference to a collection of such parables (NH I:7,35–8,11):

"Since I have already been glorified in this fashion, why do you hold me back in my eagerness to go? For after the end you have compelled me to stay with you another *eighteen days* for the sake of the *parables*. It was enough for some to listen to the teaching and understand 'The Shepherds' and 'The Seed' and 'The Building' and 'The Lamps of the Virgins' and 'The Wage of the Workmen' and 'The Didrachmae' and 'The Woman.' Become earnest about the word!"

To be sure, Gnostics could when need be take the other alternative, in claiming that Jesus even prior to Easter had taught gnostic truth, if one only had the understanding to comprehend it. For one of the things the Nag Hammadi texts are teaching us about Gnosticism is that it did not consist of the pure but largely undocumented construct that scholarship had postulated, but rather that it evolved with the changing times and thus could come to expression within Christianity not only in its own pro-Gnostic categories, and not only as an interpretation of the earliest Christian position, but also as an adaptation of later pro-orthodox positions, in this case secondary to the orthodox trajectory identifying sayings of Jesus pointedly with the period prior to Easter as they are found in the canonical gospels (see below). Thus at the luminous appearance at the opening of *The Letter of Peter to Philip* (NH VIII, 135:3–8): "Then a voice came to them out of the light, saying, 'It is yourselves who are witnesses that *I spoke all these things to you*. But because of your unbelief I shall speak again.'" This approach of claiming the pre-Easter sayings for Gnosticism is used in the gnostic *Apocalypse of Peter*, a text that in various ways attacks orthodoxy, in order with this technique also to claim Peter for Gnosticism (NH VII, 72:9–26):

And he said to me, "Peter, *I have told you many times* that they are blind ones who have no guide. If you want to know their blindness, put your hands upon (your) eyes—your robe—and say what you see."

But when I had done it, I did not see anything. I said, "No one sees (this way)."

> Again he told me, "Do it again."
> And there came in me fear with joy, for I saw a new light greater than the light of day. Then it came down upon the Savior.

This secondary gnosticizing of the canonical tradition on the part of Valentinians is criticized by Irenaeus (1.1.6): "And it is not only from the writings of the evangelists and the apostles that they endeavour to derive proofs for their opinions by means of perverse interpretations and deceitful expositions; they deal in the same way with the law and the prophets, which contain many *parables* and allegories that can frequently be drawn into various senses, according to the kind of exegesis to which they are subjected."

The usual gnostic way of laying claim to the sayings of Jesus, by providing a higher spiritual interpretation at Easter, did not even find the sayings collecton really suitable to its purposes. Rather Gnosticism found it most practical to modulate from the sayings collection to the dialogue, especially the question-and-answer version. Apart from the general proclivity for brief segments of dialogue to occur in sayings collections when needed to make a saying intelligible, the shift from the sayings collection to the dialogue may have been motivated by the greater suitablity of the dialogue for the two-level interpretation constitutive of the Gnostic method. This conjecture would seem to be suggested by a survey of the use of the two-level interpretation at the opening of sayings collections.

The collection of Jesus' sayings inserted at the opening of the *Didache* begins with the format of text plus interpretation (*Did* 1:2–3):

> The Way of Life is this: "First, thou shalt love the God who made thee, secondly, thy neighbor as thyself; and whatsoever thou wouldst not have done to thyself, do not thou do another."
> Now, the *teaching* [*didachē*] of these words is this: "Bless those that curse you, . . ."

Thus the collection is presented as the "teaching" implicit in the summary of the law as love and in the (negative) Golden Rule. But much of the collection is only in a very general way such an explication, nor are the individual sayings in the "teaching" themselves subjected to such a secondary interpretation. The two-level format with which the collection is introduced is not carried through consistently and thus seems largely extraneous to the collection as such.

The Marcan apocalypse is also a sayings collection. It has at its opening a similar text-plus-interpretation format (Mark 13:1–5):

> And as he came out of the temple, one of his disciples said to him, "Look, Teacher, what wonderful stones and what wonderful buildings!"
> And Jesus said to him, "Do you see these great buildings? There will not be left here one stone upon another, that will not be thrown down."
> And as he sat on the Mount of Olives opposite the temple, Peter and James and John and Andrew asked him *privately*, "Tell us, when will this be, and what will be the sign when these things are all to be accomplished?"
> And Jesus began to say to them, . . .

Yet here too the initial warnings against thinking the time has come (vss 5–8) are followed by exhortation (vss 9–13) that does not directly interpret the cryptic saying. Though a discussion of signs follows (vs 14ff), other apocalyptic material is freely added (through vs 37), so that the apocalyptic discourse tends to lose sight of its point of departure. Nor are the specific sayings in the body of the apocalypse themselves accompanied by interpretations. Thus the text-plus-interpretation format with which the Marcan apocalypse opens does not seem to be constitutive of the sayings collection itself.

The Gospel of Thomas may also have a similar opening. Saying 1 has been adapted from the tradition (see John 8:52) to provide a hermeneutical introduction to the collection calling for a two-level approach: "Whoever *finds* the interpretation [*hermēneia*] of these sayings will not experience death." Saying 2 is not just what happened to come next by way of independent saying, loosely associated by a catch-word connection ("find"), but seems to have been intentionally chosen as an interpretation of the first saying's offer of escape from death. For it provides a step-by-step *ordo salutis* of the stages between the initial seeking and finding and the ultimate salvation: "Let him who *seeks* continue seeking until he *finds*. When he finds, he will become *troubled*. When he becomes troubled, he will be *astonished*, and he will *rule* over the All." Yet such a text-plus-interpretation relationship, even if present at the opening, does not pervade the collection as such, which moves on without any discernible overall organization other than a loose catch-word kind of association and occasional smaller clusters of sayings that may have circulated together prior to *The Gospel of Thomas*. Some sayings are in a rather primitive form, needing interpretation, others are presented in highly interpreted form, but the text-plus-interpretation format itself does not recur.

The collection of parables used by Mark also presents the two-level format at its opening (the Parable of the Sower), where the text (vss 3–8) and the interpretation (vss 14–20) stand side by side, connected by a herme-neutical comment similar to that in Mark 13:3 (Mark 4:10): "And when he was *alone*, those who were about him . . . asked him concerning the parable." Rather than being referred to as a *didachē* (*Did* 1:3) or a *hermēneia* (*The Gospel of Thomas*, Saying 1), the hermeneutical procedure in this instance would be called by a third synonym, *epilysis*, a "resolution" or "explanation." This term occurs in its substantive form frequently in the *Similitudes* of *The Shepherd of Hermas*, though in the pre-Marcan collection only in its verbal form and then only at the conclusion (Mark 4:33, 34b): "With many such parables he spoke the word to them, as they were able to hear it; . . . but privately to his own disciples he *explained* everything." Yet in spite of the conclusion thus claiming the text-plus-interpretation format, that format is limited to the first of the three parables, and so would not seem to be constitutive of the collection as such.

It may be no coincidence that this format occurs at the beginnings of such collections. This would tend to cast upon the whole collection the aura of a higher meaning latent in the text. But the *genre* of sayings collection as such is not particularly suited to implementing that implication, as these instances tend to illustrate. Nor do all sayings collections begin with that format—there is no evidence of it at the beginning of Q, and it is not characteristic of Jewish wisdom literature. The text-plus-interpretation format seems rather to be at home in the interpretation of the individual saying.

This may be illustrated by the striking parallel between the presentation of the Parable of the Sower with its interpretation and the presentation about ceremonial impurity in Mark 7:[9]

Mark 4		Mark 7	
3	"Listen!"	14	"Hear me, all of you, and understand:"
3–8	(The Parable of the Sower)	15	"There is nothing outside a man which by going into him can defile him; but the things which come out of a man are what defile him."
9	"He who has ears to hear, let him hear."	16	["If any man has ears to hear, let him hear" (variant reading relegated to a footnote)]
10	"And when he was *alone*, those who were about him . . . asked him concerning the parable."	17	And when he had entered the *house*, and left the people, his disciples asked him about the parable.
13	And he said to them, "Do you not understand this parable? How then will you understand all the parables?"	18	And he said to them "Then are you also without understanding? Do you not see that . . ."
14–20	(The interpretation)	18b–23	(The interpretation)

A somewhat less detailed instance of such a text-plus-interpretation format also occurs in Mark 10, where Jesus' response to the question concerning divorce (vss 5–9) and the appended interpretation (vss 11–12) are connected by a statement including the secrecy motif familiar from Mark 4:10; 7:17; 13:3 (Mark 10:10): "And in the *house* the disciples asked him again about this matter."

This text-plus-interpretation format is comparable to the Pesher method of Qumran, where a text of scripture is quoted and then an interpretation is appended with the introductory formula "its interpretation (*pesher*) is about . . . ," from which this kind of exegesis received its name. But such a Pesher can continue down to the end of a text, in that a verse and its interpretation are followed by the next verse and its interpretation, etc. Or in the case of longer quotations each subdivision can be recalled to introduce its specific interpretation, as in the case of the interpretation of the Parable of the Sower, or of the answers to the battery of questions posed by the apostles in *The Letter of Peter to Philip* (NH VIII, 134:18–137:13). Although a saying-by-saying

---

[9] Willi Marxsen, "Redaktionsgeschichtliche Erklärung der sogenannten Parabeltheorie des Markus," *ZThK* 52 (1955) 255–71.

commentary on a sayings collection is conceivable (and suggested by the title of Papias's five-volume *Exegesis of the Lord's Sayings*), the Gnostics did not seem ready to give up the pretense of recording an oral communication in favor of the commentary proper. They hence moved to the *genre* of dialogues of the resurrected Christ with his disciples, which thus became the distinctive gnostic *genre* of gospel. To be sure these dialogues are no longer genuine dialogues, where the discussion partners share a common innate *logos* or rationality, but rather are in the question-and-answer format of the *erotapokrisis*, where the authority figure is interrogated by the seeker.[10] Here the resurrected Christ responds to inquiries by the apostles, who either inquire as to the true meaning of the preceding saying, or pose a question at times itself rooted in a saying. This format is ideally suited to dissolving the rigidity of the given tradition and providing ample opportunity for creative innovation.

The substantive outcome of this third trajectory from Easter to Valentinus, from the sayings collection to the dialogue of the resurrected Christ with his disciples, is summarized by Polycarp (*Phil* 7.1): "Whosoever perverts the oracles [*logia*] of the Lord for his own lusts, and says that there is neither resurrection nor judgment,—this man is the first-born of Satan." Here is precisely the heresy of the second trajectory from Easter to Valentinus, denying the future resurrection presumably because it has taken place spiritually in the ecstasy of baptism, that is associated with the unorthodox trajectory of Jesus' sayings.

Now the same pair of technical terms, derived from scriptural exegesis and used by Gnosticism for its invidious distinction between the gnostic higher meaning imparted by the resurrected Christ and the lower meaning of the usual sayings tradition, recurs in the canonical Gospel of John (16:25, 29) with the minor variation that for *parabolē* the Gospel of John uses *paroimia*, a synonym, as is evident from the fact that it is used at John 10:6 in the normal meaning of parable: "'I have said this to you *in figures*; the hour is coming when I shall no longer speak to you *in figures* but tell you *plainly* of the Father.' His disciples said, 'Ah, now you are speaking *plainly*, not *in* any *figure*!'" Although this takes place at the climax of John (16:32: "The hour is coming, indeed it has come.'"), it is not quite at Easter; rather what would be expected to be located at Easter is pushed back into the parting discourses prior to the crucifixion, leaving for the Johannine resurrection appearances not much more to be said than *Shalom*.

---

[10] Kurt Rudolph, "Der gnostische 'Dialog' als literarische Genus," in Peter Nagel, ed., *Probleme der koptischen Literatur* (Wissenschaftliche Beiträge der Martin-Luther Universität Halle-Wittenberg 1968/1 [K2]; Halle [Salle] 1968) 85–107; Pheme Perkins, *The Gnostic Dialogue: The Early Church and the Crisis of Gnosticism* (Theological Inquiries: Studies in Contemporary Biblical and Theological Problems; New York/Ramsey/Toronto: Paulist Press, 1980); Stephen Emmel, "Post-Resurrection Dialogues Between Jesus Christ and His Disciples or Apostles as a Literary Genre" (1980, unpublished).

In Mark this turning point from coded to uncoded sayings is pushed still further back. Mark had appended to the collection of parables he had incorporated in chapter 4 the pointed comment (4:34): "He did not speak to them without a *parable*." But then this coded message is presented in uncoded form after Peter's confession at Caesarea Philippi in Mark 8, when Jesus begins to talk like a Christian. The first prediction of the passion is what the quest of the historical Jesus took uncritically to be a turning point in the life of Jesus rather than in the Marcan composition. Though Rudolf Otto also still attributed the shift to Jesus, he did at least recognize it as the first time Mark's frequent allusions to Jesus teaching are actually accompanied by the explicit teaching. Julius Wellhausen first recognized it as a basic shift from the time of Jesus to the time of Mark.[11] It is at this crucial juncture that Mark inserts the pointed remark (8:32): "And he said this *plainly*." Thus both Mark and John seem aware of the pair of contrasting terms, and both agree in placing the shift from one level to the other before rather than after Easter.

William Wrede overlooked this Marcan use of the pair of technical terms, understandable enough given the fact that in Mark the pair is not side by side, but widely separated. As a matter of fact the source material in which they occur side by side and thus emerge clearly as such a pair of contrasting technical terms was not yet available to Wrede. As a result Wrede in effect assimilated Mark to the view that the shift in levels took place at Easter, rather than recognizing Mark—and the canonical Gospel *genre*—to be a variant upon, indeed a corrective of, precisely that view. For the Easter timing Wrede appealed to Mark 9:9, where the resurrection is given as the time when the transfiguration is to be told. But this is more likely due to the association specifically of the transfiguration with Easter than to a general Marcan turning point at Easter. Wrede failed to recognize that Mark has, apparently intentionally, shifted that turning point back into the middle of his Gospel.

This may indeed be the key to the perennial problem of the gospel *genre*. The fact that Mark and John transfer the shift to the higher level of meaning back prior to the crucifixion may be their most explicit rationale for playing down didactic revelations at Easter and filling almost their whole books with the period prior to Easter, the period when Jesus was teaching in his physical body on earth. Luke would in his way carry this to its logical outcome in defining the qualifications of an apostle so as to include not just, à la Paul, the resurrection, but the whole period since John the Baptist (thus reaching the position made standard in the English language tradition through the idiom "public ministry" (Acts 1:21-22): "So one of the men who have accompanied us during all the time that the Lord Jesus went in and out among us, beginning

---

[11] Rudolf Otto, *The Kingdom of God and the Son of Man* (London: Lutterworth, reprint of new and revised edition, 1951) 247. Julius Wellhausen, *Einleitung in die drei ersten Evangelien* (2d ed.; Berlin: Georg Reimer, 1911) 72.

from the baptism of John until the day when he was taken from us—one of these men must become with us a witness to his resurrection."

The gospels of Matthew and Luke, by obscuring the Marcan turning point at Caesarea Philippi (they omit Mark 8:32) and by imbedding Q throughout Mark, have carried to its ultimate orthodox outcome this trend, in that the authoritative Christian sayings of Jesus are unmistakably fleshed out in the whole body of the Marcan narrative framework from the time of John the Baptist on. Rather than Easter marking a decisive shift in the truth value, authority, and quasi-canonicity of Jesus' sayings, the Evangelists' logical outcome is brought to expression in Luke 24:44: "These are my words which I spoke to you, while I was still with you." The resurrected Christ only repeats what Jesus had said prior to Easter. Or, put conversely, Jesus had always talked like a Christian.

The trajectory from Easter to the Apostles' Creed reached the somewhat paradoxical outcome in a creed omitting entirely Jesus' "public ministry" and the whole sayings tradition—or at least so it seems to us. To them it may have seemed quite the reverse: The Roman baptismal confession of the early second century was the faith of the apostles, that is to say, the whole orthodox creed was taught them by Jesus.

If the two-level interpretation of the sayings of Jesus on the trajectory from Easter to Valentinus meant exploiting the original orientation of the shift in levels to Easter as a rationale for extrapolating from the tradition new interpretations, indeed new sayings, and in the process modulated from the sayings collection, itself poorly suited to two-level exegesis, into the dialogue *genre* whose question-and-answer format invited the engendering of higher interpretations, then conversely the trajectory from Easter to the Apostles' Creed claimed both levels of meaning increasingly for Jesus prior to Easter, creating in the process the canonical gospel *genre* as a replacement for the all too ambivalent Q.

For Jesus to rise in disembodied radiance, for the initiate to reenact this kind of resurrection in ecstasy, and for this religiosity to mystify the sayings of Jesus by means of hermeneutically loaded dialogues of the resurrected Christ with his gnostic disciples is as consistent a position as is the orthodox insistence upon the physical bodiliness of the resurrected Christ, the futurity of the believer's resurrection back into the same physical body, and the incarnation of Jesus' sayings within the pre-Easter biography of Jesus in the canonical Gospels. Neither is the original Christian position; both are serious efforts to interpret it. Neither can be literally espoused by serious critical thinkers of today; both should be hearkened to as worthy segments of the heritage of transmission and interpretation through which Jesus is mediated to the world today.

8

THE USE OF EARLY CHRISTIAN LITERATURE
AS EVIDENCE
FOR INNER DIVERSITY AND CONFLICT

Frederik Wisse

At the present time, Frederik Wisse is Associate Professor of New Testament at McGill University in Montreal. Born in the Netherlands, Dr. Wisse received his theological education in the United States and eventually was awarded a Ph.D. in Religion from Claremont Graduate School. He has done post-graduate work at Tübingen and Münster, Germany.

Dr. Wisse's research interests and publications are in the areas of Textual Criticism, Nag Hammadi Studies, Coptology, and the History of Early Christianity. He is co-editor of the Nag Hammadi Studies monograph series.

Preface

The historian of early Christianity faces serious methodological difficulties in the attempt to reconstruct the inner diversity and conflicts within the church before 200 C.E. The few surviving historical accounts of the Christian movement during this period offer only partial and often questionable information, as well as a theologically biased picture of the earlier conflict situations which they include. Thus the historian must resort to other early Christian writings in order to reconstruct the actual situation. It is difficult enough to evaluate the historical information which can be gleaned from these diverse writings even if the larger historical framework were clear. In the current state of research, however, even the framework itself must be inferred from writings which are ill-suited for this purpose.

Major steps towards the reconstruction of a satisfactory historical framework were taken during the last 150 years, particularly by F. C. Baur and W. Bauer. Nonetheless, serious difficulties remain in placing many of the early texts in this framework; this is true for some canonical

177

and early patristic writings as well as for gnostic and apocryphal texts. The present essay argues that the nature of the conflict between orthodoxy and heresy during the third and fourth centuries C.E. mistakenly was assumed to apply also to the earlier period. This led to the false assumption that early Christian texts reflected the doctrinal diversity of competing factions or communities. This assumption is particularly inappropriate for gnostic texts, but it also does not apply to most other early Christian writings. In the heterodox situation which characterizes primitive Christianity, authors were not confined by community standards of orthodoxy. Thus conflicts usually arose over issues of practice and ecclesiastical authority. This recognition has profound implications for the historical analysis of early Christian and gnostic texts.

I. F. C. Baur's Categories
of Early Christian Literature

Beginning with F. C. Baur, the central importance of locating and defining individual writings in terms of diverse or competing branches of the early church has been recognized in the critical study of early Christian literature. Baur took his starting point from such occasional, polemical writings as Paul's Corinthian correspondence and letter to the Galatians, which, he thought, gave proof of a conflict between competing Christian ideologies represented by Paul, on the one hand, and Judaizing Christians on the other.[1] With this basic division in primitive Christianity established on firm exegetical grounds, it became necessary to explain why the book of Acts presents a much more harmonious picture of the same period. Baur answered this by means of *Tendenzkritik*, "tendency criticism." He argued that the author of Acts could not admit to a state of disunity and conflict in apostolic times and thus made the conflict appear relatively minor, local, and temporary.

Baur realized that there was a third category of early Christian literature which needed to be explained in terms of the two factions in the church. In addition to polemical writings like Galatians and histories like Acts, there are a significant number of early Christian writings which are not overtly polemical and thus cannot be assigned readily to either the Pauline or Petrine parties. These books he assigned to an irenic or mediating faction. He claimed that from the Jewish Christian side the letter of James shows this mediating spirit, while Hebrews and 1

---

[1] For the following summary of Baur's position see the excerpts from Baur's writings and the bibliography in Kümmel, 127–40.

Peter tried to mediate from the Pauline side. He located the Gospel of John a step beyond the fusion of the two factions into the early Catholic church.

We are indebted to F. C. Baur for a clear understanding of the task and problematics of the history of early Christianity. The standard had been set: to explain an early Christian text historically is to locate it in terms of the different movements and controversies which characterized the early church. His own reconstruction of this period remains one of the high points of historical analysis.

For obvious reasons, the polemical writings and passages have a primary claim to our attention for they present direct evidence of diversity and conflict. They set the stage; all other literary evidence must be defined with reference to them. Nonetheless, polemical writings pose a special set of difficulties for the historian. Polemics are often highly personal and limited in scope. The position defended or attacked need not involve more than one person; one cannot, without further ado, assume that it characterized a larger group or faction. Baur was well aware that Paul's polemics against the Judaizers were, to a large extent, a self-defense. His letters appear to be as much the cause of a division between Jewish and Gentile Christianity as the result thereof. Had they been written by a lesser figure, and had they remained without positive response among Gentile Christian readers, they would have become an idiosyncratic phenomenon on the fringes of primitive Christianity.

We cannot assume that the relationship between the few surviving pieces of early Christian polemical literature and the main instances of conflict and factions in the church was a simple and direct one. In most cases we lack the corroborating evidence to determine whether the conflict reflected in our literature was widespread or local, major or incidental, lasting or of short duration. The role that the writing in question played in the conflict is often obscure and open to various interpretations. The reconstruction of the larger picture of diversity and conflict from such writings is a highly speculative, if not an impossible, undertaking.

Particularly for those canonical and other early Christian writings which soon found wide acceptance and use, it is important to distinguish between the historical situation which they *reflect* and the historical situation they *created*. For the former we need clear internal or supportive external evidence to conclude that the position defended or attacked is shared by a larger group or community. Religious books are generally not written to state what *is* but what the author thinks *should* be. The historian who ignores this runs the danger of creating parties or religious communities which never existed or which did not yet exist when the book was written. Even if the polemicist refers to all those who support his position, one should evaluate such claims critically. The tendency is to portray one's own position as that of the majority and as being in keeping with the apostolic tradition, while that of the opponent is by definition aberrant and isolated.

This touches on the second problem the historian must face in evaluating polemical literature. One cannot expect that the position of the other side has been represented fairly and completely in the heat of the controversy. What is claimed about the opponents may well have been quoted out of context, misconstrued, wrongly inferred or slanderous. This well-known drawback of polemics is particularly unfortunate if, as is often the case, our knowledge of certain movements in early Christianity is limited to refutation by opponents. As a consequence our knowledge of the refuted individuals or groups may be so limited and distorted that the historian has difficulties identifying correctly surviving or newly found literature stemming from the refuted party. One is tempted to assign such writings to a previously unknown group. As a result, the ancient misrepresentation will have been compounded through the creation by a modern interpreter of a ficticious party in early Christianity.

The second category of ancient Christian literature for which the historian must account is comprised of the ancient historical accoun's. As Baur correctly recognized, these accounts are hostile witnesses to diversity and conflict within primitive Christianity, and their vision has been distorted by what the author thinks should have been. It is very modern to look at diversity as something positive, to make the necessity of change into a virtue and to stress the salutary effects of conflict. In contrast, ancient Christian historians from the author of Acts to Eusebius tended to explain diversity in terms of truth and falsehood: change was seen as falsification and conflict as instigated by demonic forces. Insofar as they were aware of diversity in the primitive church they would try to ignore it, make it look innocuous, or exploit it for their own partisan purposes. This makes such histories of dubious value for modern historians. Our knowledge of the first three centuries of the church, however, is so limited and haphazard that we cannot do without these histories. Nevertheless, this predicament is not as bad as it sounds, for if the special theological bias of these histories is taken into account, they prove to be invaluable witnesses for diversity and conflict in spite of themselves.

The third, and by far the largest, group of early Christian texts which the historian must place in the historical framework of early Christian literature are those which are not overtly involved in inner Christian polemics. This large and diverse group reflects a great variety of beliefs and practices. For this category F. C. Baur's evaluation has not proven satisfactory. He wrongly assumed that all early Christian literature was somehow related to the main conflict he perceived. Though we cannot preclude the possibility that some early Christian books intended to mediate between competing factions, such a function is far from obvious for the New Testament books he mentions. As with polemical writings, mediating literature can only be identified as such—and could only have been effective as such—if it identified itself as such. If a writing lacks the expected features and references germane to its polemical or mediating purpose, then the historian must try to explain it in some other way. The real purpose of such literature may be catechetical, homiletical, exegetical, apologetic, speculative or propagandizing rather than an attempt to mediate between opposing views.

To account historically for this group of writings is far more difficult than is generally realized. Some of them may fit comfortably into one of the factions identified on the basis of polemical and historical texts, but many do not. This is particularly true for the earliest among them. It is far from clear what the relationship of such writings was to the different theological, ethical, ritual and organizational positions current in Christian churches at the time of their writing. As in the case of polemical literature, one may not assume that the views advocated in these writings reflect the beliefs and practices of a distinct group. There are, of course, documents commissioned by a larger group which represent community views. These, however, are relatively rare and the reader is normally informed of the special background of the document. If these clues are absent from the texts the burden rests upon the historian to give sufficient reasons as to why the text in question ought to be taken as representative of a larger group or faction. In practice this means that one must show compelling reasons why the author reflects in the writing the beliefs and practices of a wider community. As we shall see, the reflection of the faith and practice of a wider community presupposes a *Sitz im Leben* "life situation" of an established "orthodoxy." If no such controlled "orthodox" environment can be assumed for a text—and this is more the rule than the exception in early Christianity—then it becomes very questionable to attribute the special features of the text to a certain, otherwise unknown, branch of early Christianity.[2]

---

[2] I have argued this in greater detail in "Prolegomena," 138–45.

II. W. Bauer's Use of Early Christian Literature

Even though F. C. Baur's reconstruction of the history of early Christianity has made the traditional view untenable, it still took more than a
century before W. Bauer gave it the *coup de grâce* in his *Rechtgläubigkeit und Ketzerei im ältesten Christentum*.[3] He proved that there is no
historical basis for the traditional claim that orthodoxy preceded heresy
logically and chronologically. The pure beginnings of the church were
not a historical fact, but a theological concept imposed on the facts by
the author of Acts, Hegesippus, and Eusebius. What the church fathers
called heresy was not necessarily a deviation from the earliest form of
Christianity. In stating this W. Bauer clarified what F. C. Baur and others
had already said, or implied.

The new contribution W. Bauer made was his use of early Christian
literature to prove that second-century orthodoxy was not the majority
view but was a view largely limited to the churches in Rome, Corinth,
Antioch, and Western Asia Minor. He argued ingeniously that elsewhere various forms of "heresy" held sway and that they were even able
to threaten the outposts of orthodoxy outside of Rome. It is not my
purpose here to question Bauer's conclusions about the various geographical areas in which the church was located. Rather, we must see
how he uses early Christian literature as evidence for inner diversity
and conflict.

Little needs to be said about Bauer's uses of polemical literature. It
was not his intention to reinterpret the literary evidence for ancient
Christian heresies nor to give a comprehensive picture of the diversity in
belief and practice during the second century. By limiting himself
largely to second-century heresies for which there is multiple attestation, such as Montanism, Marcionism, and Gnosticism, he was able to
escape the difficulties and pitfalls which early Christian polemical
literature presents to the historian.

In contrast, a reexamination of ancient Christian historical accounts is
central to Bauer's thesis. Much of his book, and especially ch. 8, is
preoccupied with questioning the chief "hostile" witness for the second
and third centuries, Eusebius' *Ecclesiastical History*, and the earlier
historical sources which it incorporates. Both Eusebius and Bauer
appeal to second-century Christian literature in order to support their
understanding of the relationship between orthodoxy and heresy, but
they come to opposite conclusions. Eusebius refers to a significant

---

[3] Bauer, *Rechtgläubigkeit*. References are to the English translation of the second
German edition of 1964: Bauer, *Orthodoxy*.

number of orthodox authors and titles from the period prior to 200 C.E.[4] It is clear from the titles that some of these books were anti-heretical but for others this is not so certain. Eusebius claims repeatedly that these orthodox writings and many others like them "are still preserved to this day by a great many brethren."[5] In other words, Eusebius gives the impression that from early days on there was a large and widely dispersed body of orthodox literature which defended the truth and refuted heresy. By comparison, the heretics of the same period stood isolated and condemned.

Bauer quite rightly questions the evidence Eusebius presents.[6] It appears Eusebius has grossly inflated the list of orthodox authors and books by repeatedly referring to "very many others" of whom he cannot recount the names.[7] His claim that these works "have reached us" and can still be examined cannot be taken seriously. Though he was associated in Caesarea with what was likely one of the most extensive Christian libraries of that time, he shows no knowledge of the contents of most of the writings to which he refers. Bauer has good reasons to suspect that they did not survive. Eusebius assumed that many more orthodox books survived. But if he had evidence for this why did he not present it?

The question remains why most of the orthodox writings of the second century did not survive until the first half of the fourth century when Eusebius wrote his *Ecclesiastical History*. Harnack suggests that these "writings were no longer suited to the later dogmatic taste."[8] Bauer proposes another reason. He believes that the orthodox writers rather than the heretics stood isolated, and that their writings were suppressed by the "heretical" majority well before the "dogmatic taste" changed.[9] Thus Eusebius' evidence is turned against him and is used to support the opposite of what he wanted to prove.

It is noteworthy that Bauer does not seriously question Eusebius' claim that the second-century writings he lists were indeed orthodox, even though Eusebius most likely knew the content of only a few of them. He shares with Eusebius the belief that second-century Christian literature was either doctrinally orthodox or heretical; there is no third option. Bauer does not challenge Eusebius' assumption that second-century authors who wrote against the heretics must have been doctrinally orthodox in their other writings. Both assume that all Christian literature

---

[4] *Eccl. Hist.* 4.8 and 21-28.
[5] *Eccl. Hist.* 4.25.
[6] Bauer, *Orthodoxy*, 149-59.
[7] *Eccl. Hist.* 5.27.
[8] *Altchristlichen Literatur*, 1/1.248.
[9] Bauer, *Orthodoxy*, 166.

of that period was in some way part of an ideological struggle between competing "orthodoxies."

A second piece of evidence which Bauer takes from the *Ecclesiastical History* and turns against its author is the curious scarcity of anti-orthodox polemics in the heretical literature.[10] Though it would appear that second-century heretical authors were far more prolific than their orthodox counterparts, they appear uninterested in refuting the orthodox position. The Nag Hammadi texts tend to confirm this impression.[11] In terms of Eusebius' understanding of the situation in early Christianity, this lack of anti-orthodox polemic would be due to the numerical and theological superiority of the orthodox, who isolated the heretics and put them on the defensive.

For Bauer the evidence points in the opposite direction. He argues that the absence of anti-orthodox polemics was due to the fact that the heretics were dominant and secure in large geographical areas during the second century.[12] There was no need for them to refute orthodox teaching. In contrast, the orthodox churches were hard-pressed, and were forced to attack the heretics wherever and whenever they could. According to Bauer, behind the anti-heretical struggle stood the church of Rome with its aggressive, imperialistic policies.[13]

III. The *ad hominem* Nature of Early Christian Polemics

There is another factor which needs to be taken into account in order to evaluate properly the evidence which early Christian literature gives of inner diversity and conflict. The focus of Christian polemics in this period is basically *ad hominem*, i.e., directed against persons, rather than *ad doctrinam*, i.e., directed against teaching. Bauer was not unaware of this,[14] but he is mainly interested in proving the numerical superiority of the heretics in most areas. This predominant focus seems strange if the conflict was mainly due to a clash between different doctrinal positions. What is easily forgotten is that at this early period there was no comprehensive and widely accepted rule of faith which could function as a standard for truth and falsehood. Hence polemics were hardly possible at the level of doctrine. As a consequence, heresy at this time was not so much a teaching that was at variance with established doctrine, as it was the teaching—any teaching!—of someone

---

[10] Bauer, *Orthodoxy*, 169f.
[11] The few cases of anti-orthodox polemic are discussed by Koschorke, *Polemik*.
[12] Bauer, *Orthodoxy*, 170.
[13] Bauer, *Orthodoxy*, ch. 6.
[14] Bauer, *Orthodoxy*, ch. 7.

who was either unauthorized by the leadership or who for some reason or other was considered unworthy and unacceptable. The converse also applies: whatever was taught by someone who was approved by the leadership, or by the author in question, was by definition orthodox.[15]

This means that "orthodoxy" must have begun as orthocracy, i.e., the truth claim of a teaching depended on the accepted authority of the person who taught it. Even at the time of the Pastoral Epistles "sound doctrine" does not appear to have had a clear and stable content, but "sound doctrine" was basically the teaching of sound people, such as the apostles of old and the official church leadership of that time. This also explains the many pseudepigraphical writings from this period. It was not just an ancient "sales gimmick" or a way of honoring an admired member of the apostolic circle; rather, it was a necessity. Since there was not yet a standard by which to judge the truth claim of a writing on the basis of its content, soundness came to depend on the reputation of the author. Thus also, conflict and refutation had to focus on the author, though not just of necessity, but more likely because the conflict itself at this early period centered on persons and their functions.

The *ad hominem* polemics which characterized conflict in early Christianity exhibit the following features:[16]

(1) The opponent was associated with villains from the Old Testament (e.g., Cain, the Sodomites, Balaam, Korah, Jezebel), or with reported opponents of the apostles (e.g., Judaizers, Simon Magus). Just as the opponent was guilty by association, so the protagonist claimed trustworthiness by associating himself with the apostolic circle and other acknowledged heroes of the past.

(2) The opponent was pictured as a fulfillment of the prophecies about the eschatological false prophets or antichrists.[17] This meant that he was a tool of Satan.

(3) Immoral practices were often attributed to the opponent. Any sign of virtue must be a pretense for deceiving unsuspecting believers. Though this claim would have been in most cases untrue, it cannot simply be called slander, since it was not considered possible for a false believer to speak the truth and live a genuinely moral life.[18]

(4) The opponent must have gotten his ideas from pagan sources, and as such was not really "of us," Falsehood could not issue from truth or from a true believer.[19]

[15] See my discussion in "Prolegomena," 139–40.
[16] See also my discussion in "Epistle of Jude," 133–43.
[17] E.g., 1 John 2:18f.
[18] See Wisse, "Die Sextus-Sprüche," 55–86.
[19] This is the basic premise on which Hippolytus based his *Refutatio omnium haeresium.*

(5) In case heretical teachings are mentioned, these tended to be the already refuted heresies of the past (e.g., Jewish law) or the denial of generally accepted truths (e.g., 1 John 2:22).

(6) Opponents are said to reject proper authority (Jude 8). For Thebutis, Valentinus, and Marcion it was claimed that they turned to falsehood because their aspirations for high church office were frustrated.[20] There can be little doubt that the recognition of authority played a central role in the conflicts of this period.

In this kind of polemic there is no need to refute the opponent's teaching. It is, therefore, also impossible to reconstruct his teaching on the basis of the polemic. The few beliefs attributed to the opponents were not really descriptive but merely part of the ad hominem attack.[21] This is even true for Irenaeus and later heresiologists who refute their opponents by exposing heretical "teaching." The idea is that to see heretical teaching is to reject it. By listing details from heretical books which most Christians would consider foreign or grotesque, the author and readers of such books have been discredited. The place of these details in the thinking of the author often remains obscure.

Even when actual refutation was attempted, the arguments the heresiologist could muster were far from conclusive. The appeal to revelation and the gift of prophecy was not limited to one side in the conflict. One could try to discredit the prophet but it was not possible to rule out prophecy. Also appeals to Scripture could not easily be falsified, since there were no established standards for interpretation, and allegorization opened up unlimited possibilities for the interpreter. The best argument would seem to be the one based on reason. It is already present in Paul's arguments against the Judaizers in Galatians and the enthusiasts in Corinth, but it is only fully developed in Irenaeus' writings.[22] The truth is characterized by coherence, inner logic, and unity, while falsehood is incoherent, confusing, and contradictory. Irenaeus' description of heretical teaching in Adversus haereses I is designed to show this.

It is only in terms of an appeal to "reason" that we can speak of orthodoxy in the true sense of the word. The rational coherence of ideas provided an internal standard of truth. Only what coheres with traditional dogma is acceptable; what does not cohere with it is heresy. What stood over against this emerging understanding of orthodoxy was not a rival or internally coherent ideology but rather heterodoxy, i.e., an open and eclectic situation allowing for wide ranging theological speculation.

---

[20] Eccl. Hist. 4.22.5; Tertullian, Adversus Valentianos, 4.

[21] I have argued this for Jude, "Epistle of Jude," 133–43.

[22] Esp. in Adversus haereses, II–V.

and tolerating diversity. This heterodoxy was firmly rooted in the charismatic beginnings of gentile Christianity. It presented a major and long-lasting threat to the emerging orthocracy. The established leadership could not tolerate theological speculation outside of its control, and heterodox "teachers" could not tolerate this ecclesiastical control. The appeal to reason presented a way to reject heterodox speculation on the basis that it did not cohere logically with generally accepted tenets of the faith, rather than that it came from an unapproved author. There was now an objective basis to evaluate "new" teaching; if it proved to cohere it was not really new but already implied in apostolic teaching and if it did not cohere it had to be heresy. The appeal to reason went hand in hand with the claim of catholicity. Some of Irenaeus' views may well have been as peculiar and novel as those of Valentinus, but insofar as he could claim that they were derived from traditional and widely accepted dogma they could be called the teaching of true believers everywhere.

IV. Implications for the Reconstruction of Early Christian History

We must now state what the implications of this reconstruction are for the relationship between early Christian literature and the diversity and conflict in the church. W. Bauer was right in arguing that "heresy" appears to precede "orthodoxy" in most areas. He continued to use, however, the traditional terms "orthodoxy" and "heresy" and thus confused the picture. He can be misunderstood to say that the traditional view of primitive Christianity was correct; only the terms must be reversed. Heresy rather than orthodoxy came first and orthodoxy is really a late foreign element which was able to win only because it had as its spokesman the powerful and aggressive church in Rome; yet, the evidence would indicate that not heresy but heterodoxy preceded orthodoxy, and that it continued to be the majority view through most of the second century except where orthocracy had been able to establish itself. Orthodoxy evolved from orthocracy as a result of the conflict with heterodoxy.

The existence of a large number of writings from this period which were not overtly polemical is no longer a problem. Bauer is not far off the mark by implying that they were written in areas where "heresy" was not challenged by "orthodoxy." The situation becomes clearer if we pose a heterodox milieu for them which was conducive to theological innovation and speculation, and in which a diversity of views was tolerated. Some of this heterodox literature found wide acceptance and became part of the New Testament canon and orthodox collections, but most of it was later considered suspect or heretical. This heterodox literature was not written within clear limits of tolerance, nor was there a need for the authors to reflect the beliefs and practices of Christian communities.

It is not really possible to separate heterodox literature into orthodox and heretical texts. Such categories apply if at all, only in retrospect. Thus it is no surprise that not much of this literature survived until the time of Eusebius. Even writings of authors who were later considered orthodox because of their heresiological reputation were unlikely to fit the fourth-century standards for orthodoxy.

If indeed most Christian literature before 200 C.E. was written in a heterodox milieu, this has major consequences for the historian. It means that the beliefs and practices advocated in these writings, insofar as they vary from those reflected in other Christian texts, cannot be attributed to a distinct community or sect. Rather, these writings were more likely idiosyncratic in terms of their environment. The "teaching" they contain was not meant to replace other teaching but to supplement. They did not defend the beliefs of a community but rather tried to develop and explore Christian truth in different directions. In this heterodox milieu there were few limits to such private speculation. There was room for the prophet and the visionary. One heterodox writing would inspire the creation of another.

Christian-gnostic literature offers us the most extreme examples of heterodox literature. The orthodox heresiologists did not understand this. They assumed that the gnostic books contained the teachings of different sects. Since no two writings agreed in their teaching, they pictured the gnostics as hopelessly divided among themselves. With generally only literary evidence available to them, they were not able to see their mistake.[23]

Because gnostic texts were produced as heterodox literature in a syncretistic situation conducive to speculative thought, they were part of a literary rather than a sectarian phenomenon. Similar in origin and function to Orphic, Neo-Pythagorean, and Middle Platonic literature, they presuppose no organized sect in the background, as is becoming increasingly clear.[24] These writings reflect only the visions and speculations of individuals and the literature they used and imitated. One expects to find such individuals among itinerant preachers, sages, magicians, ascetics, visionaries, philosophers, and holy men.

---

[23] See Wisse, "Prolegomena," 140–41.
[24] Cf. Burkert, "Craft versus Sect," 183–89.

V. Conclusion

In conclusion I want to return to the beginning. F. C. Baur discovered in Paul's writings evidence for two opposing factions in the primitive church. It would appear that this conflict arose against the background of heteropraxis, i.e., a situation in which diverse practices were tolerated. Both Gal 2:3 and Acts 15:19 agree that the leaders of the Jerusalem church allowed gentile Christians to be free from the obligations of circumcision and the law which remained valid for Jewish Christians. By implication, Paul must also have agreed to this double standard. By the time of the Antioch incident, however, orthopraxis had gained the upper hand in the Jerusalem church. Paul saw the behavior of Peter, Barnabas, and the other Jews in the church of Antioch as a breach of the earlier agreement. In the letter to the Galatians Paul in turn was no longer willing to tolerate heteropraxis, for he argues now that also the Jewish Christians are free from the law.

How the Jewish Christians were able to integrate the law and faith is unclear. Most likely they did not try to integrate them theologically. The fact that Paul does not refute a coherent Jewish-Christian theology would indicate that there was no Jewish-Christian orthodoxy at this time. The Jewish Christians from their side used *ad hominem* polemic against Paul by challenging his authority as an apostle and by claiming that he incited believers to sin (Rom 3:8). Thus the conflict appears to be between orthopraxis and Paul's idiosyncratic teaching on faith and works.

Paul did not impose a strict orthopraxis on his churches but argued for tolerance and freedom except in the case of immorality. There was no established leadership and the stress on spiritual gifts created a profoundly heterodox situation. Divergent views in the congregation were not treated as heresy, but Paul tried to curb factions by arguing that edification of the community should be the common goal. The situation has changed drastically in the Pastoral Epistles. The need for orthocracy is obvious to the author. The readers are warned against false teachers, most likely itinerant preachers who try to impress women (2 Tim 3:6) and are, among other things, adept in speculative myths. He even associates them with the "heretics" of old, the circumcision party (Titus 1:10), the teachers of the law (1 Tim 1:7), which the great apostle had already refuted. The situation is now dominated by the conflict with gnostic heterodoxy.

Thus for the earliest Christian period (i.e., before the middle of the second century C.E. in Rome and well beyond that elsewhere) it would be a mistake to try to define its remaining literature in terms of competing theological positions or the conflict between orthodoxy and heresy. In the heterodox situation which prevailed at this time there was considerable tolerance to doctrinal diversity, partly of necessity, because on most issues the theological structure needed for refutation was lacking. The relative isolation of Christian communities and the lack of knowledge about sister churches no doubt contributed to this heterodox milieu and apparent tolerance for diversity. This explains the absence of clear polemic in some of the writings from this period. W. Bauer's thesis that it was due to the fact that heresy was dominant and unopposed in most areas would appear to be an anachronistic explanation. Conflict and polemics in this early period had their basis mainly in diversity of practice, both ethical and liturgical, and claims of authority. Attributing false doctrine to one's opponents at this point is usually an *ad hominem* polemical device.

Orthodoxy arose out of the increasing conflict between heterodoxy and orthocracy. The ecclesiastical leadership in such cities as Rome, no longer willing to tolerate heterodox teachers in its midst, attached the teaching function to its own office. The heterodox side was represented mainly by Montanists and various gnostics. In this conflict, the appeals to the rational coherence of ecclesiastical teaching and its assumed catholic and apostolic nature began to play an increasing role. Only at this point can we speak of orthodoxy and heresy. Orthodox writings are those which have been written consciously within the limits of doctrinal tolerance set by the ecclesiastical hierarchy. Earlier heterodox literature becomes orthodox retrospectively if it falls within these limits of tolerance, or heretical if it does not. The disappearance of most early Christian writings by the time of Eusebius, even the non-polemical writings of reputed heresiologists, would be explained if most of these books did not meet the later standards of orthodoxy. If this reconstruction of early Christianity is correct it will set clear limits and guidelines to the use of early Christian literature as evidence for inner diversity and conflict.

7

Why the Church Rejected Gnosticism

GEORGE W. MACRAE

In discussing the history of his interest in the study of Gnosticism, the philosopher, and acknowledged master of Gnostic studies, Hans Jonas has remarked: 'I wanted to take up the question: Why did the Church reject Gnosticism? Apart from the obvious reason that many of its teachings were fantastic and not in agreement with the Gospels, why was *Gnosis as such* from Paul on rejected as a possible option? Why was Pistis chosen instead?'[1] As every student of Gnosticism knows, Jonas began his investigation with a brilliant study of the meaning of *gnōsis* and never really confronted the broader question that first interested him. And, somewhat surprisingly, no one else has systematically taken up this challenging question.

On the contrary, scholarship throughout the twentieth century has preferred to concentrate on what is virtually the opposite of this question, namely, to what extent has Gnosticism influenced the shaping of Christianity itself?[2] Efforts to detect Gnostic influence have concentrated on the gospel of John, the epistle to the Ephesians, certain passages in the Pauline correspondence, the letters of Ignatius, the development of the doctrine of the Trinity, the origin of Christian asceticism, and many other documents and doctrines. It is thus at least possible that Gnosticism, far from being rejected universally by the church, was a formative element in the evolution of Christianity itself.[3] But this is not our question, and we must leave it; yet we cannot leave it totally out of account.

Before attempting to identify some of the reasons why the church rejected Gnosticism – an enterprise which must remain very tentative at least at the outset – we must state several presuppositions and limitations of our inquiry, without taking the time to justify them in detail.

126

(1) We shall assume that Gnosticism is non-Christian in origin, leaving aside the question of a chronologically pre-Christian origin of it, and that it is more or less as old as Christianity. One cannot assume that the venerable controversy about the origins of Gnosticism has been settled, but the weight of evidence from Nag Hammadi has come down solidly on the side of those who argue against the classical Christian heresy theory.[4] In consequence, it will be possible to suggest that New Testament writers, including even Paul, are already in dialogue, not to say competition, with at least 'incipient' Gnosticism.

(2) It is essential to bear in mind that one cannot meaningfully speak of 'Christianity' or 'the church' as a monolithic entity in the early centuries of its existence. Not only the study of the New Testament, but the history of early post-apostolic Christianity abundantly affirms the essential diversity of forms of Christianity. It is now as much a dogma of scholarship as its opposite used to be: orthodoxy is not the presupposition of the early church but the result of a process of growth and development.[5] It is this very situation which poses the intricate challenge to which the McMaster Project is in part addressed and which justifies the efforts of the Project. In consequence of it, one can expect that not all of the early church rejected Gnosticism, but some branches of Christianity were indeed informed by it.

(3) It may be necessary, though difficult, to distinguish between early Christian polemic against Gnosticism and the 'real reasons' why early Christians rejected it. Polemic is in many contexts a conventional exercise, with rhetorical rules to guide it.[6] It was fashionable, for example, to charge an opposing philosophical school with venality, various forms of immorality, and logical absurdity, merely because they were opponents.[7] If they were wrong, their behaviour must have reflected their errors. The consequence of this caution is that one must do more than accept the arguments of the heresiological literature at face value.

(4) Finally, since another contribution to this volume deals with the anti-heretical argument of Irenaeus's *Adversus haereses*,[8] the earliest extant clear and explicit exposition of the church's case against the Gnostics, the present essay will assume some practical limitations. For the most part it will concentrate on arguments against Gnosticism, explicit and more often implicit, prior to Irenaeus, on the grounds that the post-Irenaean heresiological tradition is largely dependent on Irenaeus himself. In fact, we shall concentrate mainly on New Testament evidence.

127

Non-conformist ethical behaviour

One constant element of Christian anti-Gnostic polemic is the charge of libertinism, especially prominent in Irenaeus and Epiphanius.[9] To what extent is this charge based on empirical evidence? Or is it a typical example of conventional polemic? I propose to address these questions at first not by analysing the arguments of the patristic heresiologists, but by returning to the Christianity of Corinth in the time of Paul. The implications for the case made by the Fathers will become apparent.

Whether we should properly speak of Gnosticism already present in the Corinthian community when Paul wrote I Corinthians continues to be disputed.[10] The 'enthusiasm' that is generally agreed to characterize at least one element of the community is in any case well on the way to becoming a form of Gnostic theory and practice. The esteem of the Corinthians for *gnosis* is clearly at the root of the problems which Paul regards as a fundamental challenge to his gospel (I Cor. 8.1). In this light the problem of *porneia* in I Cor. 5, the case of the incestuous member of the community, merits a second look. It is increasingly recognized by interpreters that the text of I Cor. 5.3–5 must be read in its natural order, repressing as much as possible the reservations of modern translators: 'As for me, absent in body but present in spirit, I as one who is present have already judged the *one who has done this thing in the name of the Lord Jesus* . . . '.[11] The incestuous man is best understood as one who flouts the morality that is customary 'even among pagans' on religious grounds based on a Gnostic or quasi-Gnostic scorn for material existence. He believes that he is asserting his true spiritual identity, and thus his fidelity to the Lord Jesus, by showing that he transcends such merely material, bodily concerns as sexual morality. The traditionally alleged Gnostic libertine stance is perfectly illustrated not only in his behaviour, but in the community's proud tolerance of it – which is more properly the object of Paul's indignation. And what Paul objects to is a Gnostic-like disdain for a morality that is ultimately conventional. Perhaps the church's objection to Gnosticism really did lay considerable emphasis on its inability to tolerate such radical non-conformity in ethical behaviour.

Yet we must consider another trend in current scholarly assessment of anti-Gnostic polemics. The evidence that Gnostics did in fact behave in an antinomian manner is virtually confined to the Christian polemical literature. Of the Valentinians Irenaeus

128

says, in the famous passage about the gold in the mud, 'For this reason the most perfect among them freely practise everything that is forbidden'.[12] And of the Carpocratians he reports: 'They live a dissipated life and hold an impious doctrine, and use the name [of the church] as a cloak for their wickedness'.[13] The original Gnostic writings from the Nag Hammadi library, however, have contributed little or nothing to support these allegations of libertinism. To the extent that they deal with ethical practices directly, they uniformly advocate extreme asceticism. As a result, scholars have called into question the patristic charges of antinomian behaviour; if these are merely conventional polemics, then non-conformist ethical behaviour is not a reason for the rejection of Gnosticism but at most a consequence of such a rejection.

Irenaeus bases his assessment of the libertine behaviour of the Carpocratians, however, on a principle of their own which is not unlike the slogan 'all things are lawful for me' of the Corinthians: '. . . they claim to have in their power and to be able to practise anything whatsoever that is ungodly and impious. They say that conduct is good and evil only in the opinion of men.'[14] I have not found this statement as such in the Nag Hammadi writings, but a different type of formulation of the principle is to be found there, and it is quite likely that Irenaeus' observation was indeed an accurate one. *The Gospel of Philip*, for example, contains an important doctrine of the radical relativity of names and categories, including moral categories, which might serve as the justification for an ethic of at least indifference: 'In this world there is good and evil. Its good is not good, and its evil not evil.'[15] I believe a similar implication can be drawn from the identification of the divine voice of the thunder with opposites of every sort of category, including the ethical, in the Nag Hammadi work called *The Thunder: Perfect Mind*. There we find, for example: 'For I am knowledge and ignorance. I am shame and boldness. . . . I, I am sinless, and the root of sin derives from me. I am lust in (outward) appearance, and interior self-control exists within me.'[16] One could hardly expect to find Gnostic documents openly advocating libertinism, but in statements like these we may have examples of Gnostic authors' own formulations of a principle underlying such conduct.

Both Paul and Irenaeus, and of course many others, rejected Gnosticism in part on the grounds that it led to forms of ethical behaviour that were perceived as unacceptable. Whether the

129

Gnostics actually flouted the laws of ethical behaviour to any considerable extent, as the incestuous man of I Corinthians apparently did, or were merely indifferent to ethical behaviour, as some other Corinthians were (e.g. I Cor. 6.12–20), the church saw the danger of libertinism inherent in Gnostic language and speculation.

The God of this world

An almost ubiquitous charge brought against the Gnostics by the ecclesiastical writers is the blasphemy of denigrating the God of creation as an inferior, or an evil, demiurge. They interpret this basic Gnostic doctrine as an attack on monotheism, a repudiation – or at least an unacceptable interpretation – of the Bible, and an affront to reason itself. All of these interpretations, and doubtless more, were reasons why Christians rejected the Gnostics. But we may look again to Paul for a hint of a particular perspective on the anti-dualist argument that underlies a good deal of later Christian polemic as well.

The setting for Paul's argument against a duality of gods is again Corinth, and it may be more than coincidental that it is in such a context that he perceives the danger of dualistic language. In his defence of his ministry in II Corinthians, following upon the celebrated discussion of letter and spirit, Paul speaks of the devil with unusual boldness as 'the god of this world (or age)'. Referring apparently to Jews who reject the gospel and therefore 'are perishing', he says, 'In their case the god of this world has blinded the minds of the unbelievers, to keep them from seeing the light of the gospel of the glory of Christ, who is the likeness of God' (II Cor. 4.4). After a statement that the gospel he preaches concerns Jesus Christ and not himself, Paul apparently sees the danger of his own language when heard by persons inclined toward a Gnostic view of a lower 'god of this world'.[17] In verse 6 he then refutes any such interpretation of his own language by a statement which in form closely parallels verse 4 and in content offers a decisive argument against any Gnostic doctrine of a demiurge: 'For it is the God who said, "Let light shine out of darkness", who has shone in our hearts to give the light of the knowledge of the glory of God in the face of Christ.'[18]

If I am correct in interpreting the passage in this manner, it can be seen to contain a number of allusions which would be significant in the debate with Gnostic dualism: e.g. the light-

130

darkness contrast, the language of *doxa*, 'glory', and *eikōn*, 'image', the mention of *gnōsis*. But the crucial argument against a Gnostic dualist interpretation of Paul's own language about 'the god of this world' is the allusion to Gen. 1.3, 'the God who said, "Let light shine out of darkness"'. Paul is at pains to make the point – incisively, since Gnostic exegesis of Genesis is embarrassed by the creation of light in 1.3 – that the creator God is the God of enlightenment and thus of salvation. The chasm between the Old Testament and the New created by the Gnostic interpretation of Yahweh as the inferior demiurge is as abhorrent to the Christian Paul as it is to Irenaeus and others.[19] Paul's reply is to assert the continuity of salvation history, the identity of the God of creation with the God of salvation.

It is precisely this denial of identity which offends the Christian opponents of Gnosticism. That there should be a lower spiritual being who is inimical to humanity is not itself at issue. In a sense Paul is a 'dualist' of sorts in that he believes in Satan and evil spiritual powers; he can even call Satan 'the god of this world'. But he cannot tolerate a radical rupture of the salvation-historical process which is based on scripture. It is important, it seems to me, to note that the Gnostics, unlike Marcion, did not simply repudiate the scriptures of the old covenant. Instead, they derived much of their mythology from exegesis of the scriptures. And it was not simply a matter of methods of interpretation of the scriptures to which the churchmen objected. Even Paul was capable, in Galatians, for example, of methods of interpretation no less daring than those of the Gnostics. But any interpretation which disrupted the continuity of the history of salvation, that is, which denied that the God of Jesus was the God of creation and covenant and promise, struck at the heart of the Christian message and had to be struck down in turn. That this dichotomy of the divine also lay at the heart of Irenaeus' objections to the Gnostic heretics is well known.[20]

Jesus Christ has come in the flesh

It is commonplace to observe that one of the basic objections to Christian Gnosticism on the part of the ecclesiastical writers is that it is almost invariably docetic in its christology. Underlying the rejection of Gnostic docetism, however, is a good example of a broader issue, that of the influence of changing language on standards of orthodoxy. From first-century Christianity to sec-

131

ond, there occurs a remarkable shift in the connotation and importance of the concept of *sarx*, 'flesh', which culminates in the elaborate Pauline exegesis on the part of Irenaeus in *Adversus haereses*, Book V. Irenaeus is at pains to demonstrate, contrary to the evidence of the text before him, that the resurrection of the dead in Paul is in reality a resurrection of the flesh.[21] The shift in meaning of 'flesh', by no means a univocal term in the New Testament in any case, is already visible in the Johannine litera- ture, where its use may be related to the differing stances toward Gnosticism taken within Johannine Christianity.

Nowhere in the New Testament has the case for Gnostic influence on early Christianity been as strongly made as in the discussion of the Fourth Gospel.[22] This is not the place to review the history of the question, but it may be helpful to point out where the current debate lies. I do not believe that the fourth evangelist was a Gnostic, a former Gnostic, or even an opponent of Gnosticism. I regard it as very likely, however, that he was a somewhat sectarian Christian who was strongly influenced by Gnostic language and rhetoric and by the structures of Gnostic thought. A striking list of parallels to the Prologue of the Fourth Gospel has been observed in the Nag Hammadi work *Trimorphic Protennoia* and has led some interpreters to postulate a Gnostic origin for some of the key elements of the Prologue.[23] In addition, an analysis of the Gnostic revelation discourse form in *The Thun- der* and a number of other Nag Hammadi tractates suggests that the fourth evangelist was influenced, not by a 'revelation dis- course source', as Bultmann and his pupil Heinz Becker postu- lated,[24] but by the style of such Gnostic discourses.[25]

Among the things that kept the evangelist from becoming a Gnostic in the full sense was his emphasis on the incarnation: 'and the Word became flesh' (1.14). But as is well known, the word 'flesh' is not consistent in the Fourth Gospel, and the use of it in 1.14, while not exceptional, does not convey the negative overtones of 3.15 or 6.63, where it contrasts with 'spirit'.[26] In the first epistle of John, however, the term is used in a credal formula in which the confession that Jesus came 'in the flesh' (4.2) distin- guishes believers from docetic heretics. I believe the author of the first epistle, who was distinct from the fourth evangelist, had recognized the danger inherent in the language and thought of the gospel and had experienced some fellow Johannine Christ- ians who became out-and-out Gnostic docetists. He writes, therefore, in part in order to rescue the language of the gospel for

132

more orthodox purposes.[27] In so doing, he witnesses to the evolution in which 'flesh' came to be used as virtually a shibboleth in the argument against Gnostic docetists, leaving far behind the original Johannine, and *a fortiori* Pauline, understandings of the word. Docetism is rejected, not simply as a denial of the humanity of Jesus, but as a denigration of the flesh, which in Christian thought in the second century is increasingly seen as the instrument of salvation itself. The Gnostics, because of their radical dualism of spirit versus matter, are the archenemies of the flesh.

A good example of the importance of the flesh in the argument against the Gnostics may be found in the apocryphal Corinthian correspondence which has survived embedded in the *Acts of Paul* and circulating separately in Papyrus Bodmer X.[28] Not only because it circulated separately in the third century, but because it does not fit the context of the *Acts of Paul* precisely, I believe the correspondence originated apart from the *Acts of Paul* as a piece of anti-Gnostic propaganda. The 'pernicious words' of Simon and Cleobius, about whom the Corinthians complain, involve among other things a denial of the resurrection of the flesh and that the Lord has come in the flesh. The reply of 'Paul' is almost a short treatise on the importance of the flesh, though, to be sure, it also answers the other allegations of the heretics. It emphasizes the incarnation of Jesus, 'that he might come into this world and redeem all flesh through his own flesh, and that he might raise up from the dead us who are fleshly, even as he has shown himself as our example . . . in order that the evil one might be conquered through the same flesh by which he held sway. . . . For by his own body Jesus Christ saved all flesh. . . . As for those who tell you there is no resurrection of the flesh, for them there is no resurrection . . . you also who have been cast upon the body and bones and Spirit of the Lord shall rise up on that day with your flesh whole.'[29]

The question with which we began, namely, Why did the church reject Gnosticism?, has of course not been fully answered in these few pages. I have examined three reasons which I think pervaded the Christian opposition to Gnosticism from Paul, in the third case from the Fourth Gospel, to Irenaeus and have suggested that larger issues are implied in the polemical use of these reasons. Whether or not these are the 'real reasons' or the most important ones, the fact that they recur persistently in early Christian anti-Gnostic polemic warrants the attention paid them.

133

I.16.3). We shall, however, make some general observations on the character of the philosophical arguments found here and in other parts of *AH*.

Throughout his refutation, Irenaeus shows acquaintance with secular learning and especially with the rhetorical arguments and techniques of the Hellenistic schools of the second century.[6] The very order of the arguments in Books II to V betrays such an acquaintance, for it was a common rhetorical technique to hold back the decisive arguments for the later parts of the development and to present the weaker ones first. Irenaeus follows this pattern by presenting first his philosophical arguments against the Gnostics and then by offering the more decisive scriptural arguments.

More precisely, Irenaeus's rhetorical training (which he might have received in Rome) is seen in the fact that he uses almost all methods of argumentation (except the syllogism, as Reynders noted),[7] with a predilection for the dilemma and the question. The principles he uses are simple, almost commonplaces. For example: 'The one who conceives is also the one who makes'; 'cause contains effect'; 'what is prior contains what is posterior'; etc.[8] He excels in the use of irony and the technique *ad hominem*. This also shows a certain talent and training.[9]

Irenaeus's acquaintance with philosophy itself 'is somewhat superficial'.[10] He surely can formulate an argument; but what is properly philosophical in his work seems to be for the most part drawn from doxographical materials, i.e. from essentially eclectic sources.[11] The rest of his thought could be characterized as popular philosophy.[12] This is precisely the area where Irenaeus seems to be most at ease. At least that type of wisdom harmonizes well with the praise of simple faith that is found throughout *AH*. The most typical and frequent arguments of Irenaeus belong to this category of popular philosophy. Some examples might suffice to illustrate this point.

Irenaeus's favourite refrain is: the Gnostics are talking nonsense, folly; their discourse departs from good sense; they 'fall into a fit of frenzy', they propound 'fictitious doctrines'; they are seriously sick and foolish (see I.16.3). Their teaching is absurd and their exegesis, arbitrary (II.24.1–6).

The accusation that Gnostic teachings are borrowed from philosophy (II.14.2–7; see IV.33.3) is itself meant to disqualify them. Plagiarizing the philosophers is not a good recommendation in Christian matters since, for Irenaeus, philosophy is at the

176

source of wrong doctrines. There is only one passage in which Irenaeus commends a philosopher – Plato – but it is only to say that Plato is superior to Marcion (III.25.5). This surely does not amount in Irenaeus's eyes to a praise of philosophy. But Valentinian speculation is not only taken from the philosophers: it is philosophy. Gnosis describes philosophical or psychological processes which it takes for real entities (II.14.6 and 8; II.13.10; II.28.6);[13] making dangerous and excessive use of human analogies, it hypostatizes mental processes. In addition to these accusations a series of denunciations of the 'gnosis falsely so-called' is found. Gnostics contradict the facts or right reason; their teachings are recent, originating from Simon who is not only despicable, but also a *novator* (II.28.8 'recens'); they are therefore less respectable than ancient teachings; they are subtle, without simplicity;[14] Gnostics disagree between themselves and, lacking practical knowledge and virtue, they display only cowardice.[15]

Only a few of these assertions have real philosophical significance. We find many agreements between Irenaeus and Plotinus in the critique of the Gnostics; but nothing is found in Irenaeus that has the philosophical character of the argumentation put forward by Plotinus in *Enn*. II.9 (see Porphyry, *Vit. Plot.* 16). If one persists in calling Irenaeus's arguments at this point philosophical, they should be qualified as popular philosophy or popular wisdom.[16] Alone they do not constitute the overthrow of Gnosis that has been promised. Irenaeus seems to agree that his philosophical arguments are not that decisive. Had he thought differently, the rhetorician Irenaeus would not have presented them right at the outset, thus conceding their relative weakness.

Theological arguments

The more decisive arguments must be theological or scriptural. Here Irenaeus uses all the resources available to him from his predecessors and adds an original contribution.

Among the many theological arguments that Irenaeus mounts against the Gnostics there are a few that are constantly repeated. These can obviously lead us to what Irenaeus thought was at stake in the debate.

Turning against the Gnostics the accusation of ignorance they address to ordinary Christians, Irenaeus accuses them of ignoring God's dispensation, the rule of faith, scripture and tradition. In a word, they ignore the 'hypothesis' of truth, substance of the

177

Christian faith. P. Hefner has pointed out how crucial this concept of 'hypothesis' is to Irenaeus's refutation.[17] It designates the 'organic system or framework which constitutes the shape and meaning of God's revelation'. In a formal sense, it functions as the ultimate norm of truth and encompasses all other norms: it includes God's economy of redemption, is rooted in God, announced by the prophets, taught by the Lord, delivered by the apostles; it is derived from scripture and also serves to expound scripture; it resides in the community of the church and reaches the community through tradition; it is summarized in creedlike statements and can be expounded by reason. The hypothesis of truth is the ultimate authority which guides Irenaeus's criticism and to which all other authorities are subordinated.[18] Concretely applied by Irenaeus to meet the Gnostic assertions, it is in practice equivalent to the 'rule' that there is one God, Creator of the world, Father of our Lord Jesus Christ, and author of the economy (I.10.1).[19]

For this hypothesis of faith, the Gnostics substitute their own hypothesis which they 'dreamt into existence' (I.9.3). Obviously the hypothesis of faith is radically subverted if another God is conceived beyond the Creator. Thus Gnostics distort God's revelation and destroy the faith of the pious. Thereby they replace real salvific acts by their own inventions, fictions, and jugglings (I.15.5), practising a sort of theology-fiction, projecting mental processes into an atemporal framework[20] which develops into an arbitrary speculation about the Pleroma and its aeons and amounts to an utterly indiscrete *theologia gloriae*. In so doing, they not only deceive the simple believers, but also show that they do not care about the apostolic tradition which they do not possess. This leads men to despair about their salvation (IV.praef.4)[21] and ultimately to deny salvation. For the Gnostic view of salvation does not include the flesh; but if the flesh is not saved, nothing of man is saved (II.29.3; V.6-7; V.20.1).

Thus Gnostics freely subtract from and add to the hypothesis of truth.[22] This arbitrariness is not only opposed to Irenaeus's temperament and his positivist emphasis on the clear and real facts of the economy,[23] it is also blasphemy.[24]

With the accusation of 'blasphemy'[25] cast at the Gnostics by Irenaeus we come to the core of his theological objections, for this accusation, in its context, sums up what he thinks about the Valentinians: they render men 'disbelievers in their own salvation, and blasphemous against God the Creator' (IV.praef.4). In

178

addition to being guilty of blasphemy because they destroy the substance of the faith, their very thinking about God is blasphemous (IV.praef.3). This is so because it introduces divisions into God; it splits the divine and breaks its unity (II.28.2 and 8). Moreover Gnostics introduce such divisions throughout the real. They distinguish between God and the Creator, between Christ and Christ, between different 'economies', etc. The division of the divine is the point which upsets Irenaeus most;[26] it is above all expressed in the denigrating of the God of the Old Testament. Irenaeus repeatedly counters the Gnostic devaluation of the Old Testament God by insisting on the unity of God and the Creator and by affirming the truth and reality of the Old Testament God. This 'Ringen um den Status des AT Gottes'[27] is to Irenaeus of utmost importance.

The blasphemous split of the divine introduced by the Gnostics is the starting point for Irenaeus's attack against their dualistic teaching. From that point Irenaeus will investigate the many facets and expressions of Gnostic dualism. Dualism will thus become the target of his attack.

All forms of dualism will be detected by Irenaeus and rejected one by one in an attempt to make the case for unity which is truth and is in the church. First of all, he attacks the 'morcellement du divin' which we may call *theological dualism*: i.e., the split between God and the demiurge, which is the central point of his attack. He also attacks the division between the good God and the just God and the division of the divine in the Pleroma expressed by the doctrine of Aeons. 'Such divisions cannot be ascribed to God' (II.28.4); they suppress the deity (III.25.3). God is one: the identity of God the Creator and God the Father is the central article of Irenaeus's creed and the sum of his argument (see II.31.1, where he summarizes his argument).[28]

From this central article of his creed two further articles are derived: one Christ, one economy. Irenaeus sees the *christological dualism*, separating Christ from Jesus (IV.praef.3; IV.2.4; III.16.2; III.17.4; etc.), the Logos from the Saviour (III.9.3; III.16.8; IV.praef.3; etc.), the Christ above from the Christ below (III.11.1; III.17.4; etc.), as a typical Gnostic affirmation and as a blasphemy as well (IV.praef.3). This he attacks, as well as the *soteriological dualism*, whereby the universality of God's economy and will of salvation is denied.[29] There is only one economy, which is universal, and on the basis of which Christ will recapitulate all things.[30]

179

We may enumerate other forms of dualism to which Irenaeus objects: *scriptural dualism*, which separates the New Testament from the Old Testament and ultimately the God of the Old Testament from the God announced by the Saviour, against which Irenaeus affirms the unity and 'harmony' of the two covenants. *Ecclesiastical dualism*, according to which a distinction is made between simple believers and pneumatics, thus breaking the unity of the church.

> [The spiritual disciple] shall also judge those who give rise to schisms . . . and who for trifling reasons, or any kind of reason which occurs to them, cut in pieces and divide the great and glorious body of Christ, and so far as in them lies, destroy it. . . . For no reformation of so great importance can be effected by them, as will compensate for the mischief arising from their schism (IV.33.7; see IV.26.2).[31]

Social dualism, whereby some are said to be good, others evil, by nature (IV.37.2), which Irenaeus sees as contradicting the equality of all men before God's offer[32] and as threatening the unity of the church and its peace. *Practical dualism*, according to which some recommend, over against the common discipline, either the rigorism attainable only by a few or the libertinism of the so-called superior men. These forms of dualism, detected and attacked by Irenaeus, can be seen as derived from the fundamental theological dualism dividing the divine or as diverse expressions of a *metaphysical dualism* opposing the world above to the world below, spirit to matter.[33]

It may be surprising that the focus of Irenaeus's charge against the Gnostics is their dualistic outlook. It is not my intention to decide whether Irenaeus understood Gnosis from within,[34] faithfully grasped the Gnostic self-understanding,[35] or was fair to their profound concerns.[36] The fact is that in describing the mitigated dualism which is Gnosticism[37] Irenaeus perceived two essential aspects of its dynamic system: first, its emanationist scheme expressed in the doctrine of aeons and, secondly, its dualistic outlook. He describes both aspects, relying on Gnostic sources (I.praef.2).[38] But when he attacks their system, the second aspect comes to the fore almost exclusively. Why is it so? In order to account for this concentration on dualism we shall have to look at Irenaeus's non-theological motives for rejecting Gnostic claims.

180

Socio-political motives

There are a number of incidental remarks found among Irenaeus's arguments which cannot be considered as having philosophical or theological character. These constitute arguments of a third kind. In some passages they are mentioned almost casually; in others, they are only implicit in Irenaeus's refutation. Never are they treated extensively as a theme. But their presence is significant.

Having observed the opposing temperaments of Irenaeus and the Gnostics,[39] we may expect to hear from Irenaeus arguments which are not simply intellectual. And indeed Irenaeus's refutation reflects the suspicion harboured by simple Christians of a theological speculation that seemed to endanger such simple truths as the unity of God. In the confrontation with the Gnostics it is obvious where Irenaeus's sentiments lie. He imagines himself as the spokesman of the masses, strongly anchored in the tradition and in the faith of the average Christian. Thus he reflects and propounds a form of 'popular theology'[40] and is suspicious of those 'learned' theologians, the Gnostics, with their dangerous science and eloquence,[41] who in his eyes are mere philosophers, and bad ones at that. His natural propensity for unity and unanimity is shocked by their undisciplined discourse and behaviour; they endanger the welfare of individuals as well as of the Empire.[42]

This concern for peace and unity had already been expressed in Irenaeus's intervention against rigorist and encratite tendencies that could divide the church; Irenaeus sided with those who favoured tolerance and indulgence for the *lapsi*.[43] He even defended the Montanists[44] and was inclined to show them tolerance. He was ready to praise the Empire for favouring unity and was not interested in attacking the 'pagans'; such an attack lies beyond his scope and could only have contributed to jeopardize the peace of society. In fact he showed himself to be much harder on the Gnostics than on the Jews and was altogether mild on the pagans.[45] Why? Does the proximity of the Gnostics alone account for their passionate rejection?

Before writing against the Gnostics, Irenaeus enjoyed a reputation of peace-maker, tolerant, permissive. (It is significant that 'orthodoxy' generally emerged among those groups that favoured indulgence and opposed rigorism.) But his permissiveness went only so far. Where unity was seen as already broken,

181

where authority was challenged Irenaeus reacted strongly. Montanists might have represented the same threat as the Gnostics; but they were far from Gaul. Irenaeus witnessed Gnostic preaching and perceived it as a divisive element in the Christian communities which endangered the mission of the church. Irenaeus complains indeed that those who corrupt the truth 'affect the preaching of the church' (I.27.4). Concerned with the image of the church, he thinks that they bring dishonour upon it (I.25.3). Celsus had just (*c.* 178 CE) shown that it was possible to take Gnostic extravagancies as typically Christian.[46] The folly of the Gnostics could draw the attention of the civil authorities. 'Men hearing the things which they speak, and imagining that we are all such as they, may turn away their ears from the preaching of the truth; or, again, seeing the things they practise, may speak evil of us all, who have in fact no fellowship with them, either in doctrine or in morals, or in our daily conduct' (I.25.3). Clearly the reputation of the church is at stake.[47] It is imperative to stress that the Christians have nothing to do with these 'magicians' (see II.31.1–3) and instruments of Satan. Likewise, it is essential that Christians dissociate themselves from those radicals who hold 'unauthorized assemblies' (III.3.2) and pour contempt upon the martyrs (III.18.5; IV.26.3; IV.33.9) at a time when the church needs to offer a common front to a society still suspicious and not quite ready to welcome Christians as reliable social partners.[48]

Irenaeus sees that, in addition to unity in its own ranks, the authority of the church is challenged. This makes Irenaeus especially concerned and urges him to formulate a long series of complaints to that effect.[49] Gnostics relativize the authority of the presbyters (V.20.2: 'Those . . . who desert the preaching of the church, call in question the knowledge of the holy presbyters, not taking into consideration of how much greater consequence is a religious man, even in a private station, than a blasphemous and impudent sophist');[50] they criticize the church's understanding of Jesus.[51] Authorities in the church, Gnostics insinuate, are mere servants of the demiurge;[52] thus these authorities share in the demiurge's ambiguous nature and have no power over the 'children of the Father'. Scripture and tradition are freely accommodated and misused. Gnostics criticize what the whole church all over the world holds as sacred (I.10.2). They clash with all authorities and undermine them. 'They affirm that many of his disciples' were mistaken about Jesus (I.30.13).[53] If one adds to this their understanding of revelation as a direct communication

182

made to men, instead of seeing God's revelation in his histo
deeds,[54] it might be said that they reject all forms of mediatior.
N. Brox says, for the Gnostics

> Geschichte ist Unheilsgeschichte, niemals Heilsgeschichte, denn sie
> ist je das Merkmal der demiurgischen Welt, welche mit Gnosis und
> Heil nichts zu tun hat. . . . [Der Gnostiker] kennt ausschliesslich den
> vertikalen Einbruch jenseitiger Offenbarung. Die Gnosis erreicht ihn
> im Augenblick und ohne Vermittlung wirklicher geschichtlicher Über-
> lieferung oder Autorität.[55]

Irenaeus seems to have been very impressed by the disruptive
attitude of the Gnostics in his entourage and in particular to have
perceived the undisciplined and revolutionary character of their
outlook. This outlook is rooted in a 'Revolte gegen Zeit,
Geschichte und Welt. . . . Sie ist Negation des Vorhandenen und
in Geltung Stehenden'; it has revolutionary contours.[56] To him
Gnostics show radical tendencies.

Without taking sides on the issue of whether ancient heresies
were disguised social movements,[57] it has to be acknowledged
(and Irenaeus saw it) that Gnosticism had a strong revolutionary
impetus.[58] I want therefore to suggest that Irenaeus perceived the
Gnostic movement as socially subversive in addition, of course,
to being theologically so. Celsus on the other hand, who saw the
whole church as a social danger, only extended to it the accusation that Irenaeus reserved for the Gnostics.

Why then did Irenaeus attack almost exclusively the dualistic
aspect of Gnosticism and have very little to say against its
emanationist scheme, which he describes as well? The emanation
principle is not seen as socially subversive; it is only said to be
arbitrary and absurd. But the dualist outlook represents a social
threat. It spares no mundane authority, criticizes what is universally received, and challenges the *status quo*. Its potential for
disturbing peace and order knows no limit and, consequently,
Gnostics are seen as dangerous radicals.[59]

Irenaeus saw the greatest threat in the dualistic aspect of Gnosticism and decided to concentrate his attack upon that. Not only
was it unacceptable in its pessimism, but also socially disruptive
and subversive. It might be that the dualist tradition as such hides
in itself those subversive elements[60] in the same way that 'learned
theology' is often suspected by 'simple believers' of overthrow-
ing the faith.[61] In focusing his attack almost exclusively on one
aspect of Gnosticism, Irenaeus did neglect elements that are
essential to Gnostic self-understanding. He might have seen in

183

dualistic teachings social and political implications that his temperament could not put up with. These non-theological factors might well be those that gave him the ultimate motivation for writing his refutation.

Irenaeus took it upon himself to answer the Gnostic threat. He thought he was in a better position to do so than his predecessors were (see IV.praef.2). We can understand that his predecessors had not succeeded in having the Gnostics condemned and expelled. It is not certain that Irenaeus himself achieved such a final overthrow. But he surely did reinforce the polarization between the two groups that were already at odds.[62]

In trying to determine Irenaeus's motives and reasons for attacking the Gnostics, I have not meant to de-emphasize Irenaeus's theological reasoning. Nor have I intended to question the value of his theological contribution. I was rather interested in finding out what decided Irenaeus to oppose the Gnostics in the way he did. I think that his temperament accounts for part of his decision. The subversive character of Gnosis represented an instance that he could not see reconciled with the life in the church.[63] Irenaeus appears to have thought that Gnosis was aiming at destroying all that the apostolic tradition had transmitted and that constituted the foundation of the church. His attack was against a life-enemy.

Irenaeus thus contributed to the formation of definite fronts. After him, the Christian community did not step behind the point he fixed. Dualist ideologies have been combatted throughout the centuries with consistency, although they never completely disappeared. In the twelfth century Gnostic dualism was still the chief enemy of the church,[64] important not in number (Cathars and Bogomils were only small minorities), but for the threat they represented to an institution based on the principle of authority.

Irenaeus's contribution to the exclusion of the Gnostics surely deprived the church of colourful tendencies. Theologians were told to avoid dangerous speculations and to bow before authority and the majority. But this rejection also meant that Gnostic anticosmism and antisomatism[65] were said to be irreconcilable with the Christian view of salvation. It meant further that discrimination among men was attacked in favour of equality of all before God's universal plan of salvation. Such assertions certainly struck a responsive chord among the simple believers who constituted the majority. In retrospect, the fact that Irenaeus came forward at this time and in the way he did helped Christianity

184

save its identity in the Graeco-Roman melting pot.[66] That in turn prevented Christianity from being a marginal movement in the Western world.[67]

But with the triumph of Irenaeus's ideas in Rome[68] and with the triumph of the Roman theology in the fourth century, a conservative impetus was to set the pace. Irenaeus's part in the rejection of *gnosis* in favour of *pistis* contributed to the choice of an authoritarian structure in Christianity. An authoritarian pattern was devised to meet heretical challenges,[69] the essential features of this pattern being the criterion of antiquity (apostolicity) and that of consent (majority). This pattern was to be the *obligato* for centuries of Christian development, while Irenaeus's style became a standard element in Christian polemic for centuries.

185

Acknowledgments

Nock, Arthur Darby. "Gnosticism." *Harvard Theological Review* 57 (1964): 255–79. Copyright 1964 by the President and Fellows of Harvard College. Reprinted by permission. Courtesy of *Harvard Theological Review*.

Yamauchi, Edwin. "Pre-Christian Gnosticism, the New Testament and Nag Hammadi in Recent Debate." *Themelios* 10 (1984): 22–27. *Themelios* is an international journal for theological students, expounding and defending the historic Christian faith. Reprinted with the permission of the Universities and Colleges Christian Fellowship of Evangelical Unions. Courtesy of *Themelios*.

Armstrong, Arthur Hilary. "Gnosis and Greek Philosophy." In Barbara Aland, ed., *Gnosis: Festschrift für Hans Jonas* (Gottingen: Vandenhoeck & Ruprecht, 1978): 87–124. Reprinted with the permission of Vandenhoeck und Ruprecht. Courtesy of Yale University Sterling Memorial Library.

Dahl, Nils A. "The Arrogant Archon and the Lewd Sophia: Jewish Traditions in Gnostic Revolt." In Bentley Layton, ed., *The Rediscovery of Gnosticism: Proceedings of the International Conference on Gnosticism at Yale, New Haven, Connecticut, March 28–31, 1978; Volume Two: Sethian Gnosticism* (Leiden: E.J. Brill, 1981): 689–712. Reprinted with the permission of E.J. Brill. Courtesy of Yale University Cross Campus Library.

Pearson, Birger A. "Use, Authority and Exegesis of Mikra in Gnostic Literature." In Martin Jan Mulder, ed., *Mikra: Text, Translation, Reading and Interpretation of the Hebrew Bible in Ancient Judaism and Early Christianity* (Assen: Van Gorcum, 1988): 635–52. Reprinted from *Mikra*, edited by Martin Jan Mulder, copyright 1988 by Stichting Compendia Rerum Iudaicarum ad Novum Testamentum. Used by permission of Augsburg Fortress. Courtesy of Augsburg Fortress.

Wilson, R. McL. "Simon and Gnostic Origins." In J. Kremer, ed., *Les Actes des Apôtres. Traditions, rédaction, théologie*" (Bibliotheca Ephemeridum Theologicarum Lovaniensium, 48) (Leuven: University Press; Gembloux, J. Duculot, 1979): 485–91. Reprinted with the permission of Publications University de Louvain. Courtesy of Yale University Divinity Library.

Green, Henry A. "Gnosis and Gnosticism: A Study in Methodology." *Numen* 24 (1977): 95–134. Reprinted with the permission of E.J. Brill. Courtesy of Yale University Sterling Memorial Library.

Wisse, Frederik. "Flee Femininity: Antifemininity in Gnostic Texts and the Question of Social Milieu." In Karen L. King, ed., *Images of the Feminine in Gnosticism* (Philadelphia: Fortress Press, 1988): 297–307. Reprinted with the permission of Augsburg Fortress Press. Copyright 1988 The Institute of Antiquity and Christianity. Courtesy of Augsburg Fortress Press.

Samuel, Alan E. "How Many Gnostics?" *Bulletin of the American Society of Papyrologists* 22 (1985): 297–322. Reprinted with the permission of Scholars Press. Courtesy of Yale University Sterling Memorial Library.

Stead, G.C. "In Search of Valentinus." In *The Rediscovery of Gnosticism: Proceedings of the International Conference on Gnosticism at Yale, New Haven, Connecticut, March 28–31, 1978; Volume One: The School of Valentinus* (Leiden: E.J. Brill, 1980): 75–95. Reprinted with the permission of E.J. Brill. Courtesy of Yale University Cross Campus Library.

Turner, John D. "Sethian Gnosticism: A Literary History." In Charles W. Hedrick and Robert Hodgson, Jr., eds., *Nag Hammadi, Gnosticism, & Early Christianity* (Peabody, MA: Hendrickson Publishers, 1986): 55–86. Reprinted with the permission of Hendrickson Publishers. Courtesy of Yale University Sterling Memorial Library.

MacRae, George W. "The Ego-Proclamation in Gnostic Sources." In Ernst Bammel, ed., *The Trial of Jesus: Cambridge Studies in Honour of C.F.D. Moule* (London: SCM Press, 1970): 122–34. Reprinted with the permission of SCM Press 1970. Courtesy of Yale University Divinity Library.

Wilson, R. McL. "Ethics and the Gnostics." In Wolfgang Schrage, ed., *Studien zum Text und zur Ethik des Neuen Testaments: Festschrift zum 80. Geburtstag von Heinrich Greeven* (Berlin: Walter de Gruyter & Co., 1986): 440–49. Reprinted with the permission of Walter de Gruyter & Co. Courtesy of Yale University Sterling Memorial Library.

Wilson, R. McL. "Alimentary and Sexual Encratism in the Nag Hammadi Tractates." In Ugo Bianchi, ed., *La tradizione dell'enkrateia: Motivazioni ontologiche e protologiche* (Rome: Edizioni dell'Ateneo, 1985): 317–32. Reprinted with the permission of Edizioni dell'Ateneo. Courtesy of Yale University Sterling Memorial Library.

Pagels, Elaine H. "What Became of God the Mother? Conflicting Images of God in Early Christianity." *Signs* 2 (1976): 293–303. Reprinted with the permission of the University of Chicago Press, publisher. Copyright 1976 by the University of Chicago. All rights reserved. Courtesy of Yale University Sterling Memorial Library.

Perkins, Pheme. "Sophia and the Mother-Father: The Gnostic Goddess." In Carl Olson, ed., *The Book of the Goddess Past and Present: An Introduction to Her Religion* (New York: Crossroad, 1985): 97–109. Reprinted with the permission of The Crossroad/Continuum Publishing Group. Courtesy of David M. Scholer.

Tripp, David H. "'Gnostic Worship': The State of the Question." *Studia Liturgica* 17 (1987): 210-20. Reprinted with the permission of Liturgical Ecumenical Center Trust. Courtesy of Yale University Divinity Library.

Robinson, James M. "Jesus from Easter to Valentinus (or to the Apostles' Creed)." *Journal of Biblical Literature* 101 (1982): 5–37. Reprinted with the permission of the *Journal of Biblical Literature*. Courtesy of Yale University Sterling Memorial Library.

Wisse, Frederik. "The Use of Early Christian Literature as Evidence for Inner Diversity and Conflict." In Charles W. Hedrick and Robert Hodgson, Jr., eds., *Nag Hammadi, Gnosticism, & Early Christianity* (Peabody, MA: Hendrickson Publishers, 1986): 177–90. Reprinted with the permission of Hendrickson Publishers. Courtesy of Yale University Sterling Memorial Library.

MacRae, George W. "Why the Church Rejected Gnosticism." In E.P. Sanders, ed., *Jewish and Christian Self-Definition, Volume One: The Shaping of Christianity in the Second and Third Centuries* (Philadelphia: Fortress Press, 1980): 126–33. Reprinted with the permission of Augsburg Fortress Press. Copyright 1980 E.P. Sanders. Courtesy of Augsburg Fortress Press.

Vallée, Gérard. "Theological and Non-Theological Motives in Irenaeus's Refutation of the Gnostics." In E.P. Sanders, ed., *Jewish and Christian Self-Definition, Volume One: The Shaping of Christianity in the Second and Third Centuries* (Philadelphia: Fortress Press, 1980): 174–85. Reprinted with the permission of Augsburg Fortress Press. Copyright 1980 E.P. Sanders. Courtesy of Augsburg Fortress Press.